Making Men, Making History

Making Men, Making History
Canadian Masculinities across Time and Place

Edited by Peter Gossage and
Robert Rutherdale

UBCPress · Vancouver · Toronto

27 26 25 24 23 22 21 20 19 18   5 4 3 2 1

Printed in Canada on FSC-certified ancient-forest-free paper
(100% post-consumer recycled) that is processed chlorine- and acid-free.

ISBN 978-0-7748-3563-3 (hardcover)
ISBN 978-0-7748-3565-7 (pdf)
ISBN 978-0-7748-3566-4 (epub)
ISBN 978-0-7748-3567-1 (mobi)

Cataloguing-in-publication data for this book is available from Library and Archives Canada.

Canada

UBC Press gratefully acknowledges the financial support for our publishing program of the Government of Canada (through the Canada Book Fund), the Canada Council for the Arts, and the British Columbia Arts Council.

This book has been published with the help of a grant from the Canadian Federation for the Humanities and Social Sciences, through the Awards to Scholarly Publications Program, using funds provided by the Social Sciences and Humanities Research Council of Canada.

Printed and bound in Canada by Friesens
Set in Helvetica Condensed and Minion by Artegraphica Design Co. Ltd.
Copy editor: Robert Lewis
Proofreader: Helen Godolphin
Indexer: Celia Braves
Cover designer: Martyn Schmoll

UBC Press
The University of British Columbia
2029 West Mall
Vancouver, BC V6T 1Z2
www.ubcpress.ca

To the memory of Myra Rutherdale (1961–2014)
to whom we owe the idea for this anthology ...
and much else besides.

Contents

List of Figures / x

Acknowledgments / xiii

Introduction / 3

Part 1: Expertise and Authority / 27

1 Medical Men, Masculine Respectability, and the Contest for Power
in Mid-Nineteenth-Century Quebec / 29
Lisa Chilton

2 Accident Prevention in Early-Twentieth-Century Quebec and the
Construction of Masculine Technical Expertise / 46
Magda Fahrni

3 "The Spiritual Aspect": Gordon A. Friesen and the Mechanization
of the Modern Hospital / 64
David Theodore

4 "I am still the Supt. in this plant": Negotiating Middle-Class Masculinity in
Edmonton Packinghouses in an Era of Union Strength, 1947–66 / 85
Cynthia Loch-Drake

Part 2: Masculine Spaces / 107

5 The Place of Manliness: Architecture, Domesticity, and Men's Clubs / 109
Annmarie Adams

6 "As Christ the Carpenter": Work-Camp Missions and the Construction of Christian Manhood in Late-Nineteenth- and Early-Twentieth-Century Canada / 132
Norman Knowles

7 An Open Window on Other Masculinities: Gay Bars and Visibility in Montreal / 150
Olivier Vallerand

Part 3: Performing Masculinities / 173

8 Scales of Manliness: Masculinity and Disability in the Displays of Little People as Freaks in Ontario, 1900s–50s / 175
Jane Nicholas

9 Claiming "Our Game": S<u>k</u>w<u>x</u>wú7mesh Lacrosse and the Performance of Indigenous Nationhood in the Early Twentieth Century / 195
Allan Downey

10 Sea Shepherds, Eco-warriors, and Impresarios: Performing Eco-masculinity in the Canadian Seal Hunt of the Late Twentieth Century / 218
Willeen G. Keough

11 The New Quebec Man: Activism and Collective Improvisation at Petit Québec Libre, 1970–73 / 236
Eric Fillion

Part 4: Boys to Men / 255

12 Men's Business: Masculine Adolescence and Social Projection in Selected Coming-of-Age Novels from Interwar Quebec / 257
Louise Bienvenue and Christine Hudon

13 Boys and Boyhood: Exploring the Lives of Boys in Windsor, Ontario, during the Postwar Era, 1945–65 / 275
Christopher J. Greig

14 Heroes on Campus: Student Veterans and Discourses of Masculinity in Post–Second World War Canada / 293
Patricia Jasen

15 Constructing Canadianness: Terry Fox and the Masculine Ideal
in Canada / 312
Julie Perrone

Part 5: Men in Motion / 331

16 Tough Bodies, Fast Paddles, Well-Dressed Wives: Measuring Manhood
among French Canadian and Métis Voyageurs in the North American
Fur Trade / 333
Carolyn Podruchny

17 "The Moral Grandeur of Fleeing to Canada": Masculinity and the Gender
Politics of American Draft Dodgers during the Vietnam War / 347
Lara Campbell

18 Rebellion on the Road: Masculinity and Outlaw Motorcycle Clubs
in Postwar Ontario / 364
Graeme Melcher

Part 6: Faces of Fatherhood / 383

19 Celebrating the Family Man: From Father's Day to La Fête des Pères,
1910–60 / 385
Peter Gossage

20 "I'm a lousy father": Alcoholic Fathers in Postwar Canada and the Myths
of Masculine Crises / 409
Robert Rutherdale

Afterword / 427

List of Contributors / 434

Index / 439

Figures

3.1 Gordon A. Friesen, ca. 1970 / 65

3.2 Women working in Etobicoke General Hospital, 1973 / 66

3.3 The patient tower at the University of Cologne Medical Center, 1966 / 68

3.4 The lobby of the Kitchener-Waterloo Hospital, 1951 / 70

3.5 Scarborough Centenary Hospital, 1967 / 71

3.6 The process of centralized dispatch in the United Mine Workers hospitals, 1956 / 72

3.7 Friesen's own invention, the "Nurserver," 1964 / 74

3.8 Supplies circulation in a Friesen-concept hospital, 1970 / 75

3.9 Scarborough Centenary Hospital floor plan, 1967 / 77

3.10 The administrative communication centre on a floor of Scarborough Centenary Hospital, 1970 / 77

4.1 Canada Packers plant, Edmonton, 1937 / 86

4.2 Office entrance of Canada Packers plant, Edmonton, 1937 / 86

4.3 Canada Packers plant, front office, 1941 / 88

4.4 Beef kill floor, Canada Packers plant, Edmonton, 1952 / 88

4.5 Average hourly meatpacking wages, 1948–79 / 100

5.1 University Club, Montreal / 113

5.2 Plan for the ground floor of the University Club, Montreal, 1913 / 114

5.3 Ladies' dining room, University Club, Montreal / 115

5.4 Mount Royal Club, Montreal, ca. 1905 / 116

5.5 Plan for the ground floor of the Mount Royal Club / 117

5.6 Reception hall, University Club, Montreal, 2013 / 121

5.7 Longitudinal section of the University Club, Montreal, 1913 / 122

5.8   Reception hall, Mount Royal Club, Montreal, 2013 / 122

5.9   Plan for second floor of the University Club, Montreal, 1913 / 125

5.10 "Les sabreurs, Leo Nunes and Percy Nobbs" / 127

5.11 Billiards room, University Club, Montreal / 128

7.1   Two examples of late 1970s gay bars / 152

7.2   Gio's, Winnipeg, 2010 / 153

7.3   Pedestrian Sainte-Catherine Street in Montreal's Village, 2010 / 156

7.4   Complexe Bourbon, 1570–1592 Sainte-Catherine Street East, Montreal, 2009 / 158

7.5   Le Club Sandwich, 2009 / 159

7.6   Plans for Complexe Bourbon, ca. 2000 / 161

7.7   Olympia Building seen from corner of Sainte-Catherine and Amherst Streets, 2009 / 162

7.8   K-Lub with décor elements from previous Parking Nightclub, 2010 / 163

7.9   Rough finishes from previous occupants left visible in the Parking Nightclub hallway, 2010 / 165

8.1   A postcard of the Marechal Midgets performing with the Johnny J. Jones Exposition / 187

8.2   The Johnny J. Jones Midgets with their managers and local authorities / 188

8.3   A posed heterosexual couple and other performers in the "World's Smallest Home" show at the Canadian National Exhibition, c. 1937–1941 / 189

9.1   Andy Paull and the Squamish Indians lacrosse team, ca. late 1920s or early 1930s / 205

9.2   The 1936 North Shore Indians lacrosse team / 211

11.1 Reimagining the "Old Patriot of 1837" and the "baby's bottle," *Le p'tit Québéc libre,* 1971 / 243

11.2 Yves Charbonneau, Patrice Beckerich, and Jean Préfontaine, 1973 / 246

15.1 Terry Fox stamp, 1982 / 316

15.2 Terry Fox Monument, Thunder Bay, Ontario, 2007 / 319

19.1 Father's Day promotion, *Le Soleil,* 1924 / 388

19.2 "For Public Hero No. 1 on Father's Day," *Montreal Gazette,* 1936 / 390

19.3 "Le Père – Defenseur du Foyer!" *La Patrie,* 1942 / 393

19.4 Eaton's Father's Day ad, *Montreal Gazette,* 1958 / 395

19.5 Dupuis Frères Father's Day ad, *La Patrie,* 1954 / 397

19.6 "The Ideal Father," *Sherbrooke Daily Record*, 1951 / 399

19.7 "18 Juin: Jours des Pères," *La Gazette du nord*, 1950 / 400

19.8 "La Fête des Pères, 19 Juin," *L'Action catholique*, 1955 / 402

19.9 "La Fête des Pères chez Jean Duceppe," *La Patrie*, 1960 / 403

Acknowledgments

THIS BOOK BEGAN WITH Myra Rutherdale's suggestion that the two of us join forces to assemble in one volume some of the best original work in the history of Canadian masculinities. She thought it would be a good idea and that we would enjoy working together. And she was right, as usual, on both counts.

Our journey as co-editors has been eventful and enriching and we have accumulated many debts along the way which we are happy to acknowledge here. We are grateful in the first place to the many historians who responded to our call for submissions, especially (but not only) those whose work made its way into this anthology. Their creative scholarship made this book possible and we thank them for their contributions, their confidence in us as editors, and their patient commitment to a project that took rather longer to complete than we expected.

We are deeply grateful to many dedicated professionals at UBC Press who helped us along the way. Darcy Cullen extended a warm welcome and guided us through the assessment process with grace, clarity, integrity, and a deep respect for ideas and research in the humanities: qualities that we now recognize as her hallmarks. Ann Macklem coordinated the production of a substantial volume involving two co-editors, twenty-one contributing authors, twenty-eight individual texts, and dozens of illustrations with characteristic skill, energy, and efficiency. We thank them most sincerely, as well as Martyn Schmoll for his striking cover design, Robert Lewis for his careful work as copy editor, Nadine Pedersen for her many small favours and constant good humour, and countless others working behind the scenes in Vancouver to help make this book a success.

UBC Press solicited assessment reports from two anonymous readers and we thank them sincerely for their time and effort, their deep engagement with the material, their welcome encouragements, and their well-placed criticisms. These thoughtful and challenging critiques encouraged us to sharpen the focus of the volume, to re-think its organization, and to offer a more rigorous and straightforward statement of the theoretical and historiographical perspectives from which it emerges. We are grateful for all of that and also for the insights of Jane McGaughey, who kindly took time from a maternity leave to offer a fresh perspective on the project and some useful signposts for an ambitious introductory essay that was in need of further clarification and streamlining.

This book benefited from financial assistance from Concordia University which, through a strategic partnerships agreement with the *Centre interuniversitaire d'études québécoises,* ultimately paid for the translation of two chapters on Quebec topics into English. Steven Watt's skills as a historical translator are second to none and we were privileged to work with him on these chapters, thereby bringing some important work by francophone scholars of masculinity to a wider audience. Concordia also provided an Aid to Research Related Events, Publication, Exhibition and Dissemination Activities (ARRE) grant to offset part of the production cost. We are grateful as well to the Awards to Scholarly Publication Program (ASPP) of the Canadian Federation for the Humanities and Social Sciences for its support of this project and its continuing commitment to scholarly publishing in Canada.

As co-editors, we have been accompanied throughout this journey by our gifted editorial and research assistant, Lisa Moore. Lisa did so much for this project – from corresponding with authors to securing copyright permissions to assembling complex grant applications – that it is perfectly true to say that we couldn't have done it without her. So we extend our warm and heartfelt thanks to Lisa, along with our best wishes for her continued success as a doctoral candidate at Concordia and an emerging gender historian in her own right.

We are fortunate to be surrounded by friends and colleagues who sustain and support us in projects like this, and who provide us with a vital sense of community. At our respective universities, Concordia and Algoma, we enjoy the company of scholars and friends who make our lives and our work better by their support, their encouragement, and not infrequently by their inspiring example. We thank them sincerely, without forgetting the broader community of historians to which we belong, especially those who gather annually in the spring for the Canadian Historical Association meetings. It is as members of this marvellous moveable village that we began to imagine and develop this project and, indeed, to learn about much of the new, exciting work that found its way into this collection. So we salute the men and women of our professional community, from close friends to casual acquaintances, from distinguished professors emeriti to the bright- or bleary-eyed graduate students we once were, for their shared sense of collegiality, their inspiring ideas, and their unwavering support for meaningful historical scholarship.

We are both historians of gender and family, and it is to our families that we owe our greatest debts. We thank our parents, siblings, and extended families for the grounding they gave us early on and for the sense of belonging that still sustains us, especially through the rough patches. And we thank Annmarie, Myra, Andrew, Charlie, and Katie for their support, their understanding, their encouragement, their trust, their faith in us as husbands and fathers, and most of all their deep and unfailing love.

Making Men, Making History

Introduction

As a comparatively recent and powerful category of historical research, masculinity continues to inspire new questions and inquiries by students of gendered relationships in the past. Masculinity historiography took shape in the 1990s, as the work of Raewyn Connell, Michael S. Kimmel, John Tosh, and others was quickly taken up by historians moving beyond studies of women and gender.[1] This was a major advance in gender history, as a series of new questions, inquiries, and debates emerged from logical, if not inevitable, roots in studies of the mapping of women's gender power in patriarchal societies.[2] That it is today a fresh and vibrant field speaks to the multiple approaches that scholars have pursued and to the important fact that masculinity histor*ies* are plural and relational, even as they apply to the masculine power men exert over other men. They are constructed with crucial connections to place, class, ethnicity, life stage, health, expertise, and a matrix of varied power relationships shaped by historical context. Masculine categories emerge, as historians have taken pains to reveal, in the everyday flow of making gendered boundaries, and they do so in response to male identities that are communicated and experienced individually and collectively over time.[3]

From the beginning, Canadian experiences of manhood and masculinity have been part of this conversation. Yet there have been few attempts to take stock of the major contributions or to outline directions for further discussion and research.[4] *Making Men, Making History* seeks to fill that gap by offering both a wide-ranging, collective exploration of historical masculinities in Canada and a thematic framework in which to situate the ongoing work. Our project began as a call for submissions in 2012 and took shape over the next several years as we received proposals and invited authors to prepare and later revise their essays. From the outset, the goal was to identify *emerging themes* in masculinity history in Canada – specific directions in which this diverse and growing body of scholarship seemed to be heading. As the project progressed, we came to detect, define, and then refine the six themes that link the chapters and structure the book; we have named them expertise and authority, masculine spaces, performing masculinities, boys to men, men in motion, and faces of fatherhood. The idea of "emerging themes" is by its nature a moving target, of course, especially for a project that has played out over a six-year span in which the scale of the enterprise has grown apace. Yet we are struck by the salience of these themes, which lend structure to a diverse body of scholarship and, we maintain, represent some of the major axes along which masculinity history in Canada has emerged and continues to flourish.[5]

We return to our six emerging themes toward the end of this introduction, where we present the twenty chapters that comprise this anthology. Before we get there, however, it is worthwhile to pause and consider some fundamental questions that will help to situate both this collection and the field of masculinity history as a whole. First, how has the category of masculinity been applied to the evidence of the past? Why was this a necessary project, one that emerged from women's and then gender history? Second, and connected to this, how and why did masculinity as a category of human experience attract such a significant body of research? What has been its appeal, historiographically, as a relatively new category? Finally, by way of a brief status report, what is the current standing and reputation of the discipline, both in a wider context internationally and, for the purposes of this volume, in Canada?

Masculinity as a Category of Historical Analysis

The terms "masculinity," "manliness," and even "manhood" are comparatively modern, twentieth-century concepts when applied to widely held understandings of what it means to be a boy, or a boy becoming a man, or a man in society. Although the etymology of the English-language term "masculine" has roots in French usages of "masculinité" – which, as Sonya Rose notes, appeared in French dictionaries as far back as the mid-eighteenth century – language, rather than historical understandings, was dominated by distinctions of virility and manful power that stood in contrast to feminine traits.[6] At the same time, and well into the twentieth century, much of the history written about nation and empire building or disintegration, about war and revolution, about race and conquest, and about the actors who moved such narratives forward overwhelmingly took the form of "manmade" historical accounts. The deeds of men were equated with the deeds of all history. Women, when they did appear, were embodied in notions of sexual difference; men were not. Men made history; history did not create men as a distinct category. "Mankind," "man," and "his" place in the universe were for historians, until recent times, conflated with historical change, pivotal events, and even society as a whole. From studies of men working in groups, often in productive ways, to the negative histories of patriarchy, violence against women, or the new emphasis on "toxic masculinity" – which refers to the ways that patriarchy itself can be harmful to both men and women in terms of its predisposition toward violence, sexually aggressive behaviour, or unemotional detachment – significant new areas have opened up, prompting fresh readings of the evidence from the past.

Masculinities arise both in specific historical contexts and through their effects on the subjective experiences of particular communities that make up the wider social fabric. Since the rise of second-wave feminist scholarship, gender has been approached as a fluid construct, the outcome of power struggles that divide men from women, or more broadly the masculine from the feminine, which led to historical studies of masculinity in the first place. But a glaring oversight had long endured. By the 1990s, the time had come to introduce the specific category of masculinity into historical analysis. Men as men or boys as boys, as masculine beings, were now being approached more consistently as historically constituted, whether in relation to specific contexts or as the outcomes of struggles among masculine actors. In retrospect, a salient absence of masculinity analysis in much of the relevant literature prior to the 1990s should be placed on a historiographical timeline, one that starts with path-breaking studies on women's history in the 1970s and leads toward gender history in the 1980s, before moving on to a growing number of key works on masculinity history by the end of the 1990s.[7]

Some concern among feminist historians was expressed, in these early years, that masculinity history would prove to be a continuation of men's history, with little critique of patriarchy included.[8] This seemed a legitimate worry. Too much of history had centred on the deeds of men; too much, as well, had been written by men. But it soon became obvious that masculinity scholars, especially those who focused on the power of patriarchy, were closely allied with feminist critiques and sensibilities. John Tosh's work in England on the Victorian family and masculinity, Robert Griswold's work in the United States on the history of fatherhood, and Raewyn Connell's work in Australia on sociologically based theories of "hegemonic masculinity" led the way toward further scholarship in masculinity studies that was keenly aware of its conceptual roots in both women's and gender history.

In assessing key works and advances internationally, we might begin with the first publication and edition of Lynne Segal's *Slow Motion: Changing Masculinities, Changing Men* (1990). In many respects, this book served as a feminist indictment of the exercise of masculine power by men in many roles: as absent fathers, as rapists, and as perpetrators of violence in both the home and public sphere. As a polemic, Segal's work did two things: it identified areas where masculinity had run amok over the lives of women and children; and it shed light on how this had been an outcome of an oppressive set of gender powers. In so doing, Segal's work raised questions about how, precisely, masculinity as a category of human relationships can operate and can be improved. Beginning with examples drawn from the 1950s, she showed how men, as well as women, can fall victim to the enormous weight of masculine identities. "Sometimes in the life of every man," Segal wrote in a chapter calling for the reconstruction of "good" fatherly practices, "the weight of male tradition must prove burdensome. We are now used to hearing of some of these burdens: men die younger than women; they are more prone to coronary disease; they find it difficult to seek help when they need it – regarding illness, for example, as a sign of weakness: something to be denied."[9] Segal also took pains to enter the debate over the making of masculinities by stressing their relational component, that making men masculine happens in relationship, or in response, to notions of the *feminine,* from womanly behaviours to the effeminate man castigated by his macho rivals. "To be 'masculine,'" she wrote, "is *not* to be 'feminine,' *not* to be 'gay,' *not* to be tainted by any marks of 'inferiority' – ethnic or otherwise."[10] In an important way, Segal picked up on Natalie Zemon Davis's insistence in much of her foundational work,[11] taken up by feminist historians since, that women's oppression has to be understood in the context of a masculine gender politics.

Masculinity, however, is often constructed without reference to femininity or to women at all. Competition to assert physical and mental competence, if not dominance, between men rather than between men and women, in fact, was one of the first areas to attract research, especially in studies of "manhood" (equated with acquiring the status of *adult* male behaviours according to widely accepted gendered ideals), which is but a part of the wider category of "masculinity" (equated with acquiring the status of being male at various ages according to gendered ideals). Mark C. Carnes and Clyde Griffen's *Meanings for Manhood: Constructions of Masculinity in Victorian America* (1990), in examining industrializing societies across the social classes, recognized the importance of masculinity as a relational construct among and between men. In recognizing the roots of historians' concerns with masculinity in feminist-inspired critiques of patriarchal societies, and the importance of relationships between the sexes, Carnes and Griffen sought to select works that "analyze the evolution of cultural definitions of what it means to be male," often as a result of male associational life.[12]

Meanings for Manhood drew from a growing number of gender historians who were then at the point of making significant contributions to masculine historical topics, scholars such as E. Anthony Rotundo, Robert Griswold, and Margaret Marsh. Constructions of masculinity took place, they recognized, wherever and whenever men came into association with each other. They also highlighted the potential for insightful and revealing research on all-male networks of labour and leisure, or as they put it, essays that "focus on formal institutions, such as lawyers' associations, psychiatric hospitals, fraternal orders, or labor unions."[13] "The absence of essays on blacks and homosexuals," they wrote in introducing their anthology, "is glaring."[14] These early efforts, nonetheless, indicated key and inviting openings in the field that have now progressed considerably.[15]

American historians joined with a growing number of British and continental scholars throughout the rest of the 1990s to map, survey, and present fresh work in a field that was clearly on the rise by the end of the decade. Writing in the mid-1990s, Kimmel pointed to the paucity of masculinity histories among the work being produced at that time by many gender historians.[16] This was a significant gap in gender history but one that was rapidly closing, as indicated for instance by the publication of Rotundo's *American Manhood: Transformations in Masculinity from the Revolution to the Modern Era* (1993). Rotundo offered a compelling outline of changing definitions of American masculinity – with attention paid to transitions from a communal sense of manhood in eighteenth-century New England contexts to an individual sense of self-made manhood in the nineteenth and twentieth centuries – and illustrations, from many parts of the country, of how masculinity was experienced and shaped from boyhood to manhood.[17] By this time, insightful new approaches that centred on "hegemonic masculinity" were making their way into historical debates on masculinity as a social category. Published in 1995, Connell's *Masculinities* became famous for its explication of this pivotal concept, which combined Antonio Gramsci's notion of "hegemony" as a process of class domination with the new attention that patriarchal gender relations were receiving from a host of scholars. Connell argued that "hegemonic masculinity can be defined as the configuration of gender practice which embodies the currently accepted answer to the problem of patriarchy, which guarantees (or is taken to guarantee) the dominant position of men and the subordination of women." It has never been seen as a stable category of gender relations. As Connell conceived it, hegemony, or for that matter hegemonic masculinity, "is a historically mobile relation." Plotting its "ebb and flow," she argued, lent direction to her work.[18]

Meanwhile, Leonore Davidoff and Catherine Hall's *Family Fortunes: Men and Women of the English Middle Class, 1780–1850* (1987) had clearly broken new ground as a study of both masculine and feminine identity formation during a period of rapid change.[19] What they saw as a salient retreat into "separate spheres," dividing men in the public worlds of work from women in the private worlds of domestic home lives, established a basis for subsequent historians to test the applicability of this defining structure for masculinity and femininity in modernizing times, especially for the emerging middle class.[20] Class, economic development, and the gendered politics of the family, in effect, connected private life to the public realm of the wider society. Victorian middle-class men came increasingly to identify with their breadwinning roles outside the home, whereas women came to identify with their nurturing function within it. "Masculine identity was equated with an emerging concept of 'occupation,' while women remained within a familial frame."[21] Although a narrowly deployed "separate spheres" approach to gender has attracted its critics, more nuanced and grounded assessments have followed since this work first appeared.[22]

Writing from the United Kingdom, with a research foundation very much located in the same class- and ethnic-based materials (i.e., Protestant Victorian middle class) used by Davidoff and Hall, John Tosh emerged as one of the pre-eminent practitioners of masculinity history from its earliest days. Tosh praised *Family Fortunes* as a key work, especially for its emphasis on the centrality, not merely the presence, of gender politics in class formation. "It is precisely because Davidoff and Hall structure *Family Fortunes* around masculinity and femininity," he observed, "that we now have a different view of the middle class in the early nineteenth century; their achievement is not to fill out the gender attributes of a class we already know about, but to place gender at the centre of class formation itself."[23] Tosh himself made a considerable contribution with *A Man's Place: Masculinity and the Middle-Class Home in Victorian England* (1999),[24] which was followed by his periodic reflections on debates in the field. In his work, Tosh emphasized the relational basis on which masculine boundaries and identities are formed, with the implication that historians should resist "the tendency to study masculinity in isolation."[25] This marked a turning point in broad acceptance of the relational aspects of masculinity. Among the prominent connections that must be considered are masculinity in relation to femininity; heterosexual masculinity in relation to homosexual masculinity; working-class masculinity in relation to middle-class masculinity; masculinity and race; and masculinity, nation, and empire.

Tosh embraced Connell's concept of hegemonic masculinity, while acknowledging its limits when applied to all historical periods. But when consideration turns to the salience of patriarchy, particularly since the end of the nineteenth century, it is impossible to proceed without some notion of its historical presence and force. "Hegemonic masculinity," Tosh argued, "is a convenient phrase because it reminds us that masculinity carries a heavy ideological freight, and that it makes socially crippling distinctions not only between men and women, but between different categories of men – distinctions which have to be maintained by force, as well as validated through cultural means."[26] Tosh also recognized that "any system of hegemony is by definition liable to insecurity."[27]

Threats to masculine hegemony imply threats to manhood altogether, something that much of the discourse of the modern era has confronted as a "crisis of masculinity," especially but not exclusively since 1945.

Challenges to patriarchy and to virtually all forms of male privilege, from comparisons between boys' and girls' scholastic performance to the gender wars in contemporary political life, often attract the anxious cries of commentators who invariably ask the question "Whither masculinity? Whither modern boyhood or modern manhood?" As traditional forms of masculinity become blurred, what does it mean to be a "real man"? Often more manufactured than real, these "social panics" themselves reveal the significance and salience of very real gender power struggles; they also help to bring into focus the lines that are drawn around such all-encompassing historical trends as childhood and adolescence, immigration, colonization, industrialization, and globalization. The idea of a mid-century masculinity crisis in the United States, for instance, was addressed by James Gilbert in *Men in the Middle: Searching for Masculinity in the 1950s* (2005). Gilbert used societal fears of emasculated men as a launching point for individual chapters on the sociologist David Riesman, the sexologist Alfred Kinsey, the evangelist Billy Graham, the sitcom star Ozzie Nelson, and the playwright Tennessee Williams. "In some respects," Gilbert wrote,

> gender malaise was deemed a national calamity during the 1950s and projected backwards into a reinterpretation of American history. It found innumerable expressions, first in the attack on powerful, emasculating mothers and women, then in a critical literature deploring humiliating corporate work, fears of spies and homosexuals in government, distrust of youth and worries about juvenile delinquency, and a tense film culture which lionized war heroes, misfits, cowboys, and wandering poets.[28]

Gilbert found that these stereotypes did not reflect a broader, richer, and in many ways more inspiring search for masculine authenticity carried out by his protagonists, who studied, acted, preached, and lived fully as masculine beings in a world that was indeed undergoing fundamental changes but not one that was leaving men behind.[29]

Masculinity has now become a firm, arguably indispensable category that must be addressed in historical studies on topics ranging from local community formation and family life to imperial exchange and global transformation. Comparing dominant representations of masculinity with the evidence of lived experience has also attracted sustained interest, and historians now regularly assess both the signs and the practices that form the most striking discourses of masculinity in a given historical setting. In exploring the dissonance between representations of masculinity, on the one hand, and masculinity as lived experience, on the other, our contributors seek to reposition a variety of histories – from the social to the architectural, the professional, and the iconic – around the dynamics of being and becoming a man.

Canadian Masculinities

Canadian studies of manhood and masculinity began in the early 1990s and have maintained a constant and maturing output ever since. We can trace the origins of the current, multifaceted inquiry into Canadian masculinities back more than a quarter-century to the publication of Joy Parr's *The Gender of Breadwinners* (1990), which widened the field of gender studies by centring it not just on women and work but on men and work as well. With her dual focus on female workers at Penman's Limited, a knit-goods company in Paris, Ontario, and on male workers at Knechtel Furniture Company in Hanover, Ontario, over a long period of industrial change, Parr explored the relationship between gender formation and breadwinning.[30] Parr pointed out that the "entitlements of the single fellow and the family man emerge as distinctively as those of man and woman, the behaviours of husbands and single girls as starkly different between the two communities."[31] In an essay published five years later, Parr pushed the feminist-inspired concept of hegemonic masculinities to embrace discussion of how "some masculinities are marginalized among the powerful." With reference to class and racial identities, she observed that "whereas some masculinities are forged in relationships between men and women, others are defined by their difference from other masculinities."[32] Her entreaty was timely and has since resonated in subsequent research in Canada that continues to the present and has inspired many of the authors whose work is collected in this volume.

The emerging class- and ethnic-specific models of manhood that Andrew Holman, for instance, described for the southern Ontario Victorians he studied were calculated, measured responses to modernity – to the rise of professional expertise, to the norms of conformity and self-confidence, and to widely recognizable standards of self-aware behaviour, which ordinary middle-class men, as ideal exemplars, reinforced. These emerging masculine moderns exerted their power through expressions of competence, restraint, and resistance to temptations of the senses. They also displayed an ability to set goals directed at logical, often economic, ends. New norms for modern manhood seemed ensconced in the settled worlds of hegemonic masculinity associated with imperial nationalism and with the class-based and racial assumptions of the latter nineteenth century that served to justify it. But this could go only so far. Holman's comprehensive portraits of the Victorian middle-class man show that he projected a style of masculinity that in the first half of the twentieth century faced a series of disruptions that challenged the power of serene, purpose-driven, disciplined comportment.[33] Victorian masculinity became outmoded when faced with terrifying displays of technology on the modern battlefields of the First World War, the rise of what George L. Mosse has called "fascist man,"[34] anonymous forces that disrupted market exchange systems during the Great Depression, and the horrors of mass violence and death, which, by the end of the Second World War, had brought with them a disquieting realization of the fragility of civilization itself.

Beginning in the late 1980s, a growing number of historians in Canada embarked upon specific studies of work, leisure, and masculine camaraderie in various settings. Stephen Maynard's essay "Rough Work and Rugged Men: The Social Construction of Masculinity in Working-Class History" (1989) helped to adjust the focus toward intersections of gender and work.[35] While Maynard went on to complete studies of gay culture and history, and was joined in this work by Gary Kinsman, masculinity histories in Canada continued to map out the contours of both work and leisure.[36] Thomas Dunk's *It's a Working Man's Town: Male Working-Class Culture in Northwestern Ontario* (2003) is a good example.[37] Joy Parr and Mark Rosenfeld's ground-breaking collection *Gender and History in Canada* (1996) – by including Elizabeth Vibert's study of masculinity evident in the Plains Buffalo hunt, Colin Howell's work on early baseball in the Maritimes as a "manly" sport, and Stephen Penfold's contribution on work and masculinity in the Cape Breton coalmines of the early 1920s – showcased the new interest that social historians of work and leisure were taking in masculinity.[38] Along lines similar to Gail Bederman's American-based study of masculinity and hunting cultures,[39] Tina Loo's sophisticated article "Of Moose and Men: Hunting for Masculinities in British Columbia, 1880–1939" (2001) offered a nuanced interpretation of the contrasting masculinities that hunting as sport imbued. Sportsmen constructed themselves as masculine and bourgeois, with identities that displayed both sexualized and racialized traits; their Indigenous guides, in contrast, displayed the characteristics of the Trickster figure and carried out their services on the basis of deceiving their prey. It was a complicated game of competing masculine powers.[40]

Ceremonies, too, attracted renewed attention through the lens of masculinity. In an important article published in 2002 in the *Canadian Historical Review*, for example, Carolyn Podruchny examined the rituals of French Canadian voyageurs in the Montreal fur trade, showing how symbolic "baptism" ceremonies, involving a whiskey toast, were performed to confirm into manhood the novices who travelled with seasoned paddlers.[41] Craig Heron's 2005 study of the increased restrictions on working men's patronage of Hamilton's public drinking establishments also appeared in the *Canadian Historical Review*, shining a similarly powerful light on masculinity, class, and drinking rituals.[42] Julia Roberts's *Mixed Company: Taverns and Public Life in Upper Canada* (2009) extended consideration of drink and masculinity back to the first half of the nineteenth century.[43] Each is an excellent example of how masculinity was deployed to explain the origins and patterns of male behaviour in particular historical contexts. So, too, is Tim Cook's 2013 study of the "trench slang" favoured by men in the ranks of the Canadian Expeditionary Force, which took seriously the swearing and related colloquialisms used by fighting men in the horrific circumstances of trench warfare during the First World War.[44]

Masculinity has also been associated with men's responses to risk, particularly in the workplace and in sport. It was obvious by the end of the horrors of the Second World War that the *risks* of modern – if not "mass" – society, defined by unprecedented levels of industrial production and consumption and by the unparalleled power of the state by 1945, would necessitate yet another set of masculine responses, built around new notions of gendered conformity to postwar conditions. Christopher Dummitt addressed these dynamics in *The Manly Modern: Masculinity in Postwar Canada* (2007), an influential study of the intersections of masculinity, risk, and modernity from the end of the Second World War until the late 1960s. Regulatory bureaucracies to mitigate myriad economic, workplace, and mass transit dangers – from veteran reestablishment to mountain climbing, mental health and crime, and driving accidents – were fashioned as masculine responses, "manmade" solutions to "manmade" problems. "Canadians put men at the centre of the modernist project," Dummitt wrote.[45] "Modern life created new risks and demanded a great deal of trust in the engine of progress. One of the ways that this trust was consolidated was by coding as masculine the expertise needed to ensure successful risk taking and risk management."[46] Since bureaucratic, engineering, and urban-planning measures required rational approaches to risk management aimed at increasing public confidence and bolstering trust in new systems as they came into being, they were inherently exercises of masculine endeavour. They were, in short, the responses of the "manly modern."

Recent work in Canada also demonstrates, as noted above in a broader context, that manhood – the state of being or becoming a fully mature male – has to be approached as a specific aspect of masculinity rather than as a synonym for masculinity itself. Doing so recognizes, as Christopher Greig did in *Ontario Boys: Masculinity and the Idea of Boyhood in Postwar Ontario, 1945–1960* (2014), that boyhood masculinity – the stages through which boys move from childhood to adolescence – presents an inviting opportunity for historians to explore the perceptions and experiences of boyhood cultures in countless historical settings. With a focus on the postwar years, the same historical period in which Dummitt located the bulk of his work, Greig explored the ways that anxieties about boys' growth and development in Canada's largest province shaped public policy responses and much of the public discourse on boyhood.[47] Fears of juvenile delinquency were expressed in combination with concern over a regression in educational standards and in youth recreational opportunities. Although girls were part of the picture, the prime focus was on boys. In this sense, the postwar "crisis of masculinity" was extended to include boys as well as men, although the problems of boys were seen as part of the challenge of dealing with what were considered normal or "ideal" growth and development. The framing of ideal boyhood was explicitly masculine in orientation, as educators and allied social reformers and commentators sought solutions to the perceived challenges that Ontario boys faced based on ideal conceptions of what it *should* mean to be a boy growing up in the postwar years.[48]

It has been more than a quarter-century since Parr's *The Gender of Breadwinners* appeared. In that interval, the category of masculinity in history has assumed prominence across a considerable array of Canadian-based doctoral dissertations, historical monographs, and journal articles that investigate the gendered experiences of being or becoming a man. Masculinity research in Canada has reached a critical mass, so to speak, and the body of scholarship we have just described continues to inspire and inform further work in Canadian contexts. From earlier studies in Canada on work, family life, boyhood, and leisure, the contours of how masculinity has intersected with class, ethnicity, and the life cycle have begun to appear. This volume advances our understanding of this powerful category of analysis by undertaking to identify the areas of research currently attracting the most attention and to present fresh contributions in a widely accessible form. The time has come to consider the historical category of masculinity broadly in Canada, applying the most innovative research methods, from architectural analysis to oral history, in order to cast light on a wide spectrum of masculine experiences across time and place, from middle-class fathers raising their families in the suburbs to leather-clad bikers out on the road "raising hell."

Six Emerging Themes
From the rugged paddlers of voyageur days and the buttoned-down company men of mid-twentieth-century Canada to a courageous Terry Fox in the 1980s, these men and the diverse constructions of masculinity they represent are the focus of this anthology. Except for two chapters that have appeared elsewhere in French, these are all entirely *new* contributions to the emerging field of

masculinity history, some by established scholars and others gleaned by younger historians from their recently completed dissertations. The theoretical and empirical groundwork laid by Connell, Tosh, Parr, Dummitt, and others has inspired and informed our authors; yet their questions, approaches, sources, and conceptual frameworks are as varied as their subject matter. Amidst this diversity, we have identified six emerging themes, connecting these chapters to each other and to new and innovative areas of masculinity dynamics in Canadian history.

Expertise and Authority

If certain constructions of masculinity are understood to be dominant in a given place and time, then others, whether based on race, ethnicity, social class, age, ability, sexual orientation, or something else, must necessarily be framed as secondary, subaltern, subjugated, or even oppositional. This is one of the key lessons of Connell's path-breaking work on hegemonic masculinity and an important premise, as we shall see, for many of the chapters throughout this volume. The four assembled under the heading "Expertise and Authority" throw these dynamics into sharp relief, sharing as they do a focus on accomplished, powerful, generally white men: professionals, managers, and technical experts whose reputations and authority depended to a large extent on their ability to demonstrate expertise, judgment, and high ethical standards in their business and professional lives.

As Dummitt has emphasized, hegemonic masculinity in postwar British Columbia was wrapped up in discourses of professional and technical expertise, especially the effective management of risk.[49] This concern with expertise and risk management was shared, to at least some extent, by middle-class managers and professionals in other places and times in Canadian history, whereas the hegemonic masculinity of the later twentieth century stands in sharp contrast to the various and competing ways that medical *manhood*, for instance, was understood and performed in the mid-nineteenth century. In Chapter 1, Lisa Chilton shows this distinction in her study of the Quebec Marine and Emigrant Hospital, focusing on doctors like James Douglas, an accomplished hunter and angler who, as a physician, was widely recognized for his surgical skill, speed, and efficiency. But his many critics considered this the wrong set of manly qualities for a leadership role, in which "control of temper, good social judgment, and dignity without arrogance" might be more valuable. In Chapter 2, focusing on the same province but a century later, Magda Fahrni looks at risk-management discourses, organizations, and proponents in interwar Quebec. Her discussion of masculine expertise within the emerging accident-prevention movement reveals a transitional situation, one in which the "reasoned expertise" of the high-modern postwar era "clearly coexisted with other forms of masculinity rooted in experience and on-the-job training."

In Chapters 3 and 4, David Theodore and Cynthia Loch-Drake move us forward into the postwar years and offer fresh perspectives on the "manly modern" described by Dummitt, with its dominant tropes of technology and risk. Theodore's essay is about a Canadian best known for his application of automation and Fordist principles to the design, construction, and management of hospitals. Theodore unpacks Gordon A. Friesen's vision for the twentieth-century hospital, a project that both "prescribed a crucial role for women in a vast, mechanized, masculine architecture" and incorporated a "spiritual vision of care," which has most often been missed in treatments of postwar, modernist masculinity. Conflicting expressions of male managerial authority are the focus of Loch-Drake's chapter on the Alberta meatpacking industry after the Second World War. As with so many contributions to this anthology, the emphasis here is on individual men – in this case, the mid-level managers who implemented the directives of senior executives and who, most importantly for present purposes, represented "a technocratic ideal of middle-class masculinity" that accompanied and helped to legitimize the new technologies that so profoundly affected the power relations between capital and labour in this industry. We are a long way, of course, from the colourful and fractious Quebec City physicians of the previous century introduced by Chilton. These essays, nonetheless, are linked by their emphasis on patterns of leadership in the workplace, which drew on specific bundles of masculine characteristics and which certainly changed over time as the dynamics of patriarchy shifted from one generation to the next.

Masculine Spaces
From its inception, gender history has been replete with spatial metaphors, beginning with the "separate spheres" image used by Davidoff and Hall, among many others, to describe men's and women's gendered roles and identities. The ideological and cultural distance between a male-dominated public sphere and a private sphere peopled and managed largely by women often corresponds to a physical boundary, such as the exterior wall of a private home. Gender historians, however, have usually been more interested in socially and ideologically constructed spaces and boundaries than in those built of bricks and mortar. Yet there is room, we submit, for a more physical reading of the history of gendered space, some exciting examples of which can be drawn from the neighbouring disciplines of architectural history and historical geography.[50]

By studying the physical spaces designed and occupied by particular groups of men, especially for work and leisure, we can learn much about the particular sets of gendered ideals that informed their conception and use. These *masculine spaces* must certainly include the stately men's clubs examined here by Annmarie Adams in Chapter 5, which adroitly juxtaposes gender and social class while revealing a particular concern with the ways that historians can move beyond spatial metaphors in order to "link real architectural spaces with changing cultures of masculinity." The contemporary mining and logging camps discussed by Norman Knowles in Chapter 6 were as distant as one can imagine, in social and economic terms, from the grand private clubs of Montreal's famed Square Mile. Yet in the Canadian context, it would be difficult to find a more quintessentially masculine space, one with its own mix of class, ethnic, and religious dynamics and one where rough and respectable notions of appropriate manhood were in constant contact and competition. The study of masculine space in Canada, furthermore, must surely attend to all manner of bars, taverns, and nightclubs, from Joe Beef's iconic canteen on the Montreal waterfront[51] to the late-twentieth-century gay bars of the same city, as Olivier Vallerand reminds us in Chapter 7. Although the contrast with the private clubs of the Square Mile is dramatic, the focus persists on same-sex sociability in leisure spaces reserved for men but defined now in terms of sexual orientation – and, increasingly, the politics of sexuality – rather than social class.

Performing Masculinities

Since the 1990s, Judith Butler's thesis about the performative character of feminine and masculine identities has been part of the stock-in-trade of gender studies across North America and beyond. Butler's ideas are complex and their implications far-reaching. But her key insight – that "gender reality is created through sustained social performances" – can be stated quite simply and is all the more powerful and influential for that reason.[52] From this perspective, masculinity involves an active process of performing attributes and expectations that are coded male. That these characteristics vary from place to place, among social classes and ethnic groups, and across time – both over the life course and through historical time – makes their study all the more rewarding for historians. As with the best new work on ethnicity, the essays in this section reveal that masculine identities must be performed – like the traditional German folk songs performed during the lager-enlivened singing festivals of nineteenth-century Waterloo County – in order to be real and meaningful and, indeed, to be understood or decoded by others.[53]

Taken together, these four contributions remind us that the performative character of Canadian masculinities – hegemonic and otherwise – must be studied in a wide range of temporal, social, and cultural settings. In Chapter 8, aptly titled "Scales of Manliness," Jane Nicholas's examination of the performance of a particular nonhegemonic masculine identity – that of little people on display in the fairgrounds and sideshows of twentieth-century Ontario – leads her to some fascinating insights, especially as she juxtaposes physical stature with gender expectations. Nicholas reveals how "midget" scripts and identities were framed by the familiar tropes of family, ethnicity, and social class. In Chapter 9, Allan Downey develops similar themes with respect to racialized men, describing how Aboriginal lacrosse players in British Columbia reappropriated an activity that was imposed on them by British Canadian colonizers. Ultimately, the S̲k̲w̲x̲wú7mesh people took pride in the sport's Iroquoian origins and absorbed it into their own culture, at a time when the Indigenous traditions of their own region, the potlach in particular, were under attack. In Chapter 10, Willeen Keough explores three distinct expressions of contemporary "eco-masculinity" in late-twentieth-century anti-sealing campaigns, revealing another set of competing but complementary masculinities, the performance of which – whether out on the Labrador pack ice or in the glare of television lights – could be dramatic indeed. Finally, in Chapter 11, Eric Fillion introduces readers to a little-known group of nationalist jazz musicians whose unbridled improvisations provided a metaphor and a distinct voice for their utopian project of a politically and socially liberated Quebec. Especially through the performance of their music and their communal lifestyle, the members of Petit Québec libre offered an unexpected critique of the breadwinner-homemaker model and of the dissipated, often violent, politically inert working-class masculinities that they explicitly located in one of the province's most sexist institutions: the tavern.

Boys to Men
Youth, particularly the emotionally fraught passage from boyhood into manhood, is a time of life where the weight of social and cultural expectations can be intense, not least around what Christopher Greig calls standards of "appropriate" masculinity.[54] Yet youth and its associated physical grace, strength, and beauty, as Julie Perrone reminds us in her chapter on Terry Fox, are also key elements in many constructions of an *ideal* masculinity. This is especially the case for those variants – and they are legion – that emphasize athleticism and physical ability, whether in an attempt to run across the country on a prosthetic leg or on the field of battle, as with the returning veterans of the Second World War studied by Patricia Jasen. So the fourth part of this anthology explores youthful masculinities, focusing in particular on twentieth-century performances, expressions, and experiences – anxious, heroic, and otherwise – of

boyhood, adolescence, and nascent manhood. It begins with Louise Bienvenue and Christine Hudon's exploration in Chapter 12 of three coming-of-age novels of the 1920s and 1930s. These works share not only a focus on male adolescence but also a common setting, as each of the protagonists has been a student at one of Quebec's classical colleges. The authors situate this chapter within their broader exploration of identity formation in these all-male educational spaces, where the sons of the French Canadian elite were trained not just in literature, history, and catechism but also in a particular code of Catholic, middle-class masculinity.[55] From interwar Quebec and its boarding schools, the focus then shifts westward to Windsor, Ontario, forward several decades to the post-war era, and from novels to another kind of story altogether. Chapter 13 is built around Christopher Greig's oral-history interviews with nine men who grew up in this working-class factory town in the immediate postwar years of 1945–1960. Their memories of boyhood are rich in detail and interconnected through masculine tropes such as aggression, sports, independence, and freedom – in this case, symbolized by the bicycle – but also through fears and anxieties rooted in "the intensified homophobia of the postwar period."

The tension between postwar ideals and anxieties is also present in Jasen's discussion of student veterans of the Second World War. In Chapter 14, however, the narrative is about returning soldiers negotiating the transition from the heroic, hyper-masculinity of the victorious fighting man to the "normalcy" of civilian manhood, specifically as university students preparing for white-collar careers while benefiting from the educational provisions of the Veterans Charter. Another, more recent expression of youthful, heroic masculinity, finally, is at the heart of Chapter 15, where Perrone looks at the commemoration of Terry Fox and his 1980 Marathon of Hope. Her insight here is to approach Fox's heroism through the process of its construction – that is, through a broad range of commemorative tributes, including books, articles, films, physical monuments such as statues and postage stamps, and much more – with an emphasis on the particular masculine archetype that the Marathon of Hope reflected and revealed.

Men in Motion
Terry Fox was also the quintessential "Man in Motion," although the phrase itself is associated with another Canadian athlete, Rick Hansen.[56] The active tropes of travel, movement, exploration, and adventure are certainly coded male in Canadian history and culture, whether linked to the selflessness and courage of Fox and Hansen pushing their bodies for medical research in the 1980s, to the young boys of the 1950s exploring the streets, parks, and vacant lots of towns like Windsor on their cherished two-wheelers (CCMs, Gliders,

and Raleighs), or to the beat nihilism of a Jack Kerouac, the son of French Canadian parents born in 1920s Massachusetts, whose iconic 1957 novel *On the Road* is evoked so often in our culture, including in the title of Graeme Melcher's chapter on outlaw motorcycle clubs in postwar Ontario. Performing a surprisingly wide range of masculinities through movement and travel, or taking Canadian manhood "on the road," is another emerging theme for Canadian scholars working in this area. As the authors in this part of the book show, the social, cultural, and political meanings attached to a long paddle, a raucous road trip, or a self-imposed exile can be as compelling as the journeys themselves.

The travellers examined here used the transportation technologies of their time – from the birchbark canoes of the fur trade era discussed by Carolyn Podruchny in Chapter 16 to the customized "choppers" and "bobbers" ridden by the bikers Melcher discusses in Chapter 18 – reminding us of another strong connection evoked in other chapters in this collection as well, namely between men and their machines. Central to biker culture was an idealized masculinity that, as with the voyageurs, had more to do with physical power, individual merit, disdain for authority, and personal freedom than with, in the case of the bikers, the postwar, middle-class, domestic, and white-collar masculinities against which these road warriors were rebelling so loudly. The northward journey of the draft dodgers discussed by Lara Campbell in Chapter 17, similarly, was widely understood as an act of rebellion against the power of an American "establishment" that embodied hegemonic masculinity every bit as much as it did wealth, racial whiteness, or political conservatism. In this way, they were not unlike Fillion's revolutionary-nationalist jazz heads; they shared an era, a rebellious spirit, and a willingness to hit the road with Melcher's outlaw bikers – although as peace-loving members of the Woodstock generation, they performed their masculinity quite differently.

Faces of Fatherhood
Canadian masculinities, finally, can be located in domestic settings as profitably as they can in the country's workplaces and clubs, in its fields and streams, or on its streets and highways. Toward that end, scholars currently use a variety of sources and methodologies to focus on the full range of experiences associated with fatherhood in this country.[57] Gone are the days when the study of fatherhood could be conflated with a kind of "recovery effort" for neglected and embattled family men, overwhelmed by the weight of their responsibilities and in need of greater understanding, including by historians.[58] Today's approaches are richer, more varied, and more attentive to persistent patriarchal power than this assessment would have allowed. They include efforts to understand the shifting ideologies and prescriptions that underlie widely circulated discourses

around men as parents, as with Chapter 19 by Peter Gossage on the rise of Father's Day celebrations in Quebec. They also include textured studies grounded in oral history and life writing, such as Robert Rutherdale's discussion in Chapter 20 of failed fatherhood in postwar Canada, seen through the particularly troubling lens of alcoholism. The contrast between these two chapters illustrates both the range of experiences and narratives that can be included under the heading "Canadian fatherhoods" and the scope for continued study along several promising avenues in this area.

Running through all six themes and all twenty chapters, finally, are the constant tensions and interactions between hegemonic ideals on the one hand and personal, everyday experiences and narratives on the other. There is a sense, then, in which all of the essays in this volume invite reflection and discussion about *ideal* masculinity. The general notion that an ideal of Canadian manhood might exist somewhere in the popular imagination will create a dissonance for many – just as we were flummoxed in 2004 when the Canadian Broadcasting Corporation asked us to vote on the greatest Canadian of all time. This was not explicitly, of course, a poll about Canada's great *men* – although it may as well have been given that only four women, Laura Secord and three singers (Shania Twain, Céline Dion, and Avril Lavigne), made it into the top fifty.[59] But it makes a useful point about masculine ideals just the same: that there is nothing fixed or monolithic about them and that, depending on the context, the rough, testosterone-driven pugnacity of a Don Cherry (ranked seventh) is perhaps as likely to be deemed an "ideal" masculinity as the calm, principled, and approachable paternalism of a Tommy Douglas (ranked first).

At the same time, the agency expressed by individual men and boys in the conduct of their own lives and in the performance of their identities *as* men and boys is one of the strongest recurring motifs in this entire anthology. *Making Men, Making History,* in other words, is really about the nineteenth-century fur trader and recorder of extraordinary voyageur tales Alexander Ross; the Montreal architect, fisherman, and Olympic fencer Percy Nobbs; the Skwxwú7mesh residential school survivor, athlete, and lacrosse promoter Andy Paull; the reluctant and insecure Alberta slaughterhouse manager Bill McLean; the intrepid schoolteacher Henry Ferguson, also from Alberta, whose life of financial insecurity and domestic tension ultimately dissolved into alcoholism and liver disease; the radical nationalist jazz musician and utopian commune member Yves Charbonneau; and the interview subject identified only as "James" who grew up black and gay in postwar Windsor, surrounded by racial prejudice and homophobia. Who were these men, and how did they come to understand and perform their identities *as* men at various times and places in Canadian history? These are the questions that inform and propel this project as much as any other. We have been privileged to get to know these men, and dozens of others, through the talented and thoughtful work of our contributors. It is a privilege that we value deeply and are now most pleased to share with a broader readership.

Notes

1 Since the late 1980s, Connell's work as a sociologist and theorist has provided key arguments on the power dynamics that create masculine identities and boundaries. See, especially, Raewyn (R.W.) Connell, *Gender and Power: Society, the Person, and Sexual Politics* (Stanford, CA: Stanford University Press, 1987), *Masculinities* (Cambridge, UK: Polity, 2005), and *Gender* (Cambridge, UK: Polity, 2005). Most of Connell's work was published under the initials R.W. or her former first name, Robert, before her transsexual transition relatively late in life. This transition, in part, inspired her to write "Transsexual Women and Feminist Thought: Toward a New Understanding and New Politics," *Signs: Journal of Women in Culture and Society* 37, 4 (2012): 857–81. (In referring to Connell and her work, we have elected to use feminine pronouns throughout this volume, even with respect to work produced prior to her transition.) The foundational work of Michael S. Kimmel also offers a key introduction to the meaning and experience of masculine identities. See Michael Kimmel, *Manhood in America: A Cultural History* (New York: Free Press, 1996). John Tosh is among the leading British historians in this area. See John Tosh, *A Man's Place: Masculinity and the Middle-Class Home in Victorian England* (New Haven, CT: Yale University Press, 1999); and John Tosh, *Manliness and Masculinities in Nineteenth-Century Britain: Essays on Gender, Family, and Empire* (Harlow, UK: Pearson Education, 2005). Other foundational works include Gail Bederman, *Manliness and Civilization: A Cultural History of Gender and Race in the United States, 1880–1917* (Chicago: University of Chicago Press, 1996); and Angus McLaren, *The Trials of Masculinity: Policing Sexual Boundaries, 1870–1930* (Chicago: University of Chicago Press, 1997).

2 On recent work that moves from the critiques of patriarchy in women's histories to new studies grounded in the category of masculinity history, see John H. Arnold and Sean Brady, eds., *What Is Masculinity? Historical Dynamics from Antiquity to the Contemporary World* (Basingstoke, UK: Palgrave Macmillan, 2011). That collection features essays originally presented at the conference "What Is Masculinity?" held at Birkbeck College, University of London, in May 2008. John Tosh's contribution demonstrates the vitality of recent masculinity histories and offers suggestions for research methods that focus on lived experiences of masculinity rather than on the prescriptive discourses they generated in any given period. See John Tosh, "The History of Masculinity: An Outdated Concept?" in *What Is Masculinity? Historical Dynamics from Antiquity to the Contemporary World*, ed. John H. Arnold and Sean Brady, 17–35 (Basingstoke, UK: Palgrave Macmillan, 2011). Recent national and regional collections on masculinity history include Ann Rubenstein and Víctor M. Macías-González, eds., *Masculinity and Sexuality in Modern Mexico* (Albuquerque: University of New Mexico Press, 2012); Craig Thompson Friend, ed., *Southern Masculinity: Perspectives on Manhood in the South since Reconstruction* (Athens: University of Georgia Press, 2009); and Heather Ellis and Jessica Meyer, *Masculinity and the Other: Historical Perspectives* (Newcastle-upon-Tyne, UK: Cambridge Scholars, 2009), which is comprised of select papers presented at the interdisciplinary

conference "Masculinity and the Other," held at Balliol College, University of Oxford, in 'August 2007.

3 See Joan W. Scott, "Gender: A Useful Category of Historical Analysis," *American Historical Review* 91, 5 (1986): 1053–75, which can be compared to her assessment nearly two and a half decades later, "Gender: Still a Useful Category of Analysis?" *Diogenes* 57, 1 (2010): 13.

4 Christopher J. Greig and Wayne J. Martino's 2012 anthology is a testament to the growing momentum around masculinity studies in Canada. But Greig and Martino's volume is more centrally concerned with *contemporary* perspectives on manhood and masculinity in Canada, with historical essays and interpretations present but squarely in the minority. Christopher J. Greig and Wayne J. Martino, eds., *Canadian Men and Masculinities: Historical and Contemporary Perspectives* (Toronto: Canadian Scholars' Press, 2012).

5 For some further thoughts on the process of assembling this collection and articulating its major themes, see our discussion in the Afterword.

6 Sonya O. Rose, *What Is Gender History?* (Cambridge, UK: Polity, 2010), 57. For a useful survey of the origins of masculinity as a historical category, see Rose's fourth chapter, "Men and Masculinity," 56–79.

7 Michael S. Kimmel, *The History of Men: Essays in the History of American and British Masculinities* (Albany, NY: SUNY Press, 2005), ix. For an early statement from a women's historian on the need to address masculinity, see Natalie Zemon Davis, "'Women's History' in Transition: The European Case," *Feminist Studies* 3, 3–4 (1976): 90.

8 See, for instance, Kathryn McPherson, Cecilia Morgan, and Nancy Forestall, eds., *Gendered Pasts: Historical Essays in Femininity and Masculinity in Canada* (Toronto: Oxford University Press, 1999), 5–6.

9 Lynne Segal, *Slow Motion: Changing Masculinities, Changing Men,* 2nd ed. (New Brunswick, NJ: Rutgers University Press, 1995), 26. See also Lynne Segal, *Slow Motion: Changing Masculinities, Changing Men,* 3rd rev. ed. (Basingstoke, UK: Palgrave Macmillan, 2007), 26.

10 Segal, *Slow Motion,* 2nd ed., x, original emphasis.

11 Davis, "'Women's History.'"

12 Mark C. Carnes and Clyde Griffen, eds., *Meanings for Manhood: Constructions of Masculinity in Victorian America* (Chicago: University of Chicago Press, 1990), 6.

13 Ibid., 5. See also E. Anthony Rotundo, *American Manhood: Transformations in Masculinity from the Revolution to the Modern Era* (New York: Basic Books, 1993); Robert L. Griswold, *Fatherhood in America: A History* (New York: Basic Books, 1993); and Margaret S. Marsh, *Suburban Lives* (New Brunswick, NJ: Rutgers University Press, 1990).

14 Carnes and Griffen, eds., *Meanings for Manhood,* 6.

15 Note that the present anthology includes studies of gay and Indigenous men, suggesting that inattention to sexual and racialized minorities no longer characterizes the field, or at least not to the extent that it did a quarter-century ago. On the origins of salient twentieth-century masculine stereotypes in Europe, including "Fascist Man," "Soviet Man," and masculinity models in contemporary consumerism, see George L. Mosse, *The Image of Man: The Creation of Modern Masculinity* (Oxford: Oxford University Press, 1996).

16 Kimmel, *Manhood in America,* 1–2.

17 Rotundo, *American Manhood.*

18 Connell, *Masculinities,* 77. Connell's work on hegemonic masculinities underscored the pervasiveness of gender relationships that empower men over women, something that later attracted debate concerning its essentializing potential when applied to changing gender dynamics. For a useful discussion of the limits and potential of this concept, see R.W. Connell and James W. Messerschmidt, "Hegemonic Masculinity: Rethinking the Concept," *Gender and Society* 19, 6 (2005): 829–59.

19 Leonore Davidoff and Catherine Hall, *Family Fortunes: Men and Women of the English Middle Class, 1780–1850* (Chicago: University of Chicago Press, 1987), 30.
20 Ibid.
21 Ibid.
22 For a critique of this concept, see Robert B. Shoemaker, *Gender in English Society, 1650–1850: The Emergence of Separate Spheres?* (London and New York: Longman, 1998).
23 John Tosh, "What Should Historians Do with Masculinity?" in Tosh, *Manliness and Masculinities*, 42.
24 Tosh, *Man's Place*.
25 Tosh, "What Should Historians Do?" 4.
26 Ibid., 44.
27 Ibid., 45.
28 James Gilbert, *Men in the Middle: Searching for Masculinity in the 1950s* (Chicago: University of Chicago Press, 2005), 32.
29 Ibid., 33.
30 Joy Parr, *The Gender of Breadwinners: Women, Men, and Change in Two Industrial Towns* (Toronto: University of Toronto Press, 1990).
31 Ibid., 10.
32 Joy Parr, "Gender History and Historical Practice," *Canadian Historical Review* 76, 3 (1995): 371.
33 See Andrew C. Holman, *A Sense of Their Duty: Middle-Class Formation in Victorian Ontario Towns* (Montreal and Kingston: McGill-Queen's University Press, 2000), 160.
34 Mosse, *Image of Man*, 155.
35 Stephen Maynard, "Rough Work and Rugged Men: The Social Construction of Masculinity in Working-Class History," *Labour/Le Travail* 23 (1989): 159–69.
36 Gary Kinsman, *The Regulation of Desire: Homo and Hetero Sexualities*, 2nd rev. ed. (Montreal: Black Rose Books, 1996).
37 Thomas Dunk, *It's a Working Man's Town: Male Working-Class Culture in Northwestern Ontario* (Montreal and Kingston: McGill-Queen's University Press, 2003).
38 See Elizabeth Vibert, "Real Men Hunt Buffalo: Masculinity, Race and Class in British Fur Trader's Narratives," in *Gender and History in Canada*, ed. Joy Parr and Mark Rosenfeld, 50–67 (Toronto: Copp Clark, 1996); Colin Howell, "A Manly Sport: Baseball and the Social Construction of Masculinity," in Parr and Rosenfeld, *Gender and History in Canada*, 187–210; and Stephen Penfold, "'Have You No Manhood in You?' Gender and Class in the Cape Breton Coal Towns, 1920–26," in Parr and Rosenfeld, *Gender and History in Canada*, 270–93.
39 Gail Bederman, *Manliness and Civilization: A Cultural History of Gender and Race in the United States, 1880–1917* (Chicago: University of Chicago Press, 1996).
40 Tina Loo, "Of Moose and Men: Hunting for Masculinities in British Columbia, 1880–1939," *Western Historical Quarterly* 32, 3 (2001): 296–319.
41 Carolyn Podruchny, "Baptizing Novices: Ritual Moments among French Canadian Voyageurs in the Montreal Fur Trade, 1780–1821," *Canadian Historical Review* 83, 2 (2002): 165–95.
42 Craig Heron, "The Boys and Their Booze: Masculinities and Public Drinking in Working-Class Hamilton, 1890–1946," *Canadian Historical Review* 86, 3 (2005): 411–52.
43 Julia Roberts, *Mixed Company: Taverns and Public Life in Upper Canada* (Vancouver: UBC Press, 2009).
44 Tim Cook, "Fighting Words: Canadian Soldiers' Slang and Swearing in the Great War," *War in History* 20, 3 (2013): 323–44.

45 Christopher Dummitt, *The Manly Modern: Masculinity in Postwar Canada* (Vancouver: UBC Press, 2007), 13.

46 Ibid., 21.

47 This focus on postwar Canada is a strong trend in the literature and one to which we return in the Afterword to this volume.

48 Christopher J. Greig, *Ontario Boys: Masculinity and the Idea of Boyhood in Postwar Ontario, 1945–1960* (Waterloo, ON: Wilfrid Laurier University Press, 2014).

49 See Dummitt, *Manly Modern,* esp. ch. 3.

50 Notable, for example, is the exciting work of geographers Deryck Holdsworth and Julie Podmore and of architectural historians Paula Lupkin and Tania Martin. See Deryck Holdsworth, "'I'm a Lumberjack and I'm OK': The Built Environment and Varied Masculinities in the Industrial Age," in *Gender, Class, and Shelter: Perspectives in Vernacular Architecture V,* ed. Elizabeth Collins Cromley and Carter L. Hudgins, 11–25 (Knoxville: University of Tennessee Press, 1995); Julie Podmore, "Lesbians in the Crowd: Gender, Sexuality and Visibility along Montreal's Boul. St-Laurent," *Gender, Place and Culture: A Journal of Feminist Geography* 8, 4 (2001): 333–55; Paula Lupkin, *Manhood Factories: YMCA Architecture and the Making of Modern Urban Culture* (Minneapolis: University of Minnesota Press, 2010); Tania Martin, "Housing the Grey Nuns: Power, Women, and Religion in Fin-de-siècle Montréal," in *Perspectives in Vernacular Architecture VII,* ed. Annmarie Adams and Sally McMurry, 212–29 (Knoxville: University of Tennessee Press, 1997).

51 Peter DeLottinville, "Joe Beef of Montreal: Working-Class Culture and the Tavern, 1869–1889," *Labour/Le Travail* 8–9 (1981–1982): 9–40.

52 Butler writes, "If gender attributes ... are not expressive but performative, then these attributes effectively constitute the identity they are said to express or reveal. The distinction between expression and performativeness is crucial. If gender attributes and acts, the various ways in which a body shows or produces its cultural signification, are performative, then there is no pre-existing identity by which an act or attribute might be measured; there would be no true or false, real or distorted acts of gender, and the postulation of a true gender identity would be revealed as a regulatory fiction. That gender reality is created through sustained social performances means that the very notions of an essential sex and a true or abiding masculinity or femininity are also constituted as part of the strategy that conceals gender's performative character and the performative possibilities for proliferating gender configurations outside the restricting frames of masculinist domination and compulsory heterosexuality. Genders can be neither true nor false, neither real nor apparent, neither original nor derived. As credible bearers of those attributes, however, genders can also be rendered thoroughly and radically *incredible.*" Judith Butler, *Gender Trouble: Feminism and the Subversion of Identity* (New York: Routledge, 1990), 180, original emphasis.

53 Barbara Lorenzkowski, *Sounds of Ethnicity: Listening to German North America, 1850–1914* (Winnipeg: University of Manitoba Press, 2010).

54 Greig's term in Chapter 13 is "appropriate boyhood," but the idea seems to apply just as much to teenagers and young men negotiating their coming-of-age experiences.

55 See Christine Hudon and Louise Bienvenue, "Entre franche camaraderie et amours socratiques: L'espace trouble et ténu des amitiés masculines dans les collèges classiques (1840–1960)," *Revue d'histoire de l'Amérique française* 57, 4 (2004): 481–507; Christine Hudon and Louise Bienvenue, "Des collégiens et leurs maîtres au tournant du 20ᵉ siècle," *Globe: Revue internationale d'études québécoises* 8, 2 (2005): 41–71; and Louise Bienvenue and Christine Hudon, "'Pour devenir homme, tu transgresseras ...': Quelques enjeux de

la socialisation masculine dans les collèges classiques québécois (1880–1939)," *Canadian Historical Review* 86, 3 (2005): 485–511. Along with Ollivier Hubert, these authors recently collected these and other essays into a capstone volume for their project. See Louise Bienvenue, Ollivier Hubert, and Christine Hudon, *Le collège classique pour garçons: Études historiques sur une institution québécoise disparue* (Montreal: Fides, 2014).

56 Hansen's wheelchair tour of thirty-four countries from 1985 to 1987 raised awareness about spinal cord injuries as well as $26 million for medical research in that area. Rick Hansen Foundation, https://www.rickhansen.com/About-Us/About-the-Foundation.

57 For a recent literature review that focuses special attention on Quebec, see Peter Gossage, "*Au nom du père?* Rethinking the History of Fatherhood in Quebec," *American Review of Canadian Studies* 44, 1 (2014): 49–67.

58 In 2006 Jeffery Vacante made essentially this argument about the general state of masculinity history in Quebec. See Jeffery Vacante, "Liberal Nationalism and the Challenge of Masculinity Studies in Quebec," *Left History* 11, 2 (2006): 96–117, where he advances the claim that most scholars in this area "have tended to focus on the ways that men have suffered under the weight of patriarchal expectations" (106). A pioneering study that seems to conform to the pattern criticized by Vacante is Cynthia S. Fish, "Images and Reality of Fatherhood: A Case Study of Montreal's Protestant Middle Class, 1870–1914" (PhD diss., McGill University, 1991).

59 See "Who Is the Greatest Canadian? CBC Viewers Respond," https://www.jjmccullough.com/greatest%20Canadians.htm.

Part 1
Expertise and Authority

THE STUDY OF MASCULINE *expertise and authority* prompts us to think about powerful white men – including middle-class professionals, consultants, and managers – from a fresh perspective. Canadian scholarship in this area draws on the work of Raewyn Connell, Michael S. Kimmel, and others to explore hegemonic masculinities and their ebb and flow over time, as "the currently most honored way of being a man"[1] changes from generation to generation. Professional expertise – a combination of specialized knowledge, physical skill, and the mastery of increasingly sophisticated technology – is an important part of that discussion, as Christopher Dummitt has shown for postwar British Columbia.[2] In addition, Canadian scholars have been carefully unpacking the various components of professional and managerial power, which are inevitably rooted in regional realities and in diverse and evolving patterns of class, ethnic, and gender dynamics.

The four essays assembled here do exactly that, and in an interesting range of historical contexts. In Chapter 1, Lisa Chilton explores competing notions of masculine authority in what must surely be understood as a premodern setting: the scandal-ridden Quebec Marine and Emigrant Hospital from the late 1830s to the early 1850s. These scandals pitted physicians against each other, leading to a series of inquiries that provide Chilton with a fascinating set of sources, revealing much about standards and expectations for men at that time in positions of trust and authority. Although the setting is a century later, Magda Fahrni's discussion in Chapter 2 of the rise of an "accident-prevention infrastructure" in early-twentieth-century Quebec is similar in some key respects.

Expertise and leadership, especially in the workplace, are once again at the heart of the discussion. And the focus remains on the individual men, such as factory inspector Louis Guyon and coroner Edmond McMahon, who possessed and embodied specific masculine traits, especially the "reasoned expertise" (a concept borrowed from Dummitt) that drove and informed the provincial safety movement. With David Theodore's discussion in Chapter 3 of Gordon A. Friesen, a quintessentially modern *expert* by any definition, we return to the world of the hospital – which, as a workplace and as a technology for healing, had changed enormously in the century since the period discussed by Chilton.[3] As this chapter and its protagonist remind us, forms of male authority and expertise expanded alongside the planning and design of twentieth-century medical infrastructures – a modernist risk-management project par excellence. Theodore's chapter on Friesen hospitals as "machines for healing" leads nicely, if ironically, into Cynthia Loch-Drake's discussion in Chapter 4 of postwar management practices in Edmonton's meatpacking houses. These were modern food-processing plants that, arguably, given the new technologies and more centralized work processes in use, could increasingly be described as "machines for killing."[4] In particular, Loch-Drake shows that the industry shifted toward greater concentration, more technology, and a centralized system of collective bargaining. In the process, the expertise and authority that guided these operations – what Loch-Drake terms a "technocratic image of masculine corporate leadership" – replaced older, rougher notions of masculinity, rooted in the ideals of independence, individualism, and the self-made man.

Notes

1   This thumbnail definition can be found in R.W. Connell and James W. Messerschmidt, "Hegemonic Masculinity: Rethinking the Concept," *Gender and Society* 19, 6 (2005): 832.

2   See Christopher Dummitt, *The Manly Modern: Masculinity in Postwar Canada* (Vancouver: UBC Press, 2007), which was discussed in the Introduction and is cited by several authors in this section.

3   For a skilled exposition of this process in the Canadian context, see Annmarie Adams, *Medicine by Design: The Architect and the Modern Hospital, 1893–1943* (Minneapolis: University of Minnesota Press, 2008).

4   Both of these phrases are essentially riffs on Le Corbusier's iconic characterization of modernist houses as "machines for living."

1

Medical Men, Masculine Respectability, and the Contest for Power in Mid-Nineteenth-Century Quebec

Lisa Chilton

IN THE MIDDLE OF THE nineteenth century, the Quebec Marine and Emigrant Hospital was considered one of the most desirable medical-training institutions in the British Empire. Aspiring doctors from across North America fought to gain poorly paid and voluntary positions at the Marine and Emigrant Hospital both because it afforded an unusually wide range of opportunities for dissection and medical experimentation and because it boasted the educational leadership of some of the continent's most innovative and skilled practitioners.[1] Yet this hospital was not known solely for its impressive staff and (sometimes) impressive medical record. It also gained a notorious identity during this period. The Marine and Emigrant Hospital was a poorly managed and inadequately funded institution situated within a colonial context that was undergoing significant social and economic changes. Relationships among the hospital's medical staff and members of the larger community of Quebec's doctors were often tense and at times openly antagonistic, with the result that during the first three decades of its existence, the hospital became the focus of a series of public scandals involving malpractice suits, large-scale graft, accusations of unethical proselytizing, and sexually explicit slander and counter-slander.

Public scandals offer possibilities for the study of social behaviours and attitudes at particular moments in the past that might otherwise be difficult to access.[2] The five official investigations into the management of the Marine and Emigrant Hospital that were conducted between 1839 and 1853 were largely instigated by doctors, some of whom worked at the institution and some of whom did not. The resulting documents consist of hundreds of pages of witness statements, commissioners' reports, and privately published open letters and memoirs.[3] As a set, they provide a rich source of information about doctors' contests for power, representations of self and other, and everyday life in Quebec City's medical community at mid-century. Through an exploration of these documents as they relate to three prominent doctors – James Douglas, William Marsden, and Joseph Painchaud – this chapter provides a case study of the gendered nature of masculine identity making at the middle of the nineteenth century. The three individuals in question recorded characterizations of each other as ethnically and religiously suspect, inherently corrupt, and untrustworthy in their positions of authority, and in so doing, they both attacked each other's masculine credibility and confirmed their own behaviour as reflecting a superior form of masculinity.

In the introductory chapter of his book *The History of Men* (2005), Michael S. Kimmel neatly encapsulates masculinity as follows:

> Masculinities are constructed in a field of power: 1) the power of men over women; 2) the power of some men over other men. Men's power over women is relatively straightforward. It is the aggregate power of men as a group to determine the distribution of rewards in society. Men's power over other men concerns the distribution of those rewards among men by differential access to class, race, ethnic privileges, or privileges based on sexual orientation.[4]

Although one might question the "relatively straightforward" nature of men's power over women, the basic point of Kimmel's summary of how masculinities work serves as a useful starting point for a discussion of the behaviour of the doctors associated with the Quebec Marine and Emigrant Hospital in the mid-nineteenth century. In the records produced by and about these doctors, these men's efforts to demonstrate their own masculine credibility and to concurrently undermine that of doctors with whom they competed for work and for public favour are clearly in evidence. The three men studied here held approximately the same status in their community: they were all white, middle-class, relatively successful medical professionals. They were all highly motivated, ultimately well-celebrated doctors who did much to expand the power of mainstream male doctors in Canada. Yet as this chapter demonstrates, their understandings of the masculine ideal varied in significant ways.

Understanding the context within which the Marine and Emigrant Hospital staff functioned is essential for an appreciation of the nature and significance of these doctors' contests for power. Quebec City was a troubled urban space in the middle decades of the nineteenth century. It had been the administrative heart of the French Empire in North America for more than a century when New France was taken over by the British in 1763. Quebec continued to house the colony's government during most of the British North American period, and its leading citizens felt strongly that it ought to continue in that role. But already by the middle of the nineteenth century, it was clear that the focus of British North America's administration was shifting farther west, hastened by the westward focus of the economy. Economically, the city was superseded first by Montreal and then by Toronto. Quebec's declining fortunes made for much anxiety in the city's population, as jobs became scarce and businesses went bankrupt, all at the same time as large-scale immigration was fundamentally altering the city's demographic profile.[5] Franco-Canadians' convictions that Anglo-Canadian elites were working to reform Quebec to their own advantage added more specific grievances to the already simmering mix of ethnically based tensions.[6] French Canadian nationalism versus British imperialist agendas and Catholic versus Protestant rivalries featured strongly in the political discourse surrounding local and regional elections held during the middle decades of the century.[7] Major disasters in the form of epidemics and devastating fires[8] further undermined the stability of Quebec City's society. The city witnessed riots ignited by elections, competition for employment, and epidemics during the 1820s through the 1860s. The city's doctors would all have witnessed these troubles first-hand, although from significantly different perspectives.

The socio-political context within which Quebec City's doctors lived and worked was bound to produce behaviour that reflected the larger community's ongoing anxieties. Further contributing to the hostile social dynamics at the hospital was the aggressive professionalization of the field of medicine that was occurring at this time.[9] The middle of the century was still witness to contests for authority among various forms of medical practice. It was not until later in the century that orthodox medicine was able to effectively muscle homeopathy, osteopathy, and traditional female midwifery out of the field of legitimate medical practice. This meant that all mid-century medical practitioners would periodically feel the need to defend their practices and beliefs.[10] There was no medical school in British North America when the doctors at the centre of this study were receiving their training, which meant that doctors who trained within the region would have less impressive credentials than their colleagues who had trained at medical colleges in the United States, Britain, or Europe.[11] Such markers of professional standing became increasingly important in the middle decades of the nineteenth century. The move to professionalize medicine also resulted in efforts to establish medical associations and publications that would promote "appropriate" forms of medical practice. For ambitious doctors, taking on leadership roles in medical education, in professional associations, and in communicating research findings through publications served to elevate their own professional status.[12] All three of the doctors in this case study were heavily involved in these forms of professionalization.

The community of relatively ambitious doctors practising in Quebec City at mid-century was not very large. They worked together in a multitude of institutional settings, they established medical practices in combination, and they served on boards and on investigative commissions to oversee and review each other's work. Quebec City's most prominent medical men were also some of the city's most actively engaged public figures during this period. As a group, doctors were overrepresented in elected government positions.[13] Whereas the hospital's patients, nurses, domestics, and other menial staff were typically recently arrived emigrants from the British Isles, especially Ireland, the physicians and administrators were typically more closely tied to the host community. Some of the doctors were born in England or Scotland, but they were well-established members of Quebec society by the time of their engagement at the hospital. Social ties established through blood and marriage, mentorships, and long-term friendships connected the doctors with various competing local, regional, and imperial networks of influence and power. These social connections added extra challenges to colleagues' relationships, which were already strained by differences in ethnicity, religion, and political views.

The personnel at the Marine and Emigrant Hospital changed frequently during the 1830s and 1840s, especially at the lower levels of the institutional hierarchy. But by 1839 the leadership of the medical team was largely stable. Joseph Painchaud and James Douglas shared responsibility at the head of the hospital's group of visiting physicians throughout the period under study here. Technically, Douglas oversaw the surgical side of the practice, whereas Painchaud led work related to women's and children's maladies. Supervision of all other medical complaints was divided between them. In addition to Douglas and Painchaud were four visiting doctors, equal to each other in status, who had been selected for their positions on the basis of their reputations within the profession. All six visiting doctors were associated with this hospital only on a part-time basis; all had private practices and other institutional affiliations on the side. The live-in house surgeon was outranked by all of the hospital's visiting physicians. He worked most closely on a daily basis with the live-in apothecary, who was usually a doctor-in-training. Also attached to the hospital were students who followed in the wake of Douglas and Painchaud as they performed their on-site medical duties. Members of the male medical community at this hospital were all fully aware of how they fitted within the group's power structure. Although those who considered themselves bullied by the men above them clearly resented their superiors' abuse of power, it was evident to all that it was professionally suicidal to complain too loudly. Passing through a period of training or early-career practice at the Marine and Emigrant Hospital was a masculine rite of passage for dozens of medical professionals in Quebec City. William Marsden, the third doctor studied in this chapter, had no formal relationship with the Marine and Emigrant Hospital, although he took a keen personal interest in its affairs.

James Douglas served as the institution's principal surgeon from 1837 through the early 1850s. An emigrant from Scotland, Douglas arrived in Quebec in 1826 in his mid-twenties with significant professional qualifications. Having served a five-year apprenticeship in England, Douglas studied for and obtained a diploma for surgery from the Royal College of Surgeons in Edinburgh, after which he studied at and received a diploma from the Royal College of Surgeons in London. After an extensive period of travel and medical practice on a whaling ship, in India, and in Central America, he moved to the United States, where he worked as a lecturer on anatomy and surgery at the medical college in Auburn, activities for which he was awarded an honorary doctorate in medicine by Williams College in New York State.[14]

William Marsden had some basic characteristics in common with James Douglas. He was a British emigrant with a Protestant background. Born in Lancashire, England, Marsden settled in Lower Canada with his family in 1812 at the age of five. Like Douglas, he received his medical education on the other side of the Atlantic, first in London and then as a postgraduate student in Paris. By the end of his career, Marsden had also gained an impressive reputation within the medical profession.[15] But although Marsden and Douglas may have had similar backgrounds, their behaviour and attitudes differed in significant respects, and these differences made for conflict. The foundations of Marsden's animosity toward Douglas and his colleagues at the Marine and Emigrant Hospital are relatively easy to trace. In the late 1830s the doctors at the hospital had taken the unusual step of banning Marsden from the institution. So strongly did they feel that Marsden ought not to be allowed into the hospital that they used the fact that his brother-in-law, Dr. Andrew, had permitted Marsden's entry into the hospital wards against their orders as part of their justification for Andrew's dismissal from his post as house surgeon.[16] The humiliation associated with this earlier experience was obviously a driving force behind Marsden's vitriolic denunciations of the hospital's medical staff in the 1840s and early 1850s.

Born in 1787 in Quebec City, Joseph Painchaud was older than Douglas and Marsden, and he was fully immersed in the Lower Canadian Catholic community. Unlike his colleagues, who had had the benefit of transatlantic experience and medical college educations, Painchaud's educational credentials ended with the completion of his apprenticeship under Quebec garrison surgeon James Fisher. That Fisher was a very well-respected, influential member of Quebec's medical community served Painchaud well in the early years of his profession, in part because this early period of training had him establishing solid relationships with other students of Fisher who were more closely associated with the

Anglo-Canadian social world of Quebec. Painchaud's relative lack of certifica-
tion, compared with doctors like Douglas and Marsden, did not seem to hold
him back. He became a powerful figure within the medical teaching community of Quebec, and through his extensive organizational work, he gained
prestigious positions within local and regional medical associations.[17] However, Painchaud's comparatively provincial training and experience would be
duly alluded to in the war of words waged by members of his profession during
the course of the various investigations into the work of the Marine and Emigrant
Hospital.

Of all of the doctors associated with the hospital, James Douglas had the
most formidable reputation. Douglas was a physically large individual, with a
personality to match. He had a reputation for being strong-willed and arrogant.
In the words of his son, who wrote a glowing introduction to Douglas's posthumously published *Reminiscences*, "when he undertook any public work or
advocated any public measure ... he threw his whole strength into the enterprise
or its advocacy, with such impulsive energy that he bore down all opposition
and carried his point by sheer force of attack."[18] According to his son, Douglas
had a soft side:

> Though overbearing, there lay in his nature a depth of tenderness, which never
> came to the surface more attractively than in the presence of pain. While intoler-
> ant of disobedience or querulousness on the part of his patients, many a sufferer
> lay in unrest for hours waiting for his visit and for the luxury of being lifted and
> turned by his strong arms, and encouraged by his unfaltering and sincere
> opinion.[19]

Unlike many of his fellow practitioners, Douglas believed strongly that medical
service and politics ought not to mix. As a doctor, he felt that his first duty was
to his patients and that engaging in politics would merely serve as a distraction
from his more important medical responsibilities.

Although Douglas was critical of colleagues who engaged in politics on the
side, he was convinced that physical distractions from the stress of a doctor's
daily work were essential to the maintenance of one's own health and thus,
ultimately, to the service of one's patients. In his autobiography, Douglas outlined
his understanding of the usefulness of physical activity – in his case, fishing and
hunting – as a restorative "when mind or body, or both, are exhausted by long
continued strain upon their energies."[20] Douglas's description of his fishing and
hunting expeditions emphasized the physicality and close-to-nature aspects of
his pursuits. His daily fishing excursions involved a lengthy hike via an "Indian
trail" to fishing grounds well beyond the area used by most other anglers from

town where he could sport with trout whose "size and game qualities would have delighted old Isaac Walton."[21] Douglas represented himself as a man who had a strong connection with the First Nations communities of the region, and he drew upon compelling images of Native men in the imagery he associated with himself. He knew where to find the best fishing grounds because of their shared insights, and his hunting expeditions were with his Huron friends. In the aftermath of a particularly draining period of medical practice, Douglas chose to retire from civilization for some manly recuperation. "I thought that perhaps the best mode, or the mode best suited to my natural tastes, would be to throw physic to the dogs for a few days and explore the virgin forests, among the hills to the North of Quebec," he wrote. Some of the hunters of the Huron of Lorette had discovered moose resident about 50 miles north of Quebec, and Douglas "agreed to accompany them to the hunt as soon as the snow was sufficiently deep."[22] Needless to say, the hunting expedition was a success![23]

Although women ran Douglas's home, it was decorated to convey the owner's masculine identity. Edward D. Worthington, who had studied medicine under indenture to Douglas, and later under both Douglas and Painchaud at the Marine and Emigrant Hospital, included descriptions of both doctors in his reminiscences. These descriptions demonstrate how both Douglas and Painchaud made a show of their privileged positions in society, if in very different and rather eccentric ways. Douglas lived on Mountain Hill in a spectacular home that would later serve as a hotel. Although the house itself was impressive, it was the "huge stuffed moose, with immense horns, a trophy of the Doctor's skill as a hunter," which stood sentry at the bottom of the circular staircase in the drawing room, that gained the most respect from Douglas's visitors. According to Worthington, "nearly every celebrity of the day who visited Quebec called and asked permission to see the moose."[24]

James Douglas's reputation as a doctor was even more impressive than his temper and his skills as an outdoorsman. Edward Worthington reflected the general opinion of the medical community when he wrote, many years later, that Douglas was an absolutely brilliant operator: "It was not only that he did his work quickly, but he did it well, and his operations were simply splendid." Douglas's superior abilities were clearly demonstrated when he joined another surgeon to perform the simultaneous amputation of both of the legs below the knees of a sailor who had suffered serious frostbite. In the case of the amputation performed by Douglas, "From the instant the point of the knife entered, till the leg was on the floor was *one minute and forty-two seconds* ... The vessels were tied and the wound dressed inside of three minutes." The other leg, removed by Douglas's colleague, was not quite stitched up after a half an hour.[25] As Martin Pernick's classic study of surgery during the period of transition to the use of anesthesia demonstrates, speed and effectiveness as a surgeon who was working with conscious patients required a significant amount of physical strength and a serious lack of squeamishness.[26] It is thus hardly surprising that descriptions of Douglas's success as a surgeon emphasized his masculine physicality and decisiveness of action.

Even William Marsden, who clearly despised Douglas, avoided criticizing his professional skills when commenting upon Douglas's inadequacies. According to Marsden, Douglas was not worthy of his position as the hospital's highest medical authority because he was not capable of leading or educating those under him with the necessary degree of tact and diplomacy required of the position. Rather than possessing too little masculinity, Douglas was presented by Marsden – and others associated with the hospital who questioned Douglas's right to his position – as lacking the *right sort* of masculine traits: control of temper, good social judgment, and dignity without arrogance. For Marsden, Douglas's tendency to be overbearing, domineering, and contemptuous of others indicated that he should not be allowed to hold a leadership position at this particularly important hospital.[27] The conclusions of the committee tasked with the investigation of the Marine and Emigrant Hospital in 1853 agreed, although the committee found it impossible to dismiss Douglas from his post. Douglas chose to spend less and less time working at the hospital in the aftermath of the investigation. As his son put it, he continued to work there only long enough to show that he had not been pushed out.[28]

In his work on the evolution of masculine identities and behaviours over the course of the eighteenth and nineteenth centuries, John Tosh has highlighted the increasing importance of the concept of self-control. As Tosh notes, men's abilities to channel their responses to provocation away from physical aggression were central to middle-class reformulations of appropriate male behaviour. Instead of physical contests among men trying to prove their honour, men proved their masculine credentials through shows of character.[29] In the doctors' representations of themselves and others, the subject of relative self-control was regularly in the foreground. Just as Marsden criticized Douglas for his temper and his tendency to ridicule others, in Douglas's comments about the shortcomings of Marsden, the subject of restraint and discipline played a central role. Whereas Marsden considered Douglas to be a tyrant, Douglas made it clear that he felt that Marsden (and his discharged brother-in-law, Dr. Andrew) drank too much to be worthy of a position of authority at any public institution. A determined abstainer himself, Douglas had no patience for men he considered to be drunkards.[30] In Douglas's opinion, Andrew had been fully exposed as an untrustworthy, morally corrupt doctor when it became evident that he had falsified a medical certificate for a ship's captain so that the captain would not be fined and dismissed from his position on account of his intemperance.[31] He held Marsden partly responsible for Andrew's faulty moral compass. Douglas claimed that a significant change in the general tenor of the institution was evident during Andrew's term as the hospital's house surgeon: "The Hospital [became] the scene of brawls, noises, disturbances by night, and very indecorous behaviour, not so much on [Andrew's] part, as on the part of his relative and friend, Dr. Marsden." Douglas referred to Marsden as Andrew's "coarse" company, a man lacking decency and self-restraint.[32]

Although James Douglas was scathingly critical of Marsden's morals, he could be enthusiastic in his praise of Marsden's professional skills. One such instance of praise related to Marsden's abilities as a mesmerist. According to Douglas, Marsden possessed "considerable mesmeric power," as was demonstrated during an operation performed by Douglas to excise half of a man's lower jaw. "The patient was a powerful, a strong minded, and a sensible man, about fifty years of age," a factor that no doubt contributed to the success of the undertaking as far as Douglas was concerned. "Dr. Marsden mesmerised him thoroughly," wrote Douglas, "while I removed the diseased bone, an operation, which from its peculiar nature, occupied a much longer time in its performance, than an amputation of a limb."[33] As described by Douglas, this exercise certainly demonstrated that Marsden was a man of impressive mental strength despite his fatally flawed moral character.

Historians of gender have had much to say about the establishment of men's and women's separate spheres. Since the publication of Leonore Davidoff and Catherine Hall's *Family Fortunes: Men and Women of the English Middle Class, 1780–1850* (1987), which promotes the idea that a central tenet of middle-class life in the nineteenth century was the separation of home and work, historians have been working to nuance this understanding in order to show how in fact the private and the public were more integrated, in various ways, than the findings of *Family Fortunes* and other studies like it might suggest. According to Tosh, "recent scholarship has done more than adjust the balance between public and private; it has called into question the validity of the distinction itself."[34] Yet whatever the reality of lived experience, the concept of gendered spheres heavily influenced personal and public identities. Domestic relations could be critical to masculine identities in the middle of the nineteenth century, although the relationship between domesticity and masculinity was not without its contradictions and resulting tensions.[35]

James Douglas's memoirs, written well after the events of the 1840s and 1850s, are striking for the absence of any reference to familial matters or private concerns. They read like a typically heroic narrative of manly actions and observations. Douglas was predeceased by two wives, and he had at least three children, two of whom died as infants, yet the women and children in his life do not receive any notice in these pages. Likewise, the private sufferings of his brother, George, who committed suicide after the death of his wife and the loss of his position as head doctor at Grosse Isle Quarantine Station, are not given space in Douglas's written reminiscences. He brought two younger brothers (one of whom was George) over from Scotland to help him with his own medical practice in the early years of his career, so he was clearly willing to combine family and business when it suited him to do so. But he was adamant that family and work should not mix in a public institution like the Marine and Emigrant Hospital.[36]

An exploration of documents pertaining to Marsden and Painchaud suggests that, unlike Douglas, these men could not keep their private lives separate from their professional identities, with the result that they opened themselves up to charges of flawed masculinity. Both men received professionally oriented criticism – although ultimately, it seems, little professional penalty – for how they conducted themselves in relation to matters that might be considered private. For example, when the hospital's house surgeon, Charles Eusèbe Lemieux, was accused by Marsden of establishing a prohibited sexual relationship with one of the hospital's nurses, Lemieux fired back that Marsden could have no legitimate grounds for making such a claim and that his own reputation would not stand up to scrutiny: "Is he not, in fact, notorious ... for his immorality? Does not the public know, that although a married man, he is the fancy-man and the bully of a house of ill-fame? Has he not been seen walking, without shame, through the streets of the city, with the ignoble mistress of the bawdy-house which he patronises?"[37] Other witnesses insinuated that Marsden's relationships with female patients were also highly questionable. He chose to spend off-hours time socializing in the women's wards at a hospital where he did not have the right to practise. Of particular note was Marsden's obvious interest in spending time with an attractive young woman whom the other doctors thought to be infected with syphilis.[38] Marsden's extramarital interactions with women were clearly noteworthy for the public record, as far as his colleagues were concerned. But as in the parallel world of contemporary Lower Canadian politics, whatever private stigma there may have been associated with Marsden's extramarital relations, they would not significantly impact his professional standing.[39]

In a privately published and extensively circulated pamphlet, Marsden made his own accusations about the sullied natures of his detractors. The animosity between Douglas and Marsden was not conveyed in subtle terms; he made it clear that between himself and Douglas, "not the slightest sympathy" had existed for several years, a claim that was well supported in evidence given by Douglas at various meetings over the years with the hospital's commissioners. Yet Marsden's dislike of Douglas's *Canadien* associates at the hospital, especially Painchaud, led to even more rhetorically violent exchanges. Marsden described Painchaud as corrupt of mind and "recreant in both morals and professional character and standing,"[40] and he was emphatic in his opinion that all of the other French Canadian doctors at the hospital were as poorly suited to their positions as Painchaud. Marsden's criticism of Painchaud was especially heated when it related to subjects that suggested a blurring of lines between Painchaud's domestic life and professional identity.

For his interventions to have his son serve as the house surgeon of the hospital, and then for his protests against Douglas's tyranny over his son once he was in that position, Painchaud was roundly criticized by both Douglas and Marsden. Painchaud was Marsden's senior by twenty years, and the younger doctor clearly resented the extent to which Painchaud had exerted influence over the workings of the hospital and beyond during the course of his career. In Marsden's opinion, "The Marine and Emigrant Hospital [had] been under gallic dominion from the day the trickey doyen [Painchaud] entered it until now: he having exercised the 'banal' right of officering it exclusively: either from his family, his relatives or his students."[41]

Marsden described Painchaud's familial-centred nepotism as a form of professional corruption. In his representation of Painchaud's medical practice related to female patients, he was even more explicit about the gendered nature of his own superiority over Painchaud. Marsden described Painchaud as "a man whose very breath is pollution, occupying the high position of Lecturer on Midwifery ... where, 'out of the fullness of heart,' *every lecture* to the listening student is charged with some foul or filthy joke or anecdote, so vile that he would not be allowed to occupy a like chair in any school in Europe for a week."[42] Donning the mantle of protector of female virtue, Marsden described in shocked tones how Painchaud's total lack of understanding of chivalric decency permitted him to treat women in childbirth as on-show exhibits for large groups of male students. As evidence, he cited the example of Bridget McDermot, who was so intimidated by her audience of twenty-four students and two doctors that her labour was delayed by as much as a day and a half.[43]

Marsden was explicit that Painchaud's ethnic identity was at the root of his uncouth behaviour and that this doctor's "papist" religious affiliation alone should be enough to warrant his removal from the hospital. Painchaud was not the only French Canadian doctor at the Marine and Emigrant Hospital to receive this sort of critical review from Marsden. In fact, by 1853 Marsden seems to have made it a personal mission to eliminate *Canadien* and Catholic influence from this hospital altogether. In a privately published open letter to the hospital's new commissioners, Marsden noted that *Canadiens* had no innate European sensibility and thus unwittingly insulted patients on a regular basis. He asked the officials to bear in mind, when considering how the hospital should be staffed, "that the patients are British and Irish, and that their natural feelings and sympathies are the same."[44] It is difficult to assess to what extent Marsden's opinions of the francophone members of the medical community were shared by his anglophone colleagues, but it is evident that many doctors within the community were relatively comfortable working within an ethnically mixed environment. For example, Douglas established long-lasting and very close professional partnerships with francophone Lower Canadians. Painchaud was Douglas's choice for a partner with whom to serve as head doctor when he was hired at the institution in 1837, and these two men worked closely together for over fifteen years at the hospital. It was only when Douglas was seen to be actively undermining the confidence and reputation of Painchaud's son that there was a falling out between the men. Douglas also worked closely with Dr. Charles-Jacques Frémont, a man he considered an exceptionally capable doctor and "an honest, an upright, and a high-minded gentleman,"[45] and the fact that the house surgeons and apothecaries at the Marine and Emigrant Hospital were francophone and Catholic does not seem to have troubled Douglas.

The documents reviewed here do not contain physical descriptions of Marsden. A small photograph published in a biographical sketch of the doctor suggests that he likely chose to visually represent himself as solidly, respectably mainstream.[46] Douglas's physical persona has already been discussed. The physical descriptions and extant photographs of Douglas suggest that he, too, ably fitted the mould of the mid-nineteenth century, unflamboyant professional male that is detailed in Jan Noel's study of masculinity and male attire in Montreal. Noel suggests that although Franco- and Anglo-Canadians originated in cultures that had different attitudes toward clothing and gendered behaviour, these differences had been seriously undermined by the 1840s. "The French have never shared the Anglo-American conviction that makes the fashionable the opposite of the serious," writes Noel. Yet the nineteenth-century portraits of her case studies indicated that "French colonials fell victim to London's male fashion dictates, just as their nineteenth-century Parisian cousins did." Noel's conclusion is that "their common masculinity drove [the two cultural groups of men] together more than their cultures drove them apart, both in concepts of manhood and in dress."[47] Thus, by the mid-1840s, severe black suits and white starched collars had completely replaced the ruffles, colours, and silky fabrics of men's clothing of an earlier era.

Painchaud's visual representation of masculinity serves as an alternative to the men reviewed in Noel's work. He clearly ignored the mid-nineteenth-century expectation that respectable professional men would shun fun and frivolous attire for the serious black wear, devoid of ornamentation, that was presumably being donned by his colleagues. As described by Edward Worthington, Painchaud performed his medical house calls "resplendent in waistcoats, worn almost as loose as a blouse – of purple or bright scarlet silk, and most exquisitely got up shirt frills. Wellington boots he wore with trousers strapped tightly down, silver spurs and chains, and in his 'fob' he carried a heavy bunch of seals." He did most of his visiting of patients around Quebec City on an exceptionally well-trained, unusually large horse that had "evidently been a Military Charger." When a visit was concluded and Painchaud called for his horse, which had been allowed to wander freely in his absence, "the horse marched up, got his lump of sugar, wheeled his left side to the sidewalk for the Doctor to mount, and off he went prancing, to the great admiration of the [neighbourhood's] small boys."[48] Painchaud clearly aimed for visual display when he was on his medical rounds!

Although it appears that Worthington remembered Painchaud's flamboyant appearance with some amusement, he was otherwise respectful of his former medical instructor. Painchaud's penchant for flashy clothing does not seem to have had any negative impact on his professional standing. In Worthington's opinion, Painchaud had the largest francophone practice in Quebec City,[49] and according to Painchaud's biographer, he "had considerable influence with his *confrères*, governments, and in councils and medical societies." One of the posts that Painchaud was assigned as a mark of his high status in the medical community was that of "commissioner responsible for supervising the application in the Quebec region of 'the ordinance to prevent unlicensed persons from practising medicine and surgery in the province of Quebec or midwifery in the cities of Quebec or Montreal.'" It was a position that would see him contribute substantially to the masculinization of the medical profession by shutting down female midwives' work in this field.[50]

Over the past couple of decades, historians of masculinity have substantially expanded our understandings of how men's behaviour and identities have changed over time. Within the historiography on masculinity, the Victorian period has been the subject of particular interest. Recent emphases in studies of Victorian masculinity have confirmed the central importance of work, public service, domesticity, and the development of "character" to middle-class men's identities during this period. Although the evidence reviewed here that relates to the identities of three doctors who obtained a significant amount of professional success in Quebec City in the middle decades of the nineteenth century certainly fits these criteria, the specific context within which they lived and worked, and the men's personal orientations within that context, clearly impacted how each expressed his masculinity.

Quebec City was situated within a colonial context in which colonized Franco-Canadians, settled Anglo-Canadians, and British newcomers struggled to establish themselves in uncertain relationship with each other.[51] They lived in a colony that was undergoing a period of painful political, administrative, and economic transition. And as medical practitioners, these men were involved in a process of professionalization that required significant personal investment. With Quebec City still predominantly French-speaking and overwhelmingly Catholic in religious affiliation, but with positions of power increasingly dominated by men associated with Anglo-Canada, the potential for antagonism where different elements of the community came together was great. The Marine and Emigrant Hospital was certainly one such context. Not only did it contain residents and visiting physicians from a wide variety of backgrounds, but it was also a highly visible public institution that lay at the centre of many ambitious doctors' efforts to gain greater professional legitimacy and power. These efforts generated conflicts that were fought out through gendered representations of middle-class respectability and authority. In their relationships with other colleagues and with the larger public, Douglas, Marsden, and Painchaud established three notably different masculine identities. In spite of their shared class and professional occupation, these were men who held fundamentally different understandings of how men of their class and professional standing ought to behave. As a result, their battles with each other, stemming from perceptions of injured pride and honour, involved public pronouncements of character flaws most closely associated with a lack of appropriate masculinity.

Notes

1 For this reason, many officials felt that no remuneration was necessary for the institution's visiting doctors; the increased status and associated growth of the doctors' private practices were considered payment enough. Evidence of this attitude may be found in documents throughout the investigations used in this study. A short but interesting history of the hospital may be found in Sylvio LeBlond, "The Marine Hospital of Quebec," *Historical Bulletin* 21, 2 (1956): 33–35.
2 Kirsten McKenzie makes this point well in her book *Scandal in the Colonies: Sydney and Cape Town, 1820–1850* (Carlton: Melbourne University Press, 2004). The documents produced in the course of the government's examination of the scandals at the Quebec Marine and Emigrant Hospital in the 1840s and 1850s also served as the base for my article on the experiences of a nurse who became a prime focus of gossip at the institution during this period. See Lisa Chilton, "Sex Scandals and Papist Plots: The Mid-Nineteenth-Century World of an Irish Nurse in Quebec," *Journal of Women's History* 27, 3 (2015): 109–31.
3 Documents pertaining to the five official investigations may be found in the following locations: for the first investigation (1839–1840), see Library and Archives Canada (LAC), RG4, C1, Provincial Secretary, Canada East, Numbered Correspondence Files, 1839–1840; for the second investigation (1846–1847), see LAC, RG4, C1, vol. 124; for the third and fourth investigations (1849–1851), see the *Appendix to the 10th Volume of the Journals of*

the Legislative Assembly, Canada, 20th May to 30th August, 4th Session, 1851 (hereafter *1851 Report*); and for the fifth investigation (1853), see *Report of Drs. Nelson and MacDonnell, and Zephirin Perrault, Esq., Advocate, of the Quebec Marine and Emigrant Hospital* (Quebec: John Lovell, 1853) (hereafter *1853 Report*). See also William Marsden, *Facts and Observations connected with the Management of the Marine and Emigrant Hospital, Quebec, including a Report of the Trial and Acquittal of Thomas Burke ...* (Quebec: n.p., 1852).

4 Michael S. Kimmel, "Inside Masculinity," in *The History of Men: Essays in the History of American and British Masculinities* (Albany, NY: SUNY Press, 2005), 6–7.

5 For details on immigration and its impact on Quebec City during this period, see John A. Dickinson and Brian Young, *A Short History of Quebec and Canada,* 4th ed. (Montreal and Kingston: McGill-Queen's University Press, 2008), 112; Robert J. Grace, "A Demographic and Social Profile of Quebec City's Irish Populations, 1842–1861," *Journal of American Ethnic History* 23, 1 (2003): 55; and Fernand Ouellet, *Lower Canada, 1791–1840: Social Change and Nationalism,* trans. Patricia Claxton (Toronto: McClelland and Stewart, 1980), 61.

6 Perceptions of related injustices led to open resistance on the part of some Franco-Canadians. See Dickinson and Young, *Short History,* chs. 4 and 5; Ouellet, *Lower Canada,* esp. ch. 7; Michael Ernest McCulloch, "The Defeat of Imperial Urbanism in Quebec City, 1840–1855," *Urban History Review/Revue d'histoire urbaine* 22, 1 (1993): 17–29.

7 David De Brou, "The Rose, the Shamrock and the Cabbage: The Battle for Irish Voters in Upper-Town Quebec, 1827–1836," *Histoire sociale/Social History* 24, 48 (1991): 305–34.

8 Lorne Green, *Chief Engineer: Life of a Nation-Builder – Sandford Fleming* (Toronto: Dundurn, 1993), 7.

9 The professionalization of medicine was, by this point, very much a masculine enterprise. See C. Lesley Biggs, "The Case of the Missing Midwives: A History of Midwifery in Ontario from 1795–1900," *Ontario History* 75, 1 (1983): 21; Mary Walsh, *Doctors Wanted, No Women Need Apply: Sexual Barriers in the Medical Profession, 1835–1975* (New Haven, CT: Yale University Press, 1977); and Constance Backhouse, "The Celebrated Abortion Trial of Dr. Emily Stowe, Toronto, 1879," *Canadian Bulletin of Medical History* 8, 2 (1991): 159–87.

10 For examples, see documents related to the efforts of Dr. Andrew to defend himself against charges of malpractice in 1839, located in LAC, RG4, C1, Provincial Secretary, Canada East, Numbered Correspondence Files, 1839–1840, vol. 6, no. 1214, 5; and the case of the deceased seaman discussed in Marsden, *Facts and Observations.* For further discussion of the unstable nature of the medical profession in mid-nineteenth-century Canada, see Geoffrey Bilson, "Canadian Doctors and the Cholera," in *Medicine in Canadian Society: Historical Perspectives,* ed. S.E.D. Shortt (Montreal and Kingston: McGill-Queen's University Press, 1981), 118–23.

11 McGill was the first university to open a medical school in Lower Canada. Its first semester of classes took place in the fall of 1823, after most of the doctors discussed here had completed their studies.

12 For a tight summary of the history of the profession, see Jacques Bernier, *Disease, Medicine and Society in Canada: A Historical Overview* (Ottawa: Canadian Historical Association, 2003), esp. 3–12 on the period under discussion. For more thorough overviews of the professionalization of medicine, see W.F. Bynum, *Science and the Practice of Medicine in the Nineteenth Century* (New York: Cambridge University Press, 1994); and Paul Starr, *The Social Transformation of American Medicine: The Rise of a Sovereign Profession and the Making of a Vast Industry* (New York: Basic Books, 1982).

13 For example, see De Brou, "Rose, the Shamrock."

14 Sylvio Leblond, "James Douglas," *Dictionary of Canadian Biography*, vol. 2 (1982), 270–1.
15 A summary of Marsden's accomplishments is communicated in A.D.K., "Our Forgotten Man," *Canadian Medical Association Journal* 96, 22 (1967): 1485–86. Marsden was clearly impressed by the need to convey his professional rank in his written critiques of his fellow doctors. In his self-published condemnation of the medical staff of the Quebec Marine and Emigrant Hospital, Marsden signed himself "Governor of the College of Physicians and Surgeons of Canada East." Marsden, *Facts and Observations*.
16 LAC, RG4, C1, Provincial Secretary, Canada East, Numbered Correspondence Files, 1839–1840.
17 Charles-Marie Boissonnault, "Joseph Painchaud," *Dictionary of Canadian Biography*, vol. 10 (1871–1880).
18 James Douglas Jr., "Introduction," in James Douglas, *Journals and Reminiscences of James Douglas, M.D.* (New York: n.p., 1910), 11.
19 Ibid.
20 James Douglas, *Journals and Reminiscences of James Douglas, M.D.* (New York: n.p., 1910), 136.
21 Ibid., 137. Izaak Walton was a much-celebrated English authority on fly fishing.
22 Ibid., 138.
23 For a fascinating analysis of these sorts of activities by mid-nineteenth-century Anglo-Canadians, see Gillian Poulter, *Becoming Native in a Foreign Land: Sport, Visual Culture, and Identity in Montreal, 1840–1885* (Vancouver: UBC Press, 2009), esp. ch. 3. For an interesting, rather different exploration of the relationship between a retreat to nature and masculine rejuvenation, see Paul R. Deslandes, "Curing Mind and Body in the Heart of the Canadian Rockies: Empire, Sexual Scandal and the Reclamation of Masculinity, 1880s–1920s," *Gender and History* 21, 2 (2009): 358–79.
24 Quoted in Douglas, *Journals and Reminiscences*, 164–65.
25 Quoted in ibid., 170–71, original emphasis.
26 Martin Pernick, *A Calculus of Suffering: Pain, Professionalism, and Anesthesia in Nineteenth-Century America* (New York: Columbia University Press, 1985).
27 Marsden, *Facts and Observations*.
28 Douglas Jr., "Introduction."
29 John Tosh, "Masculinities in an Industrializing Society: Britain, 1800–1914," *Journal of British Studies* 44, 2 (2005): 334.
30 For discussion of the ways that during this period liquor consumption could be a "badge of manhood" yet both the source and symptom of undermined masculinity, see E. Anthony Rotundo, *American Manhood: Transformations in Masculinity from the Revolution to the Modern Era* (New York: Basic Books, 1993), 180. For similar observations regarding Quebec during this period, see Jan Noel, "Defrocking Dad: Masculinity and Dress in Montreal, 1700–1867," in *Fashion: A Canadian Perspective*, ed. Alexander Palmer (Toronto: University of Toronto Press, 2004), 81.
31 See the discussion concerning patient Millar in LAC, RG4, C1, Provincial Secretary, Canada East, Numbered Correspondence Files, 1839–1840.
32 LAC, RG4, C1, vol. 6, Provincial Secretary, Canada East, Numbered Correspondence Files, 1839–1840, Declaration of James Douglas.
33 Douglas, *Journals and Reminiscences*, 144.
34 Tosh, *Man's Place*, 2.
35 Ibid., 7. Tosh writes at length about the significance of the family for men's public identities. See especially his "Introduction: Masculinity and Domesticity," in ibid. For an

interesting case study of this subject, see Veronica Strong-Boag, *Liberal Hearts and Coronets: The Lives and Times of Ishbel Marjoribanks Gordon and John Campbell Gordon, the Aberdeens* (Toronto: University of Toronto Press, 2015).

36 Douglas was most explicit about his opinions related to this question in the investigations of 1851 and 1853.

37 *1851 Report,* statement of Charles Eusèbe Lemieux recorded on May 1, 1851.

38 See commentary on the case of Miss Jamieson in LAC, RG4, C1, Provincial Secretary Correspondence 1839–1840, #1214, copy of charges preferred against Dr. Andrew by the Visiting Physicians and his defence.

39 For some interesting context in this respect, see the discussion of George-Etienne Cartier's extramarital relationship with Luce Cuvillier in Brian Young, *George-Etienne Cartier: Montreal Bourgeois* (Montreal and Kingston: McGill-Queen's University Press, 1981), 52.

40 Marsden, *Facts and Observations,* 17–18.

41 Ibid., 30–31.

42 Ibid., 17–18, original emphasis.

43 Reference to this event is made in LAC, RG4, C1, Provincial Secretary, Canada East, Numbered Correspondence Files, 1839–1840, Copy of charges preferred against Dr. Andrew by the Visiting Physicians and his defence.

44 Marsden, *Facts and Observations,* 30–31.

45 Douglas, *Journals and Reminiscences,* 147.

46 David A.E. Shephard, "Dr. William Marsden," *Canadian Journal of Anaesthesia/Journal canadien d'anesthésie* 39, 5 (1992): 512.

47 Noel, "Defrocking Dad," 70.

48 Quoted in Douglas, *Journals and Reminiscences,* 170.

49 Quoted in ibid.

50 Boissonnault, "Joseph Painchaud."

51 For a discussion of how newcomers of a lower class fitted into the social dynamics outlined here, see Chilton, "Sex Scandals," 109–31.

2

Accident Prevention in Early-Twentieth-Century Quebec and the Construction of Masculine Technical Expertise

Magda Fahrni

"The engineer responded to the call; developed engines and machines; lifted man to a higher plane; multiplied his powers a thousandfold, and created a new era. An era, however, fraught with many new and unforeseen hazards as by-products of progress; and again man called upon the engineer to protect him against the hazards incident to these very engines and machines that had contributed so much toward the increase of his productive capacity."

– LEW R. PALMER, "HISTORY OF THE SAFETY MOVEMENT"

THIS CHAPTER IS DRAWN from my current research on changing understandings of accidents in early-twentieth-century Quebec and the building of what I call an accident-prevention infrastructure. This research is rooted in the international historiography of industrial modernity and the interdisciplinary literature on risk. Scholars working with the concept of risk have suggested that it was only under conditions of industrial modernity that accidents came to be seen as preventable rather than as the inevitable consequence of God's will or fate. They have demonstrated the ways that, armed with scientific studies and statistics, late-nineteenth- and early-twentieth-century experts set out to document and understand accidents in order to predict the likelihood of their occurrence and, where possible, prevent them.[1]

Central to the building of an accident-prevention infrastructure in early-twentieth-century Quebec was the creation of a broad-based safety movement that encompassed both state structures and associations that emanated from civil society. Quebec's provincial government, as we shall see, implemented official inspections of industrial workplaces in the late nineteenth century and, in the early twentieth century, passed legislation designed to compensate victims of workplace accidents. In the early decades of the twentieth century, citizen groups such as the Ligue de sécurité de la Province de Québec (LSPQ), founded in 1923, joined and often even spearheaded the movement.[2] The LSPQ was made up of both French- and English-speaking citizens – the majority of them residents of Montreal, the metropolis of both Quebec and Canada, a city that industrialized both early and intensively. Some of these individuals might well have been expected to take an interest in safety matters – for instance, Pierre Bélanger as the chief of police, Raoul Gauthier as the fire department chief, or William Bowie as a key actor in Montreal's parks and playgrounds movement. The LSPQ's founding general secretary was Arthur Gaboury, superintendent of the Montreal Tramways Company. The LSPQ sought to prevent accidents at work, at school, in the street, at home, and at play through what we might call "risk education." It organized conferences and talks, published a monthly illustrated bulletin entitled *Le Signal de Sécurité,* printed advertisements and produced posters in both French and English as a way of spreading its "gospel of prudence" (évangile de prudence). It bought radio time, made phonograph recordings of safety talks, and screened movies on the random dangers of everyday life. It gave talks in schools and drafted pledges to be taken by school children.[3]

In this chapter, I argue that the LSPQ and other actors in Quebec's accident-prevention movement, including civil servants and provincial factory inspectors, were building a masculine technical expertise, which was deployed and promoted in part by members of new white-collar professions. As Christopher Dummitt has argued about a slightly later period, the expertise required to manage the risks inherent to modernity – what Dummitt calls "a reasoned expertise" – was gendered masculine and seen to belong to engineers, actuaries, and purveyors of insurance.[4] This was also the case in early-twentieth-century Quebec, where accident-prevention experts included architects, engineers, building inspectors, insurance salesmen, and firemen. The precise nature of these "expert masculinities," however, bears interrogation. As we shall see, the accident-prevention movement in early-twentieth-century Quebec drew upon various kinds of expertise and upon a heterogeneous group of men from different backgrounds and with diverse sets of skills and knowledge. On the one hand, we see in this period the emergence of a white-collar masculinity anchored in professional training and "a reasoned expertise," represented by inspectors, engineers, civil servants, physicians, lawyers, and actuaries. On the other hand, the safety movement was also built by workers and their representatives: union members, labour journalists, and sympathetic factory inspectors, many of whom had been industrial workers themselves.[5] It also involved policemen and firemen – municipal employees of working-class backgrounds who did not have much formal education but who had acquired deep local knowledge of urban hazards and had developed their own methods of calculating risk. In this period, then, "reasoned expertise" clearly coexisted with other forms of masculinity rooted in experience and on-the-job training.

All of these experts, based in Montreal or Quebec City, were part of an international community of technical experts, contributing to, and benefiting from, the circulation of technical knowledge not only around central Canada and the eastern United States but also between Quebec and francophone countries such as Belgium and France.[6] Union leaders and labour journalists similarly contributed to the diffusion of internationally acquired knowledge of workplace accidents, in particular. As we shall see, the study of the circulation of this masculine technical expertise not only provides us with an innovative way of exploring what both Gérard Bouchard and Yvan Lamonde have called Quebec's *américanité* but also underlines the fact that Montreal was a hub that received and transmitted knowledge between Europe and North America.[7] It also reminds us that, contrary to a certain received wisdom, French-speaking Quebecers were active participants in scientific and technical professions well before the Quiet Revolution of the 1960s.[8]

Through an analysis of such key figures as Louis Guyon, who was a factory inspector and later Quebec's deputy minister of labour, Arthur Gaboury, who was superintendent of the Montreal Tramways Company and general secretary of the LSPQ, and Edmond McMahon, who was a long-time Montreal coroner, among others, this chapter proposes an exploration of the building of masculine technical expertise in early-twentieth-century Quebec. Sources for this study include the documents produced by the LSPQ, the archives of the Montreal Street Railway Company and the Montreal Tramways Company, the annual reports of Montreal's police department and fire department, coroners' reports, the published writings of Edmond McMahon, Wilfrid Derome, and Louis Guyon, and the various reports compiled in the federal government publication *The Labour Gazette*.

Building an Accident-Prevention Infrastructure in Early-Twentieth-Century Quebec

The accident-prevention infrastructure that was built in Quebec at the turn of the twentieth century was an ensemble of heterogeneous measures and actors. Workplace accidents were the first category of accidents to attract sustained attention from legislators and from the press, beginning with the passage of Quebec's first factory legislation in 1885. The Acte des manufactures de Québec established safety measures in industrial workplaces and provided for the inspection of these workplaces – inspections that were instituted in 1888. The outcomes of workplace accidents were still determined in the courts, however, and under the provisions of Quebec's Civil Code, workers seeking compensation for job-related accidents were required to prove that their employers were at fault.[9] This remained the case until, a quarter-century later, in 1909, Quebec adopted one of the first workers' compensation measures in North America.[10] Although the 1909 law recognized employers' responsibility for accidents even in the absence of fault, this rather limited measure was nonetheless the object of frequent, recurrent criticism by both unions and sympathetic civil servants such as Louis Guyon.[11] Regardless, from the 1880s onward, both the political and judicial arms of the state undertook sustained reflections on how to understand, regulate, and ideally prevent workplace accidents. Montreal, like Amsterdam, Paris, and New York, had its safety museum, devoted to apparatuses and equipment designed to make the workplace safer.[12] This museum, which had clear pedagogical goals, was founded and sustained – for a time, at least – by Guyon.[13]

Provincial civil servants concerned about the costs, both human and monetary, of workplace accidents found an ally in the safety movement that took root in Quebec's civil society during the early decades of the twentieth century, notably the LSPQ and, after 1931, the Association de prévention des accidents du travail de la Province de Québec (APATPQ), the LSPQ'S former industrial branch.[14] The LSPQ undertook extensive educational campaigns on workplace accidents, creating and circulating a series of bulletins, posters, advertisements, and calendars that promoted lessons such as the following: "ACCIDENTS are caused by – a <u>Man</u>, a <u>Machine</u> or a <u>Method</u> not functioning properly."[15] It relied heavily on illustrations and photographs accompanied by short didactic texts in both French and English, such as "A broken arm in PLAY – Plaisir COUTEUX. À l'ouvrage – travaillez sérieusement. At work – work seriously."[16] The LSPQ also promoted the creation of safety committees within industrial workplaces, provided examples of model factories, gave radio talks on workplace safety, organized first-aid contests within factories, and lobbied for improved provincial legislation, more careful inspections of workplaces, and the better keeping of statistics. It focused particularly on the problem of the inexperienced employee, the individual most likely to fall victim to a workplace accident.[17] And it directed a good part of its workplace safety message to foremen, those men who had moved up the ranks within the workplace and who were now centrally positioned to help prevent accidents.[18] Shortly after the APATPQ was incorporated in 1931, provincial civil servants within the Ministry of Labour complained that its members were stepping on their toes: apparently, factory owners and foremen had difficulty distinguishing visitors sent by the APATPQ from official provincial inspectors and occasionally received conflicting advice from officers of these two bodies, which represented, respectively, citizens and the state.[19]

The LSPQ was also concerned with street accidents (as we have seen, its general secretary, Arthur Gaboury, was superintendent of the Montreal Tramways Company), and members of the LSPQ gave lessons on road safety in public schools, administered safety pledges to school children, helped to implement a crossing-guard system, mounted safety-education programs for taxi drivers, and published road-safety guides for tourists.[20] Its risk-education efforts were aided, concretely, by local police departments, which found themselves, from the 1920s onward, having to deal with the consequences of increased automobile traffic in urban streets and notably with road accidents.

The LSPQ was also concerned, albeit to a lesser extent, with domestic accidents.[21] It was joined here by public health experts and by municipal and provincial health departments, which also undertook risk education around household accidents. *Bulletin sanitaire,* published by the Service provincial d'hygiène, printed regular reports on accidents, backed by statistics, warning readers of the seasonal nature of falls, drownings, and burns.[22] It also provided basic information on simple first-aid techniques.[23]

In all of these areas, international models and examples were key; the LSPQ, for example, had concrete ties with over 160 other North American and European safety leagues and met regularly with like-minded associations at congresses and conferences.[24]

The "Efficiency Experts": Architects of an Accident-Prevention Infrastructure

Anthony Giddens has argued that central to industrial modernity is trust in expertise, technical knowledge, and what he calls "abstract systems."[25] Systems based on reason, linear thinking, technical qualifications, and expertise were implemented and privileged under conditions of industrial modernity; individuals necessarily placed their trust in new experts – the "efficiency experts"[26] – those familiar with the workings of complex new systems beyond the everyday knowledge held by most lay people. It is interesting to study the architects of Quebec's early-twentieth-century accident-prevention infrastructure with this in mind. To what extent were the province's accident experts actually the product of white-collar training, knowledge, and expertise?

A broad definition of this accident-prevention infrastructure – not only the citizen-initiated safety movement but also the state infrastructure designed to manage and compensate for accidents – brings us into contact with a diverse group of individuals. There are those who are active participants in the citizen safety movement, such as Arthur Gaboury, a key figure in the LSPQ who was also involved, from the 1910s onward, in the North American Safety First movement. There are also those who are called upon to define, identify, or prevent accidents in the course of their professional work: the coroner, for example, or the forensic medical examiner who served as an expert in the application of the 1909 Loi sur les accidents du travail. The adoption of the 1909 legislation meant that physicians were increasingly called upon to determine the nature and cause of workplace accidents and to play a new, key role in the judicial system. Physicians could act as the worker's doctor, as the doctor chosen by the employer or the insurance company, or as an expert witness.[27]

Some of the individuals involved in accident prevention had considerable formal education, acquired at classical colleges and universities; others had received practical training at business colleges; and still others drew upon on-the-job informal apprenticeships and hard-earned experience. Wilfrid Derome, for example, renowned for his forensic expertise, was trained as a physician and had extensive experience assessing judicial causes for the state. The son of a farmer, he attended classical colleges in Montreal and Joliette and studied medicine at the Université Laval de Montréal and the Université de Paris. He directed a laboratory at the Hôpital Notre-Dame, was a consulting doctor at the Hôpital Saint-Jean-de-Dieu, taught at the Université de Montréal, and provided expert medical opinion in criminal cases.[28] His *Précis de médecine légale* (1920) became a reference on the topic and includes dozens of pages on accidents such as burns, firearm injuries, and electric shock.

Edmond McMahon, trained as a lawyer and the holder of a bachelor's degree in civil law, had a similarly privileged upbringing. The son of a doctor, he attended classical colleges in Sainte-Thérèse and Montreal. Called to the bar in 1881, he became magistrate of Westmount in 1894 and, in 1892, coroner of Montreal – a position that he occupied for over thirty-five years.[29] As coroner of Canada's largest city, McMahon was necessarily brought into contact with the question of accidental death. His well-known treatise *A Practical Guide to the Coroner and His Duties at Inquests without and with a Jury, in Quebec, and Other Provinces of Canada* (1907), however, highlights the fact that although coroner's inquests occasionally served to reflect upon means of preventing accidental deaths, in doing so they were in fact overstepping the bounds of their duty, as the sole official purpose of the coroner's inquest was to seek out homicide.[30] Nonetheless, despite McMahon's conviction that "it does not seem well advised to require that a Coroner or a Coroner's inquest should extend beyond the search for the homicide," several pages of his treatise were devoted to the question of various kinds of accidents – which he categorized as unquestionable accidents, excusable accidents, fortuitous cases, and accidents with or without human intervention.[31]

Members of the liberal professions such as Derome and McMahon were an integral part of state bodies and structures called upon to manage the consequences of accidents. Other early-twentieth-century Quebecers, however, made the deliberate decision to devote part of their working lives to the management, prevention, or compensation of accidents. Many of these men – for they were almost all men – came from more modest social backgrounds than Derome or McMahon. Louis Guyon, for instance, rose through the ranks as in a classic nineteenth-century tale. Born to a Franco-American family in New York State in 1853 (his father was a harness maker), he was successively a machinist, an insurance salesman, a member of the Knights of Labor, an inspector (eventually chief inspector) of Quebec's industrial establishments, and ultimately, in 1919, Quebec's deputy minister of labour. Both his experience as a machinist and that earned selling insurance had probably predisposed him to think about accident prevention and about the prevention of workplace accidents in particular. Even as deputy minister of labour, he remained a "friend to the workingman," and much of his work as a civil servant was devoted to workplace safety, notably his founding of a museum on workplace safety and his advocacy of new and improved legislation. Guyon travelled a great deal and was in contact with safety legislation and workplace innovations in the United States and in Europe, particularly in France.[32]

Other individuals involved in Quebec's safety movement, such as Arthur Gaboury and Pierre Bélanger, were also "self-made," and these up-the-ladder stories, tales of social mobility, printed in the annual *Biographies canadiennes-françaises* (Quebec's equivalent of the American *Who's Who*) have become part of the public personas of these men. Gaboury, born in 1875, studied at the Montreal Business College and entered the employ of the Montreal Street Railway in 1892, where "he began at the bottom of the ladder and successively filled each job, so as to familiarize himself with this huge organization, which has become one of the most important of its kind in America." (Il y partit du bas de l'échelle et remplit successivement tous les emplois, afin de se familiariser avec cette vaste organisation, devenue une des plus importantes du genre en Amérique.)[33] In 1907 Gaboury reached the "summit" (sommet) of this company when he was named general superintendent, a position he retained when the Montreal Street Railway became part of the Montreal Tramways Company in 1911. He first became involved with the North American Safety First movement in 1913 – perhaps as a result of having served as head of the Montreal Street Railway's claims department and as a member of the Administrative Council of the Montreal Street Railway's mutual benefits association.[34] He was the founding general secretary of the LSPQ in 1923 and the founding director-general of the APATPQ, incorporated in 1931.[35] A member of various North American railway associations, Gaboury was also a member of numerous service clubs, such as the Foresters, as well as golf clubs and automobile clubs; associational life was an important part of these men's identity building and networking.[36]

Pierre Bélanger, the son of a carpenter, was born in 1862 and attended public Catholic schools near the Quebec-Ontario border. He entered Montreal's police force in 1894 and, like Gaboury, "quickly earned his stripes" (conquit rapidement ses galons), rising from the position of a simple police officer up through the ranks to become, in turn, corporal, sergeant, lieutenant, captain, inspector, and ultimately chief of police in 1919.[37] He was active in various charitable and service organizations and in the associational life of the police force not only in Montreal but also across Canada and the United States. He was particularly active in police athletic associations, where, according to the *Biographies canadiennes-françaises*, "he was especially advantaged by his athletic abilities" (il était qualifié tout spécialement par ses personnels avantages athlétiques) (Bélanger was 6 feet and 1 inch tall and, at the time of his entry into the police force, weighed 184 pounds). Upon his death in 1939, at the age of seventy-six, obituaries noted that he had been "a powerful athlete" (un athlète puissant).[38] Such information was not simply anecdotal, as surviving records documenting both successful and unsuccessful candidates for the police force show that men judged too short, too light, too young, or too old were denied entry to the force.[39]

As chief of the police department of a large North American city in the 1920s, Bélanger was forced to deal with the rapidly increasing presence of the automobile and the consequent rise of road accidents. Historian Peter D. Norton has argued that for most urban police forces in the United States in the first quarter of the twentieth century, the automobile signified disruption, disorder, and chaos.[40] Montreal appears to bear out Norton's case; in his 1925 annual report, Chief Bélanger declared, "The regulation of traffic in Montreal continues to be one of the most difficult problems to solve. Our streets are narrow; the number of vehicles and automobiles grows unceasingly, as does the number of tourists during the summer months." (La réglementation du trafic à Montréal continue d'être l'un des problèmes les plus difficiles à solutionner. Nos rues sont étroites; le nombre des voitures et des automobiles augmente sans cesse, tout comme celui des touristes durant la belle saison.) That year, between 100 and 200 Montreal policemen were assigned to enforce traffic regulations and speed limits.[41] Bélanger had created a traffic department within the Montreal police department in 1920, and in 1924 he began appending detailed accident statistics to his annual report.[42] His accident-prevention work, including that undertaken within the International Association of Chiefs of Police, was recognized and lauded by his peers.[43] And Bélanger himself appears to have seen this accident-prevention work as among his major contributions to the changing nature of the municipal police department.[44] In the years following Bélanger's departure from the police force, the annual reports continued to include detailed accident statistics, often in the form of charts and tables, which classified accidents according to whether they were injuries or fatalities and recorded the age and sex of fatal accident victims and the seasonal nature of these accidents. Among the accidents documented and analyzed were various kinds of road accidents and collisions that involved automobiles, motorcycles, buses, streetcars, carts, trucks, trains, bicycles, horses, and pedestrians. Beginning in 1932, these annual reports also included statistical analyses of the accidents that befell members of the police force themselves while on duty.[45]

Like Pierre Bélanger, Raoul Gauthier was a municipal employee who made his way up through the ranks. Hired by the Montreal fire department in 1904, Gauthier occupied a series of functions in the department in his early twenties, before being named chief in 1928. Four years later, in June 1932, while attempting to put out a fire on the *Cymbeline,* a petrol boat docked in the harbour, he died tragically when the force of an explosion projected him into the water and he drowned. Three of his firefighters and twenty-six employees of Canadian Vickers also died in this explosion. Gauthier's official funeral was said to have drawn 50,000 mourners and even more onlookers.[46] His widow and their four young children were granted pensions by the city.[47] During Gauthier's years in the employ of the city, the fire department developed a new interest in the prevention of fires, establishing a Service de prévention des incendies, essentially devoted to the inspection of public buildings and private residences, in 1914. Gauthier's annual reports reveal an unshakable faith in the value of inspections for preventing fires, list the principal causes of fires in the city each year (among them, stoves and furnaces, electricity, defective chimneys, and children playing with matches), and are replete with graphs and tables detailing the numbers of fires dealt with by the department each year. The superintendent of the Service de prévention des incendies, Jason McIsaac, took care to outline the characteristics of competent inspectors, night watchmen, and security guards, among them good eyesight and good physical condition.[48] McIsaac's observations on fire prevention, like those of Gauthier, reveal signs of what Giddens might term a reflexive modernity – that is, an explicit recognition that industrial modernity generates new hazards but also creates the possibility of taming those hazards: "As new dangers come to light, as a new industry creates hazardous materials, we adopt the necessary measures to regulate their storage and production." (Au fur et à mesure que des dangers nouveaux sont signalés, qu'une industrie nouvelle apporte des matériaux dangereux, nous prenons les mesures nécessaires pour en réglementer le magasinage et la fabrication.)[49]

We see here, then, members of the long-established liberal professions – doctors and lawyers – whose work was changing under conditions of industrial modernity and in response to new demands by the state. We also see white-collar, technical experts, such as engineers, building inspectors, and accident claims officers within large corporations, for which accidents meant "expense in lawsuits and in settlements for damages."[50] And we see municipal officials such as police officers and firefighters. Whether obliged to consider the question of accidents in the course of their daily work or whether actively seeking to play a role in the safety movement, these individuals were lent the authority and endorsement of political figures, usually Liberal in party affiliation and liberal in philosophical inclination, such as successive premiers Lomer Gouin and Louis-Alexandre Taschereau.[51] We see, then, in the work of accident prevention, alliances such as those found in the late-nineteenth-century reform movements well known to historians, where the interests of engineers and public health physicians occasionally coincided with those of municipal "boosters."

Union members and leaders, too, had a keen interest in accident prevention, along with first-hand knowledge of the consequences of accidents for their immediate victims and for the families of these victims. In 1908, just a year before the pioneering workers' compensation legislation of 1909 was adopted, Louis Guyon argued that unions had a larger role to play in accident prevention, insisting that "it rests with organized labor to urge the legislators of every Province and State the necessity of framing compensation laws. That, in my estimation, will be the quickest solution to the problem of the introduction of special appliances to prevent accidents in mills and factories."[52] Throughout the 1910s and 1920s, union representatives did in fact lobby for legislative reform, notably improvements to the 1909 workers' compensation legislation and to the 1928 legislation that succeeded it. They deplored the fact that, until 1928, workers still had to resort to lengthy and costly procedures before the courts in order to receive compensation. They criticized the fact that Quebec legislation required employers to take out their own insurance rather than establishing state insurance, as in neighbouring Ontario; this meant that Quebec workers were at the mercy of criteria set by private insurance companies. And they criticized the fact that both the 1909 and the 1928 laws excluded industrial diseases from coverage.[53] In particular, Gustave Francq – a typographer, long-time unionist, and founder of the labour newspaper *Le Monde ouvrier* – devoted years to the campaign for better legislation around workplace accidents, drawing on his extensive knowledge of accident legislation in other provincial and national jurisdictions.[54] The comments of reform journalist Éva Circé-Côté, writing in *Le Monde ouvrier* under the masculine pseudonym Julien Saint-Michel, provide us with some idea of how labour circles viewed the accident-prevention infrastructure that was built in Quebec in the early twentieth century. Circé-Côté wrote scathingly of male accident experts, particularly lawyers, whom she depicted as intervening and mercenary, seeking to profit from the misery and misfortune of the workers placed at their mercy by the 1909 workers' compensation legislation.[55]

The Nature of This Expertise

At first glance, the work of these various individuals involved in accident prevention appears to confirm much of what Giddens writes about industrial modernity and the faith in science, reason, and technological fixes. Most of the men who are discussed here were involved in developing new systems of knowledge and management, most seem to have put their faith in science and technology, and most spoke out in favour of what they called "efficiency." And it is clear that in the context of industrial modernity, certain kinds of knowledge were increasingly valued over others. The fire that broke out in Montreal's Macdonald Tobacco factory, the largest of its kind in Canada, on April 25, 1895, taking the lives of four employees – three women aged eighteen to twenty-seven and one man aged twenty-nine, all of whom either leapt or were pushed to their deaths from their fourth-storey workplace – points to different ways of understanding danger and constructing risk in late-nineteenth-century Montreal. At the coroner's inquest that followed this tragic accident, Maria and Elmina Thibaudeau, the sisters of Alphonsine Thibaudeau, one of the young women killed, claimed that the dangers of this five-storey factory had often been a topic of dinner-table conversation. According to Maria and Elmina, the three sisters, all in their twenties, had on countless occasions deplored the absence of an outdoor staircase that would allow workers to rapidly exit the building in case of fire. The architect who had designed this state-of-the-art factory in 1875, Alexander Hutchison, dismissed the young women's fears in his postfire testimony. Defending his decision to provide the building with a wide internal staircase rather than outdoor fire escapes, he stated, "Of course a staircase is used all the time, and females out in the air, without any appearance of support are liable to lose their heads. It is very difficult to get a female to go up a few steps on a ladder in a room, let alone a building four storeys high."[56] In this instance, official – technical, scientific, authoritative – knowledge appears to have been gendered masculine, whereas the young female workers were clearly seen to be repositories of local, embodied knowledge, which was in cases such as these coded as irrational, illogical, and even hysterical.[57]

That said, the division between official knowledge and local knowledge – of which much is made, for instance, by James C. Scott in his well-known *Seeing Like a State* (1999) – was not always clear-cut.[58] As historians Tina Loo and Meg Stanley have argued in their work on dam building in twentieth-century British Columbia, experts such as engineers, geologists, and construction workers can also value, embody, create, and apply local knowledge – what Loo and Stanley call "high modernist local knowledge." This kind of knowledge is tacit and practical, is rooted in experience, and might, as Loo and Stanley point out, be termed "savoir-faire."[59] In early-twentieth-century Quebec, firemen and policemen, for example, could be seen as residing at this juncture between formal and informal knowledge, as they were called upon to apply scientific, technical knowledge but also possessed deep local knowledge, gained through patrolling the streets and entering the houses of their constituents. We need to recognize the heterogeneity not only of the individuals involved in accident prevention in this period but also of the kinds of expertise and knowledge put to use here. Some of these men possessed knowledge that might be called "artisanal" – a combination of on-the-job training and experience.[60]

E. Anthony Rotundo and others, as discussed at length in the introduction to this volume, have convincingly demonstrated that masculinity changes over time.[61] In the period that interests us here, technical, scientific knowledge was highly valued – as is evident, for instance, in the quotation from engineer Lew R. Palmer with which this chapter begins. This knowledge, based on reason, logic, and science, was gendered masculine and was actively opposed to other kinds of knowledge, gendered feminine, namely those informed by emotion, intuition, and tradition. Women were denied access not only to the formal education and training that provided technical and scientific knowledge but also to most of the professions and jobs in which they could have acquired such expertise on the ground.

The masculine expertise studied here was not identical to what Dummitt, examining the post–Second World War years of high modernity, has described as the "manly modern."[62] The industrial modernity of the turn of the twentieth century meant faith in science, technology, reason, and expertise. This was no longer – or not necessarily – the masculinity associated with craft, with physical strength, and with skill, such as that described by historian Joy Parr for the woodworkers of industrializing Hanover, Ontario.[63] But it is nonetheless a more heterogeneous mix of masculinities and of men than that evoked by Dummitt for postwar Canada. In some ways, what we see here echoes what historian Carole Srole has discovered in her study of masculinity among office workers and clerks in the nineteenth-century United States, namely that male court reporters, like "other incipient professionals, ... imposed a connection to science and technology and mixed the practical and theoretical."[64] The twelve Montreal firefighters who received first-aid training from the St. John Ambulance Association in 1934, for instance, were described as having been trained in the "science" of first aid.[65]

Central to the development of these various sets of masculine expertise was an international conversation that took place across the Canada-US border and that also spanned the Atlantic. This was a transnational masculine knowledge, constructed through congresses, conferences, official correspondence, associational life, and what we would today call "networking."[66] In some sense, this confirms what Loo and Stanley have argued about local knowledge, namely (and paradoxically) that such forms of knowledge are *mobilized* by social and intellectual networks.[67] Uniquely positioned in North America, Quebec safety experts, many of whom were French-speaking, were acutely aware of the activities of their counterparts in France, Belgium, and Switzerland. But other Quebec safety specialists, both French- and English-speaking, were plugged into American networks in the northeastern United States and the Midwest. In this sense, Gérard Bouchard and Yvan Lamonde are not wrong to insist upon the *américanité* – the essential North Americanness – of Quebec. Bouchard and Lamonde locate this *américanité* in Quebec's popular culture; I propose that we also look for it in the circulation of technical, scientific, and sometimes local knowledge, as well as in the masculine professional and associational networks studied here.

Notes

My thanks to the Social Sciences and Humanities Research Council of Canada for its generous funding of this research. I also warmly thank Geneviève Létourneau-Guillon, Jacinthe Archambault, Maude Charest-Auger, and Sophie Doucet for their research assistance over the past few years. Some of the material in this chapter was presented at the conference "Accidents and Emergencies: Risk, Welfare and Safety in Europe and North America, c. 1750–2000," held at Oxford Brookes University, September 9–11, 2013, and I thank the participants at that conference for their useful feedback.

1 Ulrich Beck, *Risk Society: Towards a New Modernity* (London: Sage, 1992); Anthony Giddens, "Risk and Responsibility," *Modern Law Review* 62, 1 (1999): 1–10; François Ewald, *L'État-providence* (Paris: Bernard Grasset, 1986); François Ewald, "Insurance and Risk," in *The Foucault Effect: Studies in Governmentality: With Two Lectures by and an Interview with Michel Foucault*, ed. G. Burchell, C. Gordon, and P. Miller, 197–210 (Chicago: University of Chicago Press, 1991). These perspectives are also reflected in the articles collected in Roger Cooter and Bill Luckin, eds., *Accidents in History: Injuries, Fatalities and Social Relations* (Amsterdam: Rodopi, 1997); and in the fascinating work by Arwen Mohun, most recently *Risk: Negotiating Safety in American Society* (Baltimore, MD: Johns Hopkins University Press, 2013).

2 Magda Fahrni, "'La lutte contre l'accident': Risque et accidents dans un contexte de modernité industrielle," in *Pour une histoire du risque: Québec, France, Belgique*, ed. David Niget and Martin Petitclerc, 181–202 (Rennes/Québec: Presses universitaires de Rennes/Presses de l'Université du Québec, 2012).

3 Arthur Gaboury, *La lutte contre l'accident: Un exposé sur la valeur sociale de l'oeuvre de la sécurité préventif accompli dans la province de Québec* (Montreal: LSPQ, 1934); "Notes sur

la sécurité et l'hygiène du travail: La Ligue de Sécurité de la province de Québec," *La Gazette du Travail* 28, 9 (1928): 1037; "La Ligue canadienne nationale de sécurité: Rapports des organisations nationale et provinciales pour 1928: Ligue de sécurité de la province de Québec," *La Gazette du Travail* 29, 3 (1929): 309–10.

4 Christopher Dummitt, *The Manly Modern: Masculinity in Postwar Canada* (Vancouver: UBC Press, 2007), 152. See also Amélie Bourbeau, *Techniciens de l'organisation sociale: La réorganisation de l'assistance catholique privée à Montréal (1930–1974)* (Montreal and Kingston: McGill-Queen's University Press, 2015).

5 Jean-Claude Dionne notes that Quebec's provincial government frequently appointed former factory workers as factory inspectors. Jean-Claude Dionne, "Les accidents mortels en milieu de travail dans le district judiciaire de Montréal de 1890 à 1930: Recension et analyse à partir des rapports d'enquête des coroners" (MA thesis, Université de Montréal, 2006), 96–97.

6 On communications and conversations between public health experts in Quebec, France, and Belgium at the turn of the twentieth century, see Nicolas Kenny, "From Body and Home to Nation and World: The Varying Scales of Transnational Urbanism in Montreal and Brussels at the Turn of the Twentieth Century," *Urban History* 36, 2 (2009): 223–42.

7 Gérard Bouchard, *Genèse des nations et cultures du Nouveau Monde: Essai d'histoire comparée*, 2nd ed. (Montreal: Boréal Compact, 2001); Yvan Lamonde, *Ni avec eux ni sans eux: Le Québec et les États-Unis* (Montreal: Nuit Blanche Éditeur, 1996).

8 Robert Gagnon, *Histoire de l'École polytechnique de Montréal: La montée des ingénieurs francophones* (Montreal: Boréal, 1991); Robert Gagnon and Yves Gingras, "Le mythe de la 'marginalité professionnelle' des ingénieurs francophones du Québec," *Journal of Canadian Studies* 31, 2 (1996): 29–44.

9 For a study of one case of judicial regulation of a workplace accident, see Magda Fahrni, "Risque et accidents dans la ville industrielle: Le cas de l'incendie de l'usine de tabac Macdonald, Montréal, 1895," paper presented at Université du Québec à Trois-Rivières, September 18, 2014.

10 For a summary of this new law, see Wilfrid Derome, *Précis de médecine légale* (Montreal: La Compagnie d'imprimerie des marchands, 1920), 75–76.

11 Éric Leroux, *Gustave Francq: Figure marquante du syndicalisme et précurseur de la FTQ* (Montreal: VLB Éditeur, 2001), 217–28.

12 Jean-Claude Dionne, "Documents pour l'étude des expositions et musées pour la prévention des accidents et des maladies du travail au Québec au début du siècle," *Labour/Le Travail* 40 (1997): 199–211.

13 "Louis Guyon," *Biographies canadiennes-françaises*, vol. 1 (Ottawa: J.-A. Fortin, 1920), 127; "Notes sur la sécurité et l'hygiène industrielles," *La Gazette du Travail* 24, 12 (1924): 1143; Violette Allaire, "Notes bio-bibliographiques sur Louis Guyon, Officier d'Académie, Ex-Sous-ministre du Travail de la province de Québec" (École de Bibliothécaires, Université de Montréal, 1953), 20–21. Historians of Canada have noted the impetus provided to public health movements by the Great War. Surprisingly, the Great War had little impact upon the accident-prevention movement, at least in Quebec. See Magda Fahrni, "La Première Guerre mondiale et l'intervention étatique au Québec: Le cas des accidents du travail," in *Le Québec dans la Grande Guerre: Engagements, refus, héritages*, ed. Charles-Philippe Courtois and Laurent Veyssière, 131–41 (Sillery, QC: Septentrion, 2015); and Magda Fahrni, "'Victimes de la tâche journalière': La gestion des accidents du travail au Québec pendant la Grande Guerre," paper presented at the conference "Mains-d'oeuvre en guerre: Régulations, territoires, recompositions," Ministère des Affaires Sociales, Paris, May 18–19, 2015.

14 "Notes sur la sécurité et l'hygiène industrielles: La ligue de sécurité de la province de Québec," *La Gazette du Travail* 27, 8 (1927): 937–38; "L'Association de prévention des accidents du travail de la province de Québec," *La Gazette du Travail* 31, 8 (1931): 909.
15 Bibliothèque et Archives nationales du Québec – Québec (BANQ – Québec), Fonds Lomer Gouin, ZC10.
16 "Ligue de sécurité de la province de Québec," *La Gazette du Travail* 28, 12 (1928): 1394; BANQ – Québec, Ministère du Travail, E24, contenant 1960–01–040/75, dossier A-71/32–33, poster, Province of Quebec Safety League – La Ligue de Sécurité Publique de la Province de Québec.
17 "Ligue de sécurité de la province de Québec," *La Gazette du Travail* 28, 12 (1928): 1394; "Comité de sécurité industrielle dans le Québec," *La Gazette du Travail* 26, 3 (1926): 290.
18 "Notes sur l'hygiène et la sécurité du travail: Le rôle du contremaître dans la prévention des accidents," *La Gazette du Travail* 29, 12 (1929): 1409–10.
19 BANQ – Québec, Ministère du Travail, E24, contenant 1960–01–040/75, dossier A-71/32–33, Arthur Gaboury to Gérard Tremblay, October 24, 1932; Gérard Tremblay to Arthur Gaboury, October 19, 1932; Alfred Robert to Gérard Tremblay, October 18, 1932.
20 Ligue de sécurité de la Province de Québec, *Cours de sécurité juvénile: Quarante leçons complètes sur la sécurité, le secourisme, l'hygiène, pour les quarante semaines de l'année scolaire* (Montreal: LSPQ, 1936); "L'enseignement de la sécurité dans les écoles de Montréal," *La Gazette du Travail* 25, 12 (1925): 1299; BANQ – Québec, Fonds Lomer Gouin, ZC10, radio talk, February 4, 1928; "Concours de sécurité chez les conducteurs professionnels d'automobiles de la province de Québec," *La Gazette du Travail* 33, 2 (1933): 185–86; Province of Quebec Safety League, *Tourist Safety Guide* (Montreal: Provincial Publishing Co., 1931).
21 "Ligue de sécurité de la Province de Québec: Première convention de sécurité du travail tenue à Montréal en mai 1929," *La Gazette du Travail* 29, 6 (1929): 672–73; *Proceedings of the Tenth Annual Safety and First Aid Congress*, Montreal, November 4–6, 1937, 47–58.
22 "Accidents et soins d'urgence," *Bulletin Sanitaire* 31, 3 (1931): 25–40; "Accidents évitables," *Bulletin Sanitaire* 38, 5 (1938): 59–60; "Les accidents d'hiver," *Bulletin Sanitaire* 39, 6 (1939): 69.
23 "Les pansements d'urgence," *Bulletin Sanitaire* 34, 4 (1934): 37–38; "Secours d'urgence," *Bulletin Sanitaire* 42, 3 (1942): 25–28.
24 Arthur Gaboury, "La ligue de la sécurité publique de la Province de Québec," *La Revue municipale* 4, 10 (1926): 343, 355; "Notes sur l'hygiène et la sécurité du travail: La Ligue de sécurité de la province de Québec," *La Gazette du Travail* 30, 2 (1930): 176–77. On the Safety First movement in the United States, see Mark Aldrich, *Safety First: Technology, Labor, and Business in the Building of American Work Safety, 1870–1939* (Baltimore, MD: Johns Hopkins University Press, 1997); and Mark Aldrich, *Death Rode the Rails: American Railroad Accidents and Safety, 1828–1965* (Baltimore, MD: Johns Hopkins University Press, 2006).
25 Anthony Giddens, *The Consequences of Modernity* (Stanford, CA: Stanford University Press, 1990).
26 Sinclair Lewis, *Babbitt* (New York: Harcourt, Brace and Company, 1922), ch. 6.
27 On the role of doctors in applying and interpreting the 1909 law, see Derome, *Précis de médecine légale*, 73, 75–76.
28 "Wilfrid Derome, M.D.," *Biographies canadiennes-françaises* (Montreal: Raphael Ouimet, 1924), 378; "Wilfrid Derome, M.D.," *Biographies canadiennes-françaises* (Montreal: Raphael Ouimet, 1927), 499; "Wilfrid Derome, M.D.," *Biographies canadiennes-françaises* (Montreal: Raphael Ouimet, 1929), 494; "Wilfrid Derome, M.D.," *Biographies canadiennes-françaises*

(Montreal: Raphael Ouimet, 1930), 422; "Wilfrid Derome, M.D.," *Biographies canadiennes-françaises* (Montreal: Raphael Ouimet, 1931), 481.

29 "Ed. McMahon," *Biographies canadiennes-françaises* (Montreal: Raphael Ouimet, 1923), 136; "Ed. McMahon," *Biographies canadiennes-françaises* (Montreal: Raphael Ouimet, 1924), 542; "Ed. McMahon," *Biographies canadiennes-françaises* (Montreal: Raphael Ouimet, 1925), 419.

30 Edmond McMahon, *A Practical Guide to the Coroner and His Duties at Inquests without and with a Jury, in Quebec, and Other Provinces of Canada* (Montreal: Wilson and Lafleur, 1907), 13–16.

31 Ibid., 84–90. See also Wyatt Johnston and George Villeneuve, "Les verdicts de la cour du Coroner du district de Montréal, pour le premier semestre de 1893, au point de vue médical," *L'Union médicale du Canada* 22, 8 (1893): 393–403.

32 "Louis Guyon," *Biographies canadiennes-françaises,* vol. 1 (Ottawa: J.-A. Fortin, 1920), 127; "Louis Guyon," *Biographies canadiennes-françaises* (Montreal: Raphael Ouimet, 1922), 558; Allaire, "Notes bio-bibliographiques sur Louis Guyon," 21–24. See also the numerous international references in Louis Guyon, "The Inspectors of Factories" and "Comparative Methods of Preventing Accidents," in *Labor Laws of the Province of Quebec,* 21–22 and 78–84 (Montreal: Mercantile Printing Co., 1908).

33 "Arthur Gaboury," *Biographies canadiennes-françaises* (Ottawa: J.-A. Fortin, 1920), 290; translation by author.

34 Archives de la Société de transport de Montréal (ASTM), "Quatrième Rapport de l'Association Mutuelle de Bienfaisance de la Compagnie de Chemin de Fer Urbain de Montréal, Rapport annuel pour l'année 1906–07, Montréal, juin 1907"; ASTM, S1/5,2, clippings from August 16, 1904, to January 18, 1905, contenant 0268A, *La Presse,* August 24, 1904, "Témoignage d'estime."

35 "L'Association de prévention des accidents du travail de la province de Québec," *La Gazette du Travail,* 31, 8 (1931): 909.

36 "Arthur Gaboury," *Biographies canadiennes-françaises* (Ottawa: J-A. Fortin, 1920), 290; "Arthur Gaboury," *Biographies canadiennes-françaises* (Montreal: Raphael Ouimet, 1922), 561; ASTM, S1/5,2, clippings from August 16, 1904, to January 18, 1905, contenant 0268A, *La Presse,* August 24, 1904, "Témoignage d'estime."

37 "Mort de l'ex-chef Pierre Bélanger," *Le Devoir,* May 15, 1939.

38 "Pierre Bélanger," *Biographies canadiennes-françaises* (Ottawa: J-A. Fortin, 1920), 399; "Pierre Bélanger," *Biographies canadiennes-françaises* (Montreal: Raphael Ouimet, 1922), 201; "Pierre Bélanger," *Biographies canadiennes-françaises* (Montreal: Raphael Ouimet, 1923), 254; Archives de la Ville de Montréal (AVM), Dossier d'employé, Bélanger, Pierre, "M.P. Bélanger, ancien chef de police, décédé," *La Presse,* May 15, 1939.

39 AVM, XCDOO, P5122, "Rapport annuel du Département de la police, 1935, Relevé des résultats se rapportant à l'examen des aspirants-policiers."

40 Peter D. Norton, *Fighting Traffic: The Dawn of the Motor Age in the American City* (Cambridge, MA: MIT Press, 2008), esp. 47–49.

41 AVM, "Rapport annuel du Département de la police, 1925."

42 AVM, "Rapport annuel du Département de la police, 1920"; "Rapport annuel du Département de la police, 1924"; and "Rapport annuel du Département de la police, 1927."

43 AVM, Dossier d'employé, Bélanger, Pierre, "Personal Tribute to Chief Bélanger," *Montreal Gazette,* July 18, 1924.

44 AVM, "Rapports annuels du Département de la police, 1919–1927." Bélanger resigned from the police force in 1928, a resignation no doubt linked to allegations of corruption and police complicity with vice made during the Coderre Inquiry of 1924–1925. Chief Bélanger

was singled out as being on the take. See Andrée Lévesque, "1924: L'Enquête Coderre," in *De la Belle Époque à la Crise: Chroniques de la vie culturelle à Montréal*, ed. Denis Saint-Jacques and Marie-José Des Rivières, 271–86 (Montreal: Nota Bene, 2015).

45   AVM, XCDOO, P5117–P5122, "Rapports annuels du Service de la Police, 1929–1935."

46   AVM, Dossier d'employé, Gauthier, Raoul; "Cinquante mille personnes forment le cortège funèbre," *Le Devoir*, June 22, 1932; BANQ – Québec, Ministère du Travail, E24, contenant 1960-01-040/75, dossier A-7/32–33, *Report of the Commissioner S.A. Baulne in the Matter of the Investigation into the Circumstances Surrounding an Explosion Which Occurred on the 17th June, 1932, in the Drydock of the Maisonneuve Plant of the Canadian Vickers Limited (29 December 1932).*

47   AVM, Dossier d'employé, Gauthier, Raoul, règlement no. 1200.

48   AVM, XCDOO, P5292–P5306, "Rapports annuels du Département des incendies, 1918–1935." McIsaac was particularly critical of religious institutions: "It is difficult to understand how, in order to save a few dollars a year, we place in the hands of the disabled elderly, the simple-minded, and even the blind, the care of buildings for which citizens are so heavily taxed; if this is done out of charity, in order that these people might earn their living, it would be less expensive to keep them idle in a hospice, and to place the safe-keeping of these buildings in the hands of men who are both physically and mentally fit." (Il est difficile de comprendre comment, pour sauver quelques dollars par année on met dans les mains de vieillards infirmes, pauvres d'esprit et même d'aveugles, la garde d'édifices pour lesquels les citoyens sont appelés à payer de si lourdes taxes; si c'est par charité, pour leur fournir le moyen de gagner leur vie, il serait moins coûteux de les garder oisifs dans un hospice, et confier à des hommes valides, physiquement et mentalement, le soin de ces édifices.) Security guards ought to be examined by physicians, McIsaac argued, in order to ensure that they had "relatively good eyesight and normal intelligence" (une assez bonne vue et une intelligence normale). AVM, XCDOO, P5297, "Rapport annuel du Département des incendies, 1924," and "Rapport du Surintendant du Service de Prévention, 26 janvier 1925."

49   AVM, XCDOO, P5297, "Rapport annuel du Département des incendies, 1924," and "Rapport du Surintendant du Service de Prévention, 26 janvier 1925."

50   ASTM, *General Rules for Conductors and Motormen Depot Clerks, Etc. Règlements généraux pour les Conducteurs et Garde-Moteurs Commis de dépôts, Etc. Montreal Street Railway Company, Montreal* (n.d.). On corporate involvement in workplace safety, see Aldrich, *Safety First;* and Aldrich, *Death Rode the Rails.*

51   BANQ – Québec, Fonds Lomer Gouin, ZC10, Arthur Gaboury to Lomer Gouin, December 30, 1927.

52   Guyon, "Comparative Methods."

53   BANQ – Québec, Fonds de la Commission d'étude sur la réparation des accidents du travail (1923–1924), E184, contenant 1970-03-001/1, dossier 1, "Réponses au questionnaire sur la Loi de compensation des ouvriers de la Province de Québec, décembre 1923 – mars 1924."

54   Leroux, *Gustave Francq*, 217–28.

55   Julien Saint-Michel (Éva Circé-Côté), "Les accidents du travail: Comment on procède dans les pays où l'en veut améliorer le sort du prolétaire," *Le Monde ouvrier*, May 20, 1916; Julien Saint-Michel (Éva Circé-Côté), "Les accidents du travail: Le taux de la réparation devrait être uniforme et basé sur des données mathématiques," *Le Monde ouvrier*, May 27, 1916.

56   BANQ – Vieux-Montréal, TP11, S2, SS2, SSS1, D417, Fonds Cour supérieure, Greffe de Montréal, Matières civiles en général, "Delle Marie B. Gélinas vs Wm. C. McDonald,

octobre 1895"; Superior Court, Montreal, "Orvis W. Finlay, Plaintiff vs W.C. McDonald, Defendant," deposition of A.C. Hutchison for the defendant, filed 1897.

57 On the female employees of Macdonald Tobacco, described as "the easiest creatures to panic" (les êtres les plus faciles à s'affoler), see also "Variétés – L'incendie de la manufacture de tabac Macdonald," *L'Union médicale du Canada* 24, 5 (1895): 278.

58 James C. Scott, *Seeing Like a State: How Certain Schemes to Improve the Human Condition Have Failed* (New Haven, CT: Yale University Press, 1999).

59 Tina Loo and Meg Stanley, "An Environmental History of Progress: Damming the Peace and Columbia Rivers," *Canadian Historical Review* 92, 3 (2011): 407, 414.

60 Candidates for Montreal's police force in the 1930s were turned down for "lack of instruction," but it is unknown exactly what level of education was required. AVM, XCDOO, P5122, "Rapport annuel du Département de la police, 1935, Relevé des résultats se rapportant à l'examen des aspirants-policiers."

61 E. Anthony Rotundo, *American Manhood: Transformations in Masculinity from the Revolution to the Modern Era* (New York: Basic Books, 1993).

62 Dummitt, *Manly Modern.*

63 Joy Parr, *The Gender of Breadwinners: Women, Men, and Change in Two Industrial Towns, 1880–1950* (Toronto: University of Toronto Press, 1990). Parr is interested in the transition from a nineteenth-century masculinity rooted in craft, skill, and physical prowess to the early-twentieth-century masculinity represented by scientific management and technical expertise. See ibid., ch. 7.

64 Carole Srole, *Transcribing Class and Gender: Masculinity and Femininity in Nineteenth-Century Courts and Offices* (Ann Arbor: University of Michigan Press, 2010), 96.

65 AVM, XCDOO, P5305, "Rapport annuel du Service des incendies, 1934."

66 See, for instance, the list of participants at the Tenth Annual Safety and First Aid Congress held in Montreal in 1937. *Proceedings of the Tenth Annual Safety and First Aid Congress,* Montreal, November 4–6, 1937, 5–10.

67 Loo and Stanley, "Environmental History of Progress," esp. 417–18, 427.

3
"The Spiritual Aspect":
Gordon A. Friesen and the Mechanization
of the Modern Hospital

David Theodore

WHEN HE DIED IN 1992, Canadian hospital-planning consultant Gordon A. Friesen (Figure 3.1) had garnered a worldwide reputation.[1] He was best known for a remarkably cogent set of ideas about how to design, construct, and manage hospitals based on automation and Fordist production-line workflows.[2] His induction for an honorary doctor of laws degree, awarded to him in 1970 by George Washington University, cited his innovative adaptations of modern technology, which were "useful to improvement in patient care."[3] Planning techniques he pioneered were quickly absorbed into part of the basic hospital-planning repertoire.[4] He developed his ideas in response to Canadian life experiences, yet he was responsible for hospital designs around the world, including key projects in the United States, Britain, Costa Rica, Taipei, and Germany, where the University of Cologne Medical Center was perhaps his biggest and most radical undertaking. His work has endured. Friesen-designed hospitals are still in use in Canada, including pavilions in the Ontario cities of Ottawa and Scarborough.[5]

The eponymous Friesen-Concept hospital prescribed a crucial role for women in a vast, mechanized, masculine architecture. Friesen's stated goal was to give nurses more time at the patient's bedside. A 1964 article about Friesen in *Canadian Hospital* took Friesen's rhetoric as a description of the field: "It is considered almost axiomatic that the only proper nursing care is that in which the nursing staff does virtually *nothing else* but minister to the patient."[6] Despite this forceful way of speaking, the images produced by the hospital-planning firm he headed from 1954 to 1976, now gathered in the Friesen Collection at Library and Archives Canada, tell a different story. They rarely depict women interacting with patients. Instead, nurses pose and work amidst sundry machines and hospital equipment in a stark industrial setting of factory-like corridors, communication posts, laboratories, kitchens, and supply rooms (Figure 3.2). The documents systematically show women as "angels" of care embedded in a medical machine built for men. As we will see, his plans depended

Figure 3.1 Gordon A. Friesen, ca. 1970. The caption reads, "The young ladies of the Friesen International staff anticipate the honorary LL.D. degree conferred upon Mr. Friesen by presenting him with their own degree on Valentine's Day." *Concepts* 4, 2 (1970): 7.

on a nursing corps that had the authority, professionalism, training, and masculinity to control the mechanized hospital. The point is not that the mere conjunction of women and machines made women masculine. Indeed, scholars of factory and office work usually point to the opposite phenomenon, namely that as women take up work with machines, the work becomes feminized.[7] Instead, Friesen's championing of women as angels challenges us to rethink the boundaries of what it means to be masculine.

In this chapter, I use the example of Friesen and Friesen-designed hospitals to explore spatial and material contributions to the production, performance, and experience of masculinity in Canada after the Second World War. I focus on a longstanding contradiction in the postwar modern hospital between the female labour force, essential to everyday hospital life, and the masculine machine environment that organized the workplace. The contradiction unfolds as the positioning of one sort of masculinity –military, religious, administrative, and entrepreneurial – against another one – material, mechanical, and spatial. Although histories of public and private life in Canada have been shaped by masculine power, the role of material culture is underexplored in the history of masculinity.[8] As Harry Brod wrote in his introduction to a 1987 edited collection on the "new men's studies," a constructionist account of masculinities seemed to offer the best approach, more specifically a "social feminist analysis of capitalist patriarchal masculinity."[9] I want to shift the history of masculinity away from the relational constructionist account of masculinity (i.e., the cultural

Figure 3.2   Women posed working in Etobicoke General Hospital. *Concepts 7*,
1 (1973): 11.

history of men's experiences as men), which ignores material matter other
than the gendered body. A particular masculinity, in this sense, is not just the
social history of gendered experience – lives lived as male persons – but includes
the material history of objects and places as they constitute or shape our actions, as ground, tool, organization, or structure.

In Friesen's hands, the objects of hospital life, from food and furniture to
buildings and campuses, do more than reflect elusive gender identities. In the
Friesen hospital, masculinity is visibly distributed between people and things.[10]

Moreover, the nurse's place in the automated hospital does not easily map onto gender identities prevalent in broader society, where what counts as masculine is structured by a set of contradictions, namely between queer and straight, clean and dirty, rotting flesh and muscularity, as well as helplessness and control.[11] Nursing was a gendered profession, female but not therefore feminine. In the early twentieth century, the nurse's gender registered neatly on the femininity of the work: women took care of the sick, whereas men cured them.[12] In the postwar automated hospital, nurses' work was not women's work but the work of angels. And angels, after all, were men in Christian mythology. Viewed this way, masculinity is not strictly a set of characteristics or behaviours linked to men's bodies or experiences. It is a performative, relational, social entity, part of an organized structure of material relations that sticks to women as easily as to men.[13]

The Spiritual Aspect

There is a further complication: Friesen's ideals and work are based on a third concern, namely religion, which unveils another facet of the history of postwar masculinity: the spiritual aspect.[14] Religious notions infused both the way Friesen worked as a consultant and the way he understood hospital work. He claimed, "We are all interested in the same basic philosophy, and that is to take care of the whole patient – the mental, physical, and spiritual aspect of the patient."[15] Throughout his career, commentators remarked on how he approached hospital planning and design as a moral endeavour, "pursuing his goal of a better hospital with an almost evangelical fervor" while delivering the "Gospel According to Friesen."[16]

The Friesen-Concept hospital was a self-conscious attempt to take advantage of modern factory life, production techniques, and management systems in order to deliver care and thus *produce* spirituality. The automated hospital and its myriad objects and systems – pneumatic tubes, push-button beds, adjustable chairs, washer-sterilizers – might seem to be part of the materialist culture Friesen decried. His most explicit statement against materialism came early in his career. In a speech given to the American Hospital Association in 1951, he claimed, "One of the reasons why the German people followed Hitler so blindly was because they had over-estimated the material things in life. They were quite willing to denounce their Christian faith in order to join the Nazi religion in which Hitler became their God. Let us not be guilty of riding on the bandwagon of materialism."[17] Friesen did not see this as inconsistent logic; the spiritual aspect was opposed to materialism but not to mechanization, not to the use of technological solutions. Consumerism (i.e., the "chain-store" hospital), car culture (Figure 3.3), supermarkets, Fordist industry, and the factory – all of

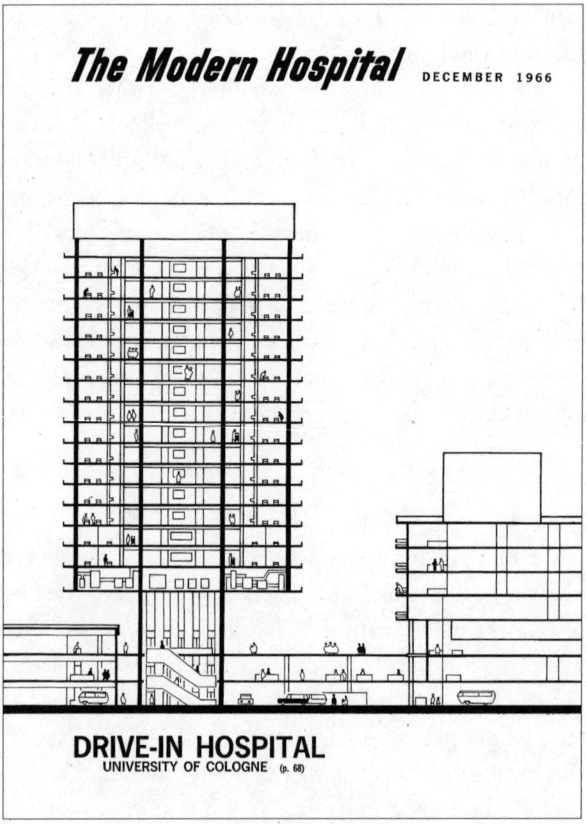

Figure 3.3 Friesen's patient tower at the University of
Cologne Medical Center, which he conceived as a "drive-in
hospital," adopting planning ideas from modern consumer
culture. *Modern Hospital*, December 1966, cover. Courtesy
of Heinle, Wischer und Partner.

these apparently materialist domains were rejigged by Friesen as the mechanical support for spiritual practices.

Friesen, as we will see, was a formidable publicist, so it is possible that the "spiritual aspect" was cant.[18] Yet throughout his career, he posed this configuration of religious care and automation as a desirable, modern configuration of humanism and efficiency; mechanical optimization was the basis of spiritual life. Machine, nurse, masculinity, and spirituality were held together by Friesen's religious conviction that humans are enlivened matter. In 1967 he wrote about how the spirit enlivened mere matter at Mercy San Juan Hospital in Carmichael, California: "As opposed to the erection of an unwieldy structure built with little regard to the modern systems which must be activated within it, this hospital is proof that from the inanimate there can be created a vibrant, living tool for patient care and treatment."[19] How did that spiritual vision of care come to be housed in the assembly-line hospital? What can the Friesen hospital teach us about the contribution that location, décor, and environment make to the constitution and practice of masculinity? In what ways was nursing reconceived as a masculine practice?

Friesen's early hospital work explicitly endorsed religion. He grew up on a Mennonite farm near Saskatoon, Saskatchewan. His first hospital-management job, as business manager at the City Hospital in Saskatoon, came in 1929 at the age of twenty-one and continued until 1937, leading to a position at Belleville General Hospital in Ontario.[20] He joined the medical branch of the Royal Canadian Air Force in 1941, where he stayed until 1946, spending the first three years as the personal assistant to the director of medical services. He was director of a camp for displaced persons that numbered 6,000 refugees in British-occupied Germany, and then in 1944 he worked as the military governor of Kreis Brilon in Westphalia. Back in Canada after the war, he became involved in the planning and construction of a new tower at the Kitchener-Waterloo Hospital. Here, the "spiritual aspect" was conspicuous in three places. In the lobby, an artist depicted the story of the Good Samaritan on pillars (Figure 3.4). The hospital included a "small but elegant" chapel. And a radio service, provided through "pillow ear phones," ensured that "patients will be able to listen regularly to religious services."[21] The "spiritual aspect" determined the physical environment and was enabled and supported through technology.

Altogether, there are a number of masculinities, a number of social roles, practical activities, and experiences constituting maleness that form a surprisingly stable configuration in Friesen's career. There is, first of all, his work fashioning the manliness of the business consultant and, in particular, his own masculinity. There is the sociological reversal in the hospital, where certain kinds of roles perceived as masculine are carried out by women. And the nurse-patient relationship, although rarely detailed in the kinds of documents Friesen has left us, demonstrates the spatiotemporal fluidity of masculine roles and identities that the automated hospital organized and supported.

The Invention of the Postwar Hospital

After the Second World War, hospital planning and construction faced challenges stemming from the consolidation of the so-called modern hospital that followed the First World War. Social and medical historians, including Charles Rosenberg and Morris Vogel, have outlined the "invention" of the modern hospital. Around the turn of the twentieth century, hospitals transformed from

Figure 3.4 The lobby of the Kitchener-Waterloo Hospital, 1951, with Christian-themed artwork and ornamentation, such as paintings of the Good Samaritan on two pillars. Courtesy of Kitchener-Waterloo Record Photographic Negative Collection, Special Collections and Archives, University of Waterloo Library.

custodial institutions, primarily concerned with the care of the sick poor, to scientific institutions, replete with laboratories, trained nurses, and newly accredited surgeons focused on curing patients from all levels of society.[22] Rosenberg calculated that the number of hospitals in the United States rose from 178 in 1873 to 4,359 in 1909. But note that the rise does not reflect a rise in popularity of the older custodial model but the rapid proliferation of the newly invented one. Most of these new hospitals were urban. Once healthcare was established as a basic service that should be available to all citizens, it became apparent that rural areas lagged far behind cities. The Hill-Burton Act in the United States and both the National Health Service and the Nuffield Provincial Hospitals Trust in Britain directly funded the research, design, and construction

Figure 3.5 Scarborough Centenary Hospital. "Distribution," *Hospital Administration in Canada* 9, 1 (1967): 20.

of hospitals in nonurban areas. In Canada the 1948 National Health Grants Program provided the provinces with matching funds for hospital construction. The postwar boom in new hospital construction was concentrated in suburban and rural hospitals.[23]

Friesen's work was rooted in these community-based hospitals. Etobicoke General Hospital, Mercy San Juan Hospital, and Scarborough Centenary Hospital (Figure 3.5) were all new institutions founded and built to serve emerging population centres outside of major cities. His early breakthrough came in the United States when he achieved international recognition as the consultant on a regional chain of ten hospitals for the United Mine Workers of America Welfare and Retirement Fund in Virginia, West Virginia, and Kentucky.[24] The hospitals opened in 1955 and 1956 to serve coalminers and their families.[25] He promoted the proposed facilities as "chain-store" hospitals; the message is that the familiar convenience and efficiencies of the consumer supply chain would work for a hospital system – and work well.[26] With the United Mine Workers hospitals, he presented four areas where automation improved the supply system: receiving, processing, storage, and dispatch (Figure 3.6). The whole system was meant to lower, if not eliminate, any time the nurse spent obtaining supplies and returning soiled items. The hope was that through the overwhelming presence of machines, both nurse and patient would find themselves in a situation where all required materials, such as bandages, food, medicines, instruments, and clothing, were ready-to-hand.[27]

Figure 3.6 The process of centralized dispatch in the United Mine Workers hospitals. Floor plan by Sherlock, Smith and Adams Architects. *Architectural Forum* 105, 5 (1956): 113.

One way to understand Friesen's program is to place him in the tradition of efficiency-oriented twentieth-century American management consultants. These figures include Henry Ford, whose ideas about automation certainly influenced Friesen's.[28] Friesen would surely also have known about the famous "scientific" management of Frederick Winslow Taylor[29] and especially about the proselytizing work of industrial engineers Lillian Gilbreth and her husband, Frank.[30] Friesen, however, saw his own concepts as a distinct advance on these older methods of improving hospital work.[31] For instance, besides not using the terms of scientific management, he never vaunted their well-known time and motion studies.[32] He argued that hospitals had already incorporated business management ideas such as "nursing activity studies, staffing patterns, development of the nursing team"; he proposed a stream of brand-new ideas "to take hospitals out of the horse-and-buggy era."[33]

The Nurse

The Friesen hospital followed a strict organization of the sexes (nurses were almost 100 percent female) but welcomed a confusion of genders.[34] In this description of the Friesen concept, the pronoun that belongs with each role is telling:

> Why is the patient always the last one to be consulted in any plan to improve hospital services? Why is the nurse the low man on the totem pole of providers of health care? Why does she sometimes spend as much as half of her eight or twelve hour shift away from the bedside finding the supplies she needs to give care?[35]

Friesen's response to this confusion was twofold. First, he elevated nurses from "low man" to team head: "I love nurses. They must be kept on the highest professional level making sure they are recognized as an important part of the medical team."[36] Second, the things in the hospital were likewise elevated. Friesen argued that the nurse should devote 100 percent of her time to the patient. This meant that the *entire* layout of the hospital – elevators, loading docks, dumbwaiters, and laundry rooms – was secondary to the nurse's ability to be present with the patient.[37] Attending to the patient's well-being required a comprehensive approach to the hospital setting, from bed to shelving to trolley to floor plan to elevator to building configuration to regional hospital network. "If we are interested in the care of the patient," he wrote, "we should take a little more care in the design of the hospital which we are building."[38]

In other words, he subordinated the hospital's technological regime to the needs of nurses. He invented an apparatus, which he called the "Nurserver," that signalled the importance of the nurse. This piece of equipment was essentially a cupboard accessible both from the corridor and from the patient's room (Figure 3.7). Employees could stock it with clean supplies and remove dirty ones without disturbing the nurse or the patient. In parallel, the nurse could attend to the patient, including dispensing food and medications, without leaving the

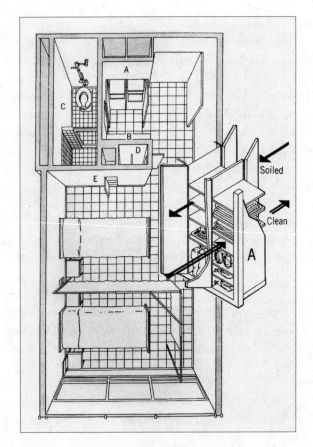

Figure 3.7 Friesen popularized his own invention, the
"Nurserver," which he devised as a way to deliver clean
supplies to and remove soiled supplies from patients' rooms.
Marijo Juzwiak, "Glimpse of the Future? The Friesen
Hospital," *RN Magazine,* October 1964, reprint, LAC,
Gordon Arthur Friesen Collection, MG31, B51, vol. 4.

room. At one scale, the Nurservers were furniture, but they also functioned as
walls, separating private patient areas inside the room from the public corridors.[39] In turn, the Nurservers required a centralized storage room on each
floor, equipped with service elevators or dumbwaiters for both soiled and clean
items. But because elevator shafts run vertically through all the hospital floors,
the placement of the storage was key to the layout of the hospital (Figure 3.8).
British architect John Weeks put it this way: "[Friesen] rationalised whole
buildings round a cluster of vertical shafts for the mechanical distribution and

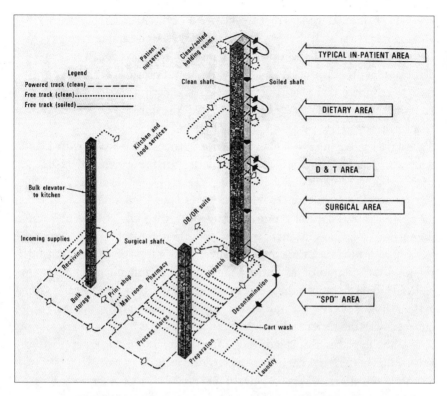

Figure 3.8 An axonometric diagram of how supplies circulated vertically in a Friesen-concept hospital. "The Interior Network," *Consulting Engineer* 34, 10 (October 1970): 112.

collection of all people using and things used in the hospital. And most hospitals now being built [1964] owe pretty much to these influences."[40]

Friesen's insistence on the importance of the nurse to the physical environment of the hospital (i.e., things and equipment) as well as to its spatial organization is strikingly different from the subordinate role for nurses that scholars have revealed in studies of the institution.[41] It differs also from the social history of nurses, which sees nursing work in hospital environments as versions of female work.[42] Scholars have argued, for instance, that in the first half of the twentieth century, hospital training schools for nurses gave women new visibility and new roles in the modern city, dedicated places in which to explore careers outside of traditional roles in the middle-class home.[43] Friesen hospitals did not counter these interpretations, but they did complicate them. For instance, Annmarie Adams has argued that women in hospitals tend to be spatially positioned in ways that associate them with nature, whereas men live and work in parts of the hospital associated with the city and technology.[44] Yet in the Friesen hospital, the nurses, the largest group of women, were explicitly associated with machinery, and the entire layout of the hospital was organized to reinforce that association. In short, the caring nurses, supported by an array of machinery, enacted and embodied "the spiritual aspect" of hospital treatment.[45]

Or did they? An interview with Friesen published in *Canadian Nurse* in 1980 carries the subtitle, "On the Side of the Angels."[46] In the accompanying images, there are pictures of three women: a nurse, a clerk or "technician," and an "aide." At issue here is Friesen's concept of "no nurses' station," a planning idea in which an administrative control centre substituted for the familiar nursing station. This arrangement was meant to free the nurse to move from patient to patient without returning each time to a centralized post.[47] It involved breaking down the ward nurses' traditional duties and redistributing them among three specialized labour functions that corresponded to three new physical and spatial systems. In the photos, the nurse (recognizable by her uniform and hat) is not engaged with the patient, although that relationship is a staple of Friesen imagery. She is pictured instead interacting with the containers in the Nurserver. In 1964 Friesen described the clerk or technician as "a secretary who also takes outside messages for patients and greets visitors. A co-ordinator, she is more than a ward clerk; she is not a ward manager – there is nothing to manage. Perhaps a Ward Secretary?"[48] The aide's responsibilities included restocking supplies and removing soiled items; this subordinate role was envisaged as part of the "teamwork" required to meet the goal of having the nurse spend 100 percent of her time with the patient. There is an important spatial differentiation between the three roles. The nurse is inside the patient's room, the aide is outside in the corridor, and the clerk is at the command centre (Figures 3.9 and 3.10). The nurses' masculinity, then, was posited in relation to space and equipment.

There were two other figures that indicated the fluidity of masculinity in a Friesen hospital: the surgeon and the patient. Friesen's planning assumed that both were male, and although his hospitals were built (i.e., it was not just a question of prescriptions about gender roles), the surgeon in the surgery was the head of a team, and the dichotomies between clean and soiled and between man and woman mapped neatly onto the dichotomy between doctor and nurse. That is, the layout of the surgery and the movements of clean and soiled supplies were dictated by hospital equipment.[49] On the ward, however, the nurse was at the top of the hierarchy, and the dichotomy between clean and soiled was joined by the dichotomies between upright and supine, mobile and immobile, as well

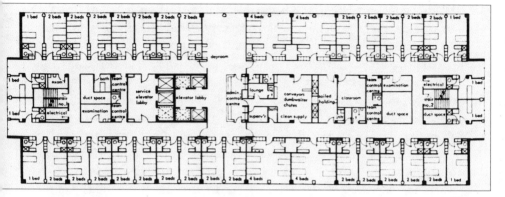

Figure 3.9 The floor plan of Scarborough Centenary Hospital, showing the spatial division of labour among the members of the nursing team. The administrative control centre at the middle of the plan is not a nursing station and does not visually survey the nurses' working areas in the patients' rooms. "Distribution," *Hospital Administration in Canada* 9, 1 (1967): 21.

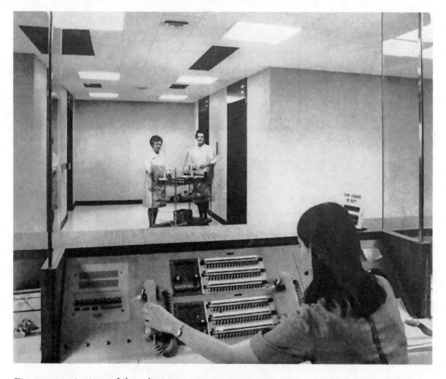

Figure 3.10 A view of the administrative communication centre on a floor of Scarborough Centenary Hospital. "The Interior Network," *Consulting Engineer* 34, 10 (October 1970): 110.

as healthy and sick. The nurse, then, was on the masculine side of the hierarchy, and the male-female dichotomy no longer registered because the actual split was female-female (i.e., between nurse and aid or between nurse and clerk).

The sick patient is temporarily sexless – and therefore male. The patient, in a situation of loss, needs protection (until restoration), not just physically but also psychically. A commentator in *Material Handling Engineering* enthused (the pronoun used is once again important): "Friesen believes in automating all around the patient. Handle his supplies mechanically. Bring his tray to the floor mechanically. But the patient's in the eye of the hurricane. He gets personalized service. Nurses always close by. Easy to communicate with. Meals when he wants them."[50] Paradoxically, nurses sustained the authority of the institution, with its masculine ideal of the surgeon as hero (and the administrator as efficiency expert, a wartime value), in fact making the helpless, passive, male patient into the controlling "king."

The Consultant

In 1954 Friesen left his work with the United Mine Workers (with the hospitals still under construction) to establish a private consultancy in Washington, DC, Gordon A. Friesen Associates (later Gordon A. Friesen International), which he sold to American Medical International in 1973. With his consultancy, he spent the rest of his career promoting proprietary notions – the Friesen Concept – of precisely how automation and workflow processes should be established in the hospital. He was always ready with a provocative comment. In 1977, in arguing for an inpatient entertainment system, he quipped, "More people die of boredom than of cardiac, cancer, etc."[51] Perhaps the best comparison is the postwar advertising maverick. When television host Frank McGee interviewed Friesen on NBC's *The Today Show* in August 1972, Friesen offered up a seamless pitch for the Friesen hospital. The interviewer's first question concerned one of Friesen's slogans: "Now, you have been quoted as saying somewhere that we are practicing 20th century medicine in 19th century facilities. What do you mean?"[52] In the short interview, Friesen was able to mention his idea for preventive health centres, single-patient rooms, the Nurservers, food preparation and delivery modelled on the blast-freeze system used by airlines, and the central dispatch system. Friesen's own in-house magazine, *Concepts*, vaunted the hospital consultant as "innovator and catalyzer."[53] Friesen was clearly good at the business of selling, relishing the masculine role of the entrepreneurial planning consultant.

Friesen thus had an unusual role in the healthcare world. He was not the client and not the administrator. And he was certainly not a medical man or architect. Architects seemed to be interchangeable in his mind; they were, after all, merely implementing his suggestions. And he cared little about central construction problems such as structural systems or the external image of hospital buildings. "He [Friesen] said that there was too much emphasis on what the hospital should be architecturally. 'Let's develop the organization first and then put a roof over it,' he advised."[54] There were some competitors and forerunners. One predecessor was Sigismund Schulz Goldwater (1873–1942), a physician, hospital superintendent, and hospital consultant, who was named hospital commissioner of New York City in 1933.[55] A more contemporary competitor was architect E. Todd Wheeler (1906–1987), who worked as an independent hospital consultant from 1942 to 1957 but spent most of his career as a hospital architect in the firm Perkins and Will.[56]

The consultant, in Friesen's terms, took risks. In a discussion of the consultant's role, an unsigned opinion column of 1966 in *Modern Hospital* raised questions, on the one hand, "about the propriety of recommending experimental departures in hospital design and function. The client hospital has to pay for the experiment, one consultant warned, suggesting that only known and tested methods should be recommended." On the other hand, medicine itself was clearly advancing through experimentation, and perhaps hospital architecture should follow suit: "Unknown improvements that will make tomorrow's hospital as much better than today's as the antibiotic is better than the mustard plaster."[57]

Finally, as a consultant, Friesen played the part of an evangelist. Becoming a preacher was a childhood dream. "When I was a young lad some three score years ago I worked in the summer on my uncle's farm in Northern Saskatchewan," he wrote. "I used to lie on the bottom of the horse-drawn hay wagon and dream about becoming an evangelist like Billy Sunday."[58] The last important part of the "spiritual aspect" of the hospital, then, was that it gave an unambiguous masculine role model for the consultant to follow:

> Friesen's own dynamics are rather considerable. He is a man of great vigor and movement, sometimes even theatrical, his arms waving a part of his message, his fingers running through a mane of long, almost pure white hair ... A visitor leaves with the assurance that Friesen is utterly devout, one might even say evangelistic, with respect to his doctrines of patient care. And as one travels the country, he is equally assured that Friesen does not want for disciples. There are, of course, those who differ with either the thrust or the emphasis of his concepts, but there is none who ignores him and more than a few who proudly preach The Gospel According to Friesen.[59]

Conclusion

In this chapter I have argued that Friesen's work manifests the interplay among three kinds of masculinities. First, there is the evangelical masculinity of Friesen himself, in the role of proselytizing hospital consultant. Second, there is the equivocal masculinity of the female nurses in their role as angels and assembly-line workers. Finally, there is the situational masculinity afforded, supported, and organized by material things, namely hospital equipment and architecture. Overall, I have claimed that masculinity is a disposition of things in the world: it has material markers and conditions that (like maleness itself) cannot be directly observed or measured but can in some way be "read off" a plan, a photograph, a trolley. Nurservers, for instance, were meant to free nurses; but they also, equivocally, constrained them, perpetuating masculine roles in the mechanical world and feminine roles in the patient's world. We are in a position to say about masculinity that it is not itself one-half of a binary couple. Instead, it is constituted within a system of binaries regarding sexuality (queer-straight), sex (male-female), occupations (nurse-doctor), and purity (dirty-clean). We know that such pairs are asymmetrical. That is, only one-half of the pair has access to both sides. For instance, a queer person has access to the experience of a straight person, but the straight person does not live in the same simultaneity. Thus the nurse has access to the masculinity that doctors perform in the hospital; nursing work, although carried out by women, can be masculine work. Yet this kind of analysis lacks material. That is, the masculine, although understood as an immaterial something that cannot be measured or directly observed, is partly constituted by material stuff. When buildings, building design, technology, and equipment are brought into consideration, the history of masculinity need no longer rely on men's experience as the centre of the narrative. Friesen's dedication to bringing nonmedical technology into the hospital helps both to highlight and to limn the history of masculinity in Canada as something extending before and beyond the life experiences of men.

Notes

1   See the interview conducted by Friesen's biographer, Donald G. Soth, "Gordon A. Friesen: An Interview," *Journal of Healthcare Material Management* 5, 4 (1987): 26–34. The unpublished manuscript is in Library and Archives Canada (LAC), Gordon Arthur Friesen Collection, MG31, B51, vol. 4.

2   See the assessment in Stephen Verderber and David J. Fine, *Healthcare Architecture in an Era of Radical Transformation* (New Haven, CT: Yale University Press, 2000), 64, passim.

3   "Honorary Doctor of Laws Degree Conferred upon Gordon A. Friesen by the George Washington University," *Concepts* 4, 2 (1970): 1.

4 In a paper presented to the Royal Institute of British Architects in 1964, British hospital architect John Weeks wrote, "And most hospitals now being built owe pretty much to [Friesen's] influences." John Weeks, "Hospitals for the 1970s," *Medical Care* 3, 4 (1965): 197.

5 On Friesen's role in the planning and operation of Ottawa General Hospital, see Patricia Teskey, "The Modern Hospital: Building for the Future," *Canadian Medical Association Journal* 125, 5 (1981): 481–82, 486–87, 490. On Scarborough Centenary Hospital, see "The Friesen Concept," *Consulting Engineer* (October 1970): 105–8.

6 "Friesen's Progress: Look! No Nursing Station," *Canadian Hospital* 41, 3 (1964): 43, emphasis in original.

7 For an account of how technology in the United States was made masculine, see Ruth Oldenziel, *Making Technology Masculine: Men, Women and Modern Machines in America, 1870–1945* (Amsterdam: Amsterdam University Press, 1999). See also Kim England and Kate Boyer, "Women's Work: The Feminization and Shifting Meanings of Clerical Work," *Journal of Social History* 43, 2 (2009): 307–40; and Delphine Gardey, "Culture of Gender, Culture of Technology," in *Cultures of Technology and the Quest for Innovation,* ed. Helga Nowotny, 73–94 (New York: Berghahn, 2006).

8 On overcoming the divisions between material and gendered bodies, see Stacy Alamo and Susan Hekman, eds., *Material Feminisms* (Bloomington: Indiana University Press, 2008), esp. Hekman's essay, "Constructing the Ballast: An Ontology for Feminism," 85–119. Michel Foucault's work on bio-power, begun in *Discipline and Punish* (New York: Random House, 1979), lies behind many attempts to theorize gendered bodies as the historical interaction between ideals/concepts and bodies/practices.

9 Harry Brod, "Introduction: Themes and Theses," in *The Making of Masculinities: The New Men's Studies,* ed. Harry Brod (Boston: Allen and Unwin, 1987), 13. For a recent Canadian version of this configuration, see Christopher J. Greig and Wayne J. Martino, "Introduction: Masculinities in Post-industrial and Neoliberal Times," in *Canadian Men and Masculinities: Historical and Contemporary Perspectives,* ed. Christopher J. Greig and Wayne J. Martino, 1–20 (Toronto: Canadian Scholars' Press, 2012). The constructionist notion was perhaps most useful as a way to grasp the historical unfolding of archetypes. See Michael Kimmel, *Manhood in America: A Cultural History* (New York: Free Press, 1996); and E. Anthony Rotundo, *American Manhood: Transformations in Masculinity from the Revolution to the Present Era* (New York: Basic Books, 1993).

10 On the intertwining of the material, medical, and social in hospitals, see Annmarie Adams, Kevin Schwartzman, and David Theodore, "Collapse and Expand: Architecture and Tuberculosis Therapy in Montreal, 1909, 1933, 1954," *Technology and Culture* 49, 4 (2008): 908–42; and Alberto Cambrosio and Peter Keating, *Biomedical Platforms: Realigning the Normal and the Pathological in Late-Twentieth-Century Medicine* (Cambridge, MA: MIT Press, 2003).

11 Aaron Belkin, *Bring Me Men: Military Masculinity and the Benign Façade of American Enterprise, 1898–2001* (New York: Columbia University Press, 2012), 36, 76, 173.

12 Kathryn McPherson, *Bedside Matters: The Transformation of Canadian Nursing, 1900–1990* (Toronto: Oxford University Press, 1996). For studies of nursing outside the hospital, see Jayne Elliot, Meryn Stuart, and Cynthia Toman, eds., *Place and Practice in Canadian Nursing History* (Vancouver: UBC Press, 2008).

13 Gail Bederman, *Manliness and Civilization: A Cultural History of Gender and Race in the United States, 1880–1917* (Chicago: University of Chicago Press, 1995); R.W. Connell, *Masculinities* (Berkeley: University of California Press, 1995); J. Beynon, *Masculinities and Culture* (Milton Keynes, UK: Open Universities Press, 2002).

14 He first used the term in Gordon A. Friesen, "The Spiritual Aspect," *Canadian Hospital* 28, 12 (1951): 27–28, 72.

15 Quoted in John Weeks, "Hospitals of the Future," *British Medical Journal* 1, 5241 (1961): 1757.

16 Booth Mooney, "U.S. Hospitals 'Largely Obsolete,'" *Constructor,* February 1968, reprint, LAC, Gordon Arthur Friesen Collection, MG31, B51, vol. 4; "The Gospel According to Friesen: A Conference at the Hospital Centre," *British Hospital Journal and Social Service Review,* November 25, 1966, offprint, LAC, Gordon Arthur Friesen Collection, MG31, B51, vol. 3.

17 Friesen, "Spiritual Aspect," 72.

18 Verderber and Fine, *Healthcare Architecture,* 64: "He would develop a prototype system or unit ... and proceed to market it with the intensity of an automobile manufacturer with a new model."

19 Quoted in Mooney, "U.S. Hospitals."

20 On his planning and construction activities in Belleville, see James Govan and Gordon A. Friesen, "Past Performance – Present Needs – Future Possibilities," *Canadian Hospital,* October 1940, 28–32, 78, 80.

21 "Novel Features Noted at New 'K-W' Hospital," *Canadian Hospital* 28, 7 (1951): 30–35, 78. The article anticipates television, too: "Operating rooms are fitted with television conduits which, it is hoped, will come into use later" (78).

22 On the rise of the modern institution (and its buildings), see Charles Rosenberg, *The Care of Strangers: The Rise of America's Hospital System* (New York: Basic Books, 1987); Allan M. Brandt and David C. Sloane, "Of Beds and Benches: Building the Modern American Hospital," in *The Architecture of Science,* ed. P. Galison and E. Thompson, 281–308 (Cambridge, MA: MIT Press, 2000); and John D. Thompson and Grace Goldin, *The Hospital: A Social and Architectural History* (New Haven, CT: Yale University Press, 1975). On Canadian hospitals, see Annmarie Adams, *Medicine by Design: The Architect and the Modern Hospital, 1893-1943* (Minneapolis: University of Minnesota Press, 2008); Denis Goulet, François Hudon, and Othmar Keel, *Histoire de l'Hôpital Notre-Dame de Montréal, 1880-1980* (Montreal: VLB Éditeur, 1993); and David Gagan and Rosemary Gagan, *For Patients of Moderate Means: A Social History of the Voluntary Public General Hospital in Canada, 1890-1950* (Montreal and Kingston: McGill-Queen's University Press, 2002).

23 And among these institutions, the university teaching hospitals had a particular role to play in integrating hospital activities into social life. The large, urban, academic health centres changed later, related to changes in medical education. These projects, such as the McMaster Health Sciences Centre, incorporated the ideas of Friesen and others in a wave after 1965. See Thomas Strickland, "Experimental Spaces: Megastructures, Medicine, and McMaster" (PhD diss., McGill University, 2012). On the University Hospital in Köln, Germany, see "Drive-In Hospital Is Planned for Cologne," *Modern Hospital* 107, 6 (1966): 68–75.

24 John Weeks wrote several influential articles assessing the United Mine Workers hospitals, including "Developments in the USA," *Hospital and Health Management* 22 (1958): 365–70; "Developments in the United States of America," *Royal Institute of British Architects Journal,* January 1959, 83–87; and "Mechanization of Hospital Design in Britain," *Architectural Design* 31, 1 (1961): 10–11.

25 The funding officially came from the United Mine Workers of America Welfare and Retirement Fund through its Memorial Hospital Association. Ivana Krajcinovi, *From Company Doctors to Managed Care: The United Mine Workers' Noble Experiment* (Ithaca, NY: Cornell University Press, 1997), 107–30.

26 "For Coal Miners and Their Families: Chain-Store Hospitals," *Modern Hospital* 81, 5 (1953): 54–61.
27 Gordon A. Friesen, "Automation in Hospital Design," *Architectural Design,* January 1961, 8–9.
28 On Ford, see John C. Wood and Michael C. Wood, *Henry Ford: Critical Evaluations in Business and Management,* 2 vols. (New York: Routledge, 2003).
29 Frederick Winslow Taylor, *The Principles of Scientific Management* (New York: Harper and Brothers, 1911).
30 For example, see Frank B. Gilbreth, "Hospital Efficiency from the Standpoint of the Efficiency Expert," *Boston Medical and Surgical Journal* 172 (1915): 774–75. Gilbreth had a direct effect on the surgical services of the American hospital. See Caitjan Gainty, "'Going after the high-brows': Frank Gilbreth and the Surgical Subject, 1912–1917," *Representations* 118, 1 (2012): 1–27.
31 Friesen marketed his services as innovative and forward-looking. Taylor's book *The Principles of Scientific Management* was published in 1911. Taylorism would thus have seemed old-fashioned, a remnant of business management from a half-century earlier. On the uptake of scientific management in nursing in that earlier generation, see Cynthia Toman, "'Trained Brains Are Better Than Trained Muscles': Scientific Management and Canadian Nurses, 1910–1939," *Nursing History Review* 11 (2003): 89–108.
32 Lillian Gilbreth continued to advise hospitals on nursing as late as 1951. See Barry T. Ross and Bopaya Bidanda, "A Brief History of Health Systems Engineering – Its Early Years through 1989: An Industrial Engineering Perspective," *IIE Transactions on Healthcare Systems Engineering* 4, 4 (2014): 217–29. Scholars align these later contributions, however, with the arrival of operations research in hospital management. See Tolu K. Abe, Benita M. Beamon, Richard L. Storch, and Justin Agus, "Operations Research Applications in Hospital Operations: Part I," *IIE Transactions on Healthcare Systems Engineering* 6, 1 (2016): 42–54.
33 "Friesen's Progress," 43.
34 In 1960 about 2 percent of professional nurses in the United States were men. See Patricia D'Antonio and Jean C. Whelan, "Counting Nurses: The Power of Historical Census Data," *Journal of Clinical Nursing* 18, 19 (2009): 2719. On the sociology of men working as nurses, see Ruth Simpson, *Men in Caring Occupations: Doing Gender Differently* (Basingstoke, UK: Palgrave Macmillan, 2009); and Ruth Simpson, "Masculinity at Work: The Experiences of Men in Female Dominated Occupations," *Work, Employment and Society* 18, 2 (2004): 349–68.
35 Quoted in Anne Besharah, *"CNJ* Interviews Gordon Friesen: On the Side of the Angels," *Canadian Nurse,* 76 (June 1980): 45.
36 Ibid.
37 On the organization of the hospital around nursing activities, see David Theodore, "'The Fattest Possible Nurse,'" in *Hospital Life: Theory and Practice from the Medieval to the Modern,* ed. S. Sheard and L. Abreu, 273–98 (London: Peter Lang, 2013).
38 Weeks, "Hospitals of the Future," 1757.
39 For a detailed study of planning a hospital around the Nurserver, see "The Friesen Concept." Nurservers are still in use at the Ottawa General Hospital, which opened in 1980.
40 Weeks, "Hospitals for the 1970s," 197.
41 Susan Reverby, *Ordered to Care: The Dilemma of American Nursing, 1850–1945* (Cambridge, UK: Cambridge University Press, 1987); Barbara Melosh, *"The Physician's Hand": Work, Culture, and Conflict in American Nursing* (Philadelphia: Temple University Press, 1992); Veronica Strong-Boag, "Making a Difference: The History of Canada's Nurses," *Canadian Bulletin of Medical History* 8, 2 (1991): 231–48.

42 Masculine authority demands women adopt roles that are sometimes unmasculine and sometimes structural, among them nurturers and victims. See Bederman, *Manliness and Civilization;* and Cynthia Enloe, *Maneuvers: The International Politics of Militarizing Women's Lives* (Berkeley: University of California Press, 2000).

43 Annmarie Adams, "Rooms of Their Own: The Nurses' Residences at Montreal's Royal Victoria Hospital," *Material Culture Review* 40 (1994): 37.

44 Ibid., 32.

45 Weeks, "Hospitals of the Future," 1757.

46 Besharah, "*CNJ* Interviews Gordon Friesen," 45.

47 Lowering the distance travelled daily by nurses is a constant preoccupation of hospital planners. See, for instance, Nuffield Provincial Hospitals Trust, *The Work of Nurses in Hospital Wards: Report of a Job-Analysis* (London: Nuffield Provincial Hospitals Trust, 1953).

48 "Friesen's Progress," 46.

49 Sister Mary Kathleen Anne Campbell, "Friesen Concept Applied to the Operating Room," *Point of View (Ethicon)* 4, 2 (1967), in LAC, Gordon Arthur Friesen Collection, MG31, B51, vol. 3.

50 "Needed: Handling Health for Hospitals," *Material Handling Engineering,* October 1969, 5.

51 Quoted in Maria R. Traska, "Planner Sees 'Supermarket' Concept for Future Hospital Center Construction," *Modern Healthcare* 7, 2 (1977): 31. Friesen had argued for modern entertainment systems as standard features in patients' rooms twenty-five years earlier; see note 21.

52 Transcript in LAC, Gordon Arthur Friesen Collection, MG31, B51, vol. 6.

53 "Special Issue, The Consultant – Innovator and Catalyzer," *Concepts* 6, 1 (1972).

54 Emma Harrison, "Electronic Nurse for 10 Patients Is Developed," *New York Times,* September 13, 1961.

55 Goldwater's writings on hospital planning and administration were posthumously collected in Sigismund Schulz Goldwater, *On Hospitals* (New York: Macmillan, 1947).

56 See Verderber and Fine, *Healthcare Architecture,* 106–7. Wheeler was known for his futuristic, speculative projects for hospital design. See E. Todd Wheeler, *Hospital Modernization and Expansion* (New York: McGraw-Hill, 1971).

57 "Looking Around," *Modern Hospital* 106, 2 (1966): 85.

58 Friesen wrote this story on two cue cards preserved at Library and Archives Canada. The words are the opening to the speech he made in 1970 while accepting an honorary doctor of laws degree from George Washington University. LAC, Gordon Arthur Friesen Collection, MG31, B51, vol. 1.

59 "The Friesen Concept," 105.

4

"I am still the Supt. in this plant": Negotiating Middle-Class Masculinity in Edmonton Packinghouses in an Era of Union Strength, 1947–66

Cynthia Loch-Drake

WHEN THE TREND-SETTING company Canada Packers Ltd. built a sleek new packinghouse in Edmonton during the depths of the Great Depression, the plant's architecture embodied corporate Canada's modernist imagination, winning the gold medal at a Toronto exhibition a year later, in 1937 (Figure 4.1).[1] It was built of brick, and its box-like, strong, lean lines effectively conveyed the corporate elite's values of industriousness, control, and hard-headed, rational efficiency, which have long been linked to white, middle-class masculinity.[2] Toronto executives positioned the office at the front of the building, with large windows stretching around the corner of two ground-floor walls to assert local management's power and status with a sweeping 180-degree view of the property (Figure 4.2). Inside the bright offices, managers, salesmen, and administrators in well-tailored suits worked in an elegant atmosphere of order and calm that contrasted starkly with the horror, gore, and apparent disorder of industrialized slaughter taking place in the bowels of the building, where male production workers sweated in the heat, humidity, and brutality of the kill floor (Figures 4.3 and 4.4).

Despite the stark class lines that elite managers tried to draw at the local level using architecture, interior design, and dress codes, by the 1950s a new era of strong unionism and centralized bargaining in the Canadian meatpacking industry had fostered an unusual degree of cross-class cooperation between local white-collar men and male unionists. Negotiations at the local level increasingly subverted head office goals of efficiency and control, particularly control over labour costs. Using Edmonton packinghouses as a lens, this chapter explores the diverse ways that local salaried white-collar men, as well as the male corporate elite in Toronto who hired and directed them, responded to this new era. It focuses on the period between the implementation of industry-wide bargaining in 1947 and the series of labour disputes that began to destabilize both the bargaining system and the industry in 1966.[3] The study examines how particular notions of middle-class masculinity were mobilized to bolster the

Figure 4.1 Canada Packers plant, Edmonton, 1937. *Royal Architectural Institute of Canada Journal* 14, 2 (1937): 158.

Figure 4.2 Office entrance of Canada Packers plant, Edmonton, 1937. *Royal Architectural Institute of Canada Journal* 14, 2 (1937): 160.

status of white-collar men and to legitimize corporate power, particularly at Canada Packers Ltd., by far the largest and most influential packing company in the country.[4] The chapter considers the practices, ideals, and strategies used by white-collar men at different levels of the corporation to protect their status and power.

I argue that packing executives, particularly at Canada Packers, invested in a technocratic ideal of middle-class masculinity that had considerable currency in the decades following the Second World War. In companies that were national in scope with branch plants in cities like Edmonton, head office managers drew on modern, highly gendered, class-based, and racialized notions of bureaucratic rationalism, technical expertise, and professionalism within an elaborate system of centralized bargaining to strengthen their authority in the new era of union legitimacy. These strategies often yielded contradictory results. Local salaried men negotiated middle-class masculinity in diverse ways, at times forging unusual levels of cross-class cooperation, yet their strategies most often reinforced dominant social hierarchies.

During the era of national pattern bargaining, each of the Big Three packing companies operated a packinghouse in Edmonton, generating hundreds of white-collar jobs.[5] These work organizations were profoundly historical and variable "sites for the reproduction of men's power and masculinities."[6] Studies of work experiences and practices have revealed many different ways of being a man based on fine "distinctions, such as those between 'mental' and 'manual,' 'skilled' and 'unskilled,' or even workers in different departments or offices."[7] During the mid-twentieth century, Canadian companies operating far-flung packinghouses from a head office often thousands of miles away were an important cultural arena where hierarchies of masculinity were constantly being elaborated, negotiated, reinforced, and challenged in complex ways that intersected with class but also with race, ethnicity, and other aspects of identity. Figures 4.3 and 4.4 make it clear that both the office and the beef kill department were male preserves. The only woman in the photographs filled the "feminine" role of switchboard operator and receptionist in the office. The photos also suggest that in comparison to the ethnically diverse working-class men on the kill floor, many of eastern or southern European heritage, those who held middle-class positions in the office were exclusively white Anglo-Celtic men, reflecting the persistence of racial hierarchies produced by global processes of colonization and slavery.

The middle class has played a central role in the making of "modern" societies that are undergoing rapid rates of industrial development and urbanization. For my purposes, modernity is identified broadly by notions of rationalism, control, and progress, which emerged during the Enlightenment,[8] but it also

Figure 4.3 Canada Packers plant, front office, 1941. Provincial Archives of Alberta, BL361/11.

Figure 4.4 Beef kill floor, Canada Packers plant, Edmonton, 1952. Provincial Archives of Alberta, BL1976/1.

refers to a "discourse of equal opportunity and its inherent assumption of un-equal outcomes," which has legitimized social hierarchies of class, gender, and race or ethnicity.[9] Recent studies challenge a dominant discourse that treats the middle class as natural, as self-evident, or even as the solution to contemporary economic, political, and social problems.[10] Mid-twentieth-century Edmonton and its important meatpacking industry were heavily influenced by the ideals of the city's middle classes as it experienced dramatic rates of industrial develop-ment and urbanization, particularly following a major oil discovery in 1947.[11]

Like being middle-class, masculinity is an aspect of identity that is often nat-uralized yet can gain importance within a particular historical context. The ex-clusion of women from all but the lowest-level office positions made masculinity a central aspect of identity for white-collar men in Edmonton packinghouses. Scholars have documented the fluid nature of middle-class ideals of masculinity in Canada.[12] R.W. Connell's concept of hegemonic masculinity describes the most "culturally exalted" ideal of masculinity in a given historical moment.[13] As David Morgan has explained, some masculinities become powerful because they are "more dominant, more valued, or more persuasive than others."[14]

The Self-Made Man

The roots of a hegemonic masculinity in the Canadian packing industry can be traced to the ideal of the "self-made man," which emerged in nineteenth-century America with the growth of a market-based economy. This masculine ideal celebrated the pursuit of self-interest and qualities like ambition and dominance as vehicles for individual achievement, particularly economic independence, which was most highly prized.[15] The entrepreneurial businessmen who founded the meatpacking companies that became successful in Canada around the turn of the twentieth century epitomized the image of the self-made man who achieved economic independence through his initiative and ability to reason. American Gustavus Swift, who founded the Swift Corporation, and Calgary-based Pat Burns, of Burns and Company, were craftsmen who parlayed their skills into a successful industrial enterprise by inventing or adopting technolo-gies and processes like the moving chain and the "disassembly line" to cut labour costs.[16] Their reputation for achieving business success through efficiencies wrought by hard work and persistence reinforced an image of the dutiful and responsible "self-made modern capitalist," earning them popular respect and entitlement to their phenomenal wealth.[17]

The men who shaped Canada Packers also conformed to the ideal of the self-made man. Joseph Flavelle, who founded the firm central to the 1927 merger of four companies that formed Canada Packers, represented a new generation of meatpacking entrepreneurs who grasped the logic of the operation but had never held a knife.[18] Using strategic efficiencies to turn his pork-packing operation into the largest in the British Empire by the First World War, Flavelle became a luminary in the Canadian modernist firmament, symbolizing the pure spirit of capitalism for many Canadians, until his public image was tarnished by allegations of wartime profiteering.[19] Similarly, James Stanley (J.S.) McLean, who engineered the 1927 merger and became the company's first president, came to represent the modern Canadian industrial maverick. McLean, who trained under Joseph Flavelle and married Flavelle's niece, was considered an accounting wizard. He single-mindedly sought ways to increase the efficiency of the operation by cutting costs, developing Canada Packers into a national company that operated packinghouses and distribution centres in most major urban centres from coast to coast.[20] McLean held a major share in and tight control of the publicly traded company until he turned over the presidency to his son William (Bill) Flavelle McLean in 1954, a month before he died.[21] The power of this masculine ideal helped these entrepreneurs to legitimize highly concentrated ownership in the Canadian meatpacking industry, despite ongoing public concern about price collusion and excessive market dominance.[22]

In early-twentieth-century Canada, the ideal of the self-made man was becoming much less attainable for the legions of white-collar salaried men who staffed the large new American and Canadian firms that were emerging. The era of monopoly capitalism that began in the late nineteenth century created fewer opportunities for ambitious middle-class men to achieve economic independence. Large corporations, finding it difficult to attract young men to white-collar desk jobs, actively cultivated an alternative, more professionalized, and bureaucratic image of middle-class masculinity. Management emphasized the higher status of nonmanual work in a clean environment, as well as the opportunities for professional designation and promotion. Being on a salary and more highly paid than production men, who were on an hourly wage, reinforced the status of white-collar men. Corporations also implemented strict hierarchies of gender and race to essentialize white-collar work as the exclusive preserve of white, Anglo men.[23] Clark Davis concludes that although a masculine ideal of boldness, individualism, and economic independence remained hegemonic, by the 1920s corporate leaders had successfully expanded constructions of middle-class manhood to encompass "ascendance up the corporate ladder" as a legitimate avenue to success.[24]

But the image of the corporate bureaucrat who was expected to develop interpersonal skills in order to become "a professional manipulator of people and a team player in the service of organizational duty" was a far cry from the hegemonic ideal of rugged individualism and economic independence.[25] As traditional codes of masculinity held fading appeal, men unable to achieve economic independence in the early twentieth century tried to remake middle-class masculinity in order to strengthen their social authority in the face of new threats from workers, women, and ethnically diverse immigrants fighting for the vote, as well as from women entering the public sphere, including corporate offices, in unprecedented numbers. Gail Bederman has demonstrated that, by 1930, "ideals like aggressiveness, physical force, and male sexuality" had gained primacy among middle-class men in America, who drew on a discourse of "civilization" and "primitiveness" in contradictory ways to assert white male superiority.[26] These manly ideals gained popularity among middle-class men, who embraced athletics and valued impulse and instinct anew to counter potential overcivilization and feminization from their sedentary jobs.

Management Strategies in the Canadian Meatpacking Industry

Demographic and anecdotal evidence suggests that these two overlapping middle-class manly ideals influenced management practices in Edmonton packinghouses during the Depression and war years. In 1936 there were no women in even the lowest management positions. Ninety-two percent of white-collar men were born in Canada, the United Kingdom, the United States, or Scandinavia, and former workers said management adhered to a strict "colour line" at even the level of foreman.[27] Depression-era managers routinely felt the muscles of men lined up seeking work each morning, treating them little differently from the livestock they slaughtered, which reinforced the class and ethnic divide.[28] White male management's ability to place a premium on male working-class bodies (many of whom they saw as nonwhite) for their brawn and endurance in a harsh work environment devalued both the work and the men who performed it by signalling exploitation, not status, in the eyes of middle-class men.[29]

The advent of strong unionism during the Second World War shifted the power dynamics for white-collar men at all levels of the packing companies. Wartime labour legislation compelling employers to negotiate with government-certified unions made it possible for workers to organize the militant industrial union United Packinghouse Workers of America (UPWA) in all three major packing companies by the end of the war. Government intervention in a national strike in 1947 also established pattern bargaining for the industry. Under pattern bargaining, the union chose one company to negotiate the "key" contract – almost always Canada Packers because it was so much larger than the others – which then set the wage standard for both Swift and Burns. The new framework for labour relations in the meatpacking industry produced a strong network of union locals across the country, which were led by a growing complement of full-time union staff who were predominantly men headquartered in Toronto.[30]

Although they initially resisted national pattern bargaining, senior executives of Canada's Big Three packing companies came to embrace it as a way to control labour costs, which were a major source of competition in the postwar era.[31] In the immediate postwar years, notwithstanding its oligopolistic structure, there were still fewer barriers to entry in the labour-intensive meatpacking industry than in some manufacturing industries, like steel or automobiles. Mid-size operations could achieve substantial economies of scale, and there was limited product differentiation by brand for fresh meats, which prevented a company from setting prices independently. As a result, the companies continued to support national pattern bargaining by consensus, not by any rule of law.[32] Centralized bargaining was particularly attractive to Canada Packers because of the economies of scale it could achieve as the largest meatpacking company in the country, which allowed it to set a high wage standard in the industry.[33]

Technocratic Masculinity

In embracing national pattern bargaining, senior packing managers drew on modern notions of bureaucratic rationalism, planning, and professionalism. They saw the complex and bureaucratic centralized system of pattern bargaining as a "technology" of rationalist planning and efficiency that would give them greater control over workers.[34] These powerful companies saw centralized collective bargaining led by professionals with specialized expertise as more efficient and reliable than the "mechanism of the labour market."[35] In an interview, former Burns vice-president William Goetz emphasized the system's logistical efficiencies, explaining that meatpacking companies with geographically scattered plants supported centralized bargaining because it settled contracts across the country "in one fell swoop" and eliminated chronic strikes at the more militant plants, which got "pulled along" by the pattern.[36]

The meatpacking corporate elite's faith in a rational system of centralized bargaining was emblematic of a highly masculinized postwar zeitgeist. Successful government direction of the war had renewed public confidence in the modern ideas of reason and planning as vehicles for "man" to control the economy, nature, society, and the self in order to achieve "progress." In Canada there was unprecedented public support for "a managed capitalism in which the state would play a major role."[37] Within this postwar context, the distinctively modern concept of risk management gained influence. As Christopher Dummitt has shown, the key values on which it is based – "expertise, instrumental reason, stoical self-control" – have long been linked to masculinity, particularly white, Anglo, middle-class masculinity.[38] After years of economic depression and war disrupted traditional gender roles by creating massive unemployment among men and then drawing an unprecedented number of women into the workforce, "those who linked ideal masculinity with the benefits of modern technology and progress provided contemporary justifications for gender hierarchies that were under threat."[39] Similarly, in the British context, Beverly Burris argues that the need to subordinate women after the gains they made in the Second World War was central to the power of particular ideas attached to masculinity after the war. She demonstrates that management shifted away from "simple" and overt forms of control and toward the use of technologies, bureaucratic processes, and professionalism.[40]

Although this technocratic image of middle-class masculinity became more persuasive in the decades following the Second World War, it did not displace the ideal of the self-made man, which E. Anthony Rotundo argues has remained hegemonic since the late nineteenth century.[41] We can see this in postwar public fears about the emasculation of men in white-collar jobs.[42] Even more compellingly, John Porter's classic 1965 study of class structures in Canadian society found that men at the top of corporations in the 1950s and early 1960s (and they were all men) preferred "charismatic qualities" and identified "initiative," "imagination," "personality," "aggressive leadership," "ambition," and performance success as most important "to get to the top," not the more bureaucratic qualities of competence, expertise, and efficiency.[43] An overlapping emphasis on reason and control in these masculine ideals, however, strengthened the appeal of a more technical and bureaucratic image of middle-class masculinity.

Negotiating Middle-Class Masculinity

Elite managers of trend-setting Canada Packers drew on these overlapping notions of middle-class masculinity strategically during the postwar era. President J.S. McLean, who had a reputation for bold, "autocratic" leadership and strongly resisted industrial unionism, won popular respect for his aggressive, hands-on, and tough-minded management style.[44] As a retired foreman in the Edmonton plant explained, J.S. McLean "was a businessman ... You've got to have sting, like a bee, to motivate people."[45] Yet developments in the postwar years suggest that the president tempered this bold and forceful management style in the new union environment by cultivating an image of reasoned and professional restraint and by turning more determinedly to new technologies in order to achieve less overt forms of control. In company annual reports, J.S. McLean struck a conciliatory tone, consistently describing labour relations as "cordial and co-operative" or even "harmonious."[46] Similarly, although there had been no major technical innovations in the Canadian meatpacking industry since the late nineteenth century, after the war J.S. McLean began developing a way to mechanize the beef kill department in order to give management more control over the pace of work and reduce labour costs.[47]

The shift to a management style focused on technological innovation, bureaucratic processes, and professional training found its fullest expression, however, under the leadership of Bill McLean, who took control of Canada Packers in 1954 upon the death of his father and ran the company until it was sold in 1990. Raised in wealth and granted the leadership of a company that enjoyed a dominant position in an expansive economy, Bill McLean did not have the experience his father gained from building the company during an economic downturn. He seemed to feel he had big shoes to fill, telling one interviewer, "We were brought up in a successful company, and you know whose fault it will be if we fail."[48] Bill McLean was a generous philanthropist, perhaps influenced by the Methodist religious convictions and practices of his father and his father's mentor, Joseph Flavelle, whom some called "Holy Joe."[49] The business community, however, saw him as someone preoccupied with avoiding any action that could be construed as "immoral or unethical." He gained a reputation for being sensitive to criticism and emotionally reactive in challenging management situations. Described as a "strong-minded, authoritarian manager with a traditional set of values," McLean expected "deference toward elders," would take "no back talk," and required that office staff wear suit jackets "at all times."[50]

Bill McLean's strict moral code and insecurity about his management skills help to explain the way that he negotiated the masculine ideals of his era. McLean eschewed the bold and decisive image of men like his father, investing instead in a more hands-off approach to management that relied heavily on notions of technical proficiency, bureaucratic rationalism, and professionalism. These management strategies often had paradoxical outcomes that discredited him as a businessman. University-educated in the sciences, McLean saw himself as more of a scientist than a businessman. Bob Joyce, who headed up the company's industrial relations team during much of the era of national pattern bargaining, acknowledged that Bill McLean was a "hell of a better researcher than a manager."[51] Under McLean's direction, Canada Packers developed a large and expensive research laboratory on the outskirts of Toronto in which he took an active interest.[52]

Bill McLean took a similar technocratic approach to a government investigation into Canada Packers' market dominance in 1955 after the company bought independent plants in Calgary and Montreal. Anxious to clear Canada Packers of any wrongdoing, he hired a team of lawyers and researchers, who spent two years gathering evidence to defend the company at enormous expense.[53] Former industrial relations director Bob Joyce felt that McLean "panicked" and could have simply sold off the two small packinghouses, one of which was of marginal value, according to Joyce. Although the government took no substantive action against the company, McLean was chastened by the knuckle-rapping and chose to continue growing the company by expanding outside the country, without significant success.[54]

This preference for bureaucratic rationalism also influenced the way McLean handled labour relations. Described by one Alberta union staffer as a "reluctant president," McLean hired a large and expensive staff to manage most of the company's industrial and human relations so that he could devote himself to scientific research. When Canada Packers was sold in 1990, the staff of roughly three hundred in these two departments was reduced to about twenty people.[55]

How did local Edmonton white-collar men respond to the growing emphasis of national executives on new technologies, bureaucratic processes, and professional expertise, which restructured their jobs in many ways? There is evidence of a significant shift in attitude locally to a more conciliatory approach to labour relations after 1947. In 1949 the union's Alberta staff representative reported that the superintendent of Canada Packers' Edmonton plant, Jim Long, took "a very stiff attitude" when challenged by members of the union's grievance committee.[56] A year later, the president of the Canada Packers union local reported that Long had tried to "intimidate" him for sharing information about the plant with the union's national office.[57] In 1951, however, the union reported a "change of attitude for Canada Packers locally" that made the superintendent more accommodating about union requests for job-rate increases.[58] This impression is reinforced by Joyce, who described Long as "kind of friendly with the union a good part of the time."[59] In 1961 the chief steward at Canada Packers in Edmonton was able to confide in a letter to the national union office that all local management agreed with him that the job rate on a new piece of equipment was too low. He cautioned, however, that the local personnel manager "was leery of me quoting him or his opinions, which could lead to criticism for him from his Toronto office people. But, the fact is that he whole-heartedly agrees with my recommendations."[60] The willingness of local managers to confide in local union leaders, and more generally to work out ad hoc solutions to local issues rather than rigidly adhering to bureaucratic processes and corporate authority, suggests that these men at times resisted the technocratic policies imposed by head office.

The logistics of the centralized system of bargaining encouraged cross-class cooperation. As one former Edmonton worker of the Swift Corporation explained, the fact that senior managers conducted negotiations many miles away near company head offices helped to foster good relations between workers and management, even when there was a labour dispute: "The supervisors are well aware that whatever brings on the strike is not their doing. It's because our negotiating people who negotiate contracts, they go to the head office back east – they're the ones that decide how a collective agreement is going to be settled."[61]

Similarly, for a number of years, the Big Three tied pay increases for salaried workers to whatever the union won in negotiations. One former Canada Packers unionist explained in an interview that this policy created a degree of affinity between unionized and salaried workers: "A lot of times when we were negotiating with them, they told us, 'Look, we have to follow the non-bargaining-unit group. We hope that you get it, in a way, but we have to fight this in the best way we can because, you know our position.'"[62] The potential for mutual understandings to develop between local managers and union leaders was also enhanced by the men's shared Depression and wartime experience. After the war, many managers at the local and even the national level had limited schooling because they had worked their way up through the packinghouse.[63] In the same way, the common experience of serving overseas during the war created a bond between some local management figures and unionized packing workers.[64]

Throughout the era of national pattern bargaining, all local managers and union leaders were men, making patriarchal values an additional source of cross-class alignment in Edmonton packinghouses. Local management was able to gain informal agreement from Edmonton union leaders for policies that reinforced women's subordinate position in the workplace. These included a prohibition against marriage for women until the late 1950s and gendered seniority lists until the 1970s, even though, according to correspondence with the national union office, UPWA officially opposed these policies.[65] Similarly, when management treated female union stewards more harshly and with less respect than male stewards, it was difficult for the women to get male union leaders to take the problem seriously.[66] In the same way, a disproportionate number of Anglo union leaders, and the increasing "whiteness" of eastern Europeans, particularly Ukrainians, in the postwar years, enhanced the potential for mutual understanding in local packinghouses.[67] For example, some local managers were willing to circumvent the head office policy of excluding Ukrainians from management positions in the 1950s and 1960s by offering a man of Ukrainian heritage a promotion to supervisor if he Anglicized his name.[68]

Nevertheless, local white-collar men had to deal with two painful realities. One was a significant loss of power over workers at the local level. A 1952 work stoppage at Canada Packers' Edmonton plant illustrates how contract and grievance structures checked the power of local managers in ways that forced them to cultivate more cooperative relations with labour. Faced with a production crisis because of a sudden influx of diseased livestock, plant superintendent Jim Long tried to negotiate with local union leaders to get the plant's entire production workforce to work overtime the next day, which was a Saturday. According to a union report, when a two-hour meeting with union leaders ended in a deadlock over unresolved grievances, Long bypassed the union and appealed directly to workers on the shop floor – until the chief steward arrived to "give the union's side of the story." Long immediately intervened, saying "I am still the Supt. in this plant and this was my meeting," but the union official persisted and told employees that in speaking directly to workers, the superintendent had violated the union contract, which alone justified the union leadership's decision not to endorse management's overtime request. Both parties filed grievances about the incident, but tellingly, only five of the roughly five hundred plant workers showed up to work overtime.[69]

The 1952 work stoppage illustrates how the machinery of the modern labour relations system circumscribed the traditional paternalistic authority of local managers. As superintendent of Canada Packers' Edmonton plant, Jim Long was the highest-ranking local manager, yet the quotation attributed to him suggests that he was struggling to assert his authority over workers and his power in relation to the union. The grievance system challenged his control over production decisions, yet senior management held him accountable for lost production. The new bargaining system, which removed negotiations to Toronto, together with the establishment of company-wide job rates, also reduced the power and control of local managers, from the superintendent down to the foreman, who previously had considerable discretion for setting local wage rates.

White-collar workers also had to make sense of the reality that by the 1960s their salary was significantly lower than the wages earned by many union men. The income gap developed after all three companies delinked salary increases from union-won wage increases to save costs and disrupt relations between local salaried men and union leaders. Local salaried men responded to the new policy in diverse and sometimes contradictory ways. William, who began working as a clerk in a local packinghouse during the Second World War at the age of sixteen and who rose into middle management during a lifetime of work in the firm, expressed bitterness about the decision, which occurred midway through his career. In an interview, he blamed union men: "After several years, the union said the salaried people are not fighting for their increase in pay, where we are, so why are you automatically giving salaried people a raise? They discontinued that, and you only got a raise on your merit." Asked how salaried workers felt about this change, he responded, "Terrible, yeah, well, you know, our grocery bills and utility bills went up the same as the union."[70]

William responded to the growing income gap, however, by drawing on an image of salaried men as rational, efficient, and self-disciplined compared to union men. He depicted himself as more frugal and responsible than union men, whom he felt earned too much: "It took me forty-three years to earn $500 a month. Some workers started at that wage."[71] William said he and his wife were able to achieve a satisfying lifestyle while raising their two children by carefully managing their modest single-family income – for example, he biked to work in all seasons for many years.[72] This implied that unionized workers who pressed for a higher income than office workers must have been profligate. With considerable passion, he also disparaged unionized workers as aggressive, irresponsible, and exploitive because they "pressured" summer students to pay union dues – among them his own two sons at one time.[73]

Yet another mid-level manager at the Swift plant coped with his low salary by closing the social distance between himself and union men. Vince Westacott took pride in the fact that he had developed such a strong relationship with production men that he was made an honorary member of the union. Westacott said packinghouse workers gave him free help and sometimes building supplies from the plant for his home and cabin, which helped to supplement an income that was barely adequate to support his wife and seven sons: "I had kind of a preference at the meatpacking plant ... I got along real well with the people at Swift. Anything I wanted ... They were real good to me." Union men's willingness to help Westacott with the material needs of his family may have stemmed in part from his status as a respectable family breadwinner with heavy responsibilities, a value they held in common. But the office worker's own gregarious personality and genuine respect for workers also seems to have been a contributing factor.[74] The affable Westacott saw himself as an exceptional mid-level manager because of his rapport with workers and explained that he would don a white packing coat and, to the amazement of his white-collar co-workers, sit down for lunch with production men in their gore-spattered work clothes on occasion because "it was the best way to know what was going on."[75] Westacott's pride in his ability to subvert middle-class norms, together with the surprise of other salaried men, affirms how deeply class lines typically divided the packinghouse.

Dummitt and others have emphasized that modern, rationally planned systems of control can create a profound sense of disconnection in individuals, an alienation from the self that gets "mapped onto other social hierarchies" of class, as well as gender and race.[76] Local white-collar workers in Edmonton packinghouses responded most often in ways that reinforced existing social hierarchies. The superintendent of Canada Packers' Edmonton plant appears to have vented his job frustrations on lower-level management figures like fore-men, who were an easy target compared to unionized workers. Canada Packers executive Bob Joyce described Jim Long as "a very loud, tough, tough guy on his staff ... He made foremen cry in front of the union men, blasted them day after day."[77] Local management also adhered rigidly to the gender segregation of white-collar jobs; although the proportion of salaried women stabilized at roughly one-quarter after the war, women continued to be ex-cluded from management and held only the lowest-level administrative pos-itions.[78] The handful of production men who were seen as black often ended up in the most difficult jobs on the kill floor. Maintaining a predominantly "white" production workforce may have become even more important in the era of national pattern bargaining when unionism compelled local management to deal with workers on a more equitable basis.

In the 1960s all three Canadian packing companies responded to rising labour costs by investing in technocratic processes and strategies that often had con-tradictory effects (Figure 4.5).[79] To disrupt a pattern of costly strategic "under-standings" between management and workers that had developed at the local level, head offices appointed new university-educated personnel to key manage-ment positions in Edmonton and limited their local autonomy.[80] This change contributed to rising tensions between management and workers that erupted into a series of costly labour disputes in 1966, 1974, and 1978. Scholars have linked rising working-class militancy in these years to the rigid and elaborate bureaucratic system of labour relations that had developed since the Second World War, as well as to the highly rational, technical, and authoritarian image of middle-class men who held its leadership positions.[81] In the packing labour disputes, senior company managers manipulated the bargaining system by using complicated strike/lock-out situations to isolate and discipline the most militant segment of the union, which created public resentment and confusion, fortify-ing a masculinist image of corporate power as impersonal, irresponsible, and dangerous. The irony is that the disputes also resulted in strong wage gains for workers. Instead of a militant section being "pulled along" by the pattern as management had reasoned, in these labour disputes the most militant section of the union was able to harness the system to its needs and drive wages higher.

Conclusion

This chapter has explored notions of middle-class masculinity that were mobil-ized within major corporations in the Canadian meatpacking industry after 1947 when a strong industrial union and an elaborate system of pattern bar-gaining threatened existing social hierarchies. National executives drew on a

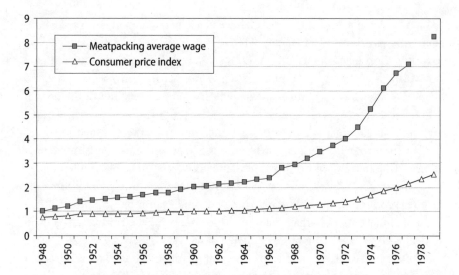

Figure 4.5 Relative increase in average hourly meatpacking wage and consumer price index, Canada, 1948–79. *Note:* Average meatpacking wages from 1974 to 1979 are for Edmonton because Canadian figures were not available. Department of Labour Canada, *Wage Rates, Salaries, and Hours of Labour, 1947–1983,* ed. Surveys Division Labour Data (1983); Statistics Canada, *Consumer Prices and Price Indexes,* series 62–010.

technocratic ideal of middle-class masculinity by investing heavily in new technologies, professional expertise, and the logic of bureaucratic processes, particularly an industry-wide system of pattern bargaining. These ideas gained power and influence in the wake of a war that many felt was won through effective large-scale government planning and through regulation and control under the leadership of civil bureaucrats, business experts, and technical professionals. This masculine ideal was particularly influential within trend-setting Canada Packers Ltd., where owner-manager Bill McLean embraced a technocratic image of masculine corporate leadership as an alternative to the hegemonic ideal of rugged individualism epitomized by his father.

White-collar men in Edmonton packinghouses responded to the modern labour relations system imposed by head office in diverse ways. Faced with a loss of power, a number of local managers cooperated strategically with union leaders at the local level, which compromised the corporate bottom line. Many also invested in social hierarchies of class, gender, and race to affirm their social authority. In the 1960s and 1970s the complex and legalistic lock-out strategies used by senior packing managers in labour disputes helped to fuel an image of corporate decision makers as hyper-rational authoritarians who were out of touch with the lives of ordinary people, which compromised their class claims.

Notes

I am grateful for the insightful comments from colleagues on an earlier draft of the paper that was presented to the Labour Studies Reading Group at University College, University of Toronto, in December 2013. The research was made possible by funding from the Ontario Graduate Scholarship program and the Ramsay Cook Scholarship at York University's Department of History.

1 Eric R. Arthur, "Canada Packers Plant at Edmonton," *Royal Architectural Institute of Canada Journal*, 14, 2 (1937): 158–60.
2 R.W. Connell, *Masculinities* (Berkeley: University of California Press, 1995), ch. 7.
3 Within this bargaining system, each company had a separate master contract but agreed to the same annual wage increase. The union negotiated the wage increase with one of the Big Three packing companies, which set the pattern for wages in the industry, much like the auto industry.
4 Canada Packers was bigger than its two largest competitors put together, which were the Swift Corporation and Burns and Company.
5 Office employees comprised roughly one-quarter of the total workforce, and the number of male office workers in Edmonton's meatpacking industry rose from 454 in 1956 to 588 in 1966. Statistics Canada, *Manufacturing Industries of Canada Section G, Geographical Distribution*, cat. 31–209 (1956–1971). This research is informed by a handful of interviews with former white-collar workers at the three largest packinghouses in Edmonton and at their head offices. It also draws on company records found randomly within union papers, interviews with former production workers and union leaders, as well as company annual reports and newspaper reports on labour disputes. See Cynthia Loch-Drake, "Unpacking 'Alberta Beef': Class, Gender, and Culture in Edmonton Packinghouses during the Era of National Pattern Bargaining, 1947–1979" (PhD diss., York University, 2013).
6 David L. Collinson and Jeff Hearn, "Men and Masculinities in Work, Organizations, and Management," in *Handbook of Studies on Men and Masculinities*, ed. Jeff Hearn, Michael S. Kimmel, and R.W. Connell (Thousand Oaks, CA: Sage, 2005), 289.
7 David Morgan, "Class and Masculinity," in *Handbook of Studies on Men and Masculinities*, ed. Jeff Hearn, Michael S. Kimmel, and R.W. Connell (Thousand Oaks, CA: Sage, 2005), 170.
8 Victor J. Seidler, *Rediscovering Masculinity: Reason, Language, and Sexuality* (London: Routledge, 1989), 15. Seidler's work makes explicit the ways that masculinity became connected to reason and control with the development of a capitalist economic system in the seventeenth century and Enlightenment thinking.
9 Barbara Weinstein, "Commentary on Part I: The Making of the Middle Class and Practices of Modernity," in *The Making of the Middle Class: Toward a Transnational History of the Middle Class*, ed. A. Ricardo López and Barbara Weinstein (Durham, NC: Duke University Press, 2012), 109.
10 A. Ricardo López and Barbara Weinstein, "Introduction," in *The Making of the Middle Class: Toward a Transnational History of the Middle Class*, ed. A. Ricardo López and Barbara Weinstein, 1–25 (Durham, NC: Duke University Press, 2012).
11 Edmonton's population boomed from 118,541 in 1947 to 371,265 in 1965. City of Edmonton, "Population History," https://www.edmonton.ca/city_government/facts_figures/population-history.aspx.
12 Joy Parr, *The Gender of Breadwinners: Women, Men, and Change in Two Industrial Towns, 1880–1950* (Toronto: University of Toronto Press, 1990); Gillian Creese, *Contracting Masculinity: Gender, Class, and Race in a White-Collar Union, 1944–1994* (Don Mills, ON: Oxford University Press, 1999).

13 Connell, *Masculinities*, 77.
14 Morgan, "Class and Masculinity," 170.
15 E. Anthony Rotundo, *American Manhood: Transformations in Masculinity from the Revolution to the Modern Era* (New York: Basic Books, 1993), 3.
16 Roger Horowitz, *Negro and White, Unite and Fight! A Social History of Industrial Unionism in Meatpacking, 1930–90* (Urbana: University of Illinois Press, 1997), 17; Henry C. Klassen, *A Business History of Alberta* (Calgary: University of Calgary Press, 1999), 89.
17 Collinson and Hearn, "Men and Masculinities," 297. This notion of modern masculinity contrasts starkly with an early-twenty-first-century "transnational business masculinity" identified by R.W. Connell as egocentric. It is characterized by "a declining sense of responsibility" and a "libertarian" attitude toward sexuality. Ibid., 295–96.
18 Michael Bliss, *A Canadian Millionaire: The Life and Business Times of Sir Joseph Flavelle, Bart., 1858–1939*, 1st paperback ed. (Toronto: University of Toronto Press, 1992), chs. 1 and 2.
19 Ibid., x.
20 Ibid., 185, 211.
21 George Athanassakos and Kenneth Harling, "Canada Packers Inc.," *Case Research Journal* 14, 1 (1994): 92.
22 Neither of two government investigations resulted in significant government action. Henry Herbert Stevens and William Walker Kennedy, *Report of the Royal Commission on Price Spreads* (Ottawa: J.O. Patenaude, Printer to the King, 1935), 56–58; Canada, Restrictive Trade Practices Commission, *Report Concerning the Meat Packing Industry and the Acquisition of Wilsil Limited and Calgary Packers Limited by Canada Packers Limited: Combines Investigation Act* (Ottawa: Department of Justice, 1961).
23 Clark Davis, "The Corporate Reconstruction of Middle-Class Manhood," in *The Middling Sorts: Explorations in the History of the American Middle Class*, ed. Burton J. Bledstein and Robert D. Johnston (New York: Routledge, 2001), 204, 206.
24 Ibid., 216. Joy Parr's work suggests that there was a similar development in the Canadian context during the interwar era. Parr, *Gender of Breadwinners*, 154–55.
25 Angel Kwolek-Folland, *Engendering Business: Men and Women in the Corporate Office, 1870–1930* (Baltimore, MD: Johns Hopkins University Press, 1994), 47.
26 Gail Bederman, *Manliness and Civilization: A Cultural History of Gender and Race in the United States, 1880–1917* (Chicago: University of Chicago Press, 1995), 19.
27 In comparison, many working-class men were immigrants or first-generation Canadians of eastern or southern European heritage, particularly Ukrainian. Dominion Bureau of Statistics Canada, *Census of the Prairie Provinces, 1936*, Tables 7, 9, and 10 (1936). Alex Goruk, "Interview Transcript," Provincial Archives of Alberta, Warren Caragata fonds, PR1980.0218/3, 1977. During the war, a man of African American heritage who looked white had his job title changed from "foreman" to "gang leader" when his family background was inadvertently revealed to management. Fred and Mary, interview with author, 2004. Interviewees identified by only a first name have been given pseudonyms.
28 George Kozak, *Interview Transcript* (Edmonton: Alberta Labour History Institute/Ground Zero, 1998); George, interview with author, 2004.
29 Ava Baron, "Masculinity, the Embodied Male Worker, and the Historian's Gaze," *International Labor and Working-Class History* 69, 1 (2006): 149.
30 There was flexibility, however, for each company to negotiate different nonwage contract terms. John Tait Montague, "Trade Unionism in the Canadian Meat Packing Industry" (PhD diss., University of Toronto, 1950); Alton W.J. Craig, "The Consequences of Provincial

Jurisdiction for the Process of Companywide Collective Bargaining in Canada: A Study of the Packing House Industry" (PhD diss., Cornell University, 1964).

31 Multiemployer bargaining was the norm in postwar Europe and Scandinavia but represented only 8 percent of collective agreements in Canada, which made centralized bargaining in the Canadian meatpacking industry unusual within the North American context. Anne Forrest, "The Rise and Fall of National Bargaining in the Canadian Meat-Packing Industry," *Relations Industrielles* 44, 2 (1989): 393.

32 Ibid., 401.

33 There was no real international competition in the immediate postwar years because the Big Four American meatpackers were dealing with the same union and had a similar system of industry-wide bargaining. See Ian MacLachlan, *Kill and Chill: Restructuring Canada's Beef Commodity Chain* (Toronto: University of Toronto Press, 2001), 272–73.

34 Michel Foucault, "The Subject and Power," *Critical Inquiry* 8, 4 (1982): 777–95.

35 Forrest, "Rise and Fall," 402.

36 William Goetz, interview with Ian MacLachlan, 1995.

37 Alvin Finkel, *Our Lives: Canada after 1945* (Toronto: J. Lorimer, 1997), 7.

38 The idea of calculating risk is distinctively modern in its assumption that by establishing "mechanisms and routines" and by rigorously studying mistakes, it is possible to reimagine dangers as risks that can be controlled through careful rational planning in order to ensure continuous "progress." Christopher Dummitt, *The Manly Modern: Masculinity in Postwar Canada* (Vancouver: UBC Press, 2007), 9, 13, 2. On modernity and risk management in discussions of Canadian masculinity, see also Magda Fahrni, Chapter 2, this volume.

39 Dummitt, *Manly Modern*, 2.

40 Beverly H. Burris, "Technocracy, Patriarchy and Management," in *Men as Managers, Managers as Men: Critical Perspectives on Men, Masculinities and Managements*, ed. David L. Collinson and Jeff Hearn (London: Sage, 1996), 66–67. For feminist debates about gendering bureaucracies, see Yvonne Due Billing, "Gender and Bureaucracies: A Critique of Ferguson's 'The Feminist Case against Bureaucracy,'" *Gender, Work and Organization* 1, 4 (1994): 179–94.

41 Rotundo, *American Manhood*; Bederman, *Manliness and Civilization*.

42 Mary Louise Adams, *The Trouble with Normal: Postwar Youth and the Making of Heterosexuality* (Toronto: University of Toronto Press, 1997), 33–34. William Hollingsworth Whyte's book *The Organization Man* (New York: Simon and Schuster, 1956) articulated this idea most effectively in the 1950s. See Deborah McPhail, "What to Do with the 'Tubby Hubby'? 'Obesity,' the Crisis of Masculinity, and the Nuclear Family in Early Cold War Canada," *Antipode* 41, 5 (2009): 1021–50.

43 John A. Porter, *The Vertical Mosaic: An Analysis of Social Class and Power in Canada* (Toronto: University of Toronto Press, 1965), 281–82.

44 Joseph Lindsey, "James Stanley McLean," *The Canadian Encyclopedia* (2012).

45 George, interview.

46 Canada Packers Inc., *Annual Report*, 1949; Canada Packers Inc., *Annual Report*, 1950.

47 The large size and delicate nature of the valuable cattle hide and carcass made the beef kill department much more resistant to mechanization than the hog kill department, which was mechanized in the late nineteenth century. MacLachlan, *Kill and Chill*, 171, 173.

48 Athanassakos and Harling, "Canada Packers," 92.

49 Bliss, *Canadian Millionaire*, 92.

50 Athanassakos and Harling, "Canada Packers," 92.

51 Bob Joyce, interview with author, 2008.
52 Ironically, it was a supervisor in the company's Winnipeg plant working with production men on the shop floor who developed arguably Canada Packers' most important and lucrative invention, the CanPak system, which mechanized the beef kill department. Bob Joyce said the man earned nothing more than his wage for an invention that the company patented and sold internationally. Ibid.
53 Canada, Restrictive Trade Practices Commission, *Report.*
54 Joyce, interview.
55 Norm Leclaire, interview with Ian MacLachlan, 1995.
56 Jack Hampson, "Alberta Staff Reports, Locals 233–422," Library and Archives Canada (LAC), Canadian Food and Allied Workers (CFAW) fonds, MG28, I-186, Packinghouse Workers Organizing Committee (PWOC) and United Packinghouse Workers of America (UPWA) series, vol. 24, 1947–50, Local 243, February 17, 1949.
57 Ibid., July 5, 1950.
58 Jack Hampson, "Alberta Staff Reports, Locals 233–511," LAC, CFAW fonds, MG28, I-186, PWOC and UPWA series, vol 24, 1951–55, Local 243, June 7, 1951.
59 Joyce, interview.
60 Harold Steele, LAC, CFAW fonds, MG28, I-186, PWOC and UPWA series, vol. 22, Canada Packers Grievances, February 9, 1961.
61 Bill, interview with author, 2004.
62 Frank and Winnifred, interview with author, 2004.
63 Craig, "Consequences of Provincial Jurisdiction," 82.
64 Two men I interviewed – a white-collar worker and a tradesman – actually met while serving in the same battalion in Europe and then encountered each other in an Edmonton packinghouse after the war.
65 Loch-Drake, "Unpacking 'Alberta Beef,'" ch. 6.
66 Gloria Kereliuk, interview with author, 2006.
67 Helen Potrebenko, *No Streets of Gold: A Social History of Ukrainians in Alberta* (Vancouver: New Star Books, 1977), 26.
68 One man refused to change his name and was never promoted, despite a long career at Canada Packers in Edmonton. Kereliuk, interview.
69 The outcome of the grievance is unknown. Local 243 Executive, "Grievance Re: Overtime Refusal by Workers," LAC, CFAW fonds, MG28, I-186, PWOC and UPWA series, vol. 20, Canada Packers Grievances, May 19, 1952.
70 William and Elaine, interview with author, 2004.
71 Ibid. This packinghouse office worker's attitude is similar to the attitude of unionized, male, white-collar workers at BC Hydro who, during the same period, ranked supervisory, mental, and manual labour in descending order of importance and argued that they should be paid at least as much as or more than male, blue-collar workers because they regarded themselves "as highly skilled and worth higher wages than their blue-collar counterparts." The male-dominated union's complicity in defining women's clerical work as low-skilled and its decision to make male breadwinner rights a higher priority than equal pay for women helped to undermine its claim that men's office work was highly skilled. Gillian Creese, "Normalizing Breadwinner Rights," in *Contracting Masculinity: Gender, Class, and Race in a White-Collar Union, 1944–1994*, 78–83 (Don Mills, ON: Oxford University Press, 1999).
72 William's wife did not work for wages throughout most of the years that the couple was childrearing.
73 William and Elaine, interview.

74 More than one union leader insisted that I include an interview with Westacott in this research, presumably because production workers respected his understanding of their position in the local industry.
75 Vince Westacott and Mary Westacott, interview with author, 2004.
76 Dummitt, *Manly Modern*, 6.
77 Joyce, interview.
78 Statistics Canada, *Slaughtering and Meat Processors. Abattage et conditionnement de la viande, 1949–79*, Manufacturing and Primary Industries Division, cat. 32-221.
79 The average wage in the Canadian meatpacking industry rose 104 percent between 1948 and 1961, compared to a 33 percent increase in the Canadian Consumer Price Index during the same period. Department of Labour Canada, *Wage Rates, Salaries, and Hours of Labour, 1947–1983*, ed. Surveys Division Labour Data (1983).
80 Nick Romanko, LAC, CFAW fonds, MG28, I-186, accession 1984-0536, box 11, Canada Packers, Current, February 21, 1963; Goetz, interview.
81 Bryan D. Palmer, *Canada's 1960s: The Ironies of Identity in a Rebellious Era* (Toronto: University of Toronto Press, 2009), ch. 7; Peter S. McInnis, "Hothead Troubles: 1960s-Era Wildcat Strikes in Canada," in *Debating Dissent: Canada and the 1960s*, ed. Lara Campbell, Dominique Clément, and Gregory Kealey, 155–70 (Toronto: University of Toronto Press, 2012).

Part 2
Masculine Spaces

THE STUDY OF GENDERED SPACE has emerged as a staple of historical geography and architectural history over the past thirty years. And Canada's social and cultural historians have been keen to take up the challenge. *Masculine spaces* are an increasingly important part of that discussion, as will already be apparent from previous chapters that focus on different kinds of workplaces: hospitals and meatpacking plants, in particular.[1] The spatial dimensions of Canadian masculinity in the past are now receiving sustained attention from a variety of scholarly perspectives, as the three studies assembled here illustrate clearly.

We begin with Annmarie Adams's discussion of men's private clubs in Chapter 5, which builds on her earlier work on gender and space in the Victorian home and the modern hospital.[2] The chapter focuses especially on Montreal's University Club on Mansfield Street, designed by the remarkable Percy Nobbs and one of several stately establishments built to serve the scions of Montreal's legendary Square Mile around the turn of the twentieth century. Here, Adams draws us into a privileged world of "homosocial domesticity" conducted in well-appointed rooms devoid of women and devoted to gossip, card games, billiards, eating, smoking, and drinking. With Norman Knowles's discussion of work-camp missions in Chapter 6, the focus shifts away from urban (and urbane) Anglo-Protestant men of privilege and toward their virtual antithesis: the miners and lumbermen toiling for meagre wages in the rural, ethnically diverse Canadian hinterland. Although the class and ethnic contrasts could not be starker, these essays share a similar chronology and a focus on masculine culture in exclusively male settings. In the case of the work camps, it was one where evangelical missionaries promoted a version of Christian manhood rooted in "self-improvement and personal regeneration" among working-class and immigrant men whose own sense of manliness was very different. In this rugged environment, men validated physical strength and competitive individualism, often expressed through "drinking, brawling, gambling, and swearing." Several generations later, we move in Chapter 7 to Olivier Vallerand's discussion of another homosocial space, the gay bars of Montreal in the final three decades of the twentieth century. Interestingly, these were spaces that reflected "mainstream gay culture's obsession with images of masculinity" and therefore often celebrated the sort of rough, hyper-masculine personas – including the cowboy, the sailor, and the lumberjack – with which the anxious missionaries of an earlier generation were having such difficulties in the distant lumber and mining camps described by Knowles.

Notes

1 We refer, of course, to Chapters 3 and 4 by David Theodore and Cynthia Loch-Drake respectively.
2 Annmarie Adams, *Architecture in the Family Way: Doctors, Houses, and Women, 1870–1900* (Montreal and Kingston: McGill-Queen's University Press, 1996); Annmarie Adams, *Medicine by Design: The Architect and the Modern Hospital, 1893–1943* (Minneapolis: University of Minnesota Press, 2008).

5

The Place of Manliness: Architecture, Domesticity, and Men's Clubs

Annmarie Adams

"His love for the association of men and their activities is attested by a life membership ... in the University Club, of which he was a founder and whose delightful club house is his work."

– JOHN BLAND, EULOGY FOR PERCY NOBBS, 1964

A PROMINENT BUILDING TYPE designed for the "association of men," the men's club was a conspicuous shaper of a North American culture of urban masculinity, especially in wealthy urban centres like early-twentieth-century Montreal. Clubs were explicitly male spaces, carefully separated from the spaces of other social classes in the industrial-capitalist city. Club architecture reveals how gender and class interacted on multiple and simultaneous levels, creating a distinctive symbol of upper-class power associated with men. Eighteenth-century London was the birthplace of the North American typology. By the beginning of the twentieth century, London boasted more than one hundred clubs, many designed by famous architects. Charles Barry, for example, best known for his work on the British Houses of Parliament, designed both the Travellers Club and the Reform Club in 1830–32 and 1838–41 respectively. Described as "the very model of a gentlemen's club," the Reform Club was "a stately palace presenting, like the palaces of Renaissance Rome, a stern front to the world."[1] Major cities in North America followed the British club tradition. The oldest is the State Club, founded in Philadelphia in 1732, and it was not long before New York became the most prominent club city on the continent. Montreal, the largest city in Canada at that time, boasted an early example with its Beaver Club of 1785. The Beaver Club membership held regular meetings at private houses and hotels rather than in a purpose-built venue, foreshadowing the close relationship of club architecture with other building types.[2]

Two purpose-built Montreal clubs designed by renowned architects and built long after the era of the Beaver Club constitute the subject of this chapter: the

Mount Royal Club, by New York architects McKim, Mead and White, founded in 1899 and constructed in 1904–06;[3] and the University Club, by Scottish-born architect Percy Nobbs (eulogized in the chapter's epigraph), founded in 1907 and built in 1913. Both clubs are in downtown Montreal, in or near the area known as the Square Mile, where it is widely reported that 70 percent of Canada's wealth lived from 1870 to 1900.[4] The two clubs are private, anglophone business clubs, with highly restrictive admissions processes and membership fees. One rather amusing link between the two clubs is that humourist Stephen Leacock, a member of the University Club, satirized the Mount Royal Club as "the Mausoleum Club" in his book *Arcadian Adventures with the Idle Rich* (1914). Leacock had a good eye for spatial codes and thus serves as a helpful witness to how club architecture functioned.[5]

The University Club is the main focus of my architectural analysis, with comparative observations on the Mount Royal Club. The intention of the study is to illustrate the usefulness of architectural evidence in the history of gender relations rather than to contribute to the social history of men's clubs, which is well covered by historians such as Amy Milne-Smith and Barbara Black.[6] How did the design of the men's club affirm codes of masculinity? What relation did the club building bear to other architectural typologies, such as the house, restaurant, and hotel? How were club architects chosen? Exclusive clubs often had no sign on the building that revealed their purpose, relying wholly on their architecture for public identity. Did architectural decisions reinforce this status as an "invisible" or "secret" urban building or help clubhouses to resist easy identification? In addition, does clubhouse architecture, as historical evidence, reveal aspects of the history of masculinity illegible in written sources?

Methodology

My approach to the study of these high-style buildings is inspired by methods of vernacular architecture research, honed since the 1980s, especially papers written by members of the Vernacular Architecture Forum and published in early issues of the journal *Perspectives in Vernacular Architecture*. In particular, I look to Deryck Holdsworth's "'I'm a Lumberjack and I'm OK'" and to William Moore's "The Masonic Lodge Room, 1870–1930," both published in the fifth volume of that journal in 1995, for inspiration on how to link real architectural spaces with changing cultures of masculinity.[7] Especially motivating for this research is how Moore analyzed the Freemasons' lodge room first as a theatre and then as a church, which allowed him to show how the Freemasons' architecture maintained a unique sense of social order in a world where masculine values were rapidly disappearing. Fifteen years later, Paula Lupkin augmented this approach considerably, arguing that the YMCA's architecture "spatially and conceptually restructured male identity, respectability, and leisure."[8] These authors assigned an active role to architecture, whereby it *structures* male identity rather than simply reflecting it, making their work especially pertinent to an exploration of how the men's club shaped masculine values.

As mentioned, the social history of the men's club is well established. Historians note that the origins of men's clubs are in coffee and chocolate houses;[9] interestingly, they have shown how private boys' schools serve as precursors to these urban business clubs; and some writers have pondered whether American fraternity houses might foreshadow the "old boys' clubs" that sometimes usurp them as privileged male students today move from college to high-paying jobs.[10]

My perspective in this chapter points to a different building type, the home, as a way to think about manliness and masculinity at this time.[11] I approach the men's club as an architecture of homosocial domesticity, a perspective that has also interested social historians. Milne-Smith writes,

> Building on this broader understanding of domesticity, ... one of the emotional
> needs being filled within the walls of the gentlemen's clubs of London was, in fact,
> a form of domesticity. Men's retreat to homosocial spaces and activities signaled
> not only an escape from the tyranny of the Victorian home, but also a search for
> a new form of emotional life.[12]

An architectural history of the club, I contend, is a fresh take, allowing us not only to refute the stereotype that men's activities are always about a "flight" from domesticity but also to redefine domesticity in order to include relations of familiarity and comfort that are based on a shared space outside the traditional house.[13]

In addition, inspirational literary scholar Martha Vicinus has pointed out how many early buildings for women – colleges, schools, and settlement houses – looked like large houses, despite their public roles. This domestic imagery was probably intended to smooth the transition of middle-class women to the world of paid work, while offering the promise of gentle protection in public. "The surroundings," Vicinus says of the first colleges for women in England, "bespoke permanence, seriousness of purpose, and the same solidity that marked the middle-class families from which the bulk of them came."[14] Nurses' residences, for example, which looked much like aristocratic houses, probably assured anxious parents that their daughters would be looked after, protected, and separated from the hospital, the street, and the city beyond.[15] Working in buildings that resemble big houses also, obviously, undermines women's power outside the home, suggesting that places where women work resemble the home in other ways.

Like these buildings designed for women, men's clubs also looked like big houses. What does this appearance of domesticity mean for our general understanding of how domestic imagery *subverts* women's power? How did club men understand the architecture of their clubhouses? Did the overtly domestic atmosphere signal an escape from the unpredictability of business and the city?

Because of this complementary relationship to women's spaces, secondary scholarship on women's spaces thus serves as a central tool for an analysis of men's sites. Architectural historians Dolores Hayden, Gwendolyn Wright, Elizabeth Cromley, Gail Lee Dubrow, Abigail Van Slyck, Marta Gutman, Cynthia Hammond, Tania Martin, and others, in roughly that order, have published an array of outstanding studies on everyday spaces designed for women: cities and suburbs, houses, big-city apartments, kitchens, preservation projects, libraries, summer camps, women's clubs, penitentiaries, and convents.[16] Vernacular architecture and everyday architecture, that is, have been at the centre of gender-space studies, with remarkably little attention paid to men. This chapter addresses this gender gap in the architectural literature.

Separation

Any architectural analysis must begin with an architectural description. The University Club is a five-bay, four-storey, red-brick structure (Figure 5.1) on Mansfield Street in Montreal, just south of busy Sherbrooke Street, a major east-west artery and the site of many of the city's most prestigious institutions: the Montreal Museum of Fine Arts, the Ritz-Carlton Hotel, McGill University, and the McCord Museum, to name only a few.[17] The club is attached to its neighbour to the north, occupying the corner of what was Burnside Place at the time and is now Avenue du Président-Kennedy. Its façade is dignified and elegant, with an elevated main floor, or *piano nobile,* that is distinguished by five large arched windows and sits on a rusticated limestone (greystone) base, punctuated by a central entry. Like many urban commercial buildings in Montreal, it occupies the site without any setback whatsoever, sitting on the edge of the sidewalk and following the line of the adjacent buildings. There is no sign identifying it as the University Club.[18] Because of its references to classical architecture – arched windows, symmetry, central entry, rusticated base, and *piano nobile* – and its use of red brick, it looks like a tasteful Georgian townhouse.

The clubhouse functions as a tool of gender separation through its two distinct front doors and distinct circulation paths. This message of separation, spoken in architecture, is clear and simple: men occupy the centre of this place; women are literally on the margins and even "behind" the men, given the subordinate location of the women's entrance. It is also notable that the women's

Figure 5.1 The University Club, Montreal, date unknown. John Bland
Canadian Architecture Collection, McGill University.

entrance is the only architectural feature to break the strict symmetry established
by Nobbs on the façade of the building.

Women visitors to the University Club had very few choices. Once entering
the ladies-only entrance hall, women were directed to two dining rooms (labelled
"private dining room" and "ladies' dining room" on the plan) on either side of
a reception room (Figure 5.2). A small women's lavatory was also located in this
special women's wing, down a staircase, at the same level as the wine cellar.
Significantly, the areas designed for women at the University Club were restricted
to the ground floor of the building, within the rusticated base of the entry level.[19]
The dictates of classical architecture call for this level to include minor and

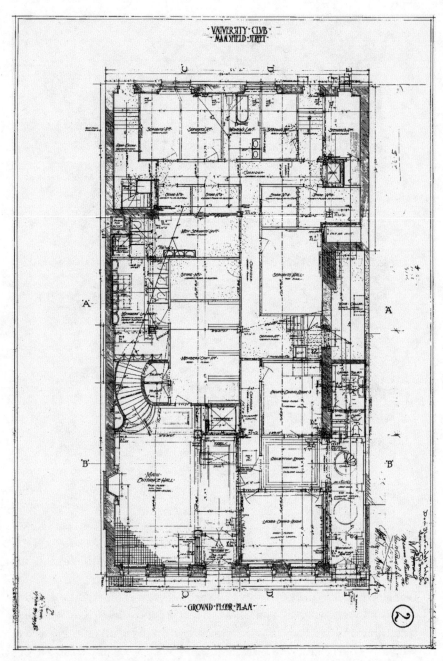

Figure 5.2 Plan for the ground floor of the University Club, Montreal, 1913. Ink on linen. John Bland Canadian Architecture Collection, McGill University.

Figure 5.3 Ladies' dining room, University Club, Montreal, date unknown. John Bland Canadian Architecture Collection, McGill University.

service rooms, although in the case of the University Club it is also the location of the all-important reception room.

A remarkable leather-bound album includes photographs (Figure 5.3) that document this sequence of spaces. The album is extraordinary because it takes the viewer on a room-by-room tour of the building, complete with hand-written captions, allowing one to revisit the rooms in sequence a century later. This is particularly valuable because the women's section of the building no longer exists, presumably renovated at the time when women were finally admitted as full members in 1988.[20] It is noteworthy, for example, that Nobbs chose to showcase the women's spaces in the album of professional photographs produced to document the building. To him, that is, these rooms were a significant feature of the architectural design, important enough to appear at the beginning of the album.

The same architectural concept of a secondary entrance for women appears at the nearby Mount Royal Club (Figure 5.4), where members entered at the

Figure 5.4 The Mount Royal Club, Montreal, ca. 1905. Wm Notman and Son, view-3344.A, McCord Museum Online Collection, http://www.musee-mccord. qc.ca/en/collection/artifacts/View-3344.A.

centre of the three-storey, limestone, neoclassical building directly from Sherbrooke Street, whereas women entered on the east from Stanley Street, a residential street located three blocks west of Mansfield Street.

Quite literally, the architecture subordinates women's social status in this place because they enter and participate in the building *obliquely* (Figure 5.5). In contrast to the University Club, the ground floor of the Mount Royal Club is a space nearly exclusively for men. After entry, women visitors ascend immediately to an upstairs parlour and dining room, spaces pushed to the rear of the building, invisible from the street, and separated vertically from most of the men's socializing spaces.

This side-door entry sequence and rear, off-axis, vertical circulation are reminiscent of the centuries-old tradition of how domestic servants entered and occupied invisible space in aristocratic houses. The spatial separation of family members and domestic servants meant that domestic labour could be largely hidden, while servants remained close at hand should family members

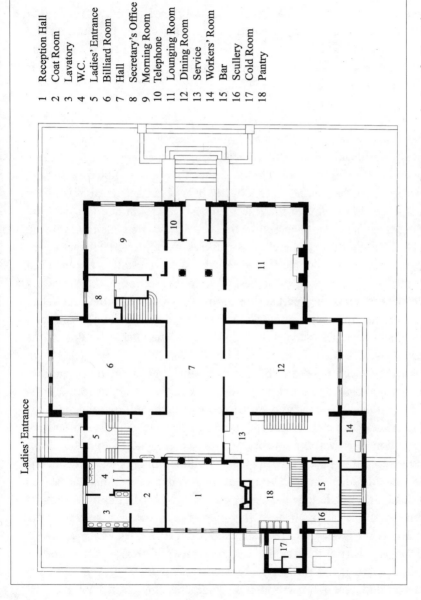

Ladies' Entrance

1	Reception Hall
2	Coat Room
3	Lavatory
4	W.C.
5	Ladies' Entrance
6	Billiard Room
7	Hall
8	Secretary's Office
9	Morning Room
10	Telephone
11	Lounging Room
12	Dining Room
13	Service
14	Workers' Room
15	Bar
16	Scullery
17	Cold Room
18	Pantry

Figure 5.5 Plan for the ground floor of the Mount Royal Club, built 1904–06, redrawn in 2017 by Jennifer Tu-Anh Phan, from a print owned by the Mount Royal Club.

need anything. In architectural terms, this was accomplished through clearly demarcated and separate entries for family members (i.e., front entrance) and servants (i.e., rear or kitchen entrance); distinct paths of circulation in the house (captured in the title of the BBC series *Upstairs Downstairs*); a wide public staircase versus the steep and narrow back stairs for servants; and attic bedrooms for servants, often located conveniently for access to children's bedrooms and nurseries. The men's club was even more complex than the aristocratic home in terms of separate circulation paths, given the tripartite separation of members from women guests and additionally from staff members, who functioned very much like domestic servants.

In fact, Percy Nobbs's architectural plan (Figure 5.2) of the University Club refers to the employees of the establishment as servants, reproducing the language associated with home at this time. Staff members entered through the rear of the building, from a laneway; their dozen or so rooms occupied a reverse-L shaped wing on the ground floor, directly behind the sequence of women's rooms described above and the club members' coatroom and lavatory. The labelling of the floor plan suggests that the staff included both men and women, as lavatories for both are included. This staff area on the ground floor at the rear comprised a T-shaped, double-loaded corridor, with four staff rooms arranged along the back or east wall; the largest room in this section of the club was a windowless servants' hall, perhaps for dining, located next to the wine cellar. In terms of its program, it resembled the servants' quarters of a large home, which would have been located in the vicinity of the kitchen and/or on the basement level.

This arrangement in men's clubs of separate entry and circulation sequences by gender and class was much more disparaging than it might seem at first glance, for it meant women and employees were excluded from the most important space of any club, the reception room. The architectural experience of the reception room was the sole prerogative of members. This paradox of an exclusive reception space has been noted by Milne-Smith in her study of London clubs: "Although modelled on great English homes and foreign palaces, clubhouses were not designed to receive guests, and thus the impressive entries are somewhat misleading. Instead, the impressive interior was reserved for a select group; the grandeur of the hall assured and reinforced a member's own importance."[21] Part of the way that this assurance and reinforcement worked was through its denial of women (and obviously of nonmembers). In an explicit architectural gesture of separation-cum-dominance, the architecture received members and excluded women. The club's "servants" could enter the reception space but only from the interior, missing out on the full ritual of "reception," which by definition would include crossing the all-important threshold by entering through the club's main door. This architectural affirmation of membership was one of the major mandates of the design of men's clubs.

Leacock captured the significance of the club's entrance in his delightful *Arcadian Adventures with the Idle Rich:*

> There are broad steps leading up to the club, so broad and so agreeably covered with matting that the physical exertion of lifting oneself from one's motor to the door of the club is reduced to the smallest compass. The richer members are not ashamed to take the steps one at a time, first one foot and then the other; and at tight money periods, when there is a black cloud hanging over the Stock Exchange, you may see each and every one of the members of the Mausoleum Club dragging himself up the steps after this fashion, his restless eyes filled with the dumb pathos of a man wondering where he can put his hand on half a million dollars.[22]

And in a hilarious description of a poverty-stricken duke entering the club, Leacock notes the important function of the reception space for the performance of class: "He wore a dinner jacket, just like an ordinary person, but even without his Norfolk coat and his hobnailed boots there was something in the way in which he walked up the long main hall of the Mausoleum Club that every imported waiter in the place recognized in an instant."[23]

Admitting women to the building at all was a signal of elite status, showing clubmen to be above all the childish nonsense of keeping women out. On special occasions, in fact, women seemed to function almost as architectural ornaments. Working-class men's clubs were far less concerned with hiding their activities from women than were the members of gentlemen's clubs. Architectural historian Abigail Van Slyck has suggested that working-class men saw themselves as women's "other," whereas elite clubmen tended to see men as women's "opposite." Working men's clubs, too, encouraged teamwork and intergenerational bonding, while elite clubs encouraged competition and provided activities that appealed to distinct generations. The elite men's club, in other words, privileged individualism, a characteristic that was ideal for succeeding in business.

Note that segregation by race operated the same way in other institutions. In hotels, golf clubs, and hybrid spaces like train cars, for example, the white masculinity of users often depended not on the absence of black masculinities per se but on their presence and subjugation. Architecture was particularly complicit in this campaign of separation. Even though segregation was never institutionalized in Canada, there are many cases of African Canadians being restricted to particular parts of buildings. The best known case, from much later in the twentieth century, is of Viola Desmond, a Nova Scotia businesswoman who refused in 1946 to sit in the balcony of a New Glasgow movie theatre, where staff members insisted she sit because of her race. The example of the theatre balcony is particularly compelling in this context because the debate focused on sightlines. The balcony would have been "invisible" to white moviegoers sitting on the main floor of the theatre, plus those in the balcony had a disadvantaged view of the screen. Indeed, Desmond insisted on sitting on the main floor so that she could have a better view of the film. Forcing black moviegoers to occupy space in this way – in the back and above the main floor – reinforced their second-class status through a language of space and vision, just as women occupied a special, highly constrained space in the urban men's club. "On ordinary days there are no ladies in the club, but only the shepherds," Leacock explained.[24]

> But at gayer times, when there are gala receptions at the club, its steps are all buried under expensive carpet, soft as moss and covered over with a long pavilion of red and white awning to catch the snowflakes; and beautiful ladies are poured into the club by the motorful ... Its broad corridors and deep recesses are filled with shepherdesses such as you never saw, dressed in beautiful shimmering gowns, and wearing feathers in their hair that droop off sideways at every angle known to trigonometry.[25]

The cultural power of the "broad corridors and deep recesses" to affirm the status of club members was thus profound, asserting members' social position by purposeful omission or inclusion, as Leacock noted.

How does architecture express manliness and power? At the University Club, the reception room (Figure 5.6) is dark and cozy, an ambience traditionally associated with men's residential spaces, such as libraries, dens, and dining rooms, which in the nineteenth century frequently showcased dark panelling, fine wooden furniture, leather upholstery, and books. The room features wooden panelling, an expensive and luxurious wall treatment associated with aristocratic mansions and fine hotels. An expansive fireplace, a built-in reception desk, fine textiles, and a centrally positioned table also added to the sumptuous atmosphere of entry.

The limits of the reception room were also powerful indicators of status, particularly Nobbs's generous, elliptical staircase, which provides access to the major socializing spaces on the prestigious level of the *piano nobile*. This staircase also marked the limit of women's penetration into the building long after Nobbs's generation. That is, even when women were allowed to visit rooms beyond the original, small entry sequence I have described, they were never permitted to take the stairs. Rather, they were expected to ascend by elevator

Figure 5.6 Reception hall, University Club, Montreal, 2013. Courtesy of Don Toromanoff.

to the second floor and were permitted to occupy only the main dining room. Never were they allowed to use the rooms on the first floor (the one just above entry), which included the reading room and billiards room. Nobbs's exquisite longitudinal cross-section (Figure 5.7) of the building showcases the importance of the staircase as a vertical connector and boundary.

Entering the men-only space of the stairway continued the filtering effect of the reception room, affirming the cultural superiority of members as they ascended to the first floor. The wide stairway invited men to ascend in pairs or on their own, taking in the especially curated stairway décor, which showcased themes of military history and war. The roundel between the ground and first floors includes the names of twenty-six members lost in the First World War, and the arched window a storey higher depicts the names of members who served. This carefully choreographed ascension through the club, with its discreet wartime illustrations, was exactly the opposite of the spatial sequence followed by women through the building, which was horizontal and steady.

McKim, Mead and White's entrance to the Mount Royal Club had a similar funnelling effect but accomplished it through different architectural means. Its reception room was much larger than that of the University Club, and it was anything but dark and cozy. Instead, it was a brightly lit, white, rect-angular room (Figure 5.8). Following the strictures of classicism, it was rigidly

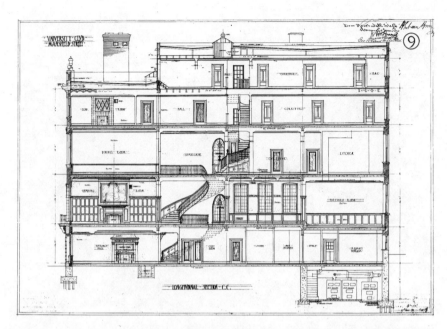

Figure 5.7　Longitudinal section of the University Club, Montreal, 1913. Ink on linen. John Bland Canadian Architecture Collection, McGill University.

Figure 5.8　Reception hall, Mount Royal Club, Montreal, 2013. Courtesy of Owen Egan.

symmetrical in plan. Members entered between a pair of classical columns; another pair marked the end of the room, which opened into a small reception area up a few stairs. This reception room followed more in the tradition of Charles Barry's British clubs, where the core of the building echoed great interior courtyards found in Roman and Florentine *palazzi*.

Club architecture reaffirmed each institution's excruciating admissions process through planning but also through scale and décor. The plans of both clubs reveal how the central programmatic functions of the typology, namely meeting, dining, reading, and playing billiards or cards, overlapped with typical upper-class houses. Mostly, these clubs were a place to meet other men and escape from the workplace, the home, and the diversity of the city; the club was a place to have whispered conversations,[26] eat fine meals, read newspapers and magazines, play card games and billiards, and very importantly, drink and smoke a lot. The scale of drinking and smoking is illustrated by the 1914 expenditures of the University Club, which used $1,594 worth of supplies, including $720 in wine and $272 in cigars.[27] After food and wine, cigars were the third highest expense. In today's age of dedicated smoking places (e.g., in airports, restaurants, and some workplaces), it is interesting to remember that smoking rooms were at the core of men's club architecture, isolating male smokers from others, including women.[28]

As Milne-Smith notes, smoking rooms were significant sites of conversation in men's clubs, which she describes as "emporia of gossip."[29] She even goes so far as to say that "the club smoking room became synonymous with such narratives." Smoke, politics, and social class were major themes in Leacock's clever characterization of the Mausoleum Club:

> Thus the members sit and talk in undertones that float to the ear through the haze of Havana smoke. You may hear the older men explaining that the country is going to absolute ruin, and the younger ones explaining that the country is forging ahead as it never did before; but chiefly they love to talk of great national questions, such as the protective tariff and the need of raising it, the sad decline of the morality of the working man, the spread of syndicalism and the lack of Christianity in the labour class, and the awful growth of selfishness among the mass of the people.[30]

Intimate conversations between and among members were facilitated by the domestic scale and atmosphere of smoking rooms; the shared activity of smoking, too, would have encouraged confidence and trust. Although the plans of both the University Club and the Mount Royal Club include no spaces labelled as "smoking rooms," archival photographs show ashtrays in other rooms. In all club rooms intended for activities other than dining (e.g., reading, cards, break-fast, etc.), comfortable seating furniture was clustered in small groups; stair-ways with landings and other circulation spaces that twisted and turned, too, invited members to pause and converse, like the ways in which vestibules and other nooks and crannies functioned in Victorian aristocratic mansions. And most importantly, each club interior's semblance of home made the institution and its members bond closely. "For men who lived so much of their lives in the public world, the ability to carve out a more private space for themselves was invaluable," Milne-Smith argues.[31]

Like smoking, eating together was an important club activity. The plan for the second floor (Figure 5.9) of the University Club shows an array of three dining rooms of various scales (one is larger than 1,200 square feet), connected to an enclosed kitchen of 1,165 square feet, ensuring that the intense labour needed to produce fine meals was invisible to members. Moreover, the plan in general features arrangements of differently sized rooms for eating, like an upper-class house. Large rooms, like the main dining room, assured that members could see other members and be seen, and they were good places to display the club's impressive art collection. Fine art, fine dining, and fine furniture were further ways that members affirmed their elevated status in society, in addition to simply being in the club building.

A further home-like aspect of the club building was the fact that members could spend a night at the club. Montreal's University Club included hotel-like rooms on the upper floors for overnight stays; some clubs, such as the Mount Royal, provided only modest rooms for members too intoxicated to get home (in the basement!),[32] emphasizing again the role of the club as a literal home away from home.

Education, Sports, War

Scale is not the only planning cue that the club building was no ordinary house. Education, sports, and war, as we saw in the central staircase, feature promin-ently in the University Club. For example, at least three interior spaces boast a display of university emblems, furnishing material evidence that the club's bringing together of these elites was upheld by an educated, structured, exclu-sive, *male* lineage. Note that although the club was physically and symbolically close to McGill University, membership was open to graduates of all universities. Nobbs included the coats of arms of the world's most prestigious universities in the billiards room. Deeply interested in heraldry throughout his career, Nobbs had designed McGill University's coat of arms in 1922, at the invitation of Principal Sir Arthur Currie.

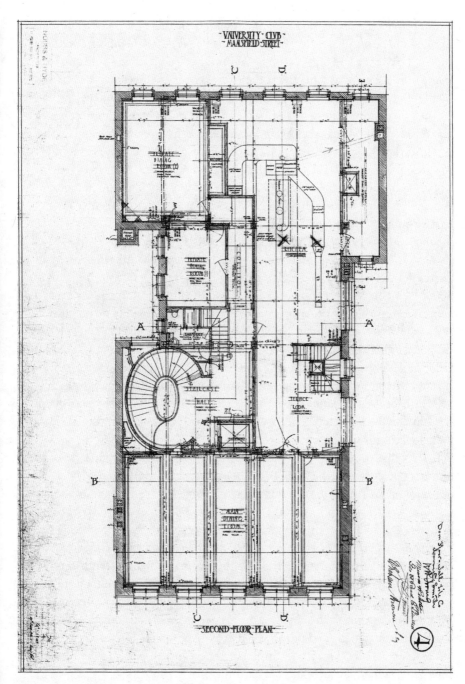

Figure 5.9 Plan for the second floor of the University Club, Montreal, 1913. Ink on linen. John Bland Canadian Architecture Collection, McGill University.

Nobbs was the ideal choice for the architect of the University Club for a number of reasons. Foremost, he was among its founding members; his role at McGill University and his Scottish background and education would also have made him the right architect. But the choice of an architect was also fundamental for attaining the manly, exclusive environment sought by men's clubs. Nobbs's professional life as a tastemaker and influential architectural educator was offset by his "vernacular" accomplishments as a fencer, angler, and hunter. Art historian Susan Wagg has pointed out that Nobbs liked adversarial sports in particular because he enjoyed testing his wits and skills.[33] He started fencing in 1901 and was a member of the Canadian Olympic fencing team in 1908. Although it is often written that Nobbs won a silver medal, there is no evidence that he got an Olympic medal during the 1908 London games.[34] Nobbs loved fencing and was even called the dean of Canadian fencing (Figure 5.10). "In all its aspects," he wrote, "as mere exercise, recreation, applied mechanics, gymnastics for the mind, and school of manners, as a training in co-ordination of action, self-control, deception, strategy and sportsmanship, this science, art and sport is too good a thing to drop from our civilization, even if we do not duel."[35]

As with his other passions, Nobbs wrote about salmon fishing and fencing, ultimately publishing *Salmon Tactics* in 1934 and *Fencing Tactics* in 1936. In his eulogy for Nobbs in 1964, colleague John Bland referred to these books on fishing and fencing as being among Nobbs's three major publications, also noting, "His love for *the association of men* and their activities is attested by a life membership ... in the University Club, of which he was a founder and whose delightful club house is his work."[36]

In the billiards room (Figure 5.11), replete with university insignia, heads of animals also decorated the walls. In her book *Becoming Native in a Foreign Land* (2009), Gillian Poulter has convincingly illustrated that sport and especially hunting were taken up by wealthy, male, anglophone Montrealers to shape a uniquely Canadian identity. Poulter uses photographs to show how *seeing* was crucial to this process of identity. Club architecture functioned the same way, almost like a three-dimensional model of an image by nineteenth-century photographer William Notman, "produc[ing] ideology rather than merely expressing it."[37] The conservative men's club building with discreet entries positioned the club in the city's centre but preserved its customs and secrets through its thick walls and purpose-built rooms. Crossing the threshold from sidewalk to reception room confirmed members' elite status, and the flowing, interpenetrating plan ensured that each member saw others and was seen by others, affirming the bonds between and among members in spatial terms. Without the building, that is, urban men's clubs were all but meaningless.

Figure 5.10 "Les sabreurs, Leo Nunes and Percy Nobbs," date unknown. Photocopy, vertical file. John Bland Canadian Architecture Collection, McGill University.

Similarly and finally, a gendered analysis of the University Club is informed by Nobbs's interest in military symbolism, which enhanced the masculinist expressions of the building in subtle ways. For example, John McCrae's famous war poem of 1915, *In Flanders Fields* (which Canadian children still memorize in school) was popularized by another member, Andrew Macphail, and is framed on the wall of the library today.[38] McCrae was a founding member of the University Club and, with Stephen Leacock, is among its most famous members. Nobbs's own military experience as a major in the First World War commingled with his architectural production throughout his career. He proposed a War Memorial Museum for Regina in 1919 (unbuilt) and was appointed adviser to the Canadian Battlefields Memorial Commission in 1920. He designed a War and Naval Memorial Chapel for St. Peter's Church in Sherbrooke, Quebec, a Naval Memorial for Point Pleasant Park in Halifax, and Currie Hall at the Royal Military College in Kingston. As both a front-line officer and a prominent architect, then, he contributed directly to Canada's rich military architectural history.

Complicating the story of the Mount Royal Club is the fact that architect Stanford White is better known for his murder in 1906 at the hands of his young

Figure 5.11 Billiards room, University Club, Montreal, date unknown. John Bland Canadian Architecture Collection, McGill University.

mistress's husband than for his athletic or military accomplishments. White was famous, nonetheless, as a seducer of young girls, so perhaps lechery was his special masculine characteristic.[39] His firm, McKim, Mead and White, also designed a number of influential men's clubs in New York.[40]

Conclusion

To conclude, the main contribution of this chapter to masculinity studies is its insistence that expectations about masculinity are encoded in the built environment. Echoing club policy, club architecture excluded women and all men but those who could afford the fees and gain acceptance as members, a highly select group. As a gender-exclusive and class-exclusive building type, then, clubs show how notions of gender and class intersect and reinforce each other. Architecture was a powerful language to express this message. As we have seen, references to the aristocratic home reinforced the overarching messages of masculine power. The chapter thus suggests the need for a new understanding of domesticity and how it relates to gender, perhaps as an atmosphere or environment that was commonly simulated outside the house. In this way, men's clubs functioned almost like prosthetic homes, in which gender absences or subordinations were structuring presences.[41] In architecture, the design of men's clubs as a "place of manliness" was largely thematic and overlaid on a floor plan that showcased house-like rooms and activities: dining, reading, and even sleeping. In addition, the reputations of the architects, not only as tastemakers but also as particular models of masculinity, enhanced the manly expression of the institutions they designed. Their buildings included material cues that constituted manliness, filtered through their own experiences and interests, especially schooling, war, and sports. In addition to a considerable expansion of the domestic realm, this manliness was attained through architectural control of entry sequences and circulation, architectural codes of belonging and unbelonging, the careful construction of interiors to accommodate male-only leisure, and subtle projections of the club architect as an exaggerated exemplar of the ideal clubman.

Notes

Thanks to McGill architecture graduate students Tania Gutiérrez Monroy and Don Toromanoff, who assisted with the research for this chapter. Also thanks to Dave Cameron, David Covo, Lucas Crawford, Owen Egan, Jennifer Garland, the John Bland Canadian Architecture Collection at McGill University, Julia Gersovitz, Peter Gossage, Cynthia Hammond, Ann Marie Holland, Julia Kampis, Juan Llano, William Moore, the Mount Royal Club, Jarrett Rudy, the University Club, Abigail Van Slyck, and Michael Windover.

1 Julian Orbach, *Victorian Architecture in Britain* (London: A&C Black, 1987), 225.
2 See Carolyn Podruchny, "Festivities, Fortitude and Fraternalism: Fur Trade Masculinity and the Beaver Club, 1785–1827," in *New Faces in the Fur Trade: Selected Papers of the Seventh North American Fur Trade Conference,* ed. William C. Wicken, Jo-Anne Fiske, and Susan Sleeper-Smith, 31–52 (East Lansing: Michigan State University Press, 1998).
3 The club was founded when twenty members of the St. James Club decided to form a new association, believing the St. James Club had become too inclusive. Kathryn Banham, "The Architecture and Painting Collection of the Mount Royal Club, Montreal, 1899–1920" (MA thesis, Concordia University, 2006), 8. The first clubhouse was on the same site, a residence that had belonged to Prime Minister John Abbott and which was destroyed by fire in 1904. In December 2017, the University Club announced its decision to vacate and sell its Mansfield Street clubhouse, discussed at length in this chapter. See Susan Schwartz, "University Club of Montreal Giving Up its Percy Nobbs Designed Downtown Digs," *Montreal Gazette,* December 21, 2017.
4 This statistic is much cited but rarely explained. It appears in many popular Montreal guidebooks today. See, for example, *Ulysses Travel Guide Montreal* (Montreal: Hunter, 2006), 86.
5 Canadian novelist Robertson Davies said Leacock was "a man set apart, who lived, worked and felt on an ampler scale than those who lacked his gift." Robertson Davies, *Stephen Leacock* (Toronto: McClelland and Stewart, 1970), 57.
6 Amy Milne-Smith, "A Flight to Domesticity? Making a Home in the Gentlemen's Clubs of London, 1880–1914," *Journal of British Studies* 45, 4 (2006): 796–818; Amy Milne-Smith, "Club Talk: Gossip, Masculinity and Oral Communities in Late Nineteenth-Century London," *Gender and History* 21, 1 (2009): 86–106; Amy Milne-Smith, *London Clubland: A Cultural History of Gender and Class in Late-Victorian Britain* (New York: Palgrave Macmillan, 2011); Barbara Black, *A Room of His Own: A Literary-Cultural Study of Victorian Clubland* (Athens: Ohio University Press, 2012).

7 William D. Moore, "The Masonic Lodge Room, 1870–1930: A Sacred Space of Masculine Spiritual Hierarchy," in *Gender, Class, and Shelter: Perspectives in Vernacular Architecture V*, ed. Elizabeth Collins Cromley and Carter L. Hudgins, 26–39 (Knoxville: University of Tennessee Press, 1995); Deryck Holdsworth, "'I'm a Lumberjack and I'm OK': The Built Environment and Varied Masculinities in the Industrial Age," in *Gender, Class, and Shelter: Perspectives in Vernacular Architecture V*, ed. Elizabeth Collins Cromley and Carter L. Hudgins, 11–25 (Knoxville: University of Tennessee Press, 1995).

8 Paula Lupkin, *Manhood Factories: YMCA Architecture and the Making of Urban Culture* (Minneapolis: University of Minnesota Press, 2010), 2.

9 Queer theorist Lucas Crawford notes that these houses were the scene for the launching of a new spate of gossip-rag publications, pamphlets, and so on. Lucas Crawford, correspondence with author, May 28, 2013. An important difference between this early form and exclusive business clubs is that anyone could partake in coffeehouse culture.

10 See for instance Caitlin Flanagan, "The Dark Power of Fraternities," *Atlantic* 313, 2 (2014): 72–91.

11 See Milne-Smith, "Flight to Domesticity?" Another good model for this study is John Potvin, "Hot by Design: The Secret Life of a Turkish Bath in Victorian London," in *Craft, Space and Interior Design, 1855–2005*, ed. Sandra Alfoldy and Janice Helland, 11–25 (London: Ashgate, 2008).

12 Milne-Smith, *London Clubland*, 111.

13 Thanks to Lucas Crawford for noting this contribution. Crawford, correspondence with author.

14 Martha Vicinus, *Independent Women: Work and Community for Single Women, 1850–1920* (Chicago: University of Chicago Press, 1985), 129.

15 Annmarie Adams, "Rooms of Their Own: The Nurses' Residences at Montreal's Royal Victoria Hospital," *Material History Review* 40 (1994): 29–41.

16 Dolores Hayden, *The Grand Domestic Revolution: A History of Feminist Designs for American Homes, Neighborhoods, and Cities* (Cambridge, MA: MIT Press, 1981); Gwendolyn Wright, *Moralism and the Model Home: Domestic Architecture and Cultural Conflict in Chicago, 1873–1913* (Chicago: University of Chicago Press, 1980); Elizabeth Cromley, *The Food Axis* (Charlottesville: University of Virginia Press, 2010); Gail Lee Dubrow and Jennifer B. Goodman, eds., *Restoring Women's History through Historic Preservation* (Baltimore, MD: Johns Hopkins University Press, 2003); Abigail Van Slyck, *A Manufactured Wilderness: Summer Camps and the Shaping of American Youth, 1890–1960* (Minneapolis: University of Minnesota Press, 2006); Marta Gutman, *A City for Children: Women, Architecture, and the Charitable Landscapes of Oakland, 1850–1950* (Chicago: University of Chicago Press, 2014); Cynthia Hammond, *Architects, Angels, Activisits and the City of Bath, 1765–1965* (London: Ashgate, 2012); Tania Martin, "Housing the Grey Nuns: Power, Women, and Religion in Fin-de-siècle Montréal," in *Perspectives in Vernacular Architecture VII*, ed. Annmarie Adams and Sally McMurry, 212–29 (Knoxville: University of Tennessee Press, 1997).

17 This prestigious location reflects the substantial wealth of the club's members, as do the annual dues for membership, which in 1915 were $1,800. See University Club of Montreal, "Statement of Operating Account for the Half-Year Ended 31st July 1915," in the John Bland Canadian Architecture Collection, McGill University.

18 Lucas Crawford notes that a range of queer spaces use similar design features to different effect, especially bars and bathhouses. So unmarked doors can be about prestige and mystery but also about protection and required seclusion. Crawford, correspondence with author.

19 Women penetrated further into the building over time. According to Louise Robertson, women could use the Humphrey Lounge and main dining room in the company of a member by the 1970s but not the stairs. Louise Robertson, "Club Life," in *University Club of Montreal, 1907–2007*, ed. Peter R.D. MacKell (Montreal: Price-Patterson, 2007), 74. I thank the club's membership and marketing manager, Julia Kampis, for sharing this centennial album and her own knowledge with me.

20 See Alex K. Paterson, "Changing Times," in *University Club of Montreal, 1907–2007*, ed. Peter R.D. MacKell (Montreal: Price-Patterson, 2007), 20–26.

21 Milne-Smith, *London Clubland*, 113.

22 Stephen Leacock, *Arcadian Adventures with the Idle Rich* (New York: John Lane, 1914), 11.

23 Ibid., 34.

24 Ibid., 12.

25 Ibid.

26 Milne-Smith, "Club Talk."

27 University Club accounting, in the John Bland Canadian Architecture Collection, McGill University.

28 Jarrett Rudy writes, "Not only were women not supposed to smoke; they were not supposed to be in places where men smoked." Jarrett Rudy, *Freedom to Smoke: Tobacco Consumption and Identity* (Montreal and Kingston: McGill-Queen's University Press, 2005), 14; see also 32–33 and, on clubs, 35.

29 Milne-Smith, "Club Talk," 93.

30 Leacock, *Arcadian Adventures*, 13.

31 Milne-Smith, "Club Talk," 95.

32 Banham, "Architecture and Painting," 26, claims these rooms were for the club manager and other staff members.

33 Susan Wagg, *Percy Erskine Nobbs: Architect, Artist, Craftsman* (Montreal and Kingston: McGill-Queen's University Press, 1982), 73.

34 This story is reported in various and ambiguous ways. In Nobbs's eulogy, however, Bland clearly states, "When he was 33 he won a silver medal for fencing in the Olympic Games of 1908." John Bland, "In Memoriam: Percy Erskine Nobbs, St. Mary's Church, Como, November 15th, 1964," 2; John Bland Canadian Architecture Collection, McGill University. Official documents from the 1908 Olympics show that he competed in the first round of the épée event, coming sixth and therefore not advancing. The confusion stems from the fact that Nobbs participated in a foil fencing display, for which he perhaps received an award.

35 Percy Nobbs, "Praise of Fencing," *McGill University Magazine*, May 1905, 239.

36 Bland, "In Memoriam," 2–3, emphasis added.

37 Gillian Poulter, "Becoming Native in a Foreign Land: Visual Culture, Sport, and Spectacle in the Construction of National Identity in Montreal, 1840–1885" (PhD diss., York University, 1999), 422. See also Gillian Poulter, *Becoming Native in a Foreign Land: Sport, Visual Culture, and Identity in Montreal, 1840–85* (Vancouver: UBC Press, 2009).

38 MacKell, ed., *University Club*, 51–52.

39 "White's Victims Confess," *Los Angeles Herald*, July 1, 1905, 1.

40 On the clubs, see Mosette Glaser Broderick, *Triumvirate: McKim, Mead and White: Art, Architecture, Scandal and Class in America's Gilded Age* (New York: Knopf, 2011), chs. 24 and 38.

41 Milne-Smith argues that clubs were attractive because men had limited power and privacy at home. Milne-Smith, "Flight to Domesticity?" 807–9.

6

"As Christ the Carpenter": Work-Camp Missions and the Construction of Christian Manhood in Late-Nineteenth- and Early-Twentieth-Century Canada

Norman Knowles

THE LATE NINETEENTH AND early twentieth centuries witnessed a growing concern within Canada's Protestant churches about the religious condition of the growing number of workers who lived and toiled in the nation's logging, mining, and construction camps. "What have the Churches done," Rev. John Duncan Byrne, the superintendent of Presbyterian Home Missions for northwestern Ontario, asked in 1910, "for the men who toil in the camps scattered across the Dominion harvesting the forests, mining the earth's riches, and building the railroads that open up the frontier?" Byrne lamented that the loggers, miners, and labourers of the work camps were Canada's "forgotten men." He warned that such neglect not only threatened the welfare of the men who lived and worked in the remote camps far removed from the "centres of civilization" and "religious influence" but also endangered the very future of Canada "as a righteous nation built upon Godly principles." "The camps," Byrne complained, were "breeding grounds for vice" and "hot beds of radicalism" in which "indifference and hostility" to religion were "permitted to flourish unchallenged." "Canada's working men," Byrne concluded, must learn to become "as Christ the carpenter."[1] As concern for the moral and spiritual well-being of these workers increased, Canada's Protestant churches created a number of special missions dedicated to the camps. This chapter examines the motivation that lay behind the creation of these camp missions, the strategies adopted by missionaries to reach the workers, and the responses of the workers to these ministrations. A close examination of camp missions reveals that the relationship between the missionary and the missionized was shaped to a large degree by competing cultures of masculinity.

For much of the nineteenth century, the religious care and instruction of the loggers and miners who worked in remote camps were left largely to individual missionaries. The inherent limitations of such individual efforts, however, resulted in calls for more systematic and sustained work in the camps. In 1869 a group of concerned Presbyterians in Ottawa founded the Lumber Mission to work among the bush workers of the Ottawa Valley. With the financial support of several prominent local businessmen in the industry, the Lumber Mission secured the services of Rev. Hugh Cameron and Rev. H.J. Borthwick to visit the camps on both the Ontario and Quebec sides of the Ottawa River. Cameron and Bothwick held religious services, distributed "suitable literature" in both English and French, and met with the men on an individual basis.[2] One of the Presbyterian clergy sent into the camps by the Lumber Mission in 1892 was a young Nova Scotian, Alfred Fitzpatrick. Fitzpatrick was appalled by the "physical discomforts of the bunkhouse," the "deadening monotony of camp life," and "the absence of culture or of any refining influence."[3] Inspired by the practical and applied social Christianity of the Social Gospel, Fitzpatrick denounced the neglect of the camps by the churches and called for immediate and concrete action to alleviate the workers' condition. In 1899 he founded the Reading Camp Association to provide workers with wholesome reading materials as an alternative to the vices of camp life. Since bunkhouses were noisy, crowded, and poorly lit, Fitzpatrick convinced camp operators to set up reading cabins where the men would gather to pass their spare time. The following year, he left regular church work and founded Frontier College. Although he was no longer directly employed by the church, Fitzpatrick believed that his camp work was no less religious. Through the college, university students were sent into the camps during the summer to work alongside the men during the day and to offer courses in the evening. Fitzpatrick believed that education was essential if the working man was to improve himself and acquire the traits of good Christian citizenship.

As the number of camps multiplied after the turn of the century, concern with the religious condition of the working man increased. Byrne identified "carrying the gospel message to the men of the camps" as "one of the big problems facing the Canadian church."[4] The Home Missions Boards of the Methodist and Presbyterian Churches responded by dispatching theological students and the newly ordained to work in the camps before completing their education or being called to serve a congregation. Anglicans adopted a different strategy. In 1908 the Missionary Society of the Church of England in Canada and the Navvy Mission Society of England jointly sponsored the creation of the Canadian Church Camp Mission to evangelize "the vast army of men scattered all over the Dominion living in lonely exile in Mining, Lumbering, Railway and Construction Camps." Under the superintendency of Rev. J.M. McCormick, the Church Camp Mission employed a dozen permanent missionaries across the country and supported another dozen temporary volunteer workers. Operating under the motto "service rather than services," the itinerant Church Camp missionaries sought to express the "Church's practical sympathy with the men in their peculiarly trying circumstances" and to do "everything possible to elevate and brighten the lives" of the workers.[5] British Columbia's geography dictated further innovation. In that province, the Anglican, Methodist, and Presbyterian Churches launched several mission boats to serve the many isolated logging and fishing camps along the coast. In addition to spreading the Gospel, the boats often provided medical services and carried mail and supplies to the camps.[6]

Organizations such as the Woman's Christian Temperance Union (WCTU) and the Young Men's Christian Association (YMCA) also became active in the camps. In 1890 Agnes Hunter of Pembroke convinced the Ontario convention of the WCTU to establish a department for the "spiritual and moral betterment" of the province's miners and loggers. Believing the men of the camps to be particularly vulnerable to the seduction of alcohol and gambling, the WCTU set out to supply these "isolated and tempted" men with wholesome reading material and comfort bags, and it hired missionaries to visit the camps and preach the gospel of temperance. Drink, the WCTU warned, robbed the worker of his wages and independence, eroded his discipline and self-control, and destroyed his strength and virility.[7] With the support of industry, the YMCA sent out camp secretaries to help companies and workers organize activities based on its commitment to a fourfold program of social, physical, educational, and religious development. The secretary typically brought with him a large supply of reading material, games, sports equipment, and records, and he stayed in the camp for about a week, organizing social activities, sports teams, lectures and classes, bible studies, hymn sings, and Sunday services. Once the various activities were under way, the secretary appointed men in the camp to continue the program in his absence. The aim of the program was to render the camps more pleasant and habitable, to create a more contented and productive workforce, to foster good relations between workers and management, and to build Christian character.[8]

In 1908 William Henderson and a group of evangelical Toronto businessmen founded the Shantymen's Christian Association to minister exclusively to the men of the camps. Born into a well-to-do Scottish shipping family, Henderson was raised as a devout Presbyterian. In 1895 he emigrated to Canada at the age of twenty-three. He settled in Hespeler, Ontario, where he became the superintendent of a woollen mill. In 1905 Henderson moved to Toronto and became publisher of a monthly religious magazine, *The Faithful Witness,* dedicated to strengthening Christians in their faith and commitment to missions. On a visit to Parry Sound, he became disturbed by the lack of any Christian influence in the lives of the men living and working in the bush and resolved to dedicate himself to bringing the Gospel to the lumber camps. From Henderson's initial efforts, the Shantymen's Christian Association spread to camps across the country.[9] The missionaries of the Shantymen's Christian Association preached a fundamentalist Protestantism that distinguished them from the more liberal Social Gospel Christianity of the mainline denominations.

Despite their differences in theological outlook and approach, all of these groups shared a common objective: the development of "strong and manly characters."[10] It was repeatedly asserted in sermons and mission literature that camp men were prone to vices that degraded their manliness. J.M. McCormack of the Church Camp Mission explained that "when men are segregated by fifties and hundreds, often at great distance from civilization there is a deadening effect upon the minds caused by the absence of diversified interests; the result in the majority of cases is a peculiar predisposition to the allurements of drink, immorality, gambling and other forms of vice." Such behaviour, McCormack asserted, endangered the "manly character" of these "strong sons of toil."[11] The "monotony of camp conditions" and the complete inattention to the "cultivation" of the workers' "mental and moral nature," Henderson insisted, turned otherwise "strong" and "healthy" men into "brute beasts."[12] Fitzpatrick warned that "to neglect the opportunity to surround these men with home-like influences and with the tools with which to fashion their characters is to leave them open to every evil influence. It is to allow their minds to be full of thoughts that sap their manhood."[13]

The missions sought to rescue the men of the camps from the primitive state into which they had fallen by imposing a higher standard of masculinity based on middle-class Protestant values that emphasized self-control and the virtues of industry, honesty, loyalty, sobriety, and thrift. Christian manliness demanded the discipline and dedication that came with faith and the self-improvement and moral responsibility that came with personal regeneration. Rev. Ebenezer E. Ross outlined the characteristics of Christian manhood in an address to the Young Men's Christian Association of Halifax. "True manliness," Ross insisted, did not "consist in any purely physical attributes." Nor was it to be found in "revelry and riot" and "the arts of the libertine." "To sing the loudest song, to drain the deepest goblet, to swear the coarsest oath, to break the obscenest jest are not the achievements it boasts," Ross continued. "Genuine Manliness," Ross maintained, "recognizes the distinction between right and wrong." The essential characteristics of Christian manhood, according to Ross, were "indomitable perseverance," "unswerving integrity," "self-denial," "self-conquest," and the "courage" to "adopt and avow and maintain the truth."[14] Similar sentiments were expressed by Rev. William Cochrane in an 1887 address on "Christian Manliness" to graduates at Queen's University. Cochrane exhorted the men of Canada "to seek after the highest qualities of true manhood, chief of which is moral and spiritual strength." "God's idea of manhood," Cochrane proclaimed, was defined by "industry," "purity of heart," "rugged honesty," "transparency of character," and "unflinching faith."[15] These ideas continued to be expressed by the Protestant clergy during the first quarter of the twentieth century in articles, sermons, and lectures with titles such as "The Whole Man," "A Young Man's Religion," "Men in the Making," and "A Challenge to Manhood."[16]

A theology of self-improvement and personal regeneration was at the heart of the message carried to the camps by the different missions. "The only true way to help a man," Henderson asserted, "is to get him to help himself."[17] Even Social Gospellers, who proclaimed the need for social transformation, insisted that reform had to begin with the individual. Methodist T.E.E. Shore insisted that "experience in mission work teaches that nothing is so essential to social redemption as individual regeneration. Salvation is the real and radical cure for the social ills of our times. It changes men. It breaks the fetters of evil habits, and takes away the appetite for sin."[18] The reformation of character and self-mastery required for personal regeneration were presented as particularly manly achievements. The capacity "to overcome inherent evil" and to "combat successfully against the temptations and wiles of a seductive world" were hailed as "the highest qualities of true manhood."[19]

"The noblest type of manhood possible on earth," asserted Alexander Sutherland, the secretary of the Methodist Missionary Society, "is that which approximates most closely to Jesus of Nazareth."[20] The late nineteenth and early twentieth centuries witnessed the publication of dozens of books on the life and character of Jesus. Many of these works reacted against the sentimental portrayals of Jesus that had become popular in the middle of the nineteenth century and emphasized Christ's masculine qualities: his strength of will, physical endurance, courage, virtuous fortitude, decisiveness, and self-sacrifice. Much was made of the fact that Jesus had been a carpenter who lived by the sweat of his brow before he became a strong and vigorous leader of men. It was this active, militant, and muscular Jesus, rather than the gentle Saviour, who was upheld as the model of Christian manhood by the camp missions. "In Jesus," asserted a missionary with the Shantymen's Christian Association,

> we have a guide to what it is to be a real man. Like Jesus, a real man does not give in to temptation. Like Jesus, a real man does not cower in the face of ridicule. Like Jesus, a real man does not shirk away from telling it like it really is. Like

Jesus, a real man is prepared to endure hardship and sacrifice all for what is right and good.[21]

Such statements make it clear that in calling the men of the camps to follow Jesus, the missions were proclaiming not only a set of religious beliefs and values but a particular code of masculinity as well.

Many of the men who worked in the camps were young and single, and they jumped from job to job as need or desire arose. These men and their behaviour challenged the middle-class Protestant ideal of the family man. In late-nineteenth- and early-twentieth-century Canadian society, the mature and responsible male was expected to marry and to become a good provider for his family. Male identity rested to a considerable degree on one's status as a breadwinner and success in supporting a family. In this culture, the home was widely revered as a sanctuary from the evils and temptations of the world where husbands and sons were exposed to the morally and spiritually elevating influence of their wives and mothers. To many middle-class English Canadians, the camps and the presence of a large number of transient single men appeared to threaten the traditional family by drawing young men away from their homes and families and exposing them to a host of evils that were then spread across the country as the men moved from job to job. "The influence of the men after leaving the camps and going into families where they are engaged as hired help for the summer has not been good," warned a Presbyterian missionary working in the lumber camps of Manitoba.[22]

Many missionaries attributed the camp workers' vices to the absence of women and the "gracious influence of the Christian home."[23] Convinced of the moral and spiritual uplift provided by women, the WCTU took the unusual step of sending women missionaries into the camps. "One cannot overrate the influence of a woman's presence on the life of the camp," the *Methodist Magazine and Review* observed. "The very sound of her voice will be a daily reminder of wife or mother or sister and of the better influence of home."[24] The churches were less willing to employ women in camp work and instead called upon companies to employ married foremen who could settle their families in the camps as a means to improve the men's behaviour and provide a good example of the benefits of family life. Alfred Fitzpatrick advised companies that they could increase production, reduce discontent, and eliminate vice and transiency by employing married men and settling them with their families in the camps.[25] Failure to expose the men of the camps to the wholesome influence of women and family, it was feared, would result in the creation of a class of shiftless drifters who threatened to erode not only the moral and social order but the sexual order as well. Implicit in Protestant middle-class anxieties about bachelorhood and camp conditions were unspoken concerns about the sexual activity of large numbers of men living in close quarters for long periods of time.[26]

Although missionaries lamented the degraded state of the workers' manly character, they insisted that the men of the camps were not beyond redemption. A Methodist missionary in northern Ontario asserted that the men's riotous behaviour "did not strain the character beyond the point of recovery." He observed that the strenuous and demanding work of the camp labourer fostered "the development of moral strength and muscular well-being." The constant danger of the job instilled "battle courage, an adventurous spirit and indomitable steadfastness," qualities that formed "the basis of character."[27] Just as work in the camps contributed to the men's physical health and to their development of many manly character traits, it was equally imperative that "these strong sons of toil" and "great muscular empire builders" develop their spiritual and mental capacities before they could be considered whole men.[28] "The man who works with his muscles," Fitzpatrick asserted, "should have an opportunity for mental and spiritual development ... Intellect, soul and body must go together to form one well-rounded personality. We can no more divorce mental exercise and worship from manual labour than we can separate soul from body. The end is death in either case."[29] Many missionaries claimed that despite their rough appearance and rugged ways, the men of the camps were not inherently hostile to religion. The proximity of the camps to nature, in fact, was believed to make the men particularly susceptible to spiritual influences. "There is pure air, open sky, and that blessed quiet in which great souls have ever been nurtured," the *Methodist Magazine and Review* observed.[30] "Never judge these men by their outward appearances or behaviour when they come to town and get under bad influences," advised a missionary with the Shantymen's Christian Association, "but learn to know them in the woods and you find them 'nature's gentlemen.'"[31] The purpose of the missions was to provide an alternative to the destructive vices of camp life and to refine the men's manly character by cultivating their moral and spiritual natures. The key to success, however, was to arouse in the men a desire for their own improvement by providing them with the saving message of the Gospel. "Rough in [his] way but good at heart," the camp worker was sure to become "a better citizen and a God fearing man" if provided with the proper spiritual guidance and practical help.[32]

The determined efforts of the missions to implant the ideals of middle-class Christian manhood in the camps often met with apathy and even hostility from many of the workers. In regular reports to their superintendents, missionaries frequently expressed frustration with the indifference and opposition they encountered in the camps. The following account of a visit to a camp in British

Columbia by a missionary with the Shantymen's Christian Association was typical:

> Stopping at Camp No. 1 we had supper and, with Gospels and tracts in our hands, sallied forth to visit the men in the different bunkhouses. Our reception was not any too warm, several of them speaking out bitterly against the church ... The majority seemed utterly indifferent, but a few asked for Gospels and appeared to appreciate the visit. Some of course were anxious to argue, but knowing the utter uselessness of argument, we endeavoured to keep to the one and only theme: Jesus Christ and Him Crucified. We held a meeting in the cookhouse but only some 12 or 15 men would come in.[33]

Some missionaries even reported being physically threatened and run out of camp, but pranks at the missionaries' expense appear to have been more common. One missionary recounted that he "asked any in the audience to put up their hand as an indication of their desire to know Jesus as their Saviour. One fellow put up his bare foot and the fellows laughed."[34] Although such incidents occurred regularly, missionaries also reported that many of the men appreciated the break in routine that their visits provided. Hymn sings appear to have been especially popular. "These men living in entire isolation," reported a missionary with the Church Camp Mission, "just love something in the form of singing to break the monotony." Another Church Camp missionary asserted that "the softer side of the 'boys' was soon revealed by the influence of music and my old violin was a golden key to their good will."[35]

Missionaries encountered their strongest opposition in camps with a large number of recent immigrants. By the end of the nineteenth century, immigrants from central and eastern Europe formed an increasingly large share of the workforce in many camps. These groups often received the missionaries with suspicion and distrust. A missionary in the mining camps of northern Ontario complained that "the Slavs and Galacians are most hostile to us and refuse to accept our tracts even when written in their own language."[36] To many immigrants, the missionaries were purveyors of an unfamiliar culture and religion that threatened their own ethnic and religious identity. Some immigrant groups carried with them a socialist tradition that openly opposed organized religion. The Finns, for example, were frequently identified by camp missionaries as socialists who were especially hostile to their efforts. A missionary working in northwestern Ontario observed that it was "exceptional" to find a Finn who was not "indifferent, suspicious and often antagonistic to God's Word and His Messenger."[37] The district superintendent of Presbyterian home missions for northwestern Ontario, John Duncan Byrne, frequently complained to both church leaders and government authorities that the Finns were dangerous Bolshevists and spreading radical and revolutionary ideas throughout the camps.[38] The influence of radicals in the camps concerned many of the missionaries. "The Reds or IWW [Industrial Workers of the World]," a Shantyman warned, "are plenteous in number to counteract the good done by the ministry of the word."[39] A Church Camp missionary in Alberta observed that many of the men "fought shy of his religion" because they had been taught by "socialists" that it was "the cult of the rich" and that the church was a "useless burden upon the workers."[40]

The close association that the missions attempted to cultivate with the companies that owned and operated the camps appeared to give credence to such accusations. In their attempts to win the support of industry for their work, mission organizations often held up the missions as a means to undermine labour radicalism and to restore order in the camps. William Henderson of the Shantymen asserted in the *Canadian Lumberman* that mission work would "help greatly to solve the labour troubles in the camps."[41] The YMCA promised management that its fourfold program would increase efficiency and improve labour relations.[42] Sensitive to the hostility that company support for the missions could produce among the labourers of the camps, missionaries were often advised to conceal any assistance they received from the operators.[43] Although a few companies contributed financially to the different mission organizations and actively sought out missionaries for their camps, the aid that industry gave to the missions was actually quite limited. The perception in the mind of many workers, however, was that missionaries were essentially agents of the company. This assumption was supported by the reception given the visiting missionary by the camp boss. It was often the camp boss who decided whether the missionary could distribute tracts and hold services and who provided the missionary with accommodation during his stay. Some bosses compelled their men to attend services and to treat the missionary with respect, confirming the men's suspicions that the missionaries were working for their employers.[44]

The opposition encountered by the missionaries in the camps was not simply a product of class and ethnic suspicions and radical politics. Much of the hostility directed toward the missionaries can be attributed to the conflict that existed between the middle-class Christian code of manhood promulgated by the missionaries and the standards that defined manliness in the camps. In his study of the northern Ontario logging industry, Ian Radforth asserts that "the bush camp was a male world, suffused in every respect with a keen sense of masculinity." The long hours of physically demanding labour combined with the rugged conditions of camp life to create a distinctive male culture that celebrated physical prowess, endurance, and hardiness. Workers took tremendous pride in putting in a full day's labour and in taking on difficult and dangerous tasks. This spirit of manly competition continued in the bunkhouse, where workers often spent their off-hours competing in arm-wrestling matches and other tests of strength. Radforth suggests that workers presented themselves as fearless "dare-devils and he-men" to compensate for the relative lack of respect and reward accorded to their work by society.[45] The competitive individualism of the camp men was accompanied by a strong sense of brotherhood. In his 1928 study of Canada's work camps, Edmund Bradwin observed that the dangers of the workplace and the close quarters of the bunkhouse demanded that the men have "a good deal of confidence in one another."[46] As a result, a strong sense of camaraderie developed among the men of the camps. Transiency was another defining characteristic of camp life. It appears that few men completed their work terms or spent an entire season in one camp. The ability to pack up and move on enabled the men to escape a corrupt or oppressive operator and particularly bad conditions. It also allowed workers to assert that they were independent at a time when technology and capitalist development had eroded the autonomy of labour.[47]

The drinking, brawling, gambling, and swearing denounced by missionaries were vital elements of the masculine culture of the camps. In addition to providing a much-needed release from the routine drudgery of work and the monotony of camp life, such rough and rugged behaviour gave expression to the physical strength, competitive individualism, and sense of brotherhood that were part of the workers' sense of self-identity. It also constituted a form of rebellion against middle-class restraints and expectations. By attacking these perceived vices, the missions challenged key aspects of the workers' masculine identity. Calls for temperance proved particularly problematic. The tavern provided men with a meeting place, and the rituals of drinking were an important source of social solidarity. Not surprisingly, the message of moral reform carried to the camps by the missionaries was resented by many workers as an assault upon their own sense of manhood. Many workers responded to the missions' efforts to impose middle-class definitions of manliness upon them by calling into question the manhood of the missionaries. In upholding their own male identity, male workers often disparaged the young men fresh out of theological college who were frequently sent to the camps by referring to them as "boys." Charles Gordon captured the attitudes of many workers toward the missionaries in several of the novels on the Canadian West that he published as Ralph Connor. In *The Sky Pilot,* Gordon portrayed the experiences of a newly ordained minister sent out to minister to the men on the western frontier. In a foothills cattle camp, the young missionary is "despised, ignored or laughed at," and dismissed as a "blankety-blank, pink-and-white nursery kid."[48] Bradwin reported similar feelings, observing that "men who have rubbed up against the raw realities, whose judgments have slowly matured under obstacles often encountered and frequent reverses, who, with the passing of years, have grubbed unaided by the fundamentals of life" were not "easily reached" by the inexperienced young men who were frequently sent into the camps.[49]

Prevailing cultural assumptions about the type of work appropriate to men and women provided another barrier to mission work. Missionaries dealt with matters of the soul and the heart and with the emotional and spiritual nurturing of others. According to the "separate spheres" ideology that dominated the discourse on gender in the late nineteenth and early twentieth centuries, matters of morality and piety as well as the care and nurture of others were regarded as innately feminine qualities. Such beliefs contributed to what Ann Douglas has described as the feminization of religion. As guardians of morality and natural nurturers, women became increasingly involved in the churches and were reputed to have formed the worshipping majority in most Protestant churches.[50] E. Anthony Rotundo suggests that the association of the clergy with women and with the traits and cultural spaces allotted to females lowered their status in the eyes of many men and contributed to male disinterest in religious matters.[51] The problem was greater than the clergy, however, and rooted in the nature of evangelicalism itself. With its emphasis on love, gentleness, and submission to God's will, traditional evangelicalism appeared to stand in opposition to the manly traits of strength, independence, and autonomy. William Cochrane acknowledged the problem in an address at Queen's University in 1898. "Meekness, gentleness and forbearance – a certain effeminacy of disposition and backwardness of action," Cochrane complained, "are recognized as the most becoming traits of Christian character."[52] Ebenezer Ross observed that many men seemed to feel that "religion may be something very excellent and very appropriate to woman, in her weakness and dependence," but that "it is by no means necessary or becoming to a man, in his power and strength. She needs the supports and comforts of the Gospel in the cloudy and dark day; but as for him the innate fortitude of his own nature may suffice, and from any intrinsic source would be a detraction from his manhood."[53]

The challenge faced by the missions was to convince the men of the camps that "the ideal Christian life and the ideal manly life are one and the same."[54] The missions developed a number of strategies to achieve this objective. The first priority was to refute the notion that there was anything effeminate or weak about the men called to mission work. The religious novel was one of the principal means of shaping popular views of mission work and missionaries in the late nineteenth and early twentieth centuries.[55] In the mission literature of the period, the missionary was typically portrayed as a virile soldier of Christ engaged in a holy war against sin and evil. Writing as Ralph Connor, Charles Gordon chronicled the adventures of brave and robust young ministers on the Canadian frontier in novels such as *Black Rock* (1900) and *The Prospector* (1904). "The men of the book," Gordon wrote in his foreword to *Black Rock*, "are still there in the mines and the lumber camps of the mountains, fighting out that eternal fight for manhood, strong, clean, God conquered. And when the west winds blow, to the open ear the sounds of battle come telling the fortunes of the fight." Such images enabled missionaries to apply masculine qualities of courage, endurance, and assertiveness to their work in the field.[56] Although novels might help to change the public's perception of the missionary, it was even more vital that the missions recruit the right type of men. "If the missions to the camps are to be successful," advised the district superintendent of Presbyterian home missions for northern Ontario, "the church must put her very strongest and best in charge of this work. For they will not be won by weaklings, subtle, suave and mild, but by men with the heart of vikings."[57] The ideal missionary for the camps was said to be strong and courageous, sure in his faith, and willing to endure danger and discomfort for the sake of the work. The Shantymen's Christian Association observed that "it takes a real man with a glorious sense of devotion to Jesus Christ his Lord to be willing to tramp the roads, ride the freights, sleep rough and feed as may be."[58]

Just as a strong masculine character was seen as essential to camp work, it was equally important that the missionary distance himself from working-class perceptions of the church as an elitist and middle-class institution. The Shantymen's Christian Association attempted to overcome such views by separating itself from the churches. On their visits to the camps, Shantymen were quick to inform the workers that they did "not represent any church in particular" and that they "had come not to preach religion but to preach Christ."[59] The Shantymen also made a point of not taking a collection during their visits and of refusing money when it was offered. Church-sponsored missionaries were advised to rid themselves of any middle-class manners or affectations likely to separate them from the men. "To know the men," the Church Camp Mission advised its workers, the missionary "becomes one of them"; he sheds his suit and clerical collar for "overalls, knee boots and a back pack" and replaces his "learned and eloquent speech" with "straight from the shoulder talk."[60] A missionary in British Columbia wrote about changing into his "war paint," which consisted of "tall boots, khaki shirt and trousers [and a] big hat," before entering a camp.[61] Alfred Fitzpatrick of the Reading Camp Association believed that much more than outward gestures would be required to win the trust and respect of the men. He was convinced that the missionary would find acceptance only after he had worked alongside and lived with the men. "To be personally popular with the shanty men," Fitzpatrick asserted, "one must handle the axe, saw and cant-hook with any of the old-time beavers, fallers, junkers, loaders and skidders."[62] Although few missionaries outside of the Reading Camp Association were able or willing to follow Fitzpatrick's advice, most recognized that their success depended on being able to find a place within the workers' own masculine self-image.

There was a great deal of "muscular Christianity" in the strategies employed by the camp missions to reach the men. Proponents of "muscular Christianity" sought to disprove that there was anything effeminate or weak about Christianity by showing that the Christian life involved an active and aggressive process of self-mastery. They believed that close contact with nature, vigorous physical activity, and participation in organized sport were the most effective means of inculcating the endurance, courage, loyalty, and cooperation that defined Christian manhood. Living in the wilderness and engaged in backbreaking work, the labourers of Canada's work camps were upheld as ideal material from which to construct the hardy Christians idealized by the propagandists of "muscular Christianity." At the same time as missionaries worried about the riotous habits of the workers, they praised their "battle courage," "adventurous spirit," and "indomitable steadfastness."[63] The challenge faced by the missions was to channel these masculine virtues into the discipline demanded by Christian commitment. The *Presbyterian Witness* advised ministers and missionaries to preach a "robust" and "virile" Gospel that was "neither weak-eyed nor maudlin." Preachers were directed to deliver a practical message with "simplicity and power" in the "plain talk" of the street and the workplace.[64] In the bunkhouse sermon, Jesus was invariably presented as "a man's man," and the men of the camps were challenged to follow his example. "The real question," a Shantyman asked the men of a camp on the West Coast, "is whether you are man enough to become true Christians. Are you man enough to acknowledge your sins? Are you courageous enough to turn around and follow Jesus? Are you strong enough to resist temptation and to remain steadfast?"[65] The language of "muscular Christianity" provided a means of commending Christian virtue to the working class by linking it with secular notions of moral and physical prowess.

In addition to the bunkhouse sermon, hymn sings were one of the principal means used by missionaries to convey their message of Christian manhood. The need to appeal to men resulted in significant changes in Christian hymnody in the late nineteenth and early twentieth centuries. Critics frequently charged that many of the hymns of the era suffered from a "nauseating sentimentality" and "otherworldliness" that many men found "unmanly." Protestant churches responded to these charges by introducing hymns and hymnals that were full of "vim and vigor" and that emphasized manly virtues of strength, courage, character, brotherhood, and patriotism.[66] The revised hymnal adopted by the YMCA provides a good illustration of this transition. In the foreword, the compilers of the hymnal explained that they had deliberately set out to select hymns "in which the emphasis is put upon the heroic, active, masculine qualities rather than upon the passive virtues and states of mind and feeling."[67] The hymns recommended for use in the camps were carefully selected to present a manly and a militant Jesus, and they often compared the Christian life to a military campaign that demanded constant vigilance against sin and aggressive action against the forces of evil. One hymn used by the Church Camp Mission challenged "the soldiers of Christ" to "wrestle and fight" the "powers of darkness." Still another called upon the Christian "to fight manfully onward" against worldly temptations and vices.[68] It was hoped that images of combat and virility would appeal to the workers' own sense of manliness. Through the use of music, camp missionaries hoped to stir men to abandon their wanton ways and to make a personal commitment to follow Christ. "For the Man of Galilee," a popular hymn from *Manly Songs for Christian Men,* effectively captured the desired impact. The hymn issued a "stirring summons" to "men of courage" and "men of purpose" to turn from their "evil ways" and become "a fellow worker" with "the man of Galilee."[69]

In its efforts to reach the men of the camps, the Shantymen's Christian Association began to publish a tabloid-style newspaper, the *Shantyman,* for missionaries to distribute on their visits to the camps. Copying the techniques of the yellow press popular with working-class readers, the *Shantyman* featured sensational headlines and large photographs on its front cover. Special editions were printed for loggers, miners, and railway section men. In these editions, pictures of workers and short articles on new machinery or operations were interspersed between inspirational stories and news of the association's activities. Conversion stories were a staple of the *Shantyman.* These stories followed a similar format: after a life of sin without God, rough and rugged men experienced a crisis that brought them face to face with their own depravity and hopelessness. Convicted of sin in their own hearts and actively seeking forgiveness, the penitent turned to God and experienced an inward transformation. A new man, the convert became obedient to God's will and dedicated to the service of Christ. Such stories repeatedly stressed that the battle against sin and temptation was a battle worthy of a true man. The corollary that followed portrayed men who succumbed to vice or rejected religion as lacking in strength and moral courage.[70]

It is difficult to determine how effective such strategies were in winning converts and reforming behaviour. Reporting on the work of the Church Camp Mission in 1912, the bishop of Algoma admitted that "the work is largely a matter of faith. Men are met and reached at odd times and at long intervals. Some word or act of kindness may touch their hearts for good. This is in God's hands. It is not possible to offer any estimate, reliable in character, as to results."[71] Rather than focusing on the uncertain rewards of the work, however, the annual reports produced by the various missions and missionaries were filled with accounts of men "saved from the power of drink and of backsliders restored."[72] There is, of course, a danger in attaching too much significance to such reports. To ensure continued support, missionaries had to show that they were making some gains. Despite the potential for exaggeration, it is undoubtedly true that the missionaries did have an impact among certain groups of workers. Missionaries reported their greatest success among young native-born workers who returned home to farms and families at the end of the work season. Although missionaries found many of these men familiar with the Christian message, they complained that the men often proved reluctant to confess their beliefs lest they find themselves ostracized by their fellow workers.[73] Failure to conform to standards of behaviour demanded by the male culture of the camps could carry a heavy price. Missionaries were most pessimistic about the chances of winning over long-time camp workers and immigrants who preferred to look to the tavern rather than to religion for relief from the drudgery and monotony of camp life.

The camp missionaries did not achieve the objectives hoped for by their supporters. That this should be so is not surprising. The resources committed to the missions did not match the enthusiasm expressed for them by the church, industry, and the middle class. As a result, missionaries rarely visited a camp more than once a year. Such fleeting appearances could not make a lasting impression upon many men. It was also unrealistic to expect that the young and inexperienced seminarians who were often sent out to the camps could connect with most of the rough and seasoned men they encountered. Despite these difficulties, converts were made; a few camp men even went on to become missionaries themselves.[74] Such men placed themselves outside of the institutions and activities that displayed and defined working-class manliness. That these men could do so owed a great deal to the resonances that existed between the Christian manliness presented by the missionaries and the standards that defined working-class manhood. Formulating manhood in this way made it possible for the convert to claim that he had become a more manly man by embracing Christianity.

Notes

1 United Church Archives (UCA), "The Camp Problem," John Duncan Byrne Papers, box 1, file 1.
2 *Report of the Mission to the Lumbermen in the Valley of the Ottawa Presented to the Synod of the Presbyterian Church of Canada in Connection with the Church of Scotland, June, 1871* (Kingston: Presbyterian Church of Canada, 1871).
3 Alfred Fitzpatrick, *The University in Overalls: A Plea for Part-Time Study* (Toronto: Hunter Rose, 1920), 5–6.
4 UCA, "Camp Problem."
5 General Synod Archives (GSA), "Pioneering: A Popular Account of the Work Done during the Year 1912 by the Church Camp Mission," 4, 16, GS75-103, series 3-2, box 57.
6 On coast missions, see Michael Hadley, *God's Little Ships: A History of the Columbia Coast Mission* (Vancouver: Harbour Publishing, 1996).
7 Sarah Powell Wright, "Missions to Lumbermen," *Methodist Magazine and Review,* July 1904, 34–39. See also Sharon Anne Cook, *"Through Sunshine and Shadow": The Woman's Christian Temperance Union, Evangelicalism, and Reform in Ontario, 1874–1910* (Montreal and Kingston: McGill-Queen's University Press, 1995) 49, 82–86.
8 Murray G. Ross, *The Y.M.C.A. in Canada: The Chronicle of a Century* (Toronto: Ryerson Press, 1951). See also *Canada Lumberman,* September 15, 1912, and March 15, 1920; and *West Coast Lumberman,* August 26, 1914.
9 On the origins of the Shantymen's Christian Association, see Douglas C. Percy, *Men with the Heart of a Viking* (Beaverlodge, AB: Horizon House, 1976), 24–30. On the work of the Shantymen's Christian Association on the West Coast, see W. Phillip Keller, *Splendour from the Sea: The Saga of the Shantymen* (Chicago: Moody Press, 1962).
10 "The Canadian Lumberman and His Social Betterment," *Methodist Magazine and Review,* January 1903, 19.
11 GSA, "The Links in the Chain of 1911," 3, GS75-103, series 3-2, box 57.
12 *Canada Lumberman,* June 1, 1910.
13 Fitzpatrick, *University in Overalls,* 9.
14 Ebenezer E. Ross, *The Manliness of Piety: A Lecture Delivered before the Halifax Young Men's Christian Association on Tuesday Evening, 31st January 1860* (Halifax: Wesleyan Conference Steam Press, 1860), 7–8, 11–14, 20, 24.
15 William Cochrane, "Christian Manliness," in *The Church and the Commonwealth: Discussions and Orations on Questions of the Day, Practical, Biographical, Educational and Doctrinal* (Brantford, ON: Bradley, Garreston, and Company, 1887), 253, 262–63.
16 *Presbyterian Witness,* August 24, 1907, 265; *Presbyterian Witness,* January 22, 1910, 8; *Methodist Magazine and Review,* June 1903 and May 1909.
17 *Canada Lumberman,* June 1, 1910.
18 *Methodist Magazine and Review,* July 1901, 52.
19 Cochrane, "Christian Manliness," 253.
20 Alexander Sutherland, *The Kingdom of God and Problems of To-day* (Toronto: W. Briggs, c.1898), 86.
21 Shantymen's Christian Association, *Summary: Field Reports* (1910).

22   *Presbyterian Record,* August 1899, 236. See also *Methodist Magazine and Review,* January 1903, 18.

23   D.M. Ramsay, *The Loggers or Pacific Coast Mission* (Toronto: Women's Home Missionary Society of the Presbyterian Church in Canada, 1914), 5.

24   "Canadian Lumberman and His Social Betterment," 18.

25   Fitzpatrick, *University in Overalls,* 64–68. By the 1920s, many companies had opted to settle families in the camps. See Richard A. Rajala, "Bill and the Boss: Labor Protest, Technological Change, and the Transformation of the West Coast Logging Camp, 1890–1930," *Journal of Forest History* 33, 4 (1989): 176–79.

26   On the challenge posed by the camps to hegemonic heterosexual masculinity, see Steven Maynard, "Rough Work and Rugged Men: The Social Construction of Masculinity in Working-Class History," *Labour/Le Travail* 23 (1989): 167–69.

27   James Allen, "New Ontario: Its Problems and How to Solve Them," *Methodist Magazine and Review,* July 1904, 55–57.

28   GSA, "Links in the Chain."

29   Alfred Fitzpatrick, "Camp Education Extension," *Methodist Magazine and Review,* September 1905, 221–22.

30   "Canadian Lumberman and His Social Betterment," 13.

31   *The Shantyman,* January 15, 1924.

32   *Canada Lumberman,* June 1, 1908.

33   Percy, *Men with the Heart,* 51.

34   *The Shantyman,* January 15, 1925. See also *The Shantyman,* July 15, 1926.

35   GSA, "The Church Camp Mission Report, 1913," 4–5, GS75-103, series 3-2, box 57.

36   UCA, "Missions to Camps," John Duncan Byrne Papers, file 1, box 1.

37   *The Shantyman,* March 15, 1925.

38   UCA, "The Finnish Paper Vapaus and the Bolshevik Campaign in Northern Ontario," John Duncan Byrne Papers, file 3, box 1.

39   *The Shantyman,* January 15, 1924.

40   GSA, "Links in the Chain."

41   *Canada Lumberman,* May 1, 1912. See also *Canada Lumberman,* March 15, 1920.

42   UCA, *Canadian Standard Efficiency Training* (Toronto: Canadian Standard Efficiency Training Committee, 1918), 3–5.

43   GSA, "Rev. C.C. Owen to the Primate," April 22, 1920, GS75-103, series 3-2, box 57.

44   *The Shantyman,* March 15, 1925.

45   Ian Radforth, *Bushworkers and Bosses: Logging in Northern Ontario, 1900–1980* (Toronto: University of Toronto Press, 1987), 8, 68–69.

46   Edmund Bradwin, *The Bunkhouse Man: Life and Labour in the Northern Work Camps* (Toronto: University of Toronto Press, 1972), 176.

47   Radforth, *Bushworkers and Bosses,* 39; Rajala, "Bill and the Boss," 170.

48   Ralph Connor (Charles Gordon), *The Sky Pilot: A Tale of the Foothills* (Toronto: Westminster Co., 1899), 43.

49   Bradwin, *Bunkhouse Man,* 220.

50   Ann Douglas, *The Feminization of American Culture* (New York: A. Knopf, 1977), 114–23.

51   Rotundo, *American Manhood,* 205–6. On the declining status of the clergy in Canada, see R.D. Gidney and W.P.J. Millar, *Professional Gentlemen: The Professions in Nineteenth-Century Ontario* (Toronto: University of Toronto Press, 1994), 268–82.

52   Cochrane, "Christian Manliness," 253.

53   Ross, *Manliness of Piety,* 5.

54   "The Young Man Problem," *Methodist Magazine and Review,* October 1905, 311.

55 Paul T. Phillips, *A Kingdom on Earth: Anglo-American Social Christianity, 1880–1940* (University Park: Pennsylvania State University Press, 1996), 122–29; Mary Vipond, "Blessed Are the Peacemakers: The Labour Question in Canadian Social Gospel Fiction," *Journal of Canadian Studies* 10, 3 (1975): 32–43.

56 Grier Nicholl, "The Image of the Protestant Minister in the Social Gospel Novel," *Church History* 37, 3 (1968): 307–27.

57 UCA, "Camp Problem." See also "The Claims of Ministry on Strong Men," *Presbyterian Witness*, August 10, 1907, 254.

58 *The Shantyman*, March 15, 1925, 10–11.

59 Percy, *Men with the Heart*, 51.

60 GSA, "Links in the Chain."

61 J.J. Callan, "At the End of Steel," *Across the Rockies*, December 1913, 356.

62 Fitzpatrick, *University in Overalls*, 119–20.

63 James Allen, *Missions in New Ontario* (Toronto: Department of Missionary Literature of the Methodist Church of Canada, 1906), 42.

64 *Presbyterian Witness*, January 22, 1910. See also W.D. Reid's address in General Assembly of the Presbyterian Church in Canada, *Acts and Proceedings* (1911), 22.

65 Shantymen's Christian Association, *Tenth Annual Report* (1918), 13.

66 *Presbyterian Witness*, January 22, 1910.

67 YMCA International Committee, *Association Hymn Book* (New York, 1907), Foreword.

68 GSA, "Hymns from the Book of Common Praise for Camp Services," GS75–103, series 3–2, box 57.

69 I.H. Meredith and Grant Tolfax Tullar, eds., *Manly Songs for Christian Men* (New York: Tullar-Meredith, 1901), 1.

70 See, for example, "The Conversion of Big Jim," *The Shantyman*, March 1927, "How Captain Couts Was Saved," *The Shantyman*, October 1927; and "Last Minute Conversion in Lumber Camp," *The Shantyman*, July 1928.

71 GSA, "Report of the Subcommittee of the Executive of the Missionary Society of the Church of England in Canada Appointed to Consider the Whole Question of the Work of the Church Camp Mission," GS75–103, series 3–2, box 57.

72 Shantymen's Christian Association, *Eleventh Annual Report* (1919), 7.

73 *The Shantyman*, January 15, 1925; GSA, "Pioneering," 10.

74 See, for example, "Lumberjack on H.B. Railway Becomes Missionary," *The Shantyman*, April 1925.

7
An Open Window on Other Masculinities: Gay Bars and Visibility in Montreal

Olivier Vallerand

BECAUSE SEXUAL ORIENTATION cannot be identified through any particular physical signs, lesbian, gay, bisexual, and transgendered people (LGBT) are sometimes identified through the spaces they visit.[1] The importance of bars as social meeting spaces for LGBT people is demonstrated, for example, by some major events in recent LGBT history being appropriately named after bars. Most famously, the gay liberation movement really gained momentum and public visibility after the Stonewall riots of June 28, 1969, named after New York's Stonewall Inn bar. In Montreal similar raids on Truxx in 1977 and Sex Garage in 1990 led to demonstrations, amendments to the Quebec Charter of Rights and Freedoms, and ultimately the first edition of Divers/Cité, Montreal's original gay pride celebration.[2] Gay bars, perceived as everyday or vernacular, are rarely discussed by architectural historians and theorists, even if they are some of the only physical – and most importantly, visible – traces of gay communities and their history.[3]

Montreal anthropologist Ross Higgins notes that LGBT histories are built from the ground up and that today's gains come from the cumulative efforts of thousands of everyday men and women who quietly fought to be who they were, to express themselves, to break free from heteronormativity.[4] As a result, and clearly so in Montreal, gay bars, as built artifacts of these communities, embody and shape the evolution of the relation between LGBT people and society at large.[5] Understanding how the characteristics of physical space affect these struggles and transformations is essential. In the context of architecture's gendered history, it is also of crucial importance to reflect on how gay bars subvert readings of public spaces as masculine and private spaces as feminine: although public in appearance, they often bring into view acts seen by many as private and therefore gain a political dimension that transcends their commercial status. They furthermore embody and stage a queer performance of masculinity through their design, which echoes some gay men's use of masculine codes.

This chapter begins with background information on the evolution of gay bars through time, then turns to the history of gay and lesbian public space in Montreal, and culminates with the emergence of the Village. At the heart of the project is an analysis of two Village bars from different generations, Complexe Bourbon and Parking Nightclub, followed by a discussion of a more recent gay-oriented night regularly held outside of the Village.

Queer Spaces in Straight Places: Forgotten Architectures of the Night

The repression of homosexuality has complicated the study of the evolution of gay spaces, both public and private, even if oral histories and judicial records help to reconstruct a landscape of early gay and lesbian meeting spaces.[6] In the case of gay bars, attempts to trace a history of their architecture is further made difficult by their ephemerality. Unfortunately, in the case of LGBT communities, bars represent some of the only traces of public social places.

Gay bars have only recently become visible (again) in the public realm. After a brief period in the early twentieth century when restaurants, bars, and clubs in large cities entertained a relatively large number of openly gay and lesbian patrons, gay and lesbian meeting places went back into hiding starting in the 1930s as a negative climate around homosexuality grew stronger.[7] Classic studies of gay spaces, such as Barbara Weightman's "Gay Bars as Private Places" and Aaron Betsky's *Queer Space*, describe a "secret geography of unsigned, inconspicuous, anonymous backstreet bars and clubs," which are not invisible but are part of a coded experience not present on any map (Figure 7.1).[8] This insider-outsider dichotomy clearly separated gay networks from the public view, keeping them out of reach both from homosexuals not yet part of this "gay world" and from the heterosexual majority. They thus reinforced both the invisibility of queers and the stereotypes associating homosexuals with underground networks of criminality.[9]

Bars initially emerged as formalized institutions in a gay network of cruising. Betsky argues that they were originally attempts to "turn the ephemeral world of cruising into something more durable and identifiable."[10] Henry Urbach further describes them as points of condensation within an urban network of homoerotic flows, artifacts of a luminal, nomadic queer culture.[11] Referencing the public experience of cruising, early bars developed labyrinthine spaces of darkness and barriers. Located in anonymous structures on the edges of town or in unidentified basements or upstairs spaces, they isolated and protected their patrons. No exterior characteristics, except sometimes the bar's name on a sign, distinguished these bars from straight taverns, their anonymity often amplified by an entrance located in a back alley. Even when a bar occupied a ground-floor space with windows, plants or unclean windows would often mask the inside

Figure 7.1 Two examples of late 1970s gay bars. The top one, situated near a railway station and a junk yard, has boarded-up windows on the more travelled street for privacy. On the bottom, a gay bar occupies the lower floor of an isolated and dilapidated building in an industrial zone. Its doors are unmarked. Photographs by Barbara Weightman, "Gay Bars as Private Places," *Landscape* 24, 1 (1980): 11–12.

use and mark the space as cut off or protected from public view.[12] Inside, subtle design elements differentiated gay bars from straight ones to both display and hide homosexuality: the provision of mirrors and "runway space" facilitated the display of bodies, bringing the rituals of public cruising inside a defined space,[13] whereas "defense mechanisms," such as steps, corridors, nooks, dark interiors, or partitions protected patrons' privacy from straight "intrusions."[14] If these anonymous bars are today less present in large North American and European cities with defined LGBT enclaves, there are many smaller cities and towns where gay bars are still close to that early model (Figure 7.2).

The June 1969 Stonewall riots gave momentum to the gay liberation movement that had emerged in the mid-1960s following the pioneering efforts of 1950s homophile activists.[15] Although the political movements appear to be separated from the social scene, the growing visibility of queers opened a space for a larger number of bars that could respond more specifically to different subcommunities. The 1970s thus saw two distinct, but not unrelated, mutations of gay spaces: derelict dance halls or unoccupied industrial spaces evolved into gay discos obsessed with technological environments, whereas smaller bars pushed role-playing as far as possible. For example, many granted access

Figure 7.2 Gio's, Winnipeg, 2010. Photograph by author.

only to patrons embodying masculine myths of cowboys or policemen, or they became radicalized into exclusively gay male sex clubs that celebrated exaggerated male bodies, bringing private acts to public spaces. Discos and smaller bars were quite different physically, but they shared a use of disorienting effects that echoed early bars' disconnection from networks of public life.[16] Gay male sexuality shaped the design, for example, with dark and labyrinthine corridors, where people could both observe and hide, or with elaborate restrooms, planned to facilitate cruising and bodily displays by taking away separations between urinals or clustering urinals around a central space.[17]

In the 1970s the popularity of discos, fuelled by their appearance of freedom and exuberance, reopened the doors of the gay clubs to a heterosexual crowd.[18] It was a return to the spirit of the exuberant and openly visible dance halls and cabarets of early-twentieth-century New York that celebrated artifice and gender parodies. The early 1980s quickly stopped this movement when the AIDS epidemic simultaneously fuelled homophobia and pushed gays and lesbians fully back into public view. These two opposite reactions prompted a sudden transformation of oversexualized gay space that still impacts today's bars, with sexual acts pushed back to exclusive sex clubs or increasingly to online networks.[19] The moving back and forth, one could even say coexistence, between visibility/acceptance and invisibility/repression places gay bars in a paradoxical context, where spaces with lucrative objectives become political.

Becoming Visible: The Emergence of Montreal's Gay Village

Most LGBT-oriented spaces in Montreal today are concentrated in the "Gay Village," with its commercial activity located on Sainte-Catherine Street between Saint-Hubert and Papineau Streets. In contrast to other well-known gay and lesbian enclaves, such as New York's Greenwich Village[20] and Toronto's Church and Wellesley,[21] Montreal's Village is a recent addition to the city's network of identity-based neighbourhoods, emerging in the early 1980s and replacing less visible downtown bars at a time when nonheterosexual people were becoming increasingly visible in public life. Its situation in Montreal, known for its bilingual identity and widely perceived embrace of sin and sleaziness, tainted the Village's development and arguably contributed to the construction of a clearly defined and publicized enclave.

The work of urban historians, sociologists, and geographers in recent years has brought forward a long and rich history of gay and lesbian life in Montreal, which unfolded long before the emergence of the current Village. They show that gay men and lesbians rarely shared space before the creation of the Village and had a different relation to public space and life.[22] Geographer Frank Remiggi divides the history of gay and lesbian public spaces in Montreal into three stages: appropriation of place, appropriation of space, and inscription in the urban landscape.[23] The first stage, lasting from the 1920s to the 1960s, saw the growth of a mostly underground network of establishments either located on Saint-Laurent Boulevard close to Sainte-Catherine Street or hidden downtown, around Peel and Stanley Streets, in the heart of the financial – at the time predominantly masculine – centre.[24] These establishments initially consisted of heterosexual bars and taverns where homosexuals were tolerated, with exclusively gay establishments starting to appear in the 1950s. Although these spaces stayed popular enough to survive until the beginning of the 1980s, the anonymity desired by a majority of homosexuals at the time prevented these establishments from creating a visible gay public space in Montreal. Spaces dedicated to homosexual encounters were thus hidden by homosocial spaces. This relative invisibility, however, did not mean that these spaces were apolitical; as Higgins reminds us, the simple fact of being in a gay-identified bar was, at the time, a sign of revolt against heteronormativity.[25]

The second stage began in parallel to changes in the social and political landscape in the late 1960s and early 1970s. It was during this period that many gay men started to see a value in being visible. This visibility, however, manifested itself more in an increased presence of "out" gays and lesbians and in a larger number of establishments than in any physical changes in the relationship between bars and the street.[26] The increased social visibility attained during this period would nonetheless profoundly affect the development of the Village and the physical characteristics of new bars.

Remiggi's third stage endures today. It is marked by the rapid emergence of the "Nouveau Village de l'Est," which radically transformed the gay scene in Montreal, prompting at once an almost instantaneous disappearance of the downtown gay bars and the decline of red-light institutions on Saint-Laurent Boulevard.[27] However, most scholarly accounts of Montreal's gay and lesbian urban history, including Remiggi's, point out that the emergence of the Village was not a relocation of previous gay and lesbian spaces. The Village appeared as previous enclaves were still being used, and they coexisted for a time, but almost all older establishments then simply closed down without relocating to the Village. This shift echoed major changes in the ways that bars were designed, as discussed below.

In stark opposition to the business-oriented downtown area, the Centre-Sud neighbourhood, where the Village developed, is still today a rundown, although increasingly gentrified, working-class neighbourhood, in similar ways to other LGBT enclaves worldwide.[28] Priape, a gay-oriented sex shop, opened in 1975,

Figure 7.3 Pedestrian Sainte-Catherine Street in Montreal's Village, 2010.
Photograph by author.

but it was not until 1982 that a significant number of bars appeared on or around
Sainte-Catherine Street, with larger institutions attracting a number of clients
sufficient to sustain smaller ones (Figure 7.3). The success of these new bars,
combined with rising rents and less visibility in the downtown area, contributed
to a rapid decline of the downtown bars, marked by the closing of the area's last
remaining major bar in 1984.[29] Unlike earlier ones, the new Village establishments were fully integrated into the city. Clearly visible and with many presenting
clear windows to the street, they entered into a direct relationship with the
public in an animated working-class neighbourhood close to a university and
three television network headquarters. Despite housing both male- and female-
oriented establishments, the neighbourhood's identity was more widely associated with male homosexuality, not only due to the highly visible presence of
advertising for gay bars or saunas depicting undressed men but also because of
the larger number of establishments catering specifically to a male clientele.

The evolution of Montreal's LGBT spaces, and more recently of the Village,
was closely linked to changes in Quebec society's attitudes toward sexual minorities. These changes were present not only socially and geographically but
also in physical and architectural transformations of LGBT meeting places such
as bars, as discussed in the following sections.

Mixing It Up at the Bourbon

Most of the initial bars and clubs that opened in the early 1980s in the Village no longer exist. The establishments of a second generation, reflecting large-scale and multifunctional developments of the early 1990s, still exist, even if they are themselves being challenged by changes in attitudes among both LGBT and non-LGBT people. Purpose-built as gay institutions, they represent a complete transformation from the early ad hoc taverns colonized by gay patrons. One of the most visible and characteristic of these establishments was Complexe Bourbon. Not only was the Bourbon a multipurpose institution that combined traditional gay spaces – bars, dance clubs, and a sauna – but it also clearly shaped a themed tourist-oriented definition of the Village. However, it presented an openness to public life rarely seen before in gay-oriented spaces. Owned and designed by heterosexuals, the Bourbon was the brainchild of Normand Chamberland, an imaginative entrepreneur who found himself almost by accident among a gay clientele and used the opportunity to create a setting that resonated with queer living.[30] This was not done without many tensions and contradictions between the queer and normative aspects of the Bourbon, many of them caused by the obvious commercial goals of the venture.

Like other gay institutions in Montreal, Complexe Bourbon gradually developed extensions, ultimately becoming a highly visible, inflated, multipurpose complex. In 1985 Chamberland bought a small tavern on Sainte-Catherine Street. As with early taverns frequented by gay men and owned by friendly heterosexuals, Chamberland realized his customers were mainly gay men only after a few months of ownership. He connected with them immediately and saw in them the perfect patrons for the transformations he had in mind. Following the success of the tavern, renamed La Taverne du Village, he opened a bar farther east on Sainte-Catherine, La Track, in 1986. From then on, he developed La Track into Complexe Bourbon, whereas La Taverne soon became Le Drugstore. Architect Simon Coquoz, also heterosexual, started his association with Chamberland around 1990 and worked on both projects until Chamberland sold them in 2005 following health and financial problems. Whereas Le Drugstore stayed a more typical large club, despite catering to an increasingly important lesbian clientele, Complexe Bourbon evolved over fifteen years into a multifunctional complex occupying an entire city block (Figure 7.4), including a presence on Gareau Street, an alley between the complex and a park. It combined under one roof a forty-room hotel, five restaurants, three bars, a sauna, a leather shop, an ice cream parlour, a chapel, and numerous terraces.[31] By clustering many smaller gay spaces, it made the whole much more visible than before. Constantly expanded and transformed, the complex was continuously

Figure 7.4 Complexe Bourbon, 1570–1592 Sainte-Catherine Street East, Montreal, 2009. Photograph by author.

reinvented by Chamberland. In contrast, the new owners were much less visible and involved in the Village scene, and the Bourbon finally closed in 2014.

Early on, the scale of the complex confirmed its place as a visible and central institution of the Village. However, the Bourbon was also remarkable and unique as a themed environment. Fascinated by Walt Disney's fantasy recreation of a nostalgic America, Chamberland used the frame provided by his architect to pay homage to the terraces of New Orleans and to the experience of the American South. He shared with Simon Coquoz a vision of New Orleans as a place of celebration of life, exterior pleasure, and dreams, which was synonymous with their vision of gay men's life and thus appropriate for a gay-oriented architecture. In the bilingual context of Montreal, it was also an apt reference to both the heritage of New France and the city's fascination with a mythical image of America (Figure 7.5).[32] Although never explicitly stated as a conscious influence, these references are consistent with mainstream gay culture's obsession with images of masculinity, often linked to working-class men or the pioneer tradition, such as the Village People's cowboy or Tom of Finland's drawings of hyper-masculine lumberjacks.[33] These drawings are for example a direct inspiration for murals displayed in the complex's bars. The juxtaposition of fantasy-themed spaces and the exaggerated visions of masculinity can be understood in the same spirit of detachment from reality exhibited by the gay discos described by Betsky.

Compared to other contemporary complexes in the Village, such as Sky and Station C, the Bourbon was physically open to the street, creating what Simon Coquoz calls "non-architecture."[34] Whereas other establishments hide their terraces on rooftops or back sides, Chamberland aspired to a complex without walls, a world of terraces blurring the separation of interior and exterior. The most visible results of these attempts to create a deconstructed building that colonized public space were the opened corner of Sainte-Catherine and Alexandre-de-Sève and the integral use of the back alley, which allowed a complete opening of the back side of the complex. Numerous anecdotes support this obsession with the blurring of public and private limits. One summer, Chamberland decided to open an uncompleted expansion and paid half-dressed handsome men to colourfully paint the structure throughout the whole summer. The Bourbon became the talk of the town, attracting both homosexuals and heterosexuals, nearby workers, and tourists. However commercial this initiative was, it still created a blurring of the former walls that separated gay space from the public. Juxtaposing the hidden world of gay bars and saunas with the public world of restaurants and terraces, which attract a large number of presumably heterosexual people, transformed the Bourbon into a powerful political tool.

Analysis of the complex's plans (Figure 7.6) reveal a web of public and private spaces that linked interior and exterior spaces. As in early gay bars, a visit to the complex felt like going through a labyrinth that acted as a filter between explicitly sexualized private and assumed-as-nonsexualized public spaces; it was, however, much more permeable than in earlier bars, where this filter had created a protective barrier. At first glance, the restaurants and bars were mostly located on the ground floor and in the basement, whereas the hotel occupied

Figure 7.5 Le Club Sandwich in 2009. Photograph by author.

the upper floors. The actual separation between the different parts was, however, not as clear. Stairs and corridors connected the hotel rooms to the dining and cruising spaces, and the public terraces were connected to a courtyard onto which hotel rooms had access. At all times, passage between all parts of the complex was possible. The terraces also permitted different levels of privacy as they wrapped around the building from public Sainte-Catherine Street to private Gareau Street. The Bourbon's spatial organization pushed formerly private sexuality into the public realm; while having lunch on the terrace, one could potentially come in contact with someone else cruising for sex in the hotel's sauna.

By constantly responding to the desires of his clientele and putting their fantasies on public view, Chamberland shaped a queer political statement. After he sold the Bourbon in the early 2000s, the queer fantasy no longer had an interlocutor, and the complex quickly declined. Chamberland and Coquoz succeeded, at least partially, in creating a queer space by designing a gay-oriented and normative architecture that paradoxically acted as a background for the ephemeral, for a transformative and evolving space, and for queer opportunities to "take place."[35]

Down in the Underground: Parking Nightclub and a New Generation of "Gay" Bars

If Complexe Bourbon exemplified a generation of purpose-built, mixed-use LGBT spaces in Montreal, more recent establishments shifted their focus, looking back at early gay bar culture in their retreat to underground spaces. Parking Nightclub was one of the most recent and popular of these clubs. No longer combining diverse functions but instead concentrating its 1,000-person space around its dance floor, Parking was much less visible from the street. Although the club's owners, Greg Thibault and Pascal Lefebvre, hired an architect and a designer to help them with technical drawings and finishing choices, they insisted that they were the ones who made all the decisions in the planning and design of the club.[36] To them, designing a club was a complex problem informed by years of experience on the club circuit and could not be successfully realized solely by an outside design consultant.

Opened in 2000 and closed in 2011 after its owners opened two new clubs in the former Station C, which is the site of one of the earliest Village bars, Parking

Figure 7.6 Plans for Complexe Bourbon, including unrealized expansion, ca. 2000. *From top to bottom:* roof, second floor, first floor, ground floor, basement. *In grey:* exterior spaces. *Hatched:* private spaces. Drawn by Simon Coquoz, modified by author. ▸

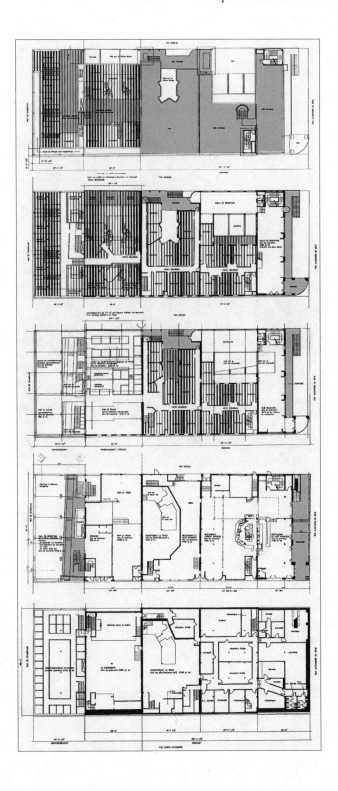

Figure 7.7 Olympia Building seen from the corner of Sainte-Catherine and Amherst Streets in 2009. Parking Nightclub occupied the highlighted zone between 2000 and 2009. Photograph by author.

hid on Amherst Street, a few metres south of Sainte-Catherine Street. Initially located in a former Consumers Distributing warehouse on the ground floor of a large mixed-use building, it moved in 2009 to an empty space in the basement of the same building (Figure 7.7). Although close to Sainte-Catherine, Montreal's main commercial street, its entrance, which served its two locations, was remote from the main traffic. It hinted at earlier times and less open communities where LGBT spaces had to be hidden. More radically, the Tunnel, a bar owned by the same men, which catered to an exclusively male clientele and was located for a short time in the space previously occupied by Parking, used as its main entrance a back door that opened onto the adjacent parking lot.

The physical situation of the bars underground and off the main street was mirrored in their names, Parking and Tunnel. In a similar approach to the Bourbon, these clubs' image – names, design, marketing – was coherent with what the owners perceived as their main clientele. As with the Bourbon, this image not only references mainstream gay male imagery of exaggerated masculinity and typically masculine space but also makes explicit references to both gay cruising space and major 1970s New York discotheques in former industrial spaces. Although the owners insist that they did not create a specifically "gay" bar but aimed instead for a large and diverse clientele, they also argue in the same discussion that they designed their dance floor and bar area with characteristics necessary to attract a "gay male" crowd. For example, Lefebvre insists that a bar catering to gay men needed a much more expansive dance floor with fewer "lounge" areas than in straight bars.

Lefebvre says that in contrast to the previous space, the design of the second Parking club was aimed less at gay men in an attempt to reach a wider clientele, while still acknowledging gay men's preferences in space configuration and décor elements. The first space included visual references to prisons, army barracks, and other places associated with masculinity that, in Lefebvre's view, gay men appreciate. Although the second space was much more neutral in its décor, traces of the old Parking persisted at K-Lub, the men-only sex club attached to Parking (Figure 7.8). Similarly, the labyrinthine layout of the former space, with

Figure 7.8 K-Lub with décor elements from previous Parking Nightclub, 2010. Photograph by author.

a large number of corners and recesses to facilitate cruising, was completely gone from the new large and unobstructed room but was still present in K-Lub.

Some of the decisions made for decorative elements at Parking were aimed at a predominantly gay male clientele. The owners wished to remind their patrons of earlier gay clubs that often colonized old warehouses or industrial spaces, as they believed this interest in reusing old spaces characterized gay men. This view echoes art historian Christopher Reed's observations on queer space's engagement with the past, which he associates with "taking place" and "camp."[37] Reed's reference to camp, usually linked to gender subversion through men's use of attributes associated with women, is here instead associated through design choices with extreme masculinities. Reed also points out the obvious metaphor linking renovation with knocking down barriers and opening up closets and further notes that it transforms what the dominant culture has abandoned, in a similar way to how queers have to rethink their lives outside of the normative expectations of heterosexist society. The club retained some of the unfinished elements left from the space's previous occupants (Figure 7.9), and new decorative elements most often consisted of rough, industrial-looking materials. Although the new club space was fairly open and uncluttered, an aspect that Lefebvre argues was also a legacy of the vast spaces used by early discotheques, clients first had to go through dark, long, and winding corridors before reaching the club itself. These corridors were designed out of necessity, as the new space had to be reached through the same door as previously; the owners, however, seemed to enjoy the scenario created by the long arrival before getting to the club space, as it once again recalled older times, although many younger patrons probably did not realize it. Tellingly, they used a similar approach in the design of their two new clubs at the former Station C.

Parking's simpler program and return to an underground location stood in contrast to Complexe Bourbon's and other large establishments' bold presence on the street. It also differed from smaller or more specialized spaces in Montreal, such as leather bars, that had their windows open to passersby for many years.[38] Even saunas, which were arguably the most private of gay-oriented public spaces because of their sexualized function, had a large presence on Sainte-Catherine Street; rather than open windows revealing the private acts inside, many saunas had windows showing large displays that clearly announced those activities. Adding to Lefebvre's insistence that Parking was not a gay bar,[39] one might even question to what extent this club was "out." Doing so, however, is somewhat unfair, as the owners' use of publicity clearly acknowledged and sought gay men as their primary patrons. Were they thus using their bar as some counter-normative space that tried to blur and reject the hetero-homo dichotomy by playing with sexual and gender expectations? In some ways, Thibault and

Figure 7.9 Rough finishes from previous occupants left visible in the Parking Nightclub hallway, 2010. Photograph by author.

Lefebvre's vision for Parking shared with queer aesthetics a desire to be situated outside of a traditional, and normative, segregation of "straight" and LGBT spaces, as discussed in the next section. Parking's first years as a space clearly for gay males and Lefebvre's comments about the club's shift toward a more mixed crowd for fundamentally commercial reasons suggest that no anti-normative agenda was at work at Parking. The shift should instead be understood as reflective of an increasing openness in Quebec society at large. The continuing success of its mixed-crowd events might also have been one of the reasons behind the increasing number of bars, both straight and gay, openly advertising hetero-homo or gay-friendly nights. However, whereas the Bourbon gained its political involvement by being boldly visible in the city, Parking's "invisibility" limited its political potential. The opening of formerly exclusively gay spaces to a larger mixed clientele was also typical of contemporary associations of gay subcultures with cosmopolitanism and a culture of cool, even if they were still often the subject of critiques regarding their openness to people who did not correspond to the typical clubgoer's image.[40]

Parking represented a paradoxical evolution from 1990s bars such as Complexe Bourbon. The limited interaction with the street – combined with the owners' insistence that their bar was not a specifically "gay" bar, even though it was largely patronized by gay men and seen by many as a gay space – clearly differs from the bold and visible 1990s gay bars that, in addition, offered separate gender-exclusive and mixed spaces. Although in appearance a step backward, this shift could also be interpreted as a large-scale societal coming-out process, in which a less visible "integration" stage followed the bold "disclosure" period.

Let's Go Outside: Temporary Queer Nights in "Straight" Land

After the emergence of clearly visible, purpose-built LGBT-oriented spaces in Montreal in the 1980s and 1990s, the first decade of the twenty-first century was marked by a shift toward a queer colonization of "straight" bars. Starting with the lesbian-oriented Meow Mix, launched by Miriam Ginestier in 1997,[41] these regular queer nights started appearing outside of the Village. Some of these nights were monthly or weekly, and others were more sporadic; some were gender-specific, and others were open to all; some were strictly for fun, and others served as fundraising events. But all shared a desire to offer an alternative to the Village. Although queer people have always been present in straight bars, until recently they most often had to hide their sexual orientation when visiting them. If homosexual public displays of affection in bars can still be unsafe due to negative reactions from other patrons or management, more and more initiatives are being implemented to "queer" straight spaces for a night. These nights, growing in number in recent years, have mostly been quite successful, once again pointing to a shift in the relation between queers and the "straight" public.[42] But if queers can now almost safely use straight bars, are there still differences between LGBT and straight bars? Does the only difference reside in how they are used? This section analyzes Mec Plus Ultra nights, an ephemeral attempt at queering space, to discuss the potential implications of such nights for the visibility of queer masculinities.

Mec Plus Ultra nights were created in November 2008 by Julien de Repentigny, Antoine Bedard, and François Guimond as an experiment parallel to other queer-driven parties seeking to create a more welcoming environment than traditional bars. Repentigny explains that Meow Mix and Faggity Ass Fridays were "more radical," whereas "we're looking for something more professional/career-oriented, there wasn't anything geared towards young professionals that aren't into that Village vibe."[43] Reaching 300 to 600 people every two weeks, Mec Plus Ultra nights were hosted by the Belmont, a Plateau-Mont-Royal tavern. Repentigny says that "despite the openness of Montreal it was hard to find a venue because many owners were worried that having a gay night would affect their clientele. It's funny because the Belmont is one of the straightest bars ever! But they were really into it and supportive!"[44]

The ephemeral nature of these events left few permanent traces of a recurrent queer occupation. At Mec Plus Ultra, physical space was used in similar ways to recent gay bars: the most important space was a large dance floor. To mark the gay appropriation of space, organizers selected a theme, usually linked to an overtly masculine or campy image, and added a few décor elements and video projections associated with that theme. It was thus an approach similar to the one implemented at Parking, where a gay male presence was symbolized mainly through visual links to a tradition of gay male spaces and camp reclamation. Unlike Parking, however, traces of the original straight use of the bar were visible amidst the "gay" traces: most explicitly, walls were covered with paintings of semi-naked women and with photographs and memorabilia of the Belmont in the 1920s and 1930s, linking the bar to a tradition of heteronormative male-only taverns. The juxtaposition of visual references to homosexuality and heterosexuality questioned both; the organizers denied any political aims, but their camp reclamation of masculinity symbols was similar to more politically inclined examples. By catering most directly to men or women respectively, both this event and Meow Mix, although officially open to all, mainly recreated alternative Village bars outside the Village. However, by focusing on the occupation of interior spaces without much presence on the street, they lacked the political potential offered by public visibility.

Temporary queer nights and the growing visible presence of queers in bars outside the Village allow us to ask whether gay bars are only a temporary "typology"? Remiggi has suggested that, like ethnic neighbourhoods, LGBT enclaves can disappear.[45] But does this mean that gay bars can also disappear? As queer users become more visible in straight bars, can the role played by gay bars' interaction with public space be replaced by social interaction and queer displays of affection in straight bars? Might visible queer uses of space in straight bars and reclamation of masculinity have an even more important political effect than bold LGBT-oriented architecture through a diffused integration of heteronormative space? It is difficult to suggest so today, as queer displays still seem to be more tolerated than integrated, but the unexpected presence of queers in straight bars might still, in smaller ways, replicate the unexpected presence of queer minorities in public space through LGBT-identified architecture. The next few years should tell us whether the current trends will continue, but gay bars might always keep a community role by creating a space of socialization for younger LGBT people.

Dancing in the Streets: A Conclusion

The architecture of gay bars presents rare public evidence of the evolution of gay communities and their relationship with society at large, which is usually assumed to be heterosexual. In Montreal's case, the geographical move from downtown to the Village, paralleled by changing public displays of gay social space through time, makes it easy to see stages in this evolution. Even since the relatively recent emergence of the Village, bars have had different functions and visibilities in public space, embodying but also shaping society's changing relation to sexual diversity.

Early downtown Montreal bars and taverns patronized by gay men were often hidden from public view and did not offer occasions for the increasingly vocal gay community to be visible. The emergence of the Village completely changed this relationship. Its bars and other commercial establishments proudly and boldly expressed their "difference," most often through explicit references to male sexuality. The 1990s generation of mixed-use complexes, exemplified by the Bourbon, juxtaposed specifically gay male space with public uses, making homosexuality clearly visible to a heterosexual audience. As a result, this architecture gained a political meaning. More recent clubs have scaled back from large mixed-use complexes to concentrate on their use as bars, thus also stepping back from public view. Their clientele, however, have been increasingly mixed, men and women, queer and straight, in parallel with an increasingly important presence of queers in straight bars. These changes document a shift in Quebec society not only toward a greater acceptance of sexual minorities but also toward a realignment of masculine symbols. Whereas early gay, lesbian, and straight (most often understood as male) bars participated in a model of segregated feminine and masculine spaces, current models bridge the gap. If gay-oriented bars were obviously not solely responsible for such changes, by exposing subverted notions of masculinity, they played a role in the transformation.

In addition to participating in the evolution of the relationship between LGBT communities and society at large, the evolution of gay bars also followed a shift away from the gay liberation and lesbian feminist movements and toward queer politics. The integration of queer politics is visible in the gradual transformation of the Village commercial establishments from places oriented toward gay men to ones that offered a broadening and mixing of different clienteles, most importantly inclusive of women. Paradoxically, the visual insistence on a certain kind of masculinity in the design and marketing of the Village and its commercial institutions created a new homonormativity that left aside other sexual minorities, such as transsexuals and bisexuals. However, this exaggerated and provocative insistence on masculinity contributed to a camp reclamation and a queer overturning of symbols associated with heteronormativity.

Notes

This chapter was developed as a master's project at McGill's School of Architecture under the very helpful supervision of Annmarie Adams. Thanks also to Simon Coquoz and Pascal Lefebvre for their generous participation in my research, as well as to the Archives gaies du Québec. The Fonds de recherche du Québec – Société et culture financially supported this research.

1 In this chapter, "gay" and "lesbian" generally refer to male and female homosexuality respectively. The terms "gay bars" and "lesbian bars" are preferred to mark the bars' specific *welcoming* of homosexuality, even if they are often open to people of other sexual orientation. "LGBT" or "queer" refer to all sexual minorities as a perceived entity, setting aside their differences. Some exceptions are made for accepted expressions, such as "Gay Village," that usually refer to more than just male homosexuality, although their degree of openness is sometimes contested. "Straight" refers to spaces perceived as not designed for or used by specifically LGBT people. A distinction is also made between "LGBT-oriented" and "queer" spaces to avoid confusion around broad political and theoretical understandings of queer space. For attempts to classify different understandings of "queer space," see Richard Borbridge, "Sexuality and the City: Exploring Gaybourhoods and the Urban Village Form in Vancouver, BC" (Master of City Planning thesis, University of Manitoba, 2007); Olivier Vallerand, "Home Is the Place We All Share: Building Queer Collective Utopias," *Journal of Architectural Education* 67, 1 (2013): 64–75; and Olivier Vallerand, "Regards queers sur l'architecture: Une remise en question des approches identitaires de l'espace," *Captures* 1, 1 (2016): http://www.revuecaptures.org/node/349/. Queer space research that has specifically discussed bars and night spaces includes Henry Urbach, "Spatial Rubbing: The Zone," *Sites*, 25 (1993): 90–95; John Paul Ricco, "Coming Together: Jack-Off Rooms as Minor Architecture," *A/R/C, architecture, research, criticism* 1, 5 (1994): 26–31; Vincent André Doyle, "Coming into Site: Identity, Community and the Production of Gay Space in Montréal" (MA thesis, McGill University, 1996); Aaron Betsky, *Queer Space: Architecture and Same-Sex Desire*, 1st ed. (New York: William Morrow, 1997); Gordon Brent Ingram, Anne-Marie Bouthillette, and Yolanda Retter, eds., *Queers in Space: Communities | Public Places | Sites of Resistance* (Seattle: Bay, 1997); David Bell, Jon Binnie, Ruth Holliday, Robyn Longhurst, and Robin Peace, *Pleasure Zones: Bodies, Cities, Spaces* (Syracuse, NY: Syracuse University Press, 2001); and John Paul Ricco, *The Logic of the Lure* (Chicago: University of Chicago Press, 2002).

2 Richard Burnett, "Montreal's Sex Garage Raid: A Watershed Moment," *Xtra!* October 23, 2009.

3 The term "community" has rightly been identified as problematical when used to describe sexual diversity, as it implies a shared cultural identification. Marianne Blidon, "Jalons pour une géographie des homosexualités," *Espace géographique* 37, 2 (2008): 175–89. However, I use "community" in this chapter, usually in plural form, to refer to some of the subcultures associated with LGBT minorities that shape bars and clubs.

4 Ross Higgins, *De la clandestinité à l'affirmation: Pour une histoire de la communauté gaie montréalaise* (Montreal: Comeau et Nadeau, 1999), 9–10.

5 If this chapter focuses on gay male spaces, Montreal's lesbian spaces have also had a rich parallel history, even if they are today much less visible. See Line Chamberland,

"Remembering Lesbian Bars: Montreal, 1955–1975," in *Gay Studies from the French Cultures: Voices from France, Belgium, Brazil, Canada, and the Netherlands*, ed. Rommer Mendès-Leite and Pierre-Olivier de Busscher, 231–69 (New York: Haworth, 1993); Julie Podmore, "Gone 'Underground'? Lesbian Visibility and the Consolidation of Queer Space in Montréal," *Social and Cultural Geography* 7, 4 (2006): 595–625; and Julie Podmore, "Lesbians as Village 'Queers': The Transformation of Montréal's Lesbian Nightlife in the 1990s," *ACME* 12, 2 (2013): 220–49.

6 See, for example, George Chauncey, *Gay New York: Gender, Urban Culture, and the Making of the Gay Male World, 1890–1940* (New York: Basic Books, 1994); John D'Emilio, *Sexual Politics, Sexual Communities: The Making of a Homosexual Minority in the United States, 1940–1970*, 2nd ed. (Chicago: University of Chicago Press, 1983); and Elizabeth Lapovsky Kenne, *Boots of Leather, Slippers of Gold: The History of a Lesbian Community* (New York and London: Routledge, 1993).

7 Chauncey, *Gay New York*, 331–60; D'Emilio, *Sexual Politics*, 9–53.

8 David Bell, "Fragments for a Queer City," in *Pleasure Zones: Bodies, Cities, Spaces*, ed. David Bell, Jon Binnie, and Ruth Holliday, 85 (Syracuse: Syracuse University Press, 2001), discussing Barbara A. Weightman, "Gay Bars as Private Places," *Landscape* 24, 1 (1980): 9–16; Betsky, *Queer Space*.

9 D'Emilio, *Sexual Politics*, 51–52; Frank W. Remiggi, "Homosexualité et espace urbain: Une analyse critique du cas de Montréal," *Téoros* 19, 2 (2000): 30.

10 Betsky, *Queer Space*, 156.

11 Urbach, "Spatial Rubbing," 90.

12 Weightman, "Gay Bars," 13; Rostom Mesli and Brian Whitener, "The Flame, the Gay Bar of Ann Arbor, MI, 1949–1998," http://outhistory.org/exhibits/show/the-flame-ann-arbor/the-flame.

13 Betsky, *Queer Space*, 159.

14 Weightman, "Gay Bars," 14–15.

15 D'Emilio, *Sexual Politics*.

16 See, for example, the description of nightclub The Saint in Betsky, *Queer Space*, 161; and Ira Tattelman, "Staging Sex and Masculinity at the Mineshaft," *Men and Masculinities* 7, 3 (2005): 304.

17 Betsky, *Queer Space*, 162.

18 Bell, "Fragments for a Queer City," 88.

19 Ricco, "Coming Together"; Urbach, "Spatial Rubbing." Ricco points out very early the changes that the Internet brings to cruising. See also Robert Payne, "Gay Scene, Queer Grid," paper presented at the conference "Queer Space: Centres and Peripheries," University of Technology, Sydney, 2007.

20 Chauncey, *Gay New York*.

21 Catherine Jean Nash, "Toronto's Gay Village (1969–1982): Plotting the Politics of Gay Identity," *Canadian Geographer/Le Géographe canadien* 50, 1 (2006): 1–16.

22 See, for example, Higgins, *De la clandestinité*; Ross Higgins, "A Sense of Belonging: Pre-liberation Space, Symbolics, and Leadership in Gay Montreal" (PhD diss., McGill University, 1997); Chamberland, "Remembering Lesbian Bars"; Julie Podmore, "Lesbians in the Crowd: Gender, Sexuality and Visibility along Montreal's Boul. St-Laurent," *Gender, Place and Culture: A Journal of Feminist Geography* 8, 4 (2001): 333–55; Podmore, "Gone 'Underground'?"; and Julie Podmore, "Queering Discourses of Urban Decline: Representing Montréal's Post–World War II 'Lower Main,'" *Historical Geography* 43 (2015): 57–83.

23 Remiggi, "Homosexualité et espace urbain," 30–31.
24 To describe this period, Remiggi refers extensively to Higgins, *De la clandestinité à l'affirmation.*
25 Ibid., 9.
26 The very few written traces of that period and the transformations that occurred after the 1980s in what used to be Montreal's gay district make it difficult to get a clear picture of the space of bars in the 1960s and 1970s. Ibid., 97.
27 From its beginnings, the Village has been entangled in Montreal's unique francophone-anglophone dichotomy. Although popular perceptions still often attribute the emergence of the Gay Village to both Quebec nationalist objectives and police repression ordered by Mayor Jean Drapeau, Remiggi argues that bar owners were instead attracted by cheap rents and existing infrastructures that dated back to the early twentieth century when the area was a centre of French Canadian entertainment. Furthermore, he notes that police repression happened a few years before the move, therefore undermining links made between both events. If it remains true that Village bars and shops are more often owned by French-speaking people than previous downtown institutions, the new Village has nonetheless always welcomed a bilingual crowd. Remiggi, "Homosexualité et espace urbain," 31; Frank W. Remiggi, "Le village gai de Montréal: Entre le ghetto et l'espace identitaire," in *Sortir de l'ombre: Histoires des communautés lesbienne et gaie de Montréal,* ed. Irène Demczuk and Frank W. Remiggi (Montreal: VLB Éditeur, 1998), 274–78.
28 See Brad Ruting, "Economic Transformations of Gay Urban Spaces: Revisiting Collins' Evolutionary Gay District Model," *Australian Geographer* 39, 3 (2008): 259–69.
29 Remiggi, "Le village gai de Montréal," 281–82.
30 Information on Chamberland, Le Drugstore, and Complexe Bourbon comes from Normand Chamberland, "Complexe-Hôtel Bourbon: Projet d'agrandissement et de rénovation," permit document presented to City of Montreal, 2002; Denis-Daniel Boullé and André C. Passiour, "Décès d'un visionnaire," *Fugues,* November 2008, 24; and Simon Coquoz, interview with author, November 19, 2009.
31 Editors' note: the author uses "terrace" throughout this chapter as equivalent to the French word *terrasse,* meaning an outdoor patio, deck, sidewalk, or other space used by bars and restaurants in warmer weather for al fresco dining and drinking.
32 In Montreal's bilingual context, it is fitting to note that most names used in the complex, in a similar way to many other Village establishments, are either English, such as Track and Body Shop, or reference place names understood by all languages, such as Bourbon and Mississippi. This use of names might be understood as an attempt to reconcile the French and English heritage of Montreal through a fascination with the United States, similar to the architectural references used (Figure 7.5).
33 In his discussion of 1970s New York gay bars, Ira Tattelman also underlines how they staged an overemphasized masculinity to transform gay male "identity." Tattelman, "Staging Sex and Masculinity," 303.
34 Coquoz, interview.
35 Christopher Reed, "Imminent Domain: Queer Space in the Built Environment," *Art Journal* 55, 4 (1996): 64; Jon Binnie, "The Erotic Possibilities of the City," in David Bell, Jon Binnie, Ruth Holliday, Robyn Longhurst, and Robin Peace, *Pleasure Zones: Bodies, Cities, Spaces* (Syracuse, NY: Syracuse University Press, 2001), 107.
36 All information on Parking Nightclub is from Pascal Lefebvre, interview with author, June 2, 2010.
37 Reed, "Imminent Domain," 67–68.

38   Remiggi, "Le village gai de Montréal," 282. Personal observations and various accounts suggest that this aspect of Montreal's Village is not common to other LGBT neighbourhoods around the world and even quite rare. Most bars and club spaces are still often hidden behind tinted glass or in basements.

39   A personal experience suggests that Thibault and Lefebvre have partially succeeded in broadening their target audience: learning that this research project would be on gay bars, a colleague told me that he realized Parking was a gay-oriented club only after his third time visiting for DJ shows, which had caused him to wonder why the crowd was predominantly male.

40   Dereka Rushbrook, "Cities, Queer Space, and the Cosmopolitan Tourist," *GLQ: A Journal of Lesbian and Gay Studies* 8, 1–2 (2002): 188–89. See, for example, Richard Florida's controversial theories on the creative class, including his use of a "diversity index," which particularly targets gays. Richard L. Florida, *The Rise of the Creative Class: And How It's Transforming Work, Leisure, Community, and Everyday Life* (New York: Basic Books, 2004).

41   Meg Hewings, "Lesbians Party On!" *Hour,* October 4, 2007; DeAnne Smith, "Montreal Ladies Love Meow Mix," *Xtra!* December 4, 2008.

42   To the examples discussed here could be added numerous other events. See Anabelle Nicoud, "Le Village encore dans le coup?" *La Presse,* July 26, 2010.

43   Quoted in Preet Bhogal, "Montreal's New Once-a-Month Gay Event, Outside the Village," *Xtra!* December 25, 2008.

44   Quoted in ibid.

45   Frank W. Remiggi, public presentation to the Archives gaies du Québec, May 13, 2010. The situation is not unique to Montreal, as pointed out, for example, in Jeff Kunerth, "For a Number of Gay Bars, It's Last Call," *Orlando Sentinel,* September 17, 2007.

Part 3
Performing Masculinities

THE PERFORMATIVITY OF GENDER identities – especially, for our purposes, *masculine* identities – is the central theme around which the next group of essays is assembled. There is a specific kind of performance located at the heart of Chapter 8, by Jane Nicholas, where the narrative is that of the little people who appeared in the "midget shows" that remained a popular sideshow entertainment in Ontario through to the 1960s. Ultimately, Nicholas argues, these shows remained popular for so long "because they reaffirmed dominant ideas of white, middle-class, heterosexual masculinity in two ways: by highlighting in miniature the appropriate family structure and by reaffirming 'normal'-bodied, white, middle-class men's expected benevolent paternal roles." The confrontation here between hegemonic and subordinate masculinities is rich and compelling, just as it is in Allan Downey's discussion in Chapter 9 of the place of lacrosse in the culture of the Skwxwú7mesh people of coastal British Columbia. There is also a central irony, inasmuch as lacrosse was an Iroquoian game that had been appropriated, adapted, and enshrined as a dimension of British Canadian identity in the nineteenth century.[1] It was then promoted among western First Nations as a way of encouraging "muscular Christianity" and Victorian, middle-class masculinity as part of a broader assimilationist project. But as Downey shows, the Skwxwú7mesh people succeeded in flipping the script on their colonizers, embracing lacrosse and its performance as expressions of both Skwxwú7mesh nationalism and what he refers to as a "pan-Indigenous identity."

With Willeen Keough's study of masculinities in the environmental movement, we return in Chapter 10 to postwar Canada and to the close analysis of
individual masculine personas. Here, the discussion is framed around specific
scripts for eco-masculinity – the shepherd, the warrior, and the impresario –
that were performed by three leading environmentalists: Robert Hunter, Brian
Davies, and Paul Watson. Keough is especially attentive to the tension within
the eco-masculine subject, showing carefully how these activists articulated
alternatives to the dominant script, even as they reinforced certain elements of
hegemonic masculinity. Alternative masculinities are also at the heart of Chapter 11, by Eric Fillion, on Petit Québec libre, an early 1970s experiment in
countercultural collective living organized around the twin principles of radical
nationalism and free-jazz improvisation. Like Pierre Vallières,[2] these activist
musicians saw clear parallels between the situation of the colonized Québécois
and the plight of African Americans in the United States. But unlike other
radical Quebec nationalists who seemed deaf to the growing demands of the
women's movement, Petit Québec libre gave voice to a trenchant critique of
traditional gender roles, promoting political independence not just for its own
sake but so that *le nouvel homme québécois* might rise, liberated, from the ashes
of his oppression.

Notes

1 On the appropriation of lacrosse as a component of the British Canadian identity project,
   see Gillian Poulter, *Becoming Native in a Foreign Land: Sport, Visual Culture, and Identity
   in Montreal, 1840–1885* (Vancouver: UBC Press, 2009).
2 Vallières was a prominent member of the Front de libération du Québec (FLQ). His book
   Nègres blancs d'Amérique: Autobiographie précoce d'un "terroriste" québécois (Montreal:
   Éditions Parti pris, 1968) became a leading text for the FLQ and for the radical independence movement as a whole.

8
Scales of Manliness: Masculinity and Disability in the Displays of Little People as Freaks in Ontario, 1900s–50s

Jane Nicholas

IN 1919, ON THE HEELS of the First World War, injured veterans appeared at the Canadian National Exhibition (CNE) in Toronto, Ontario. Their injuries made them war heroes, and they were celebrated as such. On display, their productive skills, which remained intact, allegedly *despite* their disabled bodies, were highlighted. The *Globe* ran an article that described the soldiers' work at the CNE under the title "Putting Men Together Again." The article stated,

> Happy boys who have limpsed [sic] back to Canada may be seen at the Exhibition in the Process Building ... Though badly wounded in France or Belgium, they are showing themselves to be real men still in peace. They work with real tools and machinery, and are fitting out to earn a living at a new trade – the older one no longer of use. The ladies will be simply charmed with the wonderful display of soldier-work from the hospitals, the largest collection yet ... Each pretty article aided in some soldier's cure, and the money it brings goes back to him.[1]

Metres away on the fringes of the fairground another display echoed dangerously in the heroic display of veterans: the sideshow. Necessary to ensure a profit, sideshows including so-called freaks highlighted the allegedly grotesque and seductive, not the educational and productive.[2] In earlier years, sideshow acts would have included performers like Canadian Charles Tripp, who was born without arms and found a livelihood showing paying audiences the useful things he could do with his feet, like hold a tea cup.[3] In 1919 the Midway at the CNE included a number of exhibits but not the so-called armless and legless wonders of previous sideshows.[4] Yet the proximity of the two displays – disabled veterans and sideshows – reveals much about the complicated nature of masculinities and disabilities in twentieth-century Canada. Normative, dominant masculinities were premised on ability; to work and be productive and, more generally, to be rugged, strong, and virile. Disability complicated and compromised almost the entire nature of dominant masculinity; disability meant vulnerability, dependency, and in the context of contemporary eugenics, defectiveness. Yet those complications were nuanced. Sacrificing one's body for country and empire was deemed heroic, whereas being born with a disability was to be deemed a freak of nature. If disabled veterans like those at the 1919 CNE could show their continued value by being productive, freaks exhibited on the sideshow were viewed more as performing commodities than as legitimate workers.

This chapter focuses on masculinity, disability, and the sideshow performances of little people in Ontario. I argue that although the so-called midget shows might have challenged ideals of proper able-bodied masculinity by way of their performers, they affirmed hegemonic masculinity and made it more durable in a period of economic and military crisis. These particular sideshow acts, rather than disrupting and challenging the social order, worked to assuage anxiety by providing a miniature version of the "correct" paternal and patriarchal order of the world – white, middle-class, talented, and deferent to benevolent paternal authority. As Mona Gleason has argued in regard to children's bodies, size matters, and I extend her argument to adult bodies here.[5] Although freak shows and the subordinate adult masculinities displayed by them were marginalized in the twentieth century, their popularity – measured at least by their financial viability as commercial enterprises – remained. Certain acts came and went, but few acts had the high style of the midget shows. Unlike other sideshows that were designed to evoke pity, horror, or disgust, the miniature worlds of the midget shows were ones where freaks could be beautiful, charming, or delightful. Aligned with Hollywood and its style of glamour, midget shows were popular among sideshows across North America from the 1900s to the 1950s.

Disability and what constitutes it varies, and there are real problems with labelling disability or particular people as disabled.[6] As Robert Bogdan argues in his book on the history of freak shows, "How we view people with disabilities has less to do with what they are physiologically than with who we are culturally. Understanding the 'freak show' can help us not confuse the role a person plays with who that person really is."[7] Accordingly, I use disability/disabilities as an analytical category to refer to historical practices of differentiation that considered bodies deemed and performed as different to be less than equal and/or undeserving of a fully realized masculinity based on a dominant understanding of gender.

In 1995, Raewyn Connell shaped the burgeoning field of masculinity studies by positing that there is no universal or ahistorical masculinity but rather fractured, specific, and contextually formed *masculinities*. Connell suggests a framework for understanding dominant versions of masculinities as hegemonic, with others deemed subordinate or complicit. From 1995 onward, as discussed in the introduction to this volume, masculinities developed into a lively subfield of gender and feminist studies, with Canadian scholars making significant contributions.[8] In a newer and rather less developed subfield, disability has received a modest amount of attention from Canadian historians.[9] This chapter is a preliminary attempt to bring together these two subfields in the context of the Canadian historiography by looking at some of the representations, expressions, and hierarchies of masculinities in sideshows from the 1900s to 1950s. In doing so, I explore a facet of disabilities and masculinities, working from the preliminary sociological and theoretical work of Russell Shuttleworth and colleagues on the "dilemma of disabled masculinity," in which they call for scholars to be sensitive to differences between impairments, specifically between those present at birth and those subsequently acquired.[10]

The study of the sideshow in Ontario may seem like a poor start for this project. Some people have deemed freak shows offensive. My purpose here is not to reaffirm performances of difference as freakish – or even necessarily as disability – but to explore how disability and masculinities informed each other and how the freak show worked to shore up hegemonic masculinity in a period of seemingly perpetual crisis. Although performers and other workers often defined themselves as a separate society formed of chosen families, freak shows were also commercial ventures intimately tied to consumer culture, so shows had to be responsive to shifting consumer tastes and were reflective of wider cultural patterns.

Two caveats are necessary. First, although I focus in particular on sideshows that were performed in Ontario, sideshows were transient. Shows travelled across North America, usually from the South, where they wintered, moving northward and then across Canada from west to east or east to west before returning to the United States. Canadian companies tended to winter in southern Ontario. Individual acts were also contracted to larger shows, where they might appear for a season or more before going out on their own or joining a different group, adding to the overall mobile feel of the travelling freak show. In short, although I focus on Ontario, the shows themselves were transnational and fluid. They travelled throughout Ontario, playing in cities and towns, and sometimes modified their acts to meet local standards. Conflicts with police or municipalities sometimes occurred when a show did not match a community's tastes, but overall the structure and style of the shows remained fairly consistent.

Second, I use the term "midget," as it reflects the historical language used at the time to refer to people of short stature. I recognize its offensiveness today and also use currently preferred terms like "little people" or "people of short stature." I have avoided the term "dwarfism," despite its current medical usage, both because the term historically was often used to differentiate between proportionate and disproportionate peoples of short stature and because the historical cultural meanings tied to dwarfism were different.[11] As Susan Stewart notes, "The dwarf is assigned to the domain of the grotesque and the under-world, the midget to the world of the fairy – a world of the natural, not in nature's gigantic aspects, but in its attention to the perfection of detail."[12] In a 1933 publication by the United States Eugenics Record Office, it was noted that in Midget Cities the performers were passionate about the difference they saw between dwarfs and midgets. The latter, they felt, were simply "normal" people of a smaller scale, whereas dwarfism implied deformity.[13] A 1944 *Maclean's* magazine article also noted, "Midgets resent being confused with 'dwarfs.'"[14]

Masculinity and Disability

Midway entertainment offered by outdoor amusement or carnival companies was popular across Ontario in the early and middle decades of the twentieth century, although it has received little sustained attention from Canadian historians.[15] Travelling from town to town during the summer months, companies like Johnny J. Jones Shows and Conklin Shows, among many others, toured regularly and attended to both large and small towns and cities.[16] Sometimes they exhibited independently, but other times they joined local agricultural fairs and exhibitions or were even hosted by local groups, like battalions, the Red Cross, or the Shriners, to raise money for charities, as they did in the 1920s for disabled veterans.[17] The company Canadian Victory Shows had an explicit connection to the Great War. In 1919, it opened its season in Welland, Ontario, reportedly "under the auspices of the Great War Veterans."[18] The continuing popularity of Midway shows, despite their less than wholesome reputations, meant that such charitable profit-sharing understandings were mutually beneficial. Shows got a modest boost in respectability, whereas charities and hospitals benefited financially. Exact profits are difficult to know, but certainly large companies contracted to hold Midways for big events like the Canadian National Exhibition fared better than others, even despite Toronto's reputation for being more conservative and needing only respectable shows. Indeed, in challenging the discourse of the decline of the carnival, sideshow owner Rubin Gruberg, writing in the trade publication *Billboard Magazine* in 1930, declared,

> In 13 days, at the Canadian National Exhibition, Toronto, I grossed $228,000 with my largest show, the Rubin & Cherry Shows. And in playing other fairs in the States and Canada it is nothing unusual to gross from $25,000 to $60,000 on the week. Does this appear as the carnivals are losing public interest? The business as a whole is better stabilized than any time that I can recall.[19]

The popularity and financial success of the shows were matched by public outcry from some municipalities, politicians, churches, and concerned citizens who protested their existence in the 1920s. Critics depicted sideshows as tasteless, cheap, detrimental, and offensive. Despite attempts to provoke legislative action, the calls for the end of the sideshows petered out before the sideshows did.[20] Sideshows continued in a variety of forms throughout the twentieth century. In the middle decades, sideshows were continually revamped to ensure fresh acts for large audiences. Particular acts ebbed and flowed depending on popularity, but one particular show remained continuously popular and increased in popularity: the display of little people as midgets. These shows remained popular because they reaffirmed dominant ideas of white, middle-class, heterosexual masculinity in two ways: by highlighting in miniature the appropriate family structure and by reaffirming "normal"-bodied, white, middle-class men's expected benevolent paternal roles. This worked, in part, because of the dominant way little people had been exhibited since the middle to late nineteenth century.

In the nineteenth century, little people's relationship to entertainment changed as a result of the wider cultural shift to a modern consumer culture. In the eighteenth century and earlier, some little people had been bought or otherwise acquired by European aristocracy to perform at their request. By the nineteenth century, American showmen like P.T. Barnum had refigured shows to fit the wider audiences of travelling sideshows and dime museums. Charles Sherwood Stratton, renamed General Tom Thumb, became one of the more famous and wealthy performers. In 1865 he married Mercy Lavinia Warren Bump in a spectacle that held the attention of the United States, despite the Civil War and the recently announced Emancipation Proclamation. Stratton was bought by Barnum at the age of five, and his career has been well studied, but a few details are of note here. Barnum ensured that Stratton was billed as a man in miniature – perfect otherwise in form and inoffensive to witness.[21] Stratton performed as a middle-class man, who was talented and respectable.

Stratton's name has become synonymous with midget shows because of the style of his presentation. From the nineteenth century until well into the middle decades of the twentieth century, little people were presented in what Robert Bogdan has termed a "lavish aggrandized mode." Ballyhoo biographies narrated the exceptional pedigree of performers, linking them to royalty or other high-status markers. Performers wore beautiful, extravagant costumes and sometimes showed their fine artistic skills in singing and dancing. Bogdan argues that people presented in the aggrandized mode "tended to be presented as physically normal, or even superior, in all ways except the one anomaly that was their alleged reason for fame."[22] Such shows often made claims to being clean, respectable, and in-offensive. In 1919, Johnny J. Jones Shows advertised in *Billboard Magazine* that it had the CNE contract for that year and was in need of "Two More Shows of the Highest Class for Toronto." The advertisement specified that it could place "the swellest troupe of Midgets in North America."[23] Although midget shows travelled with sideshows in Ontario in the 1910s and 1920s, they do not appear in the police reports or other files that form the significant correspondence between the attorney general's office and sideshows in the period. The protests and complaints that do appear in those files or that are recalled in showmen's memoirs are directed toward other displays, especially girl shows and trans-gender performers, or they express more general concerns about gambling and the general state of the shows.[24]

The sideshow was a place of manufactured difference where, according to some recollections, people otherwise deemed too unusual for regular society found community and family in the tented world.[25] That community and family were of a fractured kind, being based on differences of race, class, gender, and ability. Disabilities and hegemonic masculinities chafed awkwardly against each other in the world of circuses and sideshows. In her study of the circus in twentieth-century American culture, Janet Davis argues that

> the world of the circus was one of male gender flux, with androgynous acrobats, gender-bending clowns, players in drag, and animals dressed as men. Spontaneous brawls among spectators and workingmen extended these variegated masculine performances to the grounds outside the ring. As a whole, the human menagerie was a place for performative male gender play, even though the circus's deeply entrenched caste system circumscribed occupation and economic advancement within the nomadic community.[26]

The closely related world of the carnival is similar. Whereas circuses in the twentieth century worked consciously against being associated with the out-door amusements and sideshows of carnivals, the two resonated with each other, at least in much of the public's estimation. Davis's work, which focuses mostly but not exclusively on able-bodied performers – animal trainers, acro-bats, and contortionists – reveals a masculine world that challenges assump-tions of heteronormativity and the limits of the body. The place of disability in the carnival created important differences. Sideshow managers and promoters frequently defended their employees as at least finding a place in the working world and thus society with their paid performances. Many argued that it was better than being unemployed and dependent or institutionalized.[27] Sideshow folk also frequently used the metaphor of family to describe their relationships.

Yet, it should be noted, carnival families were hierarchal and not without serious tensions among members.

Owners and managers tended to be male, white, and able-bodied, whereas sideshow acts were defined by various types of disability. Rarity, mental capacity, and skill demonstrated in the performance led to differences in staging and in pay packets. Paternalistic ideas of care were common. As sideshow manager Hazel Elves recalled of her father, "Dad was a champion among many of these people who were dependent on the carnival for survival of mind and body. He protected many and came to their assistance whenever called upon."[28] Masculinity was also a defining characteristic of the scales of difference. Harry Lewiston, a freak show operator who toured with Conklin in Ontario in the period, describes his sexual escapades (in and out of the sideshows) in great detail in his autobiography, *Freak Show Man*. He notes, however, that the treatment of two white, American performers with microcephaly, referred to only as Kiki and Bobo, was different. They were billed as Albino African Pygmies and, as with other shows featuring people with microcephaly, were called "pinheads," for as Lewiston writes, "You can't tell people, 'Now, we've got these idiots here; take a good look at them.'" Lewiston admits that Bobo was always solemn and speculates that this was because they "bound his hands before putting him to bed" in order to stop him from masturbating because he was "crazy enough."[29] For Lewiston and others, disability compromised autonomy and sexuality – both being important qualities in healthy modern men.

Midget shows were defined by the use of "cute" as a commodity aesthetic, and this aspect of the shows, along with significant changes in the authority of the state to care for people deemed different or disabled, shaped the exhibition of little people. Cute as a historically constructed category was not neutral. The modern construction of "cute" came in the late nineteenth century and dovetailed with the rise of sentimental childhood, urban consumer culture, and the redefinition of gender relations. The burgeoning consumer culture of the late nineteenth century not only reshaped public, urban spaces but also provided outlets for testing Victorian gender relations. For middle-class women, shopping provided entry into public spaces and an outlet for potential activism.[30] Such changes were premised on wider shifts in industrialization and urbanization, which introduced more mechanized work for both men and women and brought people to live in cities. Concerns over these changes manifested in particularly gendered ways as Canadians debated the feminization of cities, the decline of white, middle-class manhood, and the need to fortify "the race."[31] Modernity itself was thought to be harmful to white, middle-class masculinity, and inherent in the artistic and cultural movement of anti-modernism was a desire to provide an antidote to the alleged soft and feminized modern society that seemed anathema to vigorous, robust, and healthy masculinity.[32] From "muscular Christianity" to manliness aligned biologically with soldiering, the idealized and dominant version of masculinity that emerged was tough, strong, capable, ready for war, and powerful, as well as dominated by a decisive, controlled, and skilled mind.[33] Hegemonic manliness was not cute. Rather, cute became a commercialized value associated with female maternal desire or longing and a feminized sense of empathy. As Lori Merish argues, cute became a commodity aesthetic – something that could be consumed. Cute was associated with nondominant identities and with things that could be purchased, petted, and enjoyed through display.[34] In regard to the wildly popular Tom Thumb wedding, Merish argues that it "delighted viewers because it *looked like children imitating adults,* thus assimilating the 'freak' into the familial and familiar structure of domination and hierarchy."[35] Cute was therefore also linked to stature, and small size became associated with reduced status.

The midget shows emerged and became popular in the late nineteenth century – most prominently with Barnum's exhibition of Tom Thumb and his wife, Lavinia Warren – and although they were transformed in the early decades of the twentieth century, their relationship to white, bourgeois family structures remained. Large, allegedly biological families of little people were exhibited in the 1920s, and from the late 1930s to the 1950s, organizers created so-called Midget Cities, in which little people lived on display in villages where everything from houses to fire departments was scaled for short statures.[36] Historians Gary Cross and John Walton, noting this kind of show's significance to wider changes in popular culture, argue that leisure itself was transformed in the 1920s to focus on child consumers, which changed the display of freaks:

> The freak was cutesified and passed on to children. It is no accident that the 1920s children's ride, Pleasure of Beach Express in Blackpool, [England,] used dwarfs as conductors ... Over time, "little people" were taken from the world of the bizarre to the realm of the innocent. Snow White had her cute seven dwarfs in Disney's first feature length cartoon of 1937.[37]

The association of little people with a childlike state was culturally defined. By the 1920s, the history of cute had entangled little people and children, merging the two to create a perpetually juvenile cultural construction of little people. Significantly, the feminization of the cute and the miniature happened alongside crises of masculinity and shifting notions of its relationship to disability and wage earning. Together, these factors formed a complex context for the display of little people and for the dominant messages of those displays.

From late in the nineteenth century, English Canadians had expressed concern over the state of modern masculinity. The twentieth century seemed only to sharpen the crisis: the First World War disabled bodies of soldiers and pointed to very real issues of health in wider society; the 1920s saw the rise of the Modern Girl, who challenged hegemonic masculinity by smoking, drinking, and taking up public space; the Depression seriously challenged men's roles as bread-winners; and the Second World War produced another generation of "damaged" veterans. The response by the state to these and other crises was piecemeal and largely inadequate but deeply influenced by gender and, in relation to mascu-linities, defined by entitlements to work. Welfare policy, including allowances and Workmen's Compensation Boards, was shaped by the idea that compensa-tion was due because of the loss of the ability to work. Its relationship to disability before the 1960s in Canada was largely defined by acquired impairments, notably those that resulted from military service or industrial accidents.[38]

Although in Ontario an employers' liability law had been on the books since 1886, it was the 1914 law that introduced workers' compensation.[39] The 1920s were significant in regard to the reshaping of relations between people and the state. As a number of scholars have demonstrated, the shifts in the welfare state beginning in the 1920s and continuing through the economic and political upheavals of the 1930s and 1940s were premised, at least in part, on providing a measure of security for temporary crises among male breadwinners.[40] Lara Campbell argues that "the overwhelming public and state support for the as-sociation of manhood with breadwinner status was encoded in welfare state policy."[41] Veterans of the First World War were particularly vocal in their de-mands for economic entitlement during the Great Depression. Disability and unemployment seriously challenged hegemonic masculinity, but veterans found ways to challenge the state on the masculine terms of entitlement and citizenship. Although their protests were not entirely successful, the appeal to service, patri-otic duty, and heroics did help to create changes to pensions and allowances.

Disability, however, remained an uneasy fit, and some veterans were hesitant to use discourses of disability that revealed a compromised manhood but in-stead wanted to claim sacrifice, survival, and normalcy.[42] As Mark Humphries has concluded in regard to veterans of the First World War suffering from psychological trauma, the collision of discourses of manly soldiers and dis-ability meant that some veterans were constructed as inferior, femininized, and undeserving of support.[43] Although very different disabilities were experi-enced, all ultimately challenged dominant constructions of masculinity. Sig-nificantly, however, disabled soldiers or those injured in the course of their work (regardless of the wide variety of different disabilities) were assumed to be substantively different from, and ultimately more deserving than, men who worked and performed as freaks.[44] If disabled veterans could at least appeal to the memory of their full masculinity, the same was not true of other disabled persons who were born with a disability or who acquired a disability in early childhood.

The construction and care of the disabled in Canadian history have been marked by a sense of absolute difference. In the nineteenth century, institutions housed a wide variety of people deemed to be too difficult to otherwise integrate into productive society, so the poor, the criminal, and the disabled of all ages were often institutionalized together. These earlier efforts were premised on providing society with needed protection rather than on providing care. As modern institutions emerged that were more specialized in their care, those people deemed to be disabled were separated from other groups, but the elasticity of the term "disabled" continued to pose challenges for those wanting to label, categorize, and sort people. As Veronica Strong-Boag has shown in regard to children with disabilities, class often had a profound impact on the types of care (both medical and social) available to families.[45] By the 1920s doctors had begun to encourage institutionalization, and whereas some families resisted, others could not or did not. Although the history of institutionalization in the twentieth century reveals the tragic limits of care, it did provide families with respite and the gloss of support.[46] Outside of institutions, people classified as disabled faced serious challenges in attending school, being treated as capable, and overcoming the assumptions that went along with common labels like "handicapped" or "crippled."[47] Mona Gleason has referred to mainstream treatment of children with disabilities by medical and educational professionals as a "eugenically-inspired pedagogy of failure" that lasted until the 1940s. This failure persisted in marking out the disabled as a "serious threat to individual health, public health, and the nation-state."[48]

Legislation to address disabled peoples and issues of employment was introduced first in 1937 for the blind and then in 1954 with the Disabled Persons Act.[49] Employment avenues remained limited because of assumptions about the capacity of people with disabilities. For little people, sideshows were avenues for work in a society premised on an almost singular understanding of adult body size. Although there is no hard evidence in Canada, research from the United States suggests that, in the 1930s, work in entertainment sectors was one of the more viable options for little people.[50] A 1944 *Maclean's* magazine article titled "Midget Mystery" noted, "Most midgets have been compelled to earn their living in the carnival field or in show business, but many have special talents which if they were several feet taller would equip them for business or professions."[51] Because discriminatory beliefs made finding work very difficult,

work as a midget performer was a reasonable option, which allowed performers to show off their many skills and abilities. At the same time, however, performances, which were typically narrated, managed, and staged by people other
than the performers themselves, could reinforce negative assumptions about
people of short stature.

Miniature Worlds

In this section, I focus particularly on evidence from Johnny J. Jones Shows
and Conklin Shows since they spent a considerable amount of time in Canada,
although other companies travelled across Ontario with midget performers in
the period, including Rubin and Cherry Shows and Royal American Shows.[52]
Johnny J. Jones travelled with and showed at least two different midget "families":
the Marechal Midgets and the Walter Singer Midgets. In 1920, the company
reported in *Billboard Magazine* that it was also showing the Johnny J. Jones
Midgets, whose permanent home was the Midget Castle in Orlando, Florida.
The unidentified writer also noted, "Mr. Jones' European agent has just cabled
that he has secured for him two more wonderful midgets."[53] As with many
other sideshow acts, these acts were contracted to particular shows for the
season, and the decision to travel with a particular show depended upon job
choices, financial reward, and sometimes simply opportunity. In the 1920s and
early 1930s, Johnny J. Jones Shows frequently held the CNE contract before it
was awarded to Conklin in 1937. Patty Conklin, an American by birth, who
ended up working in and largely defining the Canadian carnival scene from
the 1930s onward, owned and operated Conklin Shows. In the 1920s the operation was small, but it grew fairly consistently and included midget performers
from at least 1930.[54] In the early 1940s, Conklin Shows offered "Tiny Town,"
which featured glamorously styled performers identified as Jack Pearl and the
Duke of Tiny Town, whom advertisements declared had appeared in the 1939
film *The Wizard of Oz*. Not presented as "munchkins," they performed in tux-
edos, along with at least one female performer, identified as Lillie, who wore
fine dress and fur. In the late 1930s and early 1940s, Conklin also offered midget
shows, including "Midget Village" and "Weeny Teeny Tiny Town."[55]

In many cases, families were constructed out of a number of different performers. The narrative of family, however, worked to create a cute quality: tiny
mothers and fathers with tiny children made a cute, miniature, heterosexual
family. The Marechal Midgets were allegedly of European royalty and consisted
of Prince Dennison of France and his sisters Princess Marguerite and Lady
Little. They were shown with members allegedly of the Belgian royal family,
Duchess Leona and Baroness Simone. The troupe often included Baron Raymond as well. A 1926 newspaper article reported, "The little folk, whose average

weight is 29 pounds, carried themselves in a regal manner, befitting the clothes they had made in their native France."[56]

Perhaps of all the standard sideshow performances, midget shows were the least controversial for audiences and the least challenging to witness. Unlike with contortionists, sword-swallowers, or fire-eaters, there was no sense of risk involved in the displays, unless a little person decided to perform one of those talents separately. Girl shows relied on sex to sell (and were a success by most accounts), as did so-called "Half and Half" shows, which featured allegedly intersexed people. Other performers like Fat Ladies and the Elephant-Skinned Man appeared in states of undress to reveal their "unusual" conditions. Their differences were billed to consumers as both alluring and revolting. In contrast, the midget performances were glamorous, cute, and charming. In regard to the miniature, Stewart argues, "What is, in fact, lost in this idealized miniaturization of the body is sexuality and hence the danger of power. The body becomes an image, and all manifestations of will are transferred to the position of the observer, the voyeur. The body exists not in the domain of lived reality but in the domain of commodity relations."[57] Happy performances defined by glamour, beauty, and talent set performers with short stature apart from other freak spectacles that were intended to be jarring. Their managers also did not provoke them to make outrageous, disturbing, or angry sounds on stage.[58]

The naming of troupes indicated a degree of paternalism. The troupes were named not after the performers but after their managers. The Singer Midgets, for example, performed from 1910 into the 1940s and were named after their manager, Leo Singer.[59] Their association with cuteness as a commodity aesthetic, combined with their ownership by managers, marked them out as childlike possessions. In this way, their performances provided a miniature version of the dominant ideal of paternal authority as well as filial and managerial obedience. Paternalism here was presented as benevolent, proper, and good. The men in the midget shows who had titles and families and in most other ways mimicked white, middle-class, masculine authority had their masculinity circumscribed by scale.

The photographs of midget shows were deliberate in their construction. They were not candid shots but carefully crafted, assembled, and posed photographs designed to relay a particular message. Some of the photographs were printed as postcards, which were sold by the performers to increase their income. Patrons may have bought them as souvenirs for themselves or as gifts for friends and relatives. The photographs were also used in promotional materials like souvenir programs as well as in advertisements in newspapers or trade publications like *Billboard Magazine*. The photographs served as promotional material designed to attract positive attention and build audiences. They reveal the staging

Figure 8.1 A postcard of the Marechal Midgets performing with
the Johnny J. Jones Exposition, ca. 1920s. This was one of many
postcards for visitors to purchase as souvenirs. Circus World
Museum, Robert L. Parkinson Library and Research Centre,
Carnivals 18-2-3, box 2.

of performances and the dominant messages associated with them but little or
nothing about the actual people in them.

   Photographs of little people as sideshow performers followed particular
conventions. Unlike other sideshow workers, performers in midget shows were
almost always fully clothed in fashionable garb and adorned with makeup and
jewellery. Performers struck dignified, graceful poses. Indeed, the photographs
are in some ways unremarkable since they look like others of families or friends

Figure 8.2 The Johnny J. Jones Midgets with their managers and local authorities, ca. 1920s. Circus World Museum, Robert L. Parkinson Library and Research Centre, Carnivals 18-2-3, box 2.

gathered for the purpose of leisure or work. The photograph in Figure 8.1, reproduced as a postcard, shows the well-dressed performers arranged by height. The women, sporting fashionable clothing and hairstyles, are adorned with jewellery and makeup. The setting of scale in the photographs is significant in shaping the reading of the bodies as extraordinary. Placing a "normal"-sized man – in this case, their manager, Johnny J. Jones – in the photograph was the essential factor in showing the difference in scale. Juxtaposition was a common means of staging freaks to highlight discrepancies in scale.[60] A closer reading of some of the photographs, however, suggests a more complex staging in regard to masculinity and disability.

In Figure 8.2 the performers are lined up in front of men and a woman. The Johnny J. Jones Midgets are clearly still performing, as they are dressed in their usual garb, whereas some of the men and the woman are more casually dressed. The uniformed men behind the performers include a police constable, the chief of police, and the staff inspector. Both their dress and the authority of their stance are remarkably different. That the men stand upright, look directly forward, and appear to be strong and powerful magnifies their size. The performers,

Figure 8.3 A posed heterosexual couple and other performers in the "World's Smallest Home" show at the Canadian National Exhibition, ca. 1937–1941. Canadian National Exhibition Archives, General Photos Collection, COI, file 214, photograph by G. Hollies.

especially Prince Dennison, seem pleased and happy but appear to be literally shrinking into their married managers' protective embrace. They seem far more like children than famous adult aristocrats.

Paternalism worked to shore up ideals of middle-class heterosexual family structures. Anxiety about the modern family man's relationship to patriarchal power from the 1920s to the 1950s echoed through discourses of hegemonic masculinity, yet as Robert Rutherdale's work reveals, it did not necessarily pierce the structure of actual families in the 1950s.[61] If midget shows revealed the proper paternal managerial authority, some acts also showed paternal authority in relation to domesticity. At the CNE in the early 1940s, the sideshow included "World's Smallest Home." Although the photographic evidence may reveal some eccentricities in "home life," including a showgirl, a Hawaiian-style dancer, and a drummer, a small couple in an idealized domestic setting anchored the home (Figure 8.3).

Most of the popular midget shows deliberately mimicked middle-class or upper-class consumer and family patterns. Thus they were not threatening to audience members or authorities invested in ensuring white, middle-class values as state and social values for all. The miniature was simply a scaled-down version of "normal." The miniature was adorable, cute, and easier to identify with than other sideshow acts that reaffirmed or challenged audience assumptions in jarring or sexualized ways. These acts provided messages that were understandable and easily digestible. Like the messages they sent, they were orderly, simplified, and entertaining. Men and women dressed in fine clothing, some had the titles of the European aristocracy, and most were shown as families. Yet including the sideshow manager or owner also reinforced the childlike state of the cute bodies that feminized the spectacles and reaffirmed claims to male, middle-class, managerial authority. Here was the appropriate working of the world – a white, middle-class man with significant benevolent authority surrounded by his happy childlike workers, who clearly thought of themselves as family. Audience members could consume messages of patriarchal and paternal authority that resonated with wider messages of the need to reaffirm the white, middle-class family, anchored by hegemonic masculinity. Its respectable message and cute presentation of the paternal father figure and childlike bodies easily sold to more conservative audiences.

Conclusion

Hegemonic masculinity in Ontario in the period from the 1900s to the 1950s included powerful assumptions about ability. Although hegemonic masculinity was not static in this period, it remained fundamentally wed to particular ideas of ability in its maintenance of qualities like vigour, strength, and athleticism. For men who found themselves impaired over their life course, especially those injured in military service, their appeals to the state were premised on how their manly efforts had ultimately ended up compromising their future prospects, making them deserving of compensation. For other men like little people in the period under discussion here, their appeals to masculinity could not be the same. In the case of little people, their cultural association with the cute and the miniature feminized them regardless of their actual gender and turned them into spectacles where scale mattered in defining a subordinate masculinity that was "cute" in its mimicking of hegemonic ideals.

Notes

1 "Putting Men Together Again," *Globe*, August 23, 1919, 8.
2 I use the term "freak" throughout this chapter, but I do so following usage in critical studies of the freak show. As Susan Stewart argues, freaks are of culture, not nature. Susan Stewart, *On Longing: Narratives of the Miniature, the Gigantic, the Souvenir, the Collection* (Baltimore, MD: Johns Hopkins University Press, 1984), 109.
3 Tripp's performances continued until his death in 1930.

4 Canadian National Exhibition Archives (CNEA), *Official Catalogue of the CNE, 1919,* 43. Such performances did continue. In 1942 Conklin Shows advertised that Andrew Gawley was performing with the company. Gawley, who had lost his hands in an accident, performed with prosthetics made of steel, showing how he could write, sew, eat, and repair bicycles. North America Carnival Museum and Archives (NACMA), Conklin Scrapbook 1942, "At the Fair," Regina newspaper clipping, July 27, 1942. In 1957 Royal American Shows featured Jose de Leon, whose act included him shaving and combing his hair with his feet. "Born Without Arms, Uses Feet," *Fort William Daily Times Journal,* August 3, 1957.

5 Mona Gleason, "Size Matters: Medical Experts, Educators, and the Provision of Health Services to Children in Early to Mid-Twentieth Century English Canada," in *Healing the World's Children: Interdisciplinary Perspectives on Child Health in the Twentieth Century,* ed. Cynthia Comacchio, Janet Golden, and George Weisz, 176–202 (Montreal and Kingston: McGill-Queen's University Press, 2008).

6 In particular, I note that disability is debated among current communities of people of short stature.

7 Robert Bogdan, *Freak Show: Presenting Human Oddities for Amusement and Profit* (Chicago: University of Chicago Press, 1988), 146.

8 R.W. Connell, *Masculinities* (Berkeley: University of California Press, 1995); R.W. Connell and James W. Messerschmidt, "Hegemonic Masculinity: Rethinking the Concept," *Gender and Society* 19, 6 (2005): 829–59. Although I have used "manliness" and "masculinity" as synonyms here, I note that some of the responses to Connell's work have sought to position manliness as a separate theoretical construct differentiated from her understanding of masculinities. On the difference, see Jeff Hearn, "From Hegemonic Masculinity to the Hegemony of Men," *Feminist Theory* 5, 1 (2004): 49–72. As outlined in the introduction to the present volume, the Canadian scholarship includes Craig Heron, "The Boys and Their Booze: Masculinities and Public Drinking in Working-Class Hamilton, 1890–1946," *Canadian Historical Review* 86, 3 (2005): 411–52; Tina Loo, "Of Moose and Men," *Western Historical Quarterly* 32, 3 (2001): 269–319; Christopher Dummitt, *The Manly Modern: Masculinity in Postwar Canada* (Vancouver: UBC Press, 2007); and Christopher J. Greig and Wayne J. Martino, eds., *Canadian Men and Masculinities: Historical and Contemporary Perspectives* (Toronto: Canadian Scholars' Press, 2012).

9 A notable exception here is in regard to childhood and youth. The literature on disability in Canadian history includes specific studies of medical and psychiatric conditions, especially those arising from military conflict. The histories influenced by critical disabilities studies are fewer but include Geoffrey Reaume, *Remembrance of Patients Past: Patient Life at the Toronto Hospital for the Insane, 1870–1940* (Toronto: Oxford University Press, 2000); Mona Gleason, *Small Matters: Canadian Children in Sickness and Health* (Montreal and Kingston: McGill-Queen's University Press, 2013); and on disability in Canada, *Disability Studies Quarterly* 28, 1 (2008). For a historiographical overview of literature on disability in Canadian history, see Geoffrey Reaume, "Disability History in Canada: Present Work in the Field and Future Prospects," *Canadian Journal of Disability Studies* 1, 1 (2012): 35–81.

10 Russell Shuttleworth, Nikki Wedgwood, and Nathan J. Wilson, "The Dilemma of Disabled Masculinity," *Men and Masculinities* 15, 2 (2012): 174–94.

11 For more on the appropriate use of language, see Little People of America, "Frequently Asked Questions," http://www.lpaonline.org/faq-#Definition. For historical definitions of "midget" and "dwarf" as they were used in the sideshows, see *Howard Y. Barry Presents Singer's Midgets in a New Streamline Novelty: A Midget Circus Review* (n.p., ca. 1940s).

12 Stewart, *On Longing,* 111.

13 Quoted in Richard Howells and Michael M. Chemers, "Midget Cities: Utopia, Utopianism, and the *Vor-schein* of the 'Freak' Show," *Disability Studies Quarterly* 25, 3 (2005), http://dsq-sds.org/article/view/579/756.

14 Robert W. Marks, "Midget Mystery," *Maclean's*, October 1, 1944, 18.

15 Tina Loo and Carolyn Strange, "The Travelling Show Menace: Contested Regulation in Turn-of-the-Century Ontario," *Law and Society Review* 29, 4 (1995): 639–67; Keith Walden, *Becoming Modern in Toronto: The Industrial Exhibition and the Shaping of a Late Victorian Culture* (Toronto: University of Toronto Press, 1997); Guy Scott, *A History of Agricultural Societies and Fairs in Ontario, 1792–1992*, (Peterborough: Ontario Association of Agricultural Societies, 1992), 119.

16 Conklin Shows went through a number of modest name changes over the period. For a business history of Conklin, see NACMA, John Thurston, "Scenes from the Midway," unpublished manuscript. My thanks to Dr. Thurston for sharing his manuscript with me.

17 Communication on and between these partners can be found in Archives of Ontario (AO), RG23-26-20, file 1.11, Circuses and Travelling Shows, 1913–1917, and file 1.39, Circuses and Travelling Shows, 1919; and AO, RG56-1-1-36, Travelling Shows, 1913–1933, memorandum to Dr. J.D. Monteith, Provincial Treasurer, regarding Windsor District Maccabees Border Cities Charity, November 9, 1926. Sideshows sometimes broadcast these partnerships. See NACMA, Conklin Scrapbook 1930, "Everybody Loves Circus," newspaper clipping; and NACMA, Conklin Scrapbook 1942, "Attractions at Conklin Shows" and "Stars of Sideshows to Help Red Cross," newspaper clippings. Not all carnival-charity partnerships were financially successful. The Shriners requested a refund of the amusement tax it had paid since the sideshow did not pay the hospital charity anything. AO, RG56-1-1-36, Travelling Shows, 1913–1933, letter to Dr. J.D. Monteith, Provincial Treasurer, October 7, 1926. See also Scott, *History of Agricultural Societies*, 119.

18 *Billboard Magazine*, April 19, 1919, 43. The report refers to the Great War Veterans Association, which operated from 1917 to 1925. *Billboard* was the largest and most popular of the trade publications for circuses, sideshows, and carnivals at the time.

19 *Billboard Magazine*, March 29, 1930, 124. See also Jerry Holtman [pseud.], *Freak Show Man: Uncensored Memoirs of Harry Lewiston – the Incredible Scoundrel* (Los Angeles, CA: Holloway House, 1968), 217.

20 Loo and Strange, "Travelling Show Menace."

21 Bogdan, *Freak Show*, 149. The literature on Tom Thumb is too large to list here, but his relationship to Barnum is one of the most well-studied cases.

22 Ibid., 162, 109; see also 108–111 for a wider discussion of the aggrandized mode.

23 *Billboard Magazine*, August 2, 1919, 124.

24 AO, Attorney General's Files, Circuses and Travelling Shows, 1910–1914 and 1919–1921, RG23-26-20. See also, for example, Holtman, *Freak Show Man*.

25 Hazel Elves, *It's All Done with Mirrors: A Canadian Carnival Life* (Victoria, BC: Sono Nis, 1977), ch. 3.

26 Janet M. Davis, *The Circus Age: Culture and Society under the American Big Top* (Chapel Hill: University of North Carolina Press, 2002), 143–44.

27 Beverly Kelley, *It Was Better Than Work* (Gerald, MO: Patrice, 1982); "The Fat Man and His Friends," *American Heritage* 17, 4 (1966): 35; Elves, *It's All Done with Mirrors*, ch. 3. Society's exclusion of people with disabilities from meaningful paid employment facilitated the persistence of this argument.

28 Elves, *It's All Done with Mirrors*, 19.

29 Holtman, *Freak Show Man*, 7–13.

30 Donica Belisle, *Retail Nation: Department Stores and the Making of Modern Canada* (Vancouver: UBC Press, 2011); Cynthia Wright, "'Feminine Trifles of Vast Importance':

Writing Gender into the History of Consumption," in *Gender Conflicts: New Essays in Women's History,* ed. Franca Iacovetta and Mariana Valverde, 153–67 (Toronto: University of Toronto Press, 1992).

31 Mariana Valverde, *The Age of Light, Soap and Water: Moral Reform in English Canada, 1885–1925* (Toronto: McClelland and Stewart, 1991); Carolyn Strange, *Toronto's Girl Problem: The Perils and Pleasures of the City, 1880–1930* (Toronto: University of Toronto Press, 1995); Jane Nicholas, *The Modern Girl: Feminine Modernities, the Body, and Commodities in the 1920s* (Toronto: University of Toronto Press, 2015).

32 Patricia Jasen, *Wild Things: Nature, Culture, and Tourism in Ontario, 1790–1914* (Toronto: University of Toronto Press, 1995); Mark Moss, *Manliness and Militarism: Educating Young Boys in Ontario for War* (Don Mills, ON: Oxford University Press, 2001).

33 Moss, *Manliness and Militarism,* 56–57.

34 Lori Merish, "Cuteness and Commodity Aesthetics: Tom Thumb and Shirley Temple," in *Freakery: Cultural Spectacles of the Extraordinary Body,* ed. Rosemarie Garland Thomson (New York: New York University Press, 1996), 187–88.

35 Ibid., 194, original emphasis.

36 Howells and Chemers, "Midget Cities."

37 Gary S. Cross and John K. Walton, *The Playful Crowd: Pleasure Places in the Twentieth Century* (New York: Columbia University Press, 2005), 126. Hollywood continued to hold a limited place for little people in making movies like *The Wizard of Oz* (1939), which became a particular claim to fame among certain sideshow acts. Little people could not become members of the Screen Actors Guild until 1970. Bogdan, *Freak Show,* 163.

38 Dummitt, *Manly Modern,* chs. 2 and 3.

39 Robert H. Babcock, "Blood on the Factory Floor: The Workers' Compensation Movement in Canada and the United States," in *Social Fabric or Patchwork Quilt: The Development of Social Policy in Canada,* ed. Raymond B. Blake and Jeffrey Keshen (Peterborough, ON: Broadview, 58.

40 Lara Campbell, *Respectable Citizens: Gender, Family and Unemployment in Ontario's Great Depression* (Toronto: University of Toronto Press, 2009), 58; Nancy Christie, *Engendering the State: Family, Work and Welfare in Canada* (Toronto: University of Toronto Press, 2000); Dummitt, *Manly Modern,* ch. 3.

41 Campbell, *Respectable Citizens,* 83.

42 Ibid., 164.

43 Mark Humphries, "War's Long Shadow: Masculinity, Medicine, and the Gendered Politics of Trauma, 1914–1939," *Canadian Historical Review* 91, 3 (2010): 518.

44 Russell Shuttleworth and colleagues argue that whereas men with acquired injuries "may be perceived as 'once like us' and may benefit from an empathy as to what terrible circumstances (e.g., accident, illness) befell them, those with early-onset impairments are likely seen as more fundamentally 'other' who from an early age transgress bodily norms." Shuttleworth, Wedgwood, and Wilson, "Dilemma of Disabled Masculinity," 183.

45 Veronica Strong-Boag, *Fostering Nation? Canada Confronts Its History of Childhood Disadvantage* (Waterloo, ON: Wilfrid Laurier University Press, 2011), 55.

46 Ibid., 40.

47 Gleason, *Small Matters,* ch. 6.

48 Ibid., 19.

49 Alvin Finkel, *Social Policy and Practice in Canada* (Waterloo, ON: Wilfrid Laurier University Press, 2006), 252.

50 Betty M. Adelson, "Dwarfs: The Changing Lives of Archetypal 'Curiosities' – and Echoes of the Past," *Disability Studies Quarterly* 25, 3 (2005), http://dsq-sds.org/article/view/576/753.

51 Marks, "Midget Mystery," 18.
52 In 1932 Model Shows of America held the Midway at the CNE, which included a "City of Lilliputians," and in 1934 the Rubin and Cherry Exposition at the CNE highlighted the "Royal Russian Midgets." CNEA, *Official Catalogue of the Canadian National Exhibition, 1932*, 12, and *1934*, 6. In the early 1950s, Royal American's shows travelled the province, attending to smaller towns and cities, and they included a midget circus and Rose's Hollywood Midget Revue. See *Fort William Daily Times Journal*, August 2, 1952; and *Fort William Daily Times Journal*, August 11, 1953.
53 *Billboard Magazine*, February 14, 1920, 91, and January 17, 1920, 75.
54 NACMA, Conklin Scrapbook 1930, "Everybody Loves Circus," newspaper clipping; and Conklin Scrapbook 1935, "Versatile Dwarf Circus Feature," newspaper clipping, *Victoria Daily Times*. Conklin Shows, like other companies, often contracted out the sideshow to managers like Harry Lewiston or Sam Alexander, who would put together the sideshow acts.
55 NACMA, Conklin Scrapbook 1942, newspaper clipping; *Fort William Daily Times Journal*, August 9, 1941; CNEA, *Official Catalogue and Program, 1938*, 18, *1939*, 16, and *1941*, 18.
56 "Newsboys Think Johnny J. Jones Real Swell Guy," *Fort William Daily Times Journal*, August 13, 1926.
57 Stewart, *On Longing*, 124.
58 Holtman, *Freak Show Man*.
59 Bogdan has the performance dates of the Singer Midgets ending in 1935. Bogdan, *Freak Show*, 162. In the 1940s a promotional booklet was published as *Howard Y. Barry Presents Singer's Midgets in a New Streamline Novelty: A Midget Circus Revue* (n.p., ca. 1940s).
60 Bogdan, *Freak Show*, ch. 4.
61 Cynthia Comacchio, "'A Postscript for Father': Defining a New Fatherhood in Interwar Canada," *Canadian Historical Review* 78, 3 (1997): 385–408; Robert Rutherdale, "Fathers in Multiple Roles: Assessing Modern Canadian Fatherhood as a Masculine Category," in *Canadian Men and Masculinities: Historical and Contemporary Perspectives*, ed. Christopher J. Greig and Wayne J. Martino, 76–98 (Toronto: Canadian Scholars' Press, 2012).

9

Claiming "Our Game": Skwx̱wú7mesh Lacrosse and the Performance of Indigenous Nationhood in the Early Twentieth Century

Allan Downey

> *"The Indian never can play as scientifically as the best white players, and it is a lamentable fact, that Lacrosse, and the wind for running, which comes as natural to the red-skin as his dialect, has to be gained on the part of the pale-face, by a gradual course of practice and training ... When civilization tamed the manners and habits of the Indian, it reflected its modifying influence upon his amusements, and thus was Lacrosse gradually divested of its radical rudeness and brought to a more sober sport ... Only a savage people could, would or should play the old game; only such constitutions, such wind and endurance could stand its violence."*
>
> – WILLIAM GEORGE BEERS, *LACROSSE: THE NATIONAL GAME OF CANADA* (1869)

AS THE PRIMARY ARCHITECT of Canada's colonization of the Indigenous game of lacrosse, William George Beers set about convincing Canadians that the game – appropriated from Indigenous peoples and codified according to Victorian perceptions of sport – was an appropriate source for Canada's new national identity. Framing Indigenous masculinity and the game of lacrosse within the proverbial discourse of the bloodthirsty and noble savage, Beers was reflecting on what he and other Montrealers at the Montreal Lacrosse Club now saw as "their game." Introduced to the Haudenosaunee version of the game by the Kanien'kehá:ka from the communities of Kahnawà:ke and Ahkwesáhsne, these influential middle-class British immigrants and anglophone Montrealers formed the Montreal Lacrosse Club in 1856 and set out to control the image that lacrosse conveyed to Canadians by monopolizing it through a series of non-Indigenous organizations, a uniform code of rules, and "informative" works such as Beers's *Lacrosse: The National Game of Canada* (1869).[1] Using visual images, holiday celebrations, popular media reports, and compiled histories, the Montreal Lacrosse Club, and later the Montreal Amateur Athletic Association, recast the game within the accepted Victorian notions of Euro-Canadian masculinity and as a "performative act" of a gendered nationalism that was emulated throughout the Dominion.[2]

During the early years of this process of appropriation, Indigenous athletes continued to compete against non-Indigenous teams in central Canada; this changed dramatically in 1880 when Indigenous athletes were barred from Canadian championship competition.[3] However, Indigenous lacrosse players never defined their relationship to the sport by their ability to participate within non-Indigenous systems of organization. So despite being barred, Indigenous players and teams continued to play intercommunity and ceremonial games and even established their own Indian World Championship. Nonetheless, this race-based discrimination excluded Indigenous players from the very game they had introduced to non-Indigenous peoples, and sadly there were more injustices yet to come. Like in central Canada, Indigenous players were also barred from organized lacrosse competition in British Columbia after the province formed its own organizing body in 1890. Furthermore, the perception of the game as a reflection of a distinct Canadian identity became so pervasive that, in 1889, residential school administrators began to implement the game in residential schools as a method of cultural genocide.[4] Here, an Indigenous game, an important Indigenous cultural and epistemological element, was appropriated by non-Indigenous Canadians and embraced as a marker of national identity, civility, and masculinity that was in the end deemed "Euro-Canadian enough" to be used in the assimilation of Indigenous boys.

The appropriation of lacrosse as a marker of national identity by non-Indigenous Canadians and its subsequent use in residential schools as a tool to coercively assimilate Indigenous boys demonstrate how, throughout the history of Canadian settler-colonialism, a substantial method of instilling the performance of gender – the production, repetition, and "standardization" of gender identities – occurred through sport and recreation.[5] Colonial agents, such as Department of Indian Affairs officials, residential school administrators, and missionaries, as well as national boosters like Beers, attempted to re-engineer and replace Indigenous gender identities and epistemologies. Lacrosse games were both a site and an articulation of these gendered acts, blanketed in a discourse of Canadian nationalism.[6] Lacrosse – as well as organized sport more generally – and its fields of play were recognized for their potential to further the assimilation efforts concurrently pursued through legislation such as the Indian Act and through the residential school system. It was believed that sport could be used to replace and control Indigenous identities, epistemologies, and gender identities.[7]

One of the many Indigenous nations to experience this process was the Coast Salish[8] S̲k̲w̲x̲wú7mesh (Squamish) Nation located on the north shore of Vancouver, in Howe Sound, and in the Squamish River watershed. Although the introduction of this performance of masculinity in the form of lacrosse was imbued with a message intended to facilitate conformity within the new gendered Canadian nationalism, the message of that performance was "interrupted" by the S̲k̲w̲x̲wú7mesh's own interpretation of the game based on their understanding of their nationhood and identities.[9] Introduced to the game by non-Indigenous organizers at residential schools and in the metropolis of Vancouver during the turn of the twentieth century, the S̲k̲w̲x̲wú7mesh quickly embraced lacrosse not in the pursuit of Canadian nationalism, as was the intention of the dominant society, but as an Indigenous game and as citizens of the S̲k̲w̲x̲wú7mesh Nation.[10] Beginning in the early twentieth century, the S̲k̲w̲x̲wú7mesh took this vehicle used for Indigenous assimilation, constructed to represent the dominant society's idealistic notions of masculinity and Canadian nationalism, and redefined it for their own specific needs. Ultimately, they created a "racialized" identity through sport by using lacrosse to articulate S̲k̲w̲x̲wú7mesh nationhood and a pan-Indigenous identity. Their efforts helped to return Indigenous athletes to official championship competition in Canadian lacrosse leagues in the late 1910s, with Indigenous athletes once again becoming some of the most proficient players in Canada.

Faced with the growing settlements in and around S̲k̲w̲x̲wú7mesh territory, the encroachment of the city of Vancouver, and the "civilizing" efforts of Canada's Colonial Age[11] (i.e., residential schools, the Indian Act, and the reserve system) in the second half of the nineteenth century, the S̲k̲w̲x̲wú7mesh participated both willingly and unwillingly in one of the largest transitional eras in modern Indigenous history. British Columbia's lower mainland, including S̲k̲w̲x̲wú7mesh territory, was a region transformed from an Indigenous-controlled space into an area dominated by settler governments and colonial institutions that sought to reform the space as an extension of British – and later Canadian – imperialism.[12] In turn, the identities of the S̲k̲w̲x̲wú7mesh were challenged as they had to redefine the collective distinctiveness they held as both S̲k̲w̲x̲wú7mesh and Coast Salish. Moreover, they had to discover and place themselves within their larger, emerging, imposed – and legal – racialized identity as "Indians."[13] This is not to say they were passive victims to a wave of non-Indigenous imposition and transition. On the contrary, the S̲k̲w̲x̲wú7mesh continued to practise their long-established ceremonies, culture, and worldviews while also participating in a growing, non-Native-controlled world of wage labour and organized sport.[14] Within this changing landscape of power and cultural exchange, the Skwxwú7mesh adapted and absorbed elements of both distant Indigenous nations and non-Native cultures, just as they had always done.[15] Lacrosse is another such example of cultural innovation, but the game was not completely unfamiliar to the Skwxwú7mesh.

The Coast Salish nations of southern coastal British Columbia had known various versions of the game long before the appropriated Haudenosaunee version was introduced to their territories. In the 1930s anthropologist Homer Barnett relayed a story that described an 1820s Xʷməθkʷəẏəm (Musqueam) village on the Fraser River, neighbouring the Skwxwú7mesh, that consisted of seventy-six housing units centred around a lacrosse field.[16] The Chinook and the SqWuqWu'b3sh (Skokomish) in present-day Washington State were described by painter Paul Kane in 1855 as taking great pleasure in the stick and ball game closely related to that of the Nêhiyawak, Anishinaabeg, Dakhóta, and Lakȟóta.[17] By extension, as historian Alexandra Harmon reminds us, ideas, technology, and identities were widely circulated through diverse kinship and transnational relationships among the Coast Salish, so it is almost certain that the Skwxwú7mesh also had a stick form of lacrosse before the Haudenosaunee stick arrived in their territory.[18]

The establishment and growth of the new form of lacrosse on the West Coast was due in large part to British Columbia's entrance into Confederation in 1871.[19] As new non-Indigenous residents arrived from the east, they brought their lacrosse sticks with them and transplanted the game to the new province.[20] As lacrosse developed throughout small-town Canada, middle-class men consciously attempted to establish a cultural hegemony through the game and emulated the example set by the Montreal Amateur Athletic Association.[21] In the British colonialist ideology, as historian Gillian Poulter explains, "the belief in the value of independence, industry, self-discipline, and moral behaviour was part and parcel of middle-class Victorian respectability ... These were all qualities Victorians believed to be inculcated by sport."[22] These local "moral entrepreneurs" and sport enthusiasts were attempting to take these British colonialist understandings of sport and apply them to a game "native" to the land – legitimizing their claim to a distinctive identity connected to place – an undertaking that both differentiated the game as Canadian and maintained the Victorian understanding of sport as respectable competition.[23]

Embedded within this construction of Canadian nationalism through lacrosse was the perception that the sport was a manly pursuit. It was constructed as a place where Canadian men could engage in aggressive, physical competition while acting within the Victorian perceptions of gentlemanly accord.[24] As Nancy Bouchier articulates,

Town boosters who sought locally feasible ways in which to play sport considered lacrosse a respectable sport that enhanced the physical and moral health of local male youth; honourable pursuits like lacrosse ultimately turned boys into men. The repeated themes of boyish sport and young manhood, echoed in early writings on lacrosse, became central to its promotion locally and nationally.[25]

Hence lacrosse was transformed into a performative act showcasing the qualities that Canadians hoped to emulate as distinctly Canadian and as part of the "masculinizing project" – the Westernized cultural practice of boys becoming men, learned through sport.[26]

For non-Natives, the new organized club form of the game of lacrosse could be found from Nova Scotia to Alberta by 1883 and truly took on a national presence with the formation of British Columbia's first organizing body in March 1890.[27] The formation of the British Columbia Amateur Lacrosse Association cemented the game's presence on the West Coast, but it also continued the injustice against Indigenous peoples initiated in central Canada.[28] As a founding rule, the lacrosse association stated that "no Indians or other person of color shall be eligible for membership in the clubs of this Association."[29] Certainly, this racialized discrimination was part and parcel of the reform movements initiated in the previous decades that had attempted to recast the Indigenous territories in the image of the white-settler society.[30] For British Columbians, the game became a further site for the performance of not only masculinity but also whiteness, which was ensured by the founding rule of racialized exclusion. Although the game grew quickly and by 1900 had drawn a large following in the cities of Vancouver, Victoria, and New Westminster, the Skwxwú7mesh remained on the fringes of the sport. This exclusion, however, changed with the forced introduction of the game to Indigenous youth in 1904 and 1905.

By the end of the nineteenth century, sports and recreation played a significant role in residential schools across Canada, as administrators felt that athletics would help the process of assimilation.[31] Beyond the gendered vocational training students received, recreational activities were also infused with Victorian gender "ideals," and games deemed proper for each sex were divided accordingly. As Eric D. Anderson observes concerning the Navajo residential school experience in the United States, "With these schools came the structure and culture of colonial sports. Sports such as football, basketball, baseball and boxing were thought to produce qualities desirable to the colonizers, in that they represent masculinized territorialization through struggle and triumph against others."[32] Although sports such as baseball and later basketball were encouraged by certain schools for both sexes, administrators often limited their annual report reflections to the advantages of sport as an inculcator of disciplined masculinity.[33]

Despite the celebration and exploitation of lacrosse's Indigenous origins even while it was being appropriated, the game was perceived to be in closer proximity to its non-Indigenous advocates than to the Indigenous peoples and their understandings of physical culture. It was strongly associated with the Victorian ideals of "muscular Christianity" by non-Native enthusiasts and hence envisioned as a perfect tool with which Indigenous children could be made to embrace such ideals. Notwithstanding the game's popularity in Vancouver and the surrounding area, the new form of lacrosse was first introduced to the Skwxwú7mesh only when it appeared at the St. Mary's Indian Residential School in 1904, the Squamish Indian Residential School (also known as St. Paul's) in 1905, and the Sechelt Indian Residential School in 1906.[34] As Janice Forsyth details, "church and state attempted to replace traditional practices, like the Potlatch and Sundance ceremonies, with activities that were seemingly secular but were imbued with Christian religious ideals, and relied on Euro-Canadian sports and games to help them accomplish this task."[35]

As Skwxwú7mesh Elder Louis Miranda (Sxaaltxw) explains, the arrival of the Roman Catholic Oblates of Mary Immaculate and eventually the residential school system at first reaffirmed the Skwxwú7mesh's desire to maintain their pride and culture. However, as the missionaries' "civilizing" efforts intensified, as evidenced by the implementation of the "Durieu system"[36] and residential schools, the Skwxwú7mesh were increasingly stripped of both:

When religion first came here, they were taught that [i.e., to have pride] also, but it was a late departure. When they took the children away, that is when the people started to lose their pride ... The old man Joe Thomas, my wife's stepfather, he said before the white man came, our people were very close, and then when the white man came, we changed, we changed a little bit, and then when the priest came, we started to change altogether ... We lost our Indian culture but we still had our language. *But it was when the school came, then he says, that is when we lost everything.*[37]

Despite the introduction of lacrosse as a component of the encroachment of Vancouver's and Canada's "civilizing" efforts, it provided an arena in which Skwxwú7mesh boys and men challenged some of the colonizing endeavours, particularly discourses of assimilation that degraded Indigenous masculinity and thus denied Indigenous men's self-determination. For the Skwxwú7mesh, colonial imposition, urbanization, and sport combined to create a contested space in which an Indigenous identity was reformed from elements of their historic understanding of what it meant to be Skwxwú7mesh. At a particularly poignant time when Indigenous nations were being undermined within the colonial borders of Canada, the Sḵwx̱wú7mesh Nation used lacrosse to articulate and instill a reassertion of Sḵwx̱wú7mesh nationhood and a pan-Indigenous identity that connected it to other Indigenous nations and their players. Although lacrosse was introduced in residential schools, as it was taken up by Sḵwx̱wú7mesh players, lacrosse helped to foster a growing surge of Indigenous political activity in the early twentieth century. One residential school pupil, Andy Paull (Te Qoitechetahl or Xwechtáal)[38] experienced this first-hand, and his story illustrates the influential role the game had in facilitating Indigenous political action during this period.

From a young age, Paull had been recognized as a potential leader among the Sḵwx̱wú7mesh. At the age of seven, he was called before the Sḵwx̱wú7mesh chiefs and chosen to be among the first class of students to attend the Squamish Indian Residential School in 1899.[39] As Father Herbert Dunlop reveals, "Andy went to school and his purpose in going was not to learn how to become a white man. He went there to learn how to use the tools of the white man, and with these tools to speak for and fight for the rights of his people."[40] One of those critical tools that Andy Paull learned was the game of lacrosse, which was introduced at the residential school in 1905 while he was in attendance.[41] Temporarily, sport and recreation offered students a break from the monotonous regime of residential school life.[42] On a longer-term basis, the introduction of lacrosse offered Paull and the Sḵwx̱wú7mesh a mechanism to maintain and develop their cultural independence and identity by reappropriating an Indigenous element as their own. Through his attendance at the residential school, his subsequent tenure at the Cayley law office, and his appointment as secretary of the Squamish Council in 1911, Paull developed a working knowledge and a voice pertaining to Sḵwx̱wú7mesh political affairs.[43] As Paull was discovering his voice as a political representative of the Sḵwx̱wú7mesh Nation, he and a number of other Sḵwx̱wú7mesh leaders helped to establish a new culture element and to create a racialized identity through the sport.

The onslaught of the colonial system that Canada imposed on Indigenous peoples introduced a series of significant traumas, but it also reasserted and facilitated new responses from Indigenous peoples that were uniquely their own. Within these spaces of colonial control, Indigenous peoples carved out for themselves paths of resistance and control – however limited – and new forms of identity that would help them to establish their voice in the arenas of politics, union formation, and sport in the early and mid-twentieth century. As Kim Anderson explains, a common value held by Indigenous peoples is a "continuous process of change" in spite of, and in resistance to, settler-colonialism.[44] Lacrosse was one such example and is best understood in relation to an abridged Sḵwx̱wú7mesh creation story of progress and regeneration:

Now after the disaster the people started to multiply again but in the years [of] confusion that followed the flood, all their culture had disappeared ... Although they were the descendants of the first people, the catastrophe had made them entirely different ... A man appeared out of the air to help them rehabilitate themselves. His [name was] T-hii-ss ... [and] this man was known as the trans-former. He showed the people methods of cooking, of preserving, of hygiene and of morals and decency. Most of the people of the coast met him with great kind-ness and respect but occasionally a man would decide that he knew all he wanted to know and would take no advice ... Now, as T-hii-ss approached Vancouver he met a man who was standing in the sea scrubbing himself with a hemlock bough. T-hii-ss came to him in friendship and attempted to chat with him about the changing times. The man was surly, however, and said that he was not interested but was going to go on living as he had always done. T-hii-ss told him that no man or beast could continue to live in the world unless he changed with the times. At this, [the] man cried ... "Go and mind your own business." This made T-hii-ss so angry that he waved his wand and changed the man and his hemlock bough into "Ss-kly-ulch" or "Standing Still," to be an example till judgement day of a man who would not adapt himself to the times, and to be known to the white people as Siwash Rock.[45]

In essence, sport was an adaptation by the Skwx̱wú7mesh that enabled them to avoid becoming like the static entity "Standing Still," and it was a strategy resulting from their own progression. Stories such as "The Legend of Progress," quoted here, or the Coast Salish story of the Great Flood, as historian Keith Carlson reminds us, follow in the tradition of Coast Salish adaptation and regeneration:[46]

Such stories do much more than help contemporary Coast Salish generations come to appreciate what their ancestors experienced in the distant past. Equally important is the role they play in guiding successive generations in negotiating responses to new events and happenings ... Perceived through local Indigenous modes of history we catch glimpses of the continuity in change, as well as the causes of change in continuity.[47]

For the Skwx̱wú7mesh, lacrosse (as with baseball and soccer) was that continuity in change; it became a new means of identity reformation and an articulation of their nationhood.

The first recorded Skwx̱wú7mesh lacrosse team was organized in 1911 under the direction of Andy Paull, but there is evidence that the Skwx̱wú7mesh were organizing teams as early as 1907 for holiday celebrations.[48] For Paull and the other early organizers, lacrosse presented an opportunity not only to (re)build community pride and identity but also to establish relations with non-Natives.[49] One venue that allowed such an opportunity presented itself at the "Indian Sports Days" held each year by non-Indigenous sports promoter Con Jones. Between 1916 and 1919, during these Sports Days, the S̲k̲wx̲wú7mesh competed against a number of Coast Salish lacrosse teams in pursuit of the "Indian Championship," held each year on Victoria Day. Significantly, as Susan Neylan and I have argued elsewhere, Indian Sports Days in British Columbia became a venue in which the S̲k̲wx̲wú7mesh and other Indigenous nations subverted the Indian Act and displaced the colonial agendas that sought to assimilate them.[50] These early competitions also served as a springboard for the S̲k̲wx̲wú7mesh to begin competing in non-Indigenous lacrosse leagues, effectively ending the ban against Indigenous athletes in British Columbia.

Together with the Indian Sports Days, labour organizing also helped to foster the establishment of S̲k̲wx̲wú7mesh lacrosse teams that would go on to compete in non-Indigenous leagues. At the turn of the twentieth century, with Vancouver in the midst of its economic and industrial boom, the S̲k̲wx̲wú7mesh played an active role in the development of Vancouver's industrial economy, having established themselves as proficient longshoremen since the 1860s as well as highly successful pan–Coast Salish union organizers.[51] In 1913 the S̲k̲wx̲wú7mesh workers formed a branch of the International Longshoremen's Association (ILA), of which Andy Paull was a key member.[52] The labour organization of the S̲k̲wx̲wú7mesh and the development of athletic teams in the early twentieth century coincided with a growing articulation of Indigenous rights by Indigenous political activists. This relationship is clearly demonstrated by the direct connection that existed between Andy Paull, the ILA, and one of the first competitive S̲k̲wx̲wú7mesh lacrosse teams.

Beginning in 1919, the Squamish Indians lacrosse team, organized by Andy Paull, began competing in the modest three-team City Senior Amateur League in Vancouver. It was one of the first regularly competitive S̲k̲wx̲wú7mesh lacrosse teams to engage in official league competition.[53] Unlike the situation in central Canada, where Indigenous athletes continued to be barred from competition, the governing body in British Columbia changed its ban on Indigenous participation with the entrance of the S̲k̲wx̲wú7mesh team. The evidence as to why the British Columbia Lacrosse Association (BCLA) reversed, or at least overlooked, its ban on Indigenous players in the West suggests a connection between Con Jones (who played a role in the league's organization), Andy Paull, and the attempt by the BCLA to restore the game's former popularity. In May 1919 the BCLA began making a number of rule changes, including shortening the field, reducing intermission and period times, and curbing excessive rough play, all in an attempt "to give the spectators a big run for their money, without taking too much of their time."[54] Continuing to see the game's popularity wane in both participation and spectator attendance, the BCLA struggled to find participants for the 1919 season and was hoping to find new ways to draw fans back to the game. Enter Andy Paull and the Squamish Indians (Figure 9.1).

Until that time, Paull's team continued to compete against other Indigenous teams in "Indian Championships" at Sports Days and in exhibition games against non-Indigenous teams, but the absence of the Squamish Indians from official league competition persisted. Nearing the June start date of league competition, and with only one team confirmed, the BCLA allowed the Squamish Indians and a third organization to play in the amateur league. Beyond the shortage in teams, there was an additional factor that enabled the team to enter league competition, effectively ending the ban, namely the relationship between Andy Paull and Con Jones. It was at the Indian Sports Days in the 1910s, which Andy Paull and the Sḵwx̱wú7mesh had helped to organize, that Paull and Jones first met and struck up a relationship that eventually led to the Sḵwx̱wú7mesh entering non-Indigenous lacrosse competition. It is more than coincidental that Jones – who knew the drawing power of Indigenous athletes as "performers" for non-Indigenous audiences and had a relationship with Andy Paull – was involved in league operations and attempting to help repopularize the game in Vancouver when the Sḵwx̱wú7mesh team was included in league competition. Add to this Andy Paull, a skilled Indigenous rights activist and organizer, who was further able to convince the league to overturn or at least ignore the rule.[55]

Just as in times past, and much to the relief of Con Jones and the BCLA, Indigenous athletes continued to be a popular drawing card for the purposes of gate receipts. Paull and Jones's relationship further points to the complexity of the interactions in "contact zones" such as lacrosse. Although the vestiges of Canada's enactment of colonialism as a coordinated structure of dispossession were never absent, relationships between Indigenous peoples and non-Indigenous Canadians were not infinitely or automatically negative or destructive. Rather, as Mary-Ellen Kelm explains, "social relations in the contact zone can be surprising, atypical, carnivalesque, or they might be overdetermined by gendered, classed, sexualized, and racialized structures that emerge within them. Contact zones mark out territories within the grand narrative of nation-building and operate at the micro-historical level."[56] Sometimes those nation-building activities in "contact zones" were concerned not with Canadian nation building but with a repositioning and articulation of Indigenous nationhood. This repositioning and articulation of Indigenous nationhood through lacrosse and its networks occurred in highly gendered ways, as both Indigenous understandings of lacrosse and settler-colonial ideas about sports

Figure 9.1 Andy Paull *(first on right)* and the Squamish Indians lacrosse team, ca. late 1920s or early 1930s. North Vancouver Museum and Archives, key 11071, inventory 7119.

and masculinity sanctioned this particular "contact zone" as an arena where it was almost exclusively men who could participate directly. This male orientation, of course, had an important effect on shaping lacrosse's possibilities – and limitations – as a means of articulating Sḵwx̱wú7mesh nationhood, empowering Indigenous identities, and decolonizing intercultural encounters. The impact of lacrosse in the early twentieth century, however, went beyond the actual players and individual games, resonating in important ways through the building of Indigenous transnational networks and the shaping of communities, kinship, and identities.

Competing in the City Senior Amateur Lacrosse League for several seasons and consistently playing in front of 1,500 to 3,500 spectators, the Sḵwx̱wú7mesh team – renamed the International Longshoremen's Association (ILA) in 1920 – experienced a great deal of success and was often regarded as one of the most competitive and popular teams in the league.[57] The Sḵwx̱wú7mesh International Longshoremen's Association (ILA) union team claimed its first championship in 1921, marking the beginning of lacrosse proficiency for the Sḵwx̱wú7mesh Nation that would last until the beginning of the Second World War.[58] In 1923 the team captured the local North Shore Senior "B" title – only one level below the highest level of competition – and followed that up with five consecutive titles between 1925 and 1929 while reaching the provincial finals three times in that period.[59] Furthermore, the union lacrosse teams of the early 1920s served as a catalyst for Skwxwú7mesh players to begin playing with non-Indigenous teams and for the development of the North Shore Indians, a team that would be part of the reintroduction of Indigenous teams to Canada's top national competition at the Senior "A" level.

By 1930 some of the greatest players ever to come out of the Skwxwú7mesh Nation were competing at the highest level for the national Senior "A" championship of Canada, represented by the Mann Cup. Although Indigenous athletes were secretly competing with non-Indigenous teams in central Canada as "ringers,"[60] they remained on the fringes of Canadian national competition due to the lingering effects of the 1880 ban. On the West Coast, in contrast, Indigenous athletes were openly competing and identified as Skwxwú7mesh players. With a lacrosse stick in hand, Andy Paull helped to provide the Skwxwú7mesh Nation with a means to escape, if only temporarily, the harsh realities of the Great Depression. While the docks slowed and longshoring increasingly waned for the Skwxwú7mesh during the Depression, lacrosse became a new means for a select few men to acquire an income. Further reflecting the crossroads of lacrosse, Skwxwú7mesh nationhood, employment, and inter–Coast Salish community ties – including romantic relationships – Elder Dave Jacobs (Paitsmauk) recalls a story he heard from his uncle as a young boy:

> The majority of the lacrosse players of the '36 team were fishermen. They would get on their fish boats, and they would go up north [into Nuxalk Nation territory] to say Bella [Coola], Bella Bella, maybe Ocean Falls, and there were canneries. The Native women, they worked in these processing plants and stuff. Anyway, these guys would go up fishing, and they would come back ... My uncle Dan Baker, he got involved in lacrosse later, but he said, "When we went back up there fishing again," because he was a fisherman, "we would carry a lacrosse stick up there, and we would throw the lacrosse stick on the dock, and if they picked it up they were Skwxwú7mesh." [Laughs.] He said, "Yeah, those kids, they picked up that stick, they are Skwxwú7mesh!" [Laughs.] He was a character.[61]

Throughout the early 1930s, lacrosse audiences varied greatly in number from a few hundred to a few thousand on any given night. Once the most popular sport in Canada, the game was now struggling to survive, and the Great Depression weighed heavily on sport enthusiasts, limiting ticket sales.[62] However, as the decade rolled on, the game witnessed a rejuvenation thanks in part to the development of a new indoor form known as "box lacrosse,"[63] in which the Squamish Indians team would be a central part. In 1931 professional hockey owners in Montreal and Toronto created a new version of the game in the hopes of filling idle hockey arenas in the summertime.[64] From its outset, the development of box lacrosse in central Canada was followed closely on the West Coast, and lacrosse promoters there, including Andy Paull, wasted no time in taking the game up.

Box lacrosse made its first appearance on the West Coast on July 14, 1931, when the province's lacrosse association organized a series of games that were played throughout the summer and that included the Squamish Indians, once again organized by Andy Paull.[65] Late that summer, the Canadian Amateur Lacrosse Association voted to replace the field game with box lacrosse for the senior national championship beginning in 1932.[66] Following suit, in the spring of 1932, both the Ontario and British Columbia lacrosse associations replaced field lacrosse with box lacrosse as their official sports.[67] By 1934 games that drew thousands were pushing the limits of local arenas, and at the centre of all this attention were the Squamish Indians and the support of the team members' communities.[68] As Skwx̱wú7mesh Elders Dave Jacobs (Paitsmauk) and Andrea Jacobs (Sla'wiya) reflect, the strategy to use sports as a cultural marker and a community unifier had been with the Skwx̱wú7mesh well before the adaptation of lacrosse, but the implementation of the game had even more significance due to its Indigenous origins:

> *Paitsmauk:* Of course, all the families and communities are involved, and it's been that way ever since, and that is how – in the tough times – they got all the communities together. Of course, in those days, there was a lot of marriages from different tribes, and families getting together, which was great. The competition started building, and soccer [and lacrosse and baseball] came in and was big, and still is, in all the villages.
>
> *Sla'wiya:* It kept our community close-knit. So it's been going on for years and years, doesn't matter what sport, but when it comes to lacrosse – of course, it's a different story, we think. You know, because of the fact *it's our game!*[69]

Similar to the expression used by the Haudenosaunee, the Skwx̱wú7mesh also reference the game of lacrosse as "our game." Thanks in large part to the zealous celebration of lacrosse as an Indigenous pastime, the Skwx̱wú7mesh, who had not traditionally known the Haudenosaunee game or stick, developed a conception and ownership of lacrosse as something directly linked with Indigenous nations and Skwx̱wú7mesh nationhood. One of the players on the 1930s North Shore Indians team, Skwx̱wú7mesh chief Simon Baker (Khot-La-Cha), further emphasizes this point in his autobiography: "I like most sports, but lacrosse is *our game. Lacrosse is a real Indian game.*"[70] The use of lacrosse by the Sḵwx̱wú7mesh is an example of what Susan Neylan refers to as "cultural collaborations," and it demonstrates the "ways in which Aboriginal culture adopted and adapted colonial forms to create new kinds of performative expressions."[71] In part, the Sḵwx̱wú7mesh lacrosse team became an articulation of both Sḵwx̱wú7mesh nationhood and an "Indian" identity.

As the Sḵwx̱wú7mesh re-entered the highest level of senior indoor competition for the 1935 season, they carried with them a new name and a new contingent of players. It was in that year that Paull began recruiting Haudenosaunee athletes to play out West and renamed the team the North Shore Indians, dropping "Squamish" from the name.[72] Beginning in 1935, the team would no longer carry the Sḵwx̱wú7mesh identity alone but would instead help to solidify a pan-Indigenous identity and relationship for those who participated, their fans, the Sḵwx̱wú7mesh and Haudenosaunee, and more generally the non-Indigenous public that followed the team. As North Vancouver sports writer Len Corben states, "Paull wanted an all-Native contender for the Mann Cup and sold the club's former players on the idea of returning to his team as a matter of Native pride and responsibility."[73]

It did not take long for the North Shore Indians to begin serving as an intersection between a pan-Indigenous, national, and sporting identity. As the season wore on, the team's fan base and popularity grew immensely, and by the end of the summer, its home crowds had grown from 3,000 to over 8,000 spectators.[74] During the middle years of the Depression, the North Shore Indians arguably became the most popular team in British Columbia.[75] Filling one of western North America's greatest sports facilities, the Denman Arena – only Madison Square Garden in New York City had a greater seating capacity when the arena was built in 1911 – the team became a landmark of Vancouver and its sporting culture.[76] Often, the North Shore Indians found themselves playing in front of large, boisterous crowds, as fans from the players' communities travelled to the games.[77] Describing the cultural phenomenon that the team became for the Sḵwx̱wú7mesh and other Indigenous peoples, Father Herbert Dunlop re-emphasizes the importance of the team during the Depression:

And for the men who had not won an encounter in months [referring to Sḵwx̱wú7-mesh lacrosse fans – which included both men and women – and being down on their luck due to the Depression], sports offered a momentary substitute. Those who could find a few pennies headed for the arena and the forums and found relief in sharing vicariously victories of their favourite team. And when they lost, a responsive chord was sounded in the depths of their souls. Down on Denman and Georgia Street[s] in Vancouver, the old forum opened its arms to this generation of men whose jackets were of yesteryear, whose pants were seedy and baggy, and whose shoes were tired and worn, and in most cases recalled from retirement by way of the half sole ... Down on Denman Street, in the old forum they forgot for a few hours that the corner around which prosperity lurked was still far beyond their reach. They forgot how poor the poor were and how maddeningly rich the rich were. *They forgot these things because before them were the darlings of the lacrosse world, the Squamish Indians!* Smaller in stature than the white teams they played, how easy it was to identify with them as they moved with lightning speed and downed teams twice their size. They were always the underdogs, but underdogs that clawed their way to the top time and time again and many a man tasted with them a momentary sip of sweet triumph![78]

Throughout the middle years of the Depression, the North Shore Indians were playing for the pride of the nation, something that did not go unnoticed by the Skwxwú7mesh communities. Every summer, villagers from Skwxwú7mesh communities would make their way to Vancouver to support *their* team. As the team entered what would be its most successful season in 1936, it brought with it the support of the Skwxwú7mesh Nation. Whereas other sports such as baseball and soccer offered localized opportunities, the North Shore Indians united the nation unlike any other team in Skwxwú7mesh history, becoming embedded as one of the most important cultural developments in the twentieth century because of the team's national success – and, of course, to different people, "national" meant several different things concurrently. Game in and game out, community members from the Skwxwú7mesh villages gathered together to support their team. Although the game of lacrosse was limited to Indigenous male athletes and did not easily cross gender lines, the expression of a localized and national Indigenous identity through the sport did.[79] Watching their team practice for hours on end behind St. Paul's Roman Catholic Church on the Mission Reserve, community members from across the Skwxwú7mesh villages were brought together by the game.[80]

With the North Shore Indians once again playing at the Denman Arena in Vancouver, Paull successfully convinced a number of other Haudenosaunee players from Six Nations of the Grand River to join the team in the summer of 1936.[81] "That was one of the great things and most important things about those ... teams, it was east [Haudenosaunee] meets west [Skwxwú7mesh]."[82] Not only were the Skwxwú7mesh establishing an identity for themselves and absorbing the game into their sense of nationhood, but they were also helping to create a pan-Indigenous identity through lacrosse and to develop a relationship with eastern Indigenous communities that would blossom and extend beyond sport. For their part, the Haudenosaunee players were given the opportunity to travel and play the game that they loved with an all-Indigenous team at the highest level. Furthermore, they quickly found themselves learning a new Indigenous culture and language:

> Andy spoke fluent S̲k̲wx̲wú7mesh [S̲k̲wx̲wú7mesh sníchim], and all the players spoke fluent S̲k̲wx̲wú7mesh. When they would score a goal, they would line up and they would stop deliberately. Andy would say, "Stop and talk about your next play and what you are going to do." So they would get out to centre floor, and they would stop and start talking S̲k̲wx̲wú7mesh, the referee standing there waiting to put the ball down, and they would all be talking S̲k̲wx̲wú7mesh, and all these white guys are looking [around and asking,] "What the hell is going on? Let's get the game on." [Laughs.] So what happened was when these eastern players came in, they started to learn S̲k̲wx̲wú7mesh, the Mohawk speakers, all of a sudden they were learning words here and there ... It was Andy, he was the one, he's [canny] that guy. [Laughs.] "Stop the game and speak S̲k̲wx̲wú7mesh!" Get them wondering what they are up to. What are they going to do?[83]

For members of the North Shore Indians, such as Chief Simon Baker (Khot-La-Cha), the ability to play the game at a high level and belong to a team where they could speak their language in the face of their non-Native opponents, often tricking them, remained a lifelong highlight of their experiences:

> We were good stick handlers. That's how come we used to beat them guys, and the best part of it was that we all talked Indian and when we hollered in our language the white man would look, and when he looked the other way, we were gone. They used to really swear at us Indians [for] talking our own language.[84]

The significance of using the S̲k̲wx̲wú7mesh language during games cannot be underestimated. Here, in a sport dominated by non-Natives on the West Coast, the anomalies could not be more visible. A game appropriated by non-Natives and introduced to the S̲k̲wx̲wú7mesh in residential schools as a way to eliminate their language, culture, and identities became a public performance of defiance, unification, regeneration, and nationhood.

For the S̲k̲wx̲wú7mesh players, the quest of the North Shore Indians for the national lacrosse championship and the Mann Cup in 1936 would take a number of them to Toronto for the first time; for their part, the Haudenosaunee players were returning home. Despite their cultural differences, languages, and distance, the S̲k̲wx̲wú7mesh and Haudenosaunee were united by a common game and symbolized the pride of Indigenous peoples that followed the team. Cheering on their fellow community members, fans from Six Nations of the Grand River came out to support *their* Indigenous team (Figure 9.2).[85] Alas, although the

Figure 9.2 The 1936 North Shore Indians lacrosse team *(left to right):* Hubie Smith, Harry Newman, Beef Smith, Oscar Bomberry, Henry Baker, Cece Vanevery, Jack Squires, Stan Joseph, Dominick Baker, Ray Baker, Chief Moses Joseph, Joe Johnston. *Vancouver Sun,* September 26, 1936.

North Shore Indians put up a hard fight, they lost in the fourth game completing the best of five-game series and Orillia captured the Mann Cup. Despite losing the series, the team was a major factor in one of the grandest exhibitions of lacrosse in the history of the game. As fans were drawn to the radio broadcasts by Foster Hewitt, the newspaper coverage, and Maple Leaf Gardens to follow the all-Indigenous team, they in turn produced one of the largest audiences to ever attend the Mann Cup, at close to 31,000 spectators over the four games played.[86]

For the Sḵwx̱wú7mesh, the 1936 Mann Cup series quickly developed into a marquee moment in their nation's history, serving as a source of pride that continues to the present day. Stories of the summer of 1936 continue to be told within Sḵwx̱wú7mesh communities and beyond. The North Shore Indians were, and remain, more than a lacrosse team. The team was the pride of a nation, and as Paitsmauk explains, it was a team of Indigenous athletes that represented Indigenous communities and established an identity that all Indigenous nations could claim as their own:

I think they were very proud of their achievements for the first thing. They won the league, they got to represent the league, but they were also an Indian team. *They're also an Indian team.* So that to them is first and foremost. But, you know, we're playing the same game. Of course, our people are very very proud. That is a seed in all of our Native people, pride. There is always that pride.[87]

Although the competitiveness of the original North Shore Indians predictably waned over time, they were never forgotten, and the success of the 1936 team remains a critical identity marker attached to the Sḵwx̱wú7mesh. Following their departure from lacrosse due to the onset of the Second World War, a semi-resurgence of the North Shore Indians materialized, and a new generation of Skwxwú7mesh and Haudenosaunee players would compete for national honours.

Introduced to the game by the encroachment of the dominant society and in residential schools as a performative act of a gendered Canadian nationalism, the Skwxwú7mesh demonstrated how a sport could be reappropriated and serve as a source of identity reformation and continuity. Although this restructuring was itself highly gendered, the Skwxwú7mesh Nation quickly recognized lacrosse as an instrument for community integration, both locally and nationally, throughout the early twentieth century, creating an important articulation of Skwxwú7mesh nationhood. Furthermore, as the Skwxwú7mesh team recruited Haudenosaunee athletes and built a relationship with the nation that first sought to create the best all-Indigenous team in the country, an equally important pan-Indigenous identity was formed through the sport. That linkage would help lead to the formation of the Indigenous rights organization the North American Indian Brotherhood beginning in 1943, as Andy Paull used his sport contacts to get the organization and other political initiatives off the ground.[88] The North American Indian Brotherhood is no longer around, but the North Shore Indians can still be seen playing on summer nights in the Vancouver area.

Notes

This chapter is based on material presented in Chapter 3 of Allan Downey, *The Creator's Game: Lacrosse, Identity, and Indigenous Nationhood* (Vancouver: UBC Press, 2018). There are several people I am grateful to for their help while writing this chapter, including Dave Jacobs (Paitsmauk), Andrea Jacobs (Sla'wiya), as well as Shanon Fitzpatrick, Kim Anderson, and Susan Neylan, each of whom provided helpful comments and suggestions on earlier drafts. I am also appreciative to Robert Alexander Innes for his insights concerning Indigenous masculinities. Last but not least, I thank Robert Rutherdale, Peter Gossage, Lisa Moore, and the anonymous reviewers for all their time and consideration.

1 Nancy Bouchier, "Idealized Middle-Class Sport for a Young Nation: Lacrosse in Nineteenth-Century Ontario Towns, 1871–1891," *Journal of Canadian Studies* 29, 2 (1994): 89.
2 Gillian Poulter, *Becoming Native in a Foreign Land: Sport, Visual Culture, and Identity in Montreal, 1840–1885* (Vancouver: UBC Press, 2009) 5–6.
3 Donald M. Fisher, *Lacrosse: A History of the Game* (Baltimore, MD: Johns Hopkins University Press, 2002), 38.
4 Dominion of Canada, *Annual Report of the Department of Indian Affairs for the Year Ended 31st December 1889* (Ottawa: Department of Indian Affairs, 1889); Allan Downey, *The Creator's Game: Lacrosse, Identity, and Indigenous Nationhood* (Vancouver: UBC Press, 2018).
5 As Brendan Hokowhitu argues in his analysis of the colonization of Indigenous masculinities, "masculinity does not exist, other than through historically constructed performance." Brendan Hokowhitu, "Producing Elite Indigenous Masculinities," *Settler*

Colonial Studies 2, 2 (2012): 29. Judith Butler further articulates this point by drawing attention to the ways that "gender is in no way a stable identity or locus of agency from which various acts proceed; rather, it is an identity tenuously constituted in time – an identity instituted through a *stylized repetition of acts*." Judith Butler, "Performative Acts and Gender Constitution: An Essay in Phenomenology and Feminist Theory," *Theatre Journal* 40, 4 (1988): 519, original emphasis.

6 This was not strictly a Canadian phenomenon; as Phillip Borell details, sport was also used in the colonization of New Zealand. See Phillip Borell, "Patriotic Games: Boundaries and Masculinity in New Zealand Sport," in *Indigenous Men and Masculinities: Legacies, Identities, and Regeneration*, ed. Robert Alexander Innes and Kim Anderson (Winnipeg: University of Manitoba Press, 2015), 169.

7 Scott L. Morgensen, "Cutting to the Roots of Colonial Masculinity," in *Indigenous Men and Masculinities: Legacies, Identities, and Regeneration*, ed. Robert Alexander Innes and Kim Anderson (Winnipeg: University of Manitoba Press, 2015), 38.

8 "Coast Salish" is an anthropological term for the collective group of nations with common histories, identities, and traditions located in present-day British Columbia, Washington, and Oregon. As Keith Carlson points out, in the anthropological literature, the Coast Salish are divided into six major groupings or language families. For more, see Keith Thor Carlson, *The Power of Place, the Problem of Time: Aboriginal Identity and Historical Consciousness in the Cauldron of Colonialism* (Toronto: University of Toronto Press, 2010); Wayne Suttles, *Handbook of North American Indians*, vol. 7, *The Northwest Coast* (Washington, DC: Smithsonian Institution, 1990).

9 Here, I draw on Audra Simpson's framing of "interruption," in which, using the example of the Kanien'kehá:ka from Kahnawà:ke, Simpson argues, "They are Indigenous nationals of a strangulated political order who do all they can to live a political life robustly, with dignity as Nationals. In holding on to this, they interrupt and fundamentally challenge stories that have been told about them and about others like them, as well as the structure of settlement that strangles their political form and tries to take their land and their selves from them." Likewise, the story of early organized lacrosse serves as an example in Sḵwx̱wú7mesh history of this interruption's manifestation. The attempted introduction of the game as a gendered nationalism was itself interrupted by the Sḵwx̱wú7mesh people's understandings of their nationhood and was reconstructed accordingly. Audra Simpson, *Mohawk Interruptus: Political Life across the Borders of Settler States* (Durham, NC: Duke University Press, 2014), 3.

10 The intention of this chapter is not to measure the "authenticity" or change in Sḵwx̱wú7mesh gender identities before and after the introduction of organized lacrosse; rather, this chapter sets out to examine the Sḵwx̱wú7mesh interpretation of that gendered performance.

11 The term "Canada's Colonial Age" is used to identify the present period, which began in 1860 when the British Crown bequeathed to the Dominion of Canada, later Canada, its position and practices as a colonizer of the pre-existing Indigenous nations.

12 Cole Harris, *The Resettlement of British Columbia: Essays on Colonialism and Geographical Change* (Vancouver: UBC Press, 1997), 68; Adele Perry, *On the Edge of Empire: Gender, Race, and the Making of British Columbia, 1849–1871* (Toronto: University of Toronto Press, 2001), 194.

13 Carlson, *Power of Place*, 211.

14 John Sutton Lutz, *Makúk: A New History of Aboriginal-White Relations* (Vancouver: UBC Press, 2008), 8.

15   For example, see Wayne Suttles, "The Early Diffusion of the Potato among the Coast
     Salish" and "The Plateau Prophet Dance among the Coast Salish," in *Coast Salish Essays*,
     137–51 and 152–98 (Vancouver: Talonbooks, 1987).
16   Harris, *Resettlement of British Columbia*, 69.
17   Paul Kane, "Wanderings of an Artist among the Indians of North America," *Canadian
     Journal*, 1855, 276, quoted in Stewart Culin, "Game of the North American Indians," in
     *Twenty-Fourth Annual Report of the Bureau of American Ethnology to the Secretary of
     the Smithsonian Institute, 1902–1903* (1907; reprint, New York: Dover, 1975), 573.
18   Alexandra Harmon, *Indians in the Making: Ethnic Relations and Indian Identities around
     Puget Sound* (Berkeley: University of California Press, 1998), 8. The S̲ḵwx̲wú7mesh know
     the game as Kʼexwa7 or alternatively Skʼéxwa7. S̲ḵwx̲wú7mesh Nation member Dennis
     Joseph points out that kʼexwa7 means "stick ball," and the *Squamish-English Dictionary*
     also lists the word as meaning "to play modern lacrosse," whereas skʼéxwa7 means "lacrosse
     match." S̲ḵwx̲wú7mesh Úxwumixw (Squamish Nation), "Our Culture – 'Lacrosse,'" http://
     www.squamish.net/about-us/our-culture; *Skwxwu7mesh Snichim-Xweliten Snichim
     Skexwts/Squamish-English Dictionary* (Seattle: University of Washington Press, 2011).
19   David S. Savelieff, *A History of the Sport of Lacrosse in British Columbia* (Vancouver, 1972), 7.
20   Ibid.
21   Bouchier, "Idealized Middle-Class Sport," 89–90.
22   Poulter, *Becoming Native*, 5.
23   Ibid., 7.
24   Morgensen, "Cutting to the Roots," 51–52; Michael A. Robidoux, "Imagining a Canadian
     Identity through Sport: A Historical Interpretation of Lacrosse and Hockey," *Journal of
     American Folklore* 115, 456 (2002): 214 and 216.
25   Nancy Bouchier, *For the Love of the Game: Amateur Sport in Small-Town Ontario* (Montreal
     and Kingston: McGill-Queen's University Press, 2003), 118.
26   Robidoux, "Imagining a Canadian Identity through Sport," 216; M. Ann Hall, "Cultural
     Struggle and Resistance: Gender, History, and Canadian Sport," in *Sport and Gender in
     Canada*, 2nd ed., ed. Kevin Young and Philip White (Don Mills, ON: Oxford University
     Press, 2007), 56.
27   Gillian Poulter, "'Eminently Canadian': Indigenous Sports and Canadian Identity in Vic-
     torian Montreal," in *Hidden in Plain Sight: Contributions of Aboriginal Peoples to Canadian
     Identity and Culture*, ed. Cora J. Voyageur and David Newhouse (Toronto: University of
     Toronto Press, 2005), 364; Fisher, *Lacrosse*, 34; Library and Archives Canada, MG31, D85
     22, "Lacrosse"; Prince Albert Historical Society Archives, H-33, "Prince Albert Lacrosse
     Team," http://sain.scaa.sk.ca/items/index.php/prince-albert-lacrosse-team-2; Karen L.
     Wall, *Game Plan: A Social History of Sport in Alberta* (Edmonton: University of Alberta
     Press, 2012), 61; Alexander M. Weyand and Milton R. Roberts, *The Lacrosse Story*
     (Baltimore, MD: Garamond and Pridemark, 1965), 44.
28   Weyand and Roberts, *Lacrosse Story*, 44.
29   British Columbia Archives, NW796.347, B862a, *Constitution and Rules of the British Col-
     umbia Amateur Lacrosse Association, Adopted March 22nd, 1890, Reviewed April 8th, 1899*
     (Vancouver: Evans and Hastings Printers, 1899).
30   Perry, *On the Edge of Empire*, 196–97.
31   For more, see Janice Forsyth, "Bodies of Meaning: Sports and Games at Canadian
     Residential Schools," in *Aboriginal Peoples and Sport in Canada: Historical Foundations
     and Contemporary Issues*, ed. Janice Forsyth and Audrey R. Giles, 15–34 (Vancouver: UBC
     Press, 2013).

32 Eric D. Anderson, "Using the Master's Tools: Resisting Colonization through Colonial Sports," *International Journal of Sport* 23, 2 (2006): 249.
33 Hall, "Cultural Struggle and Resistance," 56.
34 C.H. Marchal, principal, "St. Mary's Mission Boarding School," in *Annual Report of the Department of Indian Affairs for the Year Ended 30 June 1904* (Ottawa: Department of Indian Affairs, 1904), 399; Sister Mary Amy, principal, "Squamish Boarding School," in *Annual Report of the Department of Indian Affairs for the Year Ended 30 June 1905* (Ottawa: Department of Indian Affairs, 1905), 362; Sister Theresine, principal, "Sechelt Indian Residential School," in *Annual Report of the Department of Indian Affairs for the Year Ended 30 June 1906* (Ottawa: Department of Indian Affairs, 1906), 437.
35 Janice Forsyth, "The Indian Act and the (Re)Shaping of Canadian Aboriginal Sport Practices," *International Journal of Canadian Studies* 35 (2007): 98.
36 As J.R. Miller explains it, "This regime, named after Oblate Paul Durieu, employed methods of total control over mission Indians for the purpose of effecting a permanent conversion to Christian religious values and practices. The Durieu system aimed at eradicating all unChristian behaviour by means of strict rules, stern punishments for transgressors, and use of Indian reformers and watchmen or proctors to ensure conformity and inflict punishments as necessary. The second, more positive, phase emphasized symbolism and spectacle, and treated the celebrations of Catholicism as marks of community and acceptance." J.R. Miller, *Shingwauk's Vision: A History of Residential Schools* (Toronto: University of Toronto Press, 1996), 91.
37 British Columbia Archives, Reuben Ware Collection, T4356:0014, Louis Miranda, interview with Reuben Ware, audio tape, May 4, 1979, emphasis added.
38 There are various spellings of "serpent slayer," including "Xwechtáal," "Te Qoitechetahl," and "Quoichtal." Palmer Patterson used "Te Qoitechetahl" in his 1962 biography of Paull but recent works and articles have shifted the spelling to "Xwechtáal." Palmer Patterson, "Andrew Paull and Canadian Indian Resurgence" (PhD diss., University of Washington, 1962), 39; Sla'wiya (Andrea Jacobs, Skwxwú7mesh), correspondence, March 13, 2011.
39 Herbert Francis Dunlop, *Andy Paull: As I Knew Him and Understood His Times* (Vancouver: Order of the OMI of St. Paul's Province, 1989), 24.
40 Ibid.
41 Sister Mary Amy, principal, "Squamish Boarding School," 362.
42 Paitsmauk (Dave Jacobs) and Sla'wiya (Andrea Jacobs) interview with author, Capilano Reserve, British Columbia, audio recording and transcript, August 6, 2010.
43 Patterson, "Andrew Paull," 52.
44 Kim Anderson, *A Recognition of Being: Reconstructing Native Womanhood*, 2nd ed. (Toronto: Women's Press, 2016), 14.
45 North Vancouver Archives, "The Legend of Progress (as Told by the Squamish People)," Charles Warren Cates Fonds, 1893–1960, no. 19, key 2294, box 1.
46 See Carlson, *Power of Place*, 79.
47 Ibid., 80.
48 Len Corben, *Instant Replay: A Century of North Shore Sports Stories* (North Vancouver: Little Lonsdale, 2007), 32. In 1907 the Royal Agricultural and Industrial Society of British Columbia donated a cup for the purpose of an Indian Lacrosse Championship. The "Indian Championship of British Columbia" was played each year at the Victoria Day celebrations, which featured an Indian Sports Day. "Cup for Indian Lacrosse," *Victoria Daily Colonist*, June 29, 1907.
49 Patterson, "Andrew Paull," 185.

50 See Allan Downey and Susan Neylan, "Raven Plays Ball: Situating 'Indian Sports Days' within Indigenous and Colonial Spaces in Twentieth-Century Coastal British Columbia," *Canadian Journal of History* 50, 3 (2015): 442–68.
51 Lutz, *Makúk*, 217; Andrew Parnaby, *Citizen Docker: Making a New Deal on the Vancouver Waterfront, 1919–1939* (Toronto: University of Toronto Press), 87.
52 Parnaby, *Citizen Docker*, 88–89.
53 "Nats Winners over Indians," *Vancouver Province*, June 4, 1919.
54 "Canada's National Summer Game Is Growing All Over," *Vancouver Sun*, May 25, 1919.
55 "Richmond – I.L.A. Open 1920 City League Schedule," *Vancouver Sun*, May 17, 1920.
56 Mary-Ellen Kelm, "Riding into Place: Contact Zones, Rodeo, and Hybridity in the Canadian West, 1900–1970," *Journal of the Canadian Historical Association* 18, 1 (2007): 109.
57 *Vancouver Sun*, May–August 1920.
58 "Indians to Meet Richmond Tonight," *Vancouver Sun*, June 9, 1921.
59 "Andy Paull: Chief of Sport," *North Shore Outlook*, August 16, 2007; "Indians to Meet Richmond Tonight," *Vancouver Sun*, June 9, 1921.
60 Following the 1880 ban on Indigenous lacrosse players, organizers of non-Native lacrosse teams travelled to Haudenosaunee reserves such as Kahnawà:ke and Ahkwesáhsne to find local athletes who spoke English and could pass as Euro-Canadian to secretly play for their teams. These Indigenous players have since been coined "ringers." North American Indian Traveling College, *Tewaarathon (Lacrosse): Akwesasne's Story of Our National Game* (Akwesasne, ON: North American Indian Traveling College, 1978), 50.
61 Paitsmauk (Dave Jacobs) and Sla'wiya (Andrea Jacobs), interview with author, Capilano Reserve, British Columbia, audio recording and transcript, August 12, 2010.
62 Donald M. Fisher, "'Splendid but Undesirable Isolation': Recasting Canada's National Game as Box Lacrosse, 1931–1932," *Sport History Review* 36, 2 (2005): 126.
63 Box lacrosse, as opposed to field lacrosse, is the indoor version of the game. Field lacrosse was the original form that non-Indigenous Canadians appropriated from Indigenous peoples – mainly the Haudenosaunee surrounding Montreal and Toronto – beginning in the mid-nineteenth century, whereas box lacrosse, also known as indoor lacrosse, was invented in 1931 by professional hockey team owners to help fill idle hockey arenas in the summertime.
64 Fisher, *Lacrosse*, 157.
65 "Pros Make Comeback Tomorrow," *Vancouver Sun*, July 13, 1931. See also "Braves Nose Out Old Uns," *Vancouver Sun*, July 24, 1931; "Lacrosse Has Large Night," *Vancouver Sun*, July 28, 1931; and "Indians Entering Lacrosse Battle," *Vancouver Sun*, June 23, 1931.
66 Fisher, "'Splendid but Undesirable Isolation,'" 123.
67 Ibid., 124.
68 For example, the Queens Park Arena in New Westminster had to be temporarily expanded to include a thousand additional seats in order to meet the demand of spectators. "Barons of Lacrosse to Meet Tonight," *Vancouver Sun*, July 25, 1934.
69 Paitsmauk (Dave Jacobs) and Sla'wiya (Andrea Jacobs), interview, August 12, 2010, emphasis added.
70 Verna J. Kirkness, ed., *Khot-La-Cha: The Autobiography of Chief Simon Baker* (Vancouver: Douglas and McIntyre, 1994), 89, emphasis added.
71 Susan Neylan, with Melissa Meyer, "'Here Comes the Band!': Cultural Collaboration, Connective Traditions, and Aboriginal Brass Bands on British Columbia's North Coast, 1875–1964," *BC Studies*, 152 (2006–2007): 38.
72 Paitsmauk (Dave Jacobs) and Sla'wiya (Andrea Jacobs), interview, August 6, 2010.
73 Corben, *Instant Replay*, 32.

74 *Vancouver Sun,* June–August 1935.

75 Corben, *Instant Replay,* 32. For example, see "Spectacular Struggle Goes to Indians by One Goal in Fast Display of Lacrosse," *Vancouver Sun,* September 15, 1936.

76 Daniel Francis, *L.D.: Mayor Louis Taylor and the Rise of Vancouver* (Vancouver: Arsenal Pulp, 2004), 116.

77 For example, *Vancouver Sun* reporter Jack Patterson reflected on the deafening sound of the North Shore Indians fans and their "war drums" during the 1936 playoffs. Jack Patterson, "Braves Waste No Time Eliminating Salmonbellies in Third Straight Game," *Vancouver Sun,* September 19, 1936.

78 Dunlop, *Andy Paull,* 182–83, emphasis added.

79 For more, see Allan Downey, "Engendering Nationality: Haudenosaunee Tradition, Sport, and the Lines of Gender," *Journal of the Canadian Historical Association* 23, 1, (2012): 319–54.

80 Paitsmauk (Dave Jacobs) and Sla'wiya (Andrea Jacobs), interview with author, Capilano Reserve, British Columbia, audio recording and transcript, June 26, 2011.

81 Kirkness, ed., *Khot-La-Cha,* 90.

82 Paitsmauk (Dave Jacobs), correspondence with author, March 13, 2011.

83 Paitsmauk (Dave Jacobs) and Sla'wiya (Andrea Jacobs), interview, August 6, 2010.

84 Kirkness, ed., *Khot-La-Cha,* 90.

85 Andy Lytle, "Tormenting Terriers Tear Indian Encampments Apart," *Toronto Star,* October 3, 1936.

86 Fisher, *Lacrosse,* 106.

87 Paitsmauk (Dave Jacobs) and Sla'wiya (Andrea Jacobs), interview, August 6, 2010, original emphasis.

88 Patterson, "Andrew Paull," 225; Billy Two Rivers, a Kanien'kehá:ka of the Kahnawà:ke community, interview with author, Kahnawà:ke, Quebec, audio recording, November 5, 2011.

10
Sea Shepherds, Eco-warriors, and Impresarios: Performing Eco-masculinity in the Canadian Seal Hunt of the Late Twentieth Century

Willeen G. Keough

IN THE SECOND HALF of the twentieth century, a growing environmental move-ment in North America provided a forum for articulating masculinities that were alternative to dominant scripts. During anti-sealing protests off the Atlantic Coast, male animal rights and animal welfare activists[1] situated themselves within a gentler, more ethical eco-masculinity. They were nurturers of the en-vironment and caretakers of other mammals on the planet. Their masculinity usually challenged a hegemonic ideal of the "self-made man,"[2] giving the en-vironment priority over individual ambition and material gain. They also es-chewed the bureaucratic inertia of the "organization man,"[3] embracing direct action and personal risk. And they positioned their masculine identities in direct contrast to hyper-masculine representations of the hunter. Yet there was a tension in their self-identity, as they also defined themselves in terms of older, more combative images of masculinity. Dressed in camouflage suits, these "shadow warriors" and "eco-warriors" raced to a "front" that had become a "battleground" for the "seal wars." And to fundraise effectively, a number became masters of branding and marketing; they also became directors of large organ-izations, with boards, mission statements, websites, and war chests that would have impressed their counterparts in the corporate world.

This chapter teases out some of these complexities of eco-masculine identity as it was performed in the theatre of the seal hunt and anti-sealing protests from the 1960s to the turn of the twenty-first century. To this end, it speaks to several recent analyses of countercultural masculinities of the period. Christopher Dummitt, for example, has discussed alienation from "manly modernism," an idealized postwar masculinity that was linked to rationality, technology, and progress, observing the development of a radical critique by men who were "opting for less certainty and reason, more risk taking, and less risk management."[4] Tim Hodgdon's examination of the hippie movement of the 1960s reveals diverse manifestations of countercultural masculinity, from the egalitarian and mystical "Farmies" to the hierarchical and competitive

"Diggers."[5] Exploring the aesthetic of Black Panther masculinity, Matthew Hughey discovers a far greater fluidity in self-representation than the more static, militant hyper-masculinity portrayed in government and mainstream media reports.[6] Eco-masculinity within the theatre of animal rights and animal welfare activism was similarly fluid in its relationship to dominant masculinity. However, despite seeing themselves as radical, none of these countercultural movements created a revolution in gender; all were male-dominated, and although they presented alternative masculinities, all reproduced the gendered relations of power, albeit in rearticulated forms, of the cultures they were hoping to change.

This chapter adds to the discussion of countercultural masculinities by examining gender performativity[7] in the self-representations of leaders of three of the most significant anti-sealing movements in the period: Robert Hunter, who co-founded Greenpeace; Brian Davies, who created the International Fund for Animal Welfare (IFAW); and Paul Watson, originally a member of Greenpeace before he broke with that organization and launched the Sea Shepherd Conservation Society. Although these case studies focus on individuals, they provide insight into experiences and attitudes shared with the broader movement. Significantly, these men embodied idealized forms of masculine eco-heroism of the late twentieth century that are worthy of scholarly interest. Furthermore, although engaged in similar work, these three activists demonstrated different ranges of masculine positionings that are quite intriguing, challenging any notion of static scripts for eco-masculinity. We can see these masculine poses both in moments of protest and in memoirs, interviews, and self-produced documentary videos. This chapter explores their self-representations of eco-masculinity, revealing contradictions as these men disrupted, yet in some ways also performed, hegemonic masculinity in their anti-sealing activities. Their experiences help us to appreciate that eco-masculinity, like the broader category of masculinity itself, is unstable, relational, and complex.

Robert Hunter

One of the first animal rights activists to arrive at the Labrador front[8] was Robert Hunter, or "Uncle Bob," as fellow activists in Greenpeace called him. Hunter was a journalist who came very early to environmental politics in Canada. He was an integral part of the "Don't Make a Wave" campaign against American nuclear testing at Amchitka in the early 1970s; indeed, he gave the campaign its name, based on the powerful image of a massive tidal wave that would be unleashed by nuclear blasts and wreak devastation on both sides of the Pacific. On September 15, 1971, Hunter and other members of the group set sail from Vancouver to Amchitka on a fishing boat, the *Phyllis Cormack*, renamed the

Greenpeace for the expedition. Although they did not stop the testing that year, their efforts generated considerable interest in the Pacific Northwest, and their campaign found resonance among other environmentalist voices of the period. The following year, the group reinvented itself as the Greenpeace Foundation and was soon engaged in anti-whaling activities, chasing down Russian whaling vessels in small Zodiacs – inflatable boats – and positioning their crafts between harpooners and the whales. By the fall and winter of 1975–76, they had initiated anti-sealing protests off the Newfoundland coast; again, peaceful direct action was an important part of their strategy as they placed themselves between sealers and animals, spray-dyed seal pups, and verbally confronted frustrated sealers and fisheries officers on the ice. The annual seal hunt became both theatre and counter-theatre for what would soon become an international audience.

In the unfolding drama, Greenpeacers situated themselves as foils to the menacing presence of the sealers. Watson would later describe the dichotomous presentation of good and evil: "Sealers in grays and blacks, methodically chopping and skinning, and Greenpeacers in orange survival suits and hoods, bright as a flame against the total whiteness and rushing forward with outstretched hands."[9] Yet the essence of combative masculinity was also part of the way male Greenpeace members represented themselves and was integrated into their rhetoric and campaign strategies. In 2000 *Time* magazine named Hunter one of the top ten environmental heroes of the twentieth century,[10] and he is credited with coining the designation "eco-warriors" for himself and fellow activists. Hunter had also described the environmental movement as "the emergence of 'Green Panthers,'"[11] invoking a connection with black, militant masculinity. Yet, like the Black Panthers and men in other contemporary countercultural groups, these green warriors relied on the existence of dominant masculinity, and often performed it, even while they struggled against it.[12] The embodiment of hegemonic and counter-hegemonic masculinities, however, varied considerably among the three animal rights and animal welfare leaders discussed in this chapter, helping us to appreciate the tensions that existed in the eco-masculinist subject.

Certainly, there was a softer, more spiritual side to Hunter's activism, for he saw greater forces than himself at work in what he termed the "cosmic organizing" of the universe.[13] Born in 1941, he was a young man in the 1960s, and he was very much a creature of that era. Like many other young men who were seeking alternative masculinities in countercultural movements, Hunter was a "child of the universe."[14] Although Greenpeace was a collective, there was an unspoken acknowledgment of authority vested in certain (male) members, and Hunter was widely recognized as the group's spiritual leader. He was the mystic, the guru, the shaman of the group. His eclectic spiritualism had a profound impact on the others; looking at photographs of them in the 1970s, speeding along the water with wooden flutes and homespun vests, we can almost smell the patchouli. Watson, who was with them in these early years, likened Hunter to an "ecological Messiah" with acolytes learning at his feet.[15] Another fellow activist, Rex Weyler, observed that Hunter "had this amazing sense of wonder about life ... To him it was magic, the world was magic ... He made us believe that miracles would happen. And, guess what, they did."[16]

Hunter and Walrus Oakenbough (David Garrick) consulted the *I Ching* before major campaigns. In 1975, as they left Winter Harbour to take on the Russian whaling fleet, their reading was Hexagram 49, "Revolutions," predicting imminent combat "between the forces of light and the forces of darkness," with footnotes urging, "The hour has come!"[17] They found the fleet a week later and began harrying the ships and photographing the kills – at times, placing themselves between harpoon boats and their prey. So the eco-warriors were engaging the enemy but doing so at the behest of universal forces more powerful than themselves. This sense of "direst necessity," Hunter said, "gave the campaign the flavor of a crusade, or *jihad,* a sacred undertaking."[18] His choice of terminology is intriguing; although neither concept necessarily involves violence, both do imply struggle and conflict in the name of a cause that is just. Thus, although their main strategy was to bear witness, Hunter and his fellow Greenpeacers were signalling their willingness to accept danger, even death, in order to defend the planet.

Hunter had no doubts about the morality of their activism, which he saw as organic, almost primordial. He referred to Greenpeace activists as "Rainbow Warriors," after an Indigenous prophecy (shared by Cree, Hopi, Sioux, and Cherokee nations) that predicted, "There will come a time when the Earth grows sick and when it does a tribe will gather from all the cultures of the World who believe in deeds and not words. They will work to heal it ... They will be known as the 'Warriors of the Rainbow.'"[19] The rainbow became an important symbol for Greenpeacers, even a touchstone of their cosmic significance, in the early years of the movement.[20] According to Hunter, it was a rainbow that ultimately pinpointed the Russian whaling fleet for the Greenpeace activists in 1975 (for the *I Ching* could provide advice but not compass bearings). Helmsman Melville Gregory saw a rainbow emerge about 15 degrees off their set course, read it as a sign, and veered their vessel toward it. Within a half-hour, the whaling fleet appeared in the distance.[21] On their return journey, their vessel encountered a fog rainbow off the coast of Oregon. "So convinced was I that it was a miracle," Hunter later wrote, that "I ripped off my clothes and plunged into the icy water and started swimming in a state of bliss toward it, my heart pounding, thinking that I was swimming into a divine embrace."[22] In 1978 Greenpeace purchased a vessel and dubbed it the *Rainbow Warrior.* Crew member Susi Newborn painted a rainbow on the superstructure, a dove on the bow, and a Kwakiutl symbol of the harmony of nature on its stack. Hunter was one-thirty-second Kwakiutl and felt quite tied to his Indigenous heritage. Usually, before boarding the vessel, he performed a namaste greeting to these symbols. This element of Hunter's masculine identity – a sense of spiritual oneness with nature, a desire for peaceful harmony with the planet – seemed at odds with his aggressive environmental strategies. He was both warrior and gentler, green man.

Perhaps nothing demonstrates this complexity of his masculine identity better than his introduction of the concept of the "mind bomb" to the Greenpeace repertoire. Here again was an image of battlefields and explosives, but in Hunter's vision of revolution, he planned to storm people's minds, not physical barricades. Following the ideas of media theorist Marshall McLuhan, Hunter wanted to use mass media to create a global experience of ecological awareness. Greenpeace would create the mind bombs – the sounds and images – that would "sail across an electronic sea" and "explode in people's minds."[23] The image of a massive earthquake and tidal wave emanating from nuclear testing was a mind bomb. Photographs of small Zodiacs confronting massive Russian whaling ships were mind bombs. And whereas some activists manipulated the media rather cynically at times, for Hunter, it was an essential part of the counter-theatre that he was producing.

Perhaps Hunter's most powerful mind bomb detonated during the first Greenpeace foray into the Labrador front in 1976. Hunter and Watson planted themselves directly in the path of a large sealing vessel, the *Arctic Endeavour*, which was cutting its way through the pack ice toward some whitecoats – newborn harp seals. The two men stood with arms crossed, eyes staring straight ahead. "This was not to be a mere game of chicken," Hunter later wrote. "We had turned our backs on the enemy, and if he wanted to split us in half, it would be entirely up to him. There would be no fight." Three times, the vessel crashed through the ice toward them with ever-increasing speed; three times, the two men did not move. Watson suggested that when the ice split around them, he should jump to the left and Hunter to the right. According to Watson, "Bob looked straight ahead and calmly said, 'I'm not going anywhere.' And he meant it." Hunter later wrote that he centred his mind on the clear light, a Tibetan Buddhist meditation technique, to drive the fear from his body. On the final charge, Watson said, "She's gonna come fast this time. It's a crummy way to die." Hunter replied, "Just don't look back, Paul." The ship stopped within mere feet of the activists. The moment was photographed.[24] Boom! Mind bomb.

In his 1979 memoir, Hunter reflected on the moment as "good guerrilla theater, and ... bound to create some great media images." But eco-masculinity was at centre stage in this performance, which both replicated and subverted hegemonic masculinity. Two men stood frozen in time, refusing to acknowledge the approach of the massive vessel, disdainful of their enemy, staring into the void of death without fear. They embodied the masculine superhero. Hunter described his

> feeling that we had tapped some fairly cosmic sources of energy in the process, that angels had guarded our back ... It seemed our bodies had grown gigantic and the ships had shrunk to the size of toys that could be pushed away at will. It was a power rush of considerable proportions. In the final few seconds before the ship had stopped, ... I had felt a blaze of anger like a blowtorch. It was righteous wrath. It brought with it absolute conviction and an ecstatic, exultant feeling of strength.[25]

Yet this same tableau also presented the sea shepherds as nurturers, posing protectively over a whitecoat in the foreground while staring down the maw of corporate greed, at one with larger forces of nature that no human could control.

Despite performances of unbendable eco-heroism, however, Hunter's confrontational activism did not bring him into the realm of physical aggression. At one point, he reflected rather bitterly, "Maybe [pacifism] was a crock of shit. Maybe it was time to buy some explosives and sink the bastards [whaling and sealing vessels]." Perhaps bearing witness and peaceful protest were not the answer: "Maybe it was time to take up guns."[26] But he never did go down that path, continuing to eschew violence in any form, whether it was directed at people or property. Indeed, he had a falling out with some Greenpeace members, including Watson, over what they saw as methods that were too tame, and the dissidents splintered off into another animal rights group. Hunter also had a capacity for compromise that was not evident in some other leaders of animal rights and animal welfare groups and was read as effeminate by his critics in the movement. For example, in 1976, he and Patrick Moore halted Greenpeace plans to spray-dye whitecoat pelts green, as they did not want to ruin markets for the landsmen seal hunt – a much smaller-scale effort that they saw as less damaging to the herd than the large-vessel commercial hunt offshore. The decision can also be read as a sound public relations move, as Greenpeace did not want to be seen as an elitist urban movement ganging up on the rural working class. But there was compassion and compromise in this decision as well.

It was this ability to see both sides, to be flexible, that made Hunter a trusted adviser throughout the wider animal rights movement. When the original Greenpeace folded in the late 1970s, in the midst of personality clashes and profound disagreements over strategies, Hunter was still highly respected by all parties. When he died in 2005, Watson spoke at one of the memorial services:

"He was a man of great love and forgiveness who never let a disagreement or political difference fester into ugliness. He could sail on a Greenpeace ship or a Sea Shepherd ship because he was a part of us both."[27] Of the three articulations of eco-masculinity discussed here, Hunter's was the most spiritual, the least competitive, and the most tolerant.

Brian Davies

The eco-masculinity of Brian Davies was perhaps more self-consciously per- formative in that it was consistently directed at an international audience. He also embodied the rationality and corporate aesthetic of hegemonic masculinity more than Hunter or Watson. Davies was born in a Welsh mining village in 1935. He immigrated to Canada in 1955 and joined the Canadian army, remain- ing until 1961, when he became field secretary of the New Brunswick Society for the Prevention of Cruelty to Animals. He and other observers went to the ice in the mid-1960s and mobilized a campaign to stop the hunting of harp seals. In 1969 he founded the International Fund for Animal Welfare; at the time of writing, he was director of the Network for Animals, headquartered in the United Kingdom.

Davies also sees and presents himself as a seal saviour. His first book on the evils of the hunt, *Savage Luxury: The Slaughter of the Baby Seal* (1970), describes his 1964 effort to rescue two whitecoats from sealers at the front; he named them Jack and Jill and kept them for some time in a bathtub at home, where he and his wife nursed them until they could be transferred to a zoo.[28] Davies talks about IFAW's work as a "crusade against cruelty." You can detect a sense of wonder mixed with sorrow when he describes the ice fields as "absolutely, stun- ningly beautiful" and how profoundly disturbing it has been to see that world and its creatures "desecrated" by humankind.[29] In the film *Peace on Ice* (1988), which Davies created for his supporters to celebrate the Canadian ban in 1987 on the commercial hunting of whitecoats,[30] he flies his helicopter into a land of pristine whiteness that extends as far as the eye can see. The ice is white; the young harp seals are white; his own snowsuit is white; even his hair is white. The only creatures adding any colour contrast to the scene are adult seals that have scurried off to blowholes but are soon filmed frolicking in the water be- cause they realize that Davies means no harm. So Davies both stages and cele- brates this moment of innocence, centring himself in the frame as protagonist and protector. His concern for the seals is palpable. But he has not embraced the sort of organic spiritualism that was central to Bob Hunter's activism. Davies is a child of industrial Britain of the 1940s and 1950s. In one four-year period in his youth, he worked at seventeen different jobs. When he came to Canada, he sold Fuller brushes before joining the army; there are no spliffs or Indigenous totems in his kitbag.

Like Hunter, Davies uses battle imagery to describe his anti-sealing activities: he sees himself as a "crusader," for example, and the core members of IFAW as a "commando group."[31] But his role at the front has been more that of a witness and public relations coordinator than an ice warrior. As he once explained to writer and environmentalist Farley Mowat, "I decided that confronting seal hunters on the ice wasn't the way to do it. That wasn't my nature anyway. But I believed that if I showed enough people what the seal hunt really was like, the overwhelming feeling of revulsion" would force the Canadian government to stop the hunt.[32] Many have suggested that he became the ringmaster of a media circus that he helped to create, and it is likely that Davies would agree with this assessment. He quickly became adept at creating and communicating images that would shock the broader public. Almost from the beginning, he did this not only to present his interpretation of the hunt but also to amass the large coffers that IFAW would require to carry out an effective animal welfare campaign worldwide. In this presentation of eco-masculinity, it has been his showmanship, business acumen, single-mindedness, and organizational and marketing abilities that have predominated. His masculine identity very much embodies both the impresario and the CEO.

Although Davies has engaged in other animal welfare campaigns, he has not allowed the anti-sealing focus of his activism to be diluted. Saving the seals has always been his priority. "It's my last thought at night, and it's my first thought in the morning," he has said, describing himself as "driven." And, unlike Hunter, he sees no room for compromise on the landsman hunt. "Look," he told me in a 2012 interview, "the reality is that the seal hunt, by vessels or by landsmen, is *inherently* a cruel business." Landsmen should find something else to do for a living, he argues, and points to the potential of eco-tourism at the front, with tourists being ferried to and from a whelping ice that could become a national park or heritage site. Davies does not approve of the Inuit hunt either, but he has avoided any confrontation with Indigenous hunters simply because it would have been "impolitic," given that they had fewer options for making a livelihood in the North.[33]

Davies has picked his battles carefully. In the 1980s, for example, he focused his efforts on achieving a Canadian ban on the large-vessel commercial hunt as a first step because he realized that Canadians were not yet ready for a complete ban on sealing. He is careful not to overextend his efforts. "One of the weaknesses of the [broader] animal welfare movement," he observes, "has been that it attempts to fight all of the battles all of the time, and the end result is that very few of the battles are ever won." So he has been a wily strategist in what he calls the "war against human rapacity."[34] He has certainly been a master at creating spectacle on the ice, flying journalists and celebrities to the hunt in the latter 1960s. Davies had quickly realized that the Canadian media were generally not on his side, so he switched his attention to "exploiting the goodwill of the international media," claiming to have a worldwide audience of some 400 million people every spring.[35] When the Canadian government prohibited chartered planes from landing near the whelping ice, Davies obtained a helicopter pilot's licence to personally ferry personnel and the media to the ice and over the hunt itself; by 1977 IFAW had a fleet of six helicopters engaged in stoking international fury against sealing activities.

By the mid-1970s the performance of binary gender on the ice was central to the media coverage that Davies courted. In 1976 Davies brought three stewardesses out to the whelping ice to attract media attention – a strategy that even he admits was "kind of tacky" but necessary because "every year you had to give them something." The stewardesses were meant to evoke feminine helplessness, echoing the plight of the young seals at the mercy of the hyper-masculinity of the hunters. And situated as a foil to both was the chivalric masculinity of the animal rights and animal welfare activists. "Three young women," he says, "facing up to these seal-hunting monsters ... They lapped it up, the media." This elixir of female sexuality, blood, and violence was served up again the following year, when Davies flew actress Yvette Mimieux to the ice and Swiss conservationist Franz Weber arrived with actress Brigitte Bardot. Although sealers and local residents were somewhat flummoxed by the presence of women at the front, Davies and Weber were embracing practices that were already well entrenched in film and advertising industries: posing, photographing, and filming women as objects and presenting them to the heteroerotic male gaze.[36] Davies knew his international audience well and was particularly good at using graphic, contrasting images in media campaigns: the whitecoat cowering from the dark-clothed sealer, the white ice covered with red blood, images of lightness and darkness, and evocations of good and evil. It was deliberate staging, he told me, "a no-brainer ... It got the job done."[37]

Several times in our interview, Davies used that rationale. He admitted, for example, that he actually liked most of the Newfoundland sealers whom he had met, indicating that, seal hunting aside, they were far less violent than sealers from the Magdalen Islands, whom he found brutish and dangerous. Yet he also portrayed Newfoundland sealers as savage and barbaric in his various media campaigns because he felt that the end justified the means. In 1976 Davies described sealing masculinity in terms of a sexual frenzy. The hunt was a "great macho thing," he told the *Ottawa Citizen*, suggesting that "these guys really get off on clubbing the seals. It's got to be some kind of sexual experience."[38] In our interview, he admitted that he should not have used such an analogy "because looking back, I don't believe it." Yet he does not regret his broader representations of all sealers as thugs, and the cultures from which they came as backward, because he believed in the higher purpose of ending what he saw as the cruelty of the hunt. In short, "It got the job done."[39]

Ever the master tactician, Davies was quite savvy in shifting ground from the icefields to the political arena early in his anti-sealing campaign, when other activists were less willing to soil their hands there. Leaving direct action on the ice to other animal rights and animal welfare groups, he maintained the "symbolic confrontation"[40] of his media campaign, which kept a steady stream of funds coming in for IFAW, while also very assertively taking on the Canadian government and the Canadian Sealers Association. Davies seems to have felt a high degree of animosity toward these opponents, and he still speaks with great disdain of the Canadian and Newfoundland politicians and industry representatives whom he encountered during talks in the early 1980s. Expecting to at least be able to convince a middle-class audience in an urban boardroom of what he saw as the inhumanity of the hunt, he found their intransigence intolerable.[41] When the Canadian government refused to budge on the issue of an outright ban on the hunt, IFAW spent a good deal of money lobbying the member states of the European Economic Community to ban seal imports. Davies had decided that the moral campaign was over and that IFAW must strike the industry and the Canadian government "where it would hurt them most – in their pockets."[42] Never quite the ice warrior, here in the economic and political arena, he was on his own turf, and he went for the jugular.

The strategy that actually brought about the ban on the whitecoat hunt in 1985 and the end of commercial offshore sealing in 1987 was IFAW's extremely well-orchestrated campaigns in the United Kingdom and the United States to boycott all Canadian fish products. Targeting major supermarket chains, IFAW's postcard and poster campaigns urged customers to advise retailers that they would not buy Canadian fish products – not even British Columbia's canned salmon. Customers of McDonald's and Burger King were asked to stop buying fish sandwiches because they were subsidizing the purchase of boats, guns, and clubs used in the seal hunt. When IFAW decided to ratchet up the pressure by threatening to release a report that suggested a massive worm infestation in all Atlantic groundfish, the organization finally forced the hand of the Canadian government. Effectively, IFAW was willing to bring the entire fishing industry in Canada to its knees. Again, Davies told me, "It got the job done." And this was not mere brinkmanship; he would have seen the strategy through. That ability to compartmentalize his anti-sealing efforts from the fallout for people who were not seal hunters was a real marker of the rational, or rationalizing, CEO at work.[43]

And he was, undoubtedly, the CEO of IFAW in mind and deed as well as on paper. The animal welfare movement, he has said, is no place for democracy: "I had no intention of submitting the purpose of the organization to the divisive behaviour that goes on at annual meetings of most animal welfare organizations world-wide."[44] IFAW had needed strong leadership, and he had provided it, in part through luck and timing, he says, but also through his own talent. By the time he retired from IFAW in 1997, 1.3 million people were on its donor list from all over the globe, and it was raising US$64 million per year for its war chest. As for the remuneration Davies received – roughly a quarter of a million Canadian dollars annually and $1.7 million upon retiring in exchange for permission for IFAW to continue to use his image – he is unapologetic. He was worth it, he argues, because his strategies worked; and he still made far less than other CEOs in the Western world. "One of the great weaknesses in this whole [animal welfare] field," he says, is that "people think ... you should take no wages." But there are only a very few people "who are so passionate about it ... that they will work for a pittance." Meanwhile, there are far more "very bright people ... that could make a difference," but they do not get involved because the pay is too low. The "businesses that are raping the environment," he continues, love it because environmental groups end up being run by "relatively mediocre people" when there is much better talent out there.[45] Davies does not have the collaborative ethos of an organization man; his identity embraces the self-made man with a strong sense of showmanship.

Paul Watson

Like Robert Hunter, Paul Watson made *Time* magazine's list of the top eco-heroes of the twentieth century, although he was ranked slightly lower, in the top twenty. As with Hunter, we see a spiritual connection with nature and all sea mammals in his environmentalism. Watson describes his work saving seals as "a passion, a lifetime commitment, and a calling"[46] – evoking a sense of religious vocation about his activism. Throughout his writings, videos, and webpages, he represents himself as a seal saviour and sea shepherd. "The seals brought me to the ice and allowed me the opportunity to be their shepherd," he once wrote. "As a shepherd I have protected them, and I will fight for them against the forces of hell if need be, and I will never abandon them."[47] When Watson broke with Greenpeace in 1977, he founded a new environmental organization called Earthforce and named his first and second vessels the *Sea Shepherd*; by 1981, his organization was known as the Sea Shepherd Conservation Society. So he has literally nailed his colours to the mast. He also has embraced an eclectic spiritualism. A broom from a Siberian witch doctor protected his first vessel; he has adopted the wolf as his totem. Watson, however, has a much harder edge than Hunter. Hunter himself understood this essential difference. "There used to be an old Sioux Indian chief who would send his medicine men to the warriors before a battle," he explained. "I was that medicine man, Paul Watson was the warrior."[48] Further, Watson says that he has chosen the earth over humankind. He dismisses any claims that he has taken work away from sealers and bread out of the mouths of their families as "trivial anthropocentric bullshit."[49] Indeed, he admits to being misanthropic, and quotes Captain Nemo in his memoirs: "I have done with Society entirely ... I do not therefore obey its laws, and I desire you never to allude to them before me again!"[50]

His uncompromising attitude and desire to push environmental activism to its limits led to his split from Greenpeace. He criticized the group's corporate mentality, bureaucratic inertia, and policy of non-violence, accusing its members of cowardice. The Greenpeace strategy of bearing witness was just an excuse for inaction, he has said, arguing that you cannot stop destruction of animal species by "hanging banners and taking pictures."[51] Indeed, he observed in his 1994 memoir that mainstream environmentalism had become a mere husk of its former self: "The bastards would talk and condemn and argue and debate until the last whale was killed. For all their self-righteous blather, they had saved nothing." They had become "hypocrites who made their living from selling misery, doom, gloom and the spectre of extinction."[52] He was clearly articulating his superior credentials for leading the animal rights movement into the next century. Certainly, he has been one of the most radical and militant of the animal rights protesters, and he epitomizes the extreme eco-warrior. He has thrown himself over whitecoats to protect them from sealers, handcuffed himself to a winch loading pelts, faced down a charging sealing vessel, and rammed and scuttled ships. He has been willing to put himself in extreme physical danger, and he expects his followers to be equally committed. Sea Shepherd activists are not passive protesters, he says, but intervenors.[53] When recruiting crew, Watson ranks passion over experience; they must be prepared to die for the species they are trying to protect.[54]

His writings and documentaries are teeming with military imagery of campaigns, tactics, field manoeuvres, assault squads, sabotage, and battlefields filled with the enemy. He portrays sealing vessels as "Goliaths of Doom,"[55] while he has become David with a sling in his hand and right on his side. He describes his double-ramming of the whaler *Sierra* and ultimate scuttling of the ship by explosives as a righteous victory on multiple fronts: "The force of a steel saviour rammed into the side of a steel killer, the explosive force of a well-placed limpet [mine] and the media force of a well-placed sound bite."[56]

In his performance of eco-masculinity, Watson presents himself as an action hero. His 2002 memoir, *Seal Wars,* for example, reads like an adventure novel, with short paragraphs and chapters, plenty of physical action, and snappy dialogue that Watson always controls with the *mot juste.* The chapter titles alone tell a narrative of persecution, noble sacrifice, and ultimate triumph of the forces of good over the forces of evil:

> It Was a Good Day to Die!
> The Sacrifice of the Lamb of God
> On the Beach
> Prelude to the Ice Wars
> Shepherds of the Labrador Front
> Goodbye, Big Mean Green Machine
> Caught Red-Handed
> Escape from the Maganderthals
> The Kamikaze Kayak Brigade
> Odyssey of Compassion
> Trial by Ice!
> The Québec Inquisition
> The Truce
> Ice Shepherds
> Seals, Lies, and Videotapes
> The Sea Shepherd Legacy for the New Millennium

He positions himself as a steward of the natural world. But he is also the warrior king of animal rights activists – in conflict with sealers, Greenpeace, Mounties, politicians, and the courts, as he endures Arctic temperatures, assaults, death threats, government harassment, and imprisonment. He invites comparisons between himself and mythical or fictional heroes such as Hercules, Captain Nemo, Odysseus, and brave Horatius at the bridge; his strategies are informed by Sun Tzu's *The Art of War.*[57]

Watson cultivates his kamikaze image. Of his 1983 blockade of St. John's, Newfoundland, when he threatened to ram any sealing vessels that attempted to leave the harbour, he writes, "They knew what I was capable of, and they were convinced that I was crazy ... An opponent without fear is a dangerous opponent, one who cannot be expected to capitulate or compromise."[58] That same year in the Gulf of St. Lawrence, he tried to ram two sealing vessels, his own ship's speakers blasting Wagner's "Ride of the Valkyries." The *Sea Shepherd* provided the perfect backdrop for his display of eco-heroism, revealing a director's eye for setting the scene. "My ship is scary enough just standing still," he later wrote, "black and powerful, jagged anti-boarding stakes on her bow, her sides draped with barbed wire, a surging white tsunami bow wave pushing ahead through the inky water, looking like huge white teeth set in the jaws of a black hole."[59] But he prefers to be in the midst of the action. In a 1995 confrontation with some Magdalen Island sealers, he entered the fray shouting "Hoka hey!" – a Lakota war cry meaning, "It is a good day to die." He took them on single-handedly, he wrote, with nothing but a stun gun and his bare hands. He had faced death before, "and I would do so here with the same resolve as any true warrior before me."[60] If he were part of the movie industry, Watson would be a box-office star. He is Sylvester Stallone as Rambo. He is Errol Flynn as Captain Blood, sailing the seven seas.

Indeed, the pirate has been perhaps his best-developed and most effective persona, or certainly at least as significant as that of the sea shepherd. Watson has built quite a following on his website, which flies a skull and crossbones in the masthead – although a careful inspection reveals one of the crossbones to be a trident and the other, a shepherd's crook. And he feeds that cult of personality, with constant updates of his every action through various social media, complete with photographs of collisions on the high seas. Another disciple of Marshall McLuhan, Watson has deployed "high drama" in his relationship with the international media. "The hint of romance and piracy or the possibility of violence guaranteed coverage," he has observed; whether that coverage was positive or negative, he could work with it.[61]

Several years ago, he wrote an epic poem about himself entitled *The Thirty Years War in Thirty Verses: August 1977 – August 2007*. In the following excerpt, we find the eco-hero, outlawed from a callous society, pursuing a sacred quest:

For three decades I have fought at sea
Under *Sea Shepherd*'s piratical flag
And seven years before that under the Greenpeace name
Thirty-seven years before the mast, sailing free
Under so many coloured and convenient national rags,
And so many bloody years playing this deadly game ...
Death and shame is the only option if we fail,
And so with this unending war I must continue to grope
To fight to save the world from the human viral pox ...
But dying quietly will not be my lot,
Nor on my knees will I expire.
From the depths of the sea I will hear the call,
And I will slide beneath the darkening waves
With absolute joy and desire.[62]

Taunting his old enemies, Watson had the poem set to music called "Dance of the Russian Sailor" and posted it on YouTube. Even in his artistic choices, he has been confrontational.

And his fame – or notoriety? – has continued to grow. On December 18, 2013, an Internet search using the phrase "Paul Watson Sea Shepherd" revealed 1,040,000 Google hits, including 208,000 YouTube items. Like Davies, Watson has long been a master of manipulating the media and has been compared to P.T. Barnum; but unlike Davies, who woos and strokes journalists, Watson grabs them by the throat and knocks them to the ground. Of criticisms from journalists about his methods, he says that the Sea Shepherd Conservation Society acts within the law and does not injure people. His response to accusations that he is an eco-terrorist? "Look, arrest me or shut up."[63]

In general, he claims, he wastes no time worrying about his critics: "To some I am a hero. To others I am a pirate, a villain, even a terrorist. The qualities that make me appear heroic to some also make me appear piratical to others. All heroes have enemies; the greater the hero, the greater, stronger, more numerous the enemies. I look forward to cultivating many more enemies in my career on behalf of the Earth."[64]

Conclusion

There is a certain irony in exploring performativity and masculinity on the whelping ice of one of the world's largest populations of harp seals. Yet the ice fields that have served as a seal nursery every spring for millennia have also become a highly masculinized space for a male-dominated commercial seal hunt and for male-led anti-sealing protests. Against this backdrop, eco-masculinity has been performed in ways that both reassure and confound the audience.

When I began the research that has informed this chapter, I assumed that male-identified animal rights and animal welfare activists of the latter twentieth century would clearly articulate their masculinity as countercultural theatre; but the eco-masculinity that I encountered in studying three leaders of these anti-sealing movements was more complex. All offered subversive readings of masculinity but with variations; all were complicit in maintaining aspects of hegemonic masculinity but to varying degrees. Aside from presenting themselves as saviours of seals and other sea mammals, they were clearly not working from the same script. Of the three, Robert Hunter came closest to negotiating a liminal space between conventional masculinity and femininity. Brian Davies rejected very little of hegemonic masculinity and projected a self-made man and showman extraordinaire. And although Paul Watson clearly rejected "manly modernism," his performance of the eco-warrior and pirate king clearly tapped into stock characters of an older, primal masculinity. Thus eco-masculinity in this context, although performative in its individual repetition to self and audience, was a multifaceted countercultural identity in the latter half of the twentieth century.

Notes

The author gratefully acknowledges funding from the Social Sciences and Humanities Research Council of Canada.

1 Although the terms "animal rights" and "animal welfare" are often used interchangeably by the general public, there is a distinction. Animal rights activists believe that animals are equal to humans as species and should not be confined or killed for the benefit of humankind in any way. Animal welfare activists accept the utilization of animals for certain human needs, such as companionship, food, clothing, and medical research, but they demand that all animals be treated in the most humane and responsible way possible.
2 Michael Kimmel, *Manhood in America: A Cultural History* (New York: Free Press, 1996).
3 William Hollingsworth Whyte, *The Organization Man* (New York: Simon and Schuster, 1956).
4 Christopher Dummitt, *The Manly Modern: Masculinity in Postwar Canada* (Vancouver: UBC Press, 2007), 143.
5 Tim Hodgdon, *Manhood in the Age of Aquarius: Masculinity in Two Countercultural Communities, 1965-83* (New York: Columbia University Press, 2007).
6 Matthew W. Hughey, "Black Aesthetics and Panther Rhetoric: A Critical Decoding of Black Masculinity in *The Black Panther*, 1967-80," *Critical Sociology* 35, 1 (2009): 28-56.
7 Judith Butler argues that gender is performative and that it is through the repetition of culturally created scripts that a body comes to be understood as gendered or sexed. Indeed, the subject cannot understand itself outside of the linguistic constructions with which it has been presented. Judith Butler, *Gender Trouble: Feminism and the Subversion of Identity*, 2nd ed. (New York: Routledge, 1999). Laura Downs suggests, however, that language is a social practice in a "life-world," creating knowledge that can be different from that produced by the Foucauldian power/knowledge axis. By looking at these "intersubjective encounters," she argues, we might find the constitution of identity "in spaces that allow subjects to reflect critically on the (often glaring) disjuncture between their own experiences and the categories of power/knowledge available to them." Laura Downs, "Reply to Joan Scott," *Society for Comparative Studies in Society and History* 35, 2 (1993): 449. I agree with Downs that the subject can be involved in a dialectic process between the self and alternative subjectivities that are negotiated within the interstices where language as social practice occurs. There is potential there for a gender identity thus constituted to be subversive and not mere mimicry. Nonetheless, gender identity, whether hegemonic or subversive, can be understood only internally and externally by the rituals of performativity that Butler has discussed.
8 The Labrador front is a major whelping ice of the harp seal, situated off the northeast coast of Newfoundland and the southeast coast of Labrador.
9 Paul Watson, as told to Warren Rogers, *Sea Shepherd: My Fight for Whales and Seals*, ed. Joseph Newman (New York: W.W. Norton, 1982), 93.
10 Frederic Golden, "A Century of Heroes," *Time*, April 26, 2000.
11 Robert Hunter, *Warriors of the Rainbow: A Chronicle of the Greenpeace Movement* (New York: Holt, Rinehart and Winston, 1979), 61.
12 Hughey, "Black Aesthetics," 31.

13 Robert Hunter, in Leigh Badgley, dir., *Greenpeace: Making a Stand*, documentary (Filmwest Associates, 2006).

14 Max Ehrmann, *Desiderata* (1927), http://mwkworks.com/desiderata.html.

15 Paul Watson, "Eulogy for Robert Lorne Hunter," May 19, 2005, https://www.seashepherd. org.au/news-and-commentary/news/eulogy-for-robert-hunter-1941-2005.html.

16 Rex Weyler, in Badgley, dir., *Greenpeace*.

17 Hunter, *Warriors*, 198.

18 Ibid., 153.

19 Hunter had read this legend in William Willoya and Vinson Brown, *Warriors of the Rainbow: Strange and Prophetic Dreams of the Indian Peoples;* see Steve Erwood, *The Greenpeace Chronicles: 40 Years of Protecting the Planet* (Amsterdam: Greenpeace International, 2011): 18–19. Versions of it continue to inform First Nations, environmentalist, and New Age blogs and websites today. See, for example, Bruce Fenton, "2012 & Beyond, Rainbow Warriors the Stars Are Calling," http://www.manataka.org/page1241.html; "The Warriors of the Rainbow Prophecy," http://www.ancient-origins.net/myths-legends/warriors-rainbow-prophecy-001577; "The Prophecy of the Rainbow Warriors and Future of Planet Earth," http://www.messagetoeagle.com/the-prophecy-of-the-rainbow-warriors-and-future-of-planet-earth/; and John Black, "The Warriors of the Rainbow," http://uplift connect.com/rainbow-prophecy/.

20 The rainbow has been a persistent symbol across cultures and through millennia. Generally, it has symbolized creation, life, peace, healing, nature, harmony, and/or divine intervention.

21 Hunter, *Warriors*, 210.

22 Ibid., 274.

23 Quoted in Rex Weyler, *Greenpeace: How a Group of Ecologists, Journalists, and Visionaries Changed the World* (Vancouver: Raincoast Books, 2004), 73, 76.

24 Paul Watson, "In memory of Robert Hunter," *New Zealand Herald*, May 3, 2005; Hunter, *Warriors*, 290–94.

25 Hunter, *Warriors*, 291–93.

26 Quoted in Frank Zelko, *Make It a Green Peace! The Rise of Countercultural Environmentalism* (New York: Oxford University Press, 2013), x–xi.

27 Watson, "Eulogy for Robert Lorne Hunter."

28 Brian Davies, *Savage Luxury: The Slaughter of the Baby Seals* (Toronto: Ryerson, 1970). The rescue was ill-fated, as the two seals died shortly after being transferred to the zoo.

29 Brian Davies, interview with author, Sanibel Island, January 18, 2012.

30 Rod Goodwin, dir., *Peace on Ice: Journey to the Canadian Winter Wonderland of Baby Seals*, documentary (Magus Films and International Fund for Animal Welfare, 1988). The ban also applied to bluebacks – newborn hooded seals – but it was the whitecoat that had generated worldwide interest.

31 Quoted in Donald Barry, *Icy Battleground: Canada, the International Fund for Animal Welfare, and the Seal Hunt* (St. John's, NL: Breakwater Books, 2005), 7.

32 Quoted in Farley Mowat, *Rescue the Earth! Conversations with the Green Crusaders* (Toronto: McClelland and Stewart, 1990), 149.

33 Davies, interview, original emphasis.

34 Quoted in Mowat, *Rescue the Earth!* 163.

35 Quoted in ibid., 152.

36 Laura Mulvey, "Visual Pleasure and Narrative Cinema," *Screen* 16, 3 (1975): 6–18. See also the documentary film series by Jean Kilbourne, dir., *Killing Us Softly: Advertising's Image of Women* (Cambridge Documentary Films, 1979, 1989, 2000, and 2010).

37 Davies, interview.
38 Quoted in Barry, *Icy Battleground*, 38.
39 Davies, interview.
40 Quoted in Barry, *Icy Battleground*, 37.
41 Davies, interview.
42 Brian Davies, *Red Ice: My Fight to Save the Seals* (London: Methuen, 1989), 77.
43 Davies, interview.
44 Quoted in Mowat, *Rescue the Earth!* 152.
45 Davies, interview.
46 Paul Watson, *Seal Wars: Twenty-Five Years on the Front Lines with the Harp Seals* (Toronto: Key Porter Books, 2002), 12.
47 Ibid., 15.
48 Quoted in John Vidal, "The Original Mr. Green," *Guardian* (London), May 4, 2005.
49 Watson, *Seal Wars*, 154.
50 Paul Watson, *Ocean Warrior: My Battle to End the Illegal Slaughter on the High Seas* (St. Leonards, Australia: Allen and Unwin, 1994), 222; Watson, *Seal Wars*, 121.
51 Andrew Revkin, "'Arrest Me or Shut Up' – Paul Watson Says He's Winning the 'Whale Wars,'" interview with Paul Watson, June 3, 2011, https://www.youtube.com/watch?v=Smeh7tpl4Kc.
52 Watson, *Ocean Warrior*, 33.
53 Revkin, "Arrest Me or Shut Up."
54 Paul Watson, "The Importance of Passion over Experience," Sea Shepherd Conservation Society video, November 5, 2012, https://www.youtube.com/watch?v=5gUydpCJyaM.
55 Watson, *Seal Wars*, 93.
56 Watson, *Ocean Warrior*, 33.
57 Watson, *Seal Wars*.
58 Ibid., 161.
59 Ibid., 171.
60 Ibid., 22.
61 Watson, *Ocean Warrior*, 24.
62 Paul Watson, *The Thirty Years War in Thirty Verses: August 1977 – August 2007*, original version at https://www.democraticunderground.com/discuss/duboard.php?az=view_all&address=103x328707. A revised version, with pictures and set to the music "Dance of the Russian Sailor," was available in 2012 at the care2 website http://www.care2.com/news/member/414211311/762765, but it has since been removed from the site.
63 Revkin, "Arrest Me or Shut Up."
64 Watson, *Ocean Warrior*, xiv.

11

The New Quebec Man: Activism and Collective Improvisation at Petit Québec Libre, 1970–73

Eric Fillion

ON THE EVENING OF July 8, 1972, Jazz libre[1] performed for an enthusiastic audience. The venue was Petit Québec libre (Little Free Quebec), a socialist commune the group had established in the Eastern Townships community of Sainte-Anne-de-la-Rochelle in early 1971. Yves Charbonneau, the group's trumpet player, returned to the stage after the concert. He explained that Petit Québec libre badly needed men who were "all together," meaning politicized Quebecers who were engaged "intellectually and culturally, and also physically, and above all emotionally."[2] Drawn from the pro-independence left, the members of Jazz libre embraced improvisation as a vehicle for collective organization. They saw the creation of a community based on their musical experiences as a way of fostering the conditions necessary for the "birth of a new Quebec man."[3] And although he would be shaped in the crucible of Petit Québec libre, this new man did not exist in a vacuum. Rather, the rural commune was an open laboratory where many of the period's revolutionary currents converged. This allowed members to reflect individually and collectively on masculinity and activism in the hope of achieving a "great, free, and socialist Quebec."[4]

The members of Petit Québec libre – seventeen men, four women, and their children[5] – did not aim to cut themselves off from Quebec society. On the contrary, they sought to transform that society by pursuing new forms of communication that could underpin new forms of solidarity, including between men and women, between workers and intellectuals, and between artists and labour activists. The commune boasted an information centre, art studios, a sugar bush, and a barn, where everyone gathered for meetings and concerts. A printing press was used to publish a newspaper, titled *Le p'tit Québec libre,*[6] as well as a manifesto:

Sons and daughters of Quebec workers, WE HOPE that our communal experience will help to achieve Quebecers' individual and collective liberation ...

The meaning and social significance of "PETIT QUÉBEC LIBRE" can be found in the fact that everything will be free; in other words, people will contribute what they want ... with the goal of ensuring no one is excluded for reasons of money or social class.
This is OPERATION SCREW THE ALMIGHTY DOLLAR! AND LONG LIVE QUEBECERS! POWER TO THE PEOPLE.[7]

Quebec's working-class families remained a central concern of commune members. A large campground was therefore provided free of charge to families interested in "politically useful vacations."[8]

The commune was atypical insofar as its male members engaged in collective self-criticism aimed at mobilizing working-class families behind the struggle for a socialist and independent Quebec. This practice makes Petit Québec libre a particularly interesting case study, one that challenges the idea of an irreconcilable tension between communal life and family life.[9] Analyzing the practices and discourses adopted at Petit Québec libre also provides an opportunity to study the performance of masculinity in a communal context. In Sainte-Anne-de-la-Rochelle, Jazz libre encouraged activists on the left to reflect on gender relations within Quebec's political culture. This focus was maintained despite the constant use of androcentric language in *Le p'tit Québec libre* and the persistence of gender inequality within the commune. The whole adventure lasted barely three years, but it raised the possibility of a more inclusive Quebec left.

In this chapter, I argue that family life and communal life are not necessarily mutually exclusive. Indeed, reconciling the needs of these two social institutions has often supported the survival of similar communal experiments.[10] In short-lived 1960s and 1970s counterculture utopias, the family may have been the object of criticism, but it also remained at the centre of efforts to imagine new forms of solidarity.[11] In the same vein, Angela A. Aidala and Benjamin D. Zablocki maintain that "communes were experiments in family. They were also experiments with alternatives in work, politics and religion, and their intersections with family life."[12] The adherence to certain aspects of the nuclear family partially explains why asymmetrical power relationships between men and women were upheld within counterculture communes.[13] Of course, gender identity is a social construct, liable to change depending on time and place. It was therefore not surprising to see alternative forms of masculinity emerge during the period. However, "Diggers," "Farmies," "playboys," and "eco-warriors" generally refused to undo the patriarchal practices condemned by their feminist counterparts.[14] By contrast, the male members of Petit Québec libre embraced the practice of masculine autocritique with the encouragement of their female allies who supported the Front de libération des femmes du Québec (FLFQ).

By analyzing the political culture fostered at Petit Québec libre, this chapter describes an alternative form of masculinity that sought to be anti-patriarchal. This masculinity was inspired by a musical-political praxis that began with personal liberation but also pointed the way to collective and ultimately national liberation. In this way, Jazz libre's communal adventure brings nuance to the idea that Quebec's pro-independence left consistently marginalized feminist activists in the 1960s and 1970s. There is no doubt that by reinforcing traditional sociological conceptions of gender, many nationalist groups hindered the emergence of a more inclusive movement during the period.[15] For example, Stéphanie Lanthier speaks in terms of the "impossible reciprocity in relations between radical nationalism and radical feminism in Quebec."[16] Likewise, Jeffery Vaçante stresses the importance of a masculinity-patriarchy-nationalism axis when he describes the period as a turning point for male Quebecers who hoped to reaffirm their male dignity:

> Decades of talk about educational reform, political modernization, and decolonization meant that ... the calls for a secular and modern state with greater power over the economy were linked with the calls for a revivified manhood. The vehicle for manly power would be the state, and for many others, the fullest expression of strong manhood would only come after the attainment of complete independence for the province of Quebec.[17]

The desire to be "masters in our own house" expressed by the architects of the Quiet Revolution, the "anti-colonial" socialism promoted by the intellectuals at the magazine *Parti pris*, and the plans of the Parti Québécois for "sovereignty association," all of these rested on androcentric positions that were hostile to feminism.[18] Petit Québec libre therefore represented a brief interlude during which Quebecers, both male and female, sought to rethink masculinity and experience it differently.

In the pages that follow, I begin by describing Jazz libre's artistic process, which helps to explain the origins of Petit Québec libre and situate the commune in relation to the nationalist ambitions of the broader Quebec left. Next, I analyze the content of *Le p'tit Québec libre* with the aim of describing, in general terms, an androcentric political culture capable of self-criticism. The presence of radical feminism in the pages of the newspaper reflected a will to overcome divisions and reconcile the various revolutionary currents circulating in Quebec in the early 1970s. The chapter concludes by highlighting the contradictions responsible for the failure of Petit Québec libre as a communal experiment. The overall study is based on a vast collection of archival documents, including correspondence, personal notes, posters, videograms, and sound recordings, as well as on interviews with former residents of Petit Québec libre and with the friends and family of Jazz libre members.

A Musical-Political Praxis

Founded in 1967, Jazz libre was a collective of improvising musicians who hoped to transform the Quebec soundscape in the wake of the Quiet Revolution. The group's founding members – Yves Charbonneau on trumpet, Jean Préfontaine on saxophone and flute, Maurice Richard on bass, and Guy Thouin on drums – had gained several years of experience playing in Montreal nightclubs.[19] Stimulated by the cultural ferment that accompanied Expo 67, they decided to embrace musical experimentation after discovering free jazz. This is how Préfontaine explained their approach: "The experiment we are embarking on is, first and foremost, musical. We have abandoned traditional structures. Everyone improvises in relation to the others. And it is spontaneous creation. From a human perspective, deepening our knowledge complements our musical unity."[20] This creative process led the four musicians to reject all forms of authoritarianism in favour of experiences based on communication and self-criticism. They abandoned structure and figurative representations while embracing a more visceral form of artistic expression that was attuned to interpersonal relationships. The group saw collective musical improvisation as a tool for cultural liberation. Préfontaine coined the expression "music-action" to describe this musical-political praxis.[21]

In large part, the free jazz that inspired Jazz libre originated in African American neighbourhoods of the American Northeast.[22] Throughout the 1960s, the genre's leading figures – Ornette Coleman, Archie Shepp, and Sunny Murray, to name just a few – vigorously rejected any stylistic constraints. They insisted on their freedom to experiment with form, instrumentation, and sound. From the start, they refused to be bound by rules of tempo and harmonic progressions. They went on to adopt an innovative musical language based on collective improvisation, a language that liberated all participating musicians, including the rhythm section. In other words, they achieved musical freedom by thumbing their noses at the expectations of critics and the entertainment industry. For many, this new form of jazz went hand in hand with the radicalization of the African diaspora in the United States; it was the musical echo of the civil rights movement, black nationalism, and the struggle for decolonization.[23]

Jazz libre's embrace of the genre was in accordance with advice offered by *Parti pris* columnist Patrick Straram, a French situationist who had been living in Montreal since 1958. During the 1960s, he called for the "necessary appropriation" of free jazz by Quebec artists. He argued that, as a French minority in North America, Quebecers were in an ideal position to let themselves be guided by the music's insurrectional power.[24] He was convinced that the spread of the genre would spur colonized Quebecers – those whom activist writer Pierre Vallières would describe as the "white niggers of America"[25] – toward revolution by forging ties of solidarity with their African American counterparts. Préfontaine agreed: "French Canadians, those white niggers of America, definitely have a gift for jazz. When I play, I want to convey my feelings. The revulsion, the joy, the gentleness, the dread of modern man, humiliated and hounded by the requirements of a life that is increasingly dehumanizing and frenzied."[26] Charbonneau explained, "I am a revolutionary first, a musician second. Instead of a machine gun, I have a trumpet. To others, I preach liberty by saying: you should also play *freely*."[27] The experience these musicians gained through collective improvisation inevitably pushed them toward social action.

By early summer 1970, they had taken the first steps in this direction by establishing an artistic community in the Laurentian village of Val-David. Open "25 hours a day from June 25 to September 25,"[28] the venture aimed to "demystify art" and "make it popular and accessible to all."[29] All summer, members of Jazz libre were joined by a number of volunteers in offering music, poetry, sculpture, and painting workshops. The season ended with a three-day festival attended by almost 3,000 young people. It was at the festival that Charbonneau and Préfontaine met Front de libération du Québec (FLQ) members Paul Rose and Francis Simard. The latter offered Jazz libre an opportunity to move to a farm in the Eastern Townships that the FLQ had previously used as a cache.[30] The only conditions were that the group establish a "politicization centre" and ensure that all activities and services remain "free of charge."[31] The two musicians accepted the offer immediately and were already working on the new site by September 1970.

The group's musical experiences inspired Charbonneau and Préfontaine to opt for a communal form of organization:

> When we try to liberate ourselves, we always make discoveries; we abandoned musical structures to show trust in the four musicians, in their ability to spontaneously create new ways of playing together that achieve unity. From the complete freedom of each member, ... we have succeeded in communicating among ourselves to create a new music that undergoes constant renewal ... It's

perfectly normal, when you have a musical experience that has such resonance in human relationships, to feel the need to transpose it into everyday life.[32]

The organization and management of the commune were therefore subject to a process analogous to collective musical improvisation: all decisions were made by the group after long discussions that sought to reconcile individual and collective voices.

A Masculine Autocritique

Members of Petit Québec libre placed their experiment squarely in the tradition of the pro-independence left. Thus they refused "to be a parallel society ... lacking any broader political or social influence."[33] Instead, they sought to distinguish themselves from the apolitical youth[34] whom the press of the period associated with communes.[35] Charbonneau and Préfontaine were hardly teenagers when they embarked on this adventure. In his mid-forties, Préfontaine was the oldest member of the group. He was convinced that collective improvisation, on stage and at Petit Québec libre, was the ideal means of promoting new forms of organization and new experiences of communication. In a piece published in *Quartier Latin*, he described it as the ideal praxis to "put into practice a socialist and revolutionary lifestyle" while discovering "the everyday life of the new man of Marx, Castro, Mao, and others."[36]

Thus Préfontaine and his associates were inspired by militants and intellectuals who had been active in the 1960s. For his part, Charbonneau wrote to François Mario Bachand, an exiled FLQ member living in Paris, seeking organizational advice. In a letter dated March 19, 1971, Bachand wrote that Petit Québec libre should avoid becoming a sanctuary for "petit-bourgeois intellectuals" from Outremont.[37] Instead, the commune needed to forge solid ties with the proletariat: "Be sure to recruit a strong core made up of sons and daughters of workers."[38] This advice was clearly well received since the manifesto of Petit Québec libre was directly addressed to the "sons and daughters of Quebec workers."[39]

However, the wording of the manifesto contrasts with the androcentric language commonly found in *Le p'tit Québec libre*. For example, Préfontaine's "modern man, humiliated and hounded,"[40] elsewhere gave way to a "new [male] Quebecer who is sick of being divided, sick of being exploited, even by his brothers, right from bottom to top."[41] The newspaper invited male "Quebec workers,"[42] their "comrades,"[43] their male colleagues,[44] their "brothers,"[45] and their "chums"[46] to denounce "the exploitation of man by man"[47] in order to recover their "dignity as upright men."[48] Likewise, a visitor who greatly enjoyed his first stay at Petit Québec libre wrote, "After two years of solitude, I found myself among brothers. Men who no longer live according to society but who live proud of themselves."[49] He added, "I am a man, I am no longer alone, I have brothers at P'tit Québec libre."[50] Meanwhile, an image of the "Old Patriot of 1837,"[51] a male figure that dominated the iconography of the pro-independence left, appeared in the background of the manifesto, as well as on the cover of some editions of the newspaper. It was presented as a symbol of the connection between male members of the commune and their "fathers"[52] from the previous century (Figure 11.1).[53]

Notwithstanding these references to a nineteenth-century insurrection, the political culture fostered at Petit Québec libre did not encourage a warlike posture or support a literal call to arms. Préfontaine was categorical: "There will be no dynamite here, no training camp."[54] According to him, terrorism had been a "necessary and sad step" that no longer had a place in the Quebec of the 1970s.[55] Charbonneau gave the same message. During an evening of music and movies at Petit Québec libre, he explained that the history of the FLQ was one of "damn nice guys ... who ended up sacrificing themselves for Quebec ... because the people weren't ready."[56] The time had come to move beyond spontaneous action and fully commit to "a period of organization ... during which all Quebecers need to be conscious of what's going on."[57] The editors of *Le p'tit Québec libre* had a similar message: "[The] liberation of the Quebec people, it's a matter of the heart."[58] They continued,

> The love part, where's that at? It sure as hell ain't at the stock exchange. You can find some among the people, the farmers, and the workers, the ones who want some because there ain't none in their lives today ... An' just wait an' see if one fine day there ain't enough, they might just look for it there where there is some: in Man.[59]

This was the "all together" man, to use Charbonneau's expression, who was starting to emerge at the beginning of the 1970s.

The birth of Charbonneau's first son inspired him to clarify what the group was trying to achieve at Petit Québec libre. He already had three daughters, but this was the first time he had been present for the delivery. He wrote a text titled "The Birth of a New Quebec Man" that described the night spent at the hospital alongside his spouse, Françoise Labonne.[60] It also drew parallels with Charbonneau's work at the commune: Petit Québec libre was like a birth. The partners had to love each other and work together. They also had to be patient and let themselves be guided by the course of events rather than "be foolish enough to want to move too fast (as Lenin wrote)."[61] Furthermore, "this birth represents heightened awareness, ceaseless work, constant questioning, and

Figure 11.1 Reimagining the "Old Patriot of 1837" and the "baby's bottle," in
Le p'tit Québec libre, 1971. Reproduced with permission of Diane Dupuis.

an entirely new culture."[62] According to Charbonneau, the experience highlighted the need for greater humility, clearer commitment, and a renewed
capacity for self-criticism.

Examples of self-criticism include an exposé on tavern culture[63] and a call for
more moderate consumption of alcohol. In fact, the first issue of *Le p'tit Québec
libre* called for a boycott of products from the Labatt brewery.[64] Commune
members accused majority shareholder Brascan Ltd. of being complicit in the
Brazilian military dictatorship. The text was accompanied by an illustration depicting a worker trapped in a beer bottle, which was shaped like a baby's bottle
(Figure 11.1). Pierre Maheu, cofounder of *Parti pris*, had previously noted how
"getting wasted is a return to the oral stage: there's a reason we call a regular at
the tavern a *biberon* [baby's bottle]."[65] He added,

When a French Canadian goes out to "get wasted" with friends, he inhabits a
special place where his personality changes. He openly claims to be tremendously
virile; he becomes effusive, talkative, and aggressive; he rants and he roars. It is a
way of achieving release and liberation. But this virility is bogus and expressing
it so noisily is merely a way of putting up a front and ignoring a lack of self-
confidence. After all, women are not allowed in taverns.[66]

Commune members pursued this analysis by condemning workers who chose to "unwind with a beer"[67] and those leftists who, "because of a feeling of guilt, go and get drunk in the name of the Patriots."[68] Granted, the members of Petit Québec libre did not advocate abstinence. However, they did maintain that "taverns numb[ed] the spirit" and harmed the revolution by preventing a responsible collective consciousness from emerging.[69]

This masculine autocritique also entailed a reassessment of traditional gender roles. After all, there was a lot of work to be done at Petit Québec libre: gathering wood, processing maple sap, repairing equipment, setting up the campground, planning activities for the daycare, organizing art workshops, printing and distributing Le p'tit Québec libre, cleaning the barn before and after concerts, preparing meals, doing dishes, and so on. Commune members depended on rotating tasks and responsibilities to promote a collective consciousness and to introduce intellectuals to manual work: "For example, each of us prepares or helps to prepare a meal, even if some of the commune members feel more involved with the kitchen because they know a bit more about it than the others."[70] The original French text uses masculine terms – chacun, communards, impliqués, and ils – that do not necessarily exclude women but indicate that men are definitely involved. This language is significant, for it suggests that Petit Québec libre sought to abandon the sexual division of labour. Indeed, on the subject of task rotation, Charbonneau explained that "the women demanded equality and, in general, they received it."[71]

However, abandoning traditional gender roles can be easier said than done. And although the permanent residents of Petit Québec libre did not practise "sexual communism,"[72] the underrepresentation of women caused problems in terms of task distribution and decision making. Diane Dupuis – Préfontaine's spouse and a sound engineer for Jazz libre – would later describe how men on dishwashing and laundry duty largely neglected their tasks. In other words, they consciously sabotaged their work in the hope of being assigned other responsibilities. "They didn't want to step outside their roles," she explained.[73] Meanwhile, female commune members had limited power because there were so few of them. Charbonneau recognized that the source of these tensions could be traced back to the very beginnings of the commune: "We failed to ensure that the sexes were balanced."[74]

Despite their smaller numbers, female commune members still succeeded in expressing themselves through Le p'tit Québec libre. Contrary to L'Action nationale, Cité libre, and Parti pris, the commune newspaper regularly served as a platform for radical feminist ideas.[75] Although most of what was published in the newspaper remained unsigned, there is little doubt that Dupuis and other women authored the articles that refer to the FLFQ.[76] One such text underscores the need to fight for the emancipation of women "after the triumph of the revolution as well as before."[77] Another explains how, whereas male members worked to mobilize fathers, female members "welcomed the mommies."[78] The women of Petit Québec libre insisted that women's liberation could not be separated from national liberation. In other words, the revolution needed to be all-encompassing:

> Long live the fight for national liberation.
> Long live a free Quebec! If we stick together, I swear we will succeed.
> Power to the people.
> Long live the Front de libération des femmes du Québec.[79]

Later on, commune members expressed their support for Lise Balcer and seven FLFQ members convicted of contempt of court. Balcer had refused to testify at FLQ member Paul Rose's trial in protest against regulations that prevented women from serving on juries. When Balcer was about to receive her sentence, the FLFQ activists stormed the jury box and were themselves convicted of contempt.[80] A first article published on these events stated that justice was not an exclusively male concern and called for the release of all eight women.[81] Next, *Le p'tit Québec libre* published a long excerpt from an interview with Balcer conducted by the magazine *Point de mire*. The activist discussed her experiences in prison and the social conditions that oppress women. She also launched a harsh critique of her male counterparts: "These leftist types, they fight against one form of exploitation. But when it comes to women, they are on the other side of the fence. A true revolutionary will fight against all forms of oppression, no exceptions."[82] With a circulation of 3,000, *Le p'tit Québec libre* was seen as an important tool for unifying the pro-independence left.

This desire to build a common front led the editors to focus their attention almost exclusively on the state of political activism in Quebec. On one occasion, the newspaper did reprint a speech by Cuban leader Fidel Castro where he discussed the important role that women could play in the revolution.[83] But otherwise, *Le p'tit Québec libre* contained no news on the activities of feminist groups from elsewhere in Canada or the United States. Likewise, both male and female commune members ignored federal government initiatives, such as the Royal Commission on the Status of Women in Canada, which had been launched in 1967, and the appointment of a minister responsible for the status of women in 1971. They were completely focused on their desire to unite Quebec's pro-independence left. For instance, during an evening discussion at Petit Québec libre, Préfontaine praised the heroism of the women who mobilized to fight Montreal mayor Jean Drapeau's "anti-demonstration" regulation on

Figure 11.2   Yves Charbonneau, Patrice Beckerich, and Jean Préfontaine, 1973. Still from the videogram *Ce soir on improvise* by Michel di Torre and Raymond Gervais. Reproduced with permission of Vidéographe Inc.

November 28, 1969.[84] He used this action by the Front commun des Québécoises (a precursor of the FLFQ) as an example of strength in unity. Advice on organizing and on the rights of the proletariat was therefore directed at both men and women. And when the editors of *Le p'tit Québec libre* threw their support behind the female workforce of the World Wide Gum factory in Granby,[85] they invited the striking workers to visit the farm for an opportunity to network, learn, and rest.

A Discordant Note

Although there were few families living at Petit Québec libre, they remained a key concern of commune members. A large campground was maintained for workers interested in visiting the countryside to relax with their wives and children. One such visitor was Patrice Beckerich, a former "gars de Lapalme"[86] who became Jazz libre's new drummer in 1972 (Figure 11.2). He first learned about Petit Québec libre from a pamphlet distributed by his union. In particular, the Conseil central des Syndicats nationaux de Montréal (CCSNM), a coalition of Montreal-area trade unions, provided support to Jazz libre. Fernand Foisy, a close associate of CCSNM president Michel Chartrand, explained that the organization "looked favourably" on artists like Charbonneau and Préfontaine.[87] It provided them with paper and sometimes printing services.[88] "We won't waste our energy and we certainly won't give up our free time or our holidays," reads one of the pamphlets distributed to union members and supporters.[89] Jazz libre also organized concerts in Montreal and the surrounding area in support of the promotional campaign.

Petit Québec libre was vast enough to welcome hundreds of visitors at once. Covering about 2 square kilometres, the site was configured in such a way that visiting families could enjoy their privacy. Campsites were assigned according to children's ages and sleep schedules. The commune also provided a childcare service and educational workshops to keep young people occupied.[90] Families that lived at the commune could also maintain a certain level of privacy by setting themselves up in the fields rather than in the house located at the entrance to the farm. This is what Beckerich chose to do, by pitching his tent next to the teepee occupied by Préfontaine and Dupuis.[91]

Nevertheless, numbers remained low. Few families visited Petit Québec libre during the summer, except to celebrate Saint-Jean-Baptiste Day and on Labour Day weekend.[92] Bachand had emphasized the need for a "core of proles,"[93] but the recruitment of new working-class members proved much more difficult than expected. For one thing, free jazz is not a very accessible form of music. Foisy mentioned that the CCSNM had some of Jazz libre's records and that the organization tried to generate interest for the music out of respect for the group's approach. However, he also recognized that playing avant-garde jazz is not necessarily the best way to mobilize workers.[94] Beckerich echoed this sentiment:

Most of the time when we played somewhere, we didn't necessarily reach the people – ordinary people, you know, workers. It wasn't what they were expecting. Workers ... weren't already familiar with jazz. And on top of that, showing up and playing atonal music, free jazz, ... they didn't know what to think and they just left. So we would show up, we would start playing to a packed house, and by the end, only about a fifth of the crowd was still there.[95]

Still, Charbonneau and Préfontaine remained convinced that their musical-political praxis was a valuable tool in the fight against political and cultural alienation.

The two musicians maintained that their music was the "real music of the people."[96] Because it relied on collective improvisation, anyone could join in. At one point, in a burst of enthusiasm, they announced that Jazz libre was breaking up to allow for the creation of a new ensemble that would include all commune members: "Jazz libre du Québec is dead! Long live the members of the Petit Québec libre commune!"[97] They went on to declare,

In the commune's ensemble, we'll have guys and girls – maybe children, who experience communal life, who work together to build Petit Québec libre, who make improvised music together several times a week, who share the same socialist ideal, and who share a vision for the future of Quebec where the exploitation of man by his fellow man is no more.[98]

But at the end of the day, Jazz libre did not break up, nor did it add any female members.

Using collective improvisation as an organizational vector also created problems, which hampered efforts to restructure the commune beginning in the fall of 1971. The spontaneous and participatory approach celebrated at the outset gave way to a "melting pot of chaos" characterized by inexperience and discord.[99] The subsequent creation of a central committee – along with an array of subcommittees for maintenance, finance, activities, coordination, information, external relations, and political action – was not enough to resolve the contradictions that afflicted Jazz libre and its commune.[100] The loss of the barn to fire[101] and the intolerable police surveillance directed at commune members[102] ultimately caused Préfontaine and Charbonneau to lose heart. They took advantage of a tour financed by the Local Initiative Program to relocate to Old Montreal. Their new project, an experimental cultural centre called L'amorce, officially opened its doors in August 1973, signalling the imminent closure of Petit Québec libre.

Conclusion

Free jazz was the soundtrack for Jazz libre's experiment in communal living. The music created a context favourable to new forms of communication that galvanized interpersonal relations at Petit Québec libre. Other groups had previously used musical practices as organizational vectors, including the eighteenth-century religious communes described by Gillian Lindt, Russel P. Getz, and Stephen Marini.[103] In these earlier communes, music helped to instill discipline or to define the roles of individuals and families. But in the case of Jazz libre, collective improvisation served to dismantle all structure and replace it with spontaneous action that was both inclusive and participatory.

Both Petit Québec libre and Jazz libre saw themselves as microcosms of an emerging "Greater Free Quebec." The commune was an experimental site with the potential to reconcile the different factions that made up Quebec's pro-independence left. The goal was to reconcile individual and collective voices in a way that could give shape and strength to a new activist political culture. The latter was informed by the androcentric discourse that dominated the 1960s, but it was also open to the kind of masculine autocritique that allowed radical feminism to take root at Petit Québec libre. Still, inherent contradictions persisted and remained difficult to ignore.

Despite concerted efforts, Jazz libre failed to balance gender relations at the commune. Nor were the promotional efforts pursued in collaboration with the CCSNM particularly successful. The new Quebec man remained a prototype because the conditions necessary for his emergence were slow to take shape. Commune members therefore came to question their capacity for building bridges with outside groups: "We are reconsidering how we communicate within the group, as well as the common and specific reason for its existence."[104] Collective improvisation allowed them to outdo themselves in terms of activism, but this musical-political praxis was also a source of confusion for outsiders, who could see no guiding principle and heard nothing but noise. Nevertheless, Petit Québec libre was a product of its time, and its cacophonic contributions provide an important contrast to the dominant discourses emanating from the Quebec left during the 1960s and 1970s.

Notes

This previously unpublished chapter was translated from the French by Steven Watt. An earlier version was presented under the title "Le nouvel homme québécois: Improvisation collective et militantisme au Petit Québec libre, 1970–1973," at the 82nd annual meeting of the Association francophone pour le savoir (ACFAS), Montreal, May 2014.

1 In addition to "Jazz libre," the group adopted various names over its eight years of activity: Quatuor du nouveau jazz libre du Québec, Quatuor de jazz libre du Québec, Jazz libre du Québec or Jazz Lib' du Kébek, Rock libre, and Communards du Petit Québec libre. To make the text more readable, I refer to the group as Jazz libre throughout the chapter.

2 Jazz libre concert at Petit Québec libre, quarter-inch magnetic tape, July 8, 1972, Centre Tenzier pour la préservation et la diffusion des avant-gardes québécoises (hereafter Tenzier), Jazz libre Collection (JLC), JLQ-P-1994-0014-0125-02. I thank Mario Gauthier for his assistance with digitizing the magnetic tapes cited in this chapter. Throughout the chapter, French quotations have been translated to make the text more readable. The original French has been reproduced in notes 7, 26, 59, and 95 to provide a sample of the more colourful colloquial expressions.

3 Yves Charbonneau, "La naissance d'un nouvel homme québécois," Le p'tit Québec libre, May 24, 1971, 2.

4 The cover of most issues of the commune's newspaper included this statement: "Ten, twenty, thirty P'tit Québec libre communes are needed to achieve a free and socialist Quebec."

5 Yves Charbonneau, summary of activities at Petit Québec libre from September 1970 to June 1972, draft, n.d., Tenzier, JLC.

6 The word petit was sometimes written out in full in the newspaper's title, Le petit Québec libre.

7 In the original French, the last line reads, "C'est l'OPÉRATION FUCK LA PIASSE! ET VIVE LES QUÉBÉCOIS! LE POUVOIR AU PEUPLE." Manifeste du Petit Québec libre, leaflet, 1971, Concordia University Library Special Collections (CULSC), Jean Préfontaine Collection (JPC).

8 Le P'tit Q libre: Centre d'activités socio-culturelles et de formation politique, pamphlet, n.d., Tenzier, JLC.

9 This theory was put forward in the early 1970s by Rosabeth M. Kanter, *Commitment and Community: Communes and Utopias in Sociological Perspective* (Cambridge, MA: Harvard University Press, 1972); Rosabeth M. Kanter, ed., *Communes: Creating and Managing the Collective Life* (New York: Harper and Row, 1973).

10 See, among others, Christoph Brumann, "All the Flesh Kindred That Ever I See: A Reconsideration of Family and Kinship in Utopian Communes," *Comparative Studies in Society and History* 45, 2 (2003): 395–421; Ruth S. Cavan, "The Family in Communes: An Overview," *International Journal of Sociology of the Family* 13, 2 (1983): 3–15; and Yaacov Oved, *Two Hundred Years of American Communes* (New Brunswick, NJ: Transaction Books, 1988).

11 William L. Smith, *Families and Communes: An Examination of Nontraditional Lifestyles* (Thousand Oaks, CA: Sage, 1999); Angela A. Aidala and Benjamin D. Zablocki, "The Communes of the 1970s," *Marriage and Family Review* 17, 1–2 (1991): 87–116; Angela A. Aidala, "Communes and Changing Family Norms: Marriage and Life-Style Choice among Former Members of Communal Groups," *Journal of Family Issues* 10, 3 (1989): 311–38.

12 Aidala and Zablocki, "Communes of the 1970s," 112.

13 This is one of the observations made by both Colin Coates and Sharon Ann Weaver. See Colin Coates, ed., *Canadian Countercultures and the Environment* (Calgary: University of Calgary Press, 2015); and Sharon Ann Weaver, "Making Place on the Canadian Periphery: Back-to-the-Land on the Gulf Islands and Cape Breton" (PhD diss., University of Guelph, 2013). See also Oved, *Two Hundred Years*, 411–26; Jon Wagner, ed., *Sex Roles in Contemporary American Communes* (Bloomington: Indiana University Press, 1982); and Pearl W. Bartelt, "Sex Roles in American Communes," in *Communal Life: An International Perspective*, ed. Yosef Gorni, Yaacov Oved, and Idit Paz, 559–84 (New Brunswick, NJ: Transaction Books, 1987).

14 For more information on these alternative forms of masculinity, see Willeen Keough, Chapter 10, this volume. See also Tim Hodgdon, *Manhood in the Age of Aquarius: Masculinity in Two Countercultural Communities, 1965–83* (New York: Columbia University Press, 2008); and Bill Osgerby, *Playboys in Paradise: Masculinity, Youth and Leisure-Style in Modern America* (New York: Berg, 2001).

15 See Anne-Marie Gingras, Chantal Maillé, and Évelyne Tardy, *Sexes et militantisme* (Montreal: Éditions du CDIHCA, 1989); Micheline Dumont, "La culture politique durant la Révolution tranquille: L'invisibilité des femmes dans *Cité libre* et *l'Action nationale*," *Recherches féministes* 21, 2 (2008): 103–25; Diane Lamoureux, *L'amère patrie: Féminisme et nationalisme dans le Québec contemporain* (Montreal: Éditions remue-ménage, 2001); and Jean-Philippe Warren, "Un parti pris sexuel: Sexualité et masculinité dans la revue *Parti pris*," *Globe: Revue internationale d'études québécoises* 12, 2 (2009): 129–57.

16 Stéphanie Lanthier, "L'impossible réciprocité des rapports politiques et idéologiques entre le nationalisme radical et le féminisme radical au Québec, 1961–1972" (MA thesis, Université de Sherbrooke, 1998), 116.

17 Jeffery Vacante, "Quebec Manhood in Historical Perspective," in *Canadian Men and Masculinities: Historical and Contemporary Perspectives*, ed. Christopher J. Greig and Wayne J. Martino (Toronto: Canadian Scholars' Press, 2012), 32.

18 Jeffery Vacante, "Liberal Nationalism and the Challenge of Masculinity Studies in Quebec," *Left History* 11, 2 (2006): 98–99.

19 Jean Préfontaine and Yves Charbonneau formed the core of the group. At various moments between 1967 and 1975, the ensemble also included Pierre Nadeau on piano, Gaby Johnston on saxophone, Tristan Honsinger on cello, Jacques Valois on bass, Jacques

Beaudoin on bass, Yves Bouliane on bass, Cyril Lepage on drums, Curly Virgil on drums, Jean-Guy Poirier on drums, Patrice Beckerich on drums, and Mathieu Léger on drums.

20 Quoted in Jacques Thériault, "Le Quatuor du nouveau jazz libre du Québec," *Le Devoir*, January 20, 1968, 11.

21 Jean Préfontaine, "Jazz libre = Musique-action," in *Musique du Kébèk*, ed. Raôul Duguay (Montreal: Éditions du jour, 1971), 157.

22 Ornette Coleman's record *Free Jazz*, released in 1961, marked the official beginning of this musical movement. For more details, see Gérald Côté, *Le jazz vu de l'intérieur* (Montreal: Nota bene, 2006); and Iain Anderson, *This Is Our Music: Free Jazz, the Sixties, and American Culture* (Philadelphia: University of Pennsylvania Press, 2007).

23 See LeRoi Jones, *Blues People: Negro Music in White America* (New York: Perennial, 2002), 235; Frank Kofsky, *Black Nationalism and the Revolution in Music* (New York: Pathfinder, 1970); and Philippe Carles and Jean-Louis Comolli, *Free Jazz/Black Power* (Paris: Champ Libre, 1971).

24 Patrick Straram, "Les divertissements: Jazz dans la vie quotidienne," *Parti pris* 1, 3 (1963), 57. For more details, see Eric Fillion, "Jazz libre: 'Musique-action' ou la recherche d'une praxis révolutionnaire au Québec (1967–1975)," *Labour/Le Travail* 77 (2016): 93–120.

25 The reference is to a book that galvanized the pro-independence left at the end of the 1960s. See Pierre Vallières, *Nègres blancs d'Amérique* (Montreal: Éditions Parti pris, 1968).

26 In the original French: "Les Canadiens français, ces nègres blancs d'Amérique, sont certainement très doués pour le jazz. Ce que je veux communiquer en jouant, ce sont mes sentiments. La révolte, la joie, la douceur, l'angoisse de l'homme moderne humilié et traqué par les exigences d'une vie de plus en plus déshumanisante et frénétique." Quoted in Gilles Ouellet, "Dans le sillage des grands démons noirs du jazz libre," *La Presse*, October 21, 1967, 22.

27 Quoted in Jacques Larue-Langlois, "Une musique jaillie de l'âme québécoise," *Perspectives*, May 10, 1969, 21, original emphasis.

28 *La Colonie artistique de Val-David*, poster, 1970, CULSC, JPC.

29 "Projet d'une colonie artistique," n.d., CULSC, JPC.

30 Louis Fournier, *F.L.Q.: Histoire d'un mouvement clandestin* (Montreal: Lanctôt Éditeur, 1998), 265–66.

31 Charbonneau, summary of activities.

32 Jean Préfontaine and Yves Charbonneau, "L'Aventure socialiste du Jazz libre du Québec," *Quartier Latin*, Fall 1970, 28.

33 Charbonneau, "La naissance," 2.

34 Jules Duchastel claims that counterculture is aligned with apoliticism, "an ideological practice whose effects are produced by decentring political action outside of the locations where power relationships are ordinarily formed and undone." He continues, "Apoliticism denies the political nature of its intervention." Jules Duchastel, "La contre-culture, une idéologie de l'apolitisme," in *La transformation du pouvoir au Québec: Actes du colloque de l'ACSALF*, ed. Nadia Assimopoulos and Association canadienne des sociologues et anthropologues de langue française (Montreal: Albert Saint-Martin, 1980), 256.

35 See Paul Henry, "30 jeunes préparent la libération pacifique," *Pop jeunesse*, January 29, 1972, 25; and Henri Goulet, "Phénomène des 'crash pads' communautaires au Québec: Les communes," *Pop jeunesse*, August 25, 1973, 16–17. For an overview of Quebec communes in the 1970s, see Jean-Philippe Warren and Andrée Fortin, *Pratiques et discours de la contreculture au Québec* (Montreal: Septentrion, 2015). See also Eric Fillion, "Jazz libre et *free jazz*," in *La contre-culture au Québec*, ed. Karim Larose and Frédéric Rondeau, 25–54 (Montreal: Presses de l'Université de Montréal, 2016).

36 Préfontaine and Charbonneau, "L'aventure socialiste," 28.
37 François Mario Bachand, *Trois textes* (Montreal: n.p., 1972), 167.
38 Ibid.
39 *Manifeste du Petit Québec libre.*
40 Quoted in Ouellet, "Dans le sillage," 22.
41 Charbonneau, "La naissance," 2.
42 "Travailleurs québécois! Le Petit Québec libre c'est à vous autres," *Le p'tit Québec libre,* May 24, 1971, 1.
43 "Au camarade," *Le p'tit Québec libre,* June 18, 1971, 3.
44 "Priorité aux travailleurs," *Le p'tit Québec libre,* 1971, 3.
45 "Le gros pick," *Le p'tit Québec libre,* 1971, 1.
46 "Aux travailleurs de la région," *Le p'tit Québec libre,* 1971, 6.
47 Pierre Vallières, quoted in *Le p'tit Québec libre,* 1971, 5.
48 "Lettre ouverte aux travailleurs," *Le p'tit Québec libre,* 1971, 2.
49 "Impression d'un premier séjour au P'tit Québec libre," *Le p'tit Québec libre,* June 18, 1971, 7.
50 Ibid.
51 This image was inspired by an illustration by Henri Julien from about 1880.
52 "Naissance d'un pays," *Le p'tit Québec libre,* 1971, 5.
53 The tenth edition of the newspaper closed with a reinterpretation of the image of the Patriot. His posture is the same, but he is reimagined as a worker armed with a machine gun. The dates "1837–1971" appear below the image. *Le p'tit Québec libre,* 1971, 7.
54 Quoted in Jacques Maher, "Le Petit Québec libre: Une maison de pêcheurs à 60 milles de Montréal," *Le petit journal,* May 16, 1971, 2.
55 Jazz libre concert at Petit Québec libre, quarter-inch magnetic tape, July 22, 1972, Tenzier, JLC, JLQ-P-1994-014-0126.
56 Jazz libre concert at Petit Québec libre, quarter-inch magnetic tape, July 8, 1972, Tenzier, JLC, JLQ-P-1994-014-0125-02.
57 Ibid.
58 "Faut libérer le Québec," *Le p'tit Québec libre,* June 18, 1971, 3.
59 In the original French: "L'Amour là-dedans de ousse qui yé? Chose certaine, yé pas à la bourse. Yé dans le peuple chez le cultivateur, chez le travailleur chez celui qui en veut parce que yen manque dans son monde d'aujourd'hui ... Pis watch ben que si un bon jour y en manque, y va l'chercher là dé ousse qui yé: dans l'Homme." Ibid.
60 Charbonneau, "La naissance," 2.
61 Ibid.
62 Ibid., 3.
63 For analyses of taverns as sites of working-class culture, see Peter DeLottinville, "Joe Beef of Montreal: Working-Class Culture and the Tavern, 1869–1889," *Labour/Le Travail* 8–9 (1981–1982): 9–40; and Anouk Bélanger and Lisa Sumner, "De la taverne Joe Beef à l'Hypertaverne Edgar: La taverne comme expression populaire du Montréal industriel en transformation," *Globe: Revue internationale d'études québécoises* 9, 2 (2006): 27–48.
64 "Boycottons la 50," *Le p'tit Québec libre,* May 24, 1971, 4.
65 Pierre Maheu, "Bilan du cléricalisme: Le Dieu Canadien français contre l'homme québécois," *Parti pris* 4, 3–4 (1966): 50.
66 Ibid., 49.
67 "Lettre ouverte aux travailleurs," 2.
68 "La critique est facile mais l'art est difficile," *Le p'tit Québec libre,* June 18, 1971, 1.
69 "Debout travailleurs," *Le p'tit Québec libre,* 1971, 6.
70 "Démocratie et participation," *Le p'tit Québec libre,* June 24, 1971, 1.

71 Yves Charbonneau, summary of activities.
72 Jean Préfontaine, quoted in Maher, "Le Petit Québec libre," 2.
73 Diane Dupuis, interview with author, L'Anse-Pleureuse, April 7, 2012.
74 Yves Charbonneau, summary of activities.
75 See Dumont, "La culture politique," 122; and Lanthier, "L'impossible réciprocité," 78.
76 For more information on this organization, see Véronique O'Leary and Louise Toupin, eds., *Québécoises deboutte!* vol. 1 (Montreal: Édition du remue-ménage, 1982); and Sean Mills, "Québécoises deboutte! Le Front de libération des femmes du Québec, le Centre des femmes et le nationalisme," *MENS: Revue d'histoire intellectuelle de l'Amérique française* 4, 2 (2004): 183–210.
77 "Pourquoi la libération des femmes," *Le p'tit Québec libre*, 1971, 1.
78 "Femmes-elles-femmes," *Le p'tit Québec libre*, 1971, 5.
79 "C'est quoi un groupe révolutionnaire," *Le p'tit Québec libre*, June 18, 1971, 5.
80 See O'Leary and Toupin, *Québécoises deboutte!* 80–88.
81 "Tout l'été en prison pour Lise Balcer," *Le p'tit Québec libre*, 1971, 5.
82 "La voix des prisons," *Le p'tit Québec libre*, 1971, 2.
83 Fidel Castro, "La révolution dans la révolution," *Le p'tit Québec libre*, 1971, 2. For more details on this speech, see Dominique Guay-Sylvestre, *Être femme à Cuba: Des premières militantes féministes aux militantes révolutionnaires* (Paris: L'Harmattan, 2006), 127.
84 Jazz libre concert at Petit Québec libre, quarter-inch magnetic tape, July 22, 1972, Tenzier, JLC, JLQ-P-1994-014-0126-A-1-A-2-L.
85 "Six mois de grève à la World Wide Gum," *Le p'tit Québec libre*, 1971, 4.
86 The "gars de Lapalme" (Lapalme boys) were a group of workers fired by Canada Post in early 1970. These union members subsequently carried out a series of actions to force their employer's hand. Their fight with the federal government was eventually supported by the FLQ. See Fournier, *F.L.Q.*, 253–54.
87 Fernand Foisy, interview with author, Montreal, May 22, 2012.
88 Jean Préfontaine also received mail and telephone messages at the offices of the CCSNM.
89 *Le P'tit Q Libre: Centre d'activités socio-culturelles et de formation politique*, pamphlet, n.d., Tenzier, JLC.
90 "Projet de la ferme du Jazz libre du Québec," proposal, November 1970, CULSC, JPC.
91 Patrice Beckerich, interview with author, Montreal, February 17, 2012.
92 Dupuis, interview; Beckerich, interview.
93 Bachand, *Trois textes*, 167.
94 Foisy, interview.
95 In the original French: "La plupart du temps quand on jouait quelque part, ça ne rejoignait pas nécessairement les gens – les gens ordinaires là, tu sais les travailleurs. Ils ne s'attendaient pas à ça. Les travailleurs ... ne sont pas déjà en contact avec le jazz. Et en plus de ça, arriver avec de la musique atonale, du free jazz, ... ils ne comprennent plus rien et ils s'en vont. Alors on arrivait, on commençait avec une salle pleine, et en dernier il en restait peut-être le cinquième de la salle." Beckerich, interview.
96 Yves Charbonneau and Jean Préfontaine, "Une nouvelle musique populaire," *Le p'tit Québec libre*, May 24, 1971, 7.
97 Ibid.
98 Ibid.
99 Yves Charbonneau, summary of activities.
100 Ibid.
101 The Petit Québec libre commune was "under close surveillance by the main police forces active in Quebec." In May 1972 police decided to set fire to the barn on the pretext that

small groups of revolutionaries were using it to plan subversive acts. This illegal act by the Royal Canadian Mounted Police was later condemned by a commission of inquiry set up following the election of the Parti Québécois. Commission d'enquête sur des opérations policières en territoire québécois, *Rapport de la Commission d'enquête sur des opérations policières en territoire québécois* (Quebec City: Ministère de la Justice, Gouvernement du Québec, 1981), 322.

102   Yves Charbonneau claimed that the problems encountered at the commune were partly the result of the presence of "police, army helicopters, infiltrators, etc." Charbonneau, summary of activities.

103   Gillian Lindt, "Moravian Family Surrogates," in *Communes: Creating and Managing the Collective Life*, ed. Rosabeth M. Kanter, 308–17 (New York: Harper and Row, 1973); Russell P. Getz, "Music in the Ephrata Cloister," *Communal Societies* 2 (1982): 27–38; Stephen A. Marini, "Hymnody in the Religious Communal Societies of Early America," *Communal Societies* 2 (1982): 1–25.

104   Members of the Petit Québec libre commune, "À propos de la libération des DINOSAURES," *Le p'tit Québec libre*, June 24, 1971, 6.

Part 4
Boys to Men

THIS NEXT SET OF ESSAYS is united by a focus on youth and on the challenges, anxieties, and opportunities associated with conceptions and experiences of boyhood, male adolescence, and the transition to manhood. In Chapter 12, Louise Bienvenue and Christine Hudon use three French Canadian interwar novels – part of an entire literary genre devoted to the coming-of-age experience – to shed interesting new light on their longstanding research topic: masculine identity formation at Quebec's *collèges classiques*. Linking the three young protagonists in these books are four common threads. To become an authentic, mature *man*, each must reject the feminized, private world of childhood; embrace his national identity as a French Canadian;[1] understand the importance of his spiritual mission as a Catholic; and do it all without the benefit of a woman's love or, indeed, of any positive heterosexual experience or education. With Christopher Greig's discussion in Chapter 13 of boyhood in Windsor, we encounter quite a different set of narratives, located in postwar, small-town Ontario rather than in the Catholic boarding schools of interwar Quebec and based on oral-history interviews rather than published fiction. But the coming-of-age theme is no less strong here, as these boyhood memories reveal an intricate pattern of pressures and possibilities, featuring both anxiety and exhilaration and deeply inflected by differences of social class, race, and sexual orientation.

With the contributions by Patricia Jasen and Julie Perrone, the concept of youthful *heroism* as a social and cultural ideal is added to the mix. The "'hero on campus' motif," Jasen points out in Chapter 14, "successfully defined the

public identity of the male ex-service students" in the wake of the Second
World War, not least by easing their adjustment to campus life and by justifying
the public expenditure on their education. "At the same time," she continues,
"it performed a disciplinary function by erecting clear boundaries around the
definition of entitlement, linking masculinity with loyalty, and discrediting
militancy even when sustained protest was a logical response to growing financial hardship." And as Perrone argues in Chapter 15, the ideal of heroism
has been clearly associated through the public memory of Terry Fox with a
number of masculine characteristics, among the most powerful of which are
physical stamina, resistance to pain, and overwhelming courage in the pursuit
of a noble cause. In Fox's case, the cause was the saving of lives through well-
funded programs for cancer research. But the journey through time and cir-
cumstance from Jasen's returning veterans – young men whose courage and
sacrifice in the defeat of Nazi aggression were similarly admired and applauded
– to Fox's Marathon of Hope is unexpected and well worth making.

Note
1 The rapprochement here with the ideas of Jeffery Vacante, who has used contemporary
   novels, political commentary, and other sources to track the rise of what he calls "national manhood" in early twentieth-century Quebec, is quite striking. See Jeffery Vacante,
   National Manhood and the Creation of Modern Quebec (Vancouver: UBC Press, 2017);
   and Jeffery Vacante, "Evolving Racial Identity and the Consolidation of Men's Authority
   in Early Twentieth-Century Quebec," *Canadian Historical Review* 88, 3 (2007): 413–38.

12

Men's Business: Masculine Adolescence and Social Projection in Selected Coming-of-Age Novels from Interwar Quebec

Louise Bienvenue and Christine Hudon

"LIKE A RIPE FRUIT, my childhood has fallen away. My teenage years are done. I am a man ... Life is opening up before me ... Everything behind me is turning to dust. I am born. From the ashes of my youth, I am born."[1] This requiem for a lost adolescence marks the closing lines of *Le beau risque*, a novel by François Hertel that was first published in 1939.[2] Having overcome a series of challenges, the protagonist, Pierre Martel, is finally ready to embrace life as a man.

In addition to *Le beau risque*, this chapter analyzes two other French Canadian novels, published between the late 1920s and the late 1930s, that chronicle the adolescent crises experienced by students attending classical colleges in Quebec. These schools for boys offered an eight-year program of secondary and post-secondary study, including courses in modern languages, Latin, Greek, religion, mathematics, and philosophy. Completion of the classical curriculum was the main pathway for Quebec students hoping to attend university. Thus Hertel's novel shares an institutional setting with *Jean-Paul*, written by Paul-Émile Farley,[3] and *André Laurence, Canadien français*, written by diplomat Pierre Dupuy.[4] All three of these books are *Bildungsromane*, or coming-of-age stories, a literary genre that narrates the adventures of a young protagonist discovering how the world works.[5] Featuring personal quests for identity, they also fall within the larger category of *romans à thèse*. As he tries to find himself, the protagonist faces a series of unforeseen events, during which he undergoes two fundamental transformations: he moves from ignorance to knowledge and from passivity to action.[6] As the story draws to a close and the protagonist arrives on the cusp of a new life, he becomes conscious of his true identity.

Novelists frequently find inspiration in the transition to adulthood and associate a variety of concepts with youth. Adolescence features roving and experimenting, dilemmas and decisions; in many coming-of-age stories, it becomes a "metaphor for social change."[7] Often, a character's quest for identity supports a specific thesis or "seek[s] to demonstrate the validity of a political, philosophical, or religious doctrine."[8] Moreover, these narratives provide particularly fascinating sources for historians. By analyzing how three young protagonists – Jean-Paul Forest, Pierre Martel, and André Laurence – experience the transition to adulthood, we seek to better explain the normative significance of the corresponding novels. In particular, we focus on aspects of identity related to gender, national belonging, religious practice, and career development. All three novels were published during the interwar period, which was marked by shifting boundaries and ideological ferment.[9] As the horrors of the First World War gave way to a period of urbanization and accelerated industrialization, the proportion of the Quebec population living in urban centres rose from just over half in 1921 to almost 60 percent a decade later.[10] Meanwhile, the effects of the Great Depression began to be felt, raising fundamental questions about the future of French Canada. Against this backdrop of upheaval, public debates raged between those who believed salvation could be achieved only through a commitment to tradition and those who enthusiastically embraced the idea of modernity. There were also a wide range of other positions whose adherents welcomed change while remaining deeply attached to religion and the traditional family.[11] In the pages that follow, we show how the three novels introduced above adopt different positions along this spectrum and how each of their young protagonists represents a unique perspective and destiny within a common field of possibilities.

The interwar period was also shaped by the emergence of youth as an active force in the public arena. As in other Western societies, Quebec saw a dramatic proliferation of youth organizations, which ranged from small circles of intellectuals to more formal or mainstream groups that offered recreational and educational opportunities.[12] The phenomenon reached all social classes and genders, although its impact was greatest among young men studying at secondary and postsecondary institutions – at the time, a relatively small elite. But despite their varying clienteles, structures, and objectives, youth organizations all contributed to giving young people a stronger voice in society and sometimes even in politics. Furthermore, the Great Depression inspired an intergenerational critique that served to further justify the presence of youth in public life. Thus the "Depression generation" portrayed itself as the victim of reckless negligence, and organizations representing young people claimed to be on an "urgent mission" to find solutions in the face of social stagnation.[13] Given that it was a time when the role of youth was on everyone's mind, the portrayal of classical college students in contemporary novels takes on a special importance.

Jean-Paul: A Traditional Approach

Jean-Paul, by Paul-Émile Farley,[14] was published in 1929. Of the three novels discussed in this chapter, it represents the most traditional approach to the question of youth. Farley was a Viatorian priest, a classical college instructor, and an experienced educational writer. The story begins as the eponymous hero embarks on a course in literature toward the end of his studies at the Minor Seminary of Joliette.[15] A gifted young man, he has been able to pursue his education thanks to sacrifices made by his family. However, he has just finished a difficult year, during which both his behaviour and his academic performance fell short of expectations. Jean-Paul has clearly entered a troubled period of his life.

As the summer holidays begin, Jean-Paul continues to be disagreeable. He shows contempt for the family farm and refuses to assist his brother in the fields. Instead, he spends his time flirting with a young female neighbour. "It can be so hard to raise boys right!" laments his worried mother. "Some days, it's like we lose touch with our older children, as if they have discovered mysteries that are far beyond our reach."[16] Unfortunately, Jean-Paul's late father is not around to support his mother as she struggles to deal with the changes in her son. This is a key similarity among the three protagonists in our study: André Laurence has also lost his father, and although Pierre Martel's father is still alive, he proves incapable of guiding his son on the journey to becoming "a man." In his diary, Jean-Paul expresses just how painful the loss of his father has been: "During my childhood, I confided in my mother. Now, things are strange! I still love her, but there are some secrets I can no longer share with her. If only I still had my father!"[17]

Like some of the novel's secondary characters, Jean-Paul risks becoming trapped in childhood because his biological mother and father cannot give him the support he needs to successfully cross over into adulthood.[18] Seeing this, Father Beauchamp, one of the priests at the college, steps in to serve as a kind of surrogate father to the young man. However, it still takes Jean-Paul a long time to admit that he needs spiritual guidance. After returning from summer holidays, he continues his errant ways and falls in with a bad crowd. For a while, he reminisces about his summer fling with his neighbour. Then he takes a shine to a younger student named René Magnan and begins slipping tender messages to this boy with a "sweet little face."[19] Over the course of a chapter titled "Other Loves," the protagonist succumbs to what was often referred to as a *chatterie*, a type of ambiguous affection shown between a senior student and a young freshman. These passages convey a touch of irony but also a large degree of indulgence on the part of the author. By portraying the relationship as a perfectly normal episode in the romantic education of a male adolescent, they reflect a widespread tolerance of such special friendships in the late 1920s. This tolerance was a far cry from the much stricter moral codes and much harsher discourses on "inverts" that would emerge after the Second World War.

"Boys will be boys," the good father seems to tell himself as he tries to bring Jean-Paul under his wing. As might be expected, the protagonist does not end up pursuing male love. He does, however, fall into a state of distress when his wild adventures take a bad turn at the start of a chapter titled "Toward the Light." The novel's turning point occurs when, after much hesitation, Jean-Paul finally decides to meet with Father Beauchamp and partake of the latter's wise counsel. The young man's discussions with the priest help him to see his life more clearly and to realize that "God could well send him hardships to purify his soul."[20] He begins to mature at an accelerated rate, suggesting that his adolescent crisis will have a happy ending.

As he turns his attention to more serious matters, Jean-Paul has a series of providential encounters that help to shape his national and religious identity. While snowshoeing in the great outdoors, he rediscovers the countryside and meets Roland Barrette, president of the college's chapter of the Association catholique de la jeunesse canadienne-française (a Catholic youth organization). Talking to Barrette, Jean-Paul recognizes the urgent need to save his "motherland draped in white that perverted sons seek to stain."[21] Shortly thereafter, as chair of the association's action committee, he begins preparing a study on foreign missions.

The study on missions serves as a catalyst for Jean-Paul's religious awakening. On Christmas evening, he has a mystical experience: "One step, one day in his life. While reading the sacred text, it was as if God were telling him a secret."[22] As he reflects on all the wrong turns his life has taken and lifts his tear-filled eyes to the altar, the young man surrenders himself to God and begins to pray "more fervently than he has in so very long."[23] These references to the past are significant insofar as the identity of the protagonist in a coming-of-age story is always revealed in childhood but remains dormant until it can be rediscovered through the initiation rites of adolescence.[24]

Having embraced his political and religious identity and with the steadfast support of his new friends, Jean-Paul once again advances to the head of his class. Ever the teacher, Farley titled the book's final chapter "The Test." In it, the protagonist experiences a shock that is at once crueller and more salutary than all the others: his mother suddenly dies.[25] It is as though she is trying to draw the man out of her son by giving him all the room he needs to mature. "Christ forges souls and then He strikes them,"[26] is Father Beauchamp's interpretation. In any case, this tragic event marks the definitive end of Jean-Paul's childish ways. After the funeral, he returns to school and begins his studies in rhetoric. However, the time is fast approaching when he must make tough decisions about his future. At Pentecost, he "sorts out" his life and abandons his plans to study medicine. Instead, he embraces his newfound passion and fulfills the hopes of his late mother by deciding to serve as a missionary with the White Fathers. Drawing strength from his patriotic zeal, confident in his faith, and committed to action, Jean-Paul successfully completes the transition from adolescence to manhood as the novel draws to a close.

Le beau risque: A Reform-Minded Approach

François Hertel[27] published *Le beau risque* in 1939, almost a decade after *Jean-Paul* was first released. But although the writing is more elegant and the characters' psychological profiles are better developed, Hertel's work still shares many characteristics with the earlier novel. To begin with, the two works have nearly identical narrative frameworks. Thus *Le beau risque* also tells the story of a classical college student, Pierre Martel, who, from all indications, is attending the Collège Brébeuf, a renowned Montreal institution. Like Jean-Paul, Pierre experiences an adolescent crisis and receives assistance from a sort of surrogate father, who helps the young man to navigate the transition to adulthood. And *Le beau risque*, like *Jean-Paul*, was authored by a teaching priest with an obvious desire to edify his readers, even if the novel was not written solely for a young audience. Nevertheless, the decidedly modern approach to Catholicism and nationalism in *Le beau risque* reflects its later publication date. It also reflects Hertel's support for the Catholic reform movement – he also published a lengthy essay in support of personalism in 1942 – a commitment he shared with many members of both the Catholic Action movement and Catholic trade unions in Quebec.[28]

Pierre is fifteen years old at the start of the story. A relatively poor student, he lacks the good looks and knowledge of the world necessary to stand out among his peers. Rather, "his truly exceptional feature is his soul ... he stands out as a leader."[29] For some time, he has been getting into more and more mischief, including skipping school to go to the cinema, dreaming of girls, and enraging the college priests by reading Zola. Furthermore, his lack of discipline reflects his troubled soul:

> Such was Pierre at the end of his fourth year. The life he was leading weighed so heavily on him – with his anxiety, his nightmares, and his compromised principles – that he prayed for a new existence. He was prematurely old but ready for the rejuvenation that comes from the direct experience of beauty. His marble had only just begun to be defined. He was, for the sculptor, the ideal material from which might emerge that incomparable shape: Man.[30]

The words chosen by Hertel to describe his protagonist's poor state of mind are significant. Indeed, the time has come for Pierre to discover his true identity.

The job of supporting this process falls to Father Henri Berthier, who teaches literature and acts as a surrogate father to the young student. Berthier instills in Pierre a humanist ideal and a steadfast conviction by introducing him to literature and history, disciplines that – through the wonder of humanist pedagogy[31] – allow him to identify his true values and discover his vocation. But the priest does not limit his teaching to intellectual and spiritual exercises. He also focuses on sport as an instrument of knowledge and personal development, celebrating the "great purification of sport" that "disrupts one's inner landscape, drives out all worries, all ideas."[32] In addition to liberating the young man's soul, sport also strengthens his body, allowing masculinity to assert itself in the senses and especially the muscles: "Pierre is enriched by strong feelings; his youthful virility affirms itself through the difficult climbs, through the compression of his muscles before a leap, through the accompanying search for harmony and balance."[33]

Kind Father Berthier, who comes across as Hertel's alter ego, is the foil to Pierre's biological father. A negative influence in his son's life, Doctor Martel is a renowned surgeon, described in the novel as a successful but superficial man. Beneath his friendly façade hides "a great void, an incurable jadedness." "Neither happy nor unhappy, he is content to simply exist. He harbours great skepticism toward his fellow man and especially toward ideas. The worries of his numerous patients and countless mundane obligations have slowly removed him from any sort of intellectual life."[34] The reader quickly understands that this man – a Rotary Club member, *Montreal Star* reader, and connoisseur of Old Orchard Beach vacations – is not equal to the challenge of guiding his son through the transition to manhood. In a candid moment, Pierre himself addresses the issue: "Sometimes I wonder if Dad wouldn't prefer it if I remained a young boy indefinitely."[35] For his part, Berthier is careful not to voice his own deeply held opinions:

I would never dare tell Pierre what I am beginning to think. Doctor Martel may be the main obstacle to his son achieving manhood.

Jaded socialites like him unconsciously prefer that their children remain carefree and charming characters who cause them no great worry. They prefer not to see that as they themselves age, these young fruits begin to ripen. They refuse to face up to responsibilities that seem too heavy.[36]

Instinctively, the protagonist removes himself from the influence of his unfit father and draws closer to Berthier. By having Pierre reject his cynical and materialistic father, Hertel symbolically highlights the intergenerational tensions of the 1930s.[37] The generation that came of age during the Depression saw itself as having been "sacrificed" by its elders.[38] In *Le beau risque*, this dynamic is also reflected in how the protagonist draws closer to his grandfather. This white-bearded and hardy landowner, a notary by profession, helps Pierre to redis-cover the rural and patriotic surroundings of his childhood.

But Pierre's return to his cultural roots is possible only after he painfully examines his conscience. "Every inch of me has been Americanized,"[39] he writes in his diary. Meanwhile, his cousin Jeanne, a young lady with a penchant for cheap amusements and cigarettes, constantly tries to lead him astray. Pierre ultimately finds himself disgusted with it all and dismisses Jeanne as little more than "flesh on offer."[40] Removing himself from the distractions and trivialities standing in the way of his development, the young man starts to better under-stand the mistakes of his father's generation. In contrast to his father's desire to "put aside questions of race,"[41] Pierre prefers the stubbornness shown by his grandfather, who dreams of living until 1937 so he can celebrate the 100th an-niversary of the Lower Canadian Rebellion.[42]

Alongside his emerging national consciousness, Pierre displays a newfound dedication to religion. Once again, this process involves severe self-criticism. Like many adolescents of his era, he practises his religion in a conformist and routine manner, essentially to please his mother. In his diary, he takes himself to task: "What a phony Catholic I am."[43] "Where am I headed with this penal code of a religion? I have neither piety nor prayer in my life."[44] Meanwhile, his grandfather provides an example of faith that is virile and unsophisticated,[45] and Father Berthier invites him to focus on Christ as the Word made flesh when he reads the Gospels. This all points Pierre toward a more authentic spiritual-ity.[46] As in *Jean-Paul*, the protagonist finally experiences his true faith at Christmastime. While attending Midnight Mass in Boucherville's old church, near his grandfather's house, Pierre has a mystical experience that engages his whole being. But despite making significant progress, he is not yet at the end of his suffering, nor is he fully protected from future relapses. "Nothing is as fickle as these young men," sighs Berthier as he watches his protégé struggle with his internal demons. The priest hopes that Pierre will seek out the light despite how, "at this age, darkness overwhelms a young man's subconscious."[47] His inner socialite is still alive, observes the Jesuit.

As in Jean-Paul's case, Pierre's transition to adulthood is accelerated by grief. First, his grandfather dies, naming him as principal heir and leaving him the family's ancestral home. Next, his favourite sister, Claire, dies unexpect-edly. She is the only female character with any depth or positive associations. Although the others – Pierre's grandmother, his mother, his other sisters, and his cousin – are not purely secondary characters, they consistently behave ac-cording to female stereotypes. In other words, they are unimportant, superficial, gossipy, or enticing. But Claire's character development moves beyond these clichés, highlighting Hertel's conception of gender during adolescence. She is presented as a chaste young lady who intuitively grasps her identity and her mission in life. Although she is the archetypical female adolescent, she does not really experience adolescence since her transition from girl to woman seems to happen naturally. She encounters none of the obstacles that inevitably obstruct the development of her male counterparts. Indeed, the author seems to imply that female characters remain in a state of nature and can therefore dispense with any crises of identity:

> [Pierre] owes something to books. He has cautiously felt his way forward. Claire pressed forward alone, by herself, like a water lily pushing its way through a rough pasture. Feminine fertility produced this miracle: a straightforward evolution, without disruption, blossoming into precocious maturity; and she owed this maturity to no one else. Or perhaps she inherited her soul from her grandmothers. But unlike men's souls, women's souls are not transmitted through words. Instead, Claire felt her grandmothers' souls spontaneously sing within her own.[48]

Such a description makes it easier to understand why coming-of-age stories published during our period of study do not have female protagonists.[49] Indeed, how could an author write a novel about a water lily that grows all by itself? Like the death of Jean-Paul's mother, Claire's death is the female sacrifice that allows Pierre to undergo his ultimate transformation. Fortifying his manliness, the ordeal also gives him an opportunity to shed his "first tears as a man."[50]

Aside from his relationship with Claire, a secondary character whose main role is to die, Pierre's progression toward manhood is an almost exclusively homosocial experience. His priestly mentor and young classmates are his true clan, among whom he begins to understand his vocation:

> For my part, I want a career that lasts, a career that involves some risk. I chose science. Others will tackle the economy, finance. Claude will be a broker. Paul is thinking about taking over the family business. Good old Albert, Albert the poet, will run his father's store. We all want our spirits to triumph as we conquer our lives. Up to the last drop of energy, we will surrender ourselves to our work for the benefit of our sons. Generations of men have made their sacrifices, and we want our sacrifice to be productive.[51]

This passage about vocations clearly highlights Hertel's commitment to reformism. Unlike Jean-Paul, Pierre has no interest in pursuing a career in the clergy.

In fact, despite his classmates' idealism, religious vocations do not figure at all among their professional ambitions. By the late 1930s, lay people had begun playing a larger role within Catholicism, and civic forms of engagement were just as valued as those expressing a rejection of modernity, if not more so. The author of *Le beau risque* also makes it clear that he no longer saw the future of French Canada in the pursuit of the liberal professions, which had been so highly valued in the past. There are no aspiring notaries, lawyers, or doctors among Pierre's classmates. Rather, they are all destined for careers in commerce, finance, and industry. By pursuing science, Pierre makes the boldest choice of all. Hertel's message is clear: French Canadians need to turn toward progress, toward economic modernity, and reject the mirage of a self-sufficient agrarian society. To serve his nation and his faith, Pierre therefore registers in the Faculty of Science. Having committed to this path, he abandons his diary: "A man does not tell his story. He lives it."[52] Thus a life begins as the novel draws to a close.

André Laurence, Canadien français: A Modern Approach

Whereas *Le beau risque* strikes a clearly reformist tone, *André Laurence, Canadien français*, which was published ten years earlier in 1930, takes an even more modernist approach. This can be partially explained by the fact that it was written by a layperson, Pierre Dupuy.[53] When the story begins, the young André Laurence is completing his studies at a Jesuit college that is clearly the Collège Sainte-Marie in Montreal. His mother wants him to follow in the footsteps of his late father by studying medicine, but André is nurturing a less conventional plan. However, no one at school is capable of helping him to achieve his dream of becoming a writer. In fact, the book is very critical of the classical college as an institution, as well as its instructors.[54] And André comes to discover his love of literature only by breaking school rules, when a classmate secretly slides him some poems to read during High Mass, including works by Alfred de Musset, Alphonse de Lamartine, Victor Hugo, Charles Baudelaire, and Paul Verlaine.

Having discovered "real" literature, the young man, who had previously been so athletic and loud, buries himself in books. His mother and teachers naively cheer this development, praising him for his earnestness.[55] Meanwhile, André's new passion transforms him. Devouring book after book, "he suddenly feels as if he has just gained the experience of several successive lifetimes."[56] Determined to develop his talent, and unknown to the college priests, André attends university lectures on literature and gets noticed by a certain Professor Dejean from Paris. The latter recognizes and encourages the protagonist's writing talent, while warning of difficulties ahead. In particular, the professor notes how North America is not a very favourable context for cultural development.

Like *Le beau risque,* Dupuis's novel involves a conflict between two sets of values personified by two different father figures. But this time, the roles have changed: the surrogate father is a layman who rejects the starched conformism of the classical college and its priests. This damning indictment stands in stark contrast to the apologia of the *Ratio Studiorum* found in the novels by Farley and Hertel. Along with his desire to become a writer – a true writer capable of saving his country's literature from "stifling provincialism"[57] – André also tells Dejean of his desire to visit Paris, a city "uplifted by the refined spirit of its men and the pleasure-seeking elegance of the women."[58] However, once the college priests learn about the young man's secret university visits, they are outraged. The principal warns him that a philosophy student must dedicate all of his time to the assigned material: "Ah! The gentleman is studying literature! ... The gentleman is already attending the university. Well then! I predict that you will end up in an asylum, just like Nelligan. But my colleagues and I refuse to be complicit. We will not let you waste your family's money. Either you abandon literature, or you leave the college."[59]

Far from being dissuaded, André continues to embrace his passion for literature. At one of Professor Dejean's lectures, he meets Jacqueline Lambert, a young woman who forces him to rethink his ideas about the other sex:

> For him, women were divided into two categories. Saintly women, including his mother and Aunt Corinne, were, in his eyes, the ideal type. They were almost all of a certain age and their femininity manifested itself through a more composed religious fervour and more affectionate generosity. They were motherly, innocent, angelic. As for the others, he had mainly encountered them in books ... They were fake, carnal, and dangerous.[60]

By contrast, Jacqueline is a "frank, spontaneous, rather unstylish" young woman whose friends and family see her as a bit of a know-it-all. Despite her passion for literature, she can only dabble in the subject because her father believes "that diplomas are not for young ladies."[61] André's admiration for Jacqueline only grows as he discovers that she has "qualities that are perhaps wrongly considered especially masculine: judgment and intelligence."[62] Eventually, she gives him the same feeling of approval that his classmates had previously provided. She shares his fascination with France, and the two sweethearts begin planning a trip to Paris, where André can study literature. Every day, they meet in the church next to the college, where they express their faith in a rather unorthodox way: "A furtive smile, and they kneel next to each other. For a few minutes, their love remains prostrate before God, and André rediscovers his fervour. This prayer is not mandatory, like so many of those he has said at the college.

Quite simply, it expresses thanks for his undeserved happiness and calls for heavenly blessings upon him."[63]

But as the reader might expect, the couple's plans are thwarted. Jacqueline's father, an Americanized and materialistic banker, sees no value in the literary ambitions of his daughter's suitor. The young Laurence finds himself faced with a dilemma: he must choose between his love of literature and his love for Jacqueline. Opting to listen to the voice of reason, he becomes a bank employee on her father's suggestion. Understanding the scope of her sweetheart's sacrifice, Jacqueline tries to distract him from the drudgery of his job by encouraging him to compose an epic poem. This persuasion is all André needs to start believing he can reconcile his love of literature with a conventional life. Filled with hope, he buys a journal and adds an inscription to the first page: "The River, by André Laurence." Clearly, Jacqueline will not be recognized as the co-author of this work, which is nevertheless a collaboration. Thus, despite giving a much more prominent role to a female character, Dupuy's novel fails to provide a particularly radical reinterpretation of gender roles.

The epic poem, which André and Jacqueline compose as a hymn to the beauty of their homeland, is what gives the novel its patriotic tone. Thus the connection between identity and country is forged through the act of literary creation. The poem's picturesque depictions of rural life are inspired by an old couple André meets during his holidays. The Savards are stereotypical Laurentian peasants with a deep love for the river: "he, with his bony and energetic features, his tanned skin that is all wrinkled at the neck, his bright eyes that sometimes smile with cunning and mischief; she, with her round cheeks and moon-shaped and red face that is set upon the corpulent frame of a productive mother hen."[64]

At work, André adapts to a world of noise, impatience, and metal. He makes two good friends: Albert, "the flag waver," who supports the "buy local" campaign; and Paul, an Americanized ladies' man. Under their influence, André is even able to get outside of his own head. In particular, Albert encourages him to play the stock market. Intoxicated by greed, the young protagonist neglects his work at the bank and loses his appetite for writing. But he comes to his senses before losing too much. Jacqueline serves as his moral touchstone and comforts him: "My poor darling, you let yourself fall under the spell of money; like all the others, you wanted to get rich through speculation. Don't despair; it was simply an unfortunate experience. Don't we have a better way of finding freedom: poetry?"[65] But André is frustrated at having squandered his Parisian dream, and he can no longer manage to write in the evenings. His mother, worried at his decline, realizes that he is not at all suited to office work. She conspires with Jacqueline to overhaul his life: the sweethearts will get married, move into the family home, and André will enrol in the Faculty of Medicine.[66]

At first, Jacqueline is fully behind the plan. But then she begins to have second thoughts. She could never allow André to give up on his dream! Instead, she decides to give up on her own. This is the third female sacrifice in our study, albeit the least dire of the three. The young woman tells her fiancé that they have to break up and that he must leave for Paris on his own. She will wait for him, if he wants her to. André is moved by her generosity of spirit: "He thought of how delicately and tenderly she persuaded him of the need to pursue his literary vocation. She sacrificed herself simply and discreetly, so that he would have no trouble allowing himself to be convinced."[67]

Everything seems to be returning to normal when Jacqueline's father belatedly decides to offer André his daughter's hand in marriage, as well as a lucrative promotion. The young man, who thought that his path was finally clear, plunges back into doubt and heartbreak. But this time, Jacqueline is less inclined to sacrifice herself: "Now that a happy life is finally within our reach, don't you think that simple pleasures are worth more than a pipe dream, regardless of how wonderful it might be?" André offers a scathing retort: "So it turns out you're just like all the others! Beef stew, warm slippers, and eating for two ... is that really enough for you?"[68]

Overlooking the tears of his mother and fiancée, André decides to leave for the City of Lights. But having the protagonist follow this solitary path while hurting those who love him seems to raise a moral dilemma for the author. It is as though Dupuy cannot bring himself to conclude the novel on a note that is so out of tune with the values of the period. As a result, André's reasons for going to France get somewhat revised in the book's final paragraph. As his vessel leaves port and approaches the Îles de Varennes, the young man sees a worker waving from shore. The image plunges him into deep thought:

> In his daydream, André thinks of the French Canadian peasant who, long ago, bid adieu to the last French ship carrying the leaders of his country back to the land of their birth, following the Conquest ... Now, after more than a century, it was clear that the Canadian of old had bequeathed his longing to his descendants. Thus, like so many others, André feels drawn to the genius of France. And he will bring the Old Country greetings on behalf of all French Canadian youth.[69]

Apart from these closing lines, there is nothing in the novel to suggest that collective will holds such power over individual choices. It is therefore difficult to believe that André is leaving on a mission to serve his homeland and his generation. More likely, the author simply found a way to avoid making his book's message appear too bold.[70]

Conclusion

"Provide us with men!" Such was the call issued by Lionel Groulx in 1938.[71] The nationalist cleric and well-known historian was exhorting young men to embrace the challenge of rebuilding French Canada. Likewise, the three coming-of-age stories analyzed here offer different ways of "making men" out of adolescents during the interwar period. They all represent contributions to the contemporary public discourse on the future of Quebec society. Among other things, the novels' traditionalist, reformist, and modernist approaches are reflected in their protagonists' choice of vocation: Jean-Paul Forest decides to become a priest, Pierre Martel a scientist, and André Laurence a writer.

Despite the differing destinies of their protagonists, the novelists share an underlying belief about how a classical college student becomes a man: it requires an escape from the world of women. Indeed, manhood requires immersion in the public sphere, that stronghold of masculinity. From this perspective, it is significant how all three narratives are partially shaped by the influence of surrogate fathers with no blood relationship to the protagonist (Pierre's grandfather being the one possible exception).[72] In terms of diegesis, this shift from biological parentage to symbolic parentage is greatly facilitated by the fact that two of the three protagonists – Jean-Paul and André – have already lost their biological fathers.

In all three stories, the intrinsically social dimension of masculine identity is expressed through a connection to the nation. The novels directly associate a commitment to defending French Canada with the steps necessary to achieve manhood. In the context of the 1920s and 1930s, this means that a young man does not become an adult for his own sake but to serve his country. Thus he becomes a soldier committed to the protection of that which has been weakened. Even the most individualistic of the protagonists, André Laurence, writes poetry to the glory of his beautiful homeland and gives himself the mission of making a major contribution to the national literary canon. The metaphor of a "motherland draped in white that perverted sons seek to stain"[73] is a rather unsubtle expression of the gendered symbolism at play in these allusions to the national cause.[74]

Furthermore, the novels all emphasize the importance of a spiritual mission in the transition to manhood. Each of the adolescent protagonists must learn to live his faith in an adult and manly fashion rather than through suffering, servility, or lyricism. For Jean-Paul, the traditionalist, doing so means facing the heroic challenge of becoming an African missionary.[75] For Pierre Martel, the reformer, it means committing to an arduous secular career in a world corrupted by religious conformity and frivolous habits. Finally, André Laurence's modern approach to life leads him to reject the clericalism of his school's out-of-touch priests in favour of freely expressing his true inner voice. From a Freudian perspective, it is as though the protagonists of these coming-of-age stories must abandon the intuitive, emotional, and feminine world of childhood before they can enter a masculine sphere defined by reason and social relations. The depictions of mothers becoming suddenly irrelevant when their sons reach adolescence bear eloquent witness to this logic of detachment. The authors of these interwar novels seem to have viewed the maternal role as entirely focused on childhood. After that, it was time for men to take up the torch. Thus the transition into adulthood – that second birth that required the abandonment of nature in favour of culture – was an exclusively masculine affair.

Finally, the absence of positive heterosexual emotional guidance is another important indication that confirms this vision of the masculine path to maturity. The love of a woman is not an ingredient that forms part of this determining passage in life, nor does it support it. Rather, it is by spurning a woman that a boy becomes a man. Thus Jean-Paul quickly stops courting his fickle neighbour in order to strengthen his commitment to gaining the maturity needed to enter the priesthood, a celibate profession if there ever was one. For Pierre's part, although he does flirt with his voluptuous cousin from Boucherville, her superficial nature quickly puts him off the idea of courting her. Finally, André's relationship with Jacqueline goes smoothly as long as she exhibits "manly" qualities. It comes to an end because she ultimately reveals herself to be bound by dominant feminine models. André therefore must abandon her in order to more fully pursue his destiny. All in all, then, in the late 1920s and early 1930s, becoming a man in novels set at classical colleges was truly men's business!

Notes

This chapter was translated by Steven Watt. It was originally published in French as "Une affaire d'hommes: Adolescence masculine et projections sociales dans quelques romans d'apprentissage de l'entre-deux-guerres," in *Nouvelles masculinités (?): L'identité masculine et ses mises en question dans la littérature québécoise*, ed. Isabelle Boisclair, with Carolyne Tellier, 23–47 (Montreal: Nota bene, 2008). A condensed version, again in French, titled "Des collégiens dans les romans: Un regard sur l'adolescence masculine dans l'entre-deux-guerres," appeared in Louise Bienvenue, Ollivier Hubert, and Christine Hudon, *Le collège classique pour garçons: Études historiques sur une institution québécoise disparue*, 369–88 (Montreal: Fides, 2014).

Translator's note: None of the three novels discussed in this chapter have been published in an English-language edition. All quoted passages are therefore my translations from the original French.

1 François Hertel, *Le beau risque* (1939; reprint, Montreal: Fides, 1961), 122.
2 *Le beau risque* was republished on multiple occasions, by Éditions Bernard Valiquette and Édition de l'ACF in 1939 and by Fides in 1942, 1945, and 1961.

3 Paul-Émile Farley, *Jean-Paul* (Montreal: Clercs de Saint-Viateur, 1929).
4 Pierre Dupuy, *André Laurence, Canadien français* (Paris: Plon, 1930).
5 They are also called "novels of education." This genre first gained popularity in the eighteenth century, "at the same time as the novel established itself as the bourgeois epic and the epic of the individual." *Dictionnaire des genres et notions littéraires* (Paris: Encyclopeadia Universalis and A. Michel, 1997), 656–58.
6 Susan Rubin Suleiman, *Authoritarian Fictions: The Ideological Novel as a Literary Genre* (New York: Columbia University Press, 1983), 7.
7 This expression is borrowed from Luisa Passerini, "La jeunesse comme métaphore du changement social," in *Histoire des jeunes en Occident*, vol. 2, *L'époque contemporaine*, ed. Giovanni Lévi and Jean-Claude Schmitt, 339–408 (Paris: Le Seuil, 1996).
8 Suleiman, *Authoritarian Fictions*, 7.
9 Fernand Dumont, Jean Hamelin, Fernand Harvey, and Jean-Paul Montminy, eds., *Idéologies au Canada français*, vol. 2, *1920–1929* (Sainte-Foy: Presses de l'Université Laval, 1974); Fernand Dumont, Jean Hamelin, and Jean-Paul Montminy, eds., *Idéologies au Canada français*, vol. 3, *1930–1939* (Sainte-Foy: Presses de l'Université Laval, 1978).
10 Paul-André Linteau, René Durocher, Jean-Claude Robert, *Histoire du Québec contemporain*, vol. 1, *De la Confédération à la crise (1867–1929)* (Montreal: Boréal, 1989), 406.
11 The entire social Catholicism movement can be interpreted as an attempt to reconcile tradition with modernity. See, for example, Jean Hamelin and Nicole Gagnon, *Histoire du catholicisme québécois: Le XXe siècle*, vol. 1, *1898–1940* (Montreal: Boréal, 1984), 357–451; and Dominique Foisy-Geoffroy, *Esdras Minville: Nationalisme économique et catholicisme social au Québec durant l'entre-deux-guerres* (Sainte-Foy: Septentrion, 2004).
12 Meanwhile, the Canadian Youth Congress was established in Toronto in 1935. The organization portrayed youth as an age group with a common political vision to express, adopting the intergenerational rhetoric typical of the period. Cynthia Comacchio, *The Dominion of Youth* (Waterloo, ON: Wilfrid Laurier University Press, 2006), 202–3.
13 Roger Brossard, *L'impérieuse mission de la jeunesse* (Montreal: L'œuvre des Tracts, 1938), 4–5. On the emergence of youth as actors in the public sphere during the 1930s and 1940s, see Louise Bienvenue, *Quand la jeunesse entre en scène* (Montreal: Boréal, 2003), 294.
14 Although he also worked as a teacher and prefect, Farley was primarily known as an author of history textbooks. He went on to serve as the superior of the Seminary of Joliette in the 1920s and 1930s. Michel De Grandpré, "*Jean-Paul*, roman du père Paul-Émile Farley," *Dictionnaire des oeuvres littéraires du Québec*, vol. 2, 603–5 (Montreal: Fides, 1987).
15 Several classical colleges that sought to cultivate a priestly vocation among their students were designated *petits séminaires* (minor seminaries).
16 Farley, *Jean-Paul*, 15.
17 Ibid., 160.
18 In *Jean-Paul*, the character Gaston Gervais embodies this negative figure; he is ultimately expelled from school due to his immaturity. Ibid., 142.
19 Ibid., 83.
20 Ibid., 125.
21 Ibid., 170.
22 Ibid., 148. This moment provides an opportunity for a look back. Upon starting at the college, Jean-Paul had prayed to become better. "How could it be that, subsequently, he had become less pious, less confident, even less virtuous? Alas!" Ibid., 149–50.
23 Ibid., 151.
24 Suleiman, *Authoritarian Fictions*, 84.

25 A prayer said by Jean-Paul's mother at the outset of the crisis had foreshadowed this development: "What promise was she making to God? What sacrifice was she agreeing to make? Would she go so far as to offer her own life for the salvation of her dear son?" Farley, *Jean-Paul*, 44.

26 Ibid., 206.

27 A well-known essayist, poet, and novelist, François Hertel (a pseudonym of Rodolphe Dubé) also worked as a classical college instructor during his time with the Jesuits. France Ouellet, *Répertoire numérique du fonds François Hertel* (Montreal: Bibliothèque nationale du Québec, 2003), 11. For preliminary reflections on this novel, see Louise Bienvenue, "Crise d'adolescence et projections sociales dans le roman: Le Beau risque de François Hertel," in *La jeunesse au Canada français: Formation, mouvements et identités,* ed. Michel Bock, 245–53 (Ottawa: University of Ottawa Press, 2007).

28 Before leaving the Jesuits, Hertel declared himself a strong supporter of the Catholic reform movement, which was championed by the French literary magazine *Esprit* and by *La Relève* in Quebec. See Stéphanie Angers and Gérard Fabre, *Échanges intellectuels entre la France et le Québec (1930–2000): Les réseaux de la revue* Esprit *avec* La Relève, Cité libre, Parti pris *et* Possibles (Sainte-Foy: Presses de l'Université Laval, 2004); and Marie Martin-Hubbard, "François Hertel, témoin et participant des grands débats des années trente au Québec" (MA thesis, University of Ottawa, 2004).

29 Hertel, *Le beau risque*, 37.

30 Ibid., 20–21. During this period, the theme of anxiety figured prominently in Hertel's thought. He was an avid reader of Henri Daniel-Rops, author of *Notre inquiétude* (1926). Hertel also published an essay on youth titled *Leur inquiétude* (1936). In some ways, *Le beau risque* echoes this earlier work, which describes the unique turmoil faced by the 1930s generation as well as an agenda for change. However, the novel met with much greater success: 18,000 copies were printed, a large number for the French Canadian market of the period. On the novel, see Kenneth Landry, "*Le beau risque,*" *Dictionnaire des oeuvres littéraires du Québec,* vol. 2, 135–37 (Montreal: Fides, 1987).

31 Like *Jean-Paul, Le beau risque* champions a *Ratio Studiorum* portrayed as being perfectly adapted to the needs of young minds on the cusp of adulthood. On this topic, see Claude Corbo, *Les Jésuites québécois et le cours classique après 1845* (Sillery: Septentrion, 2004).

32 Hertel, *Le beau risque*, 40–41.

33 Ibid., 42.

34 Ibid., 18.

35 Ibid., 32.

36 Ibid.

37 These intergenerational tensions are even more explicit in the description on the book's back cover: "François Hertel describes the blossoming of modern youth. Faced with a lack of understanding from his elders and a climate of stifling conformism, the hero nevertheless manages to persevere and embark on a promising life, thanks to the love of his skilled educators."

38 On intergenerational dynamics in 1930s Quebec, see Bienvenue, *Quand la jeunesse entre en scène;* and Karine Hébert, "Une generation, entre opposition et affirmation," in *Impatient d'être soi-même: Les étudiants montréalais, 1895–1960,* 129–82 (Montreal: Presses de l'Université du Québec, 2008).

39 Hertel, *Le beau risque*, 47.

40 Ibid., 80.

41 Ibid., 90.

42 It is not clear exactly when the novel is set. However, it must be after 1926 since Pierre's father mentions the papal condemnation of the magazine *L'Action française*, which was issued in late December 1926. Ibid., 31.

43 Ibid., 48.

44 Ibid., 104.

45 For instance, Pierre observes how his grandfather followed the Stations of the Cross "without any exaggerated or ecstatic postures." Ibid., 82.

46 Ibid., 42.

47 Ibid., 52.

48 Ibid., 114–15.

49 Susan Suleiman makes a similar argument based on observations by Georg Lukács, *The Theory of the Novel* (London: Merlin, 1971). Suleiman, *Authoritarian Fictions*, 65. We have been unable to find any exceptions, even ones that might prove the rule, in the French Canadian literature of the period. Female coming-of-age novels appear much later, after the feminist period. See, for example, France Théoret, *Laurence* (Montreal: Les Herbes Rouges, 1996), published in English as *Laurence* (Toronto: Mercury, 1998).

50 Hertel, *Le beau risque*, 114.

51 Ibid., 128.

52 Ibid., 122.

53 Although *André Laurence, Canadien français* was Pierre Dupuy's only novel, it earned him the Prix David as one of Quebec's best writers. Trained as a lawyer, Dupuy began his diplomatic career in 1922. He continued to work as a diplomat almost until his death in 1969. Arsène Lauzière, "André Laurence, Canadien français," *Dictionnaire des oeuvres littéraires du Québec*, vol. 2, 44–46 (Montreal: Fides, 1987).

54 Publishing the novel in Paris certainly made it easier for Dupuy to adopt a more critical tone.

55 Dupuy, *André Laurence*, 17.

56 Ibid., 18.

57 Ibid., 34.

58 Ibid., 96.

59 Ibid., 14. The brilliant Montreal poet Émile Nelligan (1879–1941) was institutionalized for mental illness in 1899 and spent most of his life in the Saint-Jean-de-Dieu psychiatric hospital.

60 Ibid., 40.

61 Ibid., 43.

62 Ibid., 48–49.

63 Ibid., 60.

64 Ibid., 157.

65 Ibid., 188.

66 Ibid., 214.

67 Ibid., 234.

68 Ibid., 240.

69 Ibid., 246.

70 André Laurence's journey stands out from those of the two other protagonists because of its modernity, which is also reflected in his doubts about the relevance of his chosen path: "And now it was his turn, he was the one heading out to sea, toward Paris ... but he was still not convinced he had made the right choice. He was suddenly being assailed by so many different emotions!" Ibid., 245. He is solely responsible for choosing his destiny and

is overcome by the burden. In contrast to André's uncertainty, the other two protagonists embrace their newfound identity with the certainty of Truth.

71 Lionel Groulx, *Faites-nous des hommes: Préparation des jeunes à leurs tâches prochaines* (Montreal: Les Éditions de la J.I.C., 1938).

72 Susan Suleiman writes, "What is striking is that the father-donor, if he is present, is rarely the hero's biological father. He is, rather, a spiritual, elective father, whom the hero chooses as his own." Suleiman, *Authoritarian Fictions*, 81.

73 Farley, *Jean-Paul*, 170.

74 On female representations of the nation during the period, see Michel Demers, "Vive la Canadienne! Les représentations de l'identité féminine dans le défilé de la Saint-Jean-Baptiste à Montréal (1924–1961)" (MA thesis, Université de Sherbrooke, 2001).

75 The interwar period saw an increase in the number of foreign missions undertaken by the Canadian Catholic Church, allowing the latter to expand its influence throughout the world. From this perspective, the novel is perfectly in tune with the period when it was written. See Lucia Ferretti, *Brève histoire de l'Église catholique* (Montreal: Boréal, 1999).

13
Boys and Boyhood: Exploring the Lives of Boys in Windsor, Ontario, during the Postwar Era, 1945–65

Christopher J. Greig

IN THIS CHAPTER I explore how boyhood was experienced by a small group of men who grew up in Windsor, Ontario, during the immediate postwar period of 1945–1965. This research was conducted through semi-structured interviews with men who were born between 1935 and 1953 and who are now in their late fifties, sixties, or seventies. The men were asked to talk about their childhood experiences during the 1940s and 1950s. Individually, their testimonies were commonplace reflections on boyhood; but pieced together, they began to reveal common themes. One theme that quickly emerged was the way that boys carefully navigated between "acceptable" and "unacceptable" boyhood masculinities. The key distinctions between acceptable and unacceptable versions of boyhood were often based on a boy's capacity to engage in sports such as ice hockey or to be physically tough. Certainly, an acceptable boyhood was also built on heterosexuality, as being perceived to be a homosexual was something for boys to avoid at all costs. Yet, despite a cultural emphasis on "compulsory heterosexuality," some men's testimonies, as this chapter shows, demonstrated that heterosexuality among boys was not so straightforward.

Drawing on newspapers, popular magazines, and other published work, this small-scale study relies on formal interviews conducted in 2008 with nine men and three women who grew up in Windsor, Ontario, during the postwar period and who were selected to represent a diversity of cultural backgrounds based on race, sexual identity, and social class. The ethno-cultural makeup of the respondents reflected to a degree the ethno-cultural classed backgrounds of Windsor residents at that time. Seven of the men – Albert, William, David, Bill, Dennis, Harry, and Ken – were of Anglo-European heritage but came from varying class backgrounds. The other two men, Henry and James, identified as black. James was the only "visible/invisible" minority, being both black and gay. Unfortunately, despite the significant historical presence of

Aboriginal communities in the Windsor-Essex context, there were no Aboriginal men enrolled in the study.

For this chapter, I do not draw heavily on the voices of the three women I interviewed. These women described the boys they grew up with, including their brothers and male friends, what activities those boys pursued, and what advantages or disadvantages they perceived in being a boy compared to being a girl. Pseudonyms are used to refer to participants and others throughout this chapter.

Windsor, Ontario, 1945–65

Windsor lies in the most southwestern point of Ontario and is just a few minutes' drive from downtown Detroit by either the Detroit-Windsor Tunnel or the Ambassador Bridge. The Detroit River separates Windsor from Detroit. During the postwar period, Windsor was Ontario's fourth largest city and was well known as an industrial centre, being the location of the Ford Motor Company of Canada, Chrysler Canada, and a number of "affiliated auto foundries like Auto Specialties, Walker Metal Products and Malleable Iron." As the name of the city suggests, Windsor has its origins in British tradition, although this white Anglo-Protestant tradition was integrated with Windsor's longstanding French Canadian and black communities.[1] Although Windsor's postwar population was to become increasingly diverse as immigration patterns changed, including a large influx of eastern Europeans and Italian immigrants after 1945, it was a community structured and divided by class and race.

When it came to race relations during the postwar period, Windsor was not unlike other Ontario communities in that a racial hierarchy functioned to situate white Anglo-Protestants at the top, new immigrants such as those with eastern European, Italian, and Chinese backgrounds somewhere in the middle, and blacks at the bottom. In this context, "white flight" to the suburbs found in communities such as Tecumseh and LaSalle accelerated in the 1940s and 1950s, leaving Windsor increasingly divided by race. Between 1941 and 1956 the suburban population grew by 304 percent and the city by only 16 percent.[2] For example, Les Dickirson, a member of the executive committee for the Windsor Council on Group Relations during the postwar period, described race relations in Windsor this way:

> The patterns of discrimination in the City of Windsor in the late 1940s were, for the most part, indistinguishable from those found in most other Canadian communities. While discriminatory practices, in one form or another, were extended to every racial, religious and ethnic group in Windsor, it was the Black community in particular which bore the brunt at every level.[3]

It is clear that the lives of those individuals who were not white Anglo-Protestants were directly and negatively shaped by the effects of racism, their lives being situated within structures and relations of Windsor's racialized hierarchies. Yet, despite the various populations that were targets of racism, it was black Windsorites who were disproportionately discriminated against.

In short, shaped by a race-based hierarchy that privileged whiteness, non-white Anglo-Protestants in Windsor experienced significantly more difficulties than other populations when it came to personal freedom and mobility, had greater difficulties using recreational facilities, and were often segregated in lower-paying service jobs.

At the point where whiteness and social class oppression met, blacks and other nonwhites in Windsor were situated in mostly semi-skilled and unskilled labour.[4] For example, according to a 1947 report issued by the Windsor Interracial Council, "97.8% of all Blacks were employed as common labourers."[5] Henry, for example, whose father worked as a bellhop in a local Windsor hotel, recalled his mother also rising early for work many mornings. The house where Henry grew up was in the black enclave of what was known as the McDougall Street Corridor. At the time, the McDougall Street Corridor was, as historian Peggy Bristow points out, a site that had been the centre of the black community in Windsor since the late 1800s.[6] According to Henry, his mother would board a bus and ride across the Ambassador Bridge, the border crossing linking Canada and the United States, to the wealthy, white enclave of Grosse Pointe, Michigan.[7] Henry's mother served as a maid for wealthy Americans, as job opportunities for blacks in Windsor at that time were very limited. In fact, it wasn't until 1955, as Bristow points out, that the City of Windsor hired its first "black female secretary."[8] And, even a decade or so later, when few working-class blacks like Henry were able to secure a rare higher-paying unionized job at General Motors or Chrysler Motor Corporation, for example, they continued to be subjected to overt acts of racism and discrimination, including, as Henry related, being given the more labour-intensive and dirtier duties.

Yet, despite the overwhelming evidence of the visible effects of racism on the lives of black Canadians and eastern European, Italian, and Chinese immigrants, a few of the men saw their boyhood experiences growing up in Windsor with a sense of colour-blindness. For these few, their sense of colour-blindness seemed to lie in an imagined world that the racially privileged men interviewed shared with other racially privileged men. David and Dennis seemed unaware of the "worlds within worlds" that existed during their boyhood years and that were clearly present in their everyday midst.[9] It was certainly the case that Windsor had areas of ethnic and racial concentration, with racialized minorities frequently living in older, less desirable areas of the downtown core, including Little Italy and the McDougall Street Corridor. Despite this, David, for example, who grew up in a largely all-white neighbourhood, recalled that as a boy and later as an adolescent, he knew "nothing of racism."[10] In some ways, Windsor's black population at times seemed to occupy an urban working-class space all but unknown to the world of some white boys. Nonetheless, the claim that race did not matter during the period under study is undermined by the weight of historical evidence that shows how powerfully it shaped Windsor's history, influencing where families lived, what restaurants they frequented, where mothers and fathers worked, and where children went to school.[11]

For some boys who grew up in Windsor during the postwar era, social class structured their lives and shaped where they would play. Some of the men recalled with clarity the wealthy neighbourhoods in Windsor, such as Walkerville. Their memories, however, did not reveal a warm sense of nostalgia but seemed to suddenly flash across a deep crevice of social class. Albert, for example, recalled how he and his friends would "avoid the area of Hall, Moy, and Gladstone," streets that ran through Walkerville. Asked why he avoided Walkerville, Albert mentioned that those homes "were the rich people's houses ... We didn't go over there ... I don't know why ... We just didn't go over there."[12] Walkerville was named after well-known American distiller Hiram Walker and contained some of the mansions that wealthy industrialists and professional men in Windsor owned at the turn of the twentieth century and before. Ken, who described his own family as "dirt poor," likewise never went to Walkerville or made friends with boys from that community.[13]

Yet, for some boys, race and class barriers were not overly deterministic but were at times fluid and complex. Henry, for example, who grew up in a working-class, largely black neighbourhood located in downtown Windsor, recalled that his family "never had any money." Despite his class location and racialized identity, Henry's best friend was white and wealthy and lived on Victoria Avenue, one of the more prestigious streets in Windsor. Despite the differences in racial and class backgrounds, Henry recalled spending much of his boyhood at Sam's house, largely because Sam had a "house full of toys."[14] The memories of Albert and Ken highlight the saliency of class as a historical, social, and political factor in establishing boyhood practices in terms of where they chose to play and the friendships they chose to form. At the same time, Henry's experience with a white, wealthy family reflected the complexity around issues of race, class, and boyhood experiences.

Along with race and social class, a theme that emerged from the men's recollections of their boyhood experiences was violence. It is to this theme that I now turn.

Boyhood Violence

Postwar psychological discourse taught the reading public that "real boys" were assumed to be developing normally if they were active and aggressive, as well as preferred sports over other activities such as reading. Drawing from postwar psychological discourse, social and cultural commentators also taught the public that a "real boy" would never run away from a fight with another boy; to do so would, and should, they argued, raise questions about a boy's masculinity.[15] Although such conduct in the face of violence had been a standard of appropriate masculinity since the turn of the twentieth century or longer, during the postwar period it intensified. This phenomenon helped to establish a clear expectation that was used to set apart a perceived real boyhood from an inferior boyhood, an appropriate boyhood from a perceived feminized one. To some degree, this broader social discourse shaped the lives of boys in Windsor.

Bill, for example, remarked that the boys he knew from his neighbourhood fought "all the time." Similarly, when asked whether there was fighting between the boys in his working-class neighbourhood, Ken quickly responded, "Oh yes, all the time." When asked why boys fought, he simply replied, "We'd fight about anything."[16] Ken elaborated on one incident that stuck out in his mind when it came to his own experiences with fighting as a boy:

> I think one of the worst fights I ever had was over a catcher's mask. One of the other guys wanted to be the catcher, and I wanted to be the catcher, and we started struggling over a catcher's mask. We had one heck of a fight. I got knocked in the mouth, too, and I got a bloody lip, and that night I was playing my first band job, I think I was thirteen, and I played the saxophone ... and it wouldn't stop bleeding. I had blood all over the reed and the mouthpiece.[17]

Certainly, the conquest and disciplining of boys by other boys was wrapped up in the threat of violence. The threat of violence by those boys who wielded the most social and physical power not only provided a defence of their own actions but also naturalized a gender regime that was filled with uncertainty and required constant negotiating in order to reduce the risk to themselves – all of which amounted to an ongoing friction for boys between safety and danger. As Albert recalled,

> Because of the neighbourhood I grew up in, it was important not to get picked on. It was also important to have a reputation in order not to get picked on. You knew who the one [boy] was to be afraid of. The boy, his name was Fred ... was unpredictable ... so you were never friends with them, but maybe you hung around them in order to keep an eye on them.[18]

So for Albert, who was born in 1941 in what he described as a "working-poor" neighbourhood of Windsor, the threat of violence from other neighbourhood boys such as Fred necessitated acquiring among his male friends positive "respect" based on aggression and physical strength. Albert learned that once this kind of masculine respect was earned, a boy could simply ward off potential violence without ever having to actually fight:

> It wasn't so much fighting but more a matter of establishing who you were in the neighbourhood. If I can beat Jimmy up, or Jimmy can beat me up, and you ran into Gary and found out that Gary was afraid of someone you beat up, then Gary ended up at the bottom ... It was like the monkeys, it really was, the hierarchy was there![19]

For Albert, social relations among boys were better thought of as a "pecking order" where the toughest and strongest boys were situated safely at the top. For some of these boys, winning a place within the pecking order meant escaping personal oppression and gaining personal status. Fortunately, boys such as Dennis, who described himself as rather tall and muscular as a boy, were largely exempt from violence brought on by other boys because of their recognized physical size and strength. Nonetheless, Albert's comments reveal, to a certain measure, the endless work – assessing, evaluating, and negotiating – boys did with other boys to avoid violence and to position themselves safely, yet tentatively, within the gender landscape of their boyhood. So, in the end, the relationship between and among Windsor boys was often filled with uncertainty and anxiety since most boys never really knew for certain whether they would be at the top of the gender hierarchy or be thrown to the bottom.

Yet, for some Windsor boys, violence in the form of fighting was simply a parental expectation, something an "appropriate" boy should do if, for example, a female member of his family experienced male violence. William's recollection of one boyhood incident illustrates this point:

> I mean, you had to protect your family. I remember when my sister got hit by a neighbourhood guy, probably just a little bit younger than me, probably by three or four months. I don't know what happened. They were in some kind of an argument, and he hit her across the head with a stick. And all I remember was ... pounding on him, and my older sister screaming at me, pulling me off.[20]

Despite William's physical action in avenging his sister, he still received punishment from both his mother and father, not because he was fighting but because his sister was hit in the first place: "When I got home ... I got a strip torn off me because I didn't protect my sister ... That was a given, you know, when you're walking to school, ... [something] you're supposed to do."[21] Within the hardscrabble Windsor context, there was a gendered ethic that created a positive obligation among boys to meet male violence with male violence if it was enacted in the protection of a female. Situated in the gender order of the era, the castigation of William by his parents is not surprising and clearly points to a major social basis of the dominant version of boyhood at that time: the subordination and protection of women. Yet, although a boy's neighbourhood was often a key site for conflict and physical skirmishes between and among boys, it was by no means the only site. For some boys, school was also a context where violence occurred.

School for some boys was a gendered site where they would encounter various forms of violence. James, for example, talked about how spending time at school brought with it an explicit fear of homophobic violence, a point I discuss below, whereas for others like William, it was the time spent walking to school that provided the greatest opportunity for violence to occur:

> There was always this friction. I mean, we always had to walk against the traffic [other children] going to Gordon McGregor [elementary school], so there was always this battle on the sidewalk between the kids going to St. Bernard and the kids going to Gordon McGregor. And there was always [among boys] pushing and shoving and fighting, you know, every day [going] to school.[22]

Along with physical skirmishes between and among boys, responses of some of the men also conveyed how they experienced violence at the hands of male educators. In fact, one of David's strongest memories was of the violence he experienced as a Grade 3 student. Although David noted that his school experience was positive overall, making special mention that "teachers were excellent in those days," he still retained some vivid memories of how he encountered institutional male power in the form of his principal: "He was an awfully miserable man. He used to use the strap often. He is long gone now and I am glad of it. He gave me the strap a lot of the time for spelling ... He would whip out that old black strap, and he was going to beat it [spelling] into me."[23] For David, this experience with violence and the overall petty tyranny of the male principal appeared to be fresh in his mind, although the incident had happened over half a century ago. For example, the consequential accumulation of resentment and anger over the incident became clear as David went on to mention that, as an adult, he "was very glad to read in the local newspaper when he [the principal] died."[24] Dennis, too, encountered male violence at school but far more frequently. Dennis remembered, for example, being strapped "every day" as a Grade 3 student by his classroom teacher and a few times by the school principal. To withstand this physical and physiological violence, Dennis apparently internalized a standard of normative masculinity where toughness, power, and a refusal to be dominated by other males were central. For Dennis, the violence he experienced as a child "didn't matter" because, he stated unequivocally, the teacher and principal "could not hurt me."[25]

The gendered nature of school and its undercurrent of violence shaped boys' reading practices. Harry, who mentioned that he "excelled" academically in school, also recalled that "being smart causes trouble" with other boys. Asked to elaborate on his point, Harry revealed the effects of postwar gender politics on his boyhood and the way that he had to carefully navigate his school's gendered terrain: "When you're a guy and you like books, it is kind of hard. Everyone else is out punching each other up or playing basketball. I wasn't interested in that and I knew that, but I didn't want to be labelled [homosexual]."[26] Although Harry's comment reveals the way that boys actively positioned themselves to avoid being labelled a homosexual, it also shows a conflict and struggle between the dominant and the subordinate understandings of postwar masculinity within boys themselves. A boy may have loved to read, but showing this interest publicly would have placed him in physical and psychological jeopardy due to prevailing, narrow standards of an "appropriate" boyhood.

Harry remembered an incident in one of his English classes that further illuminates other complex rules around gender and boys' reading practices at that time: "We had to stand in line [in class] and tell her [the teacher] what book we were reading. So I had this book and I showed it to her and she said, 'Good for you.' Everyone in the class could hear. And I turned beet-red because it wasn't something about a baseball hero or any macho stuff."[27] Certainly, for many boys, literary genres such as poetry were simply off limits, as their reading interests were circumscribed by the application and policing by other boys of the hegemonic heteronormative understandings of masculinity. This was clearly evident in the following statement by Harry: "I didn't have an interest in poetry, but I knew enough to stay away from poetry or else you would get laughed at. Girls could [read poetry], but guys couldn't."[28] In Windsor, where to a great extent athleticism had become a self-conscious pursuit among many of the boys in the study, the coercion, fear, and possible humiliation that bound boys together clearly did not escape Harry. In short, it appears that some Windsor boys simply adhered to the crude and implicit injunction that being an "appropriate" boy meant avoiding conflict with the interests and views prescribed by the prevailing postwar understandings of boyhood.

The fear of being labelled a homosexual haunted the childhood world of some Windsor men. In light of the intensified homophobia of the postwar period, for some boys, avoiding the mundane tyrannies of gender violence required carefully navigating the gendered landscape of their communities in general and their schools in particular. In some instances, doing so included being aware of how homophobia was colour-coded. The men discussed, for example, how on Thursdays they would avoid wearing the colours green and yellow together at school, lest one be thought a homosexual. Ken, Albert, and Harry all remembered Thursdays at their different Windsor elementary schools being designated by other students as "green and yellow day," a day that was regulated by the impact of homophobia. Ken, for example, recalled, "If you wore green on a Thursday, you were a fairy."[29] Despite failing to know where the colour-coded homophobic tradition originated or how he acquired knowledge of this gender rule, Harry remembered that it was well known by most every child that if you were a boy, you simply "didn't wear green or yellow on Thursday." When asked why, Harry mentioned that Thursday "was fairy day ... I remember that in public school, you're a fairy because that was fairy day." Yet, although boys knew not to wear the "wrong" colours on Thursdays because of their close association with homosexuality, they often knew little about what exactly homosexuality was, apart from a label to be avoided and an expression of some hostility. As Harry explained, "We didn't know what [homosexuality] was but we knew it wasn't good."[30]

In the postwar period, the cry went out to adults and boys alike to be on the lookout for signs of effeminacy in boys. Clearly, in the 1940s and 1950s, males perceived to be effeminate and homosexual were outcasts with diminished characters. Yet some Windsor boys worried less about their characters per se and more about seemingly insignificant missteps that could activate the haunting homophobic terror of being perceived or found out to be homosexual. James, for example, discussed how one of his older male relatives mentored him when he was fourteen years old on how to "pass" as an "appropriate" boy in order to survive secondary school: "My older cousin taught me how to walk. He showed me how I was walking and said, 'You will never survive high school if you walk like that. And [James], that's not how you should carry your books either.'"[31] The cultural conditions that shaped James's everyday experience in school were equally present in the broader social and political sphere. Concurrent with the anti-homosexual purges of the McCarthy era in the United States, various state and other governmental committees in Canada were established to ferret out homosexual men from the civil service.[32] And although James never touched on the broader political atmosphere, which was so clearly about the regulation of sexual identities and desire, he did note that during his time in elementary school and high school, he hid his sexuality in fear of the physical and emotional consequences that were all too evident.

Yet some men recalled how the visibility of men in their community who were, or were thought to be, homosexual brought about mixed feelings; boys' homosexual interest, curiosity, and desire commingled with homophobia. Situated in class relations, Albert, for example, talked about how he and his best friend, Philip, "discovered sex together." Albert talked about how, at age twelve, he and Philip, described by Albert as "working-class," were sexually curious about men:

> Philip would always find the gay guy in the neighbourhood. He would always have to have the gay experience. He led a seedier existence than I did ... just get the gay guy to see what he would do. I don't think he did anything. We almost interviewed him. The oddity of it ... the gay guy in the neighbourhood. He was a bit of a pariah in the neighbourhood ... He lived just one block away.[33]

Curiosity about what it was like to be a homosexual appears largely to be the subtext of Albert's comment, revealing the way that sexual desire was more complicated than most adults imagined when it came to postwar understandings of normative boyhood. Yet Albert went on to note that Philip most likely had sex with men for money, perhaps revealing the way that economic conditions and social class may have intersected with gender and a boy's sexual experiences.

Yet, although boyhood was marked at times by violence and oppression in and out of school, particularly for those boys who did not display the characteristics and attributes of normative boyhood, it was also a period that was, for some boys, marked by freedom and power.

The Power and Freedom of Boyhood

Not all boys were bicycle riders, and not all bicycle riders were boys. The fit was certainly not perfect. But unlike for girls, the association between boys and bicycles in Windsor was strong, and most importantly from the perspective of a historian of boyhood and gender, the link between the bike and the boy reveals much about the construction of masculinity. The domination by men of automobile technology has its origins in childhood, and in many cases the association begins with toy cars and moves from there to bikes and then to actual cars. In this sense, the significance of the bike to boyhood, like the significance of the car to manhood, was simply taken for granted as an accoutrement of an appropriate postwar masculinity. David, for example, recalled that when he was a boy, "playing with [toy] cars was a big thing." In fact, David, who as an adult would become an automobile enthusiast, excitedly remembered the exact type of toy car that he preferred as a boy: "high-quality," die-cast, miniature cars and trucks by Dinky Toys. These specific toys were manufactured in England and came at a relatively high cost. David said, "I remember my Dad and I going down to the hobby shop on Tecumseh Road. There was a Dinky dump truck that I wanted that cost $2.20, which was a lot of money back then. At that time, that was probably an hour's work for him. Eventually, though, my Dad bought it for me."[34] The ubiquity of motor vehicle toys in the testimonies of the men emerged as an obvious theme, but less obvious was the link between an earlier interest in toy cars and a serious later interest in automobiles. David, a toy car collector and enthusiast as a boy, recalled,

> One of the things that I remember that impressed me to this day, and I still re-member – when I was small, probably eight years old, my uncle in Detroit knew a fellow ... Mandrake the Magician ... My uncle knew him and brought him over to our house. He came over with a brand-new white Cadillac convertible with red leather seats ... Well, that car impressed me to no end, and I was just young. And that is the car that I drive now and have for many years.[35]

Situated in Canada's premier car town and in a socio-political culture where cars were codified as masculine, the bicycle was constructed as something of a key boyhood accoutrement, a symbol of power and freedom. Similar to a car, bikes afforded boys a sense of excitement and power, as well as a level of free-dom from adult authority and geography. For example, David remarked that "no-one knows the neighbourhood like a boy on a bike," expressing that some boys in Windsor had the freedom and power to explore the geography of the city in general and his neighbourhood in particular.[36] For others, such as Harry, a bike also afforded him and his young friends the opportunity to escape do-mestic confines and parental supervision: "We got the hell out of the house. We all had bicycles. We would go away all day and I am only ten. I was two miles away and my parents didn't know where I was."[37] In a similar way, David re-membered that he and his friends had "a lot of freedom" from parents and other adults as young boys. For David and his little "band of cutthroats," as he described his boyhood friends, the city was simply an open space to be explored by bike: "We would get on our bikes and we would be all over this city. Like I said, no-body knows a town like a boy on a bike. I would be all over this city. A kid on a bike has all afternoon. Don't come home until suppertime or when the street lights come on."[38] Freedom for most boys often meant mobility, independence, excitement, power, and the ability to roam and ride across the city at will. William recalled, "Everyone in our neighbourhood was pretty independent. We would ride our bicycles everywhere. There was no limit as to where we went. I remem-ber one time we rode our bicycles to Point Pelee." This would have been no small task for William and his boyhood friends, as Point Pelee, now a national park, is approximately 75 kilometres away from Windsor.

Yet it would also be a mistake to generalize about boys and bikes based on David's and William's middle-class experiences. For boys such as Albert and Ken, bikes were a rarity, especially new bikes. For these two working-class boys, it was only "from time to time" that they had a bike, and neither boy ever once acquired a "new bike." Hinting that his boyhood was limited by the actions of his authoritative father and by a lack of economic means, Ken was simply not afforded the degree of freedom that other boys enjoyed with their bikes. Ken remembered, "Well, we would travel around [on bikes] but we didn't get too far in the neighbourhood. We wouldn't go pedalling down to the [Detroit] river or anything like that. We basically stayed in our own community."[39] Understanding how race functioned to limit a boy's movements and opportunities, Henry recalled riding his bike but noted that he never ventured "too far" from his home in the McDougall Street Corridor. For other boys, such as Albert, who grew up in a working-class neighbourhood, the bike was far less about freedom and enjoyment and more a matter of economic necessity. For Albert, who worked delivering goods for a local drug store, "the bike was really important because it meant a job." Albert went on to mention that it was his uncle who bought the bike "for me."[40]

Despite an era marked by Cold War anxiety and uncertainty, some of the men recalled only easy freedoms and a childhood without terror or fear. To a certain measure, men's recollections about freedom during their boyhood were surprisingly similar whatever their neighbourhood or class background. William recalled that he was never at home under parental eyes. Rather, "we were out on the streets playing 'til dark, and then we'd go to bed." For many boys such as William, this arrangement represented unlimited freedom. Yet, although men such as David, William, and Dennis recalled having much freedom as boys, there were other men who saw unlimited freedom from their parents' watchful gaze during boyhood in more complicated ways.

Growing up in a working-class family, Bill remembered that his father, who worked at Ford Motor Company, and his mother, who worked part-time at a local jewellery store located in downtown Windsor, simply provided too much freedom and not enough parental supervision. "I had too much freedom, that was the problem," recalled Bill. He went on to note that, as a boy, "I was brought up to just do my own thing." And while Bill did his "own thing," his "parents, they were doing their own thing." Clearly still feeling some hurt after a significant amount of time had passed, Bill recalled that his mother and father, rather than spending time with him, simply pursued their own leisure and recreational activities:

My parents bowled and played golf ... and, well, my dad coached and was one of the first members of AKO [a local minor football club]. He was brought up, kind of, in a neighbourhood with a bunch of guys on a football team, and then they started a club from that. So he was real good at sports. He played football, baseball, softball ... He was one of the best softball catchers. I think he used to play for the all-star team.[41]

His father's full-time job and masculine sporting pursuits meant that Bill was left largely by himself: "I would just come home at night, come in and listen to the radio, go to bed and get up early in the morning, and then take off again."[42] That his parents left Bill largely to his own devices and did not provide him with "a whole lot of discipline" seems to run contrary to the 1950s, middle-class, postwar "domestic ideal," which increasingly promoted parental supervision as a way to effectively regulate childhood behaviour.

When it came to physical and social freedoms, however, boys had more than girls. Mary recalled that she and her brother "had two different lifestyles." For Mary, her "brother had freedom. He could go where he wanted to go." This sense of freedom was not available to Mary. She was, as she recalled, largely restricted to the small geographical area centred on her neighbourhood street. But it wasn't just geography that was gendered; it was also the amount of time a girl or boy was allowed outside the house. Mary recalled how she "had to be in when the street lights went on," whereas her "brother was supposed to be in" then, too, but rarely was. To explain the difference in curfew times, Mary simply stated that her brother "was a boy." For Mary, "boys had their freedom and girls were protected."[43] Individual respondents invariably made a distinction between the historical experience of boys and that of girls when it came to freedom, which was a social state that afforded interaction with others, structured time, benefited social identity and status, and, for boys, produced a growing sense of being connected to wider public purposes.

But it was not just an expanded sense of freedom that helped to define the contours of an appropriate boyhood. An appropriate boyhood was, in no small measure, determined by a boy's interest in sports.

Boyhood and Sports

Boys who did not like sports such as hockey, baseball, and football or who did not demonstrate a requisite amount of sporting prowess were thought lacking in the proper boyhood bona fides, thus raising the spectre of homosexuality. For example, in an interview conducted a few years before he died, Mark Goodson, a well-known American television producer during the 1950s and beyond, re-marked on the "problem" that had plagued him from boyhood to manhood:

I've decided to come out of the closet. It is not an easy decision to admit openly that I really don't like sports. There – I've said it. Do you know what it's like to be a man who is not a sports fan? Who not only doesn't care who wins the World Series but who is never exactly sure which teams are playing? Who never, but never, reads the sports section? I approach this subject with a light touch, but in truth it has been a problem that has plagued me for most of my life, particularly when I was a young boy. For to be a boy not interested in sports was, particularly back then, to run the risk of being thought a homosexual.[44]

Broadly speaking, Goodson's comment reveals the way that an "appropriate" heterosexual masculinity and sport were invariably and deeply linked in the postwar period. Within the Canadian context, in his book *Along Olympic Road* (1951), well-known radio broadcaster and writer Foster Hewitt conflates sport and an "appropriate" boyhood by describing the hockey rink as an "outdoor nursery" for Canadian boys.[45]

Given the postwar emphasis on the link between sport and an "appropriate" boyhood, it is not surprising that Dennis, when asked about what kind of boyhood activities he liked most, responded without hesitation with a sporting trinity of his own: "hockey, baseball, football."[46] For Dennis and other men such as William, it was sport, particularly hockey, that tied them to their fellow boys, filled their days and minds with excitement and joy, and was an important and enduring source of their masculine, white, working- and middle-class culture and identity. Sports provided them, as young boys, with a reason to gather together and engage with other boys in male-only spaces, thus helping to define what separated boys from girls.

Not surprisingly, for boys such as Dennis, the city-run outdoor hockey rink was their key gathering point during the winter: "Every day, every day ... That was back in the day when the city would make rinks in all of the parks. And so the rinks were already there, all flooded, ready to go. All we did was get our hockey stuff on and get to the park."[47] For some, it was older males who provided the initiation into the world of informal, unsupervised hockey. William, for example, remembered being about eight or nine years old when he was given "a hockey stick from one of the guys on the street, for my birthday."[48] Not only did older boys see fit to organize and initiate younger boys into traditional male pastimes by providing resources such as hockey sticks, but they also contributed an enormous amount of informal gender-work by demonstrating to the smaller boys how to build an elaborate and sophisticated outdoor ice rink, including handmade nets. William recalled, "The house across the street, the two houses side by side, we used to build – mainly, I was one of the younger guys on the street, and so when I say 'we', there's always more older guys – but they would build a rink across the two backyards, complete with boards and benches."[49] In the dead of a cold Ontario winter, when backyard ice rinks were not to be found, other methods were used to create homemade ice rinks. William, for example, remembered using a stolen wrench to open up a fire hydrant in order to flood his street so that he and his friends could skate or play hockey: "When we were selling my mother's house, my brother found the fire hydrant wrench that we had stolen off of the utility truck ... We used it to flood our street. I'd skate on the street."[50]

The same kind of fond memories of playing hockey can be found in the way that the men talked about their hockey sticks. Although it was well over forty years ago, Dennis remembered the type of hockey stick he had owned: "I know exactly. I used a Koho and it was left and it was light as a feather. I love those things. This is exactly what I bought."[51] Whereas boys such as Dennis, who grew up in a middle-class family, had little difficulty acquiring toys or other material goods like hockey sticks, others boys were not so fortunate. For example, with few economic resources readily available to him as a boy, Ken remembered that saving his own money to buy a hockey stick had required a significant amount of time and effort:

> I saved and saved for a hockey stick, and we bought our hockey sticks at a local
> hardware store, it was just around the corner on Drouillard, because we didn't
> have the large places at the time. So I saved and saved and finally I got enough
> money, I think it was about eight dollars, and got this hockey stick, and at that
> time it was a lot of money.[52]

Although sport was the glue that socially bound many boys together, it also functioned as a method to separate out those boys who were unwilling to contribute to a certain hysteria about sport. As Bill explained, "Some of the boys were, um, some of them were intelligent. They would be talking about atoms and, you know, ... they were good people, just socially they didn't get along. They probably didn't play sports."[53] Windsor boys who were good at sports profited from this fact socially and otherwise, whereas other boys – the awkward or scholarly – were positioned to some degree as social outcasts.

The Windsor boys' attitudes toward athletics were consistent with research findings of the day. A study of high school students carried out in the late 1950s reflected the high value that boys placed on being athletically successful above all else. The study found that, whereas academic excellence counted for little among the boys, being an athlete counted for much. In ten schools examined for the study, nearly all the boys said that they wanted to be remembered not as a "brilliant student" or a "popular student" but as the "ideal of a star athlete."[54]

Conclusion

The men's narratives of boyhood convey some of the lived texture of men's childhood experiences. Certainly, much of what it meant to be a boy rested on gender relations infused by patriarchal understandings of masculinity as it intersected with social class and race. And, despite their multiplicity, the various forms of masculinity were continually and actively being sublimated under one form of masculinity that became "boyhood." To be sure, this version of "boyhood" required boys to participate in sports, particularly hockey. It also required a heterosexual identity from an early age. The cultural knowledge that seems to have informed boys' understandings of the "green and yellow days" in elementary school, for example, reveals the way homophobia was inscribed in the daily fabric of boys' lives. James, a self-identified gay man, who experienced and carefully negotiated playground and school violence, mostly through avoidance, highlighted the way that boys often wore straitjackets of heteronormative self-discipline. This is not to say that boys did not transgress the boundaries of heteronormativity, as some experimented sexually with other boys or men for a variety of reasons, including economics. In this sense, some of the men elaborated a multiplicity of masculine identities, as their testimony also highlighted that the contours of sexuality were, at times, ambiguous.

For many boys growing up in Windsor, Ontario, freedom was important, especially if we understand freedom as a metaphor for power. Some boys had the power to literally roam free in Windsor and beyond, far away from the watchful gaze of adults. This freedom illuminates some of the benefits that were derived both literally and symbolically from white, middle-class, patriarchal privilege. Although machines and hegemonic masculinity have been linked in research, this relationship took on a deeper meaning within the context of postwar Windsor, Ontario. The city was home to Chrysler of Canada, Ford Motor Company, and General Motors. The Big Three North American automakers influenced, to one degree or another, the lives of these men. Many of them talked about their deep love of cars, the popular heterosexualized machines that they and their male friends would use "to prowl," as David mentioned, for girls when they became older. The personal testimonies of some men also included a deep sense of distrust of other boys and adult males, including an expectation that they could be physically attacked by other males and therefore needed to be prepared and constantly on guard, revealing the effects of hegemonic masculinity.

Notes

1 Rudolf A. Helling, "*The Position of Negroes, Chinese and Italians in the Social Structure of Windsor, Ontario*" (Ottawa: Ontario Human Rights Commission, 1965), 1–7.
2 Trevor Price and Larry Kulisek, *Windsor 1892–1992: A Centennial Celebration* (Windsor, ON: Chamber, 1992), 74.
3 Les Dickirson, "Windsor: The Struggle for Human Rights," *Currents*, 1987, 18.
4 Ibid., 13.
5 The Windsor Interracial Council, *How Does Our Town Add Up?* (Windsor: Sumner, 1947), 3.
6 Peggy Bristow, "A Duty to the Past, a Promise to the Future: Black Organizing in Windsor – The Depression, World War II, and the Post-War Years," *Journal of Black Canadian Studies* 2, 1 (2007): 25.
7 Henry, interview with author, July 24, 2008.
8 Bristow, "Duty to the Past," 34.
9 Cheryl I. Harris, "Whiteness as Property," *Harvard Law Review* 106, 8 (1993): 1711.
10 David, interview with author, May 29, 2008.
11 Bristow, "Duty to the Past."
12 Albert, interview with author, August 4, 2008.
13 Ken, interview with author, June 25, 2008.
14 Henry, interview.
15 In his seminal work on children and childhood, Neil Sutherland notes that "girls fought less often than boys." Neil Sutherland, *Growing Up: Childhood in English Canada from the Great War to the Age of Television* (Toronto: University of Toronto Press, 1997), 252.
16 Ken, interview.
17 Ibid.
18 Albert, interview with author, July 26, 2008.
19 Ibid.
20 William, interview with author, June 25, 2008.
21 Ibid.
22 Ibid.
23 David, interview with author, May 29, 2008.
24 Ibid.
25 Dennis, interview with author, July 20, 2008.
26 Harry, interview with author, May 15, 2008.
27 Ibid.
28 Ibid..
29 Ken, interview.
30 Harry, interview.
31 James, interview with author, June 12, 2008.
32 Gary Kinsman and Patrizia Gentile, *The Canadian War on Queers: National Security as Sexual Regulation* (Vancouver: UBC Press, 2010). See also Gary Kinsman, "The Canadian Cold War on Queers: Sexual Regulation and Resistance," in *Love, Hate, and Fear in Canada's Cold War*, ed. Richard Cavell, 108–32 (Toronto: University of Toronto Press, 2004).
33 Albert, interview, July 26, 2008.
34 David, interview.
35 Ibid.

36 Ibid.
37 Harry, interview.
38 David, interview.
39 Ken, interview.
40 Albert, interview, July 26, 2008.
41 Bill, interview with author, May 2, 2008.
42 Ibid.
43 Mary, interview with author, July 25, 2008.
44 Mark Goodson, "Lousy at Sports," *New York Times*, May 11, 1986, SM48.
45 Foster Hewitt, *Along Olympic Road* (Toronto: Ryerson Press, 1951), 21.
46 Dennis, interview.
47 Ibid.
48 William, interview.
49 Ibid.
50 Ibid.
51 Dennis, interview.
52 Ken, interview.
53 Bill, interview.
54 James S. Coleman, "Athletics in High School," *Annals of the American Academy of Political and Social Science* 338, 1 (1961): 35–36. See also James S. Coleman, "The Adolescent Subculture and Academic Achievement," *American Journal of Sociology* 65, 4 (1960): 337–47.

14
Heroes on Campus: Student Veterans and Discourses of Masculinity in Post–Second World War Canada

Patricia Jasen

TENS OF THOUSANDS OF ex-service students, the great majority of them male, converged on Canadian campuses as the Second World War drew to a close, their higher education funded by the Veterans Charter. From the start, it was understood that the Charter was a tool in the postwar nation-building project; "the leaders of Canada in the future must come from those who volunteered for active service," the public was told.[1] Although these veterans' presence transformed the culture of the universities, their experience remains largely unexamined outside of institutional histories and those focused on the workings of the Charter itself. Here, I hope to contribute to an understanding of how shifting discourses of masculinity, aimed at both valorizing and disciplining the veteran population, were used to construct the identity of the ex-service student as one who embodied the modern ideal of civilian manhood. In one sense, the student veterans represented a "culturally exalted" masculinity, to borrow R.W. Connell's phrase,[2] in that they were a privileged elite, presumably the most intellectually able or ambitious segment of the veteran population. But it was also true that this bright future had yet to materialize, and as long as the veterans remained students, they were dependent upon public largesse for their financial survival and were under the close supervision of government and university officials. The rhetoric justifying their access to education cast them as heroes, but their designation as deserving recipients of support rested upon their speedy transition to a domesticated understanding of manly citizen- ship that was rooted in individual initiative rather than in the group psychology of the military or any sense of special status. As the inadequacy of the Charter's provisions for students became evident, they had to decide whether to confront authorities of the Department of Veterans Affairs or to find a strategy for survival that would preserve the image of the mature and appropriately grateful veteran who had the nation's best interests at heart. Although this chapter focuses on the relationship between ex-service students and the bureaucratic powers that regulated their lives, it also considers how female students and veterans' wives, as more marginal elements of the "national self," were cast in subordinate roles in the process by which the veteran's identity was moulded.[3] This remasculinization of the university meant that it would remain a "man's world," both culturally and numerically, well into the Cold War years.

The "postwar emphasis on returning to normal," as Christopher Dummitt puts it, must be read as "an attempt to re-establish dominant notions of masculinity" on the civilian stage.[4] In both the United States and Canada, going to war had allowed millions to reverse the humiliating effects of Depression-era unemployment by taking on the hyper-masculine image of the man in combat. It had also given societies as a whole the opportunity to re-establish "the primacy of masculinity" as they transformed themselves into warring nations and directed women to take on identities usually reserved for men on the home front.[5] The postwar task, then, was twofold: to carry this masculine image of the nation into peacetime while also reversing the erosion of gender roles caused by women's wartime entry into nontraditional jobs and positions of influence. The organized effort to displace women at the end of the war and direct them toward the private sphere reinforced gender divisions in both public and private life that had weakened throughout the 1930s and early 1940s.[6] Just as women were expected to re-embrace the identity of helpmeet, so too were male veterans expected to conform to a particular ideal of masculinity that would suit Canada's nation-building agenda.

Central to the postwar reconstruction project was the concept of the deserving veteran. It is easy to invoke an image of the male veteran as hero, valorized in public discourse and rewarded through the many programs created by governments to ease his assimilation into civilian life. But on closer examination of the postwar project, a more complex process of managing the veteran's identity comes to light. For one thing, a clear hierarchy emerged, for it was those who had placed themselves at risk in combat overseas who found themselves at the top of the ladder of entitlement in what Dummitt calls the "discourse of deservedness."[7] As well, governments soon decided that they must handle this notion of deservedness with care; veterans had a right to assistance because they had risked their lives and were therefore heroes, but they also posed a danger to national stability through their very presence and numbers and could not be allowed to embrace notions of entitlement on a lasting basis. If, for example, they were awarded the distinction of belonging to an elevated veteran class but their expectations of reward were not met, they might become resentful, alienated, and radicalized.[8] Dummitt's case studies explore the Canadian government's felt need to temper deservedness with discipline by requiring veterans' conformity to an image of manliness that embodied toughness, self-discipline, reasonableness, a resolve to look to the future rather than to the past, a trust in the material rewards of progress, and a dedication to building a modern post-war nation. He points out that benefits provided under the Charter had a dual goal: to recognize and reward "manly sacrifice,"[9] a traditional concept that many veterans embraced, while also managing the dangers posed by the veterans' return by guiding them into socially appropriate roles and a peacetime masculine identity that conformed to public expectations – an agenda they sometimes resisted.[10]

By moulding an image of the manly veteran, civil authorities, with the help of the media, hoped to avoid the kind of turmoil that followed the First World War and the ongoing demands for compensation that had continued to grow during the Depression years. "After the last war there was a tendency to think of 'aid' in terms of doles, handouts, pensions," the Canadian public was reminded. "This time the accent is different – it's on building up the man, setting him on his own feet as fast and as firmly as may be."[11] Part of the "long shadow" cast by the First World War was the fear that large numbers of veterans would succumb to the mental trauma caused by war and, unmanned by the dependency it induced, fail to live up to their civilian obligations.[12] Predictions of psychiatric casualties found a receptive audience in a population familiar with shell shock and fascinated by psychiatry in general; Canadian mental hygienists recalled how, through movies and other media, the language of psychiatry had "crept into the everyday conversation and jokes of the people" before the end of the war.[13] But this vision of returned men unhinged by war threatened to undermine the idealized image of the manly veteran, and a counter-narrative quickly emerged that railed against such feminizing or infantilizing rhetoric. During the winter of 1944–45, for example, the CBC ran a series of radio programs called *The Soldier's Return*. Civilians were treated to reassuring talks by psychiatrists and psychologists and to the scornful reactions of enlisted men against all the journalistic "tripe" that made them out to "look like wild-eyed neurotics, strange creatures full of moods and impulses, always flying off the deep end."[14] As the end of war approached, more was heard about the ex-serviceman's mounting annoyance at the deluge of "When He Comes Home" articles in which he was "treated as though he were a pregnant woman" or "an emotional and sentimental adolescent."[15] The consensus was that the homecoming veteran should be seen as a normal person quite able to adjust to civilian life "without special coddling."[16]

At the same time, the media pressed home the need for women to understand the supportive, behind-the-scenes role they were to play in their men's postwar return to normalcy. In some respects, this resembled the morale-booster image expected of women during the Depression and war years, but it went much further in the economic and psychological demands placed upon women.[17] Not only were they to make way for the returned men by relinquishing wartime jobs and responsibilities, but, in the private realm, wives who may have been living independently for years were also to ensure a healthy readjustment to civilian life by creating just the right home environment for their husbands' resumption of masculine authority.[18] Timothy Shuker-Haines notes that in the United States "coming home" advice literature reflected "a societal emphasis on the wife's duty in adjusting to the husband rather than vice versa,"[19] and the same was true in Canada. Leading military psychologist William Line counselled that "coming back when it is all over will be easy or difficult, very largely depending on *you.*" And another advised, "You won't find him very talkative till he accepts you. You will have to make up your mind that it is his privilege to accept you and not yours to accept him, if you want to get to know him."[20]

The process of reification and management of a certain kind of manliness, supported by women who understood their own place in Canada's reconstruction, was duplicated within the self-contained community of the university campus. The focus in this chapter upon male student veterans does not imply that no ex-service women attended university; rather, it reflects the fact that they went largely unremarked as the postwar campus was abruptly restored as a masculine preserve. After a decline during the Depression, the proportion of female students had risen as men were drawn into the armed forces, but that trend had reversed by 1945.[21] It was true that both ex-service women and men approved by the Department of Veterans Affairs (DVA) could have their tuition paid and receive a living allowance for a length of time equal to their service, with universities receiving payment for each veteran they enrolled.[22] The overwhelming gender imbalance on the postwar campus occurred not only because there were many times more male veterans but also because of the multiple pressures on women to return to traditional occupations and domestic roles.[23] Jennifer Stephen has documented the double-speak embodied in DVA policies toward women veterans interested in the training opportunities they were promised. Equality was the watchword, but under the absolute authority of DVA counsellors, most were directed toward traditional pursuits on the grounds that "the sexual division of labour" was "not only natural ... but rational" – the best guarantee that the postwar nation-building project would succeed.[24] Meanwhile, women's entry to university after high school met a new obstacle because the shortage of classrooms and instructors also meant that many civilian students were turned away. Although a DVA report noted that it "was not practicable to exclude completely *all* non-veteran freshman entrants," the priority was to ensure spots for veterans.[25] Such a policy shifted the gender balance by giving priority to a body of veterans who were predominantly male. Expectations that women would place marriage and childbearing above career goals would shrink their university attendance further throughout the late 1940s and the 1950s.[26]

Glimpses of undergraduate culture also suggest a firming-up of gender divisions in keeping with wider postwar social trends. Student newspapers not only chronicled events and opinions from a student point of view but also helped to set the tone of campus life. After the war, these papers evoked common images of the female student – longing for marriage and motherhood, subordinate in her role on campus. At the same time, men's insecurities over whether women would comply with these expectations were openly displayed. As reported by the *Varsity* at the University of Toronto, male students at University College debated women's postwar obligations two years' running, concluding each time that the welfare of families and society, including the prevention of juvenile delinquency, required mothers to stay at home.[27] But this need not mean that the female student was not welcome on campus, an editorial explained. An arts degree was a fine preparation for motherhood because a "liberally-educated woman will know *why* she is washing diapers"; it was only if she sought a career that "she really lowers herself."[28] On occasion, women contributors colluded in producing an image of the cooing co-ed preoccupied with snagging a hypermasculine veteran. "The men are all so big and brawny and hard-headed," drooled one writer in the *Sheaf* at the University of Saskatchewan; another was overwhelmed by the "MEN! MEN! MEN!" available in all the "latest shapes and sizes, new fall shades of windburnt rose and tropical tan."[29] Other female students, meanwhile, protested their ongoing or renewed subordination to a male-dominant campus culture, their lesser roles in student governance, and their exclusion from certain places and activities, including access to Hart House at the University of Toronto.[30]

If a particular notion of femininity suffused postwar campus culture, its complement was the image of the returned man training to take his part in building the modern nation. The university was to be a world where the new arrivals would learn to comply with the bureaucratic construct of the ideal veteran as emotionally stable, mature, compliant, grateful, and devoted to the task at hand. One graduate recalled being received at the registrar's office as a "brand-new war hero to shape, mold, push and pull into a career."[31] Long before their arrival on campus, all potential student veterans faced an authoritarian selection process that was intended to exclude anyone likely to fall short of the ideal. Journalist Blair Fraser explained that each serviceman had a "farewell chat" with a Veterans Affairs personnel officer who assessed his physical and mental health and produced a summary of his qualities and abilities, which was then used in deciding whether he was the sort of man wanted on campus.[32]

Whether any veterans with a recorded history of psychological disability were
knowingly granted funding to go to university is hard to discover, but given the
DVA's inclination to see "battle exhaustion" as a sign of personal weakness, it
seems unlikely.[33] This may also have been the point at which those whose sexual
orientation was in question were supposed to be weeded out, for a mere suspicion of homosexuality could be reported even if a man was honourably discharged.[34] Gay men were not wanted among the nation's future leaders, nor
were they wanted on university campuses.[35]

As for the fields of study they entered, much has been made in institutional
histories of veterans' no-nonsense preference for professional programs such
as commerce and engineering. Those who wanted to take arts courses faced
some opposition at first, but bureaucrats soon discovered that to admit as many
veterans as possible, arts faculties would need to receive their share.[36] In contrast
to wartime, when arts courses were considered "nonessential" to the national
interest, they could now be justified as the means whereby veterans could
understand their war experience and prepare to serve as "custodians of the
future."[37] The meaning of being an arts student was thus constructed differently
according to gender. Female students were expected to benefit from their studies
as a preparation for domestic life and citizenship on the local level, whereas the
male veteran, as one English professor put it in true Arnoldian fashion, "wishes
to acquire all that is best and most broadening in his course, so that he may
become, in the best sense of the word, useful to the fullest degree as a citizen
of the world."[38]

Despite efforts to make the whole process rational and sufficiently exclusion-
ary, authorities worried about how veterans would adapt to civilian and campus
life.[39] One strategy was to provide counseling for the "normal" problems they
faced while dismissing the fear that psychiatric casualties were invading aca-
deme. Universities were required to set up advisory bureaus, in cooperation
with the DVA, by the fall of 1945. At the University of Toronto, President Sidney
Smith wanted it to be very clear that the newly opened bureau had nothing to
do with the "nonsense" about veterans being "psychiatric cases." He allowed
that although they certainly would not "*be* problems," they might "*have* problems in becoming oriented within the institution after years with the Armed
Forces."[40]

The bureaus were staffed by faculty members and others who had served
during the war. They counselled students about their rights as veterans, referred
them for aptitude tests, helped with housing and other practical matters,
and strove to ensure conformity to campus norms and to dampen discontent.[41]
The scope and approach varied, and two models seem to have prevailed. Most
of the bureaus saw themselves mainly as providers of information and firm,

sometimes paternalistic, guidance. At the University of Saskatchewan, Major H.H. Ferns, a mathematics professor and veteran of both world wars, became adviser to veteran students in the fall of 1945.[42] He introduced himself with a sharp warning to the first crop of veterans, who had apparently blamed their poor grades on being unable to "settle down to studying because of the war." None of that nonsense would be tolerated now, he said, and veterans would be watched with a close eye: "You will have neither Hitler nor Mussolini to call to the witness-box this time."[43] At the University of Manitoba, advisers invited ex-service students to bring any and all problems to the bureau, but the advisers' priorities were to engender "a sane, analytical attitude" in veterans' minds and to tame expectations of privileged treatment. "It is felt that the sooner the ex-serviceman adapts to the outlook of the average citizen, rather than that of a special case for which everything possible is being done, the better will be the result for both the student and the country," read one internal report. Confidentiality between counsellor and veteran was not assured, and the bureau provided authorities with information drawn from private interviews when veterans' performance came "under faculty consideration."[44]

At the University of Toronto, by contrast, there was more emphasis on the therapeutic goal of the encounter and on the counsellors' independence from administration, even though the ultimate purpose was the veterans' readjustment to campus life. Psychologist William Line was well qualified to run the advisory bureau, and he drew on his own experiences after the First World War, his interwar involvement in the mental hygiene movement, and his intimate knowledge of psychological assessment processes (and their shortcomings) gained during the Second World War.[45] Veteran students were invited to "discuss in strictest confidence any matter of a vocational, financial or personal nature," although there was to be no "mollycoddling."[46] Line referred to the counselling relationship as "a neutral zone" where anything could be said without fear of consequences, and he won praise for his nonjudgmental approach.[47] "The quiet room, plus its retiring occupant, has lulled many an ex-service student into talking about his problems," wrote one admirer.[48] The University of Toronto was also unusual in creating a psychiatric unit within its Health Service to which both veterans and nonveterans could be referred.[49] One exceptionally frank comment by the Health Service's director reveals that veterans did, in fact, seek psychiatric help and in greater numbers than regular students. During the academic year of 1946–47, of those diagnosed with anxiety, "unstable personalities," and psychoses, well over half were "ex-service personnel who form only 40 per cent of the registration."[50]

The consensus, however, was that the returned men, en masse, were fine. *McGill News* journalist Robert Fetherstonhaugh confirmed how the student veterans had exploded the myth about their fragile mental state; they simply "did not suffer from problems of psychological adjustment, about which the civilian population had been so dramatically warned."[51] In both public discourse and university records, there was virtually no legitimization of issues that might not be construed as "normal" aspects of veterans' rehabilitation, nor was there acknowledgment that any psychological trauma arising from the war affected students during their university lives. One satisfying measure of how well ex-service students were able to conform to the image of the competent, rational, and responsible man was their academic success, and Dalhousie University's veterans' adviser was able to report that "the first mid-term results brought enthusiastic reports from the length and breadth of the continent," even though their margin of superiority was overstated.[52] Survival as students meant performing well, as failing grades in a course and the supplementary examination would mean loss of the DVA grant – a deliberate strategy to ensure that universities did not become "houses of refuge in which the unemployed will bide their time."[53]

Authorities were still left with the question of how, after making the case for the deservedness of veterans, they could discourage them from feeling special and failing to assimilate into campus life. Ex-service students were in an anomalous position in that they instantly constituted a new and powerful community on campus but one that was supposed to dissolve rapidly into the main. From the start, both government and university officials stressed that veterans' postwar entitlements must not undermine the individual's sense of masculine independence by fostering a need to cling together; military psychiatrist Brock Chisholm warned that any tendency toward the "segregation of returned servicemen would be an indication of their failure to become citizens."[54] Those who favoured separate classes thought that the "initial rustiness of the returned man" might be embarrassingly obvious if he were compared with "the younger boys straight from school," but those who argued successfully for "the melting pot" maintained that any such accommodation would make veterans feel "that they were a race apart and that their interests were special ones."[55] In virtually all matters related to the veterans at university, including their social life, the emphasis was on integration, on how they should blend into the undergraduate body and become "club members, fraternity members, and campus 'joe-boys,'" despite the gaps in age and experience between themselves and the younger students.[56]

Some university administrators were therefore leery of the veterans' associations and Royal Canadian Legion branches that were formed on many campuses as soon as ex-service students began to arrive, fearing they might interfere with the assimilationist agenda.[57] Like the advisory bureaus, such organizations were intended to ease students' return to civilian life, but their leaders saw this as a collective process rather than a purely individual one. At the University of Saskatchewan, for example, the veterans' association helped with ex-service students' particular problems, organized social activities, negotiated with university authorities, and strove to preserve "the spirit of comradeship and co-operation" that many veterans missed after leaving the forces.[58] The University of Toronto discouraged veterans' associations, but the Ex-Service Committee of the Students' Administrative Council performed a similar function, and a Legion branch was also eventually created.[59] At the University of British Columbia, the Legion offered "returned men a mental meeting ground" but soon found itself accused of being inward-looking and creating "a cleavage between servicemen and non-servicemen."[60] Although not opposed to its presence, President Norman A.M. MacKenzie warned veterans to put duty to nation before self-interest. "When you leave the service you become members of the public," he said. "You become concerned with the general good as well as your own good."[61]

Before long, the shortcomings of the Charter gradually became more obvious, and a sense of losing out in the postwar recovery became part of many student veterans' self-image. Making matters worse, as mature undergraduates, their civilian experience of full, adult citizenship was more or less on hold. As long as they were students, they were under the tutelage of others, they were not self-supporting, they were not making their anticipated contribution to the nation, and they were aware that the country might fall into economic depression before they could share in the promised postwar prosperity.[62] Their sense of grievance was fuelled mainly by the housing shortage and by the unchanging level of the living allowance, which had been set low enough to discourage triflers and, for many, was barely sufficient for survival. Playing the role of the grateful, toiling scholar was acceptable up to a point, but as *Canadian Forum* columnist Samuel Roddan warned, initial enthusiasm would fade to desperation if their pursuit of degrees forced them into "an intolerably low standard of living." He predicted that they were unlikely to remain "docile or subservient" as the winter wore on, and he was right.[63] The growing tensions pitted the authorities who had defined the ideal qualities of the student veteran against those who were expected to embody that ideal, thus bringing to light a major disjuncture in the whole concept of manly deservedness. As they organized themselves into a National Conference of Student Veterans (NCSV) and began lobbying in earnest, however, veterans found that they did not necessarily speak with one voice regarding their goals and strategies.

The least divisive issue was housing, for this was a problem shared with other veterans that could easily be portrayed as a danger to the whole postwar recovery process. The collapse of the building industry during the 1930s, a continuing lack of materials, and a bulging population had produced a situation that, as critics presented it, threatened to expose the hollowness of veterans' entitlement, doom the rehabilitation plan to failure, undermine family life for a generation, and leave veterans open to "subversive elements."[64] Ex-service students were especially disadvantaged due to their low incomes and the fact that many of them had to combine family living and academic work within the confines of one small room. In some centres, veterans were simply told to leave their wives behind when coming to university.[65] While the NCSV lobbied the government for rent controls, emergency housing, and a building program, campus organizations and Legion branches campaigned to find local residents able to provide accommodation and to expose homeowners who inflated rents and discriminated against the married veteran.[66] At the University of Alberta, for example, the *Gateway* reported that infants "are viewed by prospective landlords as a form of bubonic plague," an attitude that violated the postwar imperative that linked fatherhood with nation building.[67] Those fighting such discrimination drew upon the rhetorical strategies embodied in the ideal of fighter turned family man in an effort to shame homeowners into doing their peacetime duty. At the University of British Columbia, the *Ubyssey* told the story of one student whose English bride and son were about to arrive in Vancouver. He thought he had found a home but was "shown the door" when the owner's son learned of the baby. His plight was portrayed as especially egregious because he was a "real" veteran who had gone overseas in 1941, landed in France on D-Day, engaged in the liberation of Europe, and at the end of the war, undertaken the task of apprehending and questioning "saboteurs, war criminals, Gestapo members, and German 'were-wolves.'" If this war hero could not find accommodation, he was going to forgo his right to higher education and return to his parents' home in Chilliwack, British Columbia, thus defeating the purpose of the Veterans Charter.[68]

Pressure from veterans' organizations, including the early left-wing leadership of the NCSV, eventually brought a response, and the Canada Mortgage and Housing Corporation supported the creation of "veterans' villages" in disused government buildings or groups of huts on university grounds.[69] These were reserved for families and were prized despite their basic nature; those at the University of Manitoba, which were unfinished and uninsulated, encircled three "ablution huts," each containing a single washing machine and lavatories.[70] Residents typically organized themselves into self-governing communities, with elected councils, shared kitchens and cooking routines, nurseries and baby-sitting services, and common spaces for recreation. In contrast to the ethic of self-sufficiency idealized in the postwar nuclear family, these communities apparently thrived through the practice of mutual aid and were (oddly enough) praised in *Saturday Night* magazine for "proving the possibility of communal living."[71] Gender divisions were maintained in keeping with postwar norms. Women took care of household work and tried to stay out of the way; student newspapers announced teas and bridge parties to keep them amused while "friend hubby" concentrated on his studies.[72] However, many veterans' wives also worked, for they were expected to supplement their husbands' grants if there were no children, although until 1948 there was a ceiling on their earnings that, if exceeded, would negate a portion of their wages.[73] Women also helped their husbands by researching and writing essays, a practice common enough to attract instructors' attention. University of Alberta veterans later admitted that "sometimes we thought the wives should get the degree rather than the man ... It took a lot of dedication on the part of the wives to get the husbands through."[74] Toward the end of the veteran years, the *Ubyssey* praised understanding wives for standing "shoulder-to-shoulder with their men-folk in the battle for education," cheerfully resigning themselves to buying "books instead of tea-cups," and accepting the role of sympathetic helpmeet.[75]

"Homes fit for heroes" was a unifying sentiment that the government could support and that veterans across the political spectrum could agree upon. By contrast, the amount and the very meaning of the veterans' maintenance allowance was an issue that brought the more militant NCSV delegates into sustained conflict with Veterans Affairs authorities, raised questions about the moral fibre of those who presumed to ask for more money, and divided ex-service students along political lines. In 1944 the government had established the level of the grant at $60 for single students and $80 for married students, with an additional stipend for each child. Based on the results of a survey showing that hundreds of veterans would be "unable to complete their courses on present income," delegates to the 1945 conference voted to ask the DVA to increase the monthly grant by $20 and $40 for single and married students respectively.[76] Taking on jobs during term, they pointed out, brought the risk of academic failure, and high unemployment meant that summer jobs were hard to find. Hitting close to the bone with respect to postwar values, the NCSV reported that the married veteran would rather leave university "than inflict hardship on his family" and that unmarried veterans were "discouraged from marrying" at all. "Increased grants are urged," the report added, "not as a reward – for the reward is already generous – but on grounds that the 'National Education Scheme' is an ideal which ought to be achieved" for the benefit of the whole country.[77]

The authorities' response was a flat "no" to any increase, and their reasoning opened up a key question: were veterans entitled to full support in recognition of their sacrifice and future value to the nation, or had it always been understood that the educational grant was only a leg-up that they had to supplement through their own initiative? In the words of Major-General Burns, director-general of rehabilitation, the "allowances were never intended to cover the whole cost of subsistence and education. The student has to make a contribution himself." Equally important to Burns was the question of what the very act of requesting more support signified about a veteran's personal worth. Manliness, in his view, was exhibited not through making demands but through cheerful compliance and self-help. He told students that their return to university was a "character test" and that the veteran not willing to supplement his allowance through his own efforts "is not the sort of veteran we want to go to University."[78] Students seized on these words, arguing that it would be harmful to the economy for Canada to make veterans risk failure, that men were "entitled to an adequate standard of living, and not just a parsimonious handout to keep the boys from starving," and most importantly, that the rules of the game had changed along the way. They pointed to the booklet distributed in 1944 called *Back to Civil Life*, which had promised the veteran a grant that "would enable him to keep alive – and live – while he attended University."[79]

The authorities took heart from the fact that ex-service students were increasingly divided over goals and strategies, and they attempted to ally themselves with the "sound and reasonable" majority.[80] Accusations flew over Communist influence in the NCSV, and many veterans sought to distance themselves from the taint of disloyalty and to prove that they had embraced the self-help ideology of civilian citizenship.[81] In one *Toronto Globe* report, the spectre of Communists plotting to "sneak" their way in was set against the image of a student veteran and Military Cross recipient who had allegedly thwarted their efforts.[82] Shortly after the *Globe* noted that the ousting of McGill University's Len Starkey from the NCSV leadership in December 1946 was praised by the DVA for showing that most veterans appreciated the assistance given to "those who are willing and able to help themselves," and the editor also described how, as "tomorrow's leaders," they had proven their loyalty to the national community.[83] Some veterans echoed such language by emphasizing their own "growing sense of self-responsibility," which each year brought them "nearer to being civilians and a step farther from being servicemen."[84]

As they attempted to manage public opinion, those who continued to argue for grant increases revised their strategy in the face of government intransigence. Instead of pursuing a flat increase, they engaged in a long campaign for a bonus that would restore their allowances to 1944 levels, pointing out that during the war and postwar years, while inflation had soared and veterans' standard of living had plummeted, civil servants in Veterans Affairs had enjoyed a series of cost-of-living bonuses.[85] Rather than present all ex-service students as equally needy, they stressed the plight of the veteran as family man, the embodiment of the postwar ideal. "Undoubtedly, the married student with a child or children is suffering great hardship, for the increase in the living cost affects him by a multiple of the number of dependents he has," advocates argued.[86] During a Hart House debate early in 1947 at the University of Toronto, Minister of National Defence Brooke Claxton agreed that "the standard of living of the families of married student veterans is desperately low." Invoking memories of the "long shadow" cast by the First World War, he warned that if conditions did not improve, "the married veteran with children will inevitably, justifiably feel bitterness," leading to the creation of a class of "professional veterans," which would threaten the very process of integration and undermine the sturdy independence that was at the core of postwar masculine identity.[87] The government finally announced an increase in living allowances for married veterans in February 1948, leaving the single students to make their own case.[88]

Conclusion

To a great extent, the "hero on campus" motif successfully defined the public identity of the male ex-service students. It rewarded their sacrifice, eased their entry into university life, and justified, to the taxpayer, the government's expenditure on their education as essential for national recovery. At the same time, it performed a disciplinary function by erecting clear boundaries around the definition of entitlement, linking masculinity with loyalty, and discrediting militancy even when sustained protest was a logical response to growing financial hardship. Nigel Moses has examined the wider postwar student movement in Canada as a "Cold War battlefield" and concluded that, for its part, the NCSV avoided militancy because veterans' needs were different; they were well cared for by government benefits, and university administrators "responded adequately ... to campus veterans' issues."[89] I argue, instead, that the image of the deserving student veteran analyzed here played a significant part, as it was meant to do, in discouraging a militant campaign to secure a better deal. Masculinity, in this construct, was equated with stoic gratitude and citizenly duty, whereas protest, far from being construed as a manly defence of one's rights, implied either a lack of character or collusion with dangerous subversives. Challenging this dominant image threatened to undermine the very real benefits of being cast as no-nonsense men of reason and self-sacrifice, on the cusp of becoming the voices of authority in postwar Canada. More lastingly, the postwar strategy of associating the mission of the university with the needs of the state buttressed the Cold War obsession with Western technological supremacy – an aspect of "manly modernism" that deserves further attention.[90] In addition, because women's roles had been so clearly defined in relation to the needs of the returned men and the Canadian nation, the much higher value placed upon the latter's education for professional and public life persisted well beyond the veteran years. The university of the 1950s remained, statistically and culturally, a man's world, where male undergraduates outnumbered women students by a ratio of over three to one and where women's share of undergraduate degrees did not recover to prewar levels until 1962.[91] Although the postwar remasculinization of the Canadian university was a complex process, it was made to appear rational and natural through the discourses that shaped the veteran's identity on campus.

Notes

1 Government of Canada, *Back to Civil Life*, 2nd ed. (Ottawa: Minister of Pensions and National Health, 1944), 21.
2 R.W. Connell, *Masculinities* (Berkeley: University of California Press, 1995), 77.
3 Stefan Dudink, Karen Hagemann, and John Tosh, "Editors' Preface," in *Masculinities in Politics and War: Gendering Modern History*, ed. Stefan Dudink, Karen Hagemann, and John Tosh (Manchester, UK: Manchester University Press, 2004), xiv.
4 Christopher Dummitt, *The Manly Modern: Masculinity in Postwar Canada* (Vancouver: UBC Press, 2007), 29–30.
5 Timothy Shuker-Haines, "Home Is the Hunter: Representations of Returning World War II Veterans and the Reconstruction of Masculinity, 1944–51" (PhD diss., University of Michigan, 1994), 21. On the effects of the Great Depression on masculine "self-worth," see Lara Campbell, *Respectable Citizens: Gender, Family, and Unemployment in Ontario's Great Depression* (Toronto: University of Toronto Press, 2009), 59–60; Christina S. Jarvis, *The Male Body at War: American Masculinity During World War II* (DeKalb: Northern Illinois University Press, 2010), 15–16.
6 Dummitt, *Manly Modern*, 2–5; Robert Francis Saxe, *Settling Down: World War II Veterans' Challenge to the Postwar Consensus* (New York: Palgrave Macmillan, 2007), 16.
7 Dummitt, *Manly Modern*, 30.
8 Ibid., 30–36; Saxe, *Settling Down*, 14–15.
9 Dummitt, *Manly Modern*, 21.
10 Ibid., 42–43.
11 Blair Fraser, "When the Boys Come Marching Home," *Maclean's*, April 15, 1944, 18; J.C. Meakins, "The Returning Serviceman," *Canadian Medical Association Journal* 551, 3 (1944): 198; Peter Neary, *On to Civvy Street: Canada's Rehabilitation Program for Veterans of the Second World War* (Montreal and Kingston: McGill-Queen's University Press, 2011), 57.
12 Mark Humphries, "War's Long Shadow: Masculinity, Medicine, and the Gendered Politics of Trauma, 1914–1939," *Canadian Historical Review* 91, 3 (2010): 503–31. See also Terry Copp, "From Neurasthenia to Post-Traumatic Stress Disorder: Canadian Veterans and the Problem of Persistent Emotional Disabilities," in *The Veterans Charter and Post–World War II Canada*, ed. Peter Neary and J.L. Granatstein (Montreal and Kingston: McGill-Queen's University Press, 1998), 148–50; Samuel Roddan, "Preparing the Fighter for Civvy Street," *Canadian Forum*, March 1945, 280–81; and Fergus Glenn, "Fighter's Return – To What?" *Canadian Forum*, January 1945, 235.

13 Doug Owram, "Canadian Domesticity in the Postwar Era," in *The Veterans Charter and Post-World War II Canada*, ed. Peter Neary and J.L. Granatstein (Montreal and Kingston: McGill-Queen's University Press, 1998), 216; John Griffin and William Line, "Trends in Mental Hygiene," *Review of Educational Research* 16, 5 (1946): 397. On cinema, see William Friedman Fagelson, "'Nervous out of the Service': 1940s Cinema, World War II Veteran Readjustment, and Postwar Masculinity" (PhD diss., University of Texas, 2004).
14 CBC, *The Soldier's Return*, radio series transcript (Toronto: CBC, 1944–45), 18–20.
15 Samuel Roddan, "The Veteran Looks Around," *Canadian Forum*, May 1945, 39.
16 "The Boys Come Back," *Canadian Forum*, August 1945, 105; Paul Corbett, "Homecoming Veteran Is Puzzled but Normal," *Saturday Night*, April 6, 1946, 12–13.
17 Ruth Roach Pierson, *They're Still Women After All: The Second World War and Canadian Womanhood* (Toronto: McClelland and Stewart, 1986), 43.
18 Jeffrey A. Keshen, *Saints, Sinners, and Soldiers: Canada's Second World War* (Vancouver: UBC Press, 2004), 267–71.
19 Shuker-Haines, "Home Is the Hunter," 23.
20 CBC, *Soldier's Return*, 30–31, 12–13, original emphasis.
21 Veronica Strong-Boag, *The New Day Recalled: Lives of Girls and Women in English Canada, 1919–1939* (Markham, ON: Penguin, 1988), 25; Paul Axelrod, *Making a Middle Class: Student Life in English Canada during the Thirties* (Montreal and Kingston: McGill-Queen's University Press, 1990), 91, 117–19; Nancy Kiefer and Ruth Roach Pierson, "The War Effort and Women Students at the University of Toronto, 1939–45," in *Youth, University and Canadian Society*, ed. Paul Axelrod and John G. Reid, 161–83 (Montreal and Kingston: McGill-Queen's University Press, 1989); Keshen, *Saints, Sinners, and Soldiers*, 148–49; Martin L. Friedland, *The University of Toronto: A History* (Toronto: University of Toronto Press, 2002), 373.
22 By the fall of 1945, enrolments at many universities had doubled, and the number of veterans would reach approximately 35,000 in 1946. See Gerald Anglin, "Colleges in a Jam," *Maclean's*, March 1, 1946; and Peter Neary, "Canadian Universities and Canadian Veterans of World War II," in *The Veterans Charter and Post-World War II Canada*, ed. Peter Neary and J.L. Granatstein (Montreal and Kingston: McGill-Queen's University Press, 1998), 110, 118–22, 129–30.
23 Magda Fahrni, *Household Politics: Montreal Families and Postwar Reconstruction* (Toronto: University of Toronto Press, 2005), 83–84; Pierson, *They're Still Women*, 79–80; Peter Neary and Shaun Brown, "The Veterans Charter and Canadian Women Veterans of the Second World War," *British Journal of Canadian Studies* 9, 2 (1994): 259–72.
24 Jennifer A. Stephen, *Pick One Intelligent Girl: Employability, Domesticity, and the Gendering of Canada's Welfare State, 1939–1947* (Toronto: University of Toronto Press, 2007), 151, 145–62; Mary Louise Adams, *The Trouble with Normal: Postwar Youth and the Making of Heterosexuality* (Toronto: University of Toronto Press, 2003), 18–23.
25 Neary, *On to Civvy Street*, 205, emphasis added. See also Walter H. Johns, *A History of the University of Alberta, 1908–1969* (Edmonton: University of Alberta Press, 1981), 208–15; Friedland, *University of Toronto*, 372–74; University of Alberta Alumni Association, "History Trails: The Returned Men," 1995, https://www.ualberta.ca/ALUMNI/history/traditions/95summen.html. Policies varied; see Robert Collins, *You Had To Be There: An Intimate Portrait of the Generation that Survived the Depression, Won the War, and Reinvented Canada* (Toronto: McClelland and Stewart, 1997), 106.
26 See Alison Prentice, Paula Bourne, Gail Cuthbert Brandt, Beth Light, Wendy Mitchinson, and Naomi Black, *Canadian Women: A History* (Toronto: Harcourt Brace Jovanovich,

308 *Patricia Jasen*

1988); A.B. McKillop, *Matters of Mind: The University in Ontario, 1791–1951* (Toronto: University of Toronto Press, 1994), 555–56; and Susan M. Hartmann, *The Home Front and Beyond: American Women in the 1940s* (Boston: Twayne, 1982).

27 "Women's Post-War Duties," *Varsity*, February 3, 1944; "Women Should Stay Home," *Varsity*, March 1, 1945; "A Woman's Place," *Manitoban*, January 4, 1946; "Marriage and a Career," *Manitoban*, November 11, 1947.

28 "She Stoops to Conquer," *Varsity*, December 16, 1945, original emphasis.

29 "Women's Page New Feature," *Sheaf*, September 27, 1945; "Dear Mom," *Sheaf*, October 12, 1945; "I'd Like One of Those And–," *Sheaf*, October 26, 1945; "Canadian Campus: More Men So Co-eds Coo," *Varsity*, October 19, 1945.

30 "Feminine Protest," *Manitoban*, November 11, 1947. In the *Varsity*, see "Equality for Women," March 14, 1947; "Victoria Female Element Fails in Attempt to Gain Male Executive Position," January 22, 1948; "Co-educational Hart House," February 19, 1945; "SAC Office Splits," January 11, 1946; and "Hart House Ban Still Operates," October 8, 1947.

31 Barry Broadfoot, *The Veterans' Years: Coming Home from the War* (Vancouver and Toronto: Douglas and McIntyre, 1985), 197.

32 Fraser, "When the Boys Come," 18, 36.

33 Dummitt, *Manly Modern*, 44–47. Peter Neary notes that the DVA archival record is not transparent regarding the admissions process. Neary, "Canadian Universities," 142.

34 Paul Jackson, *One of the Boys: Homosexuality in the Military during World War II* (Montreal and Kingston: McGill-Queen's University Press, 2004), 64.

35 Gary Kinsman and Patrizia Gentile, *The Canadian War on Queers: National Security as Sexual Regulation* (Vancouver: UBC Press, 2010); Catherine Gidney, "Under the President's Gaze: Sexuality and Morality at a Canadian University during the Second World War," *Canadian Historical Review* 82, 1 (2001): 36–54. In reality, gay veterans established their own social networks on Canadian campuses; one recalled, "I found out that universities could have their gay people too, and I made a lot of contacts there." Quoted in Gary Kinsman, *The Regulation of Desire: Homo and Hetero Sexualities* (Toronto: University of Toronto Press, 1987) 156–57.

36 Frederick W. Gibson, *Queen's University*, vol. 2, *1917–1961: To Serve and Yet Be Free* (Montreal and Kingston: McGill-Queen's University Press), 243; Friedland, *University of Toronto*, 373; Johns, *History of the University of Alberta*, 213–19; "Arts Courses Not Favoured," *Varsity*, November 14, 1944; "Veterans," *Varsity*, November 15, 1944; Neary, "Canadian Universities," 121.

37 Michael Stevenson, *Canada's Greatest Wartime Muddle: National Selective Service and the Mobilization of Human Resources during World War II* (Montreal and Kingston: McGill-Queen's University Press, 2001), 63–65; Corbett, "Homecoming Veteran," 12.

38 C.L. Bennet, "What the Veteran Student Is Teaching the Universities," *Dalhousie Review* 27, 3 (1947): 318.

39 National Conference of Canadian Universities, *Report of the NCCU on Post-War Problems*, June 13, 1941, 23. See also Keith W. Olson, *The G.I. Bill, the Veterans and the Colleges* (Lexington: University Press of Kentucky, 1974), 32–33.

40 Quoted in "Smith Applauds Service Bureau," *Varsity*, October 11, 1945, original emphasis.

41 A.J.B. Hough, "Student Counselling Services at the University of Alberta," University of Toronto Archives, A1993-002/002; *Report of the President of the University of British Columbia for the Academic Year Ended August 1st, 1946*, 9, University of British Columbia Archives, UBC Subject File Collection, box 12, file 15, https://www.library.ubc.ca/archives/pdfs/presidents/1946.pdf.

42 James Thomson, "Report of Committee on Post-War Problems," file 134, Presidential Papers, series II B-134, University of Saskatchewan Archives; Faculty Biographies, Dr. Herman Harvey Ferns, University of Saskatchewan Archives.
43 "Major Ferns," *Sheaf,* September 9, 1945, 2.
44 Veterans Advisory Bureau, "Report for the Year 1947–8," 9, 3, folder 28, UA20, box 99, University of Manitoba Archives.
45 Paul Babarick, "Psychologists in Profile: William Line (1897–1964)," *Ontario Psychologist* 8, 5 (1976): 58.
46 "Committee Releases Statement" and "Trouble-Shooting Clinic," *Varsity,* October 11, 1945; "Do You Need Advice?" *Varsity,* January 15, 1946; "Problems of All Kinds Solved," *Varsity,* September 30, 1947; W.C. Jones, "Relationship of Advisory Services to Other University Services," University Advisory Services Conference, 1948, University of Saskatchewan Archives.
47 Quoted in Jones, "Relationship of Advisory Services."
48 "Psychologist Talks on Industrial Woes," Clipping File, William Line, University of Toronto Archives, A73-0026/235(01).
49 "Psychiatric Service," *Varsity,* October 2, 1947.
50 C.D. Gossage, "Report of the Director of the University Health Service," in *University of Toronto President's Report for the Year Ending June 1947* (Toronto: University of Toronto Press, 1947), 75. https://archive.org/details/presidentsreport1947univ.
51 R.C. Fetherstonhaugh, *McGill University at War* (Montreal: McGill University, 1947), 345.
52 Bennet, "What the Veteran Student," 314–19. For extravagant praise of veterans, see Johns, *History of the University of Alberta,* 218; Gibson, *Queen's University,* 251; Peter B. Waite, *The Lives of Dalhousie University,* vol. 2, *1925–1980: The Old College Transformed* (Montreal and Kingston: McGill-Queen's University Press), 150; Charles Johnston and John Weaver, *Student Days* (Hamilton: McMaster University Alumni Association, 1986), 74–75; and Friedland, *University of Toronto,* 372.
53 "Veterans' Education," *Varsity,* January 9, 1945.
54 Chisholm, in "Soldier into Citizen," CBC, *Soldier's Return,* 8.
55 National Conference of Canadian Universities, *Report of the NCCU,* 22.
56 "Canadian Legion," *Ubyssey,* October 20, 1945, 2.
57 "Canadian Campus," *Varsity,* February 2, 1945, 2.
58 "Are Veterans Apathetic?" *Sheaf,* February 8, 1946.
59 "Arts Course Not Favoured" and "Student Veteran's Group," *Varsity,* January 4, 1946; "Ex-Service at a Glance," *Varsity,* October 14, 1947; "First Meeting Campus Legion," *Varsity,* October 31, 1947.
60 "Legion Plans Help for ALL Veterans," *Ubyssey,* September 29, 1945; "Canadian Legion," *Ubyssey,* October 20, 1945, 2; Tony Greer, "Letter to the Editor," *Ubyssey,* October 23, 1945.
61 Quoted in "MacKenzie Praises Objects of Legion," *Ubyssey,* January 29, 1946.
62 "Soldier's Return" and "Grants Are Not Adequate," *Manitoban,* December 14, 1945; "Veterans to Discuss Conference," *Sheaf,* December 14, 1945; "Disillusioned Vets," *Sheaf,* January 18, 1946; "Veterans Request Allowance Boost," *Manitoban,* January 8, 1946; Broadfoot, *Veterans' Years,* 185–86.
63 Samuel Roddan, "Nothing Was Too Good for the Soldier," *Canadian Forum,* January 1946, 242–43.
64 Owram, "Canadian Domesticity," 210–11; "The Boys Come Back," 105–6; "Soldier's Return," *Manitoban,* November 2, 1945; Alvin Finkel, *Our Lives: Canada after 1945* (Toronto: James Lorimer, 1997), 41–42; "NCSV Brief" and "Legion Brief," in *The 2nd Annual Conference*

of Student Veterans, ed. Roger Beaufroy (1947), file 66-27-4, vol. 1, box 270, Veterans Affairs, RG38, Library and Archives Canada (LAC).

65 Sylvia Irwin, "The Veteran Student," *Culture* 7 (1946): 229–30; "The Husband Student," *Varsity*, November 28, 1945; "Vet Housing Vile," *Ubyssey*, November 27, 1945; Gibson, *Queen's University*, 250.

66 "Emergency Loan Fund," *Varsity*, November 30, 1945; "Housing Problem," *Ubyssey*, September 29, 1945; "Vet Housing Vile," *Ubyssey*, November 27, 1945; "Pre-fab Homes Legion's Goal," *Ubyssey*, January 24, 1946.

67 University of Alberta Alumni Association, "History Trails." See also "Rehab Students Discuss Housing," *Gateway*, October 12, 1945; "CURMA Sets Up Central Housing Agency," *Gateway*, October 19, 1945; "Accommodation Shortage," *Gateway*, September 21, 1948; and Robert Rutherdale, "Fathering in Multiple Roles: Assessing Modern Canadian Fatherhood as a Masculine Category," in *Canadian Men and Masculinities: Historical and Contemporary Perspectives*, ed. Christopher J. Greig and Wayne J. Martino (Toronto: Canadian Scholars' Press, 2012), 79.

68 "Young Vet," *Ubyssey*, October 23, 1945.

69 Norman Wright, "Veterans' Council," *Manitoban*, December 6, 1946; Johns, *History of the University of Alberta*, 214; Gibson, *Queen's University*, 249; Melynda Jarratt, *War Brides* (Toronto: Dundurn, 2009), 192–93.

70 "Fort Garry Housing," *Manitoban*, September 28, 1946.

71 University of Manitoba Veterans Advisory Bureau, *Report for 1947–48*, 4–5, University of Manitoba Archives; "Veteran's Life at U.B.C.," *Varsity*, October 8, 1948; Alan Phillips, "Saskatchewan's Students Enjoy Life," *Saturday Night*, June 22, 1946.

72 "Vets' Wives Tea," *Ubyssey*, November 15, 1945; "WUS Tea for Veterans' Wives," *Ubyssey*, February 5, 1946; "Progress Seen at Veterans' Village" and "Veterans Imitate Pioneer Ancestors," *Manitoban*, November 28, 1947.

73 Keshen, *Saints, Sinners and Soldiers*, 276; "Discussion ... on DVA Policy and Interpretation," University Advisory Services Conference, 1948, University of Saskatchewan Archives. Many wives found jobs on campus; see "Job Bureau Open to All," *Ubyssey*, October 3, 1946; and "Applicants Must Be Veterans' Wives," *Ubyssey*, January 21, 1948.

74 University of Alberta Alumni Association, "History Trails"; Broadfoot, *Veterans' Years*, 188; Lloyd Swick, *Stories from the Veterans Village* (Winnipeg: University of Manitoba, 2005), 26, 33, 146–47.

75 "Wives and Studies Do Mix," *Ubyssey*, November 25, 1948.

76 "Student Veteran's Group," *Varsity*, January 4, 1946.

77 "Report of the National Conference of Student Veterans, Montreal, December 27–29," File 66-27-4, volume 1, Box 270, Veterans Affairs, RG 38, LAC.

78 Quoted in "A Word to the Vets," *Manitoban*, March 5, 1946.

79 "Inadequate Grants," *Manitoban*, January 25, 1946. That the veterans misunderstood the intention of the Charter became the government's mantra. See "Ministers Meet Vet Delegates ... Underwriting of Costs Never Intended," *McGill Daily*, November 29, 1946.

80 Burns to Deputy Minister Woods, December 31, 1945, file 66-27-4, vol. 1, box 270, Veterans Affairs, RG38, LAC; see also further correspondence in this file.

81 "Increased Grants: The Student Veteran's Predicament," *Manitoban*, February 12, 1946; "Veterans Air Views," *Manitoban*, October 22, 1946; "NCSV," *Varsity*, January 9, 1948; "Veterans Not Motivated by Mere Greed," *Varsity*, January 15, 1948; "McGill Students Veterans," file 66-27-4, vol. 1, box 270, Veterans Affairs, RG38, LAC.

82 "Communist Pressure on Campus Charged," *Toronto Globe*, December 13, 1946. See also Neary, "Canadian Universities," 135–36; "Student-Veterans Confer," *Manitoban*, January 14, 1947.

83 Editorial, *Toronto Globe*, January 4, 1947.

84 "Report of the NCSV, McGill University, December 28–29, 1946," file 66-27-4, vol. 1, box 270, Veterans Affairs, RG38, LAC.

85 "Campus Legion Urges Cost-of-Living Bonus," *Varsity*, November 4, 1947; "Grant Increase Proposed," *Ubyssey*, November 21, 1947; "The Next Act?" *Varsity*, December 11, 1947; "Ex-service Committee Brief," file 66-27-4, vol. 1, box 270, Veterans Affairs, RG38, LAC.

86 "NCSV," *Varsity*, January 9, 1948; "Veterans' Conference," *Manitoban*, December 18, 1947; "Student Vets," *Manitoban*, January 9, 1948.

87 "Professional Veteran," *Varsity*, January 24, 1947.

88 "Allowances Increased for Married Veterans," *Varsity*, February 17, 1948; "Ex-service Committee Asks Bonus to Aid Single Vets," *Varsity*, February 18, 1948; "The Single Veteran," *Manitoban*, February 26, 1948; "The Single Vet," *Manitoban*, September 28, 1948.

89 Nigel Roy Moses, "Canadian Student Movement on the Cold War Battlefield, 1944–1954," *Histoire sociale/Social History* 39, 78 (2006): 381–82.

90 Dummitt, *Manly Modern*, 9.

91 Statistics Canada, "Table W504–512: Degrees Awarded by Canadian Universities and Colleges, by Sex, Canada, Selected Years, 1831 to 1973," http://www.statcan.gc.ca/pub/11-516-x/sectionw/4147445-eng.htm#3. On female students' experience in the United States, see Linda Eisenmann, "'Honorary Men' and Incidental Students: Women in Post–World War II American Higher Education," in *Women in Higher Education, 1850–1970: International Perspectives*, ed. E. Lisa Panayotidis and Paul Stortz, New York: Routledge, 2016).

15
Constructing Canadianness:
Terry Fox and the Masculine Ideal in Canada

Julie Perrone

TERRY FOX STARTED HIS Marathon of Hope on April 12, 1980, in St. John's, Newfoundland.[1] In the company of Doug Alward, a long-time friend, Fox, a kinesiology student at Simon Fraser University, wanted to be the first Canadian to run across the country on an artificial leg. A native of Winnipeg, Manitoba, but raised in Port Coquitlam, British Columbia, the twenty-one-year-old amputee had lost a leg to cancer three years earlier. Marked by his experience in a cancer treatment unit, where he saw much younger children succumb to the seemingly incurable disease, he decided to help by collecting funds for cancer research in Canada. He set out on his journey almost ignored by the media, dipping his artificial leg in the Atlantic Ocean in front of a few onlookers and a reluctant journalist. After difficult times in eastern Canada and an even more dreadful passage in the province of Quebec, Terry Fox arrived in Toronto transformed into a national phenomenon. By the time he passed away in June 1981, he had become an officially recognized national hero.

After seeing Fox run in her hometown in July 1980, an enthralled onlooker declared, "You know, they say the United States is built on a history of heroes while Canada has none to look up to. But when I looked down the street today and saw Terry, I said, 'There's a hero.'"[2] This comment that Fox is one of our only heroes in Canada was certainly not exceptional then; the discourse about the young runner in 1980 and 1981 was (and arguably still is today) all about how surprised Canadians were (and are) that this country could actually produce heroism and something akin to devotion to it. As journalist Roy MacGregor mused in 1989, "Canadians aren't very comfortable with heroes. They're more used to cutting down than building up, more expectant of failure than success whenever a fellow citizen dares to raise his or her head above the field."[3] If we agree with the premise that "we're just not hero-worshippers in Canada,"[4] it is surprising and historically significant that a young man like Terry Fox was able to attain such an exalted status.

Although a nation's heroes may be their most celebrated characters, they are also often the least examined, at least critically. Fox has been an important figure in Canadian history, and he has come to represent for many the image of courage, determination, and selflessness. However, as a *Vancouver Sun* reader aptly put it in 1981, "here we are, a nation in mourning for a young man we never really knew except for a single accomplishment."[5] Canadians may not know much about "one of Canada's greatest heroes,"[6] but there also seems to have been limited academic interest in learning more about him. Hence my research has focused on how Terry Fox became a hero and how the heroic narrative of his life has been constructed – first by the Canadian media[7] and then through commemorative materials – and ultimately remembered by Canadians. In looking at the construction of Terry Fox as a national hero, I found several dominant discourses at play in the dissemination and commemoration of his story. In the following pages, I focus on how the discourse about masculinity has been shaped, conveyed, and perhaps even imposed through the story of Terry Fox.

This study of the different material forms of memory points to characteristics deemed important by those who had the means to initiate and support commemorative efforts, whether they were journalists, writers, filmmakers, or politicians. What I found to be the most significant elements of the masculine imagery in the commemoration of Terry Fox are his youth and physical beauty, his athleticism, his whiteness, his sexuality, and his disability, all of which are examined here through the framework of hegemonic masculinity. Since Terry Fox was quite rapidly hailed a Canadian hero, and if he indeed "personified how we as Canadians feel about ourselves,"[8] I argue that these characteristics should be construed as an expression of hegemonic masculinity discourse, an illustration of what the ideal Canadian man ought to be.

As discussed in the general introduction and by several other contributors to this volume, hegemonic masculinity combines Antonio Gramsci's understanding of bourgeois power and Michel Foucault's discursive construction analysis. In her ground-breaking work on masculinity, R.W. Connell has shifted Gramscian hegemony from social class to gender: instead of the bourgeois class inculcating the general population with its way of life, she sees a masculine archetype imposing its specific traits and characters on all men but also, almost necessarily in opposition, on women. Donald Sabo and Michael Messner, among the many who have used the concept of hegemonic masculinity as a frame of study, describe it indeed as "a structure of dominance and oppression in the gender order as a whole."[9] And although Gramsci did not acknowledge the constructed nature and imagined homogeneity of the bourgeois class, Connell argues that hegemonic masculinity is based on an ideal that does not necessarily exist: "Hegemonic masculinities can be constructed that do not correspond closely to the lives of any actual men. Yet those models do, in various ways, express widespread ideals, fantasies and desires."[10] Primarily the expression of a white heterosexual ideal, the North American image of masculinity usually illustrates such core male values as "violence and aggression, emotional restraint, courage, toughness, risk-taking, competitiveness, and achievement and success."[11]

The concept of hegemonic masculinity emerged in response to, or at least following, the "cultural and political project of the reformulation of masculinity [which] started immediately alongside the second-wave women's movement in the 1970s."[12] The 1970s and 1980s witnessed what some call a crisis in masculinity: the redefinition of gender roles on an unprecedented scale, which challenged the well-encrusted notion of patriarchy. Although some scholars have argued against the idea of a crisis,[13] including Robert Rutherdale, what one can safely suggest is that the concept of masculinity came under considerable criticism in the 1970s and 1980s, most effectively through a new wave of feminism. As this particular situation was indeed unprecedented, I argue that this period witnessed a profound redefinition of masculinity (and of the very concept of gender, for that matter).

In Canada the Royal Commission on the Status of Women was established in 1967 in response to the increasingly vocal women's movement across the nation. Examining issues such as equal pay, maternity leave, and birth control, the commission made 167 recommendations, which for the most part had been at least partially achieved by the 1980s.[14] Hence the implementation of some of these recommendations during the 1970s and 1980s would certainly have challenged the patriarchal structure of Canadian society and, in this sense, necessitated efforts in the redefinition of masculinity. That Canada in the 1980s saw significant challenges to a masculine-dominant order explains efforts to define and impose a hegemonic masculine archetype, as we see in the immediate commemoration of Terry Fox. Let us now look at the characteristics of this constructed masculine archetype: youth, physical beauty, athleticism, whiteness, sexuality, and disability.

Terry Fox, the Kid: Relationship to Age and Time

Terry Fox was "a young fella that wanted to do something courageous" and who truly "embodied the 'Canadian boy' image," remembers former CBC radio host Fred Walker.[15] At twenty-one years old, Fox was hovering between being a boyish athlete or a fine young man, although to be sure both images follow a similar model of hegemonic masculinity. Fox is indeed described in terms of what are perceived to be masculine values and characteristics specific to boys or men, as the rest of this chapter demonstrates. As for youth specifically, suffice it to say that Terry Fox was, as Gary T. Barker describes masculine youth, a young man "crossing the socially defined space between childhood and adulthood," putting him on the threshold of a moment in time where he would be called on to "tak[e] on more complex and demanding roles in society."[16] Whichever side of the proverbial fence Fox was considered to be on, or considered himself to be on, was irrelevant in the development of commemorative materials, for his youth was more often than not reshaped or, might we say, regressed to something closer to childhood.

For example, Leslie Scrivener described her first meeting with Fox and recalled how shockingly young he looked: "Although he was five feet ten inches, he seemed smaller, certainly smaller than his news photographs had shown him, and therefore more childlike."[17] Scrivener described Fox as showing the endearing carelessness of youth as he sat in Government House in his wet shorts, drinking a glass of orange juice brought to him on a silver tray: "Fox did not feel out of place."[18] He was, to be sure, the youngest person ever to receive the Order of Canada.[19] His childlike nature was highlighted in the many published pictures of the ceremony, showing Fox in his most formal outfit, a dark-blue velvet suit, his youth even more enhanced by the stuffiness of the award ceremony in Port Coquitlam, British Columbia.[20]

In the 1983 Terry Fox Story, directed by Ralph Thomas, the innocence and youth of Terry Fox are constantly illustrated. The first talking scene shows Fox arriving for supper at the family home, where he is told by his mother to "go make his bed" after getting a slap on the hand for trying to touch the food being prepared. After announcing his plans to run across Canada, Fox hides on the staircase of his house, listening to his parents discuss the issue, just as a young child would do. The movie generally depicts Fox as playful but immature,[21] alternating between scenes supposed to produce sheer admiration and others seeking to humanize him. This alternating between laudable hero and regular boy serves to contrast in a very vivid manner the youth of Terry Fox with his achievement, something that was consciously captured in the Terry Fox stamp design: "The youth of Terry Fox made his heroic achievement all the more admirable, and Vancouver artist Friedrich Peter ... has conveyed both these ideas in his dramatic stamp design" (Figure 15.1).[22]

That Fox was so young when he died definitely made his death all the more tragic because he had been "struck down almost at the beginning of his life."[23] The 1983 movie shows a frail and childlike Fox crying alone after hearing that the cancer has spread, his innocence dramatically highlighted by the baby-blue hospital gown floating on his body. Dying at such a young age crystallized the

Figure 15.1   Terry Fox stamp, 1982.

image of the runner as an eternal child, illustrating "the picture of youthful nerve and determination," a hero who, by his sacrifice, will be "permanently young."[24] In their examination of boys' representations in movies, Murray Pomerance and Frances Gateward noticed that, beginning with the first silent pictures, boys were, and often still are, depicted as "unruly tikes" who usually turned out as "symbols of the collapse of the civilized forces of nature."[25] Fox is indeed depicted as "unruly" in many instances in Scrivener's book and Thomas's movie. But juxtaposing this unruliness against the ravages of cancer, which effectively humanized Fox, emphasized in a very real way how the "forces of nature" could sometimes be ruthless, unfair, powerful, and dangerous.

One can notice the dominant discourse at play here. Fox's story was strongly focused, and still is, on how terribly young he was to get cancer twice and ultimately die. It was shaped in commemorative materials as a story that provided a model to a younger generation, a way for parents to set standards on how one could live his or her youth. The narratives on statues, in movies, and in books overwhelmingly emphasize boyhood over adulthood, despite the fact that Fox could have well been considered an adult. He was completing a university degree, drove his own car, was quite independent-minded, and demonstrated organizational and entrepreneurial skills that showed great maturity. But these "grown-up" characteristics were neither discussed nor depicted extensively in comparison to those that made him seem younger.

Terry Fox, the Hunk: Relationship to the Body

It seems odd to discuss Terry Fox as a "hunk" because this particular side of him is not mentioned in his commemoration and certainly is not part of the more recent narratives of his life. This is in significant contrast not only with the media coverage of the time but also with the early commemoration of Fox. Consider, for example, Leslie Scrivener's description of Fox in the first few pages of her book. In 1981 she wrote of Fox that he was "better-looking than most with a well-scrubbed, intelligent face, straight teeth, and an Adonis-like profile – which would make older women feel maternal and teenagers feverish – [and he] had only one leg."[26] Her revised description in 2000 put much less emphasis on his beauty, stating simply that "he had a handsome face, perfect teeth, and curly hair. And he had only one leg."[27]

Picturing Terry Fox today as an "Adonis-like" figure is quite difficult, but we should remember that he was adulated, at the time of the Marathon of Hope, and his good looks certainly endeared him to a legion of teenage girls. In the 1983 movie, Fox's physical attributes are definitely an important part of the character, especially at the beginning. The movie opens with close-up shots of Fox's half-naked, sweaty, and athletic body, moving and twisting as he is playing basketball. A tender moment with his girlfriend, Rika Noda, in the park shows Fox without his shirt again, the camera lingering on his muscular shoulders as Noda wipes his entire body for him.

Although these images may seem at odds with how Fox is remembered today as a pure, almost asexual hero, they were undoubtedly accepted and unquestioned in the immediate years after his passing. One characteristic extensively depicted in Scrivener's book and Thomas's movie but also in most, if not all, commemorative materials is Fox's blond locks. One movie critic described his hair as cupid's curls,[28] and a journalist talked of the "the blond, curly haired athlete."[29] In the movie itself, Fox is extremely protective of his hair, becoming quite angered when his girlfriend throws water at it. He explains, "When they cut off my leg, I thought that was it. But when I started losing my hair, that was really hard."[30] Somehow losing his hair was more difficult to cope with, perhaps because it was more complicated to hide than a prosthetic leg.

There are two possible interpretations of this focus on Terry Fox's physical beauty, especially in the early commemorative years. On the one hand, the emphasis on Fox's good looks could have been a means to avoid discussing his disability. By describing or depicting his blond curls, his freckled face, and his perfect teeth, memory producers in effect reduced the importance of his artificial leg by keeping the viewer's attention focused on his other physical features. In his examination of sexuality and disability, André Dupras notes this inclination in depictions of disabled individuals: "The absence of legs emphasizes the opposite part of the body, the head. The beauty of the person without legs is found especially on her face."[31] Here, we see traces of a dominant discourse about the importance of physical beauty as a sort of compensation for disability. Francine Saillant points to this tendency in the press coverage of Fox, noting that "despite the prosthesis, what is highlighted is rather the grace of a young and resplendent body."[32] Commemorative materials thus refocus the image of Fox on what is deemed "palatable" and, more indirectly, on what is perceived as hegemonic. And one could argue that as disability became more readily accepted in Canadian society and, parallel to this, as Fox became a venerated hero, the focus of the story gradually changed.

Terry Fox, the Athlete: Relationship to Sport

One key component of hegemonic masculinity discourse is the relationship between men and sport. As Susan Cahn found in her examination of gender and sexuality in 1920s America, "Sport remains a key cultural location for male dominance, a site where traditional patriarchal values are upheld in response to changes in the broader society."[33] The area of sport is indeed a locus of enhanced masculinity and entrenched reactionary values, but it is also the place where the meanings of masculinity, as well as gender roles, can be negotiated. Cahn has shown how gender relations and norms can be effectively modified through participation in sport: "As they manipulated the gender norms and concepts of their day, athletes frequently introduced subtle revisions that stretched or even subverted conventional gender distinctions."[34] But in the Fox story, sport serves only to make Fox into a model of athletic masculinity, a "jock in a family of jocks."[35]

The great feat of Fox the national hero was essentially a physical one: he was admired for what he was capable of doing with his body in order to motivate us to give to cancer research. According to Susan Elizabeth Hart, monuments to Fox and to men like hockey great Maurice Richard focus primarily on the "physical aspects of their achievements,"[36] which demonstrate that Fox's physical prowess is a crucial part of his story and memory. Indeed, Fox's statue in Thunder Bay – and this is the case for every Fox statue – depicts him as he is running, muscles bulging from the effort, sweat dripping down his face (Figure 15.2). What we know Fox for is his running, which is why all his statues represent him in the middle of a physical performance, just like Rocket Richard's statues always show him on his skates. And we find that the model of athleticism he is made to embody is one in which resistance to pain and a high level of stamina are essential features of masculine identity.

The pain Fox felt throughout his Marathon of Hope made his mission that much more heroic, and it also ensured that pain would be an integral part of

Figure 15.2 Terry Fox Monument, Thunder Bay, Ontario, 2007. Photograph by Richard Keeling.

the Fox story. Press coverage devoted considerable time to describing how excruciating Fox's running must have been: "Determination is etched in his features but he looks tired, and as he walks toward the intersection it becomes startlingly obvious just how difficult his run must be."[37] And his pain is indeed captured in his commemorative materials. For example, the Fox stamp design was chosen for its depiction of "a pathetic vision of suffering and courage."[38] In a pictorial tribute, Fox is described with "sweat pouring from his limbs, his stump frequently aching painfully, sores and cysts building from the constant punishing motion."[39] Even in Maxine Trottier's children's book, it looks like pain is glorified: "The prosthesis rubbed his stump raw and bloody, his bones were bruised, his foot blistered badly and he lost toenails, but he wouldn't give up."[40]

Fox's statue in Thunder Bay manages to show his pain by the sweat dripping on the side of his face and by his clenched fists. In the 1983 movie, pain is present throughout, either etched in Fox's face or part of conversations with his mother, his girlfriend, his doctor, or his friend Doug Alward. And most of these conversations are usually about Fox's anger caused by people's concerns over blood dripping or dizzy spells. Hence pain was, and still is, an important part of Fox's image and an important characteristic of the masculine model he has been set to embody. According to Don Sabo and Michael Messner, pain and sport are deeply embedded in the masculine ideal: "Sports are just one of the many areas in our culture where pain is more important than pleasure. Boys are taught that to endure pain is courageous, to survive pain is manly."[41] The emphasis on Fox's resistance, then, represented efforts in illustrating how a man should act. It was also a representation of how a man should react to pain. As Wendy Jane Gagen suggests in the case of wounded soldiers' expected resistance to pain, "toughness and resolve to deal with pain stoically may indicate a masculine desire to be capable of either transcending pain or manfully ignoring it."[42]

Terry Fox, White Canadian: Relationship to Race

Another (albeit more subtle) iteration of hegemonic masculinity discourse found in the Terry Fox story and memory is that of whiteness. Gail Bederman, in *Manliness and Civilization* (1995), has convincingly linked masculinity and race in America during the late eighteenth and early nineteenth centuries, arguing that "as white middle-class men actively worked to reinforce male power, their race became a factor which was crucial to their gender."[43] Showing that whiteness and masculinity influence each other's definition, she demonstrated that white manhood was understood as answering to higher standards. The story of Terry Fox does not have racist undertones, nor does it really include any issue related to colour or to persons of colour. But the very absence of race in the story and commemorative materials is suggestive of the 1980s Canadian context. Canada had implemented its multicultural policy in 1971, included a section against racism in its Charter of Rights and Freedoms in 1982, and created a House of Commons Special Committee on Visible Minorities' Participation in Canadian Society in 1983. Canadians were increasingly aware of racial inequalities but less conscious of how deeply embedded white privilege was in their society. As Barbara J. Flagg argues, "The white person has an everyday option not to think of herself in racial terms at all. In fact, whites appear to pursue that option so habitually that it may be a defining characteristic of whiteness: to be white is not to think about it."[44]

This particular form of dominant masculinity discourse differs from those examined in the previous sections because we are in effect looking for something that is not there. We are looking for traces of what Joyce E. King calls "dysconscious racism," which is "a form of racism that tacitly accepts dominant white norms and privileges" while uncritically accepting "certain culturally sanctioned assumptions, myths, and beliefs that justify the social and economic advantages white people have as a result of subordinating others."[45] This racism is what we can see, or rather what is concealed, in the Fox narrative. Fox's whiteness is part of his physical beauty. According to Richard Dyer, being blond with blue eyes is the epitome of whiteness, "white within white."[46] Even the focus on Fox's freckles in some ways has the effect of emphasizing his whiteness.

Fox came from a middle-class family, had an uneventful childhood, went to school, and then attended university. This background in itself was perhaps a privilege. But more significant is that Fox may have been able to pursue his unorthodox way of collecting money for the Canadian Cancer Society in part because he was white. As Dyer argues, "the right not to conform, to be different and get away with it, is the right of the most privileged groups in society."[47] One wonders how a Marathon of Hope would have fared if Fox had not been a white male. Pushing this reflection further, one might wonder whether Terry Fox could have become a national hero and icon if he had not been white and, further, whether he would have enjoyed the same level of popular and media support as he did.

Besides Fox's whiteness, race is not very present in his commemoration, even when looking at Scrivener's book, the few children's books, and the movie about him. In the rare instances when a nonwhite person is featured, it is usually in a minimal role, if any. For example, in the 1983 movie about Fox, the only person from a racialized minority is Fox's girlfriend, Rika Noda, a worker at the rehabilitation clinic where his therapy sessions took place. That Fox's girlfriend was Asian could be seen as an indication of the increasingly open nature of Canadian society. But Noda was not very present in the commemoration of Fox, and she is now almost completely obliterated from the story, which sends a mixed message about attitudes on race in Canada. With the exception of Noda, there are no visible minorities in the movie, besides a very small number scattered in the crowd, which is, in effect, overwhelmingly white. In the children's book *The Value of Facing a Challenge* (1983), all the drawn characters are white, expect for one African American wheelchair athlete and "Indians": "One day there was nobody to be seen until a pick-up truck loaded with Indians from a nearby community passed by. The Indians waved and cheered."[48]

By not acknowledging that Fox was white and by arguing for his overall representativeness, the commemorative materials indirectly impose a vision of what a Canadian should be and of who should be excluded by default. If Fox is supposed to represent Canadians – if we can say of him that "he became an embodiment of the way we would all like to see ourselves"[49] and hence also the "norm" against which all Canadians are measured – it should not be overlooked that he was white. It is a crucial part of the hegemonic masculinity discourse at play in the story and the commemoration. As Dyer has stated, "As long as race is something only applied to non-white peoples, as long as white people are not racially seen and named, they/we function as a human norm. Other people are raced, we are just people."[50]

Terry Fox, Heartbreaker: Relationship to Women and Sexuality

If we are looking at manifestations of hegemonic masculinity discourse, it is only natural to discuss women and sexuality given that the ideas of virility and domination over women are an integral part of these manifestations. This section elaborates upon some of the considerations in the previous section's discussion of race. In effect, to talk about women in the Fox story is to talk about two very specific roles: that of the mother, Betty Fox, and that of the girlfriend, Rika Noda. Besides these two women, not many others have been part of the story, so we are indeed talking about what is, for the most part, either absent or silent. These images of a protective matron and a confident flirt create two very different images of Fox: the obedient son or the desirable boyfriend. Over time, the role of Noda has consistently been diminished, to the point that she is not even mentioned in the 2000 movie remake of Fox's life. Hence the contradictions of the masculine ideal presented by Fox in the 1980s will eventually be "resolved" by simply forgetting about them.

It seems clear that the heavy presence of Terry Fox's mother in his life, and especially in his commemoration, ensures that we continue to see Fox as a boy rather than a young man. She made sure that Fox's memory was well guarded, and she worked tirelessly to ensure his legacy was kept alive: "It is an incredible legacy of one young man, overseen primarily by his loving mom."[51] The role of mother is a significant part of the Fox story, showing both the strength and the pain entailed in raising children (and for her, in losing one). But despite the fact that by the time she passed away in 2012 she was the leading figure of the Terry Fox Foundation, her role in the life of her son was traditional: she worried about his health, about how much (and what) he ate, and about how tired he looked. In fact, the 1983 movie shows that Fox's mother was much less supportive than his father. When Fox tells his mother about his plans to run across Canada, she screams at him and forbids him to go. When Betty Fox's character later on announces this plan to the father, his only response is to ask, "When?"[52] The father in the movie is stronger and less emotional, and he certainly commands respect with his authoritative masculine silence.

The other image of women in the story is provided by Rika Noda, the subdued yet quite forward girlfriend of Terry Fox. Mentioned a few times in the press coverage of the day, Noda was a very important character in the 1983 movie, was interviewed extensively for the "making of" documentary, and was also very present in Scrivener's book. In the 1983 movie, Noda is portrayed as outgoing and confident: she kisses Fox on their first date as Fox is struggling to muster up a few coherent words; she tries to get close to him physically in a park while Fox refuses to let her touch his leg; and she kisses him again in a car ride after the Prince George Marathon but gets a "not in front of everyone" comment. Fox asks her to write the letter to the Canadian Cancer Society, and she is the first person he calls when he receives his second cancer diagnosis.[53] According to Noda, she was also the first person to learn about his plans to run across Canada.[54] Scrivener spends some time discussing the relationship but concludes that "Rika was finding her relationship with Terry enormously taxing. She was in love with him, but realized he didn't feel the same way. He told her he didn't have the time to spend with a girlfriend because he wanted to concentrate totally on his running."[55]

That Fox had a girlfriend but was willing to lose her in order to complete his mission showed strength of character, emotional distance, and a very mature focus on his goals. But although the memory materials show that Fox was interested in the opposite sex, they also highlight Fox's restraint, almost asexuality. Scrivener does indeed make sure to mention in her book that Fox and Noda had a "chaste romance."[56] But during the run, Fox was not indifferent to women. A woman named Marlene, whom he met in Ontario, was deemed special enough by Fox to go on a few dates at night after his gruelling runs, and the pair "may have briefly contemplated a romance." Fox also thought seriously about inviting another to travel with him during the run.[57] As Scrivener recalls, "Young women were intensely attracted to him, and once in a while, one might join the Marathon of Hope for a day or two along the road, but Terry said he never fell in love."[58]

The sexual attractiveness of Fox was something that could be acknowledged in the years immediately following the end of the Marathon of Hope and the end of Fox's life. The Fox movie released in 1983 has several moments of sexual tension between Noda and Fox, and it also shows what may have been the daily life of Fox in Ontario, as girls run to him for autographs and one of them says, "Why don't you come back with me, I have my own place."[59] But Fox's apparently constant refusal of female advances allowed for his image to project the values of purity, restraint, and devotion to a cause. The promotion of these values may have been in part a reaction to rapidly changing social mores and roles, with the use and reuse of Terry Fox's "squeaky-clean" image serving to show how young males should behave.

Terry Fox, Amputee: Relationship to Disability

Until this point, we have seen how the Terry Fox story and his commemoration promoted a certain masculine ideal by using hegemonic masculinity discourse. But what about disability? How can one reconcile this overwhelmingly masculine image with the fact that Fox was disabled? I argue that the way Fox approached his disability and the way it is depicted in his commemorative materials are consistent with the dominant discourse being transmitted and perpetuated about Fox.

The 1970s and 1980s were crucial years for the disabled in Canada, primarily because many policies and laws were implemented to secure their rights and ensure their well-being. For example, Canada Pension Plan Disability Benefit was implemented in 1970, the Human Rights Act in 1977, the Charter of Rights and Freedoms in 1982, the Disabled Persons Participation Program in 1985, and the Employment Equity Act in 1987. In 1981, the year that Fox died and the International Year of Disabled Persons, Canada saw the creation of a House of Commons Special Committee on the Disabled and the Handicapped, responsible for identifying the "problems facing the disabled in Canada."[60] But according to Jane Crossman, the people who did the most to increase awareness of the disabled, not only their challenges but also their talents, were Fox and wheelchair athlete Rick Hansen, who "genuinely transformed people's perceptions of disabled athletes' abilities and capabilities through their unparalleled achievements of elite physical performance."[61]

R.W. Connell notes that since masculinity is a concept so entrenched in physical performance, disability is problematic in sustaining the "gender order": "The constitution of masculinity through bodily performance means that gender is vulnerable when the performance cannot be sustained – for instance, as a result of physical disability."[62] Being a disabled man, then, had the potential to reduce one's own sense of masculinity because of the normalization of physical prowess as "proof" of male power and identity. As Thomas Gerschick confirms, "The bodies of men with disabilities serve as a continual reminder that they are at odds with the expectations of the dominant culture."[63] Hence the focus on physical performance in the case of Terry Fox certainly looks like a way to minimize his disability and, at the same time, to solidify his image as a masculine ideal. An internal document of Canada Post effectively summarizes what the commemorative materials have tried to do in committing Fox to memory: "It is necessary to show his infirmity without highlighting it."[64]

Despite the many advances of the disability movement in the late 1970s and 1980s, the general reactions to disability continued to include uneasiness and discomfort, hence the need to emphasize Fox's abilities rather than disability. Some journalists masked their discomfort with humour when they interviewed Fox, including Ted Withers on CBC Radio, who cheekily said to Fox, "At least you can carry extra legs with you, most of us can't do that,"[65] and reporter Joe Mullins, who chuckled when asking Fox, "Do you have an extra leg, so to speak?"[66] Others seemed outright repulsed by Fox's disability. Prince Charles, during his visit to Canada, expressed his admiration for Fox as such: "The Canadian hero accomplished much 'despite his hideous handicap.'"[67]

Fox's own attitude to disability was not positive, to say the least. While the growing disability movement was vying for more rights and acceptance for the disabled in Canada, Fox spent considerable time denying he was disabled.[68] He argued that his disability was not permanent or in any way limiting: "I can beat my disability."[69] But as much as Fox tried to deny his disability, and as much as his commemoration makes this aspect of the Fox story secondary, it remains that he is remembered for attempting to run across Canada on one leg. If he had possessed two functioning legs, it would surely have been even harder to convince journalists to show up in St. John's, Newfoundland, to wish him well on his mission. Hugh Gallagher's examination of Franklin Delano Roosevelt points to a similar conclusion: "No matter how much he denied it – to himself and to the world – he was, indeed, a crippled man. The attack of polio that caused his condition was the central event of his life; his illness and lengthy rehabilitation shaped and altered his character."[70] In very similar ways, Roosevelt and Fox were publicly constituted as disabled persons, and it was not possible, despite their incessant efforts, to distance themselves from that image. In effect, Fox went beyond denial of his disability by overcompensating for it and/or actively trying to will it out of existence. He projected the image, as does his commemoration, of what has come to be called a "supercrip." As Clive Seale explains, "'supercrip' images that idealize disabled people as heroes (or others that show them to be the innocent victims of evil or misfortune) are as common as negative stereotypes."[71] Fox himself is quoted as saying that people should in no way pity him because "you could take my real leg away and I'd probably be even stronger than I am now with one."[72]

This narrative certainly contributed to transforming Fox into a national hero in the eyes of many, a figure who was supposed to be a model for all Canadians, including the disabled. But the attitude of Terry Fox toward his disability set a standard that is quite difficult for most disabled people to emulate and that can thus prove counterproductive. By acting as though he were not disabled and did not need special treatment, Fox did little to encourage greater accessibility programs. Moreover, such a model may actually make some feel even less able-bodied than they actually are: "A lot of ordinary disabled people are made to feel like failures if they haven't done something extraordinary ... Do we have to be supercrips in order to be valid? And if we're not super, are we invalid?"[73]

The supercrip theory is the framework we use to link disability and masculinity in the Terry Fox story because, as Dale Stevenson argues, "the supercrip version of masculinity is very similar to hegemonic masculinity in that there are rules that are often unattainable to the majority of people with disabilities."[74] Hence Fox's disability, including the way that it is taken up and represented in the public imagination, in no way contradicts my argument that the Fox story promotes – and actually confirms – a very specific type of hegemonic masculinity.

Conclusion

The Terry Fox story and commemoration show the widespread use of hegemonic masculinity discourse, the main purpose of which is to illustrate the ideal Canadian male. By reiterating that Fox was supposed to represent us all, the commemorative materials present a skewed, but perhaps hopeful, vision of a healthy, athletic, attractive, white male as the epitome of Canadianness. Even when depicting, describing, or illustrating Fox's disability, the materials under study manage to minimize it, focusing the viewer's attention instead on his physical performance. If masculinity is a "defensive category,"[75] it follows that the use of hegemonic masculinity in the commemoration of Terry Fox may have been a response to changing times. Hence despite the context of the 1980s, when significant changes occurred both in the ways that people viewed discrimination based on race, sex, or disability and in the willingness of society to acknowledge, accept, and include difference, the elaboration of a national model like Fox sought to confirm and uphold a more traditional view of masculinity and, indirectly, the social status quo.

However, it cannot be too surprising that official authorities and the mass media so readily adopted a masculine archetype as national hero. After all, masculinity and nationalism are deeply intertwined concepts: "The culture and ideology of hegemonic masculinity go hand in hand with the culture and ideology of hegemonic nationalism."[76] The ultimate sacrifice that Fox made for his cause is in itself a vivid illustration of idealized masculinity. As George Mosse muses, "heroism, death and sacrifice on behalf of a higher purpose in life become set attributes of manliness."[77] By adopting Fox so readily, so quickly, and so unquestionably, the Canadian government was setting its sights on a hero who promised to embody how Canada should be: strong, dedicated, courageous, and selfless but also white, abled, and male. As Eva Mackey argues, "the term 'virile' as an ideal term for a nation – in opposition to 'subservient and dependent' – indicates the belief that a nation, to be a proper nation, must have the male-gendered characteristics of virility."[78]

Notes

This essay is an abridged version of a chapter in my doctoral dissertation, "Constructing a National Hero: Cancer Politics, Masculinity and National Identity in the Terry Fox Story" (Concordia University, 2013).

1 For more on Terry Fox, see Leslie Scrivener, *Terry Fox: His Story* (1981; reprint, Toronto: McClelland and Stewart, 2000). Also interesting are the two movies about Fox. See Ralph L. Thomas, dir., *The Terry Fox Story* (HBO, 1983); and Don McBrearty, dir., *Terry* (Shaftesbury Films, 2005).

2 Quoted in "Doctors Diagnose Lung Cancer, Terry Fox's Marathon Run Ends," *Halifax Chronicle Herald*, September 3, 1980, front page.

3   Roy MacGregor, "A Pause Where Terry Stopped Series: MacGregor on the Road," *Ottawa Citizen,* July 16, 1989, F1.
4   Doug Ward, "Terry Fox More Than Just a Subject for Sculptor," *Vancouver Sun,* September 15, 2001, http://www.sfu.ca/terryfox/about/sculpture.html.
5   "Letters to the Editor," *Vancouver Sun,* June 29, 1981, 4.
6   Department of Canadian Heritage, "Minister Moore Announces Major Partnership to Honour One of Canada's Greatest Heroes: Terry Fox," press release, July 4, 2013, https://www.canada.ca/en/canadian-heritage.html.
7   For a detailed analysis of the role of the Canadian media in the construction of the Terry Fox story, see Julie Perrone, "Constructing a National Hero: Cancer Politics, Masculinity and National Identity in the Terry Fox Story" (PhD diss., Concordia University, 2013), 25–61.
8   Bill Vigars, quoted in Bruce Ward, "Terry's Marathon of Hope Brought the Country Together," *Ottawa Citizen,* April 12, 2005, A1.
9   Donald Sabo and Michael Messner, *Sport, Men and the Gender Order: Critical Feminist Perspectives* (Champaign, IL: Human Kinetics, 1990).
10 R.W. Connell and James W. Messerschmidt, "Hegemonic Masculinity: Rethinking the Concept," *Gender and Society* 19, 6 (2005): 838.
11 Danielle M. Soulliere, "Promoting Hegemonic Masculinity: Messages about Manhood in World Wrestling Entertainment Programming," paper presented at the Annual Meeting of the Michigan Sociological Association, October 22, 2005, 3.
12 Eric Magnuson, *Changing Men, Transforming Culture: Inside the Men's Movement* (London: Paradigm, 2007), 2.
13 See, for example, Christopher E. Forth, *Masculinity in the Modern West: Gender, Civilization, and the Body* (New York: Palgrave MacMillan, 2008), 3; and Stephen M. Whitehead, *Men and Masculinities: Key Themes and New Directions* (Oxford: Oxford University Press, 2002), 55.
14 Cerise Morris, "Royal Commission on the Status of Women," *Canadian Encyclopedia,* http://www.thecanadianencyclopedia.com/en/articles/royal-commission-on-the-status-of-women-in-canada.
15 Fred Walker, interview with author, May 15, 2012.
16 Gary T. Barker, *Dying to Be Men: Youth, Masculinity and Social Exclusion* (New York: Taylor and Francis, 2005), 9.
17 Scrivener, *Terry Fox* (1981), 94.
18 Ibid., 115.
19 See Terry Fox Foundation, "Honours," http://www.terryfox.org/terrys-story/honours.
20 See photograph at http://www.collectionscanada.gc.ca/cool/002027-2106-e.html.
21 Fox is depicted as playful most notably when he "moons" the journalists following him during a day at the beach. Thomas, dir. *Terry Fox Story.*
22 Postes Canada, "Notice de timbre commémoratif, 30 sous," Fonds Denis Masse, Library and Archives Canada (LAC), R7426-9-24, vol. 9-24, no. 000915, dossier 1, 1982–1996, Terry Fox, April 13, 1982.
23 Dr. K. George Pedersen, "Memorial Service for Terry Fox," July 2, 1981, Simon Fraser University Archival Fonds, F-160-1-0-8, Terry Fox file.
24 Mark Sutcliffe, "Terry Fox's Legacy Greater Than He Could Have Imagined," *Ottawa Citizen,* September 7, 2008, D8.
25 Murray Pomerance and Frances Gateward, "Introduction," in *Where the Boys Are: Cinemas of Masculinity and Youth,* ed. Murray Pomerance and Frances Gateward (Detroit: Wayne State University Press, 2005), 5.

26   Scrivener, *Terry Fox* (1981), 7.
27   Scrivener, *Terry Fox* (2000), 4.
28   Jay Scott, "A Glimpse of the Boy behind the Legend: Film Restores Reality to the Terry Fox Story," *Globe and Mail*, May 27, 1983.
29   Henry Ginger, "Terry Fox, Canadian Hero Dies: Ran in Marathon Despite Cancer," *New York Times*, June 29, 1981, A1.
30   Thomas, dir., *Terry Fox Story.*
31   André Dupras, "Sexualité et handicap: De l'angélisation à la sexualisation de la personne handicapée physique," *Nouvelles pratiques sociales* 13, 1 (2000): 175; translation by author.
32   Francine Saillant, "Les aspects culturels de l'expérience du cancer en contexte clinique moderne" (PhD diss., McGill University, 1986), 316; translation by author.
33   Susan K. Cahn, *Coming on Strong: Gender and Sexuality in 20th Century Women's Sport* (New York: Free Press, 1994), 278.
34   Ibid., 239.
35   Douglas Coupland, *Terry* (Vancouver: Douglas and McIntyre, 2005), 16.
36   Susan Elizabeth Hart, "Sculpting a Canadian Hero: Shifting Concepts of National Identity in Ottawa's Core Area Commemoration" (PhD diss., Concordia University, 2008), 181.
37   Sue Vohanka, "Terry's a Hit in East," *Vancouver Sun*, July 11, 1981, front page.
38   Denis Masse, "1ere émission de LIVRAISON SPÉCIALE – Terry Fox: Une leçon de courage pour tous les Canadiens," Fonds Denis Masse, Library and Archives Canada (LAC), R7426-9-24, vol. 9-24, no. 000915, dossier 1, 1982–1996.
39   Jeremy Brown and Gail Harvey, *Terry Fox: A Pictorial Tribute to the Marathon of Hope* (Toronto: Brownstone, 1980), 5.
40   Maxine Trottier, *Terry Fox: A Story of Hope* (Toronto: Scholastic Canada, 2005), 13.
41   Michael Messner and Donald Sabo, *Sport, Men and the Gender Order: Critical Feminist Perspectives* (Champaign, IL: Human Kinetics, 1990), 86.
42   Wendy Jane Gagen, "Remastering the Body, Renegotiating Gender: Physical Disability and Masculinity during the First World War, the Case of J.B. Middlebrook," *European Review of History* 14, 4 (2007): 530.
43   Gail Bederman, *Manliness and Civilization: A Cultural History of Gender and Race in the United States, 1880–1917* (Chicago: University of Chicago Press, 1995), 5.
44   Barbara J. Flagg, "The Transparency Phenomenon, Race-Neutral Decision-Making and Discriminatory Intent," in *Critical White Studies: Looking behind the Mirror*, ed. Richard Delgado and Jean Stefancic (Philadelphia: Temple University Press, 1997), 220.
45   Joyce E. King, "Dysconscious Racism: Ideology, Identity and Miseducation," in *Critical White Studies: Looking behind the Mirror*, ed. Richard Delgado and Jean Stefancic (Philadelphia: Temple University Press, 1997), 128.
46   Richard Dyer, *White* (New York and London: Routledge, 1997), 44.
47   Ibid., 12.
48   Ann Donegan Johnson, *The Value of Facing a Challenge: The Story of Terry Fox* (La Jolla, CA: Value Communications, 1983), 49.
49   Editorial, *Toronto Star*, June 29, 1981, A6.
50   Dyer, *White*, 11.
51   "A Mother and Her Son's Legacy," *Thunder Bay Chronicle-Journal*, June 21, 2011.
52   Thomas, dir., *Terry Fox Story.*
53   Ibid.
54   Canadian Press, "He Left Girl behind to Accomplish Goal," *Ottawa Citizen*, June 29, 1981, 14.
55   Scrivener, *Terry Fox* (1981), 60.

56 Ibid., 66.
57 Ibid., 125.
58 Ibid.
59 Thomas, dir., *Terry Fox Story*.
60 Jane Crossman, ed., *Canadian Sport Sociology* (Toronto: Thomson Nelson, 2007), 66.
61 Ibid.
62 R.W. Connell, *Masculinities* (Berkeley: University of California Press, 1995).
63 Thomas J. Gerschick, "Coming to Terms: Masculinity and Physical Disability," in *Men's Lives*, ed. Michael Kimmel and Michael Messner (Boston: Allyn and Bacon, 1995), 313.
64 Postes Canada, "Réunion du comité de consultation des timbres postes, 18 mars 1981," Fonds Denis Masse, LAC, R7426-9-24, vol. 9–24, no. 000915, dossier 1, 1982–1996.
65 Ted Withers, "Terry Prepares for His Run," radio interview with Terry Fox, CBC Radio, April 11, 1980, http://www.cbc.ca/archives/entry/terry-prepares-for-his-run.
66 Joe Mullins, "Reliving Terry Fox's Marathon of Hope: Day 20 near Corner Brook, N.L.," television interview with Terry Fox, CBC TV, May 1, 1980, http://www.cbc.ca/archives/entry/reliving-terry-foxs-marathon-of-hope-day-20.
67 Charlotte Montgomery, "Quiet Diana Elicits Wolf-Whistle Chorus," *Globe and Mail*, June 23, 1983, 9.
68 Scrivener, *Terry Fox* (1981), 69.
69 John Ritchie, dir., *A Dream as Big as Our Country: The Life and Times of Terry Fox*, documentary (Force 4 Entertainment and The Terry Fox Foundation, 1998).
70 Hugh Gregory Gallagher, *FDR's Splendid Deception* (New York: Dodd, Mead and Co., 1985), 213.
71 Clive Seale, *Media and Health* (London: Sage, 2008), 109.
72 Brown and Harvey, *Terry Fox*, 10.
73 Alan Toy, quoted in Jack A. Nelson, "The Invisible Cultural Group: Images of Disability," in *Images That Injure: Pictorial Stereotypes in the Media*, ed. Paul Martin Lester (West Port, CT: Praeger, 1996), 122.
74 Dale Stevenson, "Paralympic Masculinities: Media and Self-Representation of Athletes at the 2008 Paralympic Summer Games" (MA thesis, University of Manitoba, 2010), 16.
75 Christopher Dummit, *The Manly Modern: Masculinity in Postwar Canada* (Vancouver: UBC Press, 2007), 19.
76 Joane Nagel, "Masculinity and Nationalism: Gender and Sexuality in the Making of Nations," *Ethnic and Racial Studies* 21, 2 (1998): 249.
77 George Mosse, *The Image of Man: The Creation of Modern Masculinity* (New York and Oxford: Oxford University Press, 1996), 51.
78 Eva Mackey, *The House of Difference: Cultural Politics and National Identity in Canada* (London and New York: Routledge, 2002), 41.

Part 5
Men in Motion

RIVERS, LAKES, AND STREAMS were the roads and highways of early Canada. So it is fitting, as we turn our attention to Canadian masculinities *on the road*, to begin with Carolyn Podruchny's discussion in Chapter 16 of French Canadian and Métis voyageurs and their adventures *on the water*. The strength, skill, and endurance of these legendary paddlers were just some of the manly traits about which they boasted, in their old age, to Alexander Ross, who included their stories in the three volumes he published about his life in the Canadian Northwest as a trader and explorer. There is a premodern and pre-industrial hyper-masculinity outlined here in fascinating detail, as Ross's "superannuated sons of the wilderness" reminisce about long journeys freighting furs from Fort William through Sault Ste. Marie on their way to Montreal and brag about their virility, courage, and freedom. The contrast with Ross's own notions of responsible, respectable, Victorian manhood could not be more striking.

From the voyageurs and their boastful tales of backcountry conquest, the focus shifts to more recent times and to an entirely different group of adventurers on the move: the tens of thousands of American draft dodgers who crossed into Canada between 1965 and 1974 to avoid military service in the jungles of Vietnam. In Chapter 17, Lara Campbell explores the wide range of meanings attached to draft dodging, with particular emphasis on what it "meant to ideas about national citizenship, political duty, and manhood." Excoriated for unmanly acts of cowardice, immaturity, and disloyalty by conservative pundits in both the United States and Canada, draft dodgers were also accused of "copping out" by many within the antiwar movement. Yet as Campbell shows, their journey north of the border might also be constructed, especially from the left, as an act of courage cloaked in "moral grandeur" and part of the heroic struggle against "imperialism, racism, and savagery" in the United States.

The outlaw bikers studied by Graeme Melcher in Chapter 18 shared an era and a rebellious, anti-establishment ethos with the young American expatriates studied by Campbell. But that, surely, is where the similarities end. The aggressive, hyper-masculine biker culture that emerged in California and spread throughout North America in the 1950s and 1960s contrasts starkly with that of the peace-loving draft dodger, preoccupied with the wider antiwar social movement that sought social justice on a global scale. The performance of biker identity, Melcher argues, involved "public displays of shared identity and rebellion" that combined a number of material elements (including the powerful Harley-Davidson machines themselves) and that celebrated a proud, fraternal, aggressive, territorial, and frankly misogynist version of working-class masculinity – "a tough, brawling manliness that was proved through physical prowess and individual merit." Whether this construction of manliness is to be admired or vilified, especially given the level of deadly and criminal violence in which biker gangs have been involved since the 1960s, is beside the point. Understanding the hyper-masculine biker culture on its own terms, rather, is the ultimate goal.

16

Tough Bodies, Fast Paddles, Well-Dressed Wives: Measuring Manhood among French Canadian and Métis Voyageurs in the North American Fur Trade

Carolyn Podruchny

TRAPPING FURBEARING ANIMALS and trading their pelts in North America to fashion felted hats and to trim clothing in Europe dominated the early modern mercantile economy of the land that was eventually colonized as Canada starting in the early seventeenth century and continuing to the end of the nineteenth century – after which the industry shifted northward to smaller-scale commercial enterprises focused on luxury clothing.[1] Thousands of men from a variety of backgrounds worked in this industry, from those in the high-status managerial positions, who financed trade goods and decided where to build trade posts, to those in the low-status labouring positions, who built the forts and carried the trade goods vast distances all over northern North America as they travelled back and forth between the posts and central depots both in Montreal and on the coast of Hudson Bay. Men from a variety of places and ethnic groups came to work in the trade, including large numbers of Orcadians from northern Scotland, who laboured in the trade based out of Hudson Bay, and French Canadians from the St. Lawrence Valley, who were indentured to companies in Montreal.[2] This chapter explores how men who worked for Montreal-based companies, and travelled thousands of kilometres across northern North America transporting trade goods, fashioned masculine ideals that helped them to cope with the environments through which they travelled. Our view of these working men comes mainly from the writings of their bosses (usually called bourgeois or masters), such as the Scotsman Alexander Ross (1783–1856), who produced copious amounts of letters and reports in his position as a manager for a variety of fur trade companies and who eventually published long books about his experiences. We need to understand the lens of manhood through which masters perceived their servants in order to glimpse those who could not write and left few records yet dominated the working space of the fur trade over its long centuries of existence.[3]

A former fur trader, explorer, sheriff, and justice of the peace, Alexander Ross was no slouch. While working for a handful of fur trade companies from 1810 to 1825, he endured stormy sea journeys on the Pacific Coast, gruelling expeditions over mountains, and long winters running trading posts of the Continental Interior. By the time he settled down to become one of the Red River settlement's most prominent citizens, Ross had experienced his share of hardship and toil. Turning to writing, he chronicled his life experiences in three meaty tomes. One of these outlined his voyage to the Columbia River area on the Northwest Coast and his work for the Pacific Fur Company, a second described the Interior fur trade, and a third detailed the history of the settlement at the forks of the Red and Assiniboine Rivers (present-day Winnipeg).[4] The second, a two-volume work titled *The Fur Hunters of the Far West* – published in 1855 but probably composed over decades – was devoted to his experiences as clerk and master in the North West Company and the Hudson's Bay Company (HBC) up to 1825. It chronicled the lives of the trade's men and women, dedicating over four pages to a group of aged men who had devoted their lives to the fur trade. In the early 1820s, not long after the North West Company had merged with the HBC, Ross hired this motley crew, forced out of the service as a result of HBC governor-in-chief George Simpson's downsizing efforts, to take Ross and his party from Norway House to the Red River settlement. These "superannuated sons of the wilderness,"[5] as Ross called them, were talkative, high-spirited, and independent, and they had long yarns to tell about their lives. Ross was favourably disposed to those he considered loyal French Canadian servants in the fur trade, noting that they merited "the highest praise" for their abilities to endure arduous labour,[6] so he listened to their stories and, fortunately for us, chose to record them.

The eldest voyageur, over seventy years old, who acted as the leader of his crew, shared with Ross some reflections on his life, which Ross seemingly recounted in the voyageur's own words. He bragged that he had been in "the Indian country" for forty-two years. Although he was old, he could do anything requested of him – steer, row, or sail – proclaiming that he had been "brought up to voyage."[7] For twenty-four years, he was a "light canoe-man" and hardly slept, easily paddling for fifty songs a day – after which he probably worked as a servant at Interior fur trade posts.[8] He announced that no portage was too long for him and that the end of his canoe had yet to touch the ground. He saved the lives of his masters and was always the favourite because he never paused at rapids or even waterfalls, claiming that "no water, no weather, ever stopped the paddle or the song." This aged voyageur also bragged about other accomplishments: he had married twelve times and had once owned fifty horses and six running dogs. He said,

No Bourgeois had better-dressed wives than I; no Indian chief finer horses; no white man better-harnessed or swifter dogs. I beat all Indians at the race, and no white man ever passed me in the chase. I wanted for nothing; and I spent all my earnings in the enjoyment of pleasure. Five hundred pounds, twice told, have passed through my hands; although now I have not a spare shirt to my back, nor a penny to buy one. Yet, were I young again, I should glory in commencing the same career again ... There is no life so happy as a voyageur's life; none so independent; no place where a man enjoys so much variety and freedom as in the Indian country.[9]

Ross quoted these old voyageurs at length in several places in the volume, and indeed he liked to quote Indigenous people and other fur trade masters as well, so one wonders whether he developed a habit of recording their stories while he was travelling with them. Masters usually did not paddle with their servants unless the crew was short-handed or battling a storm, so Ross may have written while he was a canoe passenger. It was not unusual for fur traders to carry around paper and ink because they constantly recorded their manifests and accounts, and many were in the habit of composing narratives of their experiences.[10] I suspect that Ross took extensive notes while he travelled throughout the Northwest and used these to compose his books. He may have sometimes recorded speeches on the spot, but he probably reconstructed most from memory when he sat down to write, probably at meals or the end of a day of travel, away from the danger of water damage and using candles for light.

What happened between the stage of his rough notes and the published volume? Ross would have had to pick and choose from his notes to compose the book. By then, his memory of events may have changed, causing him to embellish his recounting of them. Editor Kenneth A. Spaulding found that the first published edition of *Fur Hunters* "was extensively revised by the 1855 editor to make it conform to accepted rhetorical practices current in mid-nineteenth century England."[11] A rough draft of the book, written in Ross's hand, with a fair amount of editing, can be found in Yale University's Beinecke Rare Book and Manuscript Library.[12] The draft copy of the pages devoted to the crew of aged voyageurs was not altered dramatically in the published book, but we cannot know the extent to which Ross may have adjusted this draft from his original notes. Later in the chapter, Ross chided the voyageurs for not being able to handle his sailboat (they all claimed to be more experienced with canoes and paddles than with sails and oars), for resorting to prayers when fighting a storm, and for dreaming about building themselves houses when they were so poor.[13] Ross may have included the extensive quotations to highlight the ridiculous nature of the men's boasting. Indeed, the draft in the Beinecke Library includes an observation that was deleted before it could reach the published version: "Whether true or false, he [the old voyageur who led the crew] had got into the habit of telling [the story] so often, that at last he finally believed it himself to be true. A sad example of vice and profligacy in an old man."[14] But at the same time, the extensive quotations are very specific and echo other traces of voyageurs' voices that we can glean from the historical record. It is likely that in recording and publishing these long quotations, Ross was simultaneously performing at least three actions: expressing his own prejudices toward men who did not share his masculine ideals of efficiency and education, meeting audience expectations by chiding the voyageurs, and revealing his admiration for voyageurs with his careful and extensive quotations.

If we accept the spirit of Ross's annals, without worrying about precise word choices that may have been altered by him at a later date or by an editor during the publication process, we find that his recordings of voyageurs' speeches are full of revelations about voyageur values and especially about qualities that detail an idealized masculinity. This chapter shows how a single source examined in careful detail can reveal a great deal about masculine ideals in the fur trade. In this method of assessment, all of our evidence about voyageur masculinity must be filtered through Ross's view of an ideal man, which is woven throughout the book. How does he imagine himself acting as a man in the world; how does he imagine the voyageurs he is constructing in his representations and memories; and how do these two images collide, coalesce, overlap, and fit together? Let us first think more broadly about masculine ideals in history.

As discussed in the introduction to this volume, studies of the history of masculinity have developed extensively in the past twenty years, growing out of the innovative field of women's and gender history in response to calls that men needed to be gendered too.[15] Although masculinity was not explicitly defined as a cultural ideal in all past times and places, viewing men's beliefs and actions through a lens of masculinity as a social and cultural construction reveals one of anthropologist Clifford Geertz's webs of signification that helps to explain past mentalities and behaviours.[16] Alexander Ross's ideals of masculinity, which involved being a leading citizen who brought elements of European community organization to a colonial setting, can be compared to voyageurs' ideals of strength and success as indentured servants in a mercantile economy.

Joan Wallach Scott suggests that masculinity and femininity work in conjunction with one another and urges historians not to simply describe the roles assigned to men and women but to interrogate the construction of sexual difference itself.[17] When French Canadian peasants entered the primarily male workforce of voyageurs, they left behind well-defined social, cultural, and economic roles played by men and women, and they had to perform what were considered women's duties in the French settlements in the St. Lawrence Valley. Their tasks included food preparation (even if they ate simple provisions that required little preparation), cleaning their workspaces (even in their small areas in canoes and camps), mending their own clothing, and so on. The mere absence of women created a vacuum where the carefully balanced social roles disappeared. This chapter argues that voyageurs reacted to this change by creating hyper-masculinized practices, which enabled men to perform their manhood in exaggerated ways so that it became visible and demonstrable away from the contrast provided by the presence of women.

Of course, women were not absent from the fur trade. Indigenous women encountered while travelling along fur trade routes at Interior trading sites became important people in the successful functioning of the trade, as Sylvia Van Kirk, Jennifer S.H. Brown, and Susan Sleeper-Smith have so convincingly demonstrated.[18] Indeed, Ross's crew included the voyageurs' wives, who were either First Nations or Métis women.[19] But the initial shock of leaving mothers, sisters, wives, and daughters behind upon entering the trade – regardless of whether one grew up in the St. Lawrence Valley, Detroit, Michilimackinac, St. Louis, or the Red River settlement – created a space where hyper-masculinity flourished.

This chapter further argues that voyageurs' evolving masculine ideals were shaped not solely by the workplace absence of the women they knew but also by the groups of men surrounding them, especially their fur trade masters, known as bourgeois, and the Indigenous men they encountered in the Continental Interior.[20] The voyageurs hired by Alexander Ross to transport him from Norway House to the Red River settlement did not simply reflect a list of attributes they held dear. Rather, they performed a masculine identity as a way to communicate to Ross, to one another, and to themselves that they had power and held worth. Ross may have both mocked and marvelled at their outrageous boasting, but he was sufficiently impressed by their actions and stature to record some form of their words.

We need to pause for a moment to consider the tricky questions of race and ethnicity among voyageurs. Ross described the crew of "North-Westers" he hired as an "invalid class ejected from the service ... infirm and superannuated servants of the Company ... taken from the different posts and left at Norway House."[21] These may have been French Canadians working lifelong in the trade, or they may have been children of French Canadian voyageurs and Indigenous women, who grew up around a fur trade post or in a mixed-heritage or Métis community. Only four pages earlier in the volume, Ross commented that there were very few French Canadians left in the service.[22] Our main character mentioned being in "this country" for forty-two years, placing his birth roughly between 1755 and 1765. He could have been a French Canadian from the St. Lawrence Valley or just as easily a Métis from a Great Lakes fur trade community. Ross himself regarded "Canadiens" – French Canadian voyageurs from the St. Lawrence Valley – as the most impressive of voyageurs but only if they remained loyal servants working for a fur trade company. He disparaged those who ended their labour contracts to become freemen – independent trappers and traders who occasionally worked for companies on short-term or even just daily contracts.[23] He painted a very unflattering portrait of the Métis, whom he called "Half-breeds" or "brulés," describing them as designing, daring, dissolute, indolent, thoughtless, improvident, licentious, unrestrained, sullen, proud, restless, clannish, and vain, while nonetheless observing that they were ingenious, hardy, enterprising, fit, vigorous, brave, sage, and so on.[24] The ambiguity in this long list of adjectives may have been due to Ross's own mixed-heritage children.[25] He implied that all voyageurs were French Canadian, but this was most certainly not the case, and one wonders about the extent to which voyageurs themselves distinguished between ethnic categories, especially if they shared language and religious practices.[26] Ross may have thought of those voyageurs he liked as French Canadians and those he did not like as Métis; he noted of the old voyageur whom he quoted extensively, "We could not help admiring the wild enthusiasm of the old Frenchman."[27] For the purposes of this chapter, it is safest to assume that the voyageurs were from a variety of locations and heritages and that they included French Canadians, Métis, Iroquoians, Hawaiians, and other First Nations men.[28] Most crews worked in groups determined by their language, so Iroquoians generally worked together, as did Hawaiians, but in the context of the fur trade, Métis usually spoke a variety of languages – Michif, Bungee, Nêhiyawewin (Cree), Anishinaabemowin (Ojibwe), English, and French – and so could easily have worked with crews of French Canadian habitants from the St. Lawrence Valley.

Thinking about language leads to another important question: in what language did Ross speak with the voyageurs from Norway House? As Ross was raised in Scotland, English was probably his mother tongue, but he may have had some familiarity with Scottish Gaelic. Some time around 1815, he married a Syilx woman of the Okanagan Nation, named in the records as Sally, and remained with her for the rest of his life, so he likely learned some of her language. Most English-speaking masters in the fur trade had to learn at least a smattering of French in order to direct their mainly French-speaking crews, and successful men like Ross, who went on to become civil servants in the multilingual Red River settlement, likely became proficient in French. Ross used some French terminology in his books,[29] and he liked to record Indigenous terms, names, or phrases in Indigenous languages.[30] This practice gives us some confidence that Ross would have understood the elderly men he hired at Norway House in the early 1820s if they were speaking French. Men who had been working in the trade for decades under English-speaking masters would also have likely learned a great deal of English and may even have told their stories to Ross in English.

In the passage quoted earlier, the leader of the aged voyageurs indicated that the tools of the transporting occupation – canoes, horses, and dogs – held a significant place as prized possessions. They were coveted, well cared for, and decorated. These tools reflected voyageurs' masculine virtues, so canoes, dogs, and horses had to be tough, fast, and strong, just like their owners. Covering vast distances also contributed to voyageurs' masculine capital. Voyageurs showed respect for those who travelled the farthest west and north in the fur trade and distinguished them from others by means of particular terms: Porkeaters were those who travelled between Montreal and the western tip of Lake Superior during the summer months, Northmen were those who wintered in the Continental Interior, and Athabasca Men were those who had the difficult task of transporting goods and furs across Methy Portage south of Lake Athabasca in the summer months. Those of lesser social distinction, based on their geographic experience, deferred to those who had travelled farther, signifying their greater skill and experience.[31] Geographic breadth in travelling for work was one area where the masculine ideals of fur trade masters and their servants obviously overlapped. Only those masters who wintered in the Interior, and thus did not return to Montreal at the end of the trading season, could join the exclusive Beaver Club, a men's dining group, in Montreal.[32]

The old voyageur quoted extensively by Ross measured his prowess against First Nations men, fur trade masters, and his fellow voyageurs. The man reflected that he was usually an obedient servant, but he wanted to show that he was stronger and more capable than his master. Indeed, he bragged that he had "saved the lives of ten Bourgeois."[33] Voyageurs had a complex relationship with their masters, who were dependent on voyageurs for survival in the Interior. The hegemonic master-servant relationship was based on both masters and voyageurs agreeing to the power structure, but voyageurs liked to invert this whenever possible in order to remind masters of their obligations.[34] Masters often reported with awe the amazing feats of strength and endurance performed by their men in the service. While describing their journey past what is today called in English Death Rapids, or Dalles des Morts, on the Columbia River, Ross commented, "In the portage, the road by land is no less difficult, and but little dangerous, than the passage by water; yet the adroit voyageur disregarding all dangers, overcomes all difficulties."[35]

Voyageurs competed with one another to see who could carry the heaviest loads, make it through difficult rapids, and paddle farther and faster than anyone else. One would expect that men who suffered from injuries, particularly back-related from carrying heavy packs, lost masculine capital. Yet the aged voyageurs who bragged about their masculine prowess had all suffered their share of injuries, and Ross described the men as mutilated and infirm.[36] No doubt, masculine capital was constantly in flux and depended on context. When they met on well-travelled routes, voyageurs dared other brigades to race across portages and rivers in order to increase their masculine capital. And they challenged their crewmates to competitions of strength, speed, endurance, and bravery.[37] Ross recorded an incident where his party of over sixty people, including French Canadian and Iroquoian voyageurs, was travelling through the mountains near the headwaters of the Missouri River when they became engaged in a battle with a group of Piegans (Piikáni), who were part of the Blackfoot Confederacy. Even though the fur-trading party had already lost at least six people in the fight, Ross recalled,

> At this part of the conflict, two of our own people, an Iroquois and a Canadian, got into a high dispute [over] which was the bravest man; when the former challenged the latter to go with him into the bush and scalp a Piegan. The Canadian accepted the challenge; taking each other by one hand, with a scalping knife in the other, savage like, they entered the bush, and advanced until they were within four or five feet of a Piegan, when the Iroquois said, "I will scalp this one, you go and scalp another"; but just as the Iroquois was in the act of stretching out his hand to lay hold of his victim the Piegan shot him through the head, and so bespattered the Canadian with his brains that he was almost blind; the latter, however, got back again to his comrades, but deferred taking the scalp.[38]

These competitions could be deadly. One presumes that Ross's use of the term "savage" to describe the men's fighting style implied that they were acting fiercely and cruelly, not that they were acting like Indigenous warriors, even though ironically two of the three involved in the incident were Indigenous.

A true test of strength for voyageurs was to "beat all Indians at the race" and to handle travelling through and living in rugged environments better than First Nations people. Indigenous women were thus often treated as prize trophies – who could navigate the routes, who knew the environments, and who could perform the day-to-day survival tasks – for there was no better demonstration of success in being a "son of the wilderness" than to wed one of its daughters.[39] Winning the hearts of Indigenous women signified a space for sexual and romantic pleasure, where perhaps both exploitation and love flourished. It also meant that voyageurs could attempt to live among Indigenous communities, whether First Nations or Métis, if they wished. But because women usually sought men who could meet their economic needs, the pride in having wives also signified that men valued wealth for what it could buy, as opposed to wealth for its own sake. The elder voyageur quoted at length by Ross bragged about having had twelve wives, who were better dressed than the wives of any of his masters, even though he currently had no money. We do not know whether the voyageur had more than one wife at a time, but it was clear that wives cost money and that one's worth could be measured by wives' apparel. The old voyageur listed his wives like possessions, but we know from Van Kirk, Brown, and Sleeper-Smith that these women would have been a large key to the voyageur's success, guiding him through unfamiliar terrain, teaching him how to live off the land, and providing him with important kin connections integral to developing trading ties. That a wife was well dressed could speak to a woman's skill, suggesting not simply that she was in possession of better fabric and decorations purchased by her husband but also that she was more valuable because of what she could make with fabric, skins, quills, beads, ribbon, and embroidery thread. Sherry Farrell Racette explains that in the fur trade, Métis men and women "adopted elements of European fashion and combined the innovative application of trade goods and the elaboration of indigenous garment forms to create visually distinct dress." She suggests that "a variety of factors influenced individual choices in dress and visual presentation" and that men's choices reflected occupation, social roles, and function.[40] Thus voyageurs represented their occupation through a distinctive style of dress, which usually included a colourful finger-woven sash (called a *ceinture fléchée*), a coat made from a wool blanket (called a *capot* or *capote*), a red cap, moccasins, and decorated leggings. Racette has found that voyageurs spent more of their income on clothing than did other groups working in the trade, suggesting that they placed a great deal of emphasis on dress.[41] Nicole St-Onge has suggested that voyageurs who engaged in small-scale trading on the side perhaps used their clothing as a means of branding themselves for their Indigenous clients.[42] To voyageurs, a well-dressed wife might have been both a euphemism for the most highly desired women, the ones who were the most helpful to their fur trade mates, and an advertisement for the goods voyageurs could trade. Unfortunately, Indigenous women's views of voyageurs' masculinity are mostly hidden from historians today because literate traders like Alexander Ross did not think their views sufficiently interesting or important to record.

An additional value, not overtly reflected in Ross's quotation of the "superannuated" voyageur, is fatherhood. All the voyageurs Ross travelled with on Lake Winnipeg had children, or as Ross reported, were "clogged with large families."[43] One wonders whether the number of offspring came to represent virility and wealth among voyageurs, but to date I have found no evidence to suggest this was the case. We know that at least some of the children accompanied their fathers on the voyage with Ross, as Ross noted that the youngsters teased their fathers when they lost their grip on the boat's sail during a storm and barely rowed the boat to safety.[44] It seems that children learned their fathers' vision of ideal masculine practices and that masculinity was reproduced in fur trade families. This masculine ideal may be only faintly heard in Ross's text because of his own fraught relationship with his children. In 1825 Ross moved with his long-time Syilx wife and four children to the Red River settlement and subsequently had at least nine more children. Ross regarded Indigenous people as racially inferior, even though he was married to one for most of his life, and he felt very ambivalent about his racially mixed children, whom he pressured to succeed in the settlement's Anglo-Protestant community.[45] As Ross had strained relations with his children, he probably did not dwell on the relations between voyageurs and their children. He may have felt threatened by the number of children fathered by other men working in the trade because he had only four living children by the time he left the service and settled down in the Red River settlement. But his comments about voyageurs imply that he thought the large size of their families was irresponsible given their limited means.

Returning to Ross's observations of voyageurs, he noted that the old voyageur's speech ended with a cry in praise of freedom: "There is no life so happy as a voyageur's life; none so independent; no place where a man enjoys so much variety and freedom as in the Indian country. Huzza! Huzza!"[46] Voyageurs worked as indentured servants under the control of their masters and in a foreign land where Indigenous peoples often controlled life and death. To counter their vulnerable position, voyageurs proclaimed their desire to be free; indeed, a handful followed through and became freemen. As Abbé Georges Dugas wrote in his biography of the voyageur Jean-Baptiste Charbonneau, "it was their desire to enjoy the unlimited freedom that they believed they would find in the wilderness of the West."[47] By overcoming the dangerous landscape through strength, the voyageurs could claim a stronger manhood than their British masters and Indigenous neighbours. They carved out a social space in which to assert their distinct identity, a space where canoes, horses, dogs, courage, risk, women, and freedom were central. Although Ross disparaged those voyageurs who became free, we still hear this voyageur value loud and clear in Ross's annals. Ross's prejudices did not totally obscure voyageurs' voices.

By examining the process through which French Canadian and Métis voyageurs measured manhood, as observed by fur trader Alexander Ross, who considered himself to be an ideal man of a kind different from his servants, this chapter has shown how a close cultural reading of a single source can reveal beliefs, values, and worldviews of those involved in the North American fur trade. Fur trade master Alexander Ross positioned himself as an outsider to fur hunters in the Far West, a cultural tourist who managed to control his rambunctious servants and to trade successfully with "wild" First Nations communities, to meet his masculine obligations of earning money for his companies, and to set a model of restrained and tempered hard work, perseverance, temperance, and responsibility for his servants and trading partners. Yet his fascination with voyageurs and Indigenous peoples is evident in his extensive quotations of their speeches and in his careful descriptions of their actions. His marvelling at one particular crew of aged voyageurs has revealed to us that voyageurs valued tough bodies, fast paddling, well-dressed wives, plenty of children, and freedom as markers of manhood. Certainly, the voyageurs performed their manhood for Ross through their tales of strength, endurance, skill, ownership of horses and dogs, and multiple wives. We don't know whether they were telling the truth, but what matters more is that these were the qualities that infused their boasting to Ross. Ross performed his manhood by writing his books, where he recorded these alternative masculinities in both jest and veiled admiration. By carefully examining Ross's writing, unpacking both Ross's and his subjects' assumptions and values, and interrogating the silences, we can probe the layered meanings of masculinity in the fur trade.

Notes

This chapter previously appeared in a French translation as "Robustes et rapides, avec des épouses bien vêtues: Mieux comprendre la masculinité des voyageurs canadiens-français et métis dans l'univers de la traite des fourrures en Amérique du Nord," in *De Pierre-Esprit Radisson à Louis Riel: Voyageurs et Métis,* ed. Luc Côté, Dennis Combet, and Gilles Lesage, 169–85 (Winnipeg: Les Presses universitaires de Saint-Boniface, 2014). I thank Douglas Hunter, Kathryn Magee Labelle, Brittany Luby, Stacy Nation-Knapper, Myra Rutherdale, and Nicole St-Onge for their comments on an earlier draft of this chapter. All errors are my own. I thank Ally Brantley for conducting research at Yale University's Beinecke Rare Book and Manuscript Library for me.

1 For an overview of the economic history of the fur trade, see Ann M. Carlos and Frank D. Lewis, "The Economic History of the Fur Trade: 1670 to 1870," *EH.net* (Economic History Association), http://eh.net/encyclopedia/the-economic-history-of-the-fur-trade-1670-to-1870. For the later period, see Arthur J. Ray, *The Canadian Fur Trade in the Industrial Age* (Toronto: University of Toronto Press, 1990). See also Carolyn Podruchny and Stacy Nation-Knapper, "Fur Trades," in *Oxford Research Encyclopedia of American History,* ed. Jon Butler, http://americanhistory.oxfordre.com/view.
2 Edith Burley, *Servants of the Honourable Company: Work, Discipline, and Conflict in the Hudson's Bay Company, 1770–1879* (Toronto: Oxford University Press, 1997); Carolyn

344 *Carolyn Podruchny*

Podruchny, *Making the Voyageur World: Travelers and Traders in the North American Fur Trade* (Lincoln/Toronto: University of Nebraska Press/University of Toronto Press, 2006).

3 I draw inspiration and guidance to "read beyond the words" of the literate fur traders from the essays in Elizabeth Vibert and Jennifer S.H. Brown, eds., *Reading beyond Words: Contexts for Native History*, 2nd ed. (Toronto: University of Toronto Press, 2003).

4 For an overview of Alexander Ross's life, see Frits Pannekoek, "Ross, Alexander," *Dictionary of Canadian Biography*, http://www.biographi.ca/en/bio/ross_alexander_8E.html. Alexander Ross's three books are *Adventures of the First Settlers on the Oregon or Columbia River: Being a Narrative of the Expedition Fitted Out by John Jacob Astor, to Establish the "Pacific Fur Company"; with an Account of Some Indian Tribes on the Coast of the Pacific* (London: Smith, Elder and Co., 1894); *The Fur Hunters of the Far West: A Narrative in the Oregon and Rocky Mountains*, 2 vols. (London: Smith, Elder and Co., 1855); and *The Red River Settlement: Its Rise, Progress, and Present State* (London: Smith, Elder and Co., 1856).

5 Ross, *Fur Hunters*, vol. 2, 235.

6 Ibid., vol. 1, 291. See also ibid., vol. 2, 186.

7 Ibid., vol. 2, 234.

8 This claim carries little meaning because songs could last between two minutes and an hour.

9 Ross, *Fur Hunters*, vol. 2, 236–37.

10 For a wide sampling of the literature written by fur traders, see Germaine Warkentin, ed., *Canadian Exploration Literature: An Anthology* (Oxford: Oxford University Press, 1993).

11 See Alexander Ross, *The Fur Hunters of the Far West*, ed. Kenneth A. Spaulding (Norman: University of Oklahoma Press, 1956), xxi.

12 For a rough draft of Ross's *Fur Hunters of the Far West*, see WA, MSS 408, Beinecke Rare Book and Manuscript Library, Yale University. It is incorrectly dated 1822, as the events recorded in the book go to 1824.

13 Ross, *Fur Hunters*, vol. 2, 237, 240, 243–44.

14 Yale University, Beinecke Rare Book and Manuscript Library, first copy of Alexander Ross, *Fur Hunters of the Far West*, vol. 2, 237.

15 See Joy Parr, "Gender History and Historical Practice," *Canadian Historical Review* 76, 3 (1995): 367–71; R.W. Connell, *Masculinities* (Berkeley: University of California Press, 1995); Judith Allen, "Men Interminably in Crisis?: Historians on Masculinity, Sexual Boundaries, and Manhood," *Radical History Review*, 82 (2002): 197–207; and Toby L. Ditz, "The New Men's History and the Peculiar Absence of Gendered Power: Some Remedies from Early American Gender History," *Gender and History* 16, 1 (2004): 2–3.

16 On gender as a category of historical analysis, see the foundational work of Joan Wallach Scott, "Gender: A Useful Category of Historical Analysis," *American Historical Review* 91, 5 (1986): 1053–75. See also a description of gender's impact on American history in Joanne Meyerowitz, "A History of 'Gender,'" *American Historical Review* 113, 5 (2008): 1346–56. On webs of signification, see Clifford Geertz, *The Interpretation of Cultures: Selected Essays* (New York: Basic Books, 1973), 5. For an excellent example of how these webs may be deployed, see Elizabeth Vibert, *Traders' Tales: Narratives of Cultural Encounters in the Columbia Plateau, 1807–1846* (Norman: University of Oklahoma Press, 1997), 4, 6–7.

17 Joan Wallach Scott, "Gender: Still a Useful Category of Analysis?" *Diogenes* 57, 1 (2010): 10.

18 Sylvia Van Kirk, *"Many Tender Ties": Women in Fur-Trade Society, 1670–1870* (Winnipeg: Watson and Dwyer, 1980); Jennifer S.H. Brown, *Strangers in Blood: Fur Trade Company Families in Indian Country* (Vancouver: UBC Press, 1980); and Susan Sleeper-Smith, *Indian Women and French Men: Rethinking Cultural Encounter in the Western Great Lakes* (Amherst: University of Massachusetts Press, 2001).

19 Ross, *Fur Hunters*, vol. 2, 235.

20 Joy Parr reminds us that differences in masculinities can be formed as oppositions to other masculinities. See Parr, "Gender History," 370–71. See also Ditz, "New Men's History," 3; as well as several contributions to the present volume.

21 Ross, *Fur Hunters*, vol. 2, 234–35.

22 Ibid., vol. 2, 230.

23 Ibid., vol. 1, 291–92.

24 Ibid., vol. 1, 298, 300–1.

25 Sylvia Van Kirk, "'What If Mama Is an Indian?' The Cultural Ambivalence of the Alexander Ross Family," in *The Developing West: Essays on Canadian History in Honor of Lewis H. Thomas*, ed. John Foster, 123–36 (Edmonton: University of Alberta Press, 1983); Brenda Macdougall, "The Myth of Metis Cultural Ambivalence," in *Contours of a People: Metis Family, Mobility and History*, ed. Nicole St-Onge, Carolyn Podruchny, and Brenda Macdougall, 422–64 (Norman: University of Oklahoma Press, 2012).

26 In one case, while travelling east from Fort Alexander, Ross commented, "Our new companions call themselves half-breeds." See Ross, *Fur Hunters*, vol. 2, 205.

27 Ibid., vol. 2, 237.

28 On Iroquoian men from Kahnawake working in the fur trade, see Trudy Nicks, "The Iroquois and Fur Trade in Western Canada," in *Old Trails and New Directions: Papers of the Third North American Fur Trade Conference*, ed. Carol M. Judd and Arthur J. Ray, 85–101 (Toronto: University of Toronto Press, 1980); Theodore J. Karamanski, "The Iroquois and the Fur Trade of the Far West," *The Beaver* 312 (Spring 1982): 5–13; Jan Grabowski and Nicole St-Onge, "Montreal Iroquois *Engagés* in the Western Fur Trade, 1800–1821," in *From Rupert's Land to Canada: Essays in Honour of John E. Foster*, ed. Theodore Binnema, Gerhard J. Ens, and R.C. MacLeod, 23–58 (Edmonton: University of Alberta Press, 2001); and Ross, *Fur Hunters*, vol. 1, 295–96. On Hawaiian men working in the fur trade, see Jean Barman and Bruce McIntyre Watson, *Leaving Paradise: Indigenous Hawaiians in the Pacific Northwest, 1787–1898* (Honolulu: University of Hawaii Press, 2006); and Ross, *Fur Hunters*, vol. 1, 293–95.

29 For examples, see Ross, *Fur Hunters*, vol. 1, 112, 142, 298; and ibid., vol. 2, 67, 124, 147, 186, 197, 237, 258.

30 For examples, see ibid., vol. 1, 20, 30, 41, 111, 121, 123. For a vocabulary of languages spoken by the Nimíipu (Nez Perce) and neighbouring tribes, see ibid., vol. 1, 313–23. And for a vocabulary of the Snakes (probably Shoshone or Paiute), see ibid., vol. 2, 153–54.

31 Podruchny, *Making the Voyageur World*, 58–71.

32 Carolyn Podruchny, "Festivities, Fortitude, and Fraternalism: Fur Trade Masculinity and the Beaver Club, 1785–1827," in *New Faces in the Fur Trade: Selected Papers of the Seventh North American Fur Trade Conference, Halifax, Nova Scotia, 1995*, ed. Jo-Anne Fiske, Susan Sleeper-Smith, and William Wicken, 31–52 (East Lansing: Michigan State University, 1998).

33 Ross, *Fur Hunters*, vol. 2, 236.

34 See Podruchny, *Making the Voyageur World*, 134–64.

35 Ross, *Fur Hunters*, vol. 2, 179.

36 Ibid., vol. 2, 235.

37 Podruchny, *Making the Voyageur World*, 126, 157, 185–87, 194.

38 Ross, *Fur Hunters*, vol. 2, 57.

39 See Podruchny, *Making the Voyageur World*, 152–56, 267–86.

40 Sherry Farrell Racette, "Sewing Ourselves Together: Clothing, Decorative Arts and the Expression of Metis and Half Breed Identity" (PhD diss., University of Manitoba, 2004), 92, 307.

41 Ibid., 308.

42 Nicole St-Onge, "Blue Beads, Vermillion, and Scalpers: The Social Economy of the 1810–1812 Astorian Overland Expedition's French-Canadian Voyageurs," in *French and Indians in the Heart of North America, 1630–1815,* ed. Robert Englebert and Guillaume Teasdale, 183–216 (East Lansing/Winnipeg: Michigan State University Press/University of Manitoba Press, 2013), 207.

43 Ross, *Fur Hunters,* vol. 2, 235.

44 Ibid., vol. 2, 240. For an account of when the voyageurs clutched their children to protect them in another storm close to Berens River, see ibid., vol. 2, 242.

45 Van Kirk, "'What If Mama Is an Indian?'"; Macdougall, "Myth of Metis Cultural Ambivalence."

46 Ross, *Fur Hunters,* vol. 2, 237.

47 Original French: "Pour les uns, c'était le désir de jouir de la liberté illimitée qu'ils croyait entrevoir dans les déserts de l'Ouest." Georges Dugas, *Un Voyageur des pays d'En-Haut* (1890; reprint, St. Boniface, MB: Éditions des Plaines, 1981), 27.

17
"The Moral Grandeur of Fleeing to Canada": Masculinity and the Gender Politics of American Draft Dodgers during the Vietnam War

Lara Campbell

In 1968, debates over the political repercussions of draft dodging played out in a series of articles and letters to the *Globe and Mail*. Coming to Canada, argued Yale University student Julian Patrick, was an ethical decision of great "moral passion" and a brave rejection of American imperialism. Not so, argued Harvard University students (and future Canadian historians) Michael Bliss and Robert Bothwell: "The draft dodger's decision to leave the United States for Canada is exactly analogous to the decision to escape from a city to the suburbs. The more discomforting demands of citizenship can be abandoned while the pleasant rhythm of one's habitual existence is preserved."[1] Patrick, Bliss, and Bothwell disagreed on how individual citizens and the Canadian state should understand and respond to the rising number of American draft dodgers arriving in Canada during the Vietnam War. They, along with antiwar activists, mainstream and alternative media, and the North American public struggled to understand what dodging the draft meant to ideas about national citizenship, political duty, and manhood.[2]

Although there is an extensive historiography on the Vietnam War in the United States, only a small number of sociologists and historians have analyzed the experiences of draft dodgers who immigrated to Canada, and even fewer have been attentive to the gender politics of the draft resistance movement.[3] Gender instability underlined responses to draft resistance because the category of masculinity was called into question by draft evasion. The figure of the draft dodger occupied a liminal space of both courage and cowardice. Could a real man retain his masculinity while fleeing his country to resist war? Was immigration to Canada an evasion of political action or a heroic sacrifice of home, family, and nation?

Ideas about normative masculinity were central to the experiences of – and responses to – men who dodged the draft by moving to Canada. Like other contributions to this volume, this chapter draws on historical and theoretical literature that considers masculinity to be performed within the larger context of idealized gender norms. Given the restriction of front-line military service to men and the way that soldiers and veterans were understood to exemplify patriotic citizenship, resistance to the draft evoked anxiety about men's moral character and sense of obligation to the nation-state.[4] As North Americans grappled with the meaning of draft resistance, political conservatives and supporters of the war in Vietnam attempted to define draft resistance as shameful, weak, and immoral. Supporters of the war, however, were not the only constituency critical of draft dodgers. For many antiwar activists, leaving the United States to avoid the draft was a "cop-out" and a betrayal of "authentic" political action. In response to accusations of betrayal and cowardice, dodgers and their supporters emphasized a heroic narrative of masculine resistance to a brutal American society. This narrative countered portrayals of antiwar protesters as cowards and intersected with emerging discourses of left Canadian nationalism that critiqued the sickness or "barbarity" of modern America.

Attitudes and opinions on the war in Vietnam were (and remain) complex and often contradictory. In the 1960s and 1970s, numerous venues for expressing these opinions were available, including articles and editorials in the mainstream, campus, and alternative press; pamphlets, posters, and minutes from the meetings of organizations that opposed the war and supported draft dodgers; and letters to anti-draft organizations, newspapers, and politicians. The gender politics of antiwar activism, examined through the lens of draft dodging and the transnational context of North American protest, offers a rewarding way to examine how masculinity was imbricated in state formation, nationalism, and antiwar activism.

Shame, Cowardice, and War

Throughout the 1960s, many North Americans remained highly suspicious of men who resisted the war. In both Canada and the United States, public opinion gradually shifted from an initial support of the war to a belief that American forces should withdraw from Vietnam. For the most part, members of the Canadian media, members of the civil service, and university professors portrayed American military involvement in Vietnam as largely ill-advised.[5] Yet polls indicated that Canadian public opinion on the war and war resistance was complicated and ambivalent. In March 1970, whereas a significant minority of Canadians (36.1 percent) stated that their opinion of the United States would improve if Americans withdrew troops from Vietnam, almost half (49 percent) stated that withdrawal of troops would either negatively impact – or not significantly change – their opinion.[6] Mainstream North American media publications were careful to point out diverse opinions about dodgers: some

North Americans understood them to be traitors, whereas others saw them as courageous "heroes" led by their conscience.[7] Public opinion about the war and the emigration of war resisters to Canada was shaped by multiple factors, including Canada's complicated political, economic, and cultural relationship to the United States. This might help to explain why Canadians, even if circumspect about the war, did not necessarily feel sympathy for draft dodgers.[8]

Ambivalence about draft dodgers was therefore bound up with ideas about masculinity, loyalty, and courage. Citizenship, honour, patriotism, and state entitlements were deeply connected to men's front-line war service.[9] If a soldier embodied manly courage, loyalty, and patriotism, the draft dodger's refusal to fight was conflated with cowardice, unmanliness, and treason. The tradition of equating masculinity with the courage to fight in war and feminizing resistance to military service as a form of cowardice has a long history.[10] Men who refused to fight in the Vietnam War were variously described by critics who wrote to newspapers, magazines, and antiwar organizations as "cowards" and "evaders" who were not "men enough to serve there [sic] country."[11] Leaving the country during wartime was understood by supporters of American troops as treasonous, an "act of conspiracy against our national security." But it was also seen as fundamentally selfish and immature, as well as an offence against those who had accepted the "challenge" asked of them as men.[12] As anti-draft organizations and their publications, most predominantly Toronto-based *AMEX,* enjoyed increased coverage in the American press, their members became targets of angry letters of condemnation. Extremely vitriolic responses included those from people who believed that draft dodgers should be court-martialled, jailed, permanently exiled, or executed.[13] Such accusations involved violent imaginings of the revenge that the state might enact upon the disloyal male body: Americans should "take all these lily-livered, yellow-bellied cowards and have them serve as targets for practice maneuvers." Dodgers' bodies should be physically dismembered and humiliated, the physical essence of their masculinity destroyed: they should have their "nuts [cut] out" or be "shave[d], ball[ed] and quarter[ed] in public."[14] Anger was sparked by a range of factors, including political ideology, patriotism, and anxiety about whether draft resistance denigrated the sacrifice of men who served, suffered, and died in Vietnam.

Even those Canadian observers who were ambivalent about the ethics of the war described draft dodgers as "slackers" and a "passive breed"; one journalist described them as "Zombies marking time, knowing that they are going nowhere, doing nothing."[15] The view of the dodger as a zombie was particularly harsh, as it drew on Second World War insults directed at military conscripts and evoked the image of a man marked by absence and emptiness who was neither truly alive nor actively participating in society. Mainstream media depictions often reflected this assumption that draft dodgers were a "lost generation" marked by emptiness, alienation, and loneliness.[16]

More common than these extreme responses of anger were accusations that draft dodgers were "spineless and gutless" cowards.[17] They lacked the characteristics of manly integrity, such as commitment, courage, and bravery. "Making all possible allowances for any who disapprove[d] of the Vietnam War, ... the weakest ... way to register such disapproval was by fleeing the country ... It wasn't a manly thing to do by any standards."[18] Dodging the draft was described as "running away," "fleeing," or "evading," terms that evoked the image of a fearful and emasculated man. Certainly, many men feared the material and psychological effects of war.[19] But fear was not considered a justification for resistance and was understood as selfish because it prioritized individual well-being over the needs of the nation. Fear was a cowardly rejection of the privileges afforded male soldiers rather than a conscientious decision rooted in ethical decision making; it made resisters "yellow, scared, weak."[20] Indeed, male war resisters and conscientious objectors have long faced accusations of cowardice for refusing to fight due to reasons of religious or political conscience.[21]

Concern centred on the assumption that war resistance was not etched out of an authentic conscience but was a reflection of men's weak moral character and a propensity to run away from adult responsibility. Consequently, private citizens and politicians in the United States and Canada argued that dodgers would ultimately "run out of Canada by the back door" if they were asked to uphold their masculine duty to defend the nation. "Where ... will you run to next if the heat hits here?" wrote a Canadian man to the editors of *AMEX*. "You chickenshit, bootlicking pacifists aren't wanted here ... run rabbit run, and may you die of exhaustion."[22] Conservative politicians like Vancouver mayor Tom Campbell and Canadian prime minister John Diefenbaker also shared these convictions, publicly pondering the courage and loyalty of men whom they perceived as marked by the desire to run away from service and duty. If such men refused to fight for their own country, wondered Campbell, "what are they going to do for Canada? If Canada was in trouble, they'd flee to another country."[23] Similarly, Pierre Salinger, White House press secretary to American presidents John F. Kennedy and Lyndon B. Johnson, warned that "if Canada ever gets involved in a war, you won't find him any use to you either."[24] The allegedly weak moral character of dodgers was sometimes portrayed as a kind of cancer or infection; consistent with mainstream perceptions of political dissent or non-normative behaviour in the Cold War period, many felt that this weakness, if not contained, would infect Canadian and American society with moral permissiveness and a lack of respect for national authority.[25]

This rhetoric of evasion marked the draft dodger as passive, apathetic, emasculated, and lacking in "brains, morals, character and stability."[26] In binary terms, he was an effeminate man whose "female" characteristics made him fundamentally weak. Dodgers were of "delicate nature and weak knees," and they were "effete" and "masochistic," charged American vice-president Spiro Agnew.[27] Like the appearance of hippies and members of the counterculture in general, the physical appearance of draft dodgers was closely linked to a supposedly degenerate moral character. Men's physical bodies were denigrated as both dirty and effeminate; they were criticized as "flea-ridden" "slobs" or "unkempt" hippies.[28] Draft dodger aid organizations were aware of these assumptions about appearance and character and advised potential draft dodgers to go "straight" in clothing and gender presentation because short hair and conservative clothes would result in favourable treatment by border officials.[29] Hair length was of particular concern. Men who sported long hair were not simply dirty or unclean but were "whiskered, long-haired cowards" and therefore outside of manhood itself.[30] The moral degeneracy of dodging was correlated with physical expressions of emasculation, femininity, and childish dependency. An angry letter to the editorial staff of *AMEX* was particularly clear on this correlation: "You're garbage ... traitors – hiding under long hair phony mustaches, wearing women's shoes, panties, etc."[31] The accompanying roughly drawn picture depicted a hairy, dirty, and diapered draft dodger, "mommy's little darling (spoiled)," who was suckling at the breast of his mother. Although particularly harsh, the picture was reflective of the ways that dodging was often understood as selfish and irresponsible; "skipping out" was childish and not the behaviour of responsible adult men.[32]

Some of these concerns about manly moral integrity played out in the case of Gregory Spears, a self-described pacifist who was fired as recreation coordinator in the Borough of York when his status as a draft dodger was uncovered. Local alderman James Trimbee claimed that "a lot of veterans and a lot of people in the borough ... wouldn't like his background. It's the same feeling they would have about a man who was separated from his wife."[33] Such men were morally suspect because they were understood as embodying a lack of manly integrity, which included disloyalty both to the nation and to the family.[34] The Montreal Council to Aid War Resisters accused the Canadian government of bowing to American pressure by arbitrarily turning back potential immigrants in 1969, accusing border agents of holding values similar to those of Alderman Trimbee. If a deserter was detected at the border, he would be turned back, "just as a man who deserts his family will be turned back. The Canadian government obviously shows a distaste for a deserter of any type. It is, of course, a moral judgment."[35] As David Churchill argues, although draft status could not be used to deny entry to Canada, immigration officials held discretionary power in areas involving the judgment of moral character.[36] Both desertion of the nation-state and desertion of the family were considered cowardly, unmanly, immature, and immoral.

Copping Out

It would be a mistake to assume that this language of unmanly evasion was restricted solely to that of political conservatives, right-wing patriots, and vocal supporters of the war in Vietnam.[37] Concerns about authentic political action were bound tightly with ideals of active masculinity – or the "men in motion," around whom the present section of this anthology is organized – and resonated across multiple political and ideological positions. The language of evasion was shared by liberal politicians and radical antiwar activists. Liberal politicians considered opposition to the war to be legitimate if played out within the limits of the law. Democratic senator John V. Tunney told activist, deserter, and *AMEX* editor Jack Colhoun that although he thought the Vietnam War was "abhorrent," he did not "believe the cause of peace is served by those who flee this country in order to escape the draft." Draft dodgers, he felt, had "run out on their fellow Americans who are mounting the pressure, within our political system ... [to] bring the war to an end."[38] The debate about the politics of draft dodging, discussed at the beginning of this chapter, was reflective of ongoing debates about the implications of dodging the draft as a form of resistance. Coming to Canada, argued Julian Patrick, was an ethical response to America's long history of imperialist intervention in international affairs. When Bliss and Bothwell claimed that leaving the United States was an easy way out of "the demands of citizenship," they drew on the rhetoric of collective responsibility and selfishness, arguing that it abandoned the United States to "militarists and racists."[39] "Abandoning" the fight also meant that the less privileged were left to die in Vietnam or that others were left to confront the military and the state.[40] But Bliss and Bothwell also drew on emerging discourses of left nationalism that critiqued the economic and cultural domination of Canada by the United States. A flood of immigrating American draft dodgers could potentially, they argued, "consume" Canada. This nationalist discourse of domination was framed in gendered metaphors, with the United States as the predator potentially violating Canada, the "geopolitical maidenhead north of the border."[41]

Although antiwar activists held diverse perspectives on the war, many shared the belief that draft dodging was a deeply "inauthentic" act because it was a "cop-out" that enabled them to evade their own country's process. New Left activists, argues Doug Rossinow, understood alienation as a form of estrangement rooted in injustice, which could be overcome or transcended through collective political action. An unjust society was sick and fundamentally damaging to the health of individual people as well as the larger social collective, but it could be cured of its brokenness through human compassion and activism.[42] This powerful conception of the responsibility of individuals to heal both themselves *and* the broken economic and political system in which they lived helps us to understand how activists came to see modern America as deeply sick and why leaving that society without attempting to transform its structure was seen as so problematic.

The charge of "copping out" employed a remarkably plastic term that resonated not just with conservatives who felt that dodgers were shirking their fundamental duties to the nation. In light of the desire for authenticity and social transformation, the accusation of copping out implied that men who avoided the draft were running away from what America desperately needed: men who would work passionately to build a new, just society. A commitment to antiwar values and social justice rested on transforming the militaristic culture that condemned young American men and innocent Vietnamese civilians to suffer and die in a war waged for power and profit. Folk singer and antiwar activist Joan Baez received a fair bit of coverage in North America for a similarly held position on draft resistance. To Baez, the only way to end the Vietnam War – and prevent future wars – was by shutting down the military system from within the United States. "These kids," she argued, "can't fight the Vietnam madness by holing up in Canada. What they're doing is opting out of the struggle at home. That's where they should go, even if only to fill the jails."[43] When asked by Canadian reporters what she thought about draft dodgers, her response was blunt: "Not much, really. I think they should stay here and go to jail – I mean instead of running away ... anything other than going to jail is being a cop-out."[44] Her position was bolstered by her political authenticity: she had been arrested and jailed after protesting at an induction centre in California, and her husband, David Harris, spent twenty months in jail for violating the Selective Service Act.[45] When Baez and Ira Sandperl of the Institute for Non-Violence appeared at a concert in Toronto, they challenged dodgers in the crowd to "come back and resist the draft at home." When an audience member accused Sandperl of being disrespectful of draft dodgers, he responded that "there is something bad going on in America, and just leaving won't stop it."[46] From this perspective, dodging the draft was fundamentally self-absorbed because successfully ending the war, whether through institutional structures or direct action, relied on the bodies of those same men who were leaving the country. Being willing to face imprisonment was also a badge of honour and a way to use one's body to challenge the validity of the draft. "Going to prison isn't such a horrible tragedy," wrote one war resister. As a strategic political move, it would allow the police, the public, and the media to have some "respect" for war resisters.[47] Certainly, some mainstream editorials embraced this argument: the "punks" who were "sitting it out in Canada" were cowards without conscience, whereas real objectors "behaved like men" and were willing to accept harsh consequences for their actions.[48]

For antiwar activists who explicitly linked the war to American imperialism and global capitalism, "running away" did not resolve these systemic problems. Leaving for Canada might offer some men legal protection from the draft, but to many antiwar activists, it did nothing to build a more just world.[49] At the Pan-Canadian Conference of US War Resisters held in Montreal in 1970, American activist Tom Hayden put a nationalist spin on this argument, claiming that Canadian activists did not need American war resisters to become citizens. Instead, dodgers should fight American imperialism as political exiles and return to America as "revolutionaries." "You could be," he told the crowd, "70,000 Eldridge Cleavers."[50]

By the early 1970s, draft dodger aid organizations in Canada were speaking openly about the necessity of Americans engaging politically at home and were growing increasingly concerned with problems of integration and unemployment faced by dodgers and deserters in Canada. Dodging the draft should not, claimed the Montreal Council to Aid War Resisters, be the first choice for American draft resisters since it was not the most "effective" way of ending the war.[51] Stan Pietlock, editor of *AMEX* in 1970, challenged dodgers to "take a new look at what their step North means. Is it enough to have just refused to go? Is it enough to merely be an expatriate and 'Canadianize' oneself, forgetting about the US forever ... Perhaps it is our role to lead the fight, physically, against the US from our exile."[52] These critiques about leaving the United States did not draw on ideas about masculine cowardice. Most had been developed by draft dodgers who had immigrated in an earlier period and who were deeply concerned about the racism and militarism in the United States, as well as about inequality and poverty in Canada.

For many draft dodgers and deserters, the motivating factor for resistance was escaping the draft, not ending war or engaging in an anti-capitalist revolution. Dodgers therefore struggled against conservative and patriotic rhetoric that designated them cowards and against a New Left rhetoric of aggressive masculinity that positioned "true" draft resisters (not dodgers) as hyper-masculine "risk takers" who were "confronting the war machine."[53] The accusation of "copping out" played well across a number of political positions about the war because it evoked an image of a weakened, emasculated man shirking his responsibilities: conservative patriots demanded that he fight for the nation, liberals expected him to make the United States a "better place" as an obligation of citizenship, and radicals wanted him to help dismantle American capitalism and imperialism. Despite different definitions of obligation and responsibility, these ideological positions shared the image of an active, committed, and engaged man willing to risk imprisonment, injury, or death for a larger cause.

The longstanding cultural emphasis on the connections between active political engagement and masculinity gave the charge of copping out added resonance. The decision to reject not just the current iteration of America but also the vision of a better America – one that could potentially exist with hard work and a transformative social vision – troubled a range of conservative, liberal, and radical political values.[54] Given the way that manhood in North America was so deeply tied to military service and patriotism, as well as to fundamental political engagement, it is not surprising that leaving America was understood as a cowardly act of running away or as an apathetic cop-out that did not allow for effective political action.

Reinscribing Heroic and Honourable Masculinity

The narrative of the heroic draft dodger imparted masculine markers of heroism and bravery to men whom many understood as the embodiment of cowardice. Clearly, some of these heroic tales must be understood in the context of nationalist stereotypes, such as the positioning of America as savage or dangerous and Canada as peaceable and tolerant. But part of the power of these tales lies in the way that dodgers' stories became heroic. Rather than running away, they were actively rejecting imperialism, racism, and savagery. The imagining of dodgers as brave and idealistic intersected with left-nationalist rhetoric that portrayed Canada as an alternative to the barbaric savagery of the United States.

Some contemporary writers told epic tales of courageous men bathed in the "moral grandeur" of fleeing to Canada. An honourable man did not blindly follow orders; he gave up his country and family to refuse the American war machine.[55] In some cases, dodgers were configured as the "conscience of America" and the ultimate embodiment of bravery because they sacrificed their homes and families to resist a criminal war.[56] Repositioning war resistance as the ultimate act of conscience drew in part from American traditions of dissent as patriotic – with resisters as the "true Americans" – rather than disloyal traitors.[57] "It takes courage and a brave, idealistic heart," argued a mother before the Democratic National Committee, to leave one's country for political reasons.[58] The language of moral courage and characterization of dodgers as "intelligent" and "morally strong" countered accusations about men's cowardice.[59] Leaving for Canada was "the supreme anti-war commitment" because it removed the bodies of young men from the military, where they were used as "cannon fodder."[60] For many activists, dodging was a revolutionary rejection of a corrupt and evil America, which symbolized "war and exploitation" and "racist imperialism."[61]

For this construction of manly heroism to work successfully, however, America needed to be framed as a fundamentally corrupt society. This muscular rhetoric that condemned the United States as savage and barbaric found support among antiwar activists as well as prominent left-nationalist Canadians. From this perspective, resistance to war was clothed in the forceful rhetoric of fighting barbarism, with Canada as the brave North American voice of reason and tolerance. The intersection of these arguments helped to mythologize the idea of Canada as a haven from war despite the complicated realities of its own military history and internal inequalities. These arguments about America resonated deeply because they intersected both with assertions of Canadian nationalism and with the desire to create a heroic narrative of antiwar masculinity.

In conceptualizing the United States as a barbarous and savage nation, activists posited Canada as saner, kinder, and more compassionate. But constructing this binary ran the risk of positing Canada as weak, ineffective, or unimportant. This may be one explanation for why condemnation of the United States had to be particularly vivid; if America was deeply barbaric, the Canadian national alternative was nothing less than brave. A good example is the 1966 antiwar speech given by author and Canadian nationalist Farley Mowat at the University of Toronto, in which he claimed that the United States was seeking "world power – and that it will use all means at its disposal, including the greatest and most destructive military machine the world has ever known, to achieve its unstated ends."[62] His influential speech showed up in various permutations on posters, in demands to the government, and at antiwar protests for many years. Several of the tropes that came to dominate later left-Canadian critiques of the war were evident in his speech. Mowat compared the United States to the regimes of Joseph Stalin and Adolf Hitler and explicitly named American war atrocities as racist. He also condemned Canada's dependence on the United States in gendered terms, arguing that Canada had a responsibility to publicly condemn the United States or itself risk becoming a "flaccid," "mindless" "parasite" that lived off the crimes of its neighbour.[63]

Mowat was certainly not alone in his analysis. These types of critiques were influenced by the American left's harsh critique of its own country as the embodiment of a "death culture" rooted in "unimaginable misery and absolute and total human degradation."[64] The United States, Rabbi Abraham Feinberg told the Toronto Coordinating Committee to End the War in Vietnam, was "sowing the seeds of bitterness, hate and revolution throughout the world ... [It] will become known as a country that reverted to barbarism and savagery."[65] But

Canadians gave this rhetoric a sharper spin, edged with anger and frustration, as many came to see Canada as a country colonized by America in a way reminiscent of America's colonization of the "Third World."[66]

For Canadian nationalists, the act of dodging existed within a long lineage of "idealistic" freedom seekers, like the Loyalists fleeing the American Revolution or runaway slaves, who were seen as heroes who had resisted American exploitation and found safety in Canada.[67] Both dodgers and escaped slaves, wrote one war resister, lacked power over their bodies and were subjected to the "harsh punishment" of the state for leaving America.[68] Canada is not "heaven," wrote an African American draft dodger who described himself as a modern "runaway slave," but "the air of freedom blows a little better" there than in "racist, genocidal" America.[69] Within this trajectory, draft dodgers were representatives of loyal citizenship and seekers of political freedom. Propaganda images that overturned assumptions about America as the repository of freedom helped to underline this narrative. For example, *Escape from Freedom* (1967) was the title of an immigration guide penned by draft dodger Richard Paterak and published by the Student Union for Peace Action at the University of Toronto,[70] which later inspired the *Manual for Draft-Age Immigrants to Canada* (1969), written by Mark Satin.[71] Leaving the United States was imagined as the rejection of imprisonment, and moving to Canada was a positive act leading to liberation.[72]

Critiquing the concept of Canada as a haven is necessary, but it is important to remember that for *some* draft-age men, Canada provided an escape and an opportunity to imagine themselves as active participants – perhaps even manly adventurers – in a new land. In 1973 CBC broadcaster Andy Barrie captured some of this sense of hopefulness when, speaking of his experience as a draft dodger, he stated that "the people who came to Canada found a better way ... They feel sorry for the sad scenes in the US, but ... they're too busy in the adventure of helping to shape a new society, rather than wanting to come back and get caught in the ruins of an old one."[73] Upholding Canada as a place where freedom might be achieved gave leaving America moral heft and ideological shape. Men were not running *from* America out of fear or cowardice; they were actively moving *toward* something more important and meaningful.

Conclusion

The heavy weight of gender expectations surrounding war service and the insistence that men authentically engage by not "copping out of" their political responsibilities meant that the antiwar movement needed to write a discourse of resistance to war as a story of active courage and bravery. The anti-draft movement was engaged in the large-scale creative project of writing an evocative and convincing narrative to counter that of shame and cowardice. Dodgers were courageous young men willing to leave their families and country in order to resist a barbaric society and build a better world. This was a way of conceptualizing manhood as strong and morally courageous yet still manly enough to reject the militaristic attributes of barbarity and cruelty. The draft dodger ultimately fulfilled the desire to embody masculine bravery and courage as well as the very American desire to achieve freedom and "liberation."[74]

Notes

1　Julian Patrick, letter to the editor, *Globe and Mail*, February 27, 1968, 6; Michael Bliss and Robert Bothwell, letter to the editor, *Globe and Mail*, March 6, 1968, 6.

2　Numbers vary but historians have estimated that approximately 50,000 Americans moved to Canada to resist the Vietnam War between 1965 and 1974. John Hagan, *Northern Passage: American Vietnam War Resisters in Canada* (Cambridge, MA: Harvard University Press, 2001), 3, 184, 241; David Churchill, "An Ambiguous Welcome: Vietnam Draft Resistance, the Canadian State, and Cold War Containment," *Histoire sociale/Social History* 27, 73 (2004): 3; Robert Bothwell, *Alliance and Illusion: Canada and the World, 1945–1984* (Vancouver: UBC Press, 2007), 212. Although the term "draft dodging" can have negative connotations, it was the term most commonly used in the period to refer to men who left the United States to avoid induction. War resistance is a broader category that captures those who resisted the war but were not in danger of the draft. On gender and Vietnam War resistance, see Michael Foley, "'The Point of 'Ultimate Indignity' or a 'Beloved Community'? Draft Resistance and New Left Gender Dynamics," in *The New Left Revisited*, ed. John McMillian and Paul Buhle, 178–98 (Philadelphia: Temple University Press, 2003); Barrie Thorne, "Women in the Draft Resistance Movement: A Case Study of Sex Roles and Social Movements," *Sex Roles* 1, 2 (1975): 179–95; and Lara Campbell, "Women United against the War: Gender Politics, Feminism, and Vietnam Draft Resisters in Canada," in *New World Coming: The Sixties and the Shaping of Global Consciousness*, ed. Karen Dubinsky, Catherine Krull, Susan Lord, Sean Mills, and Scott Rutherford, 339–46 (Toronto: Between the Lines, 2009). See also Brenda M. Boyle, *Masculinity in Vietnam War Narratives: A Critical Study of Fiction, Films and Nonfiction Writings* (Jefferson, NC: McFarland and Company, 2009).

3　On draft resistance and the antiwar movement in the United States, see Michael Foley, *Confronting the War Machine: Draft Resistance during the Vietnam War* (Chapel Hill: University of North Carolina Press, 2003); Sherry Gottlieb, *Hell No, We Won't Go! Resisting the Draft during the Vietnam War* (New York: Viking, 1991); Marilyn Young, *The Vietnam Wars, 1945–1990* (New York: Harper, 1991); and Jerry Lembcke, *The Spitting Image: Myth, Memory, and the Legacy of Vietnam* (New York: New York University Press, 1998). On draft dodgers and Canada, see Renée Kasinsky, *Refugees from Militarism: Draft Age Americans in Canada* (New Brunswick, NJ: Transaction Books, 1976); Alan Haig-Brown, *Hell No, We Won't Go: Vietnam Draft Resisters in Canada* (Vancouver: Raincoast Books, 1996); James Dickerson, *North to Canada: Men and Women against the Vietnam War* (Westport, CT: Praeger, 1999); Frank Kusch, *All American Boys: Draft Dodgers in Canada from the Vietnam War* (Westport, CT: Praeger, 2001); Jessica Squires, *Building Sanctuary: The Movement to Support Vietnam War Resisters in Canada, 1965–73* (Vancouver: UBC Press, 2013); David Churchill, "When Home Became Away: American Expatriates and New Social Movements in Toronto, 1965–1977" (PhD diss., University of Chicago, 2001);

Hagan, *Northern Passage;* Donald Maxwell, "Religion and Politics at the Border: Canadian Church Support for American Vietnam War Resisters," *Journal of Church and State* 48, 4 (2006): 807–29; Jay Young, "Defining a Community in Exile: Vietnam War Resister Communication and Identity in *AMEX*, 1968–1973," *Histoire sociale/Social History* 44, 87 (2011): 115–46; Matthew Roth, "Crossing Borders: The Toronto Anti-Draft Programme and the Canadian Anti-Vietnam War Movement" (MA thesis, University of Waterloo, 2008); Aisling Murphy, "Journeys to the North Country Fair: Exploring the American Vietnam War Migration to Vancouver" (MA thesis, Simon Fraser University, 2010).

4 Lara Campbell, *Respectable Citizens: Gender, Family, and Unemployment in Ontario's Great Depression* (Toronto: University of Toronto Press, 2009), 11; Nancy Fraser and Linda Gordon, "Contract vs. Charity: Why Is There No Social Citizenship in the United States?" *Socialist Review* 22, 3 (1992): 52–56; Veronica Strong-Boag, "The Citizenship Debates: The 1885 Franchise Act," in *Contesting Canadian Citizenship: Historical Readings,* ed. Robert Adamoski, Dorothy E. Chunn, and Robert J. Menzies, 69–94 (Peterborough, ON: Broadview, 2002).

5 Bothwell, *Alliance and Illusion.*

6 Carleton University, Social Science Data Archives, Gallup Poll 340, March 1970. Gallup polls can provide a general picture of public opinion, although they cannot elucidate the finer points of individual positions on the draft or the war.

7 Philip Smith, "Why They Chose Canada," *Weekend Magazine,* November 26, 1966; "Amnesty for the War Exiles," *Newsweek,* January 17, 1972; Oliver Clausen, "Boys without a Country," *New York Times,* May 21, 1967.

8 See Stephen Azzi, *Reconcilable Differences: A History of Canada-US Relations* (Don Mills, ON: Oxford University Press, 2015); Heather M. Nicol, *The Fence and the Bridge: Geopolitics and Identity along the Canada-US Border* (Waterloo, ON: Wilfrid Laurier University Press, 2015); Ryan Edwardson, *Canadian Content: Culture and the Quest for Nationhood* (Toronto: University of Toronto Press, 2008); Mallory Schwartz, "Like 'Us' or 'Them'? Perceptions of the United States on the CBC-TV National News Service in the 1960s," *Journal of Canadian Studies* 44, 3 (2010): 118–53.

9 Lara Campbell, "'We Who Have Wallowed in the Mud of Flanders': First World War Veterans, Unemployment, and the Development of Social Welfare in Canada, 1929–1939," *Journal of the Canadian Historical Association* 11, 1 (2000): 125–49; Desmond Morton, "The Canadian Veterans' Heritage from the Great War," in *The Veterans Charter and Post-World War II Canada,* ed. Peter Neary and J.L. Granatstein, 15–31 (Montreal and Kingston: McGill-Queen's University Press, 1998).

10 Marlene Epp, "Heroes or Yellow Bellies? Masculinity and the Conscientious Objector," *Journal of Mennonite Studies* 17 (1999): 107–17; Amy J. Shaw, *Crisis of Conscience: Conscientious Objection in Canada during the First World War* (Vancouver: UBC Press, 2009); Mark Moss, *Manliness and Militarism: Educating Young Boys in Ontario for War* (Toronto: University of Toronto Press, 2001); Mike O'Brien, "Manhood and the Militia Myth: Masculinity, Class and Militarism in Ontario, 1902–14," *Labour/Le Travail* 42 (1998): 115–41.

11 Wisconsin Historical Society and Archives (WHSA), *Americans in Exile (AMEX),* MSS 736, box 4, folder 5, correspondence, hate mail, letter to Gerry Condon from a mother, September 17, 1974. See also *Globe and Mail,* October 12, 1967, 5; *Globe and Mail,* May 26, 1971, 6; and *Globe and Mail,* May 10, 1972, 6.

12 *Kentucky New Era,* October 29, 1965, 11; *Montreal Gazette,* September 22, 1972, 7; *Montreal Gazette,* February 15, 1973, 8.

13 *Lakeland Ledger,* April 21, 1974, 15A; *Miami News,* October 21, 1967, 2A; *Lawrence Journal,* February 24, 1973, 1; *Reading Eagle,* March 24, 1974, 6; *New York Times,* April 6, 1974, 78; *Sarasota Herald-Tribune,* March 25, 1973, 5.

14 WHSA, *AMEX,* MSS 736, box 4, folder 5, correspondence, hate mail, anonymous, 1974; and correspondence, hate mail, anonymous, n.d.

15 *Globe and Mail,* October 12, 1967, 5; February 16, 1968, 7; and February 26, 1968, 6.

16 *Spokesman-Review,* April 6, 1968, 4–6; *Rock-Hill Herald,* January 15, 1971, 14. See articles on the "trauma" of exile in *Spokesman-Review,* January 22, 1967, 10; on the difficulties "adjusting" to Canada in *Deseret News,* January 15, 1972, A3; and on the inability to cope with fears in *Gettysburg Times,* July 11, 1973, 8.

17 Steve Chadwick, former commander of the American Legion, quoted in *Spokane Daily Chronicle,* June 9, 1969, 6.

18 WHSA, *AMEX,* MSS 736, box 4, folder 5, correspondence, hate mail, letter to Jack Colhoun et al. from Arthur G. Grafflin, September 18, 1974.

19 On the fear of both killing and being killed, see Hagan, *Northern Passage,* 26.

20 WHSA, *AMEX,* MSS 736, box 4, folder 5, correspondence, hate mail, anonymous, September 17, 1974; and letter from Suzanne Reynold, September 18, 1974.

21 Epp, "Heroes or Yellow Bellies?"; Shaw, *Crisis of Conscience;* Marlene Epp, "Alternative Service and Alternative Gender Roles: Conscientious Objectors in B.C. during World War II," *BC Studies,* 105–6 (1995): 139–58; Frances Early, *A World without War: How U.S. Feminists and Pacifists Resisted World War I* (Syracuse, NY: Syracuse University Press, 1997).

22 *Globe and Mail,* October 12, 1967, 5; Jack Coyne, letter to editor, *AMEX* 1, 16 (1969): 2.

23 *AMEX* 2, 5 (1970): 26. Diefenbaker claimed that draft dodgers were useless because they had refused to "defend" their own nation. See also *Globe and Mail,* July 4, 1969, 6; and *Montreal Gazette,* October 5, 1970, 1.

24 Clausen, "Boys without a Country."

25 *Rock Hill Herald,* December 7, 1971, 4; *Spokane Daily Chronicle,* June 9, 1969, 6; *The Peak* 11, 6 (1969): 1. On containment in the Cold War, see Elaine Tyler May, *Homeward Bound: American Families in the Cold War Era* (New York: Basic Books, 1988); and Patrizia Gentile and Gary Kinsman, *The Canadian War on Queers: National Security as Sexual Regulation* (Vancouver: UBC Press, 2010).

26 WHSA, *AMEX,* MSS 736, box 4, folder 5, correspondence, hate mail, letter, "Honky US Citizen," n.d.

27 *Pittsburgh Press,* March 19, 1966, 10; *Globe and Mail,* October 20, 1969, 4; *Globe and Mail,* July 4, 1969, 6. See also Shaw, *Crisis of Conscience,* 123–24.

28 See Stuart Henderson, *Making the Scene: Yorkville and Hip Toronto in the 1960s* (Toronto: University of Toronto Press, 2011); Marcel Martel, "'They smell bad, have diseases, and are lazy': RCMP Officers Reporting on Hippies in the Late Sixties," *Canadian Historical Review* 90, 2 (2009): 215–45; Van Gosse, *Rethinking the New Left: An Interpretive History* (New York: Palgrave Macmillan, 2005), 16; WHSA, *AMEX,* MSS 736, box 4, folder 5, correspondence, hate mail, letter, anonymous, 1974; and *Spartanburg Herald,* September 21, 1968, 8.

29 Multicultural History Society of Ontario, American Collection, Mary Paisley Burdick, interviewed January 21, 1979; and Tom Bonanno, interviewed January 1979; McMaster University Library (MU), William Ready Division of Archives and Research Collections (WR), Canadian Student Social and Political Organizations, box 9, File: Victoria Committee to Aid War Resisters, Factsheet, 1970; *Ramparts* 5, 7 (1967).

30 WHSA, *AMEX*, MSS 736, box 4, folder 5, correspondence, hate mail, letter, "Honky US Citizen," n.d.

31 WHSA, *AMEX*, MSS 736, box 4, folder 5, correspondence, hate mail, anonoymous letter and photo, n.d.

32 *Eugene Register-Guard*, March 25, 1973, 10A; *Park City Daily News*, September 19, 1965, 6. Even those who supported some form of postwar amnesty argued that draft dodgers should "earn" their way back into America by paying for their disobedience, childishness, and disloyalty. A Gallup survey of 1974 on amnesty found that 80 percent of Americans felt that dodgers, deserters, and draft resisters should be punished with mandated state service. *Lakeland Ledger*, April 21, 1974, 15A. On amnesty, see Sharon Rudy Plaxton, "To Reconcile a Nation: Gerald Ford, Jimmy Carter, and the Question of Amnesty, 1974–1980" (PhD diss., Queen's University, 1996); Hagan, *Northern Passage*; Young, "Defining a Community"; *New York Times*, February 13, 1969, 44; *New York Times*, November 27, 1971, 31.

33 *Globe and Mail*, August 2, 1968, 2. With the aid of the Civil Liberties Commission, Spears was rehired but placed on probation for a period.

34 *Toronto Daily Star*, August 29, 1968, 6; *Toronto Daily Star*, September 4, 1968, 6.

35 MU, WR, Quebec Social and Political Organizations Collection File: Montreal Council to Aid War Resisters, editorial, *Montreal Star*, February 7, 1969.

36 Churchill, "Ambiguous Welcome," 9–18.

37 Doug Rossinow, *The Politics of Authenticity: Liberalism, Christianity, and the New Left in America* (New York: Columbia University Press, 1998), 229.

38 WHSA, *AMEX*, MS 736, box 4, Folder: Correspondence, Jack Colhoun, August 1971 to December 1972, letter from Tunney to Colhoun.

39 Julian Patrick, letter to the editor, *Globe and Mail*, February 27, 1968, 6; Michael Bliss and Robert Bothwell, letter to the editor, *Globe and Mail*, March 6, 1968, 6.

40 Scott Young, "Draft Dodgers: A Passive Breed Doing Nothing and Going Nowhere," *Globe and Mail*, February 16, 1968, 7; see also *Yankee Refugee* 8 (July 1969). See also Foley, *Confronting the War Machine*; and Gosse, *Rethinking the New Left*.

41 Michael Bliss and Robert Bothwell, letter to the editor, *Globe and Mail*, March 6, 1968, 6. Gallup polls in 1968 reflected divisions in Canada about how to respond to draft dodgers, with the majority reporting that they neither "felt sympathetic" to draft dodgers nor believed the government should accept them as immigrants. Some Canadians may have shared conservative views that such men were morally suspect, whereas others may have believed that Americans had an obligation to fight the war from the United States or may have been worried about the impact of American immigration on Canadian sovereignty. Carleton University, Social Science Data Archives, Gallup Poll 332, October 1968. Among respondents, 32.4 percent sympathized with draft dodgers, whereas 46.8 percent did not, and 28.2 percent agreed that the Canadian government should accept draft dodgers as immigrants, whereas 50.6 percent did not.

42 Rossinow, *Politics of Authenticity*; Henderson, *Making the Scene*, 43–46.

43 Clausen, "Boys without a Country."

44 Quoted in *Globe and Mail*, March 9, 1967, 10.

45 David Harris, *Our War: What We Did in Vietnam and What It Did to Us* (New York: Times Books, 1996), 133.

46 *Vancouver Free Press*, January 25 to February 1, 1973. See also *Globe and Mail*, February 16, 1968, 7; October 12, 1967, 5; March 27, 1967, 3; and 18 March, 1968, 12; and Tim O'Brien, *If I Die in a Combat Zone: Box Me Up and Ship Me Home* (New York: Broadway Books, 1999).

47   WHSA, *AMEX*, MSS 736, box 3, folder 5, General Correspondence, 1975, letter from Gary
     Clausheide to people at *AMEX*, January 1975; and folder 2, General Correspondence, 1972,
     letter from Jeremy Mott to Jack Colhoun, November 2, 1972; *The Peak* 9, 13 (1968): 5;
     Donald Duncan, "Sanctuary," *Ramparts* 5, 10 (1967): 29–33.
48   *Bryan Times*, October 9, 1974, 4; *Lodi News-Sentinel*, August 20, 1974, 6.
49   Lancelot Greer, quoted in *Berkeley Barb*, January 3, 1969, 9. See also *AMEX* 1, 12 (1969):
     9; and Ken Stone, letter, *AMEX* 1, 10 (1969): 14.
50   "The Parley in Montreal," *AMEX* 2, 4 (1970): 10.
51   MU, WR, Quebec Social and Political Organizations Collection File: Montreal Council
     to Aid War Resisters, circular letter.
52   Stan Pietlock, editorial, *AMEX* 2, 4 (1970): 4.
53   Foley, "Point of 'Ultimate Indignity,'" 181–82; Ian Lekus, "Losing Our Kids: Queer
     Perspectives on the Chicago Seven Conspiracy Trial," in *The New Left Revisited*, ed. John
     McMillian and Paul Buhle, 199–213 (Philadelphia: Temple University Press, 2003); Terence
     Kissack, "Freaking Fag Revolutionaries: New York's Gay Liberation Front, 1969–1971,"
     Radical History Review 62 (1995): 105–34. Further deepening the association between
     radicalism and assertive masculinity, some antiwar activists in the United States empha-
     sized street-level confrontation and physical violence as part of a heroic and revolutionary
     struggle. See Jeremy Varon, *Bringing the War Home: The Weather Underground, the Red
     Army Faction, and Revolutionary Violence in the Sixties and Seventies* (Berkeley: University
     of California Press, 2004); Rossinow, *Politics of Authenticity*; Gosse, *Rethinking the New
     Left*, 158–59; and Sean Mills, *The Empire Within: Postcolonial Thought and Sixties Montreal*
     (Montreal and Kingston: McGill Queen's University Press, 2010). On feminist romanti-
     cized images of revolutionaries, see Judy Tzu-Chun Wu, "Journeys for Peace and Libera-
     tion: Third World Internationalism and Radical Orientalism during the U.S. War in
     Vietnam," *Pacific Historical Review* 76, 4 (2007): 575–84. See also Olivier Vallerand, Chapter
     7, and Graeme Melcher, Chapter 18, this volume.
54   Many dodgers initially formulated their antiwar politics in the context of coming to
     terms with the failed promises of a liberal America. On the failures of liberalism, see MU,
     WR, Combined Universities Campaign for Nuclear Disarmament, box 13, Petitions,
     Marches, Lobbies, etc. Publications, File: Vietnam: March on Washington, 1965, speech
     by Carl Oglesby, "Carl Oglesby Names It," and Harris, *Our War*, 38.
55   On the honour of dodging the draft, see *Globe and Mail*, March 6, 1968, 6; February 26,
     1968, 6; February 21, 1968, 6.
56   WHSA, *AMEX*, MSS 736, box 9, folder 1, 1971, Jack Colhoun; WHSA, *AMEX*, MSS 736,
     box 5, folder 14, Sympathetic Organizations, National Committee for Amnesty Now, letter
     from Marjorie Westman to Charles O. Porter of Amnesty Now, January 5, 1972.
57   *Owosso Argus-Press*, January 29, 1968, 6. On the value of dissent, see Foley, *Confronting
     the War Machine*, ix–x.
58   WHSA, *AMEX*, MSS 736, box 11, folder 1, n.d., Esther Lafferty White, before the Democratic
     National Committee.
59   *Globe and Mail*, December 10, 1968, 6.
60   WHSA, *AMEX*, MSS 736, box 4, folder 1, Correspondence, Jack Colhoun, August 1971 to
     December 1972, letter to Henry Swartzchild from Colhoun, June 3, 1972; *Owosso Argus-
     Press*, October 29, 1966, 4.
61   *Globe and Mail*, February 27, 1968, 6.
62   University of Toronto, Thomas Fisher Rare Book Library, pamphlet, Farley Mowat, "A
     Statement on Vietnam," speech presented at the conference "Canada's Role in Vietnam,"
     Toronto, February 19, 1966.

63 University of Toronto, Thomas Fisher Rare Book Library, Robert S. Kenny Collection, box 54, File: Vietnam 2, Poster: Toronto Coordinating Committee to End the War in Vietnam, n.d. See also Robin Mathews's "Centennial Song," which likens Canada to "A tired prostitute beyond her prime, dejected, hungry," in MU, WR, Canadian Student Social and Political Organizations, box 2, File: Canadian Union of Students Working Papers, 1967–69.

64 WHSA, *AMEX*, MSS 736, box 1, folder 5, Magazine Organization and Production, Copy-general, Roger Williams, "Descent into the Maelstrom: Notes on a Journey to Hell," 1971. See also Rossinow, *Politics of Authenticity*, 270; Stephen Azzi, "The Nationalist Moment in English Canada," in *Debating Dissent: Canada and the Sixties*, ed. Lara Campbell, Dominique Clément, and Gregory S. Kealey, 213–28 (Toronto: University of Toronto Press, 2012).

65 Quoted in *Globe and Mail*, August 8, 1966, 15. See also *Globe and Mail*, November 14, 1966, 17.

66 Azzi, "Nationalist Moment"; Bothwell, *Alliance and Illusion*; Churchill, "When Home Became Away." Bryan Palmer argues that left nationalism "drift[ed] in the direction of moral condemnation" of the United States. Bryan Palmer, *Canada's 1960s: The Ironies of Identity in a Rebellious Era* (Toronto: University of Toronto Press, 2009), 292. See also "For an Independent and Socialist Canada," *The Peak* 13, 4 (1969): 14; *The Pedestal*, May 1971 and February 1973; *New York Times*, January 22, 11; and MU, WR, Canadian Student Social and Political Organizations, box 1, File: Canada/Vietnam Week, poster, 1966. See also MU, WR, files of the Canadian Liberation Movement.

67 Richard J. Needham, "A Writer's Notebook," *Globe and Mail*, February 23, 1971, 6; Gabrielle B. Griffiths, letter to the editor, *Globe and Mail*, February 26, 1968, 6. Dr. Ray Hord, secretary of the United Church Board of Evangelism and Social Service, claimed that the United Empire Loyalists and dodgers left the United States for "idealistic reasons." Quoted in *Globe and Mail*, August 14, 1967, 5; see also *AMEX* 1, 10 (1969): 14.

68 Needham, "Writer's Notebook," 6.

69 Eusi Ndugu, "Black Draft Dodger Speaks Out on Canada," *AMEX* 2, 2 (1970): 21. The author grew more critical of Canadian racism.

70 Richard Paterak, *Escape from Freedom, or I Didn't Raise My Boy to Be a Canadian* (Toronto: Student Union for Peace Action, 1967).

71 Mark Satin, *Manual for Draft-Age Immigrants to Canada* (Toronto: Toronto Anti-Draft Programme, 1969); see also Hagan, *Northern Passage*, 75.

72 Cover image, *AMEX* 1, 15 (1969); Dennis A. Foley, "Draft-Dodgers in Canada See No Chance of Amnesty," *Pittsburgh Press*, March 19, 1969, 25.

73 WHSA, *AMEX*, MSS 736, box 1, folder 4, Magazine Organization and Production, Questionnare [sic] to Exiles, August 24, 1973.

74 Foley, "Draft-Dodgers in Canada," *Pittsburgh Press*, 25.

18
Rebellion on the Road: Masculinity and Outlaw Motorcycle Clubs in Postwar Ontario

Graeme Melcher

OUTLAW MOTORCYCLE CLUBS ARE largely mysterious. Many people *think* they know what a biker is, yet when pressed for details, they cannot provide anything beyond the simplistic construction of bikers as hellions draped in leather and filthy denim riding loud motorcycles.[1] This is no accident: many of the trappings of biker identity work to draw attention while discouraging deeper analysis. From the intimidating names chosen by many outlaw clubs to the intensive membership rituals used to screen prospective members and the fearsome look of the bikers themselves, everything is used to promote biker culture as something that unquestionably draws attention yet should not be studied too carefully – something too loud to ignore but too alienating to encourage greater familiarity.

Today, outlaw motorcycle clubs operate on an international scale, a far cry from the localized nature of their origins. The earliest outlaw bikers established their outsider image in 1950s North America as a way to differentiate themselves from contemporary Cold War society and to demonstrate the extent to which they rejected the trappings of consumerism and conformity that defined the era. Acting out, dressing in shabby clothes, and riding large, loud, and dangerous customized motorcycles were how they set themselves apart from the rest of the world. Outlaw motorcycle clubs in postwar Ontario – the focus of this chapter – began as a way for young men to hold on to a form of readily identifiable masculinity in a time when conceptions of masculinity were changing. The clubs and associated identities as bikers allowed young men to make sense of a world in the midst of unprecedented cultural, social, and political change by combining elements of traditional working-class masculinity with emerging forms of cultural rebellion, creating a new way of life for those who did not fit into postwar Canadian society. Once their image had been established, and was acknowledged by society, bikers capitalized on other developments of the Cold War era – including its expanding infrastructure and the increasing prominence and power of youth culture – and their presence continued to grow throughout the 1960s and 1970s. This growth was not entirely without its cost, and eventually outlaw biker culture experienced a distinct shift: what started as a culture of rebellion and marginal danger became one predicated on the violence and fear associated with outlaw motorcycle culture today. Biker culture was predicated on collective identity pursued in the name of working-class masculine identity and provides a counter-narrative to the evolution of domestic masculinity in postwar Canada.

Most people think they know what a biker is: a hellion, an outcast, a degenerate criminal on the fringe of society. But in reality, a biker is as much a product and reflection of our society as he is its antithesis. A biker is a continuation of working-class masculinity, made possible by cultural and social changes in the postwar world.

Creating the Biker

A 1909 article in *Harper's Weekly* warned of a growing threat to contemporary society: "foolish" motorcyclists who modified their exhaust systems in an effort to coax more power from the motors. A byproduct of this tinkering was a noticeably noisier engine, and the author sniffed that "what the rider will gain in power is more than lost in the harm done by public sentiment and loss of self-respect."[2] These riders were the first of a new breed of motorcyclists, a group who prided themselves on their public displays of shared identity and rebellion.

In 1935, in McCook, Illinois, the first self-styled outlaw motorcycle club was formed: the McCook Outlaws Motorcycle Club. It eventually became the Outlaws Motorcycle Club and moved its base of operations to Chicago.[3] The popularization of the biker lifestyle, and the birth of the term "outlaw biker," occurred in the small town of Hollister, California, in the summer of 1947. Things went awry at a weekend rally sponsored by the American Motorcycle Association after several attending clubs ran amok – racing their motorcycles through the streets, fighting, and generally causing chaos in the small town.[4] These early outlaw clubs had started as legitimate motorcycle clubs, but their renegade antics and reckless disregard for law and order differentiated them from other, more law-abiding clubs. The Hollister riot, as it came to be known, gained international notoriety following an article published in *LIFE* magazine, accompanied by a staged photograph.[5] The biker had become a part of postwar popular culture.

Outlaw bikers in postwar North America fell into one of two broad categories. The first group was comprised of Second World War combat veterans recently returned from active duty, painfully aware that they "didn't fit into the button-down conformity of the Truman/Eisenhower era." They lusted for a return to the glory days of their combat experiences – the adventure, danger, and brotherhood that they had left behind – so they chose to make a new society, formed on the road and in barrooms. The second group was made up of young men who felt that postwar North America promised the world but, in falling short, "left many behind."[6] This second group was made up of working-class youth who saw outlaw culture as a natural extension of their culture and traditions, as well as middle-class youth who rejected their middle-class respectability and the overwhelming conformity of postwar suburban life.[7]

Wasted Youth

The 1950s and 1960s saw the term "youth" become more than a simple qualifier of age, as it also began to denote a state of mind and a collection of attitudes about life, many of which were at odds with prevailing notions of adolescence as a time to learn how to become a responsible adult.[8] Young people rejected the idea that they had to be sheltered and protected so that they might grow into healthy and responsible adults.[9] In an age that valued strict adherence to universal norms of behaviour, youth who rebelled became deviants, incomprehensible to decent, mainstream Canadians.

But before young people could begin rebelling and creating their own culture, they needed to escape the stifling conformity of postwar suburbia. What they needed was a space free of adult supervision, with certain amenities and comforts, that was readily accessible. Along with the rise of suburbia and economic development in postwar Ontario came the proliferation of highways, fast food restaurants, and coffee shops.[10] Most of these establishments featured large signage to attract passing motorists, cheap food, and massive parking lots, which, in addition to providing parking for customers, also served as new sites of youth culture.[11] Part of this redefinition of youth sensibilities and identity involved challenging authority and acting out in antisocial ways, and restaurant parking lots after dark soon earned bad reputations, as stories circulated of young "hoodlums" fighting one another, experimenting with alcohol and drugs and even engaging in sexual activities on nearby properties.[12] Because young people were a lucrative market, restaurant owners could not ban them outright but chose instead to modify youth behaviour through other means. One restaurant owner spread rumours that he used to be a boxer, using "masculine bravado and informal negotiation" to control his clientele.[13] Middle-class suburban youth congregated in parking lots to perform identities and create new spaces of interaction, and in the process, these spaces confirmed shifting social dynamics.[14]

For some young people, these actions were nothing more than youthful dalliances, a rebellious phase that provided a sense of identity and excitement and could then be discarded in favour of pursuing more traditional postwar goals of economic and material success. However, for some young men, these teenage rebellions were the first step toward a more extreme rejection of postwar society. Inspired by the dangerous bikers they read about or saw on the roads, they cast off the respectability and safety of postwar suburbia in favour of the danger, brotherhood, and masculinity of the bikers. Biker culture, rather than forcing young men to buy into postwar consumerism and suburban conformity, allowed them to be wild and dangerous and to continue practising their youthful rejection of mainstream society.[15]

Making the Men
As Ontario's middle class grew, its willingness to buy into consumerism became a key part of postwar Canadian life. Participating in consumerism by buying new goods and buoying the market was not just an indulgence for postwar Canadians but also a rite of citizenship; a strong consumer market served as a strong marker of morality and social organization.[16] Since bikers stood in direct opposition to this attitude, they did not attempt to demonstrate their success through the acquisition of material goods, steady employment, or establishing a family but forged their own symbols of legitimacy and success: their "colours," or patches, which denoted club membership; their physical toughness; and, most importantly, their brutal motorcycles.

At the time, most men who could afford to move their families out of the cities and into the suburbs were middle-class, and many felt they had lost touch with the more traditional sense of working-class masculinity that their fathers had portrayed – men who could work with their hands, could fix anything, and exuded a general sense of competency.[17] "Do it yourself" (DIY) projects allowed suburban men to reclaim some of that lost masculinity, while also passing along skills to their sons that they had learned from their fathers.[18] DIY projects allowed a middle-class man to temporarily become the blue-collar man, rolling up his sleeves to fix a boiler or build a deck while still maintaining his middle-class respectability. Working on the house was a way for men to exercise control over their homes and to establish an image of traditional male competency.[19]

Bikers also embraced the DIY ethic but to very different ends: rather than working on a suburban house, bikers chose to customize their motorcycles. Harley-Davidson motorcycles have always been the bike of choice for outlaw bikers, as they carried an inherent element of danger, were easy to modify, and, crucially, were loud.[20] Mechanically speaking, most Harleys have always been far from perfect, but their imperfect designs actually contributed to bikers' image as tough and dangerous men. The Harleys ridden by early bikers – models from the 1940s to 1960s – were built using a rigid frame with no rear swing arm for suspension, and any front suspension was rudimentary at best.[21] The lack of suitable shock absorption made these bikes difficult to ride safely, as the motorcycle and the rider were constantly being thrown about by any imperfection in the road. Furthermore, motorcycle engines at this time had little or no shock absorption where they were mounted to the motorcycle frame, so they sent harsh vibrations through the frame even when idling. This took a toll on the structural and mechanical integrity of both the engine and the frame, to say nothing of the rider. All of these factors played to the biker image; only the toughest, craziest, and most competent motorcyclists could master these machines for any stretch of time.[22]

Bikers took pride not only in the fact that they themselves were visually distinctive from the rest of society but also in the fact that their motorcycles were unique creations. Bikers often customized their motorcycles, either in pursuit of better performance or simply for the sheer joy of riding an outrageous-looking machine. Their customized motorcycles, usually called "choppers" or "bobbers," reflected a biker's personality and desire to stand out.[23] There were many ways that a biker might customize his bike, such as increasing the rake – the angle at which the front forks extend from the frame – to stretch the motorcycle out, adding high handlebars, or customizing the exhaust to generate more noise and power.[24] As many of these modifications required parts that were difficult or impossible to procure, and expensive to boot, many early bikers instead made their own: handlebars could be made from metal lawn chair legs, foot pegs could be made from bits of scrap metal welded and cut to size, and stock seats and gas tanks could be replaced with the slimmer ones from children's scooters.[25]

Although the additions and customizations did help to make their motorcycles more individual, they were not always without consequence. As former Satan's Choice Motorcycle Club member Don Norris recalls, when he added a set of high handlebars to his motorcycle, he had to hold his arms so high and wide that he "filled out like a sail at fifty miles an hour," the result of which was a significantly less comfortable riding experience. Worse still, he was frequently harassed by the police for riding an unsafe vehicle, as the higher arm position was thought to provide the rider with less control over his motorcycle.[26] Still, like the inbuilt inadequacies of stock Harleys, the customizations made by bikers only added to their rebellious masculine image.

Bikers promoted deviancy by steadfastly refusing to pursue the usual hallmarks of success in Cold War Canada: a nice house in the suburbs, a good job, and a family. Instead, they created their own codes and symbols of success: their scars, their filthy clothing, and their motorcycles.[27] Whereas suburban men used DIY projects to enhance their homes and perform working-class masculinity while maintaining their middle-class respectability, bikers embraced the DIY mentality to set themselves even further apart from mainstream society and to continue performing the role of the outlaw.

Creating the Culture

As biker culture developed in the 1950s and 1960s, it acquired several hallmarks: uniforms, behavioural codes, and tribes. Treating masculinity as "something to drape over the body" was a common way for postwar men to reclaim or reassert a degree of traditional working-class masculine identity.[28] In keeping with this approach, bikers' public presentation and performance of masculinity can best be seen through their colours.[29] A biker's colours were an outward representation of how he saw himself: assertive, shocking, and not to be challenged. A biker's clothing also served the very practical purpose of protection: jeans and jackets or vests ensured a measure of safety when riding, and boots and heavy belts made for formidable weapons in fights.[30] Bikers dressed alike not only to project an image of unity and strength but also because their clothing fulfilled necessary purposes in "the Life."[31] A biker's colours, clothes, and generally shabby appearance spoke to his status in the biker world, just as working-class men used their bodies as markers of status and masculinity.[32]

Violence was, and continues to be, a definitive and complex aspect of outlaw motorcycle clubs. As biker culture couched itself in working-class ideals of masculine toughness, it was vital that bikers followed working-class codes of behaviour, chief among which was a refusal to back down from a challenge. Even a perceived threat had to be met with immediate retaliation.[33] As long-time biker Lorne Campbell said, "if you can be disrespected, then you can also be attacked ... hurt ... [and] killed."[34] At this time, Ontario bikers saw violence as a tool used to reinforce their masculine identities, not as a fetish or pleasure to be indulged.

Outlaw clubs paid just as much attention to choosing their club name as they did to establishing their members' reputation as tough men. In street subcultures among youth, gang names "inspired fear, or implied that a group had transcended its local circumstances."[35] This can also be seen in the names of outlaw motorcycle clubs, some of which were meant to inspire fear, such as Satan's Choice, the Outlaws, or the Hells Angels, and others that were chosen to imply a transient citizenship and a free-roaming spirit, such as the Vagabonds or the 13th Tribe. Bikers chose club names that reinforced their images as hard, working-class men who were free to come and go as they pleased.[36]

"We've got a club, a real terrific club, and we call it Satan's Choice"[37]

The 1950s saw several outlaw clubs establish themselves in and around Toronto, the most infamous being Satan's Choice and the Black Diamond Riders, better known as the Choice and the BDRs respectively.[38] According to former Choice member Don Norris, these early bikers were considered ruffians and rebels for what would today be considered relatively benign behaviour: riding shirtless, drinking while under the age of twenty-one, and largely ignoring posted speed limits.

The BDRs established itself as Ontario's premier outlaw club by forcing the Choice to disband in 1962 and then setting its sights on wiping out other Ontario clubs. One notorious incident occurred at a field day hosted by the Oshawa-based Golden Hawk Riders in the summer of 1962, when members of the BDRs descended en masse and brutally beat other bikers into submission.[39] Field days were meant to be nonpartisan affairs dedicated to recreation and fun, and by attacking other bikers at a field day, the BDRs had crossed a line.

The BDRs' unprecedented attack convinced Bernie Guindon, a member of the Golden Hawks and then the Phantom Riders, to take action. As a biker, Guindon had a lot going for him: he was only twenty years old in 1962 but was already a successful amateur boxer, and in 1965 he would be referred to as "one of the best young amateur welterweights in Canada."[40] Guindon was also a man of vision: he was tired of being victimized by the BDRs, but he was also aware that brute force was not the only way to best his opponents. Rather than relying exclusively on violence, Guindon wanted to beat the BDRs by outnumbering and outmanoeuvring its members; forcing them to surrender would be infinitely more emasculating than simply beating them up.[41] In 1965, in a move specifically designed to infuriate the BDRs, Guindon revived the Choice. Borrowing Norris's old colours to recreate the logo, Guindon and his Phantom Riders in Oshawa joined forces with three other outlaw clubs in Scarborough, Mississauga, and Kitchener, with each club setting aside its former memberships in favour of becoming four chapters of a revived Satan's Choice.[42] Guindon's move challenged the BDRs' dominance, and, in a culture that prized male dominance and control, to threaten a man's dominance was to threaten his value.[43]

The move was unprecedented but effective: the Choice instantly became the biggest club in Canada at the time and the first to have coordinated chapters operating in multiple cities. The Choice's membership and wide-ranging geographic scope put the club in charge of Ontario's burgeoning outlaw culture, allowing the club to dictate the terms of Ontario biker culture's continued existence. Rather than forcing the BDRs to disband, Guindon gave the club a choice: stop trying to shut down other clubs and fall in line or fight the Choice and face the consequences. The BDRs chose the former option. Guindon's edict was simple: respect other clubs, keep the peace, and do not draw the cops' attention. His policies worked, and Ontario's biker scene flourished, free of the excessive violence and bloodshed that would mark outlaw culture in years to come. Under Guindon's leadership, the Choice had grown to ten chapters in Ontario and Quebec by the end of the 1960s, making it the most powerful outlaw club in Canada, second only to the notorious Hells Angels globally.[44]

In a culture where violence, toughness, and assertive masculinity were so highly prized, Guindon succeeded as a leader because he was tougher and smarter than the next guy. Rather than crushing other Ontario clubs through brute force, he worked with them to preserve good relations, thus keeping the peace and ensuring that the Choice, with himself at the helm as national chairman, stayed at the top of the food chain.[45] Key to this dynamic was keeping the larger, more brutal American clubs out since their greater size and membership could destabilize the relatively peaceful Ontario outlaw scene, thereby challenging and threatening the masculine identities of Ontario bikers.

To keep relations between the Ontario clubs cordial and to prevent the American clubs' expansion, Guindon sometimes had to take action against members of the Choice, as occurred in the late 1960s.[46] The Toronto Choice chapter was becoming arrogant, acting with no thought for how it might impact relations with other Toronto outlaw clubs. In turn, other Toronto clubs, such as the Vagabonds, the BDRs, and the Para-Dice Riders, resented the Toronto Choice's sense of entitlement and disregard for outlaw codes of conduct, and violence seemed imminent. Guindon wanted to keep relations between the clubs civil, so rather than preparing for violence, he called a meeting of the Choice chapters. The Hamilton and Montreal chapters wanted to go to war with the other Toronto clubs, whereas other chapters, including Kingston, Oshawa, and Kitchener, wanted no part of Toronto's mess. Guindon's final decision was simple: rather than going to war, Guindon and the rest of the Choice descended upon the Toronto chapter to clean house, ejecting the "fight crazy shitheads" while keeping the more level-headed members. This ensured that Guindon and his fellow Choice members could continue to party and ride in Toronto without fear of attack, and it further cemented Guindon's status as one of Ontario's most feared and respected bikers.[47]

Not only did Guindon's actions ensure continued peace between Ontario bikers, but it also meant the Choice could continue to party in Yorkville, Toronto's burgeoning centre of postwar youth counterculture, which was in the Vagabonds' territory. Bikers established themselves as a unique group within Yorkville that was both apart from, yet also a crucial part of, the social dynamic of the scene.[48] That bikers were usually older, bigger, and more unified helped them to stand apart from the rest of the "Villagers," but so did their approaches to masculine identity. Although both bikers and hippies grew their hair long in defiance of traditional gender roles, bikers backed up their long hair with violence and physical dominance. Bikers were seen as working-class toughs, whereas hippies and "weekenders" were seen as predominantly middle- and upper-class youth playing at rebellion.[49] Whereas middle- and upper-class youth could back down from conflicts and keep their status and sense of self-worth relatively intact, bikers, as products of the working class, did not have this luxury.

More important than the sheer number of Choice bikers in Ontario was the geographic scope of the club's operation. The Choice had become Ontario's dominant outlaw motorcycle club almost overnight, and it was able to do this largely because of the recent improvements that had been made to Ontario's roads. Postwar Ontario saw the development of large highways designed to accommodate not only the rapidly increasing number of cars on Ontario's roads but also the distance these cars were driven.[50] Large highways were crucial to Ontario's postwar development: not only did they accommodate and stimulate economic growth, but they also showed human mastery of the natural environment. More than that, highways brought people together, both literally and symbolically, uniting distant cities through a ribbon of tarmac. In postwar Ontario, highways were not just roads but also political statements.[51]

Ontario's Highway 401, a limited-access highway known as a freeway, was a crucial piece of infrastructure in the development of Ontario and Ontario's biker culture. Parts of the 401 were open to drivers as early as December 1947, and when the highway was completed in 1968 it stretched from Windsor to the Ontario-Quebec border, running through major cities and intersecting other highways along the way.[52] It was no coincidence that the Choice established many of its chapters along major freeways and highways in Ontario and Quebec. Given how unreliable and uncomfortable the members' motorcycles could be, the ability to ride quickly from city to city would have been invaluable. With their multiple wide lanes, freeways also made it easier for bikers to carry out one of their most impressive shows of force: riding as a pack. Riding in a group had long been a favourite tactic of small local outlaw clubs, but with the advent of multilane freeways, bikers could take their show on the road, so to speak.[53] Passing motorists could not help but stare at the pack of bikers riding impossibly loud motorcycles, their backs adorned with fearsome patches.[54] Although highways were designed to promote growth and industry, bikers redefined these public spaces by using them for their own purposes, thus converting movement and travel into acts of rebellion.

Violence and Women

In 1969 Bernie Guindon was sentenced to five years in prison for indecently assaulting a fifteen-year-old girl.[55] Although Guindon insisted he was wrongly convicted, the incident brings to light one of the uglier sides of the Life: the abuse and mistreatment of women.

Part of bikers' attitudes toward women stemmed from working-class beliefs of male entitlement. The male "sacrifice" of working to support their families left them feeling entitled to special privileges or feeling that women were indebted to them for having sacrificed their "sacred" male independence.[56] Although these attitudes were not necessarily shared by all working-class men, their impact could not be denied, as women continued to be seen primarily either as objects of entertainment or as threats to male unity in outlaw clubs. Some men felt that women had to be kept around for their value as objects of entertainment while also stripping women of any power so as to keep them subservient and protect bikers' sense of masculine self-worth.[57] Violence toward, or at least a lack of respect for, women was the key to this relationship. A biker's displayed contempt for women ensured that he was not seen as weak but as rejecting sentiment and compassion in favour of aggression and conquest. "Getting a girl," or convincing a woman to engage in sexual activities, augmented a biker's reputation through sexual conquests and further demeaned the reputations both of the woman he had "gotten" and of women in general in the eyes of other bikers. For bikers, as for many working-class youth, the more girls you got, the more of a man you were.[58]

Some bikers resorted to sexual violence and gang rape, which they saw as "a working-class sex code ... in which girls 'knew' what would happen if they continued to hang out on the streets and therefore bore responsibility for it."[59] Gang rapes also allowed bikers to share a moment of twisted intimacy with one another without risking their masculine identity, as the violence of the act purged any homosexual overtones.[60] These incidents became part of the discourses through which identities were negotiated, the result of which was the elevation of the bikers' male identity at the cost of degrading and abusing women.[61]

Many bikers had wives or steady girlfriends who were treated with a measure of respect. However, this respect was not for the women themselves; rather, they were respected as the property of their men. Just as a biker would not touch another biker's motorcycle, neither would he touch another biker's "old lady."[62] At a time when women were becoming more independent, bikers sought to return to the roots of their working-class culture, using their physical power and shared fearsome identity to control women.[63]

A Change of Pace

At the dawn of the 1970s, the Life was changing. As outlaw clubs expanded and garnered greater media attention, their public profile skyrocketed. Publicly challenging a biker became an appealing way for ordinary men to elevate their own status; if they could beat up a biker, they could co-opt the biker's masculinity and toughness for themselves. For Choice member Lorne Campbell, what lay at the heart of bikers' violence against nonmembers was the reputation of the club. If Campbell was publicly challenged while wearing his colours, he knew that it was not only his own reputation at stake but also that of his entire club.[64] Bikers guarded their own reputations fiercely enough but they could be driven to ferocious lengths if they felt their club's reputation was threatened. If a biker shamed his club, not only would the club's reputation be left in tatters, but his own reputation, both within the club and as a man, would also be decimated.[65]

At the same time, more bikers were also settling down and getting married.[66] Some, such as the Choice's Rick Sauvé,[67] had a family before joining a club, and others left the Life when they got married, as Don Norris did in 1964, but many, including Guindon and Campbell, stayed in their clubs after marrying.[68] As bikers got older, the wild abandon of their younger days lost some of its appeal, and many decided to start their own families in order to provide a measure of stability and comfort away from the masculine brotherhood of the outlaw life.[69]

Money was also becoming more important to bikers. As "the novelty of poverty" began to wear thin, their youthful rejection of material culture was set aside in favour of at least a partial acceptance of the better life money could buy.[70] Some bikers translated their love of tinkering with their motorcycles into careers as mechanics or became partners in motorcycle shops. Some worked in factories or in other blue-collar fields, and some turned a profit on their size and intimidating image by working as bouncers and bartenders.[71]

Some members resorted to criminal activities to pay the bills, such as stealing motorcycles or collecting debts.[72] Although drug dealing became the crime most popularly associated with bikers, Ontario bikers who entered the drug market did so alone. At the time, rather than having a club or chapter work collectively to deal drugs, some individual members sold drugs on their own without club involvement. This is not to say that the club did not know about a member's drug dealing, just that it was an individual, rather than a collective, business.[73] Bikers were not making large profits off of drug sales at this time but were men who sold drugs because it was easier and more exciting than working a real job.[74]

And Hell Followed

Without a doubt, the biggest change to Ontario's biker culture came from America. The California-based Hells Angels Motorcycle Club was expanding more quickly than its Canadian counterparts, establishing chapters in England, New Zealand, and Switzerland by the end of the 1960s, and the Outlaws expanded and established chapters in Florida, Detroit, and the American Midwest.[75] These two American heavyweights were not on good terms, and each looked eagerly to Canada for an advantage over the other. If a large Canadian club could be patched over,[76] it would bring with it new members and more territory. Both the Outlaws and the Hells Angels were already established in strategically vital locations: the Outlaws had a strong presence in Detroit, a short ride across the Detroit River from the Choice in southwestern Ontario; and the Hells Angels, recently established in Manhattan, looked north along Interstate 87 to Montreal.[77]

When Guindon went to jail in 1969,[78] Garnet "Mother" McEwan, a member of the Choice's St. Catharines chapter, became the club's national chairman. Unlike Guindon, who had worked tirelessly to keep American clubs out of Canada, McEwan was open to relationships with American clubs and established a working relationship with the Outlaws' Detroit chapter around 1974.[79] The Choice split into two factions. One group, headed by McEwan and his supporters, pushed to increase and further develop relationships with the Outlaws. The other group wanted the Choice to stay Canadian and was put off by the Outlaws' bloodthirsty reputation.[80] In March 1977 McEwan called a secret meeting of his supporters; shortly thereafter, the Choice chapters in St. Catharines, Windsor, Hamilton, Kingston, Ottawa, and Montreal joined the Outlaws.[81] Almost overnight, the Choice went from being Canada's premiere outlaw club to a fractured organization with a handful of chapters.[82] Worst of all, the Choice's reputation and the dream of a united Ontario outlaw scene lay in tatters. In a single move, McEwan had undone a decade of work to promote unity and trust within the scene.[83]

On December 5, 1977, the Hells Angels officially set up shop in Canada, patching over Montreal's fearsome Popeyes.[84] The Popeyes were a natural choice for the Angels: they were tough, well established, and had a smart and reliable leader, Yves "Le Boss" Buteau.[85] With the Angels now in Montreal and several Choice chapters patched over to the Outlaws, the remaining Ontario bikers were surrounded, with only a handful of Choice and other club chapters standing between two massive and powerful American clubs that despised one another – precisely the situation Guindon had worked to prevent.

Canada now hosted two distinct styles of outlaw clubs, each with a radically different set of ideals: homegrown clubs and franchises of American clubs. The homegrown clubs wanted to do as they had always done: ride their motorcycles, drink beer, fight, and act rebellious. In contrast, the franchise clubs treated their clubs as organizations for making money rather than as a brotherhood of rough masculinity and individual merit. This difference in guiding principles translated into vastly different attitudes. To the homegrown outlaws, symbolism still ruled: if you were seen as weak or if you lost respect or reputation, you were ruined as a biker. These bikers used their notoriety, not drugs or money, to show that they were still tough and powerful men.[86] However, franchise clubs wanted control and membership numbers not to show that they were tough or to act out a ritual of biker identity but because that was how they made money.[87]

An American outlaw presence in Ontario meant that local politics and ideologies were swept aside by a mass-market product, and Ontario bikers found themselves facing a new approach to biker culture that was international instead of local, based on total control instead of loose alliances, and prone to murder instead of fistfights. Ontario bikers knew that times were changing, but rather than accepting that their time had come and surrendering to the powerful American clubs, the remaining members of the Choice banded together with other Ontario clubs, pledging to work together to fight back against the American outlaw presence.[88]

Three Shots at the Queen's Hotel

Increasing tension between American and Canadian clubs and the fear of further American expansion into Ontario can largely be blamed for what took place in the bar of the Queen's Hotel in Port Hope, Ontario, on October 18, 1978. Bill "Heavy" Matiyek was a local biker who rode with the Golden Hawks. The Hawks had limped along since their public humiliation at the hands of the BDRs at the infamous 1962 field day, and they openly defied the Choice by wearing their colours in Port Hope, a town the Choice considered theirs by virtue of its proximity to Choice-controlled Peterborough.[89]

On the evening of October 18, Matiyek and a fellow Hawk were drinking in the Queen's Hotel with two Choice-turned-Outlaws. Through a series of miscommunications, local Choice member Rick Sauvé was told that the Outlaws were in Port Hope to discuss patching over the Golden Hawks. Sauvé called the Toronto Choice chapter – the Peterborough chapter having been decimated by a series of arrests a few weeks earlier – looking for advice, and soon several Toronto Choice members were at the Queen's.[90] Matiyek, intoxicated on a mixture of Benzedrine and alcohol, panicked; when approached by two Choice members, he revealed that he had a handgun in his jacket pocket and would shoot anyone who threatened him. It is unclear what happened next, but when the smoke cleared, Matiyek was dead, shot three times by Choice member Lorne Campbell.[91]

Of eight Choice members charged in connection with Matiyek's death, six were found guilty of second-degree murder.[92] None of the accused admitted that Campbell was the shooter or identified anyone else who had been present that evening. The accused Choice members honoured the outlaw code, refusing to implicate their brothers-in-arms at the cost of their own freedom.[93] As they held fast to their beliefs, to the unwritten laws of the road set down decades earlier, outlaw culture around them was changing. They had no way of knowing it at the time, but in a few decades, outlaw culture would be entirely different.

Conclusion

Ontario's outlaw biker culture has changed dramatically since its early days in the 1950s, and it continues to evolve today. Whereas outlaw clubs once dreamed of being the most powerful clubs in their cities, clubs now operate on an international scale. The role of violence in outlaw culture has also changed. In the early days of biker culture, fistfights were used to demonstrate masculine identity.[94] Today, guns and bombs have replaced fistfights, and the increased violence can be targeted at anyone, from those outside of the club to fellow members who threaten the well-being and practices of a club.[95]

Biker culture in Ontario began as a way for young men to make sense of a world that was rapidly changing and to adopt an interpretation of masculinity that they saw as static and unchanging, a tough, brawling manliness that was proven through physical prowess and individual merit. Early bikers established reputations for themselves as men who lived outside of society, abiding by their own rules and standards of conduct and revelling in their status as outsiders. Violence was a crucial aspect of this lifestyle, but it was a particular type of violence used to establish reputation and define a hierarchy within a club. Despite the fears of the media, police, and state bodies, this violence was largely confined to the biker world, rarely harming or affecting those who were not involved in the Life. Although bikers committed criminal acts and broke the law, they most often did so as individuals, and only rarely were such actions organized by the clubs. Their ultimate goal was not financial profit through organized crime; rather, what bikers wanted was adventure instead of the security of postwar Ontario, the freedom to pursue their own interpretations of masculinity, and public acknowledgment of, and respect for, their identities as outlaw bikers.

Notes

1 In this chapter, a biker is anyone who is or has been a member of an outlaw motorcycle club.

2 Alfred H. Bartsch, "The Rise of the Motorcycle: Reasons for Its Growing Popularity, and Practical Advice to Users," *Harper's Weekly,* January 2, 1909, 21.

3 Note the difference between *an* outlaw motorcycle club or *an* outlaw and *the* Outlaws Motorcycle Club or *the* Outlaws. Outlaws MC World, "History," http://www.outlaws mcworld.com/history.

4 Peter Edwards, *The Bandido Massacre: A True Story of Bikers, Brotherhood, and Betrayal* (Toronto: HarperCollins, 2010), 31–32; Ralph "Sonny" Barger, with Keith Zimmerman and Kent Zimmerman, *Hell's Angel: The Life and Times of Sonny Barger and the Hell's Angels Motorcycle Club* (New York: HarperCollins, 2000), 25.

5 "Cyclist's Holiday: He and Friends Terrorize a Town," *LIFE,* July 21, 1947, 31.

6 Jerry Langton, *Fallen Angel: The Unlikely Rise of Walter Stadnick in the Canadian Hells Angels* (Mississauga, ON: John Wiley and Sons, 2006), 18, 23.

7 Doug Owram, *Born at the Right Time: A History of the Baby-Boom Generation* (Toronto: University of Toronto Press, 1996), 80, 136–40; Christopher Dummitt, *The Manly Modern: Masculinity in Postwar Canada* (Vancouver: UBC Press, 2007), 77–78, 128; Craig Heron, "Boys Will Be Boys: Working-Class Masculinities in the Age of Mass Production," *International Labor and Working-Class History* 69, 1 (2006): 13; Kenneth H. Rogers, *Street Gangs in Toronto: A Study of the Forgotten Boy* (Toronto: Ryerson Press, 1945), 20–21, 33–35, 43.

8 Stuart Henderson, *Making the Scene: Yorkville and Hip Toronto in the 1960s* (Toronto: University of Toronto Press, 2011), 15, 45.

9 Bryan Palmer, *Canada's 1960s: The Ironies of Identity in a Rebellious Era* (Toronto: University of Toronto Press, 2009), 184; Mary Louise Adams, *The Trouble with Normal: Postwar Youth and the Making of Heterosexuality* (Toronto: University of Toronto Press, 1997), 4, 166–69.

10 Lizabeth Cohen, *A Consumers' Republic: The Politics of Mass Consumption in Postwar America* (New York: Vintage Books, 2003), 199; Richard Harris, *Creeping Conformity: How Canada Became Suburban, 1900–1960* (Toronto: University of Toronto Press, 2004), 18–19.

11 Trent Frayne, "Just Look at the Old Ice-Cream Parlor Now!" in *Canada in the Fifties: From the Archives of Maclean's,* ed. Michael Benedict (Toronto: Penguin, 1999), 70–71; Steve Penfold, *The Donut: A Canadian History* (Toronto: University of Toronto Press, 2008), 64, 69; Harris, *Creeping Conformity,* 130.

12 Penfold, *Donut,* 84–85, 90–93.

13 John Clare, "The Scramble for the Teenage Dollar," in *Canada in the Fifties: From the Archives of Maclean's,* ed. Michael Benedict (Toronto: Penguin, 1999), 184, 186; Penfold, *Donut,* 95; Steve Penfold, "Selling by the Carload: The Early Years of Fast Food in Canada," in *Creating Postwar Canada: Community, Diversity, and Dissent, 1945–1975,* ed. Magda Fahrni and Robert Rutherdale (Vancouver: UBC Press, 2008), 180.

14 Eric C. Schneider, *Vampires, Dragons, and Egyptian Kings: Youth Gangs in Postwar New York* (Princeton, NJ: Princeton University Press, 1999), xvi–xvii; Penfold, "Selling by the Carload," 163.

15 Dummitt, *Manly Modern,* 2, 6–9.

16 Cohen, *Consumers' Republic,* 18–22, 113, 122–23.

17 Richard Harris, *Creeping Conformity,* 18–19; Cohen, *Consumers' Republic,* 6–8, 195.

18 Susan Faludi, *Stiffed: The Betrayal of the American Man* (New York: William Morrow, 1999), 24, 105.
19 Ibid., 9, 24; Robert Rutherdale, "New 'Faces' for Fathers: Memory, Life-Writing, and Fathers as Providers in the Postwar Consumer Era," in *Creating Postwar Canada: Community, Diversity, and Dissent, 1945–1975,* ed. Magda Fahrni and Robert Rutherdale (Vancouver: UBC Press, 2008), 248–50; Harris, *Creeping Conformity,* 35.
20 Robert F. Howe, "Wild Thing," *Smithsonian Magazine,* August 2003, http://www.smithsonianmag.com/history-archaeology/Wild_Thing.html?c=y; Don Norris, interview with author, December 28, 2011; Eric MacMillan, interview with author, May 19, 2013.
21 J.B. Nicholson, *Modern Motorcycle Mechanics and Speed Tuning* (Saskatoon: n.p., 1945), 33–34; Staff of "Motor Cycling," *The Motor Cycling Manual: The Complete Book of Motorcycling* (Los Angeles: Floyd Clymer, 1944), 53–61.
22 The infamous unreliability of early Harleys also offered bikers an unintended benefit: by always having to work on their bikes, they came to understand their machines and became reasonably competent mechanics. Sonny Barger, with Darwin Holmstrom, *Let's Ride: Sonny Barger's Guide to Motorcycling* (New York: William Morrow, 2010), 9; Mick Lowe, *Conspiracy of Brothers: A True Story of Murder, Bikers and the Law* (Toronto: Macmillan of Canada, 1988), 75.
23 Barger, *Let's Ride,* 64–65.
24 Ibid., 62–63; Don Norris, *Riding with Attitude: A Journey through Life on a Motorcycle* (Toronto: University of Toronto Press, 2005), 46.
25 Barger, *Hell's Angel,* 50, 56–59; Barger, *Let's Ride,* 63.
26 Norris, *Riding with Attitude,* 47–49.
27 Richard Cavell, "Introduction: The Cultural Production of Canada's Cold War," in *Love, Hate, and Fear in Canada's Cold War,* ed. Richard Cavell (Toronto: University of Toronto Press, 2004), 12; Rutherdale, "New 'Faces' for Fathers," 280; Harris, *Creeping Conformity,* 6.
28 Faludi, *Stiffed,* 35.
29 Peter Edwards, *Unrepentant: The Strange and (Sometimes) Terrible Life of Lorne Campbell, Satan's Choice and Hells Angels Biker* (Toronto: Random House of Canada, 2013), 108; Norris, interview; MacMillan, interview.
30 Barger, *Hell's Angel,* 26–27; Norris, *Riding with Attitude,* 38; Lowe, *Conspiracy of Brothers,* 6–7; Schneider, *Vampires, Dragons,* 148.
31 "The Life" is a term used by some bikers for their way of life. Lowe, *Conspiracy of Brothers,* 13, 29; Edwards, *Unrepentant,* 50.
32 Heron, "Boys Will Be Boys," 8.
33 Schneider, *Vampires, Dragons,* xvi–xvii.
34 Quoted in Edwards, *Unrepentant,* 118.
35 Schneider, *Vampires, Dragons,* 148.
36 One notable exception is the ludicrously named Sex Fox, an outlaw club in the Quebec village of Chibougamau in the 1970s. Pierre Tremblay, Sylvie Laisne, Gilbert Cordeau, Angela Shewshuck, and Brian MacLean, "Carrières criminelles collectives: Évolution d'une population délinquante (groupes de motards)," *Criminologie* 22, 2 (1989): 74.
37 The title of this section is taken from a song sung by Satan's Choice members in a 1965 documentary. Donald Shebib, dir., *Satan's Choice,* documentary (National Film Board of Canada, 1965).
38 Norris, interview; Norris, *Riding with Attitude,* 20–22, 36.
39 Lowe, *Conspiracy of Brothers,* 73–75; Edwards, *Unrepentant,* 17; Norris, *Riding with Attitude,* 107.

40 Norris, *Riding with Attitude,* 57; "All-Canadian Final in Bouts in Buffalo," *Globe and Mail,* February 23, 1965.

41 Edwards, *Unrepentant,* 18; Langton, *Fallen Angel,* 100; Lowe, *Conspiracy of Brothers,* 75.

42 Norris, *Riding with Attitude,* 113–14; Jerry Langton, *Showdown: How the Outlaws, Hells Angels, and Cops Fought for Control of the Streets* (Mississauga, ON: John Wiley and Sons, 2010), 28; Lowe, *Conspiracy of Brothers,* 76.

43 Faludi, *Stiffed,* 9; Schneider, *Vampires, Dragons,* xvi–xvii, 23–26; Cohen, *Consumers' Republic,* 99–100.

44 Langton, *Fallen Angel,* 32; Lowe, *Conspiracy of Brothers,* 81–82, 125; Jack McIver, "'Meaner Than a Junkyard Dog,'" *Montreal Gazette,* March 23, 1974.

45 Although each chapter operated independently, Guindon held power over all of them as national chairman. Lowe, *Conspiracy of Brothers,* 119.

46 Daniel R. Wolf, *The Rebels: A Brotherhood of Outlaw Bikers* (Toronto: University of Toronto Press, 1991), 13–14, 333.

47 Langton, *Showdown,* 30–32; Wolf, *Rebels,* 333.

48 A "scene" is a collection of people with similar ideals who redefine the spaces they inhabit. Henderson, *Making the Scene,* 7.

49 Reginald G. Smart and David Jackson, "Yorkville Subculture," in *The Underside of Toronto,* ed. W.E. Mann (Toronto: McClelland and Stewart, 1970), 116–17; Lowe, *Conspiracy of Brothers,* 78; Henderson, *Making the Scene,* 84; Stuart Henderson, interview with author, December 21, 2011; Norris, interview.

50 Penfold, "Selling by the Carload," 167.

51 Dummitt, *Manly Modern,* 56, 128.

52 Historical Committee, Public and Safety Information Branch, Ontario Ministry of Transportation, *Footpaths to Freeways: The Story of Ontario's Roads,* ed. Sharon Bagnato and John Shragge (Toronto: Ontario Ministry of Transportation, 1984), 93–95.

53 Edwards, *Unrepentant,* 13; "Yorkville Businesses Have Mixed Feelings about Limiting Licenses for Coffee Houses," *Globe and Mail,* May 28, 1968.

54 Lowe, *Conspiracy of Brothers,* 71–72.

55 Edwards, *Unrepentant,* 34; "5 Satan's Choice Members Get 5 Years for Assault," *Globe and Mail,* May 27, 1969.

56 Dummitt, *Manly Modern,* 6–9, 30; Owram, *Born at the Right Time,* 14–15; Heron, "Boys Will Be Boys," 9.

57 Dummitt, *Manly Modern,* 33.

58 Schneider, *Vampires, Dragons,* 131; Norris, *Riding with Attitude,* 22–24, 62.

59 Schneider, *Vampires, Dragons,* 134.

60 Ibid., 133–35; Faludi, *Stiffed,* 105–8; Rutherdale, "New 'Faces' for Fathers," 244.

61 Adams, *Trouble with Normal,* 16; Schneider, *Vampires, Dragons,* 25–26.

62 Lowe, *Conspiracy of Brothers,* 89; Barger, *Hell's Angel,* 97; Edwards, *Unrepentant,* 69; Schneider, *Vampires, Dragons,* 129.

63 Schneider, *Vampires, Dragons,* 107; Sidney Katz, "Going Steady: Is It Ruining Our Teenagers?" in *Canada in the Fifties: From the Archives of Maclean's,* ed. Michael Benedict (Toronto: Penguin, 1999), 116, 119.

64 Edwards, *Unrepentant,* 56–61.

65 Ibid., 28; Lowe, *Conspiracy of Brothers,* 101; Norris, interview; MacMillan, interview.

66 Peter Edwards, interview with author, July 14, 2013; Norris, *Riding with Attitude,* 22–23, 57, 61–63; Edwards, *Unrepentant,* 66–69.

67 Lowe, *Conspiracy of Brothers,* 10, 30–33.

68 Ibid., 424; Paul King, "My Club. My Bike. And My Wife and Kids. In That Order," *Canadian Magazine*, January 2, 1971, 12–15; Edwards, *Unrepentant*, 46–47.
69 Heron, "Boys Will Be Boys," 25.
70 Lowe, *Conspiracy of Brothers*, 111; Norris, *Riding with Attitude*, 43; Norris, interview.
71 Norris, *Riding with Attitude*, 38, 117, 124; King, "My Club. My Bike," 12–14; Lowe, *Conspiracy of Brothers*, 5–7; Edwards, interview.
72 Lowe, *Conspiracy of Brothers*, 14; Edwards, *Unrepentant*, 47–50; Langton, *Fallen Angel*, 27, 33.
73 Lowe, *Conspiracy of Brothers*, 112–14.
74 Ibid., 114; Edwards, *Unrepentant*, 36, 44–45; Edwards, interview.
75 Hells Angels MC World, "History," http://hells-angels.com/our-club/history; Barger, *Hell's Angel*, 35; Wolf, *Rebels*, 334; Langton, *Showdown*, 40–44; Outlaws MC World, "History."
76 Patching over refers to one club joining another.
77 Lowe, *Conspiracy of Brothers*, 101; Edwards, *Bandido Massacre*, 52.
78 After being released from prison in 1975, Guindon was quickly convicted in connection with a massive drug bust, and in May 1976 he was sentenced to seventeen years in prison. "17-Year Sentence in Drug Conspiracy," *Globe and Mail*, May 17, 1976; Edwards, *Unrepentant*, 77–78.
79 Langton, *Fallen Angel*, 103; Lowe, *Conspiracy of Brothers*, 125.
80 At this time, Canadian bikers largely treated violence as a means to an end, whereas American bikers seemed more willing to indulge in acts of extreme violence. Langton, *Showdown*, 43; Maria Elena Fernandez, "13-Year Hunt Ends in Arrest Extradition Sought for Biker Wanted in Deaths of 3 Rivals," *South Florida Sun Sentinel*, June 9, 1991.
81 Edwards, *Unrepentant*, 83; Lowe, *Conspiracy of Brothers*, 125.
82 Langton, *Showdown*, 47; Edwards, *Unrepentant*, 83; Lowe, *Conspiracy of Brothers*, 125. The Choice maintained chapters in Kitchener, Toronto, Oshawa, Peterborough, and Thunder Bay.
83 Edwards, *Unrepentant*, 78–80.
84 Edwards, *Bandido Massacre*, 51–52; Norris, *Riding with Attitude*, 126.
85 Lowe, *Conspiracy of Brothers*, 101.
86 Edwards, *Unrepentant*, 56; Norris, interview; Schneider, *Vampires, Dragons*, 23, 79.
87 Lowe, *Conspiracy of Brothers*, 111–12; Wolf, *Rebels*, 334–36.
88 Langton, *Showdown*, 50; Lowe, *Conspiracy of Brothers*, 46–47, 125–26.
89 Lowe, *Conspiracy of Brothers*, 2–4; Edwards, *Unrepentant*, 87–89.
90 Lowe, *Conspiracy of Brothers*, 10–11.
91 Ibid., 18–20; Edwards, *Unrepentant*, 90–91.
92 The Port Hope shooting was later immortalized in Steve Earle's song "Justice in Ontario," on the album *The Hard Way* (MCA, 1990). Edwards, *Unrepentant*, 106–8, 189–94; Lowe, *Conspiracy of Brothers*, 332–35, 443.
93 Campbell confessed in court to killing Matiyek but was never charged. Lowe, *Conspiracy of Brothers*, 332–33.
94 Faludi, *Stiffed*, 37; Lowe, *Conspiracy of Brothers*, 39, 278.
95 Lowe, *Conspiracy of Brothers*, 431; Edwards, *Unrepentant*, 24; Norris, *Riding with Attitude*, 127.

Part 6
Faces of Fatherhood

THE HISTORICAL STUDY OF fatherhood has emerged over the past thirty years as an indispensable strategy for situating men as gendered actors within the domestic world of home and family.[1] The best work in this area remains attentive to patriarchal power, with all its ramifications, and rejects out of hand what Shawn Johansen has called a "discourse of loss" wherein "fathers fell to a peripheral status in the family as early as the mid-nineteenth century."[2] There is also an ongoing interplay between cultural and social approaches to the topic, as Laura King points out in her book on fatherhood and masculinity in Britain.[3] Scholars remain preoccupied, therefore, with the perennial tension between widely disseminated paternal models and ideals – those that appear in prescriptive literature and in the mass media, for instance – and the actual experiences of real men living in real families, as reported, for instance, in life writing and oral-history interviews.

The two final essays in this collection share a concern with fatherhood as a category of masculine identity, specifically in twentieth-century Canada. But they also reflect some of these broader trends and contrasts in the literature. In Chapter 19, Peter Gossage focuses on the performance of masculine domesticity embedded in the annual celebration of Father's Day, a new family ritual promoted in the United States, first by earnest, progressive-era women and clergymen and later by clever New York merchandising executives. The discussion hinges on when, why, and to what extent this new domestic and commercial tradition found its way into Canada and especially into French-speaking, Catholic Quebec. There was certainly a dissonance there between this imported ritual, with its strong commercial overtones, and the more traditional paternal tropes of French Canadian culture. But Quebec was also a modern, North American society that could change with the times. By the 1950s, Quebec seems to have embraced Father's Day – along with other American imports like television, pop music, fast food, and car culture – rather wholeheartedly.

In Chapter 20, Robert Rutherdale outlines three popular sets of ideas – momism, the lost man, and family togetherness – each of which helped to fuel the influential but deeply flawed thesis of a "masculinity crisis" in postwar North America. Juxtaposed against these popular theories are some dark and destructive narratives of failed fatherhood rooted in alcohol abuse. Drawn from life writing and oral-history accounts, these personal narratives are linked to the prescriptive materials through a key question: was there a "masculinity crisis" that heightened alcohol abuse among Canadian fathers? Rutherdale responds resoundingly in the negative. As their life stories reveal in poignant detail, Canadian men became "lousy fathers" for a range of reasons, related to specific life experiences and to their inability to develop sustainable spousal and parenting relationships. The dads studied here drank to excess and caused enormous pain and suffering for the women and children in their lives. But they did so for individual and situational reasons, not because they were part of a generation of lost men overwhelmed by their domestic responsibilities and in search of a more authentic masculinity.

Notes

1 For a recent literature review with emphasis on Quebec, see Peter Gossage, "*Au nom du père?* Rethinking the History of Fatherhood in Quebec," *American Review of Canadian Studies* 44, 1 (2014): 49–67.
2 Shawn Johansen, *Family Men: Middle-Class Fatherhood in Early Industrializing America* (New York: Routledge, 2001), 3.
3 Laura King, *Family Men: Fatherhood and Masculinity in Britain, 1914–1960* (Oxford: Oxford University Press, 2015).

19
Celebrating the Family Man: From Father's Day to La Fête des Pères, 1910–60

Peter Gossage

ALTHOUGH THEY DEBATE THE details and the timing, most historians of fatherhood agree that there was a new, more modern ideology of fatherhood circulating in North America in the twentieth century. Ralph LaRossa has argued that this new ideology became institutionalized in the United States in the 1920s and 1930s and portrayed the *new* father "as economic provider, pal, and male role model all rolled into one."[1] Canadian scholars have presented varied evidence for the spread of what Robert Rutherdale calls "responsible family manhood" in this country, particularly during the postwar era.[2] The idea, then, that fatherhood – a site for the expression and enactment of distinct and historically specific forms of masculinity – was rather thoroughly modernized in twentieth-century North America enjoys wide currency among historians.[3] This was for reasons that are beyond the scope of this chapter but that had to do with rising income levels, falling family size, and new approaches to childrearing and education. The broad question that drives the research reported here is whether that new paternal ideology came to influence and ultimately transform fatherhood in predominantly French-speaking, Catholic Quebec as well. If so, on what timetable? If not, why not?

There are many points of entry into this discussion. Vincent Duhaime has suggested two in his study of postwar fatherhood, based partly on oral history and partly on prescriptive literature generated by the Mouvement familial, a coalition of Catholic agencies and publications devoted to family issues. Duhaime shows that the ideas underlying the new fatherhood – ideas such as family togetherness and a father's particular duties as educator and role model – were indeed in circulation in postwar Quebec. But he also finds a good deal of tension and anxiety expressed over the new, more nurturing roles ascribed to men as fathers.[4] Elsewhere, Cynthia Fish and Guillaume Saudrais have used judicial proceedings as a prism through which to examine the social, cultural, and political understandings of paternal power, privilege, and responsibility that held sway in a somewhat earlier period.[5]

By focusing on Father's Day, the present chapter opens a different window onto the broad question of those modern ideologies of fatherhood and their adoption (or otherwise) in twentieth-century Quebec. LaRossa provides a starting point when he argues that Father's Day can best be understood as neither an "afterthought" to Mother's Day nor as a marketing scheme designed to sell more ties, socks, and cigars. It was much more than that, he suggests: a new cultural ritual, an "invented tradition" that enacted the new, more modern ideology of fatherhood, specifically in the interwar period.[6] Father's Day was "the ritual that embodied America's New Fatherhood. Through the ceremony of giving and receiving Father's Day gifts, families could 'do' or 'enact' the modernization of fatherhood. And again, *the 1930s* were the key."[7] A number of interesting questions follow for historians of family and gender in Quebec. How and on what timetable did Quebecers respond to the invented, American tradition of Father's Day? To what extent did they buy into this new ritual of consumer and familial culture? How did their resistances and enthusiasms reflect either the *américanité* or the distinctiveness of the French Canadian ideology of fatherhood, or perhaps both? And what might that mean more broadly about understandings of domestic masculinity in the decades immediately prior to the Quiet Revolution?

Part of a larger project on fathers and fatherhood in Quebec from 1900 to 1960, this chapter draws on a collection of 133 articles, advertisements, editorials, cartoons, and photographs published in Canada between 1917 and 1960 on the theme of Father's Day.[8] By design, most of these items (94 of 133) were published in Quebec,[9] but the smaller set of similar materials from out-of-province newspapers provides some useful points of comparison. This collection establishes a basis on which to form some impressions about the impact of Father's Day in Quebec, especially about its transition from a rather obscure, often ridiculed, crassly commercial, and/or ill-advised American innovation – a "humbug" to use Leigh Eric Schmidt's clever term – to a widely, if sometimes rather casually observed, annual family ritual.[10]

Honour Thy Father, 1910–29

Father's Day emerged in the United States in the first decade of the twentieth century. By most accounts, it was proposed by Sonora Louise Smart Dodd (1882–1978), supported by Protestant clergy and the YMCA, and celebrated for the first time in Spokane, Washington, in June 1910.[11] Sonora Dodd's father was a Civil War veteran and widower who had raised his six children as a single parent. Interviewed some fifty years later, Dodd remembered him as "a strict man, a real disciplinarian. But he was also a kind and loving parent who kept us together and happy. I thought it would be nice to have a day honouring him and others like him."[12] To judge by its origins, Father's Day might well be understood as something other than a clever scheme designed to generate profits for haberdashers and tobacconists. In the character of these earliest American celebrations – the public ceremonies focused on Protestant churches, for example, and the shared emphasis on living fathers and those who had gone to their rest – one sees something different from the more recent focus on leisure, consumption, and family time. But what about Canada? In particular, what about Quebec? How permeable were international and cultural boundaries to this new American ritual of filial devotion?

As far as this early period is concerned, the short answer to this question is "not very." The first mention of Father's Day celebrations I found in a Canadian newspaper was in the *Montreal Gazette* on Saturday, June 16, 1917. The article announced that Father's Day services were to be held the following day at Centenary Methodist Church in Point St. Charles. Rev. B.B. Brown would preach on the theme of "Honour Thy Father" at the morning service and, in the evening, on "The Lament of a Fond Father at the Fall of His Son in Battle." Members of the congregation were encouraged to adopt a ritual initiated by Sonora Dodd, the wearing of a rose in honour of one's father – red if he was living and white if he had died.[13] Was this the first Father's Day celebration to be held in Quebec, perhaps even in Canada, or simply the first to be captured by the research net cast here? In either case, that it was a community event with publicly performed rituals, rather than the playful, private celebration of more recent memory, bears some emphasis, as does its rather thorough novelty in war-torn 1917.

The next trace of Father's Day I found (Figure 19.1) was in the Quebec City daily *Le Soleil* in 1924, and it was of a completely different nature, bearing the hallmarks of the publicity campaigns that would spread across the United States in the interwar period. *Le Soleil* presented Father's Day as a totally new idea in 1924, as it must certainly have been for the paper's francophone, Catholic readership. "L'on a déjà la fête des mamans, des mariées," announced the subtitle, "et l'on inaugure cette année la fête du papa" (We already have special days for mothers and brides, and this year we're inaugurating Father's Day.)[14] The full-page spread featured an eight-paragraph article, surrounded by specially crafted Father's Day advertisements from ten local merchants who offered a wide range of gift ideas, from tobacco products and neck ties to studio photographs and heirloom-quality silver.[15] Following this rather lavish 1924 promotion, there is a loud silence in the Quebec sources. I found only two advertisements for the rest of the 1920s, both for local clothing stores: Rosenbloom's in Sherbrooke and Reid's in Montreal. Similarly, my quick search of out-of-province newspapers

Figure 19.1 Father's Day promotion, *Le Soleil*, June 12, 1924, 11.

yielded only two items for the 1920s. The more interesting of these was a 1927 article published in Windsor about Canadian retailers' use of Father's Day promotions to boost early summer sales. Those who engaged in such campaigns, including "the largest department store in the Dominion," were presented in this business-friendly piece as being forward-thinking go-getters, whereas those who did not had clearly missed the boat.[16]

"Commercial Oxygen," 1930–45

Although Sonora Dodd is widely credited with having proposed an annual celebration of fatherhood, Madison Avenue was responsible for its promotion and commercialization a generation later. There was also a clear shift in the United States away from Dodd's vision of a public celebration of Father's Day, featuring religious sermons and solemn ceremonies, and toward an event that was located primarily in the family home and in which gift giving took pride of place.[17] LaRossa refers to this trend as "the commercialization of honor" and locates it quite precisely in the 1930s. For it was in Depression-era New York that advertising executive Alvin Austin spearheaded efforts by retailers, especially menswear dealers, to promote Father's Day as what some described, with unbridled optimism, as a "second Christmas." Austin was the key figure in the Associated Men's Wear Retailers, based in New York, and in that capacity, he launched the National Council for the Promotion of Father's Day in 1935.[18] By 1942, when the Father's Day Council presented General Douglas MacArthur with the first "Outstanding Father of the Year" award, the annual celebration of Father's Day and its association with the giving of gifts seems to have been well established in the United States, thanks to a successful national campaign, the key to which, ironically, "was to make the commercialization of honor appear non-commercial."[19]

When not met with indifferent silence, the idea of an annual celebration of fatherhood continued during the Depression to be seen in many Canadian quarters as yet another faddish American import or indeed as an object of derision and ridicule.[20] Father's Day promotions north of the border were few and far between; careful examination of two regional newspapers and a more limited search of the *Gazette* turned up only five between 1930 and 1936. Some Canadian commentators were even moved to publicly criticize the celebration. The subject was raised twice in the editorial pages of the *Canadian Jewish Chronicle*, published in Montreal. "Poor Father," wrote an editorialist on June 23, 1933,

Father's Day came and went, but all the commercial oxygen that was pumped into this artificial respect could [not] place him on that high level of idealism which Mother's Day has given to his consort ... [I]f humanity would seek a little more enlightenment from ancient civilization rather than chasing every fad that crops up, we will be able to manage without these made-to-order days for respect.[21]

The same newspaper made a similar point in 1935, citing Father's Day as an example of "the artificial 'days' and 'weeks' that [in Canada] are set aside for the purpose of renewing our acquaintance with neglected objects."[22]

THE ROBERT SIMPSON MONTREAL LIMITED

For Public Hero No. 1

on *Father's Day*

Sunday,
June 21

For the greatest "unsung hero" the world has ever known...
Dad, who's won more battles and taken more "raps" than any
war veteran...Sunday is Father's Day! Let him know he's the
swellest Dad anybody ever had!

Figure 19.2 "For Public
Hero No. 1 on Father's
Day," *Montreal Gazette,*
June 20, 1936, 3.

As we have seen, Austin's Father's Day Council also dated from 1935, and its
promotional work made significant strides in the United Sates in the second
half of the decade. Major Canadian retailers were on board to some extent. Just
before Father's Day in 1936, the Eaton's department store chain offered to help
Gazette readers "make him King for a day" in an ad featuring not just ties and
socks but also a wide range of gift ideas, including books and fishing rods.[23]
The Robert Simpson Company took a comic approach in its advertisement,
praising fathers as "Public Hero No. 1" and featuring a kindly, prosperous,
older dad receiving stacks of parcels from an overburdened delivery man (Figure 19.2).[24] Eaton's, however, was the only retailer to promote Father's Day in
the Montreal daily *La Patrie* in 1936, representing father as a distinguished,
well-groomed, older gentleman to whom customers were invited to offer
"quelque chose [qu'il désire] vraiment" (something he really wants) from a
selection of merchandise that included dress shirts, ties, socks, and hand-
kerchiefs. Interestingly, this content was presented under the title "Jour des
Papas," a more literal translation of "Father's Day" than the one that later came
into general use and surely a hint that in the mid-1930s "La Fête des Pères" was
still at a considerable distance from becoming a widely recognized event in
French Canadian family culture.[25]

    This apparent indifference, especially among francophones, seems to have
persisted in Quebec throughout the war years, although some retailers certainly
did promote the event each June. The range of advertisers, furthermore, was

growing with Eaton's and Simpson's still setting the pace but with some French Canadian merchants, including the major Montreal department store Dupuis Frères, also getting into the act.[26] Two advertisements published in June 1942 – one in *Le Soleil* and one in *La Patrie* – seem to capture the state of Father's Day celebrations in wartime Quebec. First, the publicity for the Maurice Pollack clothing store in Quebec City reminds us of what must have been a significant obstacle to the promotion of Father's Day celebrations among French Canadians. Father's Day falls on the third Sunday in June, which is generally a few days before the feast day of Saint-Jean-Baptiste on June 24.[27] This is one reason why on Saturday, June 20, 1942, *La Patrie* contained not a single advertisement with a Father's Day theme.[28] In contrast, there were many advertisements evoking the forthcoming civic and religious holiday and promoting national pride and solidarity. This, remember, was a rather tempestuous moment in the history of French Canadian nationalism. Anti-conscription forces had just been defeated in the national plebiscite of April 1942 and were set to launch a new nationalist party, the Bloc populaire canadien, in September 1942. So a typical ad encouraged consumers to buy furniture from a "select group" of French Canadian merchants in the following terms: "Soyons fiers ... de notre race, de notre langue, de notre foi ... Prenons l'habitude d'être de vrais Canadiens français et soyons fiers de l'être" (Let's be proud of our race, of our language, of our faith. Let's make it a habit to be real French Canadians, and to be proud of it).[29]

The publicity for the Maurice Pollack store squared the circle in an interesting way. Hoping to profit from the coincidence in dates and surely, if more ambiguously, from the wartime context, the Quebec City clothing store promoted Father's Day as an opportunity to celebrate "Les Papas de la Patrie":

Honorons ce dimanche ces grands canadiens ... pour leur soumission lorsque les mamans les amènent faire le magasinage ... pour leur consentement à laisser junior utiliser l'auto le soir ... pour l'accueil réjoui qu'ils font aux chapeaux folichons de mamans ... pour les petites et grandes choses que nous pouvons attendre de la bonté de papa ... Faisons-lui une grande fête dimanche, présentons-lui des cadeaux qu'il aimera ... des cadeaux de chez Pollack.

(This Sunday, let's honour this great [French] Canadian ... for his submission when Mom takes him out shopping ... for agreeing to let Junior use the car at night ... for greeting Mom's zany hats with such joy ... for all the things we count on, big and small, thanks to Dad's goodness ... Let's throw him a big party this Sunday and offer him gifts he'll appreciate ... gifts from Pollack's store.)[30]

A second June 1942 example linked fatherhood, citizenship, and the war effort in a more solemn and explicit way (Figure 19.3). The large advertisement was placed by a group of retailers called L'Association des Détaillants Montréalais commis à la célébration de La Fête des Pères. By focusing its campaign on the theme of "Father – The Defender of the Home," the association revealed its links to Austin's Father's Day Council in the United States, which used precisely that slogan in 1942.[31] The visual materials – a young family preparing gifts and a card for Dad, who has taken the ethereal form of a mounted medieval knight – are striking, as is the text with its references to citizenship and the war effort. The result is an equation between fatherhood and patriotism similar to the one offered by Maurice Pollack, although in a much more earnest tone and with much clearer links to the Canadian war effort:

> Qu'il porte l'uniforme du soldat ou de l'aviateur, la vareuse du marin, la blouse de l'ouvrier d'une usine d'artillerie – ou qu'il soit un des milliers d'hommes d'affaires à qui fut confié la tâche de coordonner et de diriger les industries du Dominion ... Quelles que soient ses fonctions, il donne à son travail le meilleur de lui-même – il se bat ou il peine pour défendre son pays contre les sinistres théories hitlériennes, contre le carnage et la destruction. Son but est la survivance de la confiance que vous avez en lui ... Dimanche le 21 juin, Fête des Pères, donnez à ce citoyen méritoire, quelque chose utile – gage de votre respect et de votre admiration.

> (Whether he wears the uniform of a soldier or airman, a sailor's pea jacket or the blue collar of a munitions factory worker – or perhaps he's one of the thousands of businessmen entrusted with the task of managing and coordinating the Dominion's industries ... Whatever his station, he gives the best of himself to his labour – he fights or toils to defend his country against Hitler's sinister theories, against carnage and destruction. His goal is the survival of the trust you place in him ... On Sunday June 21, Father's Day, give this deserving citizen something useful – a sign of your respect and admiration.)[32]

One can only imagine the dissonance generated by such a campaign – clearly designed for a broader North American audience – in French-speaking Montreal in June 1942, with so many troubled by the federal government's approach to conscription and with preparations for the annual celebration of French Canadian identity and heritage in full swing.

Retailers were hard-pressed to sell Father's Day as a "second Christmas" during the Depression and the Second World War, no matter what marketing tactics they used, including appeals to patriotism and citizenship. There were also remarkably few articles or editorials written by Quebec journalists about the celebration, much fewer than one would expect if Father's Day had gained

Figure 19.3 "Le Père – Defenseur du Foyer!" *La Patrie,* June 14, 1942, 48.

the kind of traction it did in the United States between 1936 and 1942.[33] I found only four articles published in Quebec on the topic between 1930 and 1945. One was an ironic story printed in *La Patrie* about a fictitious father whose five or six children used a series of pretexts to dislodge sufficient funds from Papa to buy him small gifts from the tobacconist or the florist, to the great amusement of the kindly breadwinner.[34] Another was published by the *Sherbrooke Daily Record* in June 1945, just a few weeks after the end of the war in Europe. This was an enthusiastic article in which the author expressed nostalgia about "the good old days of Victoria, when Father really did rule the roost," and qualified the mid-1940s as "these disrespectful times, when the so called head of the house too often gets pushed into a corner and poked fun at." Father's Day, then, was framed as a well-deserved recognition of men's contributions to their families, a kind of symbolic reordering of a gender balance that, in this narrative, had been thrown off-kilter by the war, by women's work outside the home, and by the celebration of the maternal role in popular culture.[35]

La Fête des Pères, 1946–60

Compared with the drought of the Depression and the war years, there was a veritable flood of Father's Day materials published in both French- and English-language newspapers between 1946 and 1960. Three related trends are clear among the advertisements in this collection, above and beyond the dramatic increase in their numbers.[36] First, the range of items promoted as potential Father's Day gifts increased. Many advertisements did continue to suggest dress shirts, socks, ties, and grooming supplies, such as electric razors – all of which helped middle-class men to prepare for *work*. But there was also a clear shift toward items related to leisure pursuits, including home-improvement activities, such as gardening and woodworking, and outdoor recreation, especially golf and fishing. An Eaton's ad published in the *Gazette* in June 1958 (Figure 19.4), for example, featured outboard motors, golf carts, and fishing gear, as well as lawn mowers, garden hoses, and hedge-trimming shears, all presented in a relaxed, jocular tone.[37]

Second, while big national chains like Eaton's and Simpson's were expanding their Father's Day campaigns, smaller retailers – many owned and operated by French Canadian merchants – got into the act for the first time. Local clothing stores, such as Le Syndicat de Québec in Quebec City, J.M. Nault in Sherbrooke, and L.N. Messier in Montreal, ran Father's Day ads in 1947 and 1948.[38] And three Father's Day advertisements for smaller establishments run by francophone merchants all appeared in the same issue of *La Patrie* a week before Father's Day in 1954. These establishments were A. Bélanger's local chain of hardware stores, the O. St.-Jean jewellery store downtown, and Quincaillerie Trudeau on Saint-Laurent Boulevard, which placed an elaborate ad for boats, outboard motors, water skis, and fishing tackle.[39]

Third, visual images of fatherhood in these marketing materials were changing. Fathers were increasingly represented as younger, more casual, and more often at play than at work. The image in a 1954 Dupuis Frères ad (Figure 19.5) of a young man relaxing outdoors with his pipe and his newspaper, while showing off his new Florsheim shoes, is typical of this period and stands in contrast to the formally attired, generally older dads of the 1930s and 1940s. All of this is consistent with what historians have written about the new, more nurturing, less distant models of masculine parenthood that were in wide circulation by the postwar period.[40] Like the backyard barbecues studied by Christopher Dummitt,[41] the celebration of Father's Day – with its focus on rewarding devoted family men with gifts and relaxation – was a new ritual that, to paraphrase LaRossa, allowed families to *perform* the new ideology of fatherhood.[42]

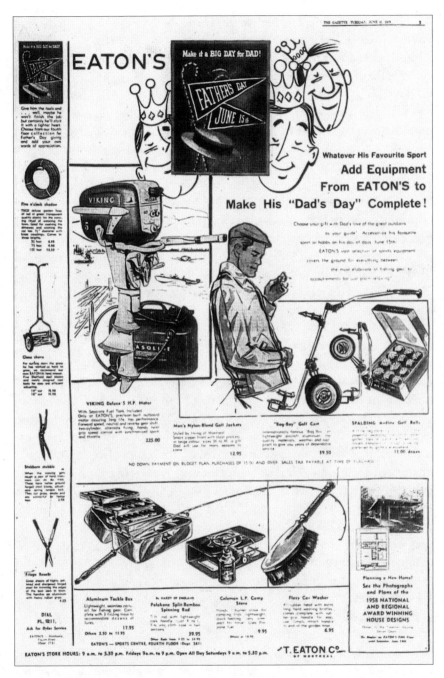

Figure 19.4 Eaton's Father's Day ad, *Montreal Gazette*, June 10, 1958, 7.

But unlike in the United States, where "the 1930s were the key,"[43] the tipping point in Quebec seems quite clearly to have come in the postwar years.

This impression is further supported by a reading of the twenty-five articles about Father's Day that I located in Quebec newspapers published between 1946 and 1960.[44] This surge in interest was focused on the years between 1947 and 1953, when more Father's Day articles were published than at any other time. Some of these articles, admittedly, contained only passing references to Father's Day. In June 1949, for instance, a small regional weekly mentioned a Father's Day celebration held at St. Damien's College in Bedford. "All present and enjoyed by all," noted the reporter, in a chatty column featuring the usual bridge parties and visitors.[45] For their part, the Montreal Royals baseball team organized their first Father's Day give-away promotion in June 1955. The reporter for *Le Petit Journal* quipped that fathers arriving for the doubleheader should not expect to receive a new car; rather, a small souvenir would be offered to all dads in attendance, the nature of which he would not divulge, except to say that "dans la plupart des cas, il n'en restera rien à la fin de l'après-midi"[46] (in most cases, there will be nothing left by the end of the afternoon).

The majority of Father's Day articles in this period, however, dealt more directly with the event itself; most were written in French, and they are the main focus here. But there was one illustrated feature published in the *Sherbrooke Daily Record* that is worth some attention, especially as a window onto prescriptions for the "new" fatherhood. This full-page spread included a brief history of Father's Day, an analysis of the word "Father" – its etymology and its use in various languages – and advertisements for leather products, clothing, electronics, and the local Canadian Tire franchise.[47] The centrepiece, however, was a cartoon depicting the "Ideal Father" of the early 1950s (Figure 19.6). Radiating out from the smiling face of a clean-cut man in his thirties is a series of ten qualities, each illustrated by a small drawing in which father and children are both represented. The ideal father, readers learn, "stresses self-respect; encourages wholesome activities; teaches tolerance and understanding; sets an example of responsible citizenship; guides spiritual growth; teaches good sportsmanship; teaches appreciation of his country's law and ideals; encourages self-reliance and independence; stresses equal rights of all; [and] takes part in school and club activities."[48]

At the same time, the growing discussion of La Fête des Pères in French-language periodicals certainly suggests the spread of its observance by francophone, Catholic Quebecers in the postwar years but also some ambivalence about it. In June 1948 *La Revue populaire* published an article announcing (incorrectly) that Father's Day would be celebrated on June 13 and describing it, along with Mother's Day, as one of those "nouvelles fêtes qui ont pour but de

Figure 19.5 Dupuis Frères Father's Day ad, *La Patrie,* June 13, 1954, 3.

resserrer les liens familiaux, tout en faisant marcher le commerce" (new cele-brations designed to strengthen family ties, while turning the wheels of com-merce).[49] The trouble, however, was that it was much easier to buy gifts for women than for men. The solution for this author was that his Father's Day present should be greater authority, trust, and affection within the household. "Je dis aux femmes," writes the author, "laissez plus d'autorité à votre mari; et aux enfants, accordez votre confiance et votre amitié à votre papa. Aucun ca-deau ne lui sera plus agréable" (I say to women ... grant your husbands more authority; and to children, give Dad your trust and your friendship. No gift will please him more).[50] A somewhat different tack was taken in an article by Paul Rochon published in 1950 in *L'Avenir Saguenayen* under the bland but revealing headline "Prenez bien note de la date; c'est le 18 juin" (Take careful note of the date; it's June 18).[51] Taking the nostalgic rhetoric of lost paternal authority to ridiculous extremes, Rochon compared contemporary mothers and fathers with their notional stone-age predecessors, asking who had the tougher job in both eras. The main idea is that whereas prehistoric women had been enslaved to club-wielding, hair-pulling men, the tables had been completely turned, and it was men who were now enslaved to women.[52]

Many of the Father's Day texts appearing in this period, however, were much more earnest and sentimental than this one. Anne Larose, for instance, framed her 1949 Father's Day contribution, published in *Le Front ouvrier*, as a story based in the village of Saint-Alexis. Larose described throngs of excited customers descending on a general store to buy up the supply of ties, socks, and similar items that the clever local merchant had bought from a commercial traveller. But the story really turns on the character of a poor child, Élise, who has recently lost her mother. Having no money with which to buy her devoted father a gift, she is assisted by a beautiful heiress who has dedicated her life to God and good works. Through the charity of this benefactor, Élise is able to buy something for Papa after all – not a flashy tie or cuff links but a book of prayers to help him cope with the loss of his beloved wife. Notwithstanding the satisfaction of the dads in the accompanying photo with their store-bought gifts, Father's Day might also (again, like Christmas) be seen as an opportunity for more universal and lasting forms of Christian charity.[53]

A Father's Day feature published in *La Gazette du nord* in June 1950 makes many of the points I have been teasing out of these materials. The absolute novelty of the celebration in the Abitibi region is clear from the replies of local residents when asked their opinion of Father's Day. "Je pense que la Fête des Pères est une bonne initiative, quoique toute nouvelle" (I think Father's Day is a good initiative, although entirely new), stated M. Morin of Malartic, for example. The rhetoric of lost paternal prestige and authority is also present throughout this item, including in the rather buffoonish cover illustration (Figure 19.7). This loss of status was often presented as symptomatic of centrifugal forces at work within the family, as in the response to an interview question by Mrs. Georges H. Dumont of Val d'Or:

Je pense qu'actuellement, l'esprit familial tend à se relâcher, les enfants sont souvent portés à s'éloigner du foyer, les papas sont également affaires [sic] et n'ont pas toujours le temps de bien penser au milieu familial, de sorte qu'une fête comme

Figure 19.6 "The Ideal Father," *Sherbrooke Daily Record,* June 12, 1951, 11.

celle des pères, contribue à rassembler tout le monde, à les rapprocher les uns des autres, et par le fait même, stimule l'esprit de famille et la compréhension.

(I think family spirit nowadays is waning, children are living further from home, dads are off at work without much time to really think about family life, so that a celebration like Father's Day serves to gather everyone together, to bring them closer to each other and, in the process, to foster family spirit and understanding.)[54]

These, of course, were exactly the same kinds of fears of family breakdown that had worried many within the Catholic Church for decades and that had given

Figure 19.7 "18 Juin: Jour des Pères," *La Gazette du nord,* June 15, 1950, 1.

rise to a well-organized Mouvement familial comprised of various agencies devoted to the promotion of conservative family values. Father's Day, then, need not be ignored or decried as a fad or as a crass materialist gimmick imported from the United States; it might also be harnessed to the ongoing Catholic campaign to reinforce "traditional" French Canadian families. "La paternité naturelle n'est pas assez respectée," wrote the author of the lead article in this feature. "La fête des pères répare cette lourde erreur, du moins partiellement" (Natural fatherhood gets too little respect, ... Father's Day corrects, at least in part, this grave error).[55]

L'Action catholique – the official organ of Quebec's Catholic Action movement – was quite slow to enter this conversation. But when it did, on Father's Day in 1955, it entered with a splash: a big feature that covered three pages, including the front cover, with four articles and three photographs, including a very modern dad looking relaxed and happy while riding double on the back of his son's bike (Figure 19.8). The image could not shout pal, role model, and therefore new fatherhood more loudly. But the rest of the material seems to articulate a more traditional model of male parenthood. There is a solemn reflection on the juxtaposition of Father's Day with Saint-Jean-Baptiste Day, which in 1955 was dedicated to the 200th anniversary of the Acadian deportation.[56] There is a parable about a mother and father, one of whom plants lettuce in a corner of their garden, whereas the other plants beans; each thinks the other's shoots are weeds, so all the plantings get pulled out. Parents who do not communicate or work together in raising their children be warned, as this is obviously not a story about vegetables.[57] And there is a recipe for turning your child into a monster, which includes "advice" like giving him everything he wants, leaving him unsupervised, punishing him for trivialities, and forgetting that parental authority derives from God.[58]

There is also, finally, a long article on "Caractéristiques propres de l'amour paternel" (the inherent characteristics of paternal love), which reads like a very conservative prescription indeed for postwar fatherhood. The main ingredients of paternal love are authority, responsibility, patience, solicitude, the ability to give of oneself, and a spirit of sacrifice. The sections on authority and responsibility are especially conservative in their tone and substance. The authors, P. and R. de Montjamant, took the view that "les notions de paternité et d'autorité aient été longtemps une seule chose et que toute autorité en ce monde puise son sens dans l'autorité paternel" (the concepts of paternity and authority had long been one and the same and that all authority in this world derives its meaning from paternal authority). Responsibility is the next most important dimension in this vision of a father's love, responsibility not only for the bodies and souls of his children but also for "ce fleuve humain – la descendance ... Le père doit [donc] assurer la race (d'où cet instinctif désir *du fils!*). La descendance de David est une illustration unique de l'achèvement d'un père en ses fils" (this river of humanity we call lineage ... The father must therefore maintain the race [hence the instinctive desire *for sons!*]. The descendants of David are a unique illustration of a father's fulfilment through his sons.)[59] We are a long way here from those modern ideologies of fatherhood that revolve around education, nurturing, and affection. That Father's Day celebrations could be harnessed to an extremely conservative ideology of fatherhood, although somewhat unexpected, is also consistent with Duhaime's thesis about the ambivalence with which some French-speaking, Catholic Quebecers embraced the new fatherhood in the 1950s.[60]

Five years later, in June 1960, *La Patrie* told quite a different story. On Sunday, June 12, a week before the event, there was no reporting or editorial comment on Father's Day. But five advertisements were published, featuring items such as luggage, Gillette's new adjustable safety razors (my own dad, born in 1927, used one of these), four models of Cavity brand pipes, and rather strangely, "lucky" cuckoo clocks from a specialty dealer on DeLorimier Street.[61] There was also an ad placed by Les Détaillants en mercerie et vêtements pour hommes du Québec Inc., which had organized a "Father of the Year" contest along the lines of those in existence in the United States since 1942 and elsewhere in Canada

Figure 19.8 "La Fête des Pères, 19 Juin," *L'Action catholique*, June 19, 1955, 1.

since 1948.[62] Participating menswear dealers offered prizes ranging from $5 gift certificates to a magnificent wardrobe worth $500 for the lucky and deserving dad crowned "Père de l'Année."[63] A week later, on Father's Day, readers of *La Patrie* could enjoy a playful cartoon in which a woman sneaks some money out of her sleeping husband's pocket, packs their toddler son off to the store, and then returns home, where the proud little boy presents Dad with what is clearly an unwelcome gift: an apron "pour laver la vaisselle et pour faire manger bébé" (for washing the dishes and feeding the baby).[64] There was also a photograph

La fête des pères chez Jean Duceppe

La joie va régner, aujourd'hui, chez Jean Duceppe, le populaire artiste de la radio, de la scène et de la télévision. Notre photo, où l'on voit Jean Duceppe et son épouse, entourés de leurs enfants : Gilles, Claude, Pierre, Louis, Monique, Anne et le tout dernier, Yves, laisse prévoir ce que sera cette fête. Chez lui, Jean Duceppe n'appartient plus au public mais à son épouse et à ses enfants. Lequel de ces garçons, de ces bambines suivra les traces du père ? Mystère que seul l'avenir dévoilera. Avec une si belle famille, la relève semble cependant assurée.

(Photo J. J. Américal)

Figure 19.9   "La Fête des Pères chez Jean Duceppe," *La Patrie*, June 19, 1960, 112.

of the popular stage, radio, and television actor Jean Duceppe, surrounded by his wife and their seven children, including their eldest, Gilles (top right), the future Bloc Québécois leader (Figure 19.9). "La joie va régner aujourd'hui," in the Duceppe family home, reads the caption in part. "Chez lui, Jean Duceppe n'appartient plus au public mais à son épouse et à ses enfants" (Joy will reign today ... At home, Jean Duceppe no longer belongs to the public, but rather to his wife and children).[65] The imperfectly domesticated dad as the butt of jokes and the curious idea that a father might *belong* to his wife and children rather than the other way around – surely, these tropes are consistent with the new images and ideologies of fatherhood circulating in North America at this time, with their emphasis on masculine domesticity, on family togetherness, and on more nurturing paternal roles.

Conclusion

Father's Day had a specific and authentic set of meanings for North American families in the twentieth century, beyond what it surely meant to the sales figures of haberdashers, tobacconists, and department stores. Over the course of the century, LaRossa argues, Father's Day was embraced and performed as the "ritual that embodied" the "New Fatherhood." In the United States, the key moment in this transformation was the later part of the 1930s, when a merchant's association based in New York began to promote the celebration and thereby to "sanctify" a tradition that had been invented about twenty years earlier but that many considered a crass commercial humbug.[66]

Evidence presented here suggests a range of Canadian responses to this new cultural and commercial event. There was a tendency in some quarters to ridicule the idea, sometimes because fathers themselves were so widely understood as breadwinners and providers whose role was to give rather than to receive. What I call the "slippery slope" argument against Father's Day was also in wide circulation, as critics asked the rhetorical question, "Where will it all end?" In 1951 Charlotte Whitton was in excellent form as she made precisely this argument in an ironic article promoting a special day for Maiden Aunts.[67] In contrast, the spread of advertising materials and editorial content makes it clear that the celebration was embraced by many Canadian families in the middle decades of the twentieth century, with important distinctions to be made, surely, on the basis of social class, ethnicity, and rural versus urban (or suburban) residence. Canadians in general seem to have adopted the American-style celebration of the modern family man by the 1950s at the latest, and many would have participated in the event much sooner than that, especially in the growing, middle-class suburbs. This is consistent, of course, with what Dummitt, Rutherdale, and others have shown in their studies of postwar fatherhood in Canada. The new, more nurturing, and more emotionally engaged model of "responsible family manhood" was widely circulated in this country – although, as Rutherdale reiterates in the next chapter, many Canadian men had considerable difficulty living up to it.

As Duhaime has already shown, however, these new ideas were not without their critics in Quebec on the eve of the Quiet Revolution. "Traditional" or patriarchal fatherhood, with its greater emotional distance and its emphasis on authority, respect, and family honour, still had its champions in the 1950s, particularly in the Catholic religious press.[68] Father's Day observance was clearly a "hard sell" in Quebec throughout the interwar period and the war years, despite the investment of Eaton's, Simpson's, Dupuis Frères, and some smaller-scale retailers in its promotion. Francophone Quebecers, it seems, remained largely impervious to these efforts for many years, embracing the celebration as a significant and welcome initiative only in the late 1940s and early 1950s.

Resistance or indifference to the invented tradition of Father's Day, in conclusion, suggests the greater persistence in Catholic Quebec of older ideologies of masculine power, couched in ancient patriarchal tropes like "God the Father" and *la puissance paternelle*.[69] From this perspective, the rise of Father's Day celebrations in the postwar period illustrates the extent to which Quebecers came to accept and indeed to celebrate a new, distinctly middle-class ideology of fatherhood that, without contesting masculine power or the patriarchal family in any substantive way, came to redefine the dad "as economic provider, pal, and male role model all rolled into one."[70] Further research into this question is underway, using different sources, including life writing, novels, and court records, and focusing on clusters of paternal discourse and experience other than those generated by Father's Day. An example is the conservative Catholic message of a strong but just father whose authority, descended directly from God, had been reaffirmed and enacted each year in the province by a much older family ritual: the *bénédiction paternelle* (paternal blessing) on New Year's Day. The slow, halting, and contested rise of modern Father's Day celebrations in the province, then, might well be read against the inexorable decline of this longstanding ritual of deference and submission to paternal authority, about which I have commented elsewhere.[71]

Notes

The research presented here was funded by the Social Sciences and Humanities Research Council of Canada and conducted with the able assistance of Abbey Mahon, Lisa Moore, Michelle Roy, Thierry Robert, and Guillaume Saudrais. Some elements of this chapter were presented at the 2011 meeting of the Canadian Historical Association in Fredericton, New Brunswick. Quoted passages from French-language sources have been translated by the author.

1 Ralph LaRossa, *The Modernization of Fatherhood: A Social and Political History* (Chicago: University of Chicago Press, 1997), 1.
2 Robert Rutherdale, "Three Faces of Fatherhood as a Masculine Category: Tyrants, Teachers, and Workaholics as 'Responsible Family Men' during Canada's Baby Boom," in *What Is Masculinity? Historical Dynamics from Antiquity to the Contemporary World*, ed. John H. Arnold and Sean Brady, 323–48 (Basingstoke, UK: Palgrave Macmillan, 2011). See also Christopher Dummitt, "Finding a Place for Father: Selling the Barbecue in Postwar Canada," *Journal of the Canadian Historical Association* 9, 1 (1998): 209–23.
3 For a recent overview of this literature with an emphasis on Quebec, see Peter Gossage, "*Au nom du père?* Rethinking the History of Fatherhood in Quebec," *American Review of Canadian Studies* 44, 1 (2014): 49–67.
4 Vincent Duhaime, "La construction du père québécois: Le discours du mouvement familial et l'expérience des pères, 1945–1965" (MA thesis, Université de Montréal, 2000); Vincent Duhaime, "'Les pères ont ici leur devoir': Le discours du mouvement familial québécois et la construction de la paternité dans l'après-guerre, 1945–1960," *Revue d'histoire de l'Amérique française* 57, 4 (2004): 535–66.
5 Cynthia Fish, "La puissance paternelle et les cas de garde d'enfants au Québec, 1866–1928," *Revue d'histoire de l'Amérique française* 57, 4 (2004): 509–33; Guillaume Saudrais, "Maris et pères devant les tribunaux civils québécois, 1900–1920" (MA thesis, Université de Sherbrooke, 2010). For my own efforts along these lines, see Peter Gossage, "On Dads and Damages: Looking for the 'Priceless Child' and the 'Manly Modern' in Quebec's Civil Courts," *Histoire sociale/Social History* 49, 100 (2016): 603–23.
6 For his seminal discussion of invented traditions and their value as objects of historical inquiry, see Eric Hobsbawm, "Introduction," in *The Invention of Tradition*, ed. Eric Hobsbawm and Terence Ranger, 1–14 (Cambridge, UK: Cambridge University Press, 1983).
7 LaRossa, *Modernization of Fatherhood*, 189, original emphasis.

8 To generate this collection, I began with a selective but systematic reading of Quebec periodicals, focusing on the months of December and, more importantly here, June. These periodicals included two daily newspapers (Quebec City's *Le Soleil* and the *Sherbrooke Daily Record*), a weekly newspaper (*Le Samedi*), two popular monthly magazines (*La Revue moderne* and *La Revue populaire*), and the Franciscan temperance monthly *La Famille*. This strategy generated a modest but interesting set of Father's Day materials. I then expanded the search in two stages. First, I queried the Google News Archive website for materials published in Canadian newspapers related to Father's Day between 1900 and 1960. Second, I conducted a brief manual search of two Montreal newspapers, *La Patrie* and the *Gazette*, in the week leading up to Father's Day for specific years in the time frame of the larger project.

9 Of these 94 items, 51 were from French-language newspapers such as Quebec City's *Le Soleil* and Montreal's *La Patrie*, and the rest were from English newspapers, especially the *Montreal Gazette* and the *Sherbrooke Daily Record*.

10 Leigh Eric Schmidt, *Consumer Rites: The Buying and Selling of American Holidays* (Princeton, NJ: Princeton University Press, 1995), 275.

11 The most thorough general account of the origins of Father's Day is in Schmidt, *Consumer Rites*, 275–92. For other useful studies of family celebrations, see John Gillis, "Making Time for Family: The Invention of Family Time(s) and the Reinvention of History," *Journal of Family History* 21, 1 (1996): 4–21; Elizabeth H. Pleck, *Celebrating the Family: Ethnicity, Consumer Culture, and Family Rituals* (Cambridge, MA: Harvard University Press, 2000); Jean-Philippe Warren, *Hourra pour Santa Claus! La commercialisation de la saison des fêtes au Québec, 1885–1995* (Montreal: Boréal, 2006); and Nancy Marando, "L'Idéal maternel: Discours, représentation et célébration des mères québécoises à l'occasion de la Fête des Mères, 1940–1980" (MA thesis, Université de Montréal, 2006).

12 Quoted in "Father's Day Idea Born in Spokane 50 Years Ago," *Calgary Herald*, June 22, 1959, 17. A competing narrative places the first Father's Day in West Virginia on July 5, 1908, when Mrs. Grace Golden Clayton organized an Independence Day tribute to all fathers, including her own, but especially those killed in a 1907 mining disaster. Thomas Koon, "The First Father's Day," *Goldseal: West Virginia Traditional Life* 26, 2 (2000): 10. My thanks to Kim Johnson of the West Virginia Division of Culture and History for providing a copy of this article. Schmidt probably has it right when he suggests that, by 1910, Father's Day was an idea whose time had come and one that was promoted independently by several progressive-era women. Schmidt, *Consumer Rites*, 275. Mother's Day is substantially older, with promotional efforts dating back to the 1860s. See Marando, "L'Idéal maternel," 1–3.

13 "Observe Father's Day: Services Tomorrow in Centenary Methodist Church," *Montreal Gazette*, June 16, 1917, 14.

14 This was surely a reference to President Calvin Coolidge's public endorsement of Father's Day celebrations that same year. "Dimanche prochain, la fête des papas," *Le Soleil*, June 12, 1924, 11.

15 Ibid.

16 "Father's Day Aid to Retail Trade," *Windsor Border Cities Star*, August 20, 1927, 36. The largest retailer in Canada in 1927 was certainly the Timothy Eaton Company of Toronto, which by 1930 boasted retail sales of $2.76 billion and a regular workforce of 25,736. See Donica Belisle, *Retail Nation: Department Stores and the Making of Modern Canada* (Vancouver: UBC Press, 2011), 39.

17 As Elizabeth Pleck has argued, family holidays in general have been increasingly privatized and commercialized since the late nineteenth century. "Advertisers and neckwear

18 I refer to this organization from here on as the Father's Day Council. Also known as the National Father's Day Committee or Council, this organization's mandate, according to LaRossa, was to "sanctify" Father's Day in the same way that the Catholic Church did Christmas. LaRossa, *Modernization of Fatherhood*, 185.

19 Ibid., 181–91, quote at 185.

20 My research located 34 items related to Father's Day dating from the period embracing the Great Depression and the Second World War (1930–45). This is not many (barely more than 2 per year) but far more than the scant 6 items I found in the previous two decades using the same methods. See note 8.

21 "Our Weekly Chat: Father's Day," *Canadian Jewish Chronicle*, June 23, 1933, 3.

22 "Our Weekly Chat: 'Sabbath Week' in Palestine," *Canadian Jewish Chronicle*, March 1, 1935, 2.

23 *Montreal Gazette*, June 19, 1936, 9.

24 *Montreal Gazette*, June 20, 1936, 3.

25 *La Patrie*, June 18, 1936, 16.

26 *La Patrie*, June 16, 1942, 28; and June 19, 1942, 28.

27 From 1939 through 1945, for example, Father's Day fell on the following dates: June 18, 16, 15, 21, 20, 18, and 17.

28 In comparison, the Saturday edition of the *Gazette* contained two Father's Day advertisements and an article about a "Father of the Year" award. *Montreal Gazette*, June 20, 1942, 5, 11, 14, 19.

29 *La Patrie*, June 20, 1942, 38.

30 *Le Soleil*, June 18, 1942, 5.

31 LaRossa, *Modernization of Fatherhood*, 191.

32 "Le Père – Défenseur du foyer!" *La Patrie*, June 14, 1942, 48. A similar advertisement was published four days later in the same newspaper. *La Patrie*, June 18, 1942, 9.

33 LaRossa, *Modernization of Fatherhood*, 187–92.

34 "La 'fête des pères' le 21 juin prochain," *La Patrie*, June 14, 1942, 66.

35 "Dad Is King for a Day Tomorrow in Recognition of Father's Day!" *Sherbrooke Daily Record*, June 16, 1945, 3.

36 Using the same sequence of methods and sources as before, I identified 93 relevant items for this fifteen-year period, of which 63 were published in Quebec newspapers, including 42 in French, and the rest in newspapers spread across the other provinces.

37 *Montreal Gazette*, June 10, 1958, 7.

38 *Le Soleil*, June 10, 1947, 6; *Sherbrooke Daily Record*, June 17, 1948, 14; *La Patrie*, June 13, 1948, 85.

39 *La Patrie*, June 13, 1954, 83, 84, 87.

40 Dummitt, "Finding a Place for Father"; Duhaime, "La construction du père québécois"; Rutherdale, "Three Faces of Fatherhood," among many other articles and book chapters, including Chapter 20, this volume.

41 Dummitt, "Finding a Place for Father."

42 LaRossa, *Modernization of Fatherhood*, 189. The performative nature of gender identities is further explored in Part 3 of the present anthology.

43 Ibid.

44 This figure contrasts with a total of seven articles in the preceding thirty-five years.

45 *News and Eastern Townships Advocate*, June 16, 1949, 3.

46 My guess is that the Royals were giving away cigars that day. "La Fête des Pères au Stade DeLormier," *Le Petit Journal*, June 19, 1955, 93.

47 *Sherbrooke Daily Record,* June 12, 1951, 11.

48 Ibid.

49 "Cadeaux pour les Papas: La Fête des Pères, 13 juin," *La Revue populaire,* June 1948, 83.

50 Ibid.

51 Paul Rochon, "Prenez bien note de la date; c'est le 18 juin," *L'Avenir Saguenayen,* June 15, 1950, 3–4. These were early times for Father's Day in Quebec, and there was still widespread confusion about the date.

52 Ibid.

53 Anne LaRose, "Conte pour La Fête des Pères," *Le Front ouvrier,* June 18, 1949, 18.

54 Both quoted in "Une bonne initiative la Fête des Peres," *La Gazette du nord,* June 15, 1950, Illustrated Section, 2.

55 "La Fête de Papa," *La Gazette du nord,* June 15, 1950, Illustrated Section, 2.

56 "La première page," *L'Action catholique,* June 19, 1955, 4.

57 "La Fête des Pères: Pour lire en tête à tête," *L'Action catholique,* June 19, 1955, 4.

58 "La Fête des Pères: Recette infaillible pour faire un monstre de votre enfant," *L'Action catholique,* June 19, 1955, 4.

59 P. de Montjamant and R. de Montjamant, "Caractéristiques propres de l'amour paternel," *L'Action catholique,* June 19, 1955, 5, original emphasis. This article seems to have been reprinted from the journal *Revue des jeunes: Organe de pensée catholique et française, d'information et d'action,* published in Paris.

60 Duhaime, "La construction du père québécois"; Duhaime, "'Les pères ont ici leur devoir.'"

61 *La Patrie,* June 12, 1960, 101, 141, 147, 108.

62 On these "Father of the Year" contests, see LaRossa, *Modernization of Fatherhood,* 191; and *Montreal Gazette,* June 20, 1942, 11.

63 *La Patrie,* June 12, 1960, 96.

64 *La Patrie,* June 19, 1960, 98.

65 "La Fête des Pères chez Jean Duceppe," *La Patrie,* June 19, 1960, 112.

66 LaRossa, *Modernization of Fatherhood,* ch. 8, quotes at 189.

67 Charlotte Whitton, "Maiden Aunt's Day," *Ottawa Citizen,* June 19, 1951, 3.

68 Duhaime, "La construction du père québécois"; Duhaime, "'Les pères ont ici leur devoir.'"

69 This principle remained in force under Quebec's civil law until it was replaced in 1977 by the gender-neutral concept of *parental authority.* The term is usually translated as "paternal power" or "paternal authority" but I would suggest that "paternal dominion" may be more accurate.

70 LaRossa, *Modernization of Fatherhood,* 1. Michelle Roy provides further support to this idea by using newspaper advertisements to document the rise of the model she calls "le père éducateur" in the postwar period. Michelle Roy, "L'évolution de la figure paternelle dans les publicités du journal sherbrookois, *La Tribune,* au XXe siècle" (MA thesis, Université de Sherbrooke, 2007).

71 See Peter Gossage, "Visages de la paternité au Québec, 1900–1960," *Revue d'histoire de l'Amérique française* 70, 1–2 (2016): 53–82, which includes a discussion of the paternal blessing based on personal memoirs and autobiographies.

"I'm a lousy father":
Alcoholic Fathers in Postwar Canada
and the Myths of Masculine Crises

Robert Rutherdale

IN THE "SECRET TRAGEDY of the Alcoholic's Wife," a national report prepared for the December 1959 issue of *Maclean's* magazine, Sidney Katz stated that "most of Canada's hundreds of thousands of problem drinkers are heads of families."[1] As fathers, they were failing.

The problem of dealing with pressures at work and at home were frequently cast as simply too much for many men. Esther L. Milwood described an ordinary case in an article published in the United Church of Canada's *The Christian Home*:

> At fifty-five, Sam is a bitter, unhappy man. His good job does little for him because it is only a job to earn money. His friends are limited because he has used friends for his own advancement and suspects them of like motives. His employees are acutely aware of his disdain for them because they were halted on the ladder of success. But most tragic of all, his family seems cruelly ungrateful for all the unsolicited wealth he has given them. One by one they have become aware of the emptiness of their life with him. Now at fifty-five he has found a partial solution, tragic as it is. He has found the oblivion of alcohol if not inner peace.[2]

But to explain why such men had failed as fathers, Katz offered a broader set of explanations. This journalist and popular social commentator, who held a master's degree in social work and was often featured in *Maclean's*, invoked three dominant fables of the postwar era: the dangers of the "lost man," the hazards of "momism," and the pressures of "family togetherness."

Alcoholic Fathers as Failed Men: A Problem of Emasculated Fathers?

The idea of lost men refers to a 1950s-based masculinity crisis expressed across those countries in the victorious, industrial West, which was then supporting a transnational baby boom, that blamed both work and home life for emasculated males: men were becoming "lost" as masculine agents because of "modern" forms of "alienation" that pitted notions of traditional male autonomy, also approached stereotypically, against the demands of work and sociability in "mass society."[3] For David Riesman, the American sociologist who was most influential in initiating this critique, lost, or "lonely," citizens – which meant men rather than both women and men – were persons who had lost their autonomy as "inner-directed" beings and had instead become "other-directed" in everyday societies of work, leisure, and family life. Ostensibly, Riesman and his collaborators, Nathan Glazer and Reuel Denny, in their hugely influential bestseller, *The Lonely Crowd* (1950), sought to cast all citizens as part of the "changing" modern character, women as well as men; but since its original publication, their work has largely been seen as anchored in the public sphere of *masculine* life in the modern era. The most basic "struggle that holds the center of the stage today," they wrote, "is that between other-direction and inner-direction."[4] Facing a masculine crisis, modern men, who had traditionally been more "inner" than "outer" directed, were fast being swallowed whole by a gaping, modern vortex that the book's title called "the lonely crowd."

Riesman's ideas, and those of his many popularizers in Canada, had strong resonance with much of the journalism on family life found in magazines like *Maclean's* and *Chatelaine*. Fatherhood themes became particularly appealing in their monthly issues during the early baby boom, especially when it came to poking holes in the middle-class myth of the so-called "good life" and critiquing the reliance on consumer products to underpin popular images of postwar domesticity. Riesman's work had a profound impact on Canadians concerned with citizenship and social change in the 1950s, including social critics like Katz.

Based originally on the writings of the American journalist Philip Wylie, "momism" introduced a formulaic and rather ugly figure: the modern "mom" as a matriarchal menace. As Wylie put it in one of his most misogynistic passages, mothers in contemporary society had become overdoting, overbearing, and overpowering in the public realm as well as in the private home.[5] Not only were traditional images of patriarchy – father-rule – dissolved, but fathers were also fast being displaced by this new busybody, built entirely on the flimsy foundation of a blatantly sexist construct. Insensitive to the violence that many married women actually experienced, some saw appealing caricatures in imagined sightings of momism in popular fiction, in comic strips, or later in television sitcoms.

Many popularizers, especially in the print media, repeatedly depicted momism as a hazardous, if not destructive, force. Family members were to be warned and to beware. As Wylie put it,

Disguised as good old mom, dear old mom, sweet old mom, your loving mom, and so on, she is the bride at every funeral and the corpse at every wedding. Men live for her and die for her, dote upon her and whisper her name as they pass away, and I believe she has now achieved, in the hierarchy of miscellaneous articles, a spot next to the Bible and the Flag, being reckoned part of both in a way.[6]

A veritable flood of fictional and journalistic discourse followed, which launched varied attacks on the misshapen figure of the postwar mom as a hyper-feminized shadow then cast upon postwar families. Unchecked, her influence extended beyond the cuckolded working father to the making of the homosexual son.

Unlike both momism and the lost man, the "family togetherness" myth was tied, often explicitly, to the messages of the producers of domestic goods, which fed the "good life" of postwar consumerism.[7] Very real material changes, like the rise of family automobile use, more suburbanization, and the increased consumption of domestic goods, which only the upper middle class could actually afford throughout most of the 1950s, led to such mythologizing. Fathers in the comparatively better times were to become successful, stalwart family providers, steady breadwinners in a national economy that favoured men's earnings over women's, despite the fact that an increasing proportion of married women were re-entering the paid workforce.

This critique was particularly pronounced in analyses of alcoholic family men in the postwar years. As a result, a new discursive industry of opinion, analysis, and prescriptive solutions appeared in both the popular media and scholarly "expert" advice, which delivered repeated warnings that ultimately contributed to the postwar incarnation of the "masculinity crises" identified here. Alcoholism was a national catastrophe. It did not begin with, but ended with, what Katz characterized as the "hundreds of thousands" of men, mostly fathers, in Canada seeking escape in alcoholic intoxication. Escape from what? Katz mixed anecdotal evidence, presented as typical stories of alcoholic abuse and failed fatherhood, to feed popular explanations of why so many fathers were failing to parent their children and to support their wives as mothers in favour of the bottle. Apart from his assessment of "lost men," who were running away from emasculating "family togetherness" threats to their masculine authority, and his assessment of the growing crisis of alcoholic fathers, Katz invoked the momist theme of "blame the wife" in his assessment of Canada's "secret tragedy": "Do their wives – while wanting to help – often unconsciously sabotage a cure?"[8]

First, the scale of the problem was revealed statistically, although it is difficult to assess its accuracy by the end of the 1950s. Katz asserted, "The plight of the problem drinker's family may add up to the most under-estimated social tragedy of our times. Five in every six of Canada's estimated 200,000–250,000 alcoholics are men, and most of them are heads of families."[9] But the sub-surface problem Katz sought to exhume was that wives and mothers often enabled and sometimes pushed their husbands toward an inebriated fate. Apart from the figure of the alcoholic father as victim, driven to his horrors by his secret life at home, the figure of the enabling wife, a cruel and misogynous construct, remained in the public sphere. Wives had to hide their husbands' drinking, especially if they were mothers living in communities shaped by gossip.

In *Booze: A Distilled History* (2003), Craig Heron compares the work of the medical experts in the postwar era – social workers and medical practitioners associated with private and public agencies, led by Toronto's Alcoholism Research Foundation, later named the Addiction Research Foundation – with the work of self-help groups for alcoholics, dominated by the growing presence, in local chapters across the country, of Alcoholics Anonymous. Serving mostly men, and many fathers, treatment centres that adhered to the hierarchical, professionalized, and medicalized approach, including Guelph's private Homewood Retreat/Sanitarium, Toronto's Bell Clinic, and the Addiction Research Foundation, stood in contrast to the democratic, alcoholic-participant approach, associated almost exclusively with Alcoholics Anonymous's "12-step" program of confession, restitution, self-help, and help to others. Founded under the name Al-Anon in 1951, this organization had a membership that comprised "more older people than young, more middle-class drinkers than working-class, and far more whites than people of colour, who were seldom made welcome in the early years (in North America, at least)."[10] Heron also points to the misogyny of self-help interactions, which most often occurred at meetings held in church hall basements or in clubroom spaces discreetly rented in the evenings, noting that the "male bonding and implicitly patriarchal and perhaps even misogynist discourse that could be at work in many of these meetings" shaped the culture. So did the "still widespread association of female alcoholism with loose morals."[11]

Such gatherings could both reflect and be reinforced by media discourses of men versus women as drunks. "Men Hate to See a Woman Drunk," Peter Davidson titled an article in *Chatelaine* in October 1946, in which he cast his imagined portrait of modern, postwar domesticity, with more than a few drinks added:

> Weren't men asking themselves more and more, what was the sense of always drinking with a herd of stags when, the way things were getting nowadays, they could perfectly well stay home and have a nice cheerful mixed party, or take their womenfolk out with them for a few quick ones? So the convivial urge was

domesticated, or expanded to include sweethearts and wives in hitherto strictly preserved ground.

But then, Davidson continued,

> came the shocking discovery. No matter how respectable she was, if a woman had too much to drink she got drunk. She staggered. She laughed, burst into tears, argued. She insisted upon telling the whole story of her life. She made everlasting friendships with total strangers in five minutes flat, and forgot them the next morning. In short, she carried on just like a man, and men took a very dim view.[12]

Men could act like men, even with a few drinks under their belts. For women, *Chatelaine* readers were warned, and they had better get used to it, a double standard was at play.

Drunken fathers, or fathers whose drinking seriously impaired their parenting roles, may have enjoyed a licence to err with prodigal drink, especially if doing so could be followed by a promise of redemption. For instance, Peg Porter (nee Martin), a suffering wife and mother invented by Sheila MacKay Russell in her short story "My Husband, My Enemy," was described in the throes of her struggle to contain her negative feelings about her husband's drinking: "She gripped the table edge and tried to control the slow, nauseating return of her anger."[13] Indeed, the "Martins of Alberta" appeared periodically in *Chatelaine* in the late 1950s:

> She must think of the children. Janey at five and Chris at two and a half were weather-wise little animals when it came to sensing the emotional climate of their parents. Janey already knew without being told when her Daddy had come home "sick" the night before. Sick, she thought bitterly. A sickness that had come nearly every Saturday night for the past year with special circumstances like the night before, thrown in for good measure.[14]

At a local banquet the previous night, Herb Porter had no doubt made quite a show. "A *few* drinks?" Peg admonished him at breakfast the next morning.

> You were sickeningly drunk. I can only thank heaven you waited until the banquet was over. You nearly broke up the dance, that's all. You reeled around telling everybody that the Martins had given you your house and your land and your wife and now all you needed was the indoor plumbing. You seemed to think you were funny. Well if that's funny, look at me. I'm Gracie Allen.[15]

Was Herb Porter a father losing his authority? A lost man? A loser? This is what readers were led to believe, at least until the happy ending in the last paragraph, when Herb promised to "work things out," to stop accepting "handouts" from his in-laws, and to stop drinking. Herb, the father of two youngsters, whose wife had, for a day, run away from home and gone to stay with her mother,

> unlatched the gate and gripped Peg in his arms, lifting her high on her toes, close to him. "We can work this out, hon! I'll work like a son of a gun, if you'll help me. But there'll be no more handouts, you hear? Oh, it isn't that I don't want you and the kids to have nice things, Peg," he said with swift pleading. "I know," Peg replied, through the gentle overflow of tears. "That's what I've come back to tell you."[16]

Such maudlin accounts in popular fiction of alcoholic fathers reconciling, promising to rehabilitate, and falling back into the embrace of understanding wives, who actually shouldered part of the blame, reflected a broader consensus in the postwar literature that placed significant blame on wives. Although in the *Chatelaine* story Herb Porter supposedly was not even a "social drinker," this was rarely the case. The darker implication facing many wives was that they should have "known better" than to marry a man already married to the bottle. Katz included a sweeping review of expert opinion on both sides of the Canada-US border that supported this popular notion.

Women who chose such men consciously, some experts claimed, "got what they paid for"; they might even be "disturbed" themselves and may have actually welcomed latching on to a "dependent" husband and future father. "As for the brides," one respondent from Toronto's Neighbourhood Workers Association reported, "most of them seem to have some psychological disturbance which led to the marriage in the first place."[17] Halifax Family Services went as far as suggesting that the "wives seem to gain satisfaction from their plight." Margaret Lewis, of the Cleveland Family Service Association, put it somewhat flatly: "The personality patterns shown by the wife are almost as familiar as the patterns of the alcoholic. She's sexually immature and suffered emotional deprivation in childhood."[18] *Maclean's* review of such professional opinion underscored that "social workers and psychiatrists are no longer surprised to meet women who have married two or three times, each time to an alcoholic."[19]

The most painstaking typology of the alcoholic's wife came from Thelma Whalen of the Family Service Agency of Dallas, Texas.[20] "After many years of observation in social agencies," Whalen was reported to have "set down a detailed account of the alcoholic's wife." Four categories of complicit personalities emerged for the wife of the alcoholic husband and, typically, father. The first was the *sufferer:* "She's the picture of uncomplaining endurance ... She chose the alcoholic so that she can always be miserable." The second was the *controller:* "She has to feel stronger than the man ... She could just have well have married a cripple or a person socially or educationally her inferior ... A more adequate man would be too threatening." The third was the *waverer:* "As long as the man can't get along without her, she feels secure. She chose a weak husband who was unlikely to leave her. Drinking increases her husband's need for her. Only when the drinking goes too far does she balk. But his pleas make her return." And the fourth was the *punisher:*

> She's like a boa constrictor with a rabbit. She doesn't ask much of her husband
> – only that he stay swallowed. He can have everything except his manhood ...
> She's aggressive, sees men as rivals ... is often a club or career woman. When her
> husband doesn't need her, she punishes him ... Since drinking is the only way he
> can assert himself, she's never free from underlying feelings of being angry.[21]

In terms of crude stereotypes, the "boa constrictor" comes closest to Wylie's matriarchal behemoth.

On a more realistic level, however, R. Margaret Cork, head of the Addiction Research Foundation's Youth Counselling Service, stated that most husbands started drinking, often heavily, before marriage. As she reported, the "majority of women knew they were marrying a drinker or a person who was insecure ... Very few of them were surprised by future developments."[22] Cork's study is important because it records the actual experiences of wives and children of alcoholics in their own words. Verbatim, explicit, and well-documented cases, combined with the life writing that looks back on this period, represent something much deeper than the speculations of social science, social psychology, and even some, but not all, social workers with front-line experience.

The Voices of Children and Wives: Turning to the Evidence of Experience

R. Margaret Cork's publication *The Forgotten Children: A Study of Children with Alcoholic Parents* (1969) reflects a broad Canadian apogee, as Heron observes,[23] of postwar efforts to medicalize alcohol abuse within the realm of applied social welfare mediation and research. "A far higher proportion of fathers than mothers," Neil Sutherland notes in his influential synthesis of childhood history in English Canada, "were alcoholics."[24] Turning to this evidence, the children with alcoholic fathers responded to Cork's questions with very poignant gendered answers and comments concerning their experiences, as girls or as boys, of failed fatherhood fuelled by alcohol abuse. Missing from their voices, almost entirely, is an overlay of the causes on which so many popular commentators and experts alike had grown accustomed to commenting. Instead, Cork actually turns to examining the children's voices carefully and critically.

To introduce the responses and testimonies of 115 children between the ages of ten and sixteen, Cork begins with a close analysis of the anonymized cases of Jerome and Sally.[25] Jerome was "a slight, intelligent youngster of twelve," the only boy in a family of three children, and the "son of a professional man." He began by stating, "I first remembered trouble in our family when I was five."[26] Asked to go on, he said, "My father mostly starts on Thursday and drinks until he gets sick. Then I have to look after him. I bring him a glass of milk and clean things up when he has been sick all over the living room."[27] Asked where his mother was "when this happened," Jerome replied, "She's at work and girls won't clean up, so I have to." But the "worse times" were "when Dad hits Mom":

One time when he was hitting her, I ran up and hit him as hard as I could with one of my toys – I don't even remember what it was – and after that it was all a blank. I don't remember what happened. Mostly when he's been drinking just a little he brings me presents. He's easier to get along with than Mom, but when he's drunk he's bad tempered and talks all the time – crazy stuff. He starts on Mom's family, says they aren't as good as his. I think he wants to hurt her when he's drunk. Maybe he wants to all the time, but he shows it most when he's loaded.[28]

Unlike *Chatelaine's* melodramatic scene of Herb Porter promising to Peg that he will no longer let her family, with booze added to the mix, come between them, this father's failure seemed a dead end, with little hope in sight. "Sometimes," Jerome said, "Dad gets all emotional."

He cries. I try to talk to him or Mom does, and he just cries some more. Then she starts and so do I. Sometimes he comes into my room and sits on my bed or lies on it when I'm in bed. He says that Mom doesn't love him, that no one does, or he says he's a lousy father. I get so upset I don't know what to say. I just cry and cry until Mom comes home. I try to push him off the bed, but he just stays there saying all these things.[29]

Sally told her story from the perspective of a fourteen-year-old girl, the second of five children, whose parents were still married, although they would later divorce. Cork also interviewed Sally's three siblings as part of her case files:

She was brought to my office by her mother. All the other children were also in the car because it was Friday and the father had already begun his weekend drinking. Although the father's earning capacity was high, the children were rather poorly dressed. Sally had a particularly neglected appearance and very poor posture. Her face seemed strained and her expression lifeless.[30]

Jerome's account can be compared to that of Sally, whose narrative is telling in terms of the tragedy that these "forgotten children" experienced as dependants of alcoholic fathers. "I always feel sad," Sally began, bursting into tears, "not just because my father drinks but because of the way he is." After she, as Cork puts it, "pulled herself together," Sally added "somewhat bitterly" that "he is always getting mad and smashing things. Once when I was little he came home late. Mother hadn't kept his supper hot so he tipped up the table with everything on it. You can never forget those times."[31] Cork asked, "Do you ever tell your father how you feel?" to which Sally replied, "No ... he'd hurt you – say mean things. You just can't talk to him about anything that matters." Sally also placed the constant, and often violent, quarrelling between her parents within a dysfunctional gendered family regime centred on the idea that her father, a salesman, could be a better provider if he did not drink part of his earnings away or waste them on otherwise needless guilt-based expenditures for his family or for his job in his sober moments: "Sometimes Dad goes out and buys us clothes, but he never asks Mother or us what we really need or want. It's just his way of playing the big shot, as though he was trying to buy us." As Sally related,

> I think he is trying to be nice to us – Mom doesn't even try – but you never know how he'll be. For instance, at Christmas he knows we want special things but he figures Mom will get them and he doesn't need to, so he drinks all his money away or gives it away. He drives people all over the city and entertains them. He spends more time and money on them than on us. It's as though he wants people to like him but he doesn't know how to be normal. It makes me feel pretty left out and sort of hopeless.[32]

With respect to her father's failure to be a good provider, Sally recalled, "He's really a great salesman." But could he really support his wife and children? Sally responded,

> He should be able to. Last month he got a thousand dollar bonus. He gave Mother money for groceries, but she never saw the rest of it. He gave it away or drank it, I guess. He never really supports us, and this makes Mom mad. I sort of think Dad holds out on Mom just to make her mad and punish her. But I

understand how he hates her to be at him. She's always at us too. She doesn't see we feel the same way.[33]

She concluded at the end of her interview that, outside the home,

I feel different from other kids. Of course, we might be more like other families if Dad didn't throw his money away. We could have things and do things like other kids. I know Dad really could afford to send me to university, but when the time comes I suppose he won't have the money. Anyway, I'd never be able to concentrate enough.[34]

Ian Ferguson's memoir of growing up during the latter baby-boom period is based on the ups and downs of his father as an unreliable family man. Following some sort of shady business deal that fell through, Henry Ferguson – or Hank, as his wife, Louise, called him – had quickly moved his family north from Edmonton to Fort Vermilion, where he found work as a teacher. Ian Ferguson's acquired hometown, as he describes, was the "third-poorest community in the country" at the beginning of the 1960s and would still remain the "fifth-poorest" by 2003, when he concludes his sometimes comical and often tragic story.[35]

His father was fired at the end of a decade of teaching in Fort Vermilion because his professional credentials to teach in the Peace River Separate School District, or in any public school in Canada, were nothing more than lies on his part. At this point, Henry, along with his wife, was rearing five children. He had for that entire time, according to his son, given up alcohol. Ian's mother had been a nurse in Edmonton when his parents met. As their son recalled,

My father had been drinking the night he crashed the social the psychiatric nurses were throwing. My mother could smell the alcohol on his breath. Since she was death on drinking, she wouldn't let him in. He tried everything he could but it was Katy, bar the door, and he wasn't getting past her. She tossed him out of the party, in fact. My mother always said she'd had to throw my father down the stairs, while he maintained he'd slipped. Either way, he seemed to take her rejection as a challenge, because the next day he showed up, sober, looking for his hat. He was carrying a single chrysanthemum, and he presented it to her along with the most heartfelt apology my mother had ever heard.[36]

Ferguson's father "had religiously attended meetings of Alcoholics Anonymous, both in Regina and Edmonton," and had made a promise at that point to Louise: "He had told her he would never have another drink again. Or, to be exact, that he would never have another drink as long as they were together."[37] Upon losing his job, he had no choice but to leave Fort Vermilion. Thus, when Ian was ten, Henry took the family to Regina so that he could attend university and gain his formal qualification to teach, which he would do by the latter 1960s. They lived in relative poverty, and Ian recalls how he and his brother were bullied: "We wore shabby clothes and we talked funny. We were fair game."[38] Up to the point of this major income setback for the family, it is clear that Henry was able to perform the role of a good father in terms of being an involved parent and providing for his family in the comparatively remote community where his children grew up. But in Regina a decade later, Ian states, "My father started coming home later and later. He was barely around. I don't remember my parents fighting during this time; they simply stopped talking to each other." He recalls how it was his sister, Margaret, who fought openly with their father: "The two of them only had to be in the same room for a few seconds before an argument would break out." Then, on one occasion, Henry was suddenly gone for a prolonged spell. As Ian relates in closing his last chapter,

> One time my father simply didn't come home. He was gone all day Saturday and all day Sunday. We were in bed asleep when the front door slammed on Monday night. It made the walls shudder. My father was trying to be quiet, but we could hear him as he came stumbling up the stairs. He went room to room to give us all a kiss goodnight. I pretended to be asleep, but could smell the alcohol on him. He went to join my mother, and they had a long hissing argument that lasted well into the morning. My father had started drinking again. He never stopped after that. He eventually died from it. Cirrhosis.[39]

If Henry Ferguson could be described as a reformed alcoholic who fell off the wagon when he lost his job, Camilla Gibb had a failed father whose alcoholism dominated her struggle to grow up in the late 1960s and early 1970s. "My father was always – to be rather British about it – somewhat peculiar," Gibb writes.[40] He certainly did not seem to have, she added, an afflicted sense of manhood that could be construed as societal but quite the reverse:

> He was never diagnosed as having anything more than an over-inflated ego and ruthlessly competitive spirit, and that assessment was not made by a health professional but by his employer at his first (and last) job in Canada. After that, he declared himself an inventor. And my mother decided she'd had enough.[41]

Throughout most of Gibb's childhood, she was tortured by a father who grossly failed to provide for his family, as he spent money he did not have on projects that could never be completed, and who literally tore things down or apart, both his family housing and his family relationships:

> He tore down a wall in the apartment he was renting. Then he tore down the ceiling as well. When the landlord tossed him out he moved to the country, where he bought a run-down farm, and promptly ripped into a hillside with a back-hoe, felled (illegally) a good number of trees in a government pine plantation and tore down three of the farmhouse's exterior walls. He lived behind tarpaulin, he lived without plumbing or heat, as did we, his children, on divorce-decreed weekends and holidays, because nothing he tore down was ever rebuilt – least of all his relationships.[42]

What Gibb reveals, in painful detail, is a search for the ultimate source of her father's failure:

> At ten, I "diagnosed" him as an alcoholic, but even then, I knew it simply wasn't the bottle. As I got older, I read in search of answers I seemed to need to label it/ him – to contain it, perhaps depersonalize it – in order to believe that I was more than a shell that might have once had the potential to become a person. And what if it was contagious or I inherited it, as I inevitably believed I would? I needed to name an illness in the hope that there was a cure.[43]

Gibb read about "manic depression," which "somewhere in my years of reading about it became bipolar disorder."[44]

Gibb claims that the quest to understand her father later inspired her as a writer in her search for "a big canvass over which to splatter" the terms, labels, explanations, and many words that might explain her failed, alcoholic father.[45]

> Throughout all of this, my father drank a litre of gin every day, turning grimmer with each sip, mutating into a mass of bitterness and paranoia. By nightfall, his transformation was complete. And we were trapped. He seethed: skewering us with profanity and insult, taking perverse pleasure in amputating any growing limbs. The more upset we became, the crueller he would get, so we learned to shrink, becoming shrivelled remnants of ourselves, hiding in cobwebbed corners with spiders and imaginary friends. We took a vow of silence. As families do.[46]

Peter Kulchyski's memories of his life growing up with his father reveal a man who could barely support his five sons. Kulchyski writes,

I was born in the small town of Bissett in northeastern Manitoba into a mining family, the fourth of five boys. Of my grandparents, I know only vague family legends. When I was five years old, my mostly Ukrainian mother courageously – this was the early sixties – left my mostly Polish father for a Métis man, earning the everlasting scorn of her family, and moved with us all to Red Lake, Ontario.[47]

However, following the tragic loss of his brother and the arrival of the first of two half-sisters, he and his remaining three brothers moved back in with their father, who drank heavily: the "second-oldest of my brothers drowned in the first year of separation; my mother gave birth to the first of two younger sisters; and we returned to the custody of my father in Bissett."[48] Kulchyski recalls being caught between his miserable past and tortured present as a youngster who was trying to grow up in what he saw as "our broken family" of father and surviving sons in the mining town of Bissett:

My mother perhaps expected that my father would tire and send us back. My father perhaps hoped that, by having us, he would force her to return. He never tired; she never returned. I have only one vague memory of ever seeing the two of them together before their break. My mother's new relationship has lasted until this day, so she found something of the happiness she needed to stay alive.[49]

When his father lost most of his income with the closing of the mine in Bissett, his drinking seemed to get worse:

Most of my life my father worked seasonally or was wholly unemployed. He drank, almost professionally. The household consisted of myself, my three brothers, my father – even our dog was male. Although by the end of my parent's marriage we had acquired one of the better houses in Bissett, within a couple of years we managed to destroy it.[50]

The actual physical destruction of their house is something both Kulchyski and Gibb, above, recall as part of growing up with a failed, alcoholic father in a home of separated, and then divorced, parents:

Without a woman in the house, it was my oldest brother's job to get us up and off to school. But there was no one to check on him, so he took to staying home. We soon discovered that he wasn't following us to school, so he lost his moral authority to compel us to go. No mother, no one to notice – no one noticed. I was in grade three at the time. After three months, we began exploring the furthest reaches of the house, finding ourselves with candles in the attic, looking for old pictures of the family in happier times, the candle wax dripping onto the wood shavings created some kind of smudge fire. In putting the fire out, the Bissett volunteer fire department chopped a hole in the roof, ran a hose through the picture window and effectively destroyed the place we were living in.[51]

It was never repaired, much like Gibb's house was never rebuilt. And neither of their fathers could do anything to turn back the clock to happier times.

Conclusion

Consideration of the period-specific discourses of "masculinity crises" and a societal approach to understanding alcoholism through parables of "lost men," or "overpowering moms," or the demands of "family togetherness" in male parenting do not help us to understand how and why some men failed as fathers. The many failures of postwar fatherhood were embedded instead in individual responses to the parenting-providing tension inherent in any father's family role, responses that come out best in family stories, often recorded in life writing. Some fathers drank and became alcoholics, but the causes were not rooted in substantial changes in family life that affected a family man's masculinity in the first three decades after 1945. Unlike much of the popular and even social-scientific writing on the subject of alcoholic fathers, life writing on the subject starkly reveals the pain and suffering caused by failed fathers who drank to excess for many reasons but not, contrary to what the experts and commentators suggested, because of failed masculinity.

What seems most clear is that some fathers' downward paths toward excessive drinking took place *within* gendered family regimes of husbands and wives, fathers and mothers, and daughters and sons but did not occur *because* of them – that is, not because a father's masculinity was being eroded. As with Ian Ferguson's father, alcoholic patterns were evident before marriages and were not the outcome of pressures on masculinity caused by becoming a father and by fatherhood through the life course. The case studies, the short stories, and the "special reports" on the "secret" tragedies of alcoholic fathers – served to readers as modern, postwar, family-life parables – help us to understand more about popular myths of period-specific masculinity crises than about being part of a real dysfunctional family parented by an alcoholic father. The evidence of these experiences, found in the voices of the children R. Margaret Cork interviewed and in the accounts of those who have since written about their lives growing up, casts a clearer light on why fathers drank to excess habitually and on how their parenting roles were diminished or destroyed as a result.

Notes

1 Sidney Katz, "The Secret Tragedy of the Alcoholic's Wife," *Maclean's*, December 5, 1959, 18.
2 Esther L. Milwood, "I Find It Good," *Christian Home*, February 1960, 34.
3 From the late 1940s onward, among the proliferation of writing on men who, as men, were becoming "lost," "alienated," or "other-directed," the text that stands out as the most influential in Western cultures is David Riesman, Nathan Glazer, and Reuel Denney, *The Lonely Crowd: A Study of the Changing American Character* (1950; reprint, New York: Doubleday, 1953), which uses the term "other-directed." Riesman himself appeared on the cover of *Time* magazine in September 1954 as the popularity of his (often misinterpreted) work caught up with the popular currents of public debate in mid-century Cold War America. In his astute assessment of Riesman's work and the influence of the idea of the "lost man" as part of postwar modernity, historian James Gilbert has pointed out that Riesman and his colleagues tended to equate social "character" with manhood and masculinity rather than drawing carefully delineated gendered distinctions between men and women as adults in modern society, although he also notes that Riesman did not ignore gender dynamics. "Reisman's foray into gender analysis," Gilbert writes, "unusual in his writings [indeed, unusual in much social commentary until the publication of Betty Friedan's bestseller *The Feminine Mystique* (1963; reprint, New York: W.W. Norton, 1997)] remains fundamentally consistent with his understanding of male and female cultural attributes. In his schema, masculine generally meant self-reliant, aggressive, and socially effective; feminine meant passive, exploited, peaceful. In some respects, these divisions coincided with his characterizations of inner- and other-direction." Increasingly evident in the popular discourse in Canada, as elsewhere, on the current state of masculinity in contemporary society was the notion that the male, or "society" construed in male-centred terms, was digressing into a less "inner-directed" and more "other-directed" existence; that is, men were becoming lost as complacent, compliant, and cooperative – indeed, feminized – beings. James Gilbert, "Lonely Men: David Riesman and Character," in *Men in the Middle: Searching for Masculinity in the 1950s* (Chicago: University of Chicago Press, 2005), 53. Prominent works of English Canadian fiction, such as Hugh MacLennan's *The Watch That Ends the Night* (Toronto: Macmillan, 1959) and Brian Moore's *The Luck of Ginger Coffee* (Toronto: McClelland and Stewart, 1960), reflected the angst of men facing postwar worlds that challenged an authentic sense of masculinity in plots that meshed with Riesman's societal analysis.
4 Riesman, Glazer, and Denny, *Lonely Crowd*, 298.
5 Philip Wylie, "Common Women," in *Generation of Vipers* (New York: Farrar and Rinehart, 1955), 184–96.
6 Ibid., 184. Wylie's bestselling *A Generation of Vipers*, which had its twentieth reprinting in 1955, was critical of what he saw as the expanding and pernicious influence of women as mothers in contemporary society. Blatantly misogynistic, Wylie's dire warnings of the growing power of women at the expense of a vibrant society crystallized around the grotesque, austere concept of "momism." In the 1955 edition, Wylie acknowledged the controversy his words had provoked: "This chapter has put the word 'momism' indelibly in our language; it has broken a path through sacred preserves into which all manner of amateur critics (along with the stateliest psychiatrists and the United States Armed Services) have since proceeded, pouring out articles, monographs, bulletins, research reports and shelves of books showing how right I was to speak as I did of a certain, prevalent sub-species of middle-class American woman; and the chapter has typed me apparently forever as a woman hater – indeed, as the all-out, all-time, high-scoring world

champion misogynist" (184). Although he particularly regretted this inevitable judgment, the simple-minded, if not lurid, appeal of his concept was unmistakable, and his
reference to an outpouring of commentary on momism, in both Canada and the United
States, is quite accurate.

7   The term the "good life" was invoked in the May 1954 issue of *McCall's* magazine, then
under the editorial direction of Otis Stiese. Stiese claimed that the happiest, most secure,
most affluent of families were learning how to live together in order to share the fruits
of the good life that the postwar world was promising. He said that "men, women, and
children were achieving it *together*. They were drafting this new and warmer way of life,
not as women *alone* or men *alone* isolated from one another but as a *family* sharing a
common experience." Quoted in Jessica Weiss, *To Have and to Hold: Marriage, the Baby
Boom, and Social Change* (Chicago: University of Chicago Press, 2000), 115, original
emphasis. In her study of family life and social change in postwar America, Jessica Weiss
notes that "the ideology of 'togetherness' sprang out of a century-long dichotomy in
prescriptions for American middle-class marriages." Ibid., 116. On the one hand, the
Victorian-era "separate spheres" notion of private and public life left the latter open only
to men and the former open only to women as mothers and wives. On the other hand, a
new "companionate" ideal arose in the latter nineteenth century that sought to draw men,
as fathers and husbands, back into the home in an atmosphere of love, companionship,
and "mutuality." As Weiss puts it, "both 'separate spheres' and 'companionate marriage'
provide historians with reductive descriptions of marital ideals rather than an accurate
portrayal of married life for most middle-class Americans in the past." Ibid., 117. And, in
Canada, some criticism of family togetherness was not altogether absent by the early 1960s
from the pages of *Chatelaine*. "Togetherness is awful," wrote June Callwood, citing a
Montreal social worker who had "vehemently" declared that marriages were now so "full
of clatter" that there was "no time for man and wife to be apart from the family." June
Callwood, "10 Reasons Why Marriages Fail," *Chatelaine*, January 1961, 63.

8   Katz, "Secret Tragedy," 18.

9   Ibid., 91.

10 Craig Heron, *Booze: A Distilled History* (Toronto: Between the Lines, 2002), 356. For an
excellent critique of medical treatments and self-help approaches from the postwar
years to the contemporary period, see ibid., 352–69.

11 Ibid., 356.

12 Peter Davidson, "Men Hate to See a Woman Drunk," *Chatelaine*, October 1946, 16.

13 Sheila MacKay Russell, "My Husband, My Enemy," *Chatelaine*, June 1959, 29.

14 Ibid.

15 Ibid., 54, original emphasis. The reference here is to the co-star stage wife in a popular
American sitcom of the time, *The Burns and Allen Show*.

16 Ibid., 64.

17 Quoted in Katz, "Secret Tragedy," 92.

18 Both quoted in ibid.

19 Quoted in ibid.

20 Thelma Whalen, "Wives of Alcoholics: Four Types Observed in a Family Services Agency,"
Quarterly Journal of Studies on Alcohol 14, 4 (1953): 632–40. For more on Whalen, see Lori
Rostoff, *Love on the Rocks: Men, Women, and Alcohol in Post–World War II America*
(Chapel Hill: University of North Carolina Press, 2002), 154. Rostoff's reading differs
somewhat from that of Katz. As she notes, "Thelma Whalen offered the most detailed
account of the alcoholic spouse's psyche. Assuming that all wives chose husbands who

would meet their underlying psychological needs, she classified alcoholics' wives into four personality types with alliterative names: Suffering Susan, Controlling Catherine, Wavering Winnifred, and Punitive Polly." A Suffering Susan selected a mate based on "her need to punish herself," a Controlling Catherine looked for a man who could be easily dominated, a Wavering Winnifred chose a husband whose "needs" would make him need her, and even more so than Controlling Catherines, Punitive Pollys simply loved to punish men. Their husbands, as Whalen constructed them, were simply amorphous "alcoholics," all with wives of these types who were complicit in their addiction. Ibid.

21 Quoted in Katz, "Secret Tragedy," 92.
22 Quoted in ibid., 91.
23 With respect to the Alcohol and Addiction Research Foundation in Toronto, Craig Heron notes, "By the early 1970s, Ontario's high-profile, internationally respected Foundation was not alone. Every province and the federal government had created some kind of government-sponsored institution to study and treat alcoholics and their problems." With considerable variation across Canada's federal system of health services administration, the "highly medicalized 'alcoholism movement'" had become well entrenched in Canada," as would remain the case into the 1980s. Heron, *Booze*, 364.
24 Neil Sutherland, *Growing Up: Childhood in English Canada from the Great War to the Age of Television* (Toronto: University of Toronto Press, 1997), 54–55.
25 R. Margaret Cork, *The Forgotten Children: A Study of Children with Alcoholic Parents* (Don Mills, ON: PaperJacks, 1969).
26 Ibid., 1.
27 Ibid.
28 Ibid., 2.
29 Ibid., 3.
30 Ibid., 12.
31 Ibid.
32 Ibid., 15.
33 Ibid.
34 Ibid., 16.
35 In socio-economic terms, introduced with a sense of irony that might reflect a gaze from southern Canada or elsewhere, Ferguson writes, "I was born and raised in Fort Vermilion, which is famous for two things. It set a record in 1911 for the lowest recorded temperature in Canada at sixty-one below, a record that wasn't beaten until 1947 by Snag, Yukon. And it was, at the time, the third-poorest community in Canada. Things have improved. Fort Vermilion is now the fifth-poorest community in the country." Ian Ferguson, *Village of Small Houses: A Memoir of Sorts* (Vancouver: Douglas and McIntyre, 2003), Foreword, n.p.
36 Ibid., 30–31.
37 Ibid., 37.
38 Ibid., 119.
39 Ibid., 120.
40 Camilla Gibb, "A Character Walks Off the Page," in *First Man in My Life: Daughters Write about Their Fathers,* ed. Sandra Martin (Toronto: Penguin, 2007), 75.
41 Ibid., 75–76.
42 Ibid., 76.
43 Ibid.
44 Ibid., 77.

45   Ibid.
46   Ibid., 76.
47   Peter Kulchyski, "Personal Dimension: Bush/Life," *Canadian Dimension*, May–June 2005, https://canadiandimension.com/articles/3639.
48   Ibid.
49   Ibid.
50   Ibid.
51   Ibid.

Afterword

As CO-EDITORS OF *Making Men, Making History,* we began this project with
a shared conviction. It was time, we believed, for a collection of essays devoted entirely to masculinity as a category of *historical* analysis in Canada.[1]
We started with a call for submissions to an anthology that would bring
together, for the first time, "original research informed by the significant potential offered by masculinity as a dimension of gendered historical experience," while "deepen[ing] our understanding of how histories of public and
private life in Canada have been shaped by masculine power."[2] Thanks mainly
to the energy and insights of our contributors, we are proud to offer a volume
that we believe meets these goals, while reflecting the current, lively state of this
rapidly progressing field of study.

From the outset, the book took shape as a collective enterprise. It began with
each contributor's individual exploration of some aspect of Canadian masculinity, framed first as a brief proposal and then fleshed out into the initial draft
of a chapter. As editors, having issued an open call, we were thus faced with a
wide range of topics and approaches. Yet we were struck by the commonalities
that unite these twenty essays, which share (among other things) a focus on innovative, often unexplored subject matter and an emphasis on masculinity as
a *relational* construct across time and space. We were also able to identify from
a very early stage the six *emerging themes* that ultimately bind this volume
together, like those few notes that state the central melody in a musical score.

Some of those themes were too clear and compelling, in our reading, to be
resisted. Such was the case, for instance, of the "active masculinity" (the phrase
is borrowed from Lara Campbell's chapter) that connects the very different
masculine cultures of Carolyn Podruchny's voyageur paddlers, Campbell's draft
dodgers, and Graeme Melcher's outlaw bikers, and which we have tried to en-
capsulate with the alliterative title "Men in Motion" (Part 5). Similarly, the sense
in which Jane Nicholas's sideshow little people, Allan Downey's Indigenous
athletes, Willeen Keough's anti-sealing activists, and Eric Fillion's nationalist

musicians were all *performing* specific masculine scripts, albeit in contrasting social and historical contexts, was too remarkable a link to be overlooked (Part 3). So we proceeded to identify the six major themes that frame this anthology, as strong connections and convergences emerged around big ideas like expertise and authority (Part 1), space (Part 2), youth (Part 4), and fatherhood (Part 6). Once this structure was in place and with some critical readings in hand, we invited the authors to revisit their work, fully aware this time of the thematic directions of the anthology and of the place each individual voice would occupy in the overall arrangement.

It is our hope that these themes will be treated as so many invitations and opportunities for focused discussion and debate, and indeed for new work among scholars, teachers, and students of Canadian gender history. At the same time, it has been interesting to reflect on certain elements that link these chapters together in different, sometimes unexpected ways – to listen carefully, as it were, not just to the recurring notes of the central melody but to harmonic variations, to clever bits of counterpoint, and even to the occasional percussive flourish. These "subdominant chords" – if we can stretch the musical analogy that far – strike us as worthy of discussion, here in this brief afterword, as we complete this phase of what we see as an ongoing project for anyone concerned with masculinity history in Canada.

Our subdominant chords begin with what must be described as an encouraging theoretical and conceptual convergence. We chose from the outset, in our call for submissions, to cast a wide net in order to encourage a diversity of perspectives rather than imposing a specific theoretical framework. Yet we have been struck by the heuristic power of certain concepts currently in wide use among masculinity historians in Canada, as represented by our contributors. Christopher Dummitt's idea of the "manly modern" is certainly in this category,[3] very much to his credit, informing Magda Fahrni's discussion of risk management, Keough's reflections on eco-masculinity, Patricia Jasen's analysis of veterans' university experience, and several other projects represented here. Raewyn Connell's idea of "hegemonic masculinity,"[4] furthermore, has mobilized research on Canadian masculinities, perhaps more than any other, and must surely continue to do so in the future. Part of the appeal of this concept is that it allows for the detailed analysis of dominant identities and discourses (Jasen, Cynthia Loch-Drake, and Julie Perrone), while leaving space for the discussion of subordinate masculinities (Nicholas), including those framed specifically as projects of resistance (Keough, Fillion, Melcher, and Olivier Vallerand). Like Judith Butler's performativity,[5] it is a powerful and useful concept that, among other things, keeps patriarchy and other hierarchies of power – based on wealth, sexual orientation, age, race, and physical ability, for example – clearly in focus.

Another subdominant chord in this arrangement is chronological rather than conceptual. *Making Men, Making History* pays more attention to postwar Canada than to any other period, with eleven of our authors situating their analysis in the four decades after 1945.[6] This emphasis, we submit, reflects the broad directions of current research in Canadian social and cultural history, as a growing number of innovative scholars turn their attention to these now receding decades between the end of the war and the 1980s.[7] Historians of masculinity have participated in this trend with enthusiasm and conviction, including Dummitt, whose exploration of the "high-modern" era in postwar British Columbia is the most influential monograph to date in the field.[8] Christopher Greig and Robert Rutherdale, who are among the leading historians of boyhood and fatherhood in Canada, have also focused their attention exclusively on the postwar experience.[9] Indeed, many of the most important insights into Canadian masculinities can be found in recent studies of the twentieth century, such as Mary-Ellen Kelm's analysis of racial and gender identities within Western Canadian rodeo culture over a long period ending in the 1970s.[10] So although there is certainly excellent research available on earlier periods, represented here in chapters by Annmarie Adams, Lisa Chilton, Norman Knowles, and Podruchny, as well as in the work of other scholars,[11] there is simply much more scholarly interest nowadays in the twentieth century, especially the postwar years. As a result, the present volume, with its strong but by no means exclusive emphasis on the period since 1945, faithfully represents the current "state of the art" in the making of Canadian masculinity histories.[12]

Another subdominant chord that we hear, in listening carefully to our twenty authors, is the growing appeal of oral history. This is another reason, surely, why the period situated within living memory – the past sixty to seventy years or so – has attracted so much attention from scholars of Canadian society and culture in general and from gender and masculinity historians in particular. "The stories that people tell matter," is the powerfully simple motto of one of the leading Canadian centres for scholarly research and community outreach in this area, reflecting the value of personal stories as eyewitness accounts of what it *felt* like, especially, to experience one's place in history.[13] From the perspective of masculinity studies, oral-history interviews provide a privileged window onto the gendered experiences of Canadian boys and men in the age of television, rock and roll, NAFTA, and the Internet. In this anthology, oral history is creatively employed in the chapters contributed by Fillion, Greig, Keough, Loch-Drake, Melcher, and Rutherdale. From anxious boyhood to failed fatherhood, by way of several fascinating political, corporate, and even gang identities, the stories shared with this anthology's oral historians inform our collective approach to a wide range of Canadian masculinities and will continue to do so.

We are particularly encouraged, furthermore, by the growing wealth of scholarship on the history of masculinities in Quebec and French Canada. In 2006 Jeffery Vacante wrote a provocative article in which he lamented the poverty of masculinity studies in Quebec, linking it to some broader trends in Québécois historiography.[14] Since then, the history of Quebec masculinities has developed to the point where we are able to include in this volume eight essays that are squarely located in Quebec settings (Adams, Chilton, Fahrni, Gossage, and Vallerand) or that that deal directly with French Canadian and Québécois conceptions of masculinity (Podruchny, Louise Bienvenue and Christine Hudon, and Fillion). Some of these chapters engage primarily with Quebec's specificities in the area of masculine identity, whereas others raise the interesting countervailing question of *américanité*, meaning the extent to which the Québécois people have incorporated broader and broadly modern North American trends, customs, and attitudes into their social and cultural vocabulary (Fahrni, Gossage). Francophone historians like Perrone, Fillion, Bienvenue, and Hudon are now offering textured studies to which we owe some of the most interesting and original insights in this volume. So the work collected here bodes well for the future of the field in Quebec, as today's masculinity historians practise their craft in both official languages (and no doubt many others) and in all parts of the country.[15]

As we read through these essays one final time, other subdominant chords began to emerge from this varied and wide-ranging composition, with its many voices sounding in several registers. As editors, we have not focused specifically, for example, on "the boys and their booze," to borrow a phrase from Craig Heron.[16] Yet alcohol and the spaces and rituals surrounding its consumption crop up again and again, notably in discussions of ritzy men's clubs (Adams), a 1970s commune (Fillion), and the edgy bars and clubs of Montreal's "Gay Village" (Vallerand), not to mention in Rutherdale's chapter on alcohol addiction and the challenges it posed to postwar fatherhood. Religion is another theme to which our authors return frequently, as with David Theodore's discussion of the "spiritual aspect" in Gordon A. Friesen's modernist hospital designs and Knowles's revealing emphasis on mission work and "Christian manhood" in the mining and logging camps he studies. Knowles's contribution also addresses the theme of social class, specifically the rough-hewn popular and working-class masculinities that are described as well in the chapters on voyageur life (Podruchny) and biker culture (Melcher). Just as prominent are the bourgeois and middle-class masculinities – informed by values like responsibility and prudent risk management – that run through discussions of medical practice in a nineteenth-century hospital (Chilton), management style in Alberta packing-houses (Loch-Drake), growing up in Quebec's *collèges classiques* (Bienvenue and Hudon), as well as the commercial and other discourses surrounding Father's Day (Gossage). A longer list of the subdominant chords that run through this volume would certainly include sport or physical activity (Downey on lacrosse; Perrone on long-distance running; Greig on the joy of cycling for small-town boys), political activism (Keough's eco-masculinities; Campbell's Vietnam-era expatriates; Fillion's free-jazz *indépendantistes*), and sexual diversity (Greig's gay male interviewee has an especially interesting perspective on growing up in postwar Windsor, while Vallerand's chapter on Montreal gay bars adds new texture to the discussion of queer masculinities). Finally, we draw attention to the masculine ideal of heroism, highlighted in at least three chapters (Jasen on returning veterans; Perrone on Terry Fox; Campbell on what she considers explicitly to be "a heroic narrative of antiwar masculinity").

It is our hope that readers will be struck by the critical power of these connections and many others as they explore and discuss Canadian histories of masculinity, both through and beyond the twenty original essays that comprise this anthology. We also hope that they might arrive at the same general conclusion to which we have been led through our journey together as colleagues, co-editors, and friends. That conclusion, in the end, is simple: It is a good time to be a historian of masculinities in Canada, with so many voices contributing stimulating insights – in harmony, counterpoint, or even collective improvisation – to the ongoing conversation about gender and power in the past.

Notes

1 The only volume that comes close is Christopher J. Greig and Wayne J. Martino, *Canadian Men and Masculinities: Historical and Contemporary Perspectives* (Toronto: Canadian Scholars' Press, 2012), which features five historical chapters, including three written by contributors to the present volume (Nicholas, Rutherdale, and Greig). The remaining thirteen chapters offer contemporary perspectives on Canadian masculinity, contributed mainly by sociologists and education scholars rather than historians.

2 Peter Gossage and Robert Rutherdale, original call for submissions to *Making Men, Making History,* distributed June 2012.

3 Christopher Dummitt, *The Manly Modern: Masculinity in Postwar Canada* (Vancouver: UBC Press, 2007).

4 See Raewyn (R.W.) Connell, *Masculinities* (Cambridge, UK: Polity, 2005); R.W. Connell and James W. Messerschmidt, "Hegemonic Masculinity: Rethinking the Concept," *Gender and Society* 19, 6 (2005): 829–59.

5 Judith Butler, *Gender Trouble: Feminism and the Subversion of Identity* (New York: Routledge, 1990).

6 Several other contributors to the present volume (including Nicholas and Gossage) embrace some of the postwar years in more broadly framed twentieth-century discussions.

7 See, for example, Mary Louise Adams, *The Trouble with Normal: Postwar Youth and the Making of Heterosexuality* (Toronto: University of Toronto Press, 1997); Magda Fahrni and Robert Rutherdale, eds., *Creating Postwar Canada: Community, Diversity, and Dissent, 1945–1975* (Vancouver: UBC Press, 2008); Sean Mills, *The Empire Within: Postcolonial Thought and Political Activism in Sixties Montreal* (Montreal and Kingston: McGill-Queen's University Press, 2010); Doug Owram, *Born at the Right Time: A History of the Baby-Boom Generation* (Toronto: University of Toronto Press, 1997); Bryan Palmer, *Canada's 1960s: The Ironies of Identity in a Rebellious Era* (Toronto: University of Toronto Press, 2009); and Joy Parr, *Sensing Changes: Technologies, Environments, and the Everyday, 1953–2003* (Vancouver: UBC Press, 2010).

8 Dummitt, *Manly Modern*.

9 Both of these authors, of course, are represented in this volume. See also Christopher J. Greig, *Ontario Boys: Masculinity and the Idea of Boyhood in Postwar Ontario, 1945–1960* (Waterloo, ON: Wilfrid Laurier University Press, 2014); and Robert Rutherdale's many articles and chapters on postwar fatherhood, which will soon culminate in a monograph.

10 Mary-Ellen Kelm, *A Wilder West: Rodeo in Western Canada* (Vancouver: UBC Press, 2011). See also Mary-Ellen Kelm, "Manly Contests: Rodeo Masculinities at the Calgary Stampede," *Canadian Historical Review* 90, 4 (2009): 711–51.

11 Among the studies that focus on Canadian masculinities in earlier periods, we should mention Mary Louise Adams, *Artistic Impressions: Figure Skating, Masculinity, and the Limits of Sport* (Toronto: University of Toronto Press, 2011); Tim Cook, "Fighting Words: Canadian Soldiers' Slang and Swearing in the Great War," *War in History* 20, 3 (2013): 323–44; Greg Gillespie, "Sport and 'Masculinities' in Early Nineteenth-Century Ontario: The British Travellers' Image," *Ontario History* 92, 2 (2000): 113–26; Craig Heron, "The Boys and Their Booze: Masculinities and Public Drinking in Working-Class Hamilton, 1890–1946," *Canadian Historical Review* 86, 3 (2005): 411–52; Robert S. Kossuth and Kevin B. Wamsley, "Cycles of Manhood: Pedaling Respectability in Ontario's Forest City," *Sport History Review* 34, 2 (2003): 168–89; Jeffery Vacante, *National Manhood and the Creation of Modern Quebec* (Vancouver: UBC Press, 2017); Marguerite Van Die, "A 'Christian Businessman': The Convergence of Precept and Practice in Nineteenth-Century Evangelical Gender Construction," in J.I. Little, *The Other Quebec: Microhistorical Essays on Nineteenth-Century Religion and Society*, 94–123 (Toronto: University of Toronto Press, 2006); and Catharine Anne Wilson, "A Manly Art: Plowing, Plowing Matches, and Rural Masculinity in Ontario, 1800–1930," *Canadian Historical Review* 95, 2 (2014): 157–86.

12 To briefly compare our anthology, once again, to the nearest equivalent published to date, three of the five historical essays in the Greig and Martino collection focus on postwar Canada, one deals with the early twentieth century, and one features a broad chronological sweep, from the late eighteenth century to the present. And this is to say nothing of the majority of the essays in their collection (13 of 18), which deal with contemporary Canada. Greig and Martino, eds., *Canadian Men and Masculinities*.

13 See the Centre for Oral History and Digital Storytelling, Concordia University, http://storytelling.concordia.ca.

14 Jeffery Vacante, "Liberal Nationalism and the Challenge of Masculinity Studies in Quebec," *Left History* 11, 2 (2006): 96–117.

15 The ongoing work of Jeffery Vacante is further evidence of this growing interest and of the range of approaches and interpretations now in play. In particular, see Vacante, *National Manhood*; and Jeffery Vacante, "Quebec Manhood in Historical Perspective," in Greig and Martino, eds., *Canadian Men and Masculinities*, 23–41.

16 Heron, "Boys and Their Booze."

Contributors

Annmarie Adams holds the Stevenson Chair in the Philosophy and History of Science, including Medicine, at McGill University, being jointly appointed in the School of Architecture and the Department of Social Studies of Medicine, where she also serves as department chair. She is the author of *Architecture in the Family Way: Doctors, Houses, and Women, 1870–1900* (1996) and *Medicine by Design: The Architect and the Modern Hospital, 1893–1943* (2008) and a co-author of *Designing Women: Gender and the Architectural Profession* (2000).

Louise Bienvenue is a professor of history at Université de Sherbrooke. Her research and teaching focus on the history of gender and youth in Quebec. With Ollivier Hubert and Christine Hudon, she is a co-author of *Les collèges classiques pour garçons au Québec* (2014).

Lara Campbell is a professor of gender, sexuality, and women's studies at Simon Fraser University. She has published on gender and the welfare state, gender and the antiwar movement, and the history of the 1960s. Her current projects include a history of gender and the antiwar movement in the Vietnam era and a history of the women's suffrage movement in British Columbia.

Lisa Chilton is an associate professor in the History Department, a member of the graduate faculty of the Master of Arts in Island Studies, and director of the Applied Communication, Leadership, and Culture Program at the University of Prince Edward Island. Her research includes studies of the history of international migrations (with a special focus on Canada) and British cultural imperialism.

Allan Downey is Dakelh, Nak'azdli Whut'en, and an assistant professor in the Department of History and Classical Studies at McGill University. He is the author of *The Creator's Game: Lacrosse, Identity, and Indigenous Nationhood* (2018) and has published articles in *the Journal of Canadian Studies*, the *Journal of the Canadian Historical Association*, and the *Canadian Journal of History*. Beyond teaching, one of his greatest passions is working with Indigenous youth, and he volunteers for several Indigenous communities and youth organizations throughout the year.

Magda Fahrni is an associate professor of history at the Université du Québec à Montréal. She is the author of *Household Politics: Montreal Families and Postwar Reconstruction* (2005) and the co-author of the 3rd edition of *Canadian Women: A History* (2011). She has also co-edited collections on postwar Canada and on the influenza epidemic of 1918–20. She is currently working on two new books: a history of families in Canada from New France to the present and a study of risk and accidents in turn-of-the-twentieth-century Montreal.

Eric Fillion is a doctoral candidate in the Department of History at Concordia University. His research focuses on the origins of Canada's cultural diplomacy and, more specifically, on the use of music in Brazilian-Canadian relations between 1938 and 1968. This project builds on the experience he has acquired as a musician and on his ongoing study of the Quatuor de jazz libre du Québec. He is also the founder and director general of Tenzier, a nonprofit organization, whose mandate is to preserve and disseminate archival recordings by Quebec avant-garde artists.

Peter Gossage is a professor of history at Concordia University in Montreal. His work on the history of family and gender in Quebec has included an exploration of fatherhood in the twentieth century, represented by a chapter in this volume. He is a co-author, with J.I. Little, of *An Illustrated History of Quebec: Tradition and Modernity* (2012) and a co-director, with John Lutz and Ruth Sandwell, of the award-winning educational website Great Unsolved Mysteries in Canadian History (www.canadianmysteries.ca).

Christopher J. Greig is an associate professor at the University of Windsor, where he teaches in the Faculty of Education and Women's and Gender Studies. He is the author of *Ontario Boys: Masculinity and the Idea of Boyhood in Postwar Ontario, 1945–1960* (2014) and a co-editor of *Canadian Men and Masculinities: Historical and Contemporary Perspectives* (2012). His most recent co-authored book is *Next to the Ice: Exploring the Culture and Community of Hockey in Canada* (2016).

Christine Hudon is a professor of history and Vice-Rector of Academic Affairs at Université de Sherbrooke. Her research focuses on religion, education, and gender history. With Louise Bienvenue and Ollivier Hubert, she is a co-author of *Les collèges classiques pour garçons au Québec* (2014).

Patricia Jasen is professor emerita at Lakehead University, where she taught in the Departments of History and English. The Social Sciences and Humanities Research Council of Canada funded her research on Canadian university student movements, gender, and mental health.

Willeen G. Keough is a professor of history at Simon Fraser University. Her research interests include gender, ethnicity, immigration, oral history, and memory. She is currently exploring conflicting articulations of masculinity during the Newfoundland seal hunt and related animal rights and animal welfare protests of the 1960s to 1990s.

Norman Knowles is a professor of history and Associate Dean of Arts and Science at St. Mary's University in Calgary. He is author, co-author, or editor of eight books and has published widely in the fields of nineteenth- and early-twentieth-century Canadian social, cultural, and religious history.

Cynthia Loch-Drake is an adjunct professor at York University in the Department of History and Schulich School of Business. She holds a doctorate in history from York University. Her research has focused on labour, gender, community, and region in mid-twentieth-century Alberta. Using a social history approach, she has explored the lives of men and women working at a pottery factory in Medicine Hat and in Edmonton's once-extensive meatpacking industry.

Graeme Melcher works at the Toronto office of a national law firm. He obtained his Master of Arts from York University in 2013 and his Juris Doctor from the Schulich School of Law at Dalhousie University in 2017. His research interests include outlaw motorcycle clubs, Cold War popular culture, and legal history.

Lisa Moore holds BA and MA degrees in history from Concordia University. In her MA thesis, she explored aspects of girls' private schooling in Montreal and she is currently preparing a doctoral dissertation on gender and juvenile justice in postwar Quebec. Lisa has extensive professional experience in the history and heritage sector, including as the Concordia-based research and editorial assistant for this project.

Jane Nicholas is associate professor at St. Jerome's University in the University of Waterloo. She is the author of *The Modern Girl: Feminine Modernities, The Body, and Commodities in the 1920s* (2015) and *Canadian Carnival Freaks and the Extraordinary Body* (2018), funded by the Social Sciences and Humanities Research Council of Canada.

Julie Perrone obtained her master of arts from the Université du Québec à Montréal and her doctorate from Concordia University. Her research interests include sports history, masculinity, national identity, and public memory. She has been working as a communications professional for a number of years in fields such as tourism, engineering, and transportation.

Carolyn Podruchny is a professor at York University. Her research focuses on the relationships created between Indigenous peoples and French colonialists in North America. Her personal and professional goal is to make sense of Canada's colonial past and to find a way forward in reconciliation by exploring the history of encounters. She is currently writing a book on the encounters of Anishinaabe and French stories in the context of the fur trade.

Robert Rutherdale is an associate professor in the Department of History and Philosophy at Algoma University. He is the author of *Hometown Horizons: Canada's Local Responses to the Great War* (2004) and a co-editor, with Magda Fahrni, of *Creating Postwar Canada: Community, Diversity, and Dissent, 1945–75* (2009).

David Theodore is an assistant professor and Canada Research Chair in Architecture, Health, and Computation in the School of Architecture at McGill University. His research focuses on architectural history, healthcare, digital technology, and social theory. He also publishes on contemporary issues, serving as a regional correspondent for *Canadian Architect* and as a contributing editor for *Azure*.

Olivier Vallerand is a visiting scholar at the University of California, Berkeley, and an architect with 1x1x1 Creative Lab. He has taught at Université Laval and the Université du Québec à Montréal. His current research on queer and feminist approaches to architectural pedagogy builds on his doctoral research, completed at McGill University, about the emergence of queer critiques of architectural domesticity.

Steven Watt is a freelance translator and editor based in St. John's, NL. He holds BA and MA degrees in history from McGill University, as well as a PhD from the Université du Québec à Montréal. His scholarly research focused on nineteenth-century political culture and the relationship between civil society and the state. Steven contributed his skills to this volume as the French-to-English translator of Chapters 11 and 12.

Index

Note: "(i)" after a page number indicates an illustration

accident prevention, 27, 59n13; citizen groups, 46–47, 49; experts and expertise, 14–15, 47, 50–52; fire, 54, 56; industrial modernity and, 46; legislation, 48–49, 55–56; road, 49–50, 53–54; union members and leaders, 55

active masculinity, 352, 427

Adams, Annmarie, 16, 75, 107, 429, 430

adolescence: female, 264; friendships, 259; initiation rites, 260; religious practice, 263; role of mothers and women, 270; transition to adulthood, 12, 18, 255, 257, 261–64, 269–70

Aidala, Angela A., 237

AIDS epidemic, 154

alcohol consumption, 36, 44n30, 430; in communes, 242–43; family service associations for, 414–15; physical violence and, 416–17; treatment centres, 412, 418, 425n23; women's, 412–13; in worker camps, 134, 141. *See also* alcoholic fathers

alcoholic fathers: children's experiences with, 415–22; emasculation and, 409–11; failures of, 384, 409, 411, 422; statistics, 411–12; wives of, 412, 413–15, 424n20

alternative masculinities, 174, 219, 220, 237, 343. *See also* eco-warriors

Alward, Doug, 312

AMEX, 349, 350, 351, 352, 354

Anderson, Eric D., 199

Anderson, Kim, 201

André Laurence, Canadien français (Dupuy), 265–68, 269–70, 273n53, 273n70

Andrew, Dr. (Marsden's brother-in-law), 33, 36–37, 43n10

Anglican Church, 133–34

Anglo-Protestants, 107, 276–77, 342

animal rights and animal welfare activism: critics, 223, 232; democracy and, 228; eco-masculinity within, 218, 219, 220, 232; media campaigns, 226–27; term distinction, 233n1

anti-sealing campaigns: Greenpeace, 220, 222–23; IFAW, 224–28, 234n30; Sea Shepherd Conservation Society, 228–30

antiwar activism, 362nn53–54, 431; American imperialism and, 354; draft dodging politics and, 347–48, 352–53; nationalist stereotypes and, 355–56; resistance to war and, 357, 358n2

appropriate masculinity, 17, 42, 279

architects, 79, 81n4, 129, 157–60; McKim, Mead and White, 110, 121, 128. *See also* Nobbs, Percy

architecture: gay-oriented, 151, 157–60, 167, 168; manliness and, 111, 128–29; vernacular, 110, 112. *See also* Mount Royal Club, Montreal; University Club, Montreal

assimilation, 196, 197, 199, 200, 294, 300

Association de prévention des accidents du travail de la Province de Québec (APATPQ), 49, 52

Austin, Alvin, 389, 390, 392
authority: biker culture and, 19; competing notions of, 27, 30; managerial, 15, 97, 189–90; moral, 421; national, 350; paternal, 176, 186, 189–90, 397–98, 401, 405, 408*n*69; of political figures, 55; social, 91, 100; youth challenging, 366
autonomy, 141, 181, 410

Bachand, François Mario, 241, 247
Baez, Joan, 353
Baker, Simon (Khot-La Cha), 207, 210
Balcer, Lise, 245
bargaining, 28, 87; cross-class co-operation in, 95–96; labour disputes, 85, 99; meatpackers national pattern, 91–92, 100, 101*n*3; multiemployer, 103*n*31; technocratic masculinity and, 92–93
Barker, Gary T., 315
Barnett, Homer, 198
Barnum, P.T., 179, 182, 192*n*21, 232
Barrie, Andy, 357
Barry, Charles, 109, 123
BC Hydro, 104*n*71
beauty, 17, 317–18, 320
Beaver Club, Montreal, 109, 339
Beckerich, Patrice, 246–47, 246(i), 250*n*19
Bederman, Gail, 11, 91, 320
Beers, William George, 195, 196
Bélanger, Pierre, 47, 53–54, 61*n*44
Belmont (bar), Montreal, 167
Betsky, Aaron, 151, 158
bicycles, 18, 284–86
Bienvenue, Louise, 18, 255, 430, 431
bikers and bike culture: American outlaws, 375–76, 381*n*80; attitude toward women, 373; clothing and colours, 369; customization of bikes, 368–69; different groups, 365–66; drug dealing, 374; Harley-Davidson motorcycles, 367–68, 379*n*22; idealized masculinity of, 19; identity, 332, 364–65, 373, 377; in Ontario, 370–72; Port Hope shooting, 376–77, 381*n*92
Billboard Magazine, 178, 180, 186, 192*n*18
binaries, 80, 356

black communities, 276–78
Bland, John, 109, 126, 131*n*34
Bliss, Michael, 347, 352, 361*n*41
Bogdan, Robert, 179, 194*n*59
Borthwick, H.J., 133
Bothwell, Robert, 347, 352, 361*n*41
Bouchard, Gérard, 48, 58
Bouchier, Nancy, 198–99
Bowie, William, 47
boyhood: acceptable and unacceptable, 275; anxieties about, 13, 18, 255, 429; appropriate, 24*n*54, 279, 282, 283, 287, 288; bicycles and, 284–86; compared to girlhood, 276, 287; homosexuality and, 282–84, 290; passage to manhood, 12, 17–18, 257–58, 261–64, 269–70; power and freedom, 285–87, 290; race and class factors of, 277–78; sports and, 287–90; violence, 279–82
Bradwin, Edmund, 141, 142
breadwinners, 17, 98, 104*n*71, 137, 404; changing roles of, 8, 10, 183, 411
British Columbia, 14, 134, 429; entrance into Confederation, 198; settler-colonialism, 17, 197, 201
British Columbia Amateur Lacrosse Association, 199
British Columbia Lacrosse Association (BCLA), 203–4
Brod, Harry, 65
brotherhood, 141, 366, 374, 376
bureaucratic rationalism, 87, 92, 94–95
Burns, Pat, 89
Burns and Company, 89, 91, 92, 101*n*4
Burris, Beverly, 93
businessmen, 93–94, 133, 134
Butler, Judith, 16, 24*n*52, 212*n*5, 233*n*7, 428
Byrne, John Duncan, 132, 133, 140

Cahn, Susan, 318
Callwood, June, 424*n*7
camaraderie, 11, 141. *See also* brotherhood
Cameron, Hugh, 133
Campbell, Lara, 19, 183, 331–32, 427, 431
Campbell, Lorne, 369, 374, 377, 381*n*93
Canada Packers Ltd.: architecture, 85, 86(i); bargaining system, 91–92; formation, 89–90, 101*n*4; front office and kill

floor, 87, 88(i), 103*n*47; management and labour relations, 93–98; social and racial hierarchies at, 98–99

Canadian Broadcasting Corporation (CBC), 20, 295, 324, 357

Canadian Historical Review, 11–12

Canadian Jewish Chronicle, 389

Canadian National Exhibition (CNE), 175–76, 180, 185, 189, 194*n*52

Canadian Nurse, 76

Canadian Victory Shows, 178

capitalism, 90, 92, 101*n*8, 354, 355

Carlson, Keith, 202, 213*n*8

Carnes, Mark C., 6–7

carnivals, 178, 180, 184, 192*n*17

Catholic Church, 274*n*75, 399–400, 407*n*18

Catholicism: fatherhood and, 400–1, 404–5; masculinity and, 18; Protestant rivalries, 31; Quebec boarding schools, 255; reform movement, 261, 264–65, 272*n*28

ceremonies, 11, 197, 200, 387, 389

Chamberland, Normand, 157–60

Charbonneau, Yves, 20, 246(i), 247, 254*n*102; birth of son, 242; L'amorce cultural centre, 248; organization of Petit Québec libre, 240–41; political activism, 236, 239, 242; on women's equality, 244

Charter of Rights and Freedoms, 150, 320, 324

Chatelaine, 410, 412–14, 416, 424*n*7

Cherry, Don, 20

Chilton, Lisa, 14, 15, 27–28, 429, 430, 431

Chisholm, Brock, 300

Christian manhood, 108, 135–38, 140, 144, 146, 430

Church Camp Mission: founding and operations, 133–34; missionary reports, 135, 139, 140, 143, 145, 146

Churchill, David, 351

Circé-Côté, Éva, 55

circuses, 180

citizenship, 183, 298, 304, 367, 410; draft dodgers and, 347, 349, 352, 355, 357; fatherhood and, 391–92, 396

classical colleges, 18, 51, 257, 258, 269, 270, 431; Collège Brébeuf, 261; Collège Sainte-

Marie, 265–66; Minor Seminary of Joliette, 259

clubs: British traditional, 109, 123; business, 111, 130*n*9; gender and class notions of, 128–29; secrecy of, 110, 130*n*18. *See also* motorcycle clubs; Mount Royal Club, Montreal; University Club, Montreal

Coast Salish, 197–98, 202–3, 206, 213*n*8. *See also* Skwx̱wú7mesh

Cochrane, William, 136, 142

Cold War, 286, 305, 350, 364, 368, 423*n*3

colonialism, 196, 201, 204, 213*n*11

coming-of-age stories: *André Laurence, Canadien français* (Dupuy), 265–68, 273*n*53, 273*n*70; female, 264, 273*n*49; identity formation in, 18, 257–58, 269; *Jean-Paul* (Farley), 258–61, 271*n*18, 271*n*22, 272*n*25; *Le beau risque* (Hertel), 261–65, 272*nn*30–31, 272*n*37, 273*n*42, 273*n*45; maternal roles in, 270; popularity, 271*n*5

communes, 237, 248. *See also* Petit Québec libre

competition, 6, 16, 119. *See also under* lacrosse

Conklin, Patty, 185

Conklin Shows, 178, 185, 191*n*4, 192*n*16, 194*n*54

Connell, Raewyn (R.W.), 3, 21*n*1, 101*n*17, 191*n*8, 293, 324; on hegemonic masculinity, 5, 7, 14, 22*n*18, 89, 176, 313–14, 428

consultants, 78–79

consumerism, 67, 68(i), 181, 367, 410

Cook, Tim, 12

Coquoz, Simon, 157–60, 161

Corben, Len, 208

Cork, R. Margaret, 415–18, 422

coroners, 28, 48, 50, 51, 56

corporations, 90, 93, 99

counterculture, 237, 351, 371; apoliticism and, 251*n*34; masculinity and, 218–19, 220, 232–33

Crawford, Lucas, 130*n*9, 130*n*18

crisis of masculinity, 9, 13, 314; disabled veterans and, 182–83; father failures and, 384, 409–11, 422

Cross, Gary, 182

Crossman, Jane, 324

Dalhousie University, 300
Davidoff, Leonore, 7–8, 15, 37
Davidson, Peter, 412–13
Davies, Brian, 174, 219, 232; anti-sealing activism, 224–27, 234*n*28; retirement and remuneration, 228
Davies, Robertson, 129*n*5
Davis, Clark, 90
Davis, Janet, 180
Davis, Natalie Zemon, 6
Denny, Reuel, 410
Department of Veterans Affairs (DVA), 296, 297–98, 300, 303, 304
Depression. *See* Great Depression
Derome, Wilfrid, 48, 51–52
deserters, 351–52. *See also* draft dodgers
Desmond, Viola, 119–20
Dickirson, Les, 276
Diefenbaker, John, 350, 360*n*23
Dionne, Jean-Claude, 59*n*5
disability: autonomy and sexuality and, 181; Canadian historiography of, 177, 191*n*9; children with, 184; legislation, 184, 324; masculinity and, 175–76, 177, 180, 183–84; physical beauty and, 317–18; term usage, 176; Terry Fox and, 323–25; veterans with, 183–84, 298; workers' compensation for, 183
discrimination, 196, 199, 276–77, 302, 326
"do it yourself" (DIY) ethic, 367, 369
doctors: francophone, 39–40; masculine identities, 14, 30, 35, 36, 41–42; practising in Quebec City, 31–34; remuneration, 42*n*1; workplace accidents and, 50–51
Dodd, Sonora Louise Smart, 386–87, 389
domesticity, 128, 412; homosocial, 107, 111; images of, 111–12, 410; and masculinity relation, 37, 365, 383; servants, 116, 118
dominant masculinity, 182, 297, 320, 322, 324; in biker culture, 370; disability and, 175–76; eco-masculinity and, 219, 220, 232; postwar re-establishment of, 294
Douglas, Ann, 142
Douglas, James: criticism of/from, 14, 36–37, 38–39; francophone colleagues, 40; home and family, 35, 37–38, 45*n*36;

hunting and fishing expeditions, 34–35; leadership role, 32; masculine identity, 29–30, 42; medical education, 33; surgical skills, 35–36; visual representation, 34, 40
Douglas, Tommy, 20
Downey, Allan, 17, 173, 427, 431
Downs, Laura, 233*n*7
draft dodgers: contradictory reactions to, 331–32, 347, 361*n*41; as freedom seekers, 357; as heroes, 355–56; masculinity and, 347–48, 351, 358; physical appearance, 351; punishment for, 361*n*32; rebellion and, 19; seen as copping out, 352–55; seen as cowards, 349–51, 357; total, 358*n*2
Duceppe, Jean, 403, 403(i)
Duchastel, Jules, 251*n*34
Dugas, Abbé Georges, 342
Duhaime, Vincent, 385, 401, 404
Dummitt, Christopher, 13, 27, 394, 404, 429; on deservedness of veterans, 294–95; on expertise, 47, 92; *The Manly Modern: Masculinity in Postwar Canada*, 12, 15, 57, 218, 428
Dunlop, Herbert, 201, 208–9
Dupras, André, 317–18
Dupuis, Diane, 244, 247
Dupuis Frères store, 391, 394, 397(i), 404
Dupuy, Pierre, 273*n*53; *André Laurence, Canadien français*, 265–68, 269–70, 273*n*70
dwarfism, 177–78
Dyer, Richard, 320–21

Eaton's store, 390–91, 394, 395(i), 404, 406*n*16
eco-masculinity, 17, 174; of Brian Davies, 224–28; counterculture identity and, 218–19, 232–33; of Paul Watson, 228–31; of Robert Hunter, 219–24
eco-warriors, 218, 220–21, 229–32
effeminacy, 142, 144, 283, 351
elite: Anglo-Canadian, 31; corporate, 85, 92; French Canadian, 18; managers, 85, 93; men's clubs, 119, 124, 126; student veterans, 293
emasculation, 9, 93, 351, 409–11
entrepreneurs, 89–90, 157. *See also* self-made man

environmental movement, 174, 218, 220, 228. *See also* animal rights and animal welfare activism; anti-sealing campaigns

Etobicoke General Hospital, 66(i), 74

ex-service students: enrolment in university, 296–97, 307*n*22; grants and living allowances, 303–5; homosexuality and, 298, 308*n*35; housing for, 301–3; identity, 256, 293, 305–6; psychiatric counselling, 298–300; veterans' associations for, 300–1; wives of, 303

exhibitions. *See* Canadian National Exhibition (CNE)

expertise: accident prevention and, 50–55; collective bargaining, 92; knowledge and, 56–58; professional, 27; reasoned, 15, 28, 47; systems of, 50; technical, 14, 47–48, 55, 63*n*63, 87

factories: automobile, 276, 290; hospitals designed as, 67; inspections and inspectors, 28, 49, 59*n*5; safety measures, 48, 49, 56. *See also* meatpacking industry

Fahrni, Magda, 14, 27, 428, 430

family: in biker culture, 374; in communes, 237, 246–47; desertion, 351–52; nuclear, 237, 302; sideshows and, 180; structures in "midget shows," 173, 179, 182, 189–90; of student veterans, 302–5; togetherness, 384, 385, 403, 409, 411, 422, 424*n*7; work-camp missions and, 137. *See also* fatherhood; momism

Family Fortunes: Men and Women of the English Middle Class, 1780–1850 (Davidoff/Hall), 7–8, 37

Farley, Paul-Émile, 271*n*14; *Jean-Paul*, 257, 258–61, 269–70, 271*n*18, 271*n*22, 272*n*25

fashion, 40–41, 341, 390

fatherhood: Catholic campaigns, 400; emasculation and, 409–11; failures, 409, 416–22; ideologies, 385–86, 394, 396, 401, 404; patriotism and, 392; responsibility, 404; son relationships, 259, 262, 266, 269; studies of, 19–20, 383; supervision and, 286–87; surrogates, 269, 274*n*72; vision of love, 401; visual images of, 394, 397(i), 410; voyageurs

and, 341–42. *See also* alcoholic fathers; Father's Day celebrations

Father's Day celebrations: advertisements and advertisers (1930–45), 389–93, 390(i), 393(i); advertisements and advertisers (1946–60), 394, 395(i), 396–99, 397(i), 399(i), 400(i), 402(i); archival materials, 406*n*8, 407*n*20, 407*n*36; Catholicism and, 399–401, 402(i); contests, 401–2; critics of, 404; early American, 383, 386–87, 406*n*12; emergence in Canada, 387–88, 388(i), 404; Jean Duceppe family celebration, 403, 403(i); new fatherhood and, 386, 401, 403; Quebec's embrace of, 20, 383–84, 387

Father's Day Council, 389, 390, 392, 407*n*18

Feinberg, Abraham, 357

femininity: animal welfare activism and, 226; campus culture and, 297; cuteness and, 182, 190; draft dodging and, 351; in relation to masculinity, 6, 7–8, 232, 336, 423*n*3; religion and, 142. *See also* women

feminism, 238, 244–46, 248, 314

feminist historians, 5–6

Ferguson, Henry, 20, 418–19

Ferguson, Ian, 418–19, 422, 425*n*35

Ferns, H.H., 299

Fetherstonhaugh, Robert, 299

Fillion, Eric, 17, 19, 174, 427, 428, 429, 430, 431

fire departments, 47, 48, 54, 57, 422

First Nations. *See* Indigenous peoples; *and specific Nation*

Fish, Cynthia, 385

Fisher, James, 33

fishing industry, 227

Fitzpatrick, Alfred, 133, 135, 137–38, 143–44

Flagg, Barbara J., 320

Flavelle, Joseph, 89–90, 94

Foisy, Fernand, 246–47

Fordist principles, 15, 67, 72

Forsyth, Janice, 200

Fort Vermilion (AB), 418–19, 425*n*35

Foucault, Michel, 81*n*8, 313

Fox, Betty (mother), 322

Fox, Terry: attitude to disability, 323, 324–25; commemorative statue and stamp, 316(i), 318–19, 319(i); as a hero, 312–13; ideal masculinity of, 17, 256, 326; Marathon of Hope, 18, 312; mother and girlfriend, 322–23; pain and, 318–20; physical beauty, 317–18; whiteness of, 320–21; youthful depictions of, 314–16, 327n21

Francq, Gustave, 55

Fraser, Blair, 297

"freaks": exhibition of, 175–77; passed on to children, 182; term usage, 190n2. *See also* "midget shows"

free jazz, 239–40, 247–48, 250n22. *See also* Jazz libre

freedom: of bikers, 377; boyhood, 285–87, 290; of draft dodgers, 357, 358; musical, 239; of voyageurs, 342

Freemasons, 110

Frémont, Charles Jacques, 40

French Canadians: Anglo-Canadian antagonism, 42; doctors, 39–41; fatherhood and, 385–86, 401; gift for jazz, 240; identity, 18, 255, 269, 392; merchants, 391, 394; nationalism, 31, 174, 391; progress and modernity and, 265, 269; traditional culture, 384, 400, 404; voyageurs, 11, 334, 337–38, 340

Friesen, Gordon A.: business management ideas, 72–73, 82n18; evangelical masculinity, 79, 80, 84n84; expertise, 28; hospital planning background, 69, 430; importance of nurses and, 73–76; photo, 65(i); private consultancy, 78–79; reputation, 64; spiritual vision of care, 15, 67–69; United Mine Workers hospitals, 71, 72(i)

Front de libération des femmes du Québec (FLFQ), 238, 244–45

Front de libération du Québec (FLQ), 174n2, 240, 241, 242, 245, 253n86

Fur Hunters of the Far West (Ross), 334–36

fur trade: ceremonies, 11; ethnicity of workers in, 333, 337–38; languages spoken, 338–39; master-servant relations in, 339; tools and travel routes, 19, 331, 339; women and family, 340–42. *See also* voyageurs

Gaboury, Arthur, 47, 48, 49–50, 52–53

Gagen, Wendy Jane, 320

Gallagher, Hugh, 325

Gateward, Frances, 316

Gauthier, Raoul, 47, 54

Gawley, Andrew, 191n4

gay bars, 16, 108, 431; Complexe Bourbon, 157–60, 158(i), 161(i), 165–66, 171n32; evolution in Montreal, 154–56, 168; importance of, 150; in/visibility of, 151, 152(i), 153, 153(i), 172n38; Le Club Sandwich, 159(i); Mec Plus Ultra nights, 166–67; Meow Mix, 166–67; Parking Nightclub, 160, 162–66, 162(i), 163(i), 165(i), 167, 172n39; types, 153–54

Geertz, Clifford, 336

gender history, 3, 4, 5, 150, 336; Canadian studies, 10–13, 428; scholarly contributions, 6–7; spatial metaphors, 15–16

Gender of Breadwinners (Parr), 10, 13, 63n63

gender roles: binaries, 80, 84n42; in coming-of-age stories, 266–67; in the fur trade, 336–37; in hospitals, 75–76, 78, 83n34; household, 303; in modern society, 423n3; at Petit Québec libre commune, 174, 237, 244, 248; public vs private life and, 7–8, 37, 424n7; redefinition of, 314; sexual difference and, 336; smoking and, 131n28; sports and, 318; in universities, 296–97; in the workforce, 93, 99, 294, 296

Gerschick, Thomas, 324

Gibb, Camilla, 419–20, 421–22

Giddens, Anthony, 50, 54, 56

Gilbert, James, 9, 423n3

Gilbreth, Lillian, 73, 83n30, 83n32

Glazer, Nathan, 410

Gleason, Mona, 176, 184

Goetz, William, 92

Goldwater, Sigismund Schulz, 79, 84n55

Goodson, Mark, 287–88

Gordon, Charles, 141, 143

Gossage, Peter, 20, 383, 430, 431

Gramsci, Antonio, 7, 313

Great Depression, 11, 85, 96, 183, 294–96; Father's Day celebrations and, 389, 392, 394, 407n20; lacrosse games and, 206, 208–9; youth and, 258, 262

Greenpeace: criticism of, 229; founding, 219–20; personality clashes, 223; rainbow symbol, 221–22, 234*n*20; sealing and whaling protests, 220, 222–24

Greig, Christopher, 17, 18, 22*n*4, 24*n*54, 255, 429, 431; *Canadian Men and Masculinities: Historical and Contemporary Perspectives*, 431*n*1, 432*n*12; *Ontario Boys: Masculinity and the Idea of Boyhood in Postwar Ontario, 1945–1960*, 12–13

Griffen, Clyde, 6–7

Griswold, Robert, 5, 6

Guindon, Bernie, 373–75, 380*n*45, 381*n*78

Guyon, Louis, 28, 48, 49, 52, 55

Hall, Catherine, 7–8, 15, 37

Hansen, Rick, 18, 25*n*56, 324

Harmon, Alexandra, 198

Hart, Susan Elizabeth, 318

Haudenosaunee, 195, 198, 207–10, 212, 216*n*60, 216*n*63

Hayden, Tom, 354

hegemonic masculinity: Connell's concept, 5, 7, 14, 22*n*18, 89, 176, 313–14, 428; disability and, 180, 183, 190; of draft dodgers, 19; eco-masculinity and, 219, 220, 222–23, 224; effects of, 290; feminist-inspired concept of, 10; generational changes in, 27; ideal masculinity and, 313–14; of "midgets" and "freaks," 176, 177, 190; self-made man and, 89–90, 93, 218, 232; sport and, 318; technical expertise and, 14; of Terry Fox, 323, 325, 326; threats to, 9, 183; Tosh on, 8; whiteness and, 320–21; women and sexuality and, 322

hegemony, Gramscian, 7, 313

Henderson, William, 134–36, 140

heroes: disabled people as, 325; draft dodgers as, 348, 355–56; environmental activists as, 219, 220, 223, 228, 230–31; Terry Fox as, 256, 312–13, 315–16, 326; veterans as, 18, 175–76, 293–94, 305; youthful, 255

Heron, Craig, 11–12, 430; *Booze: A Distilled History*, 412, 415, 425*n*23

Hertel, François, 272*nn*27–28; *Le beau risque*, 261–65, 269–70, 272*nn*30–31, 272*n*37, 273*n*42, 273*n*45

heteronormativity, 150, 155, 167, 169, 180; boyhood and, 282, 290

heterosexuality, compulsory, 24*n*52, 275

Hewitt, Foster, 288

hierarchies: in biker clubs, 377; gender, 93, 411; institutional, 32; pecking order of boys, 280; of power, 428; racial, 87, 90, 276–77; social, 87, 89, 98, 99–100, 104*n*71; veterans and, 294

Higgins, Ross, 150, 155

highways, 372

Hill-Burton Act, 70

hippies, 351, 372

hockey, 206–7, 216*n*63, 275, 288–89

Hodgdon, Tim, 218

Hokowhitu, Brendan, 212*n*5

Holdsworth, Deryck, 110

Holman, Andrew, 10–11

homophobia, 18, 20, 154, 282–84, 290

homosexuality, 151, 169*n*1, 431; exaggerated masculinity and, 158, 163, 164, 167, 168–69, 171*n*33; fear/curiosity among boys, 275, 282–84; sports and, 287–88; veterans and, 298, 308*n*35

hospitals: automation of, 71–72; consultants, 78–79; "drive-in" concept, 68(i); entertainment for patients, 78, 84*n*51; equipment and mechanization, 73–74, 74(i), 75(i); Friesen-designed, 28, 64, 71–73; masculine roles in, 66, 69, 80; postwar construction of, 69–71; role of nurses, 64–65, 67, 73, 75–76; spiritual aspect of, 67–69, 79; teaching, 82*n*23. *See also* Quebec Marine and Emigrant Hospital; *and names of individual hospitals*

Howell, Colin, 11

Hudon, Christine, 18, 255, 430, 431

Hudson's Bay Company (HBC), 334

Hughey, Matthew, 219

Humphries, Mark, 183

Hunter, Robert: anti-nuclear testing expedition, 219–20; death, 223–24; eco-masculinity/heroic performance, 174, 220, 222–23, 232; sealing vessel confrontation, 222–23; spirituality, 220–22, 229

hunting: doctors involved in, 34–35; Indigenous, 225; masculine identity and, 126; seal, 220, 223–28, 232; as sport, 11

Hutchison, Alexander, 56
hyper-masculinity, 18, 108, 294, 297; of
bikers, 332; of draft resisters, 354; of hunters, 218–19, 226; of voyageurs, 331, 337

ideal, masculine, 20, 30, 78, 431; of fathers,
396, 399(i); of managers, 94, 100; pain
and sport and, 320; of the self-made
man, 89–90, 93; of Terry Fox, 17, 322,
323–24, 326; of veterans, 294–95; of
voyageurs, 333, 336, 337, 339
identity: Anglo-Canadian, 126; biker, 332,
364–65, 369, 372, 377; Canadian national,
173, 195–96; coming-of-age and, 257–58,
260–64, 269; countercultural, 233; of
doctors, 30, 35, 41–42; French Canadian, 18, 255, 269; gay male, 171n33;
gender, 15, 24n52, 66–67, 173, 212n5,
237; masculine, 3, 6, 8, 21n1, 137, 318;
Montreal's, 154, 156; pan-Indigenous,
173, 197, 198, 200–1, 208–9, 212; performing, 16–70, 20, 337; professional vs
private, 38, 39, 45n35; racialized, 10, 11,
197, 201, 278, 429; religious, 139, 260;
sexual, 283, 290; veterans and ex-
service students, 256, 293–95, 299,
305–6; white-collar, 89; youth, 366
image of masculinity, 108, 158, 218, 294–
95; fatherhood, 394, 397(i); Terry Fox
and, 313–14, 319
immigrants: British, 195; Finns, 139–40;
Ukrainians, 96, 102n27, 104n68; in
Windsor (ON), 276, 277. *See also* draft
dodgers
imperialism: American, 332, 347, 354–55,
356; British, 197
income gap, 97–98, 104n71
Indian Sports Days, 203–4, 215n48
Indigenous peoples: athletes, 196–97,
203–6, 211, 427; identity, 173, 197, 198,
200–1, 208–9, 212; language, 210,
214n18; masculinity, 195, 200, 212n5;
women, 337, 340–41. *See also* lacrosse;
and specific Nation
individualism, 28, 90, 100, 119; competitive, 108, 141
industry: auto, 276, 290; building, 302;
Fordist, 67; logging, 133, 140. *See also*
meatpacking industry

inspections: fire safety, 54; industrial
workplace, 46, 48–49
insurance, 55
International Fund for Animal Welfare
(IFAW), 219, 224–28, 234n30
Iroquois, 17, 173, 338, 340. *See also*
Haudenosaunee

Jacobs, Dave (Paitsmauk) and Andrea
(Sla'wiya), 206, 207, 211
Jasen, Patricia, 17, 18, 255–56, 428, 431
Jazz libre: ensemble, 250n19; gender pol-
itics of, 237; musical improvisation,
236, 239–40, 247–48; organization of
Petit Québec libre, 240–41; support
and promotional efforts, 246–47, 248;
variations on name, 249n1
Jean-Paul (Farley): friendships and famil-
ial relationships, 259–60, 271n18, 272n25;
religious awakening and identity, 260–
61, 269–70, 271n22; setting, 258–59
Jesus Christ, 136–37, 139, 143, 144, 145
Johansen, Shawn, 383
Johnny J. Jones Shows, 178, 180, 185,
187(i), 188–89, 188(i)
Jones, Con, 203–4
Joyce, Bob, 94–95, 99, 104n52

Kane, Paul, 198
Katz, Sidney, 409, 410–12, 414, 424n20
Kelm, Mary-Ellen, 204, 429
Keough, Willeen, 17, 174, 427, 428, 429, 431
Kerouac, Jack, 19
Kimmel, Michael S., 3, 7, 21n1, 30
King, Joyce E., 320
King, Laura, 383
Kinsman, Gary, 11
Kitchener-Waterloo Hospital, 69, 70(i)
knowledge: cultural, 290; local, 47, 56–58;
power axis, 233n7; technical and scien-
tific, 27, 48, 50, 56, 57
Knowles, Norman, 16, 107–8, 429, 430
Kulchyski, Peter, 420–21

La Fête des Pères. *See* Father's Day
celebrations
La Gazette du nord, 398, 400(i)
La Patrie, 390–91, 393–94, 393(i), 397(i),
401–2, 403(i)

labour journalists, 47, 48, 55
labour relations: in meatpacking industry, 93–98; in worker camps, 140. *See also* bargaining; unions
lacrosse: bans, 199, 203–4, 216*n*60; box and field, 206–7, 216*n*63; British appropriation of, 17, 173, 195–96, 198; Indigenous identity and nationhood of, 197, 201–2, 204–5, 212; Indigenous origins, 198, 207–8; labour organizing, 203; spectators, 208, 211, 216*n*68, 217*n*77; teams and competitions, 202–4, 208–12, 215*n*48
L'Action catholique, 400, 402(i)
Lamonde, Yvan, 48, 58
language, 233*n*7; Indigenous, 210, 214*n*18; Métis, 338
Lanthier, Stéphanie, 238
Larose, Anne, 398
LaRossa, Ralph, 385, 386, 389, 394, 403, 407*n*18
L'Avenir Saguenayen, 398
lawyers, 55
Le beau risque (Hertel): choice of vocation, 264–65, 269; familial tensions, 262–63, 272*n*37, 273*n*45; female characters, 263–64, 270; setting, 261–62, 273*n*42; success of book, 272*nn*30–31
Le Corbusier, 28*n*4
Le Front ouvrier, 398
Le Monde ouvrier, 55
Le Soleil, 387, 388(i), 391, 406*nn*8–9
Leacock, Stephen, 127, 129*n*5; *Arcadian Adventures with the Idle Rich*, 110, 119, 120, 123
leadership: corporate, 28, 93, 100; of managers, 94; in medical practice, 29, 31, 32; of middle-class men, 99; National Conference of Student Veterans, 302, 304; workplace, 15, 28
Lefebvre, Pascal, 160, 163–65, 172*n*39
Lemieux, Charles Eusèbe, 38
lesbian, gay, bisexual, and transgendered people (LGBT): histories, 150–51; spaces in Montreal, 154–56, 160, 162, 164, 166, 169*n*5; straight bars and, 166–67; term usage, 169*n*1, 169*n*3. *See also* gay bars; homophobia; homosexuality
Lewis, Margaret, 414

Lewiston, Harry, 181, 194*n*54
Ligue de sécurité de la Province de Québec (LSPQ): educational campaigns, 49–50; founding and members, 46–48, 50, 52
Line, William, 296, 299
little people. *See* "midget shows"
Loch-Drake, Cynthia, 15, 28, 428, 429, 431
loneliness, 410
Long, Jim, 95, 97, 99
Loo, Tina, 11, 56–57, 58
lost men, 384, 409, 410, 411, 423*n*3
lumber camps. *See* work-camp missions
Lumber Mission, 133
Lupkin, Paula, 110

MacGregor, Roy, 312
MacKenzie, Norman A.M., 301
Mackey, Eva, 326
Maclean's magazine, 178, 184, 409, 410, 414
A Man's Place: Masculinity and the Middle-Class Home in Victorian England (Tosh), 8
managers: authority, 15, 87, 97; masculine ideals and, 91, 92–93; middle-class, 14; of "midget shows," 186; new technologies and, 93–94; social/racial hierarchies and, 98–99, 100, 102*n*27; union leaders and, 95–96, 100
manhood: boyhood transition to, 17–18, 255, 257–58, 261–64, 269–70; Christian, 108, 135–38, 140, 144, 146, 430; civilian, 18, 293; draft dodgers and, 331, 358; family, 404; ideal Canadian, 20; military service and, 355; of missionaries, 141; modern, 10; national, 256*n*1; on the road, 19; social character and, 423*n*3; studies of, 6–7; term usage, 4; threats to, 9; veterans and, 183
Marechal Midgets, 185, 187(i)
marriage, 32, 297; alcoholic patterns and, 414, 415, 421, 422; middle-class ideals of, 424*n*7
Marsden, William, 29, 32, 42; criticism of fellow doctors, 36, 38–39, 44*n*15; medical education, 33; mesmerist abilities, 37; opinion of francophones, 39–40; private life, 38; visual representation, 40

Martino, Wayne J., 22n4, 431n1, 432n12

masculine, etymology, 4, 423n3

masculinity histories: American and British studies, 6–10, 21n2; Canadian studies, 10–13, 22n4, 427–29, 431, 432n11; categories of, 4–6, 9, 13; emerging themes, 3–4; feminist critiques, 5–6; in Quebec, 25n58, 430

material history, 65–66

materialism, 67–68, 80

Matiyek, Bill "Heavy," 376–77, 381n93

Maurice Pollack store, 391, 392

Maynard, Stephen, 11

McCormack, J.M., 135

McCrae, John, 127

McEwan, Garnet "Mother," 375

McGill University, 42n11, 124, 126, 304

McIsaac, Jason, 54, 62n48

McKenzie, Kirsten, 42n2

McLean, James Stanley (J.S.), 90, 93–94

McLean, William (Bill), 20, 90, 94–95, 100

McMahon, Edmond, 28, 48, 51–52

Meanings for Manhood: Constructions of Masculinity in Victorian America (Carnes/Griffen), 6–7

meatpacking industry: bargaining and unions, 85, 91–92, 95–96, 101n3, 103n31; entrepreneurs, 89–90; expertise and authority, 15, 28; labour disputes, 99; management practices, 91, 93–94; middle-class ideals, 87, 89, 100, 431; office workers, 101n5, 104n71; salaries and wages, 97–98, 100(i), 101n3, 104n71, 105n79

mechanization: in hospitals, 64–65, 73–75; in meatpacking industry, 94, 103n47, 104n52

medical practice: education and training, 31, 33, 42n11, 51; female patients, 39; hierarchies and dichotomies, 32, 76, 78, 80; licences, 41; professionalization, 31, 42, 43n9; surgery, 35–36. See also doctors; hospitals; nurses

medical research, 18, 25n56, 233n1

Melcher, Graeme, 19, 332, 427, 428, 429, 431

Men in the Middle: Searching for Masculinity in the 1950s (Gilbert), 9

Merish, Lori, 182

Messner, Michael, 313, 320

Methodist Church, 133–34

Methodist Magazine and Review, 137, 138

Métis, 331, 337–38, 341, 342

microcephaly, 181

middle-class masculinity: Catholic, 18; DIY projects and, 367; economic independence, 90–91; ideals, 10, 15, 89, 90–91; in meatpacking industry, 85, 87, 89, 99–100; power and, 320; self-control and, 36; technocratic image of, 93; values, 85; Victorian, 8, 11; youth and, 366, 372

"midget shows": advertisements, 179–80; cute aspect, 181–82, 185–86, 190; Hollywood and, 193n37; middle-class family structures in, 173, 189–90; performers and performances, 184–89, 187(i), 188(i), 189(i), 191n4, 194n52; popularity of, 173, 176, 179; terms usage, 177–78

Midways, 178, 194n52

midwifery, 31, 41

Miller, J.R., 215n36

Milne-Smith, Amy, 110, 111, 118, 123–24, 131n41

Milwood, Esther L., 409

mining camps. See work-camp missions

Miranda, Louis, 200

misogyny, 332, 410, 412, 423n6

mission literature, 143

missionaries: civilizing efforts, 200; conversion failures/successes, 146–48, 215n36; hostility and opposition toward, 138–40; manhood of, 141–44; objectives, 135–36; women, 137

missions. See residential schools; work-camp missions

modernity: crisis of, 182–83; feminization of cities and, 181; industrial, 46, 50, 54, 56, 57; masculinity and, 10; middle class and, 87, 89, 191; risk and, 12, 46, 47, 92, 103n38; tradition and, 258, 271n11

momism, 384, 409, 410–11, 423n6

Montreal: bilingualism, 171n27, 171n32; fur trade, 339; Gay Village, 154–56, 156(i), 157–59, 167, 168, 171n27, 171n32; police and fire departments, 48, 53–54, 63n60; raids, 150; retailers, 394; safety

museum, 49; Square Mile, 16, 107, 110, 129*n*4; traffic regulation, 53. *See also* Sainte-Catherine Street, Montreal
Montreal Gazette, 387, 389–90, 390(i), 394, 395(i), 407*n*28
Montreal Lacrosse Club, 195
Montreal Street Railway, 48, 52
Moore, Patrick, 223
Moore, William, 110
moral character, 37, 39, 348, 350–52, 355
Morgan, David, 89
Moses, Nigel, 305
Mosse, George L., 11, 326
Mother's Day, 396
motorcycle clubs: choosing of names for, 369, 379*n*36; Hells Angels and the Outlaws, 375, 376, 378*n*3; importance of reputation, 374, 377; origins, 364, 365; Satan's Choice and Black Diamond Riders (BDRs), 370–72, 375–77
Mount Royal Club, Montreal: exterior, 116(i); floor plan, 117(i); founding and construction, 109–10, 129*n*3; overnight rooms, 124; reception room, 121, 122(i), 123; separated entrances, 115–16, 118; smoking and dining rooms, 123–24; Stanford White murder, 127–28
Mowat, Farley, 225, 356
Mullins, Joe, 324
muscular Christianity, 144, 173, 182, 200

nation-building, 204, 293, 294, 296
nationalism: draft dodgers and, 348; French Canadian, 31, 174, 391; gendered Canadian, 196–98, 212, 213*n*9; hegemonic, 326; imperial, 10; left, 352, 355–56, 363*n*66; radical, 174, 238
Nelligan, Émile, 266, 273*n*59
networks, 58; gay, 151, 154, 308*n*35
New York, 109, 154, 163, 171*n*33; merchants, 389, 403; Stonewall riots, 150, 153
Neylan, Susan, 203, 207
Nicholas, Jane, 17, 173, 427, 428
Nobbs, Percy, 20; eulogy for, 109, 126, 131*n*34; fencing and publications, 126, 127(i), 131*n*34; McGill University coat of arms design, 124; University Club design, 107, 113, 115, 118, 120–21, 126–27; war memorial designs, 127

Noda, Rika, 317, 321, 322–23
Noel, Jan, 40
Norris, Don, 368, 370, 374
North Shore Indians (lacrosse team), 206, 207–12, 211(i), 217*n*77
nuclear testing, 219–20
nurses: distances travelled by, 84*n*47; femininity and, 67; importance and needs of, 73, 75; masculinity and, 69, 76, 78, 80, 83*n*34; residences, 111; stations and administrative centres, 76, 77(i); work with machines, 64–65, 66(i), 71, 74(i), 76

office work: masculinity and, 57, 65; in meatpacking industry, 98, 101*n*5, 104*n*71
Ontario, 366, 367; employers' liability law, 183; logging industry, 140; masculinity in, 10, 13, 190; missionaries, 132–33, 138; motorcycle clubs, 19, 370–72, 375–77; sideshows, 17, 177, 178, 180, 185
oral history, 18, 20, 384, 429–30
outlaw motorcycle clubs. *See* motorcycle clubs

packinghouses. *See* meatpacking industry
Painchaud, Joseph: criticism of, 38, 39; leadership role, 32; masculine identity, 30, 35, 42; medical education, 33–34; professional partnerships, 40; visual representation, 40–41
Palmer, Lew R., 46, 57
Parr, Joy, 11, 14, 57, 345*n*20; *The Gender of Breadwinners*, 10, 13, 63*n*63, 102*n*24
Parti pris, 238, 240, 243, 244
Parti Québécois, 238, 253*n*101
paternalism, 20; authority and, 176, 186, 189–90, 397–98, 401, 405, 408*n*69; in French Canadian culture, 384, 404; love and, 401
patriarchy, 8, 15, 65, 238, 410; challenges to, 9, 314; toxic masculinity and, 5
Patrick, Julian, 347, 352
patriotism, 349, 355, 392
Patterson, Jack, 217*n*77
Paull, Andy, 215*n*38; lacrosse organizing, 20, 202–4, 205(i), 206–9, 212; at residential school, 201

performance and performativity: in biker culture, 369; Butler on, 16, 24*n*52, 212*n*5, 233*n*7, 428; in communal context, 237; of eco-masculinity, 17, 222, 224, 225, 232; of fatherhood, 394; of gender identities, 16, 20, 196, 213*n*10; of lacrosse, 198–99, 204, 212; of masculine domesticity, 383; physical disability and, 324; queer, 150

Pernick, Martin, 35

Perrone, Julie, 17, 18, 255–56, 430, 431

Peter, Friedrich, 315

Petit Québec libre: alcohol consumption, 243–44; establishment and organization, 236, 241; failure and closure, 239, 248–49, 253*n*101; families and visitors, 246–47; gender roles and feminism, 244–45; *Le p'tit Québec libre* newspaper, 238, 241–44, 243(i), 249*n*4, 249*n*6, 252*n*53; manifesto, 236–37, 241, 249*n*7; masculinities and, 17, 238; political culture, 174, 242

physicians. *See* doctors

Piegans (Piikáni), 340

Pietlock, Stan, 354

Pleck, Elizabeth, 406*n*17

Podruchny, Carolyn, 11, 19, 331, 427, 429, 430, 431

police: Montreal, 48, 50, 53–54, 57, 63*n*60; repression, 171*n*27; surveillance, 248, 253*n*101, 254*n*102

political movements: civil rights, 239; feminist, 238, 244–45, 314; gay liberation, 150, 153; Indigenous rights, 203, 204, 212; Quebec independence, 236–38, 241, 245, 248–49; student, 305. *See also* antiwar activism; environmental movement

Pomerance, Murray, 316

popular culture, 58, 182, 365, 393

Porter, John, 93

Poulter, Gillian, 126, 198

power: abuse of, 32; bourgeois, 313; corporate, 87, 99; cultural, 120; doctors' contests for, 29–30, 42; freedom and, 285–86, 290; gendered relations of, 30, 219; of managers, 27, 85, 97; masculine, 3, 5, 11, 65, 128, 404, 427; in master-servant relationship, 339; paternal,

385, 408*n*69; patriarchal, 19, 189, 383; physical, 19, 279, 324, 373; struggles, 9; United States, 356; violence and, 281–82; women's, 111–12, 423*n*6

Préfontaine, Jean, 245–46, 246(i); communal organization, 240–42; musical approach, 239–40, 247

Presbyterian home missions, 132, 133, 139, 143

Protestant churches, 132, 142, 145, 387

Protestant values, 135–37

psychiatry, 295, 298, 299–300

Quebec: *américanité* of, 48, 58, 386, 430; attitude toward sexual minorities, 156, 165, 168; fatherhood in, 385–86, 400–1; government, 30, 46; legislation, 48–49, 55; masculinity studies, 17, 430–31; modernization, 384; pro-independence left, 236–38, 241, 245, 248; Saint-Jean-Baptiste Day, 391, 400; urbanization, 258

Quebec City: administrative and economic history, 30–31, 42; medical community, 29, 31–33, 41; retailers, 391, 394

Quebec Marine and Emigrant Hospital: doctors, 14, 33–42, 42*n*1; institutional hierarchy, 32; scandals, 27, 29, 42*n*2

queer politics, 168

queer spaces: blurring of, 159–60, 164–65; engagement with the past, 164; fantasy-themed, 158; in Montreal, 154–56, 168; private to public evolution, 130*n*18, 151, 152(i), 153–54, 153(i); in straight bars, 166–67; term usage, 169*n*1. *See also* gay bars

Quiet Revolution, 48, 238–39, 386, 404

race, 87, 90, 100, 401; relations in Windsor (ON), 275–78, 286; Terry Fox story and, 320–21. *See also* whiteness

Racette, Sherry Farrell, 341

racism: dysconscious, 320; segregation, 119–20, 277; in Windsor (ON), 277–78

Radforth, Ian, 140–41

radical politics, 140, 174, 238, 244, 248, 362*n*53

Reading Camp Association, 133, 143–44

rebellion, 19, 141; in biker culture, 332, 364–65; youth, 366–67, 372

Reed, Christopher, 164

religion: assimilation, 200; conversion, 146–48, 215*n*36; evangelical masculinity, 79, 80; experiences in adolescence, 263, 269–70; hospitals and, 67–69, 430; women and, 142. *See also* Catholicism; spiritualism; work-camp missions; *and Church denomination*

Remiggi, Frank, 154–55, 167, 171*n*27

Repentigny, Julien de, 166–67

residential schools, 196, 199–201, 210

retailers, 388–92, 394, 403–4, 406*n*16

Riesman, David, 9, 410, 423*n*3

risk management, 12, 14, 28, 431; education, 49–50; modernity and, 47, 92, 103*n*38

road safety, 49–50, 53–54

Roberts, Julia, 12

Robertson, Louise, 131*n*19

Rochon, Paul, 398

Roddan, Samuel, 301

Roosevelt, Franklin Delano, 325

Rose, Paul, 240, 245

Rose, Sonya, 4

Rosenberg, Charles, 69–70

Ross, Alexander: chronicles, 20, 331, 333–36, 344*n*4; languages spoken, 338–39; masculine ideal of, 336, 342–43; observations of voyageurs, 339–42; view of French Canadians, 337–38; wife and children, 342

Ross, Ebenezer E., 135, 142

Rossinow, Doug, 352

Rostoff, Lori, 424*n*20

Rotundo, E. Anthony, 6, 7, 57, 93, 142

Roy, Michelle, 408*n*70

Royal Commission on the Status of Women in Canada, 245, 314

Rudy, Jarrett, 131*n*28

Russell, Sheila MacKay, 413

Rutherdale, Robert, 20, 314, 384, 385, 404, 429, 430

Sabo, Donald, 313, 320

safety movement: citizen involvement, 46–47, 50, 52; municipal officials in, 55; workplace accidents and, 49. *See also* accident prevention

Sainte-Catherine Street, Montreal: Complexe Bourbon, 157, 158(i), 159–60; Gay Village, 154–56, 156(i); Parking Nightclub, 162(i); saunas, 164

Salinger, Pierre, 350

Sandperl, Ira, 353

Saudrais, Guillaume, 385

Sauvé, Rick, 374, 376

Scarborough Centenary Hospital, 71(i), 77(i)

schools. *See* classical colleges; universities

scientific management, 63*n*63, 73, 83*n*31

Scott, James C., 56

Scott, Joan Wallach, 336

Scrivener, Leslie, 315–16, 317, 321, 322–23

Sea Shepherd Conservation Society, 219, 228, 232

Seale, Clive, 325

Segal, Lynne, 5–6

Seidler, Victor J., 101*n*8

self-made man, 7, 89–90, 93, 218, 228, 232

Shantymen's Christian Association, 134–35, 136, 138–39, 143; *Shantyman* newspaper, 145

Sherbrooke Daily Record, 393, 396, 399(i)

Shore, T.E.E., 136

Shuker-Haines, Timothy, 296

Shuttleworth, Russell, 177, 193*n*44

sideshows: community and family of, 180; freak shows, 175–77, 186, 190*n*2; owners and performers, 181; popularity and criticism, 179; transiency/mobility of, 177. *See also* "midget shows"

Simpson, Audra, 213*n*9

Simpson's store, 390–91, 390(i), 394, 404

Singer, Leo, 186

single men, 10, 137

Skwx̱wú7mesh: identity and nationhood, 173, 197–98, 201–2, 204–5, 211–12, 213*n*10; lacrosse teams and competitions, 17, 202–4, 205(i), 205–11, 211(i); language, 210, 214*n*18; residential schools, 200–1

Slow Motion: Changing Masculinities, Changing Men (Segal), 5–6

Smith, Sidney, 298

social class, 8, 258, 313, 430; men's clubs and, 16, 109, 118, 120, 123, 128; in Windsor (ON), 277–78

solidarity, 141, 236, 237, 240, 391
spaces, gendered: buildings for women, 111–12; in clubhouses, 112–13, 115–16, 115(i), 117(i), 118; masculine, 15–16, 107–8, 109; public and private, 150, 168. *See also* queer spaces
Spears, Gregory, 351
spiritualism, 67–69, 263, 269; of animal activists, 220–22, 224, 228–29
sports: assimilation and, 199–200; bans, 203–4, 216n60; boyhood and, 275, 279, 287–90; fencing, 126, 127(i), 131n34; hegemonic masculinity and, 318; masculine identity and, 11, 199, 205; pain and, 320; personal development and, 262; Victorian perceptions of, 195, 198. *See also* hockey; lacrosse
Squamish Nation. *See* Sḵwx̱wú7mesh
Srole, Carole, 57
St-Onge, Nicole, 341
Stanley, Meg, 56–57, 58
Stephen, Jennifer, 296
Stevenson, Dale, 325
Stewart, Susan, 178, 186, 190n2
Stiese, Otis, 424n7
Straram, Patrick, 240
Stratton, Charles Sherwood, 179, 182, 192n21
subordination: in hospitals, 73, 75, 76; masculinity and, 176, 190; of women, 7, 93, 96, 116, 281, 297
suburbs, 404; DIY projects and, 367, 369; of Windsor (ON), 276; youth rebellion and, 366–67
Suleiman, Susan, 273n49, 274n72
Sutherland, Alexander, 136
Sutherland, Neil, 291n14, 415
Swift, Gustavus, 89
Swift Corporation, 89, 91, 95, 98, 101n4

Tattelman, Ira, 171n33
Taylorism, 83n31
technocratic masculinity, 92–93, 100
temperance, 134, 141, 343
Terry Fox Story (Thomas), 315, 317, 319, 321, 322–23
Theodore, David, 15, 28, 430
Thibaudeau, Maria and Elmina, 56

Thibault, Greg, 160, 164, 172n39
Time magazine, 220, 228, 423n3
Tom Thumb. *See* Stratton, Charles Sherwood
Toronto, 178; Gay Village, 154; Yorkville, 371
Toronto Globe, 304
Tosh, Josh, 3, 5, 8, 14, 21n2; on public and private identity, 37, 44n35; on self-control, 36
Trimbee, James, 351
Tripp, Charles, 175, 190n3
Trottier, Maxine, 319
Tunney, John V., 352

unemployment, 31, 93, 183, 294, 303, 354
unions: Conseil central des Syndicats nationaux de Montréal (CCSNM), 246–47, 248, 253n88; female stewards, 96; leaders and local managers, 85, 95–97, 100, 101n5; resistance to, 93; role in accident prevention, 48, 55; Sḵwx̱wú7mesh International Longshoremen's Association (ILA), 203, 205; United Packinghouse Workers of America (UPWA), 91–92, 96; wages and, 97–98, 104n71. *See also* bargaining
United Mine Workers hospitals, 71, 72(i), 82n25
universities: campus culture and student newspapers, 297; emblems, 124; remasculinization of, 294, 306; selection process, 297–98; women's attendance, 296–97, 306. *See also* classical colleges; ex-service students; *and name of university*
University Club, Montreal: architectural design, 107, 110, 113(i), 126; billiards room, 126, 128(i); floor plans, 114(i), 122(i), 124, 125(i); location, 112; membership, 124; military symbolism, 127; reception room, 120, 121(i); servants/staff, 118; smoking and dining rooms, 123–24, 131n19; women's spaces, 112–13, 115, 115(i)
University of Alberta, 303
University of British Columbia, 301; *Ubyssey*, 302, 303
University of Edmonton, 302

University of Manitoba, 299, 302
University of Saskatchewan, 297, 299, 301
University of Toronto, 297–99, 301, 305
Urbach, Henry, 151
urban masculinity, 109
urbanization, 87, 89, 181, 200, 258

Vacante, Jeffery, 25n58, 238, 256n1, 430, 433n15
Vallerand, Olivier, 16, 108, 428, 430
Vallières, Pierre, 174, 240
Van Slyck, Abigail, 119
Vancouver, 197, 200, 203, 208–9
veterans: as bikers, 365; deservedness/ entitlement of, 294, 300–2, 305; disabled, 183–84, 298; on display at exhibitions, 175–76; enrolment in university, 296–97, 307n22; heroism of, 256; manly image, 294–95; return to civilian life, 18, 294–95; wives of, 293, 295–96, 303. *See also* ex-service students
veterans' associations, 300–1; National Conference of Student Veterans (NCSV), 301–4, 305
Veterans Charter, 18, 293, 295, 301–2, 310n79
Vibert, Elizabeth, 11
Vicinus, Martha, 111
Victorian ideals, 198, 199–200, 424n7
Victorian masculinity, 8, 173, 195–96; modernity and, 10–11; studies, 41
Vietnam War: America/Canada stereotypes and, 355–57; draft dodgers, 331, 347–48, 350; political debates on, 352–53; public opinion of, 348–49
violence: of biker clubs, 332, 365, 369, 373, 376–77, 381n80; boyhood, 279–84, 290; and nonviolence in activism, 221, 223, 226, 231; against women, 5, 373
visual masculinity, 40–41. *See also* image of masculinity
Vogel, Morris, 69
voyageurs: boasting and competition, 331, 334–36, 339–40; ceremonial practices, 11; clothing, 341; desire to be free, 342; distances travelled, 339; fatherhood, 341–42, 346n44; Indigenous women and wives of, 340–41; masculinity

and masculine ideals, 336–37, 343; performing women's duties, 337; race and ethnicity, 336–38

Walker, Fred, 314
Walton, John, 182
war resisters. *See* antiwar activism
Watson, Paul, 174, 219; fame, 232; Greenpeace activism, 220, 222–23; performance of eco-warrior, 229–32; recollections of Robert Hunter, 221, 223–24; spirituality, 228–29; split from Greenpeace, 229; *The Thirty Years War in Thirty Verses: August 1977–August 2007*, 231–32
Weeks, John, 74, 81n4, 82n24
Weightman, Barbara, 151
Weiss, Jessica, 424n7
welfare state, 183
Westacott, Vince, 98, 105n74
Weyler, Rex, 221
Whalen, Thelma, 414–15, 424n20
Wheeler, E. Todd, 79
White, Stanford, 127–28
white-collar men, 47, 93; corporations and, 87, 90; identity, 89; power and, 87, 91, 96; salaries, 97; social hierarchies and, 98; unionists and, 85, 100, 104n71
whiteness, 19, 96, 199, 277; of Terry Fox, 320–21
Whitton, Charlotte, 404
Windsor (ON), 18; elementary schools, 281–83; Father's Day promotions, 388; history and industry, 276, 290; race relations and racism, 276–78; working-class neighbourhoods, 279–80, 286
Withers, Ted, 324
women: adolescent boys and, 270; with alcoholic husbands, 411–12, 416; bikers' attitudes toward, 373; drunk, 412–13; equality, 244; in the fur trade, 340–42; Indigenous, 337, 340–41; missionaries, 137; role in religious matters, 142; shopping, 181; spaces in men's clubs, 112–13, 115, 115(i); subordination of, 7, 93, 96, 116, 281, 297; Terry Fox and, 322–23; university attendance, 296–97, 306; veterans' wives, 293, 295–96, 303; in the workforce, 89, 91, 93, 96,

245–46, 294, 411. *See also* femininity; feminism

Women's Christian Temperance Union (WCTU), 134, 137

work-camp missions: Christian manhood ideals, 135–36, 144; conversion and converts, 145–48; families and women, 137, 148*n*25; growth of, 133–35; hymn sings, 144–45; indifference and opposition, 138–40; living conditions, 133; masculine culture and, 16, 107–8, 132, 140–41; missionary challenges, 142–44; organizations involved, 134–35; spiritual development, 138

workers' compensation, 48–49, 55–56, 183

working-class masculinity, 8, 17, 367, 430; of bike culture, 332, 364–65, 369, 372, 373; men's clubs and, 119; youth and, 366

workplace: accidents and safety measures, 46, 48–49, 50–52; leadership in, 15, 28; masculinity in, 12, 65; racial discrimination, 277; women in the, 89, 91, 93, 96, 245–46, 294, 411

Worthington, Edward D., 35, 41

Wylie, Philip, 410–11, 415, 423*n*6

Young Men's Christian Association (YMCA), 110, 134, 135, 140, 145, 386

youth: heroism and, 255; identity, 366; organizations, 258, 271*n*12; rebellion, 364, 366–67, 372; of Terry Fox, 17, 314–16. *See also* adolescence; coming-of-age stories

Zablocki, Benjamin D., 237